LORD MAKE me sensitive to
your WILL TODAY ——

GUIDELINES

THE

A Mandate for the 21st Century

PENTECOSTAL

PASTOR

Compiled and edited by
Thomas E. Trask, Wayde I.
Goodall, and Zenas J. Bicket

Springfield, Missouri
02-0686

To avoid the awkwardness of *he/she* and *his/her,* the male pronouns *he* and *his* are used throughout the book to refer to the pastor. The General Council of the Assemblies of God has historically ordained women as ministers and has stated that women are eligible to fill any office in the church, including that of pastor.

2nd Printing 2000

Library of Congress Cataloging-in-Publication Data

Pentecostal Pastor / compiled and edited by Thomas E. Trask, Wayde I. Goodall, Zenas J. Bicket.
      p.   cm.
    Includes bibliographical references and index.
    ISBN 0-88243-686-4
    1. Pastoral theology—Assemblies of God. 2. Pastoral theology—Pentecostal churches. 3. Assemblies of God—Doctrines. 4. Pentecostal churches—Doctrines.
I. Trask, Thomas E. II. Goodall, Wayde I. III. Bicket, Zenas J.
BX8765.5.Z5P47 1997
253'.088' 289—dc21   97-13504

Contents

Unit 3—Preparing for Revival 5/13

Unit 4—Effective Accountability 5/16

Unit 5—Ministry to the Body *5/20, 23*

Unit 6—Spirit-Anointed Worship $MAY\ 30,\ 6/3$

6/6 FINAL

Foreword

When the church was born on the day of Pentecost, God began calling "shepherds" to lead the flocks of Christian believers that would rise up around the world. Pastors (a figurative extension of the Greek word for "shepherd") are to be responsible for the care, guidance, and teaching that a congregation receives. They are gifts to the church (Ephesians 4:11), necessary leaders who are to lead exemplary lives. Their call to the ministry is from heaven (Acts 20:28), their example is Jesus Christ, and their strength to do this incredible work comes from the Holy Spirit.

I believe that shepherds are to be Pentecostal pastors who lead Pentecostal churches. This is a mandate from God. As we live in one of the most complicated, technological ages this world has ever seen, it is critical that the leaders of the church be both filled with the Holy Spirit and led by the Holy Spirit. Peoples' lives are complex, with entanglements and bondages that only God can enable us to understand and help with. As pastors attempt to help those who have been entrapped by alcoholism, drug abuse, divorce, spouse abuse, child molestation, and countless other tragic bondages, they desperately need the power and discernment of the Spirit to minister. Methods of reaching people change; however, our message must never change. The Pentecostal message, the gifts of the Spirit, and preaching the gospel with signs and wonders following are absolutely relevant for the twenty-first century.

As pastors, we simply need the power of the Holy Spirit to guide any attempt to liberate and lead people. There are two reasons for this. The first is that at this time in history there is a critical need in people's lives; the home situations and the ills of society are perhaps greater than that of any other generation. Parallel to that is the need for the Pentecostal church to meet the demands and needs confronting it without compromising the message. We are involved in the social needs of people but our message must never become a social gospel. This generation must never water down the message that has been entrusted to us. For the church to compromise in the Pentecostal distinctives would be a travesty, thwarting the purpose for which God raised it up.

When the Scripture says, "'No eye has seen, no ear has heard, no mind has conceived what God has prepared for those who love him'" (1 Corinthians 2:9, NIV), God is speaking to the church. We need to seek God to see what He has in store for us and our ministries. I believe that we have not yet begun to scratch the surface. We must be careful not to think that just because we are Pentecostal people we have experienced all that God has. He has so much for us as we endeavor to walk in His Spirit. It is my prayer that you continually be filled with the Holy Spirit and experience all that God has for you.

This book is written by Pentecostal pastors, college presidents, and leaders. Their rich backgrounds in Christian service have brought them to a place where they can shed fresh light on the role of pastor. The various writers do not have just a theory of ministry; they have been successful in doing it—some for decades.

The first intended audience for this book is the person who shepherds a congregation, including those who might work with him as an associate pastor. To them, this book can serve as a practical theology book or a constant reference tool to turn to when the need arises.

The second intended audience is the person who is preparing for ministry. The diligent ministerial student will be keenly interested in being adequately prepared for this most valuable work. With the concern about being excellent in whatever God asks them to do, the student needs to receive advice from others who have proven ministries with great success in particular areas. We are sure that we have not covered all of the issues that will come to the pastor's attention; however, the key areas of pastoral ministry are considered. This book is intended to be a tool for the Pentecostal pastors, whether they be within the Assemblies of God fellowship or in other Pentecostal organizations.

I want to thank Dr. Wayde Goodall and Dr. Zenas Bicket for their outstanding work in compiling all of the various topics discussed, assigning and working with the writers, and editing the result. I sincerely appreciate their valuable contribution to this Fellowship through this project.

It is my prayer that "whatever you do in word or deed, [you] do all in the name of the Lord Jesus, giving thanks through Him to God the Father" (Colossians 3:17, NASB).

—THOMAS E. TRASK
General Superintendent
General Council of the Assemblies of God

List of Contributors

Gordon L. Anderson, Ph.D., President, North Central Bible College, Minneapolis, Minnesota

David Argue, Executive Presbyter, Pastor, Christ's Place Church, Assemblies of God, Lincoln, Nebraska

Don Argue, Ph.D., President, National Association of Evangelicals, Wheaton, Illinois

Tommy Barnett, Executive Presbyter, Pastor, First Assembly of God, Phoenix, Arizona

Almon M. Bartholomew, Executive Presbyter, District Superintendent, New York (1976–1996), North Syracuse, New York

M. Wayne Benson, Executive Presbyter, Assistant District Superintendent, Michigan, Pastor, First Assembly of God, Grand Rapids, Michigan

Dan Betzer, Executive Presbyter, Assistant District Superintendent, Peninsular Florida, Pastor, First Assembly of God, Fort Myers, Florida

Zenas J. Bicket, Ph.D., President, Berean University, Springfield, Missouri

Jeffrey Brawner, Pastor, Bonita Valley Christian Center, Bonita Valley, California

James K. Bridges, General Treasurer, The General Council of the Assemblies of God, Springfield, Missouri

Raymond T. Brock, Ed.D., Professional Christian Counselor, Tulsa, Oklahoma

John Bueno, Field Director, Latin America Assemblies of God, Springfield, Missouri

Warren D. Bullock, D.Min., District Superintendent, Northwest, Kirkland, Washington

Fulton W. Buntain, D.D., Pastor, First Assembly of God, Tacoma, Washington

Mark Burgund, Church Administrator, Calvary Church, Naperville, Illinois

G. Raymond Carlson, General Superintendent (1986–1993), The General Council of the Assemblies of God, Springfield, Missouri

Rob Carlson, Pastor, Bethany Christian Assembly of God, Everett, Washington

Nancie Carmichael, Author, Editor-at-Large, *Virtue,* Sisters, Oregon

David A. Cawston, Pastor, Christian Life Center Assembly of God, Bensalem, Pennsylvania

Glen D. Cole, D.D., District Superintendent, Northern California-Nevada, Santa Cruz, California

Michael D. Comer, Associate Pastor, First Assembly of God, Winston-Salem, North Carolina

Charles T. Crabtree, Assistant General Superintendent, The General Council of the Assemblies of God, Springfield, Missouri

Dennis A. Davis, President, Northwest Bible College, Kirkland, Washington

Jimmy Davis, D.Min., Evangelist/Evangelists Representative, The General Council of the Assemblies of God, Springfield, Missouri

Richard D. Dobbins, Ph.D., Founder and Director of EMERGE Ministries, Emerge Ministries, Akron, Ohio

Hal Donaldson, Editor, *Pentecostal Evangel,* Springfield, Missouri

Richard L. Dresselhaus, D.Min., Pastor, First Assembly of God, San Diego, California

Dick Eastman, D.D., International President, Every Home for Christ, Colorado Springs, Colorado

Paul Ferrin, President, The Ferrin Music Group, Inc., Colorado Springs, Colorado, Commissioner of Music, Assemblies of God, Springfield, Missouri

Richard B. Foth, Minister-at-Large to the Congressional and Diplomatic Communities of Washington, D.C., Arlington, Virginia

J. Don George, D.D., Pastor, Calvary Temple Assembly of God, Irving, Texas

Wayde I. Goodall, D.Min., National Coordinator, Ministerial Enrichment Office, Springfield, Missouri

Paul D. Goodman, District Superintendent, Montana, Billings, Montana

Dick Gruber, Associate Pastor, Bloomington Assemblies of God, Bloomington, Minnesota

Charles E. Hackett, Executive Director, Division of Home Missions of the Assemblies of God, Springfield, Missouri

Richard R. Hammar, J.D., LL.M., CPA, Legal Consultant, The General Council of the Assemblies of God, Springfield, Missouri

Scott Hagan, Pastor, Harvest Church Laguna Creek Assembly, Elk Grove, California

Randy Hurst, Evangelist, Springfield, Missouri

Charles Kelly, District Superintendent, North Carolina, Dunn, North Carolina

Robert W. Klingenberg, Evangelist, Caledonia, Michigan

Wayne Kraiss, President, Southern California College, Commissioner, Assemblies of God Christian Higher Education, Costa Mesa, California

Dale Lane, Associate Pastor, First Assembly of God, Phoenix, Arizona

William F. Leach, District Superintendent, Michigan, Farmington Hills, Michigan

H. Maurice Lednicky, D.D., President, Central Bible College, Springfield, Missouri

Donald Lichi, Ph.D., Vice-President and Director of Education, Emerge Ministries, Akron, Ohio

David Lim, D.Min., Pastor, Grace Assembly, Singapore

James D. Marocco, D.Min., Pastor, First Assembly of God, Kahului, Hawaii

Jerry G. McCamey, Pastor, Calvary Temple Assembly of God, Indianapolis, Indiana

Ronald F. McManus, D.Min., Pastor, First Assembly of God, Winston-Salem, North Carolina, Executive Presbyter (1993–1995)

J. Melvyn Ming, D. Min., Director of the Doctor of Ministry program and Professor of Church Leadership, Assemblies of God Theological Seminary, Springfield, Missouri

Jesse Miranda, D. Min., Executive Presbyter, Associate Dean, Urban and Multicultural Affairs of the C.P. Haggard Graduate School of Theology at Azusa Pacific University, Hacienda Heights, California

Ernest J. Moen, District Superintendent, Illinois (1984–1996), Carlinville, Illinois

David J. Moore, Secretary, Intercultural Ministries Department of the Division of Home Missions of the Assemblies of God, Springfield, Missouri

John M. Palmer, Pastor, First Assembly of God, Des Moines, Iowa

T. Ray Rachels, District Superintendent, Southern California, Irvine, California

E. Allen Ratta, Pastor, The Neighborhood Church, Bellevue, Washington

H. Robert Rhoden, D.Min., District Superintendent, Potomac, Fairfax, Virginia

Robert W. Rodgers, Pastor, Evangel Christian Life Center, Louisville, Kentucky

Bob Schmidgall, Pastor, Calvary Church, Naperville, Illinois, Executive Presbyter (1985–1996)

Dan Secrist, Pastor, Faith Assembly of God, Lacey, Washington

Robert H. Spence, Ph.D., President, Evangel College, Springfield, Missouri

Everett Stenhouse, Assistant General Superintendent (1986–1993), The General Council of the Assemblies of God, Rancho Mirage, California

Robert J. Strand, Pastor, Park Crest Assembly of God, Springfield, Missouri

Jerry A. Strandquist, Pastor, Bloomington Assemblies of God, Bloomington, Minnesota

Del Tarr, Ph.D., President, Assemblies of God Theological Seminary, Springfield, Missouri

Danny R. Thomas, Associate Pastor, First Assembly of God, Tacoma, Washington

Thomas E. Trask, General Superintendent, The General Council of the Assemblies of God, Springfield, Missouri

Loren Triplett, Executive Director, Division of Foreign Missions of the Assemblies of God, Springfield, Missouri

William O. Vickery, District Superintendent, Northern California/Nevada (1977–1991), Orangevale, California

Leslie E. Welk, Assistant District Superintendent, Northwest, Kirkland, Washington

Bill Wilson, Pastor, Portland Christian Center, Portland, Oregon

David A. Womack, Author, Springfield, Missouri

George O. Wood, D.Th.P., J.D., General Secretary, The General Council of the Assemblies of God, Springfield, Missouri

List of Abbreviations

BECK   —The New Testament in the Language of Today
              by William F. Beck

KJV   —King James Version

NASB   —New American Standard Bible

NIV   —New International Version

NKJV   —New King James Version

PHILLIPS   —Phillips Modern English

RSV   —Revised Standard Version

TLB   —The Living Bible

TAB   —The Amplified Bible

Unit 1

Priorities in the Pastor's Life

Introduction:
Priorities in the Pastor's Life

Thomas E. Trask

Keeping priorities in order is one of the greatest challenges pastors face. The heavy demands of the pastorate constantly pressure ministers to compromise their commitment to work, prayer, devotional life, families, and, at times, even to high moral standards.

Your priorities as a minister should be in this order: (1) your relationship with the Lord, (2) your spouse and children, and (3) your ministry and work. Look with me at some highlights of these three priorities:

Your relationship with the Lord. Your devotional life is absolutely critical. Years ago I asked the Lord to put me on a schedule, and He did. From 5:00 to 7:00 each morning I study the Bible and pray. I have carefully guarded this time—the most precious time of my day. My mother and father set the example by having early morning devotional times. Jesus' example was to pray in the first hours of the day. The psalmist David said, "My voice You shall hear in the morning, O Lord; In the morning I will direct it to You, And I will look up" (Psalm 5:3[1]). This discipline will affect everything you do.

Your relationship with your spouse and children. Some ministers get so busy they neglect the emotional, nurturing, and other needs of the family. Spouses and children can become bitter against the ministry—and even God—because the head of the home failed to minister to them. This is tragic. I determined long ago that I was not going to win everyone else's children to the Lord and lose my own. The Lord has helped Shirley and me in this priority. We have four beautiful children, and they all love God and are active in various ministries. Paul instructed Timothy, "If a man does not know how to rule his own house, how will he take care of the church of God?" (1 Timothy 3:5).

The work of the ministry. Ministers must work hard, keep focused on God's call, and function with the dynamic energy of the Holy Spirit. Paul described pastoral ministry in 1 and 2 Timothy and in Titus. As you refer to and live in these books, as you walk close to God and minister to the family He has given you, your ministry will be fulfilled with excellence.

Along with these primary personal priorities, there are secondary, but

Family VACATIONS!

PACE Self

still very important, ministry priorities. Ministers should observe these basics:

•*Give ample time to preaching God's Word.* When the people come together, they need to be fed from the Word. They are hungry for spiritual truth. As pastor, you are responsible to nourish them with a spiritually balanced diet. This means you must spend ample time in study and preparation. The early apostles understood this and determined, "'We will give ourselves continually to prayer and to the ministry of the word'" (Acts 6:4). The Bible tells us, "All Scripture is given by inspiration of God, and is profitable for doctrine, for reproof, for correction, for instruction in righteousness, that the man of God may be complete, thoroughly equipped for every good work" (2 Timothy 3:16–17).

> **Ministers have the privilege of helping laypeople find their places of ministry.**

•*Anything lasting in the church will come from prayer (and fasting).* God works in a church saturated in a spirit of prayer. D. L. Moody said, "Those who have left the deepest impression on this sin-cursed earth have been men and women of prayer. You will find that prayer has been the mighty power that has moved not only God but man."[2]

My wife and I recently attended a church whose bulletin listed numerous opportunities for prayer. No wonder this church has grown from sixty to six hundred fifty in six years. The pastor confirmed that their revival was birthed in prayer.

Fasting indicates intensity in prayer. A pattern of polite, three- to five-minute prayers will not suffice. But an intensity of prayer that sets aside the comforts and delicacies of life demonstrates the sincerity of the heart after God's own heart. Careful attention to spiritual disciplines will revolutionize a church.

•*The church must be involved in evangelism.* God designed and honors the principle of sowing and reaping—what you sow, you reap. Sowing requires some planting, or evangelism, tools such as radio, TV, literature, or door-to-door witnessing. While I pastored we witnessed door to door every Monday night year-round. God sent in people, because the church was involved in sowing.

•*The church must be involved in missions, both local and worldwide.* Missions is close to God's heart, for it means reaching the lost. God is not willing that any should perish. The church was not created to be a museum but a hospital—a soul-saving station. Therefore, opportunity must be given in every service for people to be saved at our altars. Don't assume everyone is saved or that no one is a backslider. Invitations are opportunities for people to respond to the gospel. This is critical. Demonstrate to the congregation that world missions is high in your priorities. Sponsor a missions convention. Have missionaries share in your services frequently. Give as much as you can.

•*Every church must have a discipleship program.* Discipleship is the training arm of the church. Jesus commanded, "'Go therefore and make disciples'" (Matthew 28:19). As revival energizes the body of Christ and the spiritual climate continues to rise, the need for training, teaching, and discipleship within the local church is urgent.

• *Train and involve laypeople in the work of the ministry.* Paul instructed those in leadership ministries to be continually involved in "equipping . . . the saints for the work of ministry" (Ephesians 4:12). God has placed His hand on the laity, and they want to be participants in what God is doing. The gifts of the Spirit (1 Corinthians 12 and 14) are not just for the clergy. "The manifestation of the Spirit is given to each one for the profit of all. . . . But one and the same Spirit works all these things, distributing to each one individually as He wills" (1 Corinthians 12:7,11). Ministers of the gospel have the privilege of helping laypeople find their places of ministry. Not everyone can sing in the choir, be an usher, or teach Sunday school, but there are other places of ministry. God never intended for anyone to sit and soak. He wants every member of the body of Christ involved in His kingdom work.

God has called you to this wonderful ministry of pastoring, and "'the Holy Spirit has made you overseers, to shepherd the church of God which He purchased with His own blood'" (Acts 20:28). God's sovereignty impacts your calling. When God asks us to do anything, He always gives the necessary gifts to accomplish His assignment. Understanding that brings tremendous rest.

Accountability Groups for Pastors

David Argue

The model Jesus gives us for ministry is timeless and complete. His call to those first pastors was "'Follow me'" (Matthew 8:22; 9:9). It was not esoteric. In reality, it was: "Come with me. 'Live My life.'"[1] Contemporary models for ministry are different. In training, we are heavy on the theoretical. We learn in classrooms or by self-study. We read, write, learn to speak, and become students of church polity and practice. Then we head out into actual ministry, stumbling through administration and the myriad of unexpected challenges before us. Slowly, our ability in ministry develops. Meanwhile, our personal lives tend to be just that—personal. We learn for a variety of reasons to separate personal life from ministry. And all of it—the public and the personal—is encountered largely alone.

Jesus' model for pastoral development is so different. His model includes eating with Him, foraging for a place to sleep, walking endless miles by His side, experiencing adulation and rejection with Him. All of ministry and the life surrounding it are processed together. Never are you without a colleague in ministry, even when Jesus is not physically present. To be with Him is to be asked great streams of probing questions: What do you see? Why are you thinking this? Where is your faith? How did you do? Yes, ministry development according to Jesus means a total life experience with continual accountability.[2]

Jesus knows that "each of us will give an account of himself to God" (Romans 14:12).. That truth, however, only seems to accentuate the need to prepare each day for that final examination. It is no surprise, then, to read that "when the apostles returned, they reported to Jesus what they had done" (Luke 9:10). *Reported* is from a word that means "to relate fully." It is plain. One could not remain hidden or unexamined while living next to the Son of God: Christ knew of Judas's motives and plans, confronted James and John about theirs, and continued, even after His ascension, to refine Peter. No wonder His pastors-in-training grew so strong and became so trustable. Just three years of that approach built people who, when infused by the power of the Holy Spirit, would continue to be changed—as well as change the world—for good.

Accountability is in the mix of what it means to be God's servant. Accountability means to be responsible, to give an account to others for life and ministry. The New Testament documents give at least nine major settings in which "mutually responsible relationships" are the explicit directive of God for His people in every station of life.[3] Accountability. Why do we need it?

1. Because "'the [natural] heart is deceitful above all things'" (Jeremiah 17:9) and the ego is inflatable (Galatians 6:3–4).
2. Because ministry is often discouraging (2 Corinthians 11:23–29; 2 Timothy 4:16) and is filled with complexity in every way (Philippians 1:22–24).
3. Because the enemy is on the prowl seeking to destroy (1 Peter 5:8).
4. Because the mysteries we proclaim need the clarifying light of dialogue (2 Peter 3:15–16; 2 John 12).

I find that the pressures and pace of ministry tend to propel me away from accountability rather than to it. My tendency as a pastor is to be pushed in the direction of living a less and less examined and accountable life. (An annual questionnaire for credential renewal does not really constitute accountability. In brief moments, another year of ministry is summed up, largely with Xs.) Eugene H. Peterson, a pastor for many years and now professor at Regent College in Vancouver, says it well:

> I don't know of any other profession in which it is quite as easy to fake it as in ours. By adopting a reverential demeanor, cultivating a stained-glass voice, slipping occasional words like "eschatology" into conversations. . . . not often enough actually to confuse people but enough to keep them aware that our habitual train of thought is a cut above the pew level—we are trusted, without any questions asked. . . . Even when in occasional

---

When Are You Most Likely to Face Temptation?[4]

- When you have not spent much time with God 81%
- When you have not had enough rest 57%
- When life is difficult 45%
- During times of change 42%
- After a significant spiritual victory 37%
- When life is going smoothly 30%

fits of humility or honesty we disclaim sanctity, we are not believed. If we provide a bare bones outline of pretence, they take it as the real thing and run with it, imputing to us clean hands and pure hearts.[5]

This is not Jesus' way of ministry. Accountability is Jesus' way. And if we follow Him, the rewards are overwhelming.

Accountability Groups

Accountability groups are in line for some of God's richest blessings. James promises us that when we confess our sins *to one another* healing will come (James 5:16). Jesus himself said He would be in the midst of persons who harmonize their lives; to such a group the greatest promise to answered prayer is given: "'Anything you ask for . . . will be done for you by my Father in heaven'" (Matthew 18:19). Through accountability, pastors avoid sin, strengthen character, deflect the discouragements of ministry, sharpen their grasp on truth, transform loneliness into friendship, manage grief, experience healing, energize faith, resolve problems, exchange ideas, stay balanced, expose and repulse specific attacks of the enemy, develop leadership, and keep ego in restraint. It is only when you get close enough to others that "as iron sharpens iron, so one man sharpens another" (Proverbs 27:17).[6]

Are you accountable? Who with regularity asks you probing, direct questions about your walk with Christ, your motivations, your resistance to temptation, your inner dialogue and imaginations? Who is truly representing the care and heart of Christ to you in ministry? You were not intended by God to minister alone. If married, your spouse can offer much to you in these dimensions, but there is a richness, strength, and purpose to be found in reaching beyond to brothers or sisters who walk in the same footsteps as you. Nearly all of the apostles, who give us the first model of accountability, were married. They were taught, however, to reach outside to colleagues for the additional strength and focus that come from that dimension of relationships.

Accountability is achieved only on purpose. It rarely ever "just happens"; it must be deliberately sought. It doesn't "just grow." When begun, it must be purposely cultivated. It demands priority, planning, the expenditure of energy and time. I have come to picture truly Christian accountability as five dimensions of activity that form a cycle of life.

Disclosure comes first. Disclosure means that I and every other person in the group work to become real with each other. I speak openly of my challenges, failures, hopes, disappointments, vision, and spiritual state. I speak of my family, my work, my fears, my strengths, my sins, my victories. I let the others in the group see me, just as I am. Dallas Willard, in his landmark book *The Spirit of the Disciplines,* writes of the process of disclosing to others: Disclosure nourishes "our faith in God's provision for our needs through

Accountability Questions Recommended by Charles Swindoll, Chuck Colson, Steve Farrar, and Others

1. Have you been with a woman this week in a way that was inappropriate or could have looked to others as if you were using poor judgment?

2. Have you been completely above reproach in all your financial dealings this week?

3. Have you exposed yourself to any sexually explicit material this week?

4. Have you spent daily time in prayer and in the Scriptures this week?

5. Have you fulfilled the mandate of your calling this week?

6. Have you just lied to me?

his people, our sense of being loved, and our humility before our brothers and sisters. . . . We lay down the burden of hiding and pretending, which normally takes up such a dreadful amount of human energy. . . . Nothing is more supportive of right behavior than open truth. Confession

ON CONFIDENTIALITY

If people are to open up their hearts and share their lives, not only out of their "perfection," but also out of their weaknesses, they must know that what they share will be treated with kindness and confidentiality. The group should agree to the following, clearly and up front, before opening up to one another.

1. You *cannot* share anything shared in the group with anyone outside the group. That means *anyone!*
2. You *can* share what you said about yourself to anyone outside the group. That is your information and does not cease to be yours whether you tell it in the group or out.
3. Should you desire to repeat a story or illustration from someone's sharing in the group, you must ask that person for *permission* to do so, no matter how much you think may disguise it. This holds true whether the testimony was positive or negative.
4. If something is shared in the group that constitutes a *grievous sin,* sin that is
   • continual, without lessening in force or frequency even in the clear light of

open confession and prayer, or
• acted out beyond temptations in the mind, or
• debilitating to ministry, or
• endangering to self and others
Then the person who shared such must be asked for permission to take the matter outside the group to find help. This permission should be gained before anyone outside the group is consulted in the matter.

Thus all know that they can confess their weaknesses and grow through forgiveness and encouragement without becoming the focus of judgment and gossip. Groups sharing must provide a climate of neither permissiveness nor betrayal, but one of truth and accountability *within the group.*

5. If an impasse is reached—in other words, a grievous sin is evident and the offending party will not allow it to be disclosed—then a higher law of commitment to truth and purity must prevail: Regardless of protest, to see the individual healed and restored, confidential disclosure must be made to someone who has direct responsibility for him or her.

alone makes deep fellowship possible, and the lack of it explains much of the superficial quality so commonly found in our church associations."[7] How many of our relationships as pastors are surface only, never drawing us forward into more of God? Accountability demands deep disclosure.
Enclosure is the second dimension of accountability. Enclosure means the group provides for the safety of all who disclose. Keeping confidences

is essential.[8] Acceptance, honest affirmation, gentleness in responses, and tangible commitment to help are all part of enclosure. As one in a group discloses, all others listen—really listen. We are not focused on what we will say in response. We are not mounting a defense for anything or anyone. Our focus is singular: to truly hear the message and the heart of the one who is sharing. As we listen, it may be time to "rejoice with those who rejoice," and it may as well be time to "mourn with those who mourn" (Romans 12:15).

Listening is a skill to be developed. It is easily lost by pastors who live in the continual environment of speaking and giving answers. Dietrick Bonhoeffer reminds us:

> He who can no longer listen to his brother will soon be no longer listening to God either; he will be doing nothing but prattle in the presence of God too. This is the beginnning of the death of the spiritual life, and in the end there is nothing left but spiritual chatter and clerical condescension arrayed in pious words. . . . It is the fellowship of the Cross to experience the burden of the other. If one does not experience it, the fellowship he belongs to is not Christian. If any member refuses to bear that burden he denies the law of Christ.[9]

The next dimension of accountability is prayer. Not brief, generalized, proper "closing" prayer, but prayer that captures the mosaic of life and speaks it clearly to God. It is prayer that carries the hurting in the group to the feet of Jesus. In prayer, time is given to develop and join faith. The promises of Matthew 18:19–20 can be seized now as firm ground to stand upon. Jesus truly stands among us and says, "Ask."

A fourth dimension of accountability is biblical truth. The Word of God in true accountability groups is not simply consulted in rather vague citations, but is opened and read, searched and examined. Accountability's appropriate goals come from sitting under the counsel of God's Word. All the words of the Book, both comforting and bracing, all the directions, both commonly held and uniquely striven for, are what is needed in accountability. Accountability demands the whole counsel of God. So from the Word steps are suggested for solution or response to the situations of life. It is the Word only that has the power to rebuke, reprove, correct, and instruct in every dimension of righteousness, so that we might be completely equipped (2 Timothy 3:16–17).

The final dimension in accountability is follow-up. When the group meets next time, reports are given on progress or frustrations. Jesus' kind of questions are asked, questions that draw all persons to actually give an account to the others of their lives.[10] Without this step, accountability is probably not occurring. Follow-up puts urgency and focus into place between the times the group meets. I know that I will give an account to my friends when we meet next. I am strengthened by that to act. If in the next session I have not progressed, the cycle can be run again on the same issue but at a deeper level: more complete disclosure, more intense prayer, more pointed searching of the Word. When there is progress and victory, I can open up new areas of my life for growth.

Questions That Encourage Disclosure

SPIRITUAL LIFE

1. Describe your time in the Word now and what you are learning. How frequently do you get alone with God during the week? For how long? Does this match your expectations and hopes?
2. Describe your current prayer life in reference to time, regularity, scope of prayer, and the realized presence of God as you pray. Do you live in the presence of God?
3. Describe what you sense of the anointing of the Holy Spirit on your life and ministry now. In other words, do you sense that Jesus is at work through you in tangible ways?
4. Describe where you are now in sharing your faith with those who do not know Jesus.
5. How are you following the directives: "Covet earnestly the best gifts" (1 Corinthians 12:31, KJV) and "Stir up the gift of God which is in you" (2 Timothy 1:6, NKJV)? When was the last time that you prophesied?
6. Fasting is an important spiritual discipline. Describe this dimension in your life now.

FAMILY LIFE

7. Describe the nature of your relationships now with wife and children. Include both the growth of relationships and the development of spiritual strengths.
8. What spiritual goals do you have for your family? Where are you in walking towards them?
9. What do you do as a family just for the fun of it? When did you do that last?

10. If nothing changes regarding your marriage/family relationships from this point, will you be satisfied that all will turn out well?

PROFESSIONAL/PERSONAL LIFE

11. How are you managing your time? What are your limits and how are you working with priorities, demands, pressures?
12. The fruit of the Spirit is love, joy, peace, patience, kindness, goodness, faithfulness, gentleness, meekness and self-control. What are the two strongest ones for you now? The two weakest?
13. What are your developing points in ministry now? What do you desire God to develop in you during the next month?
14. What are you reading currently? What are your learning points now?
15. How is your physical well-being? What are you doing to manage stress, weight, and age?
16. How has the enemy tried to attack you since our last meeting? How have you responded?
17. Talk about your life as a steward of the resources God has given you. How are you doing in the battle against greed, envy, and materialism? Are you walking in faith in the area of finances?
18. Are you discipling anyone at this time? Describe.
19. If God were to show up personally and say, "What can I do for you right now?" what would that be?
20. What is your vision for the next 5 years of your life?[11]

The Cycle of Accountability

In the following diagram, the full cycle of accountability is illustrated. The descriptives of the five major dimensions illustrate the inadequate (even potentially harmful) groups that result when all dimensions of true Christian accountability are not in place. For instance,

Disclosure alone often leads to great harm in the betrayal of confidences—a gossip group.

Disclosure + Enclosure (only) can result in a psychological support group that may "feel good" but will probably not lead to any significant change or growth.

Disclosure + Enclosure + Prayer (only) produces a prayer support group, but an uneven pattern of growth.

Disclosure + Enclosure + Prayer + Biblical Truth brings persons to the place of true growth but fail to close the loop and allow persons the essential dynamic that Christ calls us all to—accountability.

CHRISTIAN ACCOUNTABILITY
A Five-dimensional Cycle

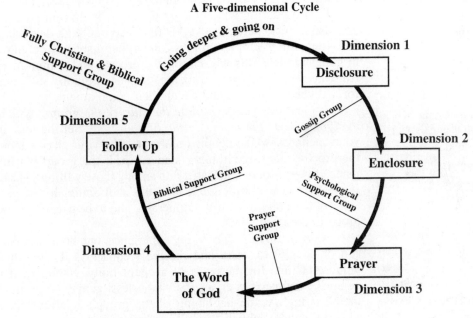

Getting Started—Some Directions

1. *Make the commitment to do it.* Don't allow this reading to be just informative. From this day on, determine that you will live out actual accountability in your life. The time to begin is now, no matter your age or stage in life and ministry.

2. *Ask God to help you find the persons to enter into accountability with.* Look for persons with an open heart, a keen desire to walk with Christ, and an ability to keep confidences. Will this group be exclusively pastors? Exclusively within one denominational setting? Exclusively married couples or just men or women? Answers to these questions affect the function of the group significantly.

Hedges for Moral Protection

Jerry Jenkins

Hedge #1: **Whenever I need to meet or dine or travel with an unrelated woman, I make it a threesome. Should an unavoidable last-minute complication make this impossible, my wife hears it from me first.**

Hedge #2: **I am careful about touching. While I might shake hands or squeeze an arm or a shoulder in greeting, I embrace only dear friends or relatives, and only in front of others.**

Hedge #3: **If I pay a compliment, it is on clothes or hairstyle, not on the person herself. Commenting on a pretty outfit is much different, in my opinion, from telling a woman she is pretty.**

Hedge #4: **I avoid flirtation or suggestive conversation, even in jest.**

Hedge #5: **I remind my wife often—in writing and verbally—that I remember my wedding vows: "Keeping you only unto me for as long as we both shall live."**

Hedge #6: **From the time I get home from work until my children go to bed, I do no writing or office work. This gives me lots of time with my family and time for my wife and me to continue to court and date.**[12]

Groups I have functioned in have required persons to travel for hours to meet. Reasonable distance is not an obstacle if the composition factors are right. As to group size, the group should be larger than two individuals or two couples but not so large as to curtail a person's opportunity to speak. Three couples or three to four individuals seems to work well (see endnote 10).

3. *Contact the persons, share this information with them, and indicate your desire for accountability.* Ask them to pray and then meet with you for a lengthy session to explore together the potentials.

4. *Hold the first meeting in a place that allows privacy and flexibility.* A restaurant is not a good choice, nor a church office, nor a home with children present. Find a place away from interruptions, noise, and scrutiny. If you must meet in a home, turn on the answering machine and turn off the phone's ringer to avoid interruptions. Spend time in the first meeting defining vision and coming to consensus on confidentiality. (See "On Confidentiality.") Decide how often the group will meet, and set a trial period during which the group can grow in transparency and also test its chemistry. At this first meeting, set a date when the group will assess its progress and either disband or commit to going further. This will clarify the process and commitment from the very start. Three to six meetings are normally sufficient for everyone to discern and weigh their commitment.

5. *If God uses you to initiate the start of the group, assume that you will be the leader at the first meeting.* Set the tone in your openness. Make people comfortable by your clarity about the process. As to continuing leadership, if the group is truly made of peers, rotate the leadership among those willing to lead. If one person is always the leader, this will diminish that person's opportunity to be truly vulnerable and to be carried by the group to the Lord's feet.

6. *Allow plenty of time.* In my experience, one hour (per person or couple) to share and receive feedback is the minimal amount of time for the cycle of accountability. Naturally, if a person or couple is in crisis, the whole session may be given to their sharing. At the beginning of the group's relationship, a longer time to establish strong foundations will pay immediate and wonderful dividends. Continuity calls for at least a monthly group meeting.

7. *Get to disclosure.* Accountability groups are part of a long journey. People will experiment with openness. Most of us move slowly into vulnerability—clamlike, opening slowly and shutting quickly if poked or betrayed. Don't give up too soon on anyone. Be patient. Provide lots of enclosure. An excellent way to begin is to allow each person to share his or her life and spiritual history. Questions that probe and push toward growth are listed on page 24; let them provide extra nerve for a group leader to heighten disclosure. Everyone should answer a question if it

is asked. All must be on equal footing.

8. *Go full cycle.* The group must be called to the Word. Open it up and read. Encourage others to do the same. The Psalmist wrote: "Your statutes are wonderful; therefore I obey them. The unfolding of your words give light; it gives understanding to the simple" (Psalm 119:129–130). Engage in prayer as often as the Spirit sensitizes you to the need; never let it be perfunctory or formal. This is the place to bear your hearts to God and agree together.

9. *Encourage prayer support between sessions.* It is helpful to sketch a note or two concerning what others have shared so that you can keep track of it for prayer between meetings and follow-up at the next meeting. A person serving as secretary in the group is most helpful in this process. Remember, it is this step that brings the group into full accountability.

As I write these closing words, the impact of my meeting with our accountability group three days ago lingers. There are three couples in our group. The men are all senior pastors, with involvements far beyond our churches in the life of our fellowship. The women are all invested deeply in ministry as well. It was our third monthly meeting. For over three hours we shared about family, trials, our search for more of God, our deep inner struggles. We complained and cajoled. We exploded in laughter at times, and then at other times we wiped tears.

As the session ended, I reflected with wonder on how much the Spirit of God had been present with us. Tangibly present. Each of us had been rejuvenated. Each of us had been used of God to speak into each other's lives. We left with fresh insight and resolve. We had been made stronger (again) through accountability. The date of our next meeting is already set.

"Live My life" is still His call. Arise, embark on the journey.

The Pastor and His Devotional Life

Leslie E. Welk

The pastor, as one expected to minister to others, must first and foremost be ministered to by God. One's personal devotional life, time spent with God, will determine the true height and depth of one's ministry.

An admirable goal for the pastor is to have an identity akin to Peter's and John's in Acts 4:13. Crowds marveled at the confidence of these uneducated and untrained men but "recognize[d] them as having been with Jesus."[1] These spiritual leaders had spent time with God, and it showed.

The English word *devotion* is defined by words like "consecration," "dedication," and "zeal." In fact, Noah Webster's 1828 edition of the *American Dictionary of the English Language* defined "devotion" largely in religious terms. Webster further described devotion as "a solemn attention to the Supreme Being in worship; a yielding of heart and affections to God, with reverence, faith and piety, in religious duties, particularly in prayer and meditation."[2] For every believer, and particularly for the pastor, devotion means daily concentration on the Scriptures and prayer. A disciplined devotional life is an intensely personal matter, and we dare not relegate it to a routine professional requirement. Before we are pastors, we are children of God, individually accountable and in need of daily spiritual nourishment. As pastors we soon learn that feeding the flock of God requires that we first be diligent students of the Word. Even so, one of the great pitfalls for the full-time Christian worker is to allow personal study time to substitute for personal devotional time. To do so can be likened to spending all week preparing a gourmet feast for invited guests without taking any time to sit down for nourishment yourself.

To help differentiate between these two approaches to God's Word, I have employed what I call the "two-chair method." Typically the chair behind my desk has served as a study chair, a counselor's chair, an administrator's chair. From this chair, people are encouraged and sermons are prepared. The chair is conveniently close to books, notepads, the telephone, and the computer. On the other hand, I have selected a different chair in my office, sometimes an entirely different location, to host my personal devotions. Each purpose is distinct, each place is distinct. Shifting between the different places reminds me of the differences between personal study and private devotions.

Pastoral Devotions "Psalm 42 Style"

Psalm 42 captures the craving of the heart of the spiritually passionate pastor. Though desiring to serve, the pastor realizes that service is not possible before meeting with the One who feeds and waters his own soul. "As the deer pants for the water brooks, So my soul pants for Thee, O God. My soul thirsts for God, for the living God; when shall I come and appear before God?" (Psalm 42:1–2). The craving of a thirsty deer for water vividly pictures the intensity of the relationship God desires. Just as thirst drives the deer to the brook, so our hunger to hear from God drives us to personal devotion and the fountain of spiritual life that flows from it. The pastor who longs no more for intimacy with God is one whose heart has grown cold. Such coldness will inevitably manifest itself in his personal and private life.

The Sons of Korah are given credit for authoring the Scripture song we call "Psalm 42." They were priests from the tribe of Levi who were "over the work of the service, keepers of the thresholds of the tent; and their fathers had been over the camp of the Lord, keepers of the entrance" (1 Chronicles 9:19). Like modern-day pastors, these priests were particularly vulnerable to being overtaken by the tasks and duties of the day.

After all, they were responsible for making sure the doors of the church were opened!

It is also noteworthy that the spiritual heritage of the Sons of Korah was nothing short of tempestuous. It was Korah and two hundred fifty other leaders who rebelled against Moses (Numbers 16). Convinced that he had gone too far in his leadership of the congregation, they chose to assert themselves. Moses, not to be intimidated, felt the Korahites had gone too far. Somewhere between their routine daily service and their rebellious pursuit of influence and control the Korahites had drifted away from God. Moses wisely suggested that the Lord should be allowed to show who was truly near to Him. The Lord's anger was unleashed against the Korahites, and the earth opened up to swallow them along with all of their possessions.

Now imagine such a heritage in your family tree and you will begin to understand the unique perspective of the Sons of Korah. Psalm 42 reflects the frustration and longing that comes with walking at a distance from the very God they hoped to serve. Korah's descendants yearned for a closeness to God they had not felt for some time. That was the sort of craving that prompted the writing of Psalm 42, the deer panting for the fresh stream.

Fostering Vulnerability

King Saul wanted David's life, but David had found security and shelter in a mountain retreat called Engedi (1 Samuel 23:29). *Engedi* means "spring of the kid." The name came from the fact that Engedi was a common watering place for the ibex, a surefooted member of the mountain goat family with an appearance and habits much like a deer.[3]

The ibex found a home in the rocky hills of the desert wilderness near the Dead Sea. No predator could negotiate the rocky crags and hills like the ibex. There it found refuge from hunters who prized its skin, horns, and meat. The mountains were its "comfort zone." However, as the desert oases dried up with the coming of the hot weather, the ibex was forced to find other vegetation and water. This would drive the animal to the hills above the Engedi springs which flowed with life-giving water.

When the thirst of the ibex became acute it would pick its way down from the security of the hills to water—and a far more vulnerable place. For centuries, hunters have known that these prized animals choose early morning to move from higher ground to the springs. At first light, hunters would lie in wait for that opportune moment when the wary ibex came to the water's edge and stooped to drink. In that most vulnerable moment the arrow would fly. The ibex became quite familiar with the stalking of the hunter. It knew it jeopardized its life each time it stole a drink from that spring. Nonetheless, its craving for water forced its becoming absolutely vulnerable. Such vulnerability is precisely what God asks of us.

Just as the deer pants for the water, the man or woman who would drink from God's fountain is driven to pursuing it at all costs, even at high risk. As thirsty followers of Jesus, we are committed to making daily prayer and meditation upon God's Word a first priority. Such pursuit of God is a regular confession of our absolute need of Him. In turn, we open ourselves to His examination at the point of our greatest vulnerability. In such surrender we will draw nearer to God.

Scheduling Time with God

As pastors we must realize that if we do not control our calendars, they will control us. Thus, it becomes necessary to schedule daily devotional time. There is no law specifying when personal time with God should be taken during the course of a day. (Of course, crisis seasons will occur, when we are driven to seek God in private devotion morning, noon, and night!) The greater issue is making certain that time is spent—and spent regularly.

Many have found the early morning watering habits of the deer a preferable model. David seemed to express that conviction when he said, "In the morning, O Lord, Thou wilt hear my voice; In the morning I will order my prayer to Thee and eagerly watch" (Psalm 5:3). It does seem logical that before we tackle each day's events we would draw strength for them by giving priority to our relationship with Jesus.

E. M. Bounds authored a classic on the preacher and prayer, *Power through Prayer.* It is one of those books worth reading and rereading over the years. Bounds had a conviction about seeking God early in the day and expressed it strongly: "The men who have done the most for God in this world have been early on their knees. He who fritters away the early morning, its opportunity and freshness, in other pursuits other than seeking God will make poor headway seeking Him the rest of the day."[4]

The Pastor's Devotional Life and Accountability

Do you struggle with the self-discipline required to maintain a consistent devotional life? Perhaps part of the solution will be found in greater levels of accountability with others who face the same challenge.

Certainly our spouses can help in holding us accountable for maintaining proper priorities in our lives, devotional life included. The husband and wife are well positioned when it comes to discerning whether each other's spiritual life is in order. Formalize being accountable, giving your spouse permission to address this critical area of your devotion to God. This will open a door for the Lord to use our spouses in holding us more accountable. One form this may take is for husbands and wives to enter into a more consistent prayer and meditation time together. Sharing devotionally as husband and wife not only provides accountability in our relationship to God, but it enhances marital bonds as well.

I was gleaning from the wisdom and experience of a veteran pastor one day and posed the question, "Looking back on your life and ministry, what three things would you change if you could do it all over again?" His answer was quick and sure, indicating that this was a subject he had thought about long before I had posed it formally. He said, "I would spend more time with Jesus. I would spend more time with my wife. I would spend more time with my children." Obviously, experience had taught him the lasting value in making a priority of these relationships. Besides, have you ever met anyone who in looking back felt that he had devoted *too much* time to God or family?

Another helpful source of accountability is other ministers who face the common challenge of sorting through priorities. Paul reminds us, "No temptation has overtaken you but such as is common to man" (1 Corinthians 10:13). We walk this path together and we can learn from the mistakes and victories of trusted friends.

Several years ago it was my privilege to be part of a self-initiated accountability group comprising six or seven area pastors from our fellowship. We would commit time from our busy calendars, lock ourselves away in a conference room of a local motel, and spend the day together. We would unburden our hearts, laugh, fellowship in the Word, build relationships, and pray.

We found strength in historic models like John and Charles Wesley. They had learned the value of accountability early in their ministerial pursuits. To assist them in the discipline of their spiritual lives they joined with eight or nine other dedicated seminarians at Oxford University. So steadfast were they in their commitments to the Lord and each other that the group became known as the "Holy Club."[5]

Those "lockdowns" with colleagues were some of the most worthwhile days I ever spent. I discovered that others struggled as I did, but that with God and each other we could find victory! Members of that group have gone separate directions, and those days are sorely missed. However, distance has not watered down the friendships, and I still feel a certain level of accountability to the members of that fraternity.

Dawson Trotman, founder of The Navigators, is another classic model of one who valued the role friends played in his exemplary life of prayer and memorization of the Word. At times his friends could not keep pace, but "Daws," as he was affectionately known, was relentless. One friend shared his memory of Daws: "He was always trying to get other young fellows to pray with him. Most of them lasted a few days or weeks. Then they would get tired. He would come to my house and throw a rock in the window to wake me up so I would go pray with him. One morning I threw the rock back out and went back to sleep. This was the only time I saw him disgusted because he believed so definitely in Matthew 18:19, the power of two praying together."[6]

Devotional Tools for the Pastor

We live in a time when resources to assist with a personal devotional life are abundant. Of course, the list of essentials is short: a person, a Bible, and the Lord. These elements must always be present to ensure devotional success.

However, there are certainly other tools that serve to bring freshness and variety into one's devotional life in God's Word and prayer. Here is but a short list of tools and ideas that may bring discipline to the pastor's devotional life.

1. Use a "One Year Bible," with its systematic daily reading plan, to keep a consistent pace.
2. Keep a personal prayer and devotional journal.

3. Include in your reading proven devotional books that lead you through Scripture and scriptural themes. Visit and revisit classic devotional books like E. M. Bounds's *Power through Prayer* or Oswald Chambers's *My Utmost for His Highest.*
4. Augment devotions by reading biographies of spiritual models and giants.
5. Employ methods like those found in Dick Eastman's material on a disciplined prayer life.
6. Reward yourself for achieving consistency in daily devotional habits by giving yourself a prize.
7. Hold yourself accountable to others.
8. Redeem driving time by listening to the Bible on cassette.
9. Acknowledge the benefits and rewards of devotion.

The Rewards of a Disciplined Devotional Life

Pastors are exposed to more than their share of human experience. We run the risk of cynically concluding with Solomon, "I have seen all the works which have been done under the sun, and behold, all is vanity and striving after wind" (Ecclesiastes 1:14). Perhaps we have seen too much. The innocence and enthusiasm with which we once ministered in the Spirit is waning. Do we cringe, are we defensive, when members of the flock comment on our apparent spiritual dryness while at the same time mentally acknowledging the absence of spiritual devotion in our lives? The craving of our hearts for God may no longer be as intense as the panting of the deer for water.

There are many rewards for faithfully pursuing God, not the least of which is giving God the opportunity to freshly anoint us. Rather than the cynicism of Solomon, we must embrace the hope and vision of Isaiah: "Do not call to mind the former things, or ponder things of the past. Behold, I will do something new, Now it will spring forth; will you not be aware of it?" (Isaiah 43:18–19).

Rewards that come with consecration to God may not be immediate, but they are certain. The promise of God concerning Kingdom investments is that "he who sows sparingly shall also reap sparingly; and he who sows bountifully shall also reap bountifully" (2 Corinthians 9:6). Deferred dividends are often the most profitable anyway!

In 1924 the United States was advancing an eight-oared crew to compete in the Paris Olympic games. They were considered certain winners of the gold medal. One of the crew members was Benjamin Spock, who would later become known as America's foremost baby doctor. Another crewman was Bill Havens of Arlington, Virginia. In addition to being in the eight-man event, Havens was also favored in the single and four-man events.

However, just a few months before the Olympic team was to leave for Paris, Havens discovered that his wife was pregnant. It was welcome news, but the athlete was immediately faced with a life-changing decision. The Havens' baby was due sometime during the two-week span that Bill was scheduled to be in Paris for the long-awaited Olympic event. After consulting with family and friends, all of whom encouraged him to go to Paris, he concluded that in the best interest of his wife and soon-to-be family he would stay home. On August 1, 1924, Frank Havens was born, a proud father at his bedside.

Bill Havens pondered his decision for years to come, wondering if it was the right one. After all, his lifetime dream of standing atop the medal-winner's platform at the Olympic Games was never realized. It would be thirty years before Havens would know he had made the best decision. A telegram from Helsinki, Finland, in 1952 confirmed it: "Dear Dad, Thanks for waiting around for me to get born in 1924. I'm coming home with the gold medal you should have won. Your Loving Son, Frank." Frank Havens had just won the gold medal in the singles 10,000 meters canoeing event.[7]

What a compelling example of deferred blessing! Bill Havens' story is Ecclesiastes 11:1 brought forward to modern times: "Cast your bread on the surface of the waters, for you will find it after many days."

Remember, many will look to your pastoral example for strength to follow God in their own devotional life. I will always cherish memories of significant people, like parents and senior pastors, who mentored me in ministry, who were faithful in seeking God each day. One of the reassuring sounds I would meet each morning upon arriving at the church as a youth pastor was the echo of my senior pastor's voice crying to God in prayer. It was an inspirational sound I will not soon forget.

Time spent in devotion to the Lord and His Word become the springboard from which spiritual initiatives are launched in our personal lives and ministry. Some today. Some tomorrow. As the deer pants for the water brook, so our souls long after the only One who can refresh our thirst!

The Pastoral Marriage

Raymond T. Brock

A primary method of presenting the gospel of Jesus Christ to the world is through the marriage of a pastoral couple. Paul tells us in Ephesians 5:32 that Christian marriage was designed by God to reveal to the world the mysterious relationship between Christ and the church. No marriage in the congregation is more important than the pastoral marriage in communicating this message—not only to believers, but to unbelievers as well. At the end of 1994, there were 31,300 credentialed ministers of the Assemblies of God. Of this number 84.8 percent were male and 15.2 percent were female. Senior pastors and credentialed church staff members accounted for 53.2 percent of ministerial assignments. Of these credentialed ministers, 89.2 percent were married, 5.9 percent were single (never married), 4.1 percent were widowed, and 0.9 percent were divorced and not remarried. At that time there were 11,144 male and 341 female senior pastors.[1]

Created for Relationships

Solomon discovered a truth that is as real today as it was three thousand years ago: "He who finds a wife finds what is good and receives favor from the Lord" (Proverbs 18:22). In addition he emphasized the importance of monogamy in marriage (Proverbs 5:18–23; Ecclesiastes 9:9), and David extolled the joys of having children who are the product of love in the marital relationship (Psalm 127:5). The Bible begins by telling us that God in relationship—Father, Son, and Holy Spirit—created man and woman to live in relationship with each other and with Him (Genesis 1:26–27). Both reflected the glory of God. Man was created first (Genesis 2:7), followed by the woman who was taken from the side of the man (Genesis 2:21–23). Woman was created because God declared: "'It is not good for the man to be alone. I will make a helper suitable for him [a helper to meet his needs]'" (Genesis 2:18).

What need did Adam have that he could not handle in the utopian Garden of Eden with its perfectly balanced ecosystem and toxic-free atmosphere? Loneliness! Loneliness was the first emotion Adam had that he could not handle. This does not mean that every adult must be married, but it does encourage marriage, especially for pastors. Singles also live in relationship with their friends and family members who embellish their lives.

> **The pastoral marriage presents the gospel to the world.**

Even though God came in the cool of the evening to converse with Adam, he needed someone like himself—another human being—with whom to communicate during the day. Woman was not created to be a sex object; rather, she was created to be a nurturing listener and active communicator. So important was this relationship that the newly created couple were instructed to teach their children to leave father and mother and cleave to each other for as long as they both lived (Genesis 2:24). This command is so important that it is repeated both in the Gospels (Matthew 19:5; Mark 10:7) and the Epistles (Ephesians 5:31). It is noteworthy that the relationship from the very beginning was a transparent one; they had nothing to hide (Genesis 2:25) until they tuned God out of their relationship and focused on the voice of Satan (Genesis 3:1–10). Living in relationships as human beings and with God is three dimensional. Jesus emphasized this in all four Gospels, the most complete description being in Mark 12:30–31: "'Love the Lord your God with all your heart and with all your soul and with all your mind and with all your strength.' The second [commandment] is this: 'Love your neighbor as yourself.' There is no commandment greater than these."

LOVE GOD

The way Jesus said to love God involves the whole person. In all of literature there is no more complete description of the human personality than this commandment. The passage Jesus was quoting (Deuteronomy 6:5) did not include the word *mind*. The Old Testament used the word *heart* to include all cognitive skills because the Hebrew language viewed man as a whole entity, a *nephesh* ("a living being").

Between Moses and Christ came the Greek philosophers who altered the thinking of the Western world from wholeness to dichotomies. They could not conceive all cognitive functions to be explained by the single word *heart*, so they created the word *mind* as the flip side of the heart concept. Using contemporary terms, the Greeks viewed heart as input and mind as output in the thinking process. Jesus was not altering the words of Moses; He was only explaining the Great Commandment in colloquial terms. Paul did the same thing in Philippians 4:7. As Jesus used it, *heart* involves the cognitive domain, which includes intelligence, knowledge, learning, and memory (Psalm 119:11,105). *Soul* involves the affective domain, which includes emotions and feelings (Psalms 25:1; 40:8). *Mind* also involves the cognitive domain but has more to do with wisdom and the application of knowledge (James 4:17). *Strength* has to do with the psychomotor domain and with behavior and actions (Ecclesiastes 9:10).

LOVE YOURSELF

This is not a narcissistic love of self or self-love, as some have taught, but a genuine accepting of yourself as a creation of God. The only way we can love our neighbor adequately is to allow the love of God to show us who we are in Christ Jesus and let His love flow through us to them.

LOVE YOUR NEIGHBOR

In marriage, our closest neighbor is our spouse. Beyond our personal relationship with God, our spouse is to be given first priority in our lives. Then come our children followed by the extended family. Our love for the church and community radiates out from our core love for God. As waves move in concentric circles from the spot where a pebble is dropped into a pool, so our love for God's creation expands. God never intended for the work of the church to get ahead of our walk with Him, which includes our loving God as well as loving our spouse and family.

Planning for Marriage

It is of vital importance for a person who feels called to Christian ministry—pastor, evangelist, missionary, or specialized service—to be extremely careful in selecting a spouse. In dating, the prospective pastor must be careful to date only those persons who are not only born-again Christians and filled with the Holy Spirit, but also have committed their life to following the Lord wherever He calls. It is also essential to be open to either home or foreign service, depending on the leadership of the Holy Spirit to the couple.[2]

Pastoral ministry begins with a personal call to ministry and requires preparation for Christian service. Half a century ago formal education was not as important as it is today. In the early part of the twentieth century, many men were called from the farm or factory into full-time ministry. They studied the Bible by night and worked by day. They prepared sermons on their knees under kerosene lamps and depended on the anointing of the Holy Spirit to inspire them as they delivered the Word of God extemporaneously. In the middle of the century the demands of ministry changed drastically. Congregations became more sophisticated and demanded more of their pastor. Preaching without notes was no longer acceptable. Preaching from the back of the *Thompson Chain-Reference Bible* was no longer tolerated. Evidence of a thorough biblical knowledge and theological training were expected, and in some cases demanded (2 Timothy 2:15; 3:15–17). Forward-thinking educators of the Assemblies of God saw the trend coming and by the 1920s were offering Bible classes in their churches. These grew into Bible institutes and then Bible colleges which now are the foundation of seminary programs preparing ministers for a broad scope of Christian ministries.

While preparing for the ministry, attention may be appropriately given to considering who will be the love for a lifetime. But a couple should consider the stress that early marriage can place on a family and an educational program. Having been involved in Christian higher education in the Assemblies of God for more than forty years, I am convinced that those who marry before graduation place an extra burden on their young marriage. Those who begin their family before they can devote adequate time to bonding with and nurturing their children are spreading themselves too thin for effective parenting. In my opinion, planning a wedding to coincide with graduation followed immediately by moving to a new ministerial assignment is extremely risky. It increases stress units to extreme proportions, for each of these events is a major stressor in life. Graduation first, then marriage or moving to the first ministerial position in either order, but both should not come within the same six-month period.

Modeling Marriage for the Congregation

There are many ways of ministering to a congregation and community. None, however, is more effective than the pastoral marriage that exemplifies to the world the mystical relationship between Christ and the Church (Ephesians 5:29–33). Paul gives the divine order of relationships in a Christian marriage. In Ephesians 5:21, the husband and wife are commanded to be mutually submissive to each other. In the rest of the chapter the husband is enjoined to initiate love to his wife and she is to submit (respond) voluntarily to his love.

The Christian husband (pastor or layman) is to love his wife as much as Christ loved the Church, extending to her the last ounce of blood and the last burst of energy if necessary. He is to give her all the privileges (material and temporal) he takes for himself (Ephesians 5:23–29). The Greek word for love in these passages is *agape,* which Donald M. Joy describes as "'targeted affection,' in which the person deliberately chooses whom to love. This is why only *agape* can be commanded. All other loves, *eros, philia,* and *storge,* are spontaneous and situated in the context of particular relationships."[3] As "head of [his] wife" (Ephesians 5:23), what does a Christian husband do? In the human anatomy, the head performs four functions: sensation, perception, cognition, and communication.

Sensation is the first function of headship. In marriage, the husband is to be sensitive to the needs of the "body" (wife and children), which means they must keep him apprised of what is going on in the family. This means no conspiracy of silence or collusion between the mother and children to keep secrets from the husband/father.

Perception involves understanding the sensations received from the body and putting them into proper perspective. Information from past experiences, current circumstances, and possible outcomes in the future are brought into focus. Then the husband has the information he needs to make a decision.

Cognition is the process of making a decision for the benefit of the family. The husband does not make decisions for his own comfort or convenience. His decisions are made for the benefit of his wife and the family.

Communication completes the cycle. Having responded to the sensations and perceptions necessary for cognition, the husband then communicates to the wife and children what he believes is most appropriate for the family. As such, he takes the initiative in communicating to the family and gives them the information and encouragement they need to enjoy the benefits of a Christ-centered marriage and family. Then the husband is appropriately the head of the house as Christ is the head of the Church.

> **"The student who marries before graduation places an extra burden on the young marriage."**

From the example of Jesus, we know He became sensitive to the needs of a lost humanity. He knew or perceived that we were lost and on our way to a devil's hell. So, a decision (cognition) was made in heaven: God not only loved the world so much He gave His only Son, but Jesus loved us so much that He came and gave His life for our salvation (John 3:16–17). The cross stands as the symbol of this communication of the love of God and His Son for us. It is this knowledge that makes the headship of the husband in the home both practical and spiritual.

Donald Joy says of the headship of the husband in Christian marriage:

> The word *kephale* which gets translated "head" has a primary meaning of "source of life or strength, or origin." So, in Colossians 1:18, Christ "is the head of the body, the church." In Colossians 2:19, Christ is the source of life who nourishes the church. In Ephesians 4:15, we are to "grow up into him who is the Head, that is, Christ." Paul sets the record straight; neither man nor woman is independent of each other. While Eve is formed from Adam, so Adam is born of Eve. And everything comes from (is derived from) God (1 Corinthians 11:11–12).[4]

Just as the husband as the head in Christian marriage is the initiator of love, so the wife is to submit or respond voluntarily and spontaneously with love to those initiatives of her husband. She becomes the recipient of the benefits derived from God's divine order of relationships. This submission is not to be forced, faked, or passive; it is to be voluntarily as unto the Lord. So Paul concludes the matter: "Let every one of you in particular so love his wife even as himself; and the wife see that she reverence her husband" (Ephesians 5:33). It is interesting that God commanded children to obey their parents and to honor them. But, where do children learn honor? From parents who are honorable. And, what is the promise to the children who honor their parents? Long life!

Wayne Warner, editor of *Heritage* magazine, made a study of longevity among ministers of the Assemblies of God. He found that as of August 24, 1995, the number of ministers age 90 or over totaled 215, the oldest being 104. In the previous fifteen-year period, 16 ministers had been 100 years old or older at the time of their death.[5] Could extended life be another way the pastoral pair witnesses to the world the benefits of a biblical marriage?

Developing Intimacy

Intimacy begins in dating, develops during courtship, matures in engagement, but does not become complete until marriage.[6]

Geographical intimacy begins as a young couple considers the influence their geographical heritage has on their marital expectations. Dating allows them to examine these differences and to consider what changes will need to be made before they "leave" and "cleave" as commanded in Genesis 2:24 (KJV).

Recreational intimacy develops as hobbies, recreations, and leisure-time activities are explored. The more the couples have in common in their dating, the easier it will be for them to enjoy their leisure time in their later years.

Intellectual intimacy involves the blending of two mental worlds in which the couple learn how to respect each other's intellectual gifts and discover how to share good books, literature, and poetry.

Aesthetic intimacy is the ability to share the world of beauty with its symmetry and form and allows the couple to share the world of art, music, and nature.

Emotional intimacy develops as the courting couple share feelings on a deep level and develop trust. They learn to laugh together as well as communicate honestly when sad, angry, or disappointed.

Spiritual intimacy continues to develop in courtship as the young couple read the Bible together, pray together, attend church together, and become involved in active Christian service activities. Both must be committed to God as the organizing basis of their relationship and to His Word for establishing their priorities, especially in any disagreements.

Financial intimacy comes as the courting or engaged couple learn to delay gratification and not buy impulsively, taking responsibility for their spending behavior. They must remember they are working for God.

Task intimacy involves discussing individual strengths and weaknesses in pastoral activities. This also includes the division of labor at home so the wife is not expected to be involved full time at church and still be in charge of all domestic and disciplinary responsibilities at home. The husband must assume his fair share of the household tasks.

Commitment intimacy grows out of sharing values and making a commitment to each other before God to maintain open communication in all dimensions of their marriage, especially in times of crisis.

Physical intimacy matures in marriage as the couple become "one flesh" (Genesis 2:23–24). They reach the purest form of intimacy when body, soul, and spirit are united in sexual intercourse in the presence of God (Genesis 2:24; 1 Corinthians 6:17; Hebrews 13:4). At this time they are able to communicate their love in a way that no words can convey. Sex in marriage is like the obbligato in a symphony—not the melody or the harmony—just the grace notes that embellish the composition.[7]

Preventing Affairs in Marriage

In the closing decades of the twentieth century, sexual affairs involving ministers increased precipitously. As a counselor I have observed several major causes of unfaithfulness among pastors. Alertness of the pastoral couple to these excuses can go a long way in avoiding marital affairs.[8]

Causes of Affairs

Invulnerability. As one pastor put it, "I began to feel I was an exception, that what I could censure in others, I could justify for myself." Another version of this excuse: "I began to believe what my people were saying about me as a person who could do no wrong."

Gullibility. David Augsburger reports a pastor's confession: "My counselee told me, 'If you really cared for me, you'd hold me.' So since caring is the essence of pastoral care, we held each other. Then we decided that much more caring was needed by us both."[9]

Warped theology. One pastor confessed having an affair with a member in his church, explaining, "After we finished making love, we both knelt beside the bed and asked God to forgive us. We knew His grace was sufficient to take care of us until the next time we got back together." Unhappy marriage—this is an age-old excuse: "My marriage is unhappy; my wife is not a good lover. Since God is good and wants me happy, it follows that I should find someone else." A survey made by *Christianity Today* discovered that only about 10 percent of the responding pastors had sought professional counseling for their sexual temptations before acting on them.[10]

Just friends. Relationships that develop beyond the limits of friendship lead to affairs. As one pastor put it, "We were just good friends. I needed someone to talk to, and she was a good listener." This frequently involves a staff member or someone who works near the pastoral office.

We fell in love. This is a take-off on the David and Bathsheba story (2 Samuel 11). As one pastor put it, "I don't know what happened. It was just the right chemistry, I guess. We fell in love. We couldn't help ourselves." This illustrates what we have learned from experience—falling is an unstable position. David could have checked his fall; so can we.

KINDS OF AFFAIRS

The avoidance affair is seldom a deep relationship. It is primarily an attempt to get the attention of the spouse, as illustrated by the seminarian who, under pressure to finish his thesis, gets involved without being aware of the causal connection between his anxiety and his sudden passion for a new lover.

In *the frustration affair* there is the conviction that the marriage denies the perpetrator the quality of experience wanted or deserved. It is a nonverbal message of dissatisfaction that becomes a way to "legitimize" leaving the marriage.

The recreational affair is essentially a one-night stand in a string of adulterous liaisons; it seldom involves emotional commitments.

The supplementary affair, on the other hand, is both sexual and emotional and may last for a considerable duration. One of my clients sustained an adulterous relationship for thirty years, until the spouse of her lover died.

The platonic affair is characterized by intellectual and emotional attachment but is seldom sexual. Perhaps a better name would be "spiritual" or "emotional" adultery.

The homosexual affair emerges when a married man develops a fixation on another male (or males) to fulfill repressed emotional needs and satisfy a longing for same-sex love he missed from an absent father.

The fill-me-up affair is a nonverbal message of a pastor-turned-womanizer who is saying, "I'm running on empty; fill me up." This is usually an attempt to compensate for an emotionally deprived childhood. The purpose of this affair is to flout convention and public morals and to get a sense of notoriety out of the events.

The exit affair is common with male pastors in burnout. He is overburdened with the pressures of ministry or disillusioned with congregational demands and secretly wants out of the ministry. He manipulates the spouse into taking responsibility for the marital breakup. Consciously or unconsciously this infidel makes sure the affair is discovered.

Summary

The purpose of marriage for pastors is not only to enjoy an intimate, loving relationship with a person of the complementary sex and to produce children. It is also to demonstrate to the world the mystical relationship between Christ and the Church. Christian marriage is a fulfillment of the purposes of creation. But the pastoral pair are wise to be alert to the potential of sexual affairs—an occupational hazard of people in helping relationships who live public lives under moral scrutiny.

Selected Bibliography

Allender, Dan B., and Tremper Longman, III. *Intimate Allies: Rediscovering God's Design for Marriage and Becoming Soul Mates for Life.* Wheaton, Ill.: Tyndale House Publishers, 1995.

Augsburger, David. "The Private Lives of Public Leaders." *Christianity Today* 31, no. 17 (1987): 23.

Brock, Raymond T. "Affairs in the Ministry." *Pentecostal Evangel,* 7 April 1988, 10–12.

_____. "Avoiding Burnout through Spiritual Renewal." *The Holy Spirit and Counseling.* Vol. 1. Ed. Marvin G. Gilbert and Raymond T. Brock. Peabody, Mass.: Hendrickson Publishers, 1985.

_____. *The Christ-Centered Family.* Springfield, Mo.: Gospel Publishing House, 1977.

_____. *Dating and Waiting for Marriage.* Springfield, Mo.: Gospel Publishing House, 1982.

_____. "The Deception of Affairs." *Pentecostal Evangel,* 24 April 1988, 6, 7, 15.

_____. *Parenting the Elementary Child.* Springfield, Mo.: Gospel Publishing House, 1995.

Brock, Raymond T., and Horace C. Lukens, Jr. "Affair Prevention in the Ministry." *Journal of Psychology and Christianity* 8, no. 4 (1989): 44–55.

Carter, Les. *The Push-Pull Marriage: Learning and Living the Art of Give-and-Take.* Grand Rapids: Baker Book House, 1983.

Conway, Jim, and Sally Conway. *Your Marriage Can Survive Mid-Life Crisis.* Nashville: Thomas Nelson Publishers, 1987.

Dobbins, Richard D. *The Believer and His Mental Health.* Munroe Falls, Ohio: Truly Alive Publications, 1982.

Doty, Sherri L. "Credentials, Marital, and Ministry Status by Gender." *Assemblies of God Ministers Report.* Springfield, Mo.: Gospel Publishing House, 1995.

Exley, Richard. *Perils of Power: Immorality in the Ministry.* Tulsa, Okla.: Harrison House, 1988.

Gangel, Kenneth. *The Family First: Biblical Answers to Family Problems.* Minneapolis: HIS International Service, 1972.

Getz, Gene, and Elaine Getz. *Partners for Life: Making a Marriage That Lasts.* Ventura, Calif.: Regal Books, 1988.

Grenz, Stanley. *Sexual Ethics: A Biblical Perspective.* Dallas: Word Books, 1990.

Grenz, Stanley J., and Roy D. Bell. *Betrayal of Trust: Sexual Misconduct in the Pastorate.* Downers Grove, Ill.: InterVarsity Press, 1995.

Harley, Willard F., Jr. *His Needs, Her Needs: Building an Affair-Proof Marriage.* Grand Rapids: Fleming H. Revell Co., 1986.

Joy, Donald M. *Bonding: Relationships in the Image of God.* Dallas: Word Books, 1985.

_____. *Rebonding: Preventing and Restoring Damaged Relationships.* Dallas: Word Books, 1986.

Joy, Donald M., and Robbie B. Joy. *Lovers: Whatever Happened to Eden?* Waco, Tex.: Word Books, 1987.

Merrill, Dean. *Clergy Couples in Crisis: The Impact of Stress on Pastoral Marriages.* Waco, Tex.: Word Books, 1985.

Minirth, Frank; Mary Alice Minirth; Brian Newman; Deborah Newman; Robert Hemfelt; and Susan Hemfelt. *Passages of Marriage: Five Growth Stages That Will Take Your Marriage to Greater Intimacy and Fulfillment.* Nashville: Thomas Nelson Publishers, 1991.

Schmidt, Jerry, and Raymond T. Brock. *The Emotional Side of Men.* Eugene, Ore.: Harvest House, 1983.

Sell, Charles M. *Achieving the Impossible: Intimate Marriage.* Portland, Ore.: Multnomah Press, 1982.

Small, Dwight H. *Christian: Celebrate Your Sexuality.* Old Tappan, N.J.: Fleming H. Revell Co., 1976.

Smalley, Gary, with John Trent. *Love Is a Decision: Proven Techniques to Keep Your Marriage Alive and Lively.* Dallas: Word Books, 1989.

Smedes, Louis B. *Forgive and Forget.* San Francisco: Harper & Row, Publishers, 1984.

_____. *Sex for Christians: The Limits and Liberties of Sexual Living.* Grand Rapids: William B. Eerdmans Publishing Co., 1976.

Stafford, Tim. "Great Sex: Reclaiming a Christian Sexual Ethic." *Christianity Today* 39, no. 14 (1987): 23–45.

Virkler, Henry A. *Broken Promises: Healing and Preventing Affairs in Christian Marriages.* Dallas: Word Books, 1992.

Warner, Wayne. "A Study in Longevity." *Assemblies of God Heritage* 15, no. 3 (fall 1995): 26–28.

Wright, H. Norman. *Holding Onto Romance: Keeping Your Marriage Alive and Passionate After the Honeymoon Years Are Over.* Ventura, Calif.: Regal Books, 1992.

_____. *Marriage Counseling: A Practical Guide for Pastors and Counselors.* Ventura, Calif.: Regal Books, 1995.

Your Relationship with the Previous Pastor

G. Raymond Carlson

The Bible has much to say regarding relationships in the body of Christ. The apostle Paul deals with the matter in several of his letters. The church at Corinth developed factions that had united behind various ministers. Some church members were becoming more attached to individual leaders than to Christ, the Head of the Church, and His Word.

Some were followers of Paul, the founder. Others linked up with Apollos, the silver-tongued orator. Then there were those who traced their loyalty to Peter. The fact that Paul uses Peter's Aramaic name, *Kephas,* rather than the Greek, *Petros,* suggests that Peter was a traditionalist. Those with Jewish tastes would respond to him. He fit their mold, for he found it difficult to separate himself from those who clung to Judaism (Galatians 2:11–13).

In response, Paul stated this great truth: one plants, another waters, but God gives the increase (1 Corinthians 3:16). Paul laid the foundation in Corinth. Others followed and built on it.

Memory takes me back to my home church. Born in a great revival, the church grew under the ministry of the founder. When the founder left to pioneer another church, many of those converts felt no one could take his place. But they yielded to the will of God and soon had an Apollos preaching to them. He was a silver-tongued orator who gained national acclaim throughout the Fellowship as a preacher. As he, in the will of God, moved on, there was a Cephas. He held rather closely to tradition— "This is the way it is done." All of these leaders made a great contribution to the church, each in his own time and way.

Then there was a fourth group in Corinth. Their claim was, "I follow Christ." That was a worthy aspiration, but a closer look indicates that this group prided themselves on their spirituality. That pride manifested itself in aloofness, snobbishness, and exclusiveness. These are the people who have secret prayer meetings claiming special revelations and experiences. To borrow a vernacular expression, they see themselves as superior to the "run-of-the-mill," that ordinary, unrefined, ungraded material.

Personality problems have plagued the church throughout its existence. When people become more attached to leaders than to Christ and His Word, division arises. Paul goes to great lengths to deal with this matter in his first letter to the Corinthians.

In 1 Corinthians 12, the apostle presents a key truth concerning the Church. He states:

- one body, but many members (vv. 12,14,20)
- one Spirit, but many gifts (v. 4)
- one purpose, but many ministries (v. 5)
- one God, but many operations (v. 6)

The Lord uses people to present and carry out His plan. He used an impulsive Peter, who often talked first and then thought afterward. Peter became the great leader presenting the gospel through the outreach of the church in Jerusalem and the Jewish world (Acts 1 through 12). The Lord used the educated Paul to plant churches and write great letters to the Gentile world (Acts 13 through 28), working out of his base at Antioch. God had a place for practical Philip, doubting Thomas, refined Luke, and thousands of others. Each had his place.

There is a function for every God-called pastor. Christ gives gifts to His redeemed Church in the sovereignty of His holy will (Ephesians 4:11). Despite their holy calling, these gifts are human "just like us" (as was said of Elijah in James 5:17). They are neither angels nor glorified saints. While there is no excuse for human failure, there must be under-standing of the ministry of the grace of God that works in the lives of His servants. A pastor is looked upon as an example of the highest principles of Christian life. His conduct in every situation is observed. How he relates to fellow ministers either commends him or condemns him.

Relating to Predecessors

How a pastor relates to his predecessor or his successor will be a strong indication of his character. Unless he pioneered the church he serves, he will follow another in the pastorate. The new leader will gain the confidence of the congregation if he will show courtesy and respect for those who previously served the church. The previous pastor will, no doubt, have many who love him dearly. Members of the congregation may even indicate their preference for a predecessor by making comparisons. Happy is the preacher who suffers neither insecurity nor jealousy.

The current pastor is wise to keep his spirit under control when members sing the praises of the former pastor. It must be remembered that his ministry was not only in the pulpit. Perhaps many members were converted under him. He baptized them in water. They were filled with the Holy Spirit while he was their shepherd. Your predecessor performed their marriage ceremonies, dedicated their children, and participated in many of their family activities. He was at their side during high points and low points. When sickness came, he was in their homes or at the hospital. During crises, the pastor was there to bring God's Word and to pray with them. When death visited their homes, the pastor was there to bring comfort, help, and encouragement. Little wonder the life of a godly pastor becomes so strongly entwined in the lives of a congregation.

To expect ties that are so strong to be forgotten by parishioners is asking too much. But that kind of relationship can be developed by you as you fulfill your role as a shepherd. Remember, while you listen to the song of praise of your predecessor, your successor will hear yours. Remember that, after all, it is a good song. Give your parishioners time and they will sing your song. Join the song. Have grace enough to avoid becoming jealous. Speak with appreciation of the previous pastor. It will please his friends and cause them to appreciate you. Let your words, however, ring with sincerity.

> **How we relate to fellow ministers either commends or condemns us.**

Paul dealt with the spiritual immaturity in the Corinthian church. Their carnality caused them to become so taken up with human channels that they lost track of God's great purpose of building a body of believers who are dedicated to Him and His eternal purpose. The apostle did not allow himself to be ruffled when those of the Apollos party or the Cephas party pressed their points of view. Paul was more interested in unity in the church. Unity in the ministry goes a long way in developing and maintaining unity in the body. There is no reference to any hard feelings between Paul and Apollos. They maintained a warm relationship, as evidenced by Paul's invitation to Apollos (1 Corinthians 16:12).

At times a predecessor may leave with a cloud over him. A moral failure of some kind may have occurred or, for one reason or another, he lost the confidence of the people. At this point, the new pastor needs to exercise great wisdom, seeking perhaps the counsel of the leadership of the Fellowship, such as the general superintendent or the district superintendent. Members may have been deeply wounded and possibly divided. They need healing. Do not become a party to criticism (there will be an overabundance) of the previous pastor. Strive to get people to "see Jesus" (John 12:21). Avoid calling attention to the faults of others. If you can help people get their eyes on the Lord, He has promised to draw all of them to himself (John 12:32).

Extend honor and consideration to the minister who preceded you. Reflecting on him either in a positive or negative way reflects on you and the Fellowship to which you both belong. Let your comments be truthful but limited to the positive. There are times when the negative must be expressed, but exercise care. The birds come home to roost. If you are not sincere, it will soon be discovered and you will be the loser.

Use the opportunities to honor your predecessor by recognizing his presence in a service. You may ask him to lead in prayer or to bring a greeting. You may also ask him to speak. Some members may ask him to officiate at a wedding, a baby dedication, or a funeral. Handle the situation with courtesy and grace.

Leaving a Pastorate

Now, a word about leaving a pastorate. Give your successor the highest accolades possible. Don't talk to people about him unless you can say good things. Pack up, move out, and stay out. The church is no longer your responsibility. If you are invited to participate in a wedding or funeral, contact the pastor. See that he has a rightful place. Avoid contacts of any kind with members who are in trouble in the church. Do not receive gifts of money. Do not criticize the methods of your successor.

For thirteen years, while serving as the Minnesota District Superintendent, I taught at North Central Bible College. One of the subjects was Pastoral Theology. Facetiously, I suggested to students that as they engaged in pastoral ministry there would be a time to move on to another church. As they prepared to make this move, I, in jest, told them to go to the best photographer in the city for the best picture possible. Supply the church with at least one picture for each family. Then as the successor would come calling, you could smile down on him from a secure position on the mantle. Your attitude toward the person who succeeds you should be one of good will. His success will be to your credit. As God helped you to lay a good foundation, the church will grow. Growth under his ministry should never be grounds for your being jealous. We must never forget—one plants, another waters, but God gives the increase.

A Perfect Predecessor

As the new pastor, you will hear much about your predecessor. He may be looked upon as just about perfect. His departure only increased the esteem in which he was held. On the other hand, others will charge him with causing everything that has been wrong. Recognize that none of us is perfect. A seminar speaker asked his audience if they had ever known or heard of a perfect person. After a pause a timid little lady raised her hand and gave this response. "Yes, I heard of such a person. It was my husband's first wife." You should be prepared for comments indicating that your predecessor was the perfect pastor.

Robert E. Lee, commander-in-chief of the Confederate army in the Civil War, was known for his exemplary Christian character. Upon being asked to give a recommendation for a certain man for a particular post, he gave a positive response. Upon hearing Lee's statement, a friend remonstrated, asking how Lee could speak so favorably concerning one who had been so critical of him. The general's response, "I was asked my opinion of him, not his of me."

The need for retaining right relationships in the ministry is illustrated in Numbers 12. Miriam, Moses' sister, held an important post in Israel. She stood at Moses' side in leadership. She grew jealous, however, when Moses married; she felt she was being replaced. Not being content with God's permissive will, Miriam began to mistrust God and her brother. Listen to Miriam's bitter complaint as jealousy possessed her. "'Has the Lord spoken only through Moses? . . . Hasn't he also spoken through us?'" (Numbers 12:2). Her bitter spirit of jealousy brought God's judgment—she became leprous.

The Bible instructs us, "Rejoice with those who rejoice; mourn with those who mourn" (Romans 12:15). At first glance that would seem easy. When someone is happy, rejoice with him. If he mourns or weeps, weep with him. But if the rejoicing is because of a brother's great success, can we rejoice with him? Phenomenal growth is the cause of his rejoicing, but you didn't experience that. Can you rejoice with him?

Jealousy brings inward deterioration. It may be fed by feelings of inferiority or of not having received due recognition. Are we more concerned about the approval of people than of our Master? Ambition that is not sanctified brings unhappiness. Guard well your ambitions lest they become selfish. May the church be delivered from ministers without ambition, but may there be a greater deliverance from the overly ambitious.

The great Corinthian church had much to commend it, but it also had much to be corrected. Throughout the Epistle there is an emphasis on the unity of the local church as the body of Christ. As the apostle Paul deals with the problems, he comes again and again to the matter of unity in the body. That unity involves people. And people need leadership. Fortunately, the various pastoral leaders in Corinth were not at war. Their followers were the guilty parties.

The central truth regarding leadership is that one plants, another waters, but God gives the increase (1 Corinthians 3:6); every minister who is called to lead a local congregation must recognize this essential truth. God works through human channels. Paul states, "There should be no division in the body, but . . . its parts should have equal concern for each other" (1 Corinthians 12:25). A good rule to follow for all in church leadership is the Golden Rule: Jesus said, "'Do to others as you would have them do to you'" (Luke 6:31).

Building Relationships in the Church and Community

Richard B. Foth

G od has a plan for humankind. It is relationship, both temporal and eternal. Nothing more and nothing less. Genesis 2:18 says, "'It is not good for man to be alone,'" and Matthew responds, "'The virgin . . . will give birth to a son, and they will call him Immanuel'—which means 'God with us'" (1:23). But what does that imply for me as a pastor? Immanuel is now with the Father and I'm slugging it out on Main Street. How does His strategy of simply being with people work in a twenty-first-century, nanosecond world?

The Fundamentals

The old axiom about not escaping death and taxes reflects the places we invest our lives: relationships and money. At first, it appears that death takes away both life and taxes. For the believer, however, relationships continue. In fact, relationships are the essence, process, and goal of God's interaction with people. From creation to consummation, the biblical story details God's attempts to establish relationship with humans, who, in response, can nurture relationships with each other. And it all goes on forever.

The Church has no other reason for being than to express what relationships look like in Christ and to attract the larger civic community to enjoy that same experience. Jesus said it this way: "'A new command I give you: Love one another. As I have loved you, so you must love one another. By this all men will know that you are my disciples, if you love one another'" (John 13:34–35).

To the degree we see the mission of the local church only in quantitative terms (e.g., "What's the attendance?"), we will dilute the essential, qualitative message of the gospel (e.g., "You are valuable to God!"). It is the greatest challenge for those of us who have some leadership role, either elected or appointed, to reflect diligently on what Jesus noted as the most significant thing God said to humankind: "'Love the Lord your God with all your heart and with all your soul and with all your strength and with all your mind'; and, 'Love your neighbor as yourself'" (Luke 10:27).

The injunction is just as valid today as it was when Jesus uttered it twenty centuries ago. Yet, it is in fact, the hardest saying in the Gospels, a truth that must be dealt with at the core of this organism called the Church. The tendency is to leapfrog that great commandment by simply acknowledging it: "Of course, that's the given, the place to begin." In reality, however, it is not the place to begin. Rather, it is the place to end. Oswald Chambers's reflection catches the thrust when he says: "What man sees as the process, God sees as the goal."

Everything about Jesus' life, death, and resurrection points us toward a reconciling union with God and humanity. The mission of the Church is then, primarily, to be a model of how loving God and loving one's neighbor works. With that in mind, when pastors turn their attention to "equipping the saints," they build relationships in the church that naturally radiate into the community. Pastors can move with great confidence here because the task is right in line with God's eternal plan for the ages and its specific implications for daily living.

A Prerequisite and a Principle

Relationship-building begins in one place and one place alone: *attitude*. A leader must want to see it happen. If a leader desires to see relationships created and nurtured, he or she already has God's full authority and support. But it takes the same attitude that the Father had toward us through Christ to get us there. The apostle Paul describes this attitude as the "mind of Christ" (Philippians 2:5, KJV). It is seen in very tangible ways in the focus of His mission and His approach with people. Reading the Gospels, one finds His mind expressed on every page. Calling the Twelve, healing the sick, feeding the hungry, identifying with outcasts, it is clear what His intention is: He wants relationship with people—anywhere, anytime, any culture, any person, any price. Whatever, therefore, mitigates against such redemptive relationships, inside or outside the church, cannot have His stamp on it.

On closer reading, the Gospels reveal a principle which expresses the thrust of Jesus' heart. Though a number of key principles are evident in His ministry, this one is pivotal: *He chooses to accept people where He meets them, just the way they are.*

The Principle Fleshed Out

When I review my life, those who have left their fingerprints on my soul, those who have had profound impact on me, are the ones who looked past my foibles, problems, and errant ways to accept me where I was. Seeing in me value that I did not perceive, they spoke into my life encouragement, which prompted me to respond positively, beyond logic or calculation on my part.

Whatever was going on in those relationships touched something so visceral and so deep that I could only think of one thing: "I want more of that." Of course, to get more of that meant spending time with those people, because their attitude towards me was more encompassing than just words. It was a kind of emotional posture, a way of approaching me with the obvious intent to be my friend. Later, I discovered that this approach came from a fundamental belief that each person on earth is absolutely valuable to God. And not just that. Each person is equally valuable to God. Every individual absolutely and equally valuable to God is both a freeing and a compelling truth.

In God's view, value comes not from intellect, gifts, performance, or a particular skill-set. Rather, it flows from spiritual heritage—eternal genes. Every person is designed in the image of God. No matter how encrusted and corroded by abuse, misuse, or disuse, that internal identity remains as the defining characteristic of each human being. The problem, of course, is that I do not intrinsically have Jesus' eyes, which immediately perceive that image. I am distracted by offending, external differences. He is drawn by the internal familial likeness to himself. I, because of my own insecurities and lack of perception, proceed from the outside in very slowly. He, in eternal confidence, proceeds from the inside out, more slowly still. To the degree that I read about Him in the Gospels and walk with Him each day, I begin to sense His mind in these matters and see why He acts the way He does.

> **Relationship-building begins in one place alone: attitude. A leader must want to see it happen.**

Jesus has gone way out of His way to connect with us. In theological circles, we call it the Incarnation. Those connections really begin by identifying things we have in common. We easily identify differences, but often have to search for things that are similar. We know that we have certain basic things in common, but they need exploration. Typically, they are human things like geography, family history, or interests not dependent on spiritual maturity. As a model, the Gospels show the way to common ground by detailing the ordinary and extraordinary events surrounding the birth and early years of Jesus. He was one of us.

I am continually impressed at how the door of privacy swings open when someone asks the simple question: "Where were you born and reared?" Everyone has a birthplace and geographic roots. The question makes no value judgment. It doesn't pry into the relationship of parents or circumstances of the family. It simply establishes a fact common to every human being and, in so doing, lays the groundwork for a very natural response.

When we view this principle in the light of a given local church or community, a question rises: "What kind of program do we need to teach the idea of unconditional acceptance?" The answer is "No program can teach this idea. Individuals can only model it." When the church struggles, it is not because it lacks clearly presented programs. It struggles because it lacks clearly modeled biblical principles.

The Pastor As a Model

It is precisely at this point that the pastor's role becomes so important. If he or she sees, fundamentally, that relationship with God and each other is the goal of our life in Christ—and that the journey of faith deals with those relationships in many stages—it affects everything, from the pastor's preaching to the internal structures of the church. For example, does the congregation get the sense that the pastor has friends beyond the congregation? Are those connections only because he is a local pastor? Or have some of them developed from a professional level into a more personal friendship—as "Fred," "Robert," or "José"—the guy next door (who just happens to be a pastor)?

People in the pew already have relationships beyond the sanctuary. They live out in the marketplace six days a week. As pastors, we venture into that arena too often as the community's spiritual paramedics, racing about saving lives. We see ourselves in that light because the work is a valid and definitive part of our pastoral response. But there are other kinds of relationships beyond those formed in crisis, outside someone's felt need. What about the relationships from involving ourselves in some form of generally recognized community service (e.g., Rotary Club or Little League)?

I ask these questions because one striking thing about Jesus' ministry is the amount of time He spent "out and about." In these days, when management-by-walking-around is seen as effective leadership, it appears that the organizational gurus have taken a page from the Gospels. Jesus was among the people where they were. To the degree that we reverse that process, having people come to where we are, we run the risk of diluting the essential methodology of the gospel: Jesus comes to where I am.

Certainly we need to gather on the Lord's Day and certainly the sanctuary, Christian education facilities, and gym need to be jammed with young and old at every opportunity for the glory of God. Those meetings are full of relational happenings and growing friendships. However, the pastor is perceived in virtually all of those events as the leader or teacher.

> **"Jesus was among the people where they were."**

That's his or her function within the community of believers. But beyond that particular setting, what would happen if you took a different role?

When we spend most of our days solving problems, shaping evangelistic strategies, and responding to human need at an incredible range of levels, how we see ourselves can become distorted—like we really do know that much, when, in reality, without Jesus we can do nothing. The problem is that many people want us to have all the answers, and in seeking to meet their needs we get confused. Dr. Lloyd Ogilvie, chaplain of the United States Senate, puts it this way: "One of the greatest challenges of the pastor is to keep the congregation from putting him on the pedestal of perfection." They need to follow Jesus, and the pastor can't handle the stress of being the perfect answer man.

I make that simple observation in order to point out the value of learning. Most effective pastors I know never stop learning—Scripture, organizational management, economics, and on and on. Another vast library, however, sits under our very noses. Not one bound in leather and recorded in the Library of Congress, it falls in that category which companies denote today as human resources. I speak of people—of all stripes and persuasions, cutting across religious, political, and ethnic lines—people who, for a thousand different reasons, would never enter our sanctuaries, but who nevertheless have a great deal to teach us. They can help us understand their backgrounds, their worlds, their ideas, their feelings. They can help us see God's world in a very different way.

> ## " Friendship is characterized by relationship, not position. "

I honestly never came to grips with (or cared much about) the political world until I began walking the halls and sitting in the offices of the United States Capitol. I could not comprehend the dynamics, tensions, pretensions, power, and pain that attend political office until we moved to Washington, D.C., in 1993 and began working in the congressional marketplace. What is shown on television and written in the press is so often a distortion. There exists a vast arena of personal need beyond the voting records and campaign speeches. There also are some wonderful people who believe that public service is exactly what it says. The public rarely gets the chance to see either up close. I think the little boy talking about his friend the garbageman had it right when he concluded: "My mommy doesn't like his smell, but then, she doesn't know him well!"

By the Lord's grace, some people entered my life over the years who were learners of people. Not students of people, learners of people. They did not consider a person an object to be studied and analyzed, but rather someone to learn from. It makes sense, really, because all of us are ignorant, just in different places. And all of us have something to offer, just in different ways. As long as we maintain a learning posture, we will get an education every bit as worthwhile as a Harvard degree, and perhaps worth more. But as we learn—exchanging thoughts and feelings, spending time together—something happens. We discover that we are both learners and teachers.

When we begin as learners, we will be invited in as teachers. The process is clearly identifiable. It is mutual; it is called friendship. In one of the most powerful statements in the Gospels Jesus says, "'I no longer call you servants. . . . Instead, I have called you friends'" (John 15:15). Friendship is characterized by lateral relationship, not vertical positioning. It sounds like Bethlehem.

With all of that in mind, many pastors would enjoy both the personal and community benefit created by befriending a handful of people in a range of settings—education, medicine, labor, business, politics—as a learner. Over time, the congregation will become aware of those friendships, and not necessarily because they are used as sermon illustrations. As a matter of fact, to make illustrations without permission could be devastating. Rather, the congregation will see subtle attitudinal changes, different perceptions, and new thoughts beginning to surface in conversation. We pastors will continue to have baptisms of clear-seeing, and our spirits will grow.

The Personal Challenge

Coming back to the original principle that Jesus accepts people where they are, let us close the loop. Voicing ideals is not difficult; practicing them is another story. Accepting someone unconditionally is at one and the same time the most difficult and most profound experience a human being can have. It must be. Jesus put it as the crown jewel of His experience with us.

To do that, however, takes something called nonjudgment. Not judging other people on the basis of the things they can't control (like place of birth or racial origin) is a tremendous leap for some of us. Not judging people on the basis of things they can control (like attitudes and personal demeanor) may be an even larger leap. We just simply have to walk through Bethlehem to the Cross again and look at how Jesus acted toward us. If He has chosen to live in us, He must be prepared to help us reflect His character and mind to a watching world. He actually says it, doesn't He? "'I am with you always, to the very end of the age'" (Matthew 28:20). That being the case, let's reflect on nonjudgment as a mechanism for expressing unconditional acceptance.

Unconditional acceptance is dependent upon the ability to bypass or diminish issues, at least in the early going, for the sake of developing a friendship. Certainly there are times when issues are so grievous as to hinder connecting with a person. However, in the vast majority of cases, that level of hindrance doesn't exist. Most of our hindrances to relationship reside inside our heads. In the general context of the church in the community, the possibilities for establishing wonderful relationships with a wide variety of people are endless.

After fifty-three years of living and more than three decades of public ministry, I am still amazed at what happens when we sublimate issues in order to understand people. Issues are like skin color. They are at the forefront of our initial perceptions and often become the litmus tests of whether we want to have a relationship or not.

Not so with Jesus. He seems to be issue blind. Actually, He has one exception: those who claim to speak for God, but are judgmental, categorical, and presumptive. He pulls no punches with them. He says, "'Woe to you, teachers of the law and Pharisees, you hypocrites! You shut the kingdom of heaven in men's faces. You yourselves do not enter, nor will you let those enter who are trying to'" (Matthew 23:13–14). Why, I ask myself, would He respond so dramatically? Why would He be so confrontational? Could it be that in their presuming to speak for God while acting so unlike Him, they deny the core of His character, loving-kindness (*chesed*)?

Now, we shouldn't be too hard on the Pharisees. Judging is the most natural thing to do. Judging is that action which allows me to feel better about myself momentarily by denigrating another individual or group. We all like to have an edge on the competition. True relationship, however, is not a matter of competition. So when a competitive element like judging is introduced, relationship does not long survive. We live in a world where looking for differences and flaws has become both legitimate and commercially profitable. But it brings out the basest instincts in humanity. Nonjudgment, on the other hand, offers value and dignity by its very silence and frees both parties to find things in common. I mean, what could Jesus have been thinking when He went to Levi's house for dinner? Levi fell so far short of accepted social standards, a Roman collaborator no less. Perhaps He was thinking of Levi as a friend, so He was going over to celebrate with Levi's other friends. But the identification was too complete for the religious leaders and they muttered their accusations to Jesus' disciples. Whereupon Jesus gave the Pharisees a homework assignment: to find out what mercy really is (Matthew 9:10–13).

Nonjudgment, then, seems to be in the mercy family. Mercy has a variety of children. Some are very active, like forgiveness for a specific offense. Some are more reflective, like not prejudging folks. By anyone's guidelines, however, mercy is life-giving. Perhaps walking in nonjudgment when it comes to making friends in the church or the community is really spreading life around. It, at the very least, allows relationship a chance to be planted and nurtured. Only time will tell the rest of the story.

Admittedly, all kinds of relationships exist in the world, relationships that focus around family, career, common interests, and myriad other connectors. Yet the kind of relationship cultivated in the church and community cuts across all of those categories. Jesus nurtures relationship for relationship's sake. Out of a relational seedbed one begins to see and follow Christ. First, He comes to our house for a celebration, and, then, we get to go to His house for another celebration . . . forever.

First Things When Coming to a New Church

Charles E. Hackett

Coming to a new pastorate is always a traumatic experience. I have pastored only two churches: one for two years and one for twenty-nine years. However, I remember very clearly the apprehension and uncertainty I felt each time I entered a new pastorate. Realizing that first impressions are sometimes lasting impressions adds to the pressure of getting started right. I have used a simple formula on many occasions, and I believe it will serve any new pastor. It is this: "Love God, love people, and use common sense." Most churches are not looking for a superman, but for someone who will bring edification, exhortation, and comfort to their lives in the midst of a troubled and confused world. I have been amazed many times at the patience and forgiveness a congregation extend to their pastor if they know he loves them.

Pastoring a church is a wonderful and exciting journey. I know of no other ministry that affords the opportunity to see people saved and then discipled into mature Christians who become lifelong "family" members. Pastoring is not a dreaded sentence from God but a high and holy calling that brings joy and fulfillment unmatched by any other profession. Some of the following suggestions may help you as you begin your journey as a pastor.

Seek God's Will

When difficult times come (and they surely will), there is no substitute for knowing that you are there because God placed you there. Woe to the pastor who uses political methods to obtain the leadership of a church. The church belongs to Jesus and He said He would build it. He does not need political schemers to do the work of the ministry. He is looking for humble servants who fast and pray, who are full of the Holy Spirit, who know how to serve as well as lead. God is looking for pastors of faith and vision who can see beyond what is currently there and can visualize a church whose builder and maker is God—a victorious church that will impact a city for God, a church of signs, wonders, and miracles where people are daily being added to the fellowship.

Call the Congregation to Prayer

There will be no spiritual victories without prayer, and leading the church to pray is the most important responsibility of any pastor. This cannot be delegated to someone else. The prayer life of the church will not rise above the prayer life of the pastor. A praying church is a healthy, growing church, free from the power struggles brought on by carnality. Nothing empowers and renews the church like prayer; in fact, when there is a lack of prayer, the load gets heavy and the task becomes impossible. The next step is confusion, burnout, and despair. But God never leads anyone into this kind of pain. He calls us to victory, not defeat.

No amount of planning or organizing will substitute for prayer. Before any strategizing is done, seek God for His direction, and success is guaranteed. Pray until you get a word from God on what steps should be taken next. You will not get that word at a conference, through a tape, or in someone's book on church growth. You get it on your knees before God. Once you have heard from God, He will very often use a conference or a book to help you flesh out what God has spoken to your heart. This process is vital to the survival and success of a new pastor.

Get as many different groups praying as possible. Set as many prayer times as possible. Use wisdom. Don't call a forty-day fast your first week, and don't use guilt as an incentive for people to pray. Remember, it is the Holy Spirit who calls us and anoints us for prayer. Don't try to take His place. Don't become discouraged if you do not see immediate results. Just keep praying, and God will give a harvest in due time.

Prepare Sermons Well

You will be judged immediately by the quality of your preaching. Remember, you are called to preach, not to bore the saints but to bless them. Reject mediocrity and dullness. Believe God for a message every time you go to the pulpit, a message that will make a difference in someone's life. Effective preaching requires much study, discipline, and constant reading. Being involved in the lives of your parishioners and the hurts of your community will add a depth to your sermons that nothing else will. Don't rely entirely on someone else's illustrations, get your own.

Every pastor should be required to listen to a tape of every sermon he preaches. It is both a humbling and a learning experience. In fact, tape the entire service, including the announcements, then evaluate it as to what would cause people to return and what would drive them away. If your sermons don't excite you, they have a similar effect on others. Quality preaching is hard but rewarding work. It should be a highlight of the week, both for preacher and parishioner.

Identify the Power Structure of the Church

Identify the influencers, the movers and shakers. They may or may not hold an office. They may be Spirit-filled people who love God and respect the office of pastor, or they may be the most unchristian people you have ever met. Many times a church has been hindered in every way by unscriptural layleaders who eventually must be removed, but don't make that your first priority. Chances are you will fail and be out of the office in a short time. Learn to give and take with them until God establishes you as the spiritual leader of the church. Then seek Him with prayer and fasting until you know what to do and the right time to do it. Many pastors have lost the battle, not because their actions were wrong, but because of bad timing.

Make every effort to develop a relationship of respect and trust with the church board. Sometimes this is a huge challenge. Remember, some of them have been hurt and bruised by previous pastoral relationships, and it is incumbent upon the new pastor to rebuild the bridges. Most board members that I know do not want tension and mistrust with the pastor, but peace and harmony. The pastor must take the initiative in building good relationships with all church leaders, no matter what his personal agenda may be. Let God establish your influence and leadership before you attempt any changes in the existing leadership structure. Also, it would be very unwise to put out old leaders unless you have qualified and trained people to take their place. A good rule to follow as you are making pastoral decisions is "do the right thing in the right spirit." Don't be hesitant to call a fellow minister friend, the local presbyter, or the district superintendent to check out the direction you believe God is leading you. I have been spared many grievous mistakes because I took the time to

> **A formula for any new pastor: 'Love God, love people, and use common sense.'**

counsel with the brethren. In the multitude of counselors there is safety, according to Proverbs.

Look for Ways to Make Improvements

Keep your improvements simple, inexpensive, and visible. Don't start a revolution, but let people see that you have a sense of direction that is blessed of God. Talk about vision, not programs or buildings. One of the surest ways to guarantee disaster is to launch a series of new programs that no one wants or understands. The only thing I can think of that would be worse is to announce a building program, especially if the present one isn't paid for or if the church is half full. Don't succumb to the hearsay that a new building will attract great crowds. It won't. People come to a church because of what God is doing, not to admire the architecture. Many pastors have had their tenure cut short because they unwisely forced an expensive and unnecessary building program upon a congregation. Our calling is to pastor, not to build buildings. A building program should be compared to major surgery—do it only if there is no other way out.

Be Fiscally Conservative

Any new pastor who immediately identifies himself as a big spender of church funds will find himself in trouble, and rightfully so. It doesn't take leadership or wisdom to bankrupt a church, and pastors who travel this road pay a high price in credibility. Learn the system for disbursing church funds and follow it. If there are changes that need to be made, be patient and wait for the proper timing. And the old theory that a church must be kept in debt in order to keep the people giving is false and unscriptural. I discovered that people would rather be giving to missions rather than paying off a mortgage.

Going to a church and personally being debt-free is a great advantage. Remaining debt-free except for a home is a powerful statement to the church and community. There is much to be gained by personally staying out of debt. There is much to lose by being burdened down with debt, especially when personal income is inadequate to cover the charges. I adopted a philosophy many years ago that has served me well: If I don't have the money, I don't buy it. It is amazing how well one can live without all the "toys."

Win the Lost

No matter what else is happening in the church, if no one is being saved and added to the family of God, then the church is failing. Having people at the altar for salvation causes even your enemies to be at peace with you. It brings life, joy, excitement, and health to the body when new people are coming in. There is no substitute for evangelism. There is not something else that is just as good. Jesus died to save the lost, not to build big cathedrals. The question must be asked over and over, "Is anyone getting saved?" Refuse to sit there week after week with the same discouraged group. Go out into the highways and hedges and find someone who needs Jesus. Don't worry about class or color. Go after the *whosoevers.* Having poor people is better than having no people even though reaching the poor and downtrodden does not carry much clout in the political structure. But it certainly pleases Jesus. Teach soul winning. Demonstrate it. Lead the congregation in reaching out to the unchurched, and your job as pastor will be much easier.

Pastoring is an exciting and challenging ministry. May we be found faithful in this calling.

How the District Office Can Help the Local Church

William O. Vickery

What is the origin of the district office? A district office is born when a district council is formed. A district council is formed on the initiative of the ordained and licensed ministers and the duly elected delegates from the General Council affiliated assemblies within a defined geographical area. The initiative, when formalized, must be prepared in compliance with Article 10 of the Constitution and Article 5 of the Bylaws of The General Council of the Assemblies of God. The initiative is then submitted to the General Council of the Assemblies of God for approval.

To exist as a legal entity, a district council usually adopts articles of incorporation as a religious, not-for-profit corporation (sometimes called a charter). When approved by the state, the newly recognized corporation (the church) must name its corporate officers and give the address of its principal office. This assumes a meeting of the membership of the newly formed corporation will be called for the purpose of adopting its constitution and bylaws and electing its corporate officers as provided therein.

It is important to understand that a district council is formed and a resulting district office is birthed on the initiative of the ministers and delegates. The purpose of a district office is to provide supervision and services for those through whose efforts it has been brought into being. Clearly, a district office is born to serve. It is equally clear that if a district office is to serve well, it must keep the support and cooperation of those who birthed it and benefit from its services.

The district office is people—a "who," not a "what." The district office staff comprises the elected officers and the personnel they employ to help serve. When thinking of and praying for the district office, visualize people, not buildings.

Diversities among District Offices

The number of executive and departmental officers elected to serve in a district office will vary from district to district. The size of the geographic area, the number of ministers and churches, and the amount of finances available are the dominant variables. These variables will have a direct bearing on the ability of a district office to provide services. Therefore, all districts may not be able to provide all of the services described below.

Keeping Records and Maintaining Legal Documents

The church, having initially adopted articles of incorporation and a constitution and bylaws, must see that they are kept current. The need for amending the corporate articles is most frequently necessitated (1) by changes in the State Corporation Code enacted by the state legislature and (2) by the church choosing to enter into activities not provided for in its current articles. The district office can assist in the preparation and adoption of certificates of amendment to the articles of incorporation in compliance with current provisions of the law.

It is equally important for the church to keep its constitution and bylaws current through proper and timely amendments, which require careful attention to detail. Proposed amendments (1) should be worded in the language style of the document it is intended to amend, (2) should conform to itself, i.e. should not contradict other provisions within the document, and (3) should be in conformity with the constitutions and bylaws of the district council and the General Council. The district office can provide the church with wise counsel when changes and amendments to the constitution and bylaws are needed. From their many years of experience the district officers can help the pastor and church avoid errors and embarrassments frequently encountered by those unfamiliar with the process.

Keeping financial records and managing the budget are extremely important to the local church. Some district offices provide a simplified (but adequate) set of accounting programs or records for their churches, especially the smaller ones. Instructions for how to use accounting records and set up and manage the church budget may also be available. Complying with the current Internal Revenue Code is essential to keeping your tax-exempt status as a local church and protecting those who contribute to the church. This information is usually available from your district office.

Recording the minutes of (1) regular and special business meetings of the church, (2) the official board meeting, and (3) other boards and committees meetings is essential to the integrity of the church. The district office can suggest or recommend minute books and sample formats. Due to the litigious nature of our society, minutes of all business meetings of the church and its boards and committees must be accurately maintained. One should know what information is required for minutes to be legal and use discretion when including more information than is legally required. It is very important that all minutes be approved. Remember, in a court of law the minutes can be subpoenaed and used as evidence. Check with your district office if there is any question about the form or wording of your church's official minutes

Developing the Ministries of the Local Church

Local churches are not all the same size, nor the same age, nor have they all reached the same level of maturity in ministry and outreach; therefore, all churches do not need the same helps. The district office thus becomes a resource center somewhat like a supermarket. A pastor can select from those resources the particular programs or materials needed to further develop the ministries of the church. Such materials include the following areas of interest.

The district Christian education department provides guidance for starting and developing Sunday schools, including organization, curriculum selection, teacher training, extension Sunday schools, and an introduction to missions for the children through the Boys and Girls Missionary Crusade (BGMC). There is an array of adult elective courses to choose from.

The district youth ministries department provides guidance for starting and developing youth groups in the local church, promoting youth involvement in missions and evangelism, and personal spiritual growth and development through youth conventions, youth camps and retreats.

The district men's ministries department provides helps for starting men's ministries in the local church and promoting men's activities with outreaches in missions, evangelism, personal spiritual growth, and the sponsorship of Royal Rangers, an auxiliary program for boys.

The district women's ministries department provides guidance for women's ministries in the local church, promoting women's activities with emphases on missions, benevolences, evangelism, personal spiritual growth, and the sponsorship of Missionettes, an auxiliary program for girls. Retreats, conferences, and regional and sectional rallies also provide encouragement and enrichment for local church women.

The district world missions department coordinates the foreign missions and home missions ministries in the district. The district director of missions (or missionary secretary) can assist the pastor in planning missionary conventions by providing promotional and thematic helps, furlough schedules for foreign missionaries, and the needs of home missions personnel and projects within the district.

The district office also encourages and enriches its ministering families and local church leaders through minister's institutes and retreats, ministry spouses conferences, MK-PK retreats, district-wide and regional leadership conferences, and family camp meetings and retreats.

Unseen and Unsung Helps for the Local Church

Every church benefits from the unseen and unsung help the district office provides in the certification of its ministers. Although all credentials are granted by the Credentials Committee of the General Council of the Assemblies of God, every candidate for credentials must first be recommended by a district credentials committee and the application processed through a district office. When it has been determined that the candidate has met the credentials requirements in Article 7 of the Bylaws of the General Council of the Assemblies of God, the district office endorses the application and forwards it to the general secretary for approval by the General Council Credentials Committee.

In the unfortunate event that allegations or complaints made against a credentialed minister might affect his standing in the Fellowship, the district office has responsibility for investigation and due process. The local church is relieved of all responsibility in matters affecting ministerial relations. One should pray that such matters are dealt with as discreetly as possible in the hope of safeguarding the church, the minister, the district, and the Fellowship. A district office also supervises all rehabilitation programs approved by the General Council for ministers in its district.

Vacancies in Pastoral or Pulpit Supply

If a church needs a pastor, the district office can help the congregation and its official board or pastoral search committee. For example, most district offices are aware of mature ministers with proven records who are or could be available for short assignments as an interim pastor without being interested in becoming a candidate. Having an interim pastor often keeps continuity in the pulpit as well as takes the pressure off the pastoral search committee to have someone in the pulpit from week to week.

When requested by the board or committee, the district office can provide information that may help the church in seeking candidates. For example, most district offices are aware of ministers who are interested in a change. On the other hand, some ministers may inquire directly of the official board or pastoral search committee. In those instances, the board or committee may wish to consult the district office for additional references or recommendations. If the minister is from another district, and to safeguard their assembly, the board or committee may ask their district office to determine if the minister has left, or is leaving, his pastorate in good order.

Assistance in Business Meetings

Usually, chairing business meetings of the church and meetings of the board are duties of the pastor or president, according to the local church bylaws. At times, however, the pastor may want assistance, or, in the absence of a pastor, the board may want an officer to chair a meeting. In either case, the district office can provide advice and counsel. There are a number of circumstances for which it would be wise to have a knowledgeable, neutral party in the chair, for example, the election or reelection of the pastor, the discussion of agenda items by the pastor without requiring the neutrality of the chair, when the pastor is on the defensive, when addressing sweeping constitution and bylaws changes or issues that have brought division. District officers are experienced and knowledgeable in chairing such meetings and will provide any assistance requested by the pastor or the board.

Assistance in Mediation

Grievances or disputes between individuals or groups within the local church can often be resolved informally through mediation. A district officer may be acceptable to both parties to assist in the mediation process. If more than one person is desired to assist in mediation, the district office can arrange for two or three qualified persons to serve in that capacity while still dealing with the matter informally within the local church.

If the matter cannot be resolved informally, the pastor should request that it be handled formally, according to district council policy. The district council policy for the resolution of disputes is usually found in the district council bylaws and should be found in the bylaws of the local church.

Assistance with Administrative Gridlock

From time to time situations develop when the board or the church loses the ability to manage its affairs. An excellent way to alleviate that problem is for the church to temporarily relinquish its administrative control to the district executive committee or district executive presbytery; this body would arrange for an interim pastor, if necessary, and appoint a local advisory committee through which the affairs of the church may be administered. As soon as unity and stability have been restored sufficiently to allow the church to again elect its officers, the church may, by vote of the congregation, request the return of administrative control. Appropriate legal documents essential to this entire process should be available from the district office.

Other Helps Available

As has been noted, because of the diversity among districts, helps are not likely to be uniformly available. A minister moving into a new district will need to contact the district office to determine what specific helps are available.

Some districts provide for enrollment in a ministers burial fund. This is not a form of insurance; rather, it is an organized benevolence for the benefit of those who enroll. The enrollees make a modest contribution to the fund on being notified of the death of another enrollee. The specific amount to be contributed is commensurate with the death benefit to be received. These modest sums are available immediately to the beneficiary. The contributions made to the fund are not tax deductible because there is a benefit to the enrollee.

Some districts have arranged for various forms of group insurance, such as fire and casualty for church buildings and group health insurance with options for dental, vision, and prescription drugs. Some districts pay all or a portion of the life insurance premium for ministers enrolled in the Group Life Insurance Program of the General Council.

The Common Bond

Perhaps one of the best helps the district office can provide for a church is its officers, available to the pastor as mentor, counselor, encourager, burden sharer, or simply a trusted friend to whom the pastor can bare his soul without fear of exposure. We noted earlier that the district office was born to serve the ministers and churches within its boundaries. Those who serve at the district office measure success in terms of the successes of those churches. District officers are somewhat like the Levites of the Old Testament; they had no personal inheritance in Canaan but their joy in ministry rose and fell with the fortunes of the other tribes they ministered to. In the same way, the local church and the district office are to be one in calling, one in commission, one in purpose, and one in the hope.

Working with All Kinds of People

Hal Donaldson

P astoring would be the greatest job in the world if I didn't have to deal with some kinds of people." Those were the words of a minister who had just tangled with Bill—a difficult member of his church.

Bill had grown weary of the pastor's sermons, wardrobe, management style, and his expectations for the congregation. So in frustration the member let the pastor have it: "You're the worst pastor this church has ever had!"

The pastor's jaw tightened as he quoted to himself, *A soft answer turneth away wrath.*[1]

Bill continued his assault. "This was a great church before you came."

Clearing his throat to signal his self-control was waning, the pastor asked, "In my eighteen months here isn't there something I've done that you've liked? The church has grown. We've seen people won to Christ. Isn't there even one church service you've enjoyed?"

Without hesitation, the man replied, "Yeah, the Sunday you were on vacation."

The pastor risked a curious smile. "Tell me, Bill, how did we get off on the wrong foot?"

Bill paused. "When you came here and started asking me and everyone else to do things."

"Like what?"

"You expected us to attend everything from work days to fellowship meetings; then you had us doing your job of visitation."

The pastor sighed. "Well, Bill, I'm sorry you feel that way."

"I am too," Bill snapped. "My family and I are changing churches and going where the preacher understands that people are busy these days and don't have time to do what he's paid to do."

Experiences such as these can send pastors in retreat. To avoid conflict with parishioners and entice them to attend church, some pastors refrain from placing expectations on them. They escort attenders to a comfortable pew each Sunday, then dare to preach messages that dodge Christian responsibility. The remainder of the week these pastors attempt to be one-man crews. They preach, sing, visit, mow, type, and pray—alone. This pattern leads to overwhelmed pastors, ineffective laity, and unreached communities.

Effective pastors learn to involve all kinds of people in the life of the church. This is more challenging today because, for many, church loyalty and involvement are no longer viewed as virtues. As one pastor noted, "Years ago people were like palm trees having shallow roots; today it seems they're more like tumbleweeds going wherever the wind blows." So how does a pastor in this culture of shifting values develop productive, lasting relationships with members of the congregation? How does one assimilate people into church life without alienating them in the process? And how does one integrate people of diverse backgrounds—bearing different spiritual gifts and levels of spiritual passion—into the ministry of the church?

Productive Relationships

Productive, lasting pastor-parishioner relationships tend to form when senior pastors fully understand their responsibility as "executive shepherds."[2] Their duties can be compared to those of shepherd boys who manage flocks in the foothills of Bethlehem. There they keep the flock together by tapping their rods on rocks *(encouraging cohesion and cooperation)*; they prepare the sheep for impending danger by casting stones along the perimeter of the pack *(discipling)*; they establish a course and keep the flock moving in a proper direction by shouting commands *(supplying vision)*; they offer care and nourishment by leading them to where there is food *(providing compassion and teaching)*; and, on occasion, they discipline with delicate, well-placed swats *(offering correction)*.

But even shepherd boys have limitations. They are incapable of carrying their entire flock across the rocky terrain, nor can they force the sheep to graze. Likewise, pastors cannot support the entire congregation on their shoulders or coerce them into spiritual growth. They must lead without trying to force-feed. They must serve without losing nerve.

Parishioners' expectations of the pastor can transform him into a plumber, banker, taxicab driver, physician, and more. But pastors cannot afford to become master impersonators, transformed by the unreasonable expectations of parishioners. Pastors can solidify their job description, nullify criticism, and nurture productive relationships with parishioners by following these steps:

Have a *board-approved job description* in writing for both the pastor and parishioner.

Model ministry and a good work ethic. People are less likely to place unreasonable demands on a pastor who is visibly active and displaying a passion to reach a community. (See Proverbs 10:4–5.)

Delegate to laity. Do not hesitate to ask parishioners to assist other members of the church or fill needed positions. (See 1 Corinthians 12; Ephesians 4:12.)

Productive pastor-parishioner relationships require church members to follow the shepherd. Laity are more likely to follow when they have confidence in the shepherd—his ability, vision, integrity, motives, work ethic, family life, prayer habits, intimacy with God, and his concern for the flock. This level of trust cannot be developed from the pulpit alone; it must be nurtured one-on-one and in small group settings, thus requiring the pastor to bridge the chasm that often exists between pulpit and pew. Here are ways pastors can extend their hand and develop meaningful relationships with layleaders.

1. Frequently mention the names of laity in sermons.
2. Open church services by greeting the congregation from the altar area (off the platform). This, symbolically, lets the people know the pastor sees himself on their level.
3. Step from the platform and, with a roving microphone, solicit testimonies and conduct casual interviews with parishioners. Again, this shows a desire to be among the people.
4. Invite laity home for a meal on special occasions (e.g., wedding anniversary, birthday).
5. Play golf or participate in another hobby together.
6. Attend a conference or seminar together. Or send layleaders to seminars related to their ministry in the church and ask them to report back to you.
7. Ask laity for their opinion on important church issues.
8. Take special interest in their children.
9. Ask a layleader to attend an important function in your place.
10. Pray together.
11. Give correspondence a personal touch with handwritten notes.

Assimilation, Not Alienation

Every church should have an assimilation plan. Certainly there are those who will enter the life of the church regardless of assimilation efforts. There are also habitual spectators—whose favorite hymn is "I Shall Not Be Moved"—who will refuse to participate. Yet most are in the valley of decision, still pondering their level of commitment.

The process of assimilation begins the moment visitors enter the church. They determine rather quickly if they intend to return and, if so, at what level of involvement. Thus, deliberate steps must be taken to guide them into participation and acceptance. That process is complicated when they dash from a church service declaring, "Last one to the car is a rotten egg." This challenge has inspired many churches to offer membership classes and get-acquainted dinners, where newcomers can get to know the pastors and ministry leaders. In these settings people discern whether they are really important to the church. They ask:

- Is the pastor interested in my attending here for what I can do for him, or is he genuinely interested in helping me and my family reach our spiritual potential?
- Do I fit? Can I really be an integral part of this church and find fulfillment?
- Can I be proud of this church and its pastor?

Membership classes and get-acquainted functions are effective if they answer these questions and lead a person, from the outset, to make a commitment to service. Laity must be taught that participation in the life of a church leads to spiritual growth; inactivity, on the other hand, can lead to spiritual atrophy and dissatisfaction. During the orientation classes, the parishioner's portfolio should be communicated. They should know what is expected of them as a member of the church.

Parishioner's Portfolio

As a faithful parishioner, you are asked to

1. Pray daily for your family, church, pastor, city, and country.
2. Care for your family's physical and spiritual needs, thus strengthening the church.
3. Serve in at least one area of ministry in the church.
4. Affirm church leaders and workers.
5. Take special interest in children, senior citizens, widows, etc.
6. Encourage always; refuse to participate in destructive conversation.
7. Discuss dissatisfaction with church leaders rather than complaining to others. Commit the issue to prayer rather than engage in criticism.
8. Accept the fact that different forms and styles of worship can be pleasing to God.
9. Pay tithes and participate in special offerings.
10. Make church attendance a priority.
11. Witness to friends and neighbors, inviting them to attend church.
12. Provide help for parishioners in special need.
13. Ensure that pastor and staff are well cared for. Don't place unreasonable demands on them.
14. Come to church with a sense of anticipation.
15. Feel free to submit ideas to the pastor, but do not take offense if a suggestion is not implemented.
16. Forgive those who have not asked for forgiveness. Make unity and cooperation more important than penance.
17. Model the Christian life for others.
18. Acquire a basic understanding of the fundamental truths of the faith.
19. Observe Communion and water baptism.
20. Do not expect the church to provide all your spiritual nourishment; spend time in God's Word and prayer throughout the week.

Ministry leaders should learn how to evaluate the spiritual gifts and readiness for ministry of newcomers. Once an evaluation is completed, parishioners should then be encouraged to select from a menu of ministry opportunities. First Peter 4:10 says, "Each one should use whatever gift he has received to serve others, faithfully administering God's grace in its various forms." When a person is introduced to the church, the pastor should also announce the ministry this person has chosen to be involved in. This permits the congregation to celebrate this person's decision to be a producer rather than a consumer, a leader rather than a looker.

Churches with an assimilation plan find that their people are more faithful. They give financially and attend regularly because this is *their* church. Through their participation they have taken a healthy ownership of the church.

Diversity and Discovery

Effective pastors celebrate their congregation's diversity. They routinely applaud the handiwork of God as shown in His creation—people of different races, backgrounds, tastes, styles, and more. And they remind the congregation of the church's desire to capitalize on their diversity to reach and minister to the needs of all kinds of people.

These pastors realize it is not their duty to discard those who do not fit the mold. Instead, they create a mold or ministry opportunity that matches the gifts and spiritual passions of their people. The pastor or leader should ask these questions when determining what ministry suits the individual:

1. Is the person living a Christian life? Does he or she ascribe to the basic tenets of the faith?
2. In what areas does the person have ministry or professional experience?
3. What are the person's people skills?
4. Does he or she have abilities that need to be nurtured?
5. What group of people in the church or community need what the person has to offer?
6. What ministry is the person *unsuited* for? Is success or failure in a particular ministry inevitable?
7. What is the person's level of understanding of the gospel and Christian living?
8. Will the person remain faithful to his or her ministry commitment?
9. Does the person have the time and freedom to fulfill his or her commitment? Is there a family issue that will be compounded by his or her participation in a ministry?
10. What ministry does the person have a passion to participate in?
11. Is there a new ministry or position that should be created to take full advantage of the person's abilities and desires?

Keeping Morale High

Morale is high in congregations where people are committed to a common purpose. They have a clear vision and each participant knows he or she is playing an important role in fulfilling the vision. The pastor states and restates the church's vision and frequently displays the fruit of the church's labor. He shows members they are accomplishing their goals— supplying evidence that they are participating in more than a public relations campaign, belonging to more than a religious glee club. The pastor understands the importance of symbols. If he maintains that the church's vision is reaching the lost, there must be examples of people finding Christ through the congregation's efforts. If he proclaims the church is a caring congregation, there must be examples of compassion in action. Otherwise, members begin to question their involvement, and their loyalty can wane.

Today persons select churches as they do neighborhoods. They scrutinize shepherds as corporations evaluate executives. They want to worship in a safe, nurturing church community; at the same time, they want to work with a shepherd who is committed to accomplishing something significant for God. When they see God at work through a pastor and congregation, they are more likely to join the team . . . and stay joined.

The Pastor, His Office, and His Schedule

William F. Leach

Time is a critical part of our lives. The opening words of the Bible are "In the beginning [of time] God . . ." (Genesis 1:1). From the dawn of this world's history, events have been measured by time. Benjamin Franklin, a pioneer in the modern subject of time management, wisely noted, "Dost thou love life? Then do not squander time, for this is the stuff life is made of."[1]

In *A Strategy for Daily Living,* Art Kiev writes, "A successful life does not result from chance nor is it determined by fate or good fortune, but from a succession of successful days."[2] A genuinely successful life is found in Jesus' prayer to His Father in John 17:4: "I have brought you glory on earth by completing the work you gave me to do." If this is to be our testimony, we must manage our time wisely. In other words, we must learn to manage ourselves.

Max Lucado recounts a delightful story of two paddleboats that left Memphis about the same time, traveling down the Mississippi River to New Orleans. In the course of their journey, sailors from one vessel made some pointed comments about how slowly the other boat was moving.

A race ensued. Competition and emotions became intense as the two paddleboats flew over the water. One ship began to lag behind. It was running low on fuel. There had been sufficient coal for the journey but no one had anticipated a race. As the boat lost steam, one entrepreneurial sailor seized some of the vessel's cargo and threw it into the boiler. When the crew realized the stores burned as well as the coal, they fueled their boat with the goods they were responsible to deliver. They won the race, but burned their cargo.[3] God has made us responsible for cargo. We must see that it reaches its destination.

It doesn't take long for a pastor to recognize that the demands on time and life are incredible. To be effective, a pastor must establish three important priorities. First is a commitment to a growing, intimate relationship with God. Second is a commitment to a growing, intimate personal relationship with one's family. Third is a commitment to provide effective visionary leadership to the church and community of God's call. The secret to success or failure lies in how these priorities are fleshed out in a practical way in the pastor's life and schedule.

Establishing Priorities in the Pastor's Schedule

We read an interesting statement in Luke 4:16: "On the Sabbath day he went into the synogogue, as was his custom." Another custom of our Lord was to absent himself from people in order to spend time with His Father in prayer. Everything Jesus did grew out of His relationship with His Father.

What are the customs and practices that characterize our lives? Do they fit the priorities we have prayerfully established? My first priority is to know God. Dick Eastman, author and teacher on prayer, reminds us that our most important appointment each day is our appointment with God. I often say that to my reflection in the mirror as I start my day. My first task each morning is to be alone with God. I have been challenged by Jesus' words to His disciples in the garden: "'Could you . . . not keep watch with me for one hour?'" (Matthew 26:40). My goal (though I am not always successful) is to spend at least one hour each day in prayer. This is followed by Bible reading.

My second priority is my family. God has given me a wonderful wife and two fabulous children. I need to spend significant time with them. Their interests, programs, ball games, and concerts are important. Those events go on my calendar first. I build all my other schedule commitments around this priority.

The third priority of being an effective pastor consumes the majority of my work schedule. Good communication is important. The church board, other key leaders, and the body as a whole must understand our priorities, our philosophy of ministry, our dreams, and how these affect our schedule. The pastor is a "vision caster" and a role model. What we preach and teach and the way we structure ministry testify to what is really important in our lives. The pastor's example helps families develop healthy lifestyles. It also creates an atmosphere so your people understand and support you in your priorities.

Developing the Pastor's Schedule

One thing predictable about a pastor's schedule is its unpredictability. The shepherd does give his life for the sheep. Careful planning becomes that much more vital because any day can be filled with a myriad of interruptions that call for ministry. These are the divine appointments that God gives to prove His mercy and love.

In planning your work week, think of it in twenty-one segments (morning, afternoon, and evening for seven days). As a pastor my workweek began on Tuesday and climaxed on Sunday. (Monday was my day off.) Dr. Archibald Hart, author of the book *Adrenaline and Stress,* urges pastors not to take Mondays off. Because Sunday is a day of heavy stress, there is a massive draw of adrenaline, leaving the pastor tired, irritable, and mildly depressed. The body needs time to recover.[4] Monday should be used to do low-level, routine maintenance activities. It's the day to clear your desk, go over attendance and financial reports. Later in the week—when your energy level is good and you are feeling alive—is the time, the prime time, to give your family quality attention.

Following prayer and Bible reading, Tuesday morning (when I taught Sunday school) was spent preparing my lesson. It was helpful to me to shut myself in a room, far away from the telephone and other interruptions, until I finished my study time. I gathered all my study materials and hid in a far Sunday school room with instructions to my secretary to interrupt me only for a genuine emergency. If you do not have a secretary, place a message on a telephone answering machine that states you are in study and will return all calls between 1:00 and 1:30 (or whatever times you choose). If the call represents an emergency, leave another telephone number of someone who will volunteer to come to the church and inform you of the need. Perhaps a schedule can be established with several volunteers.

Tuesday afternoon was focused on reviewing financial and attendance reports from Sunday, calling visitors, administrative responsibilities, returning telephone calls, answering mail, hospital visitation, etc. It was my goal several days a week to exercise. I enjoy jogging, playing basketball, or using various exercise machines. At least one Tuesday evening per month was the regular meeting of the official board.

Wednesday morning began with prayer and staff meeting. Jesus said, "My house will be called a house of prayer" (cf. Matthew 21:13). The church sanctuary was open at 6:00 A.M. Monday through Friday for people on their way to work to drop in and pray. All morning, individuals would come to the sanctuary to seek God. Each member of our pastoral team was assigned a specific morning to open the church and pray with those who arrived early. This was not a structured meeting. It was simply a time to pray.

On Wednesday the entire pastoral team assembled. We prayed from 6:00 A.M. until at least 7:00 A.M. After prayer, we gathered at a local restaurant for breakfast and staff meeting. We cleared calendars, dis-

> **One thing predictable about a pastor's schedule is its unpredictability.**

cussed ministry issues, reviewed Sunday's absentees, and divided the list for visits, calls, and follow-up. We also discussed the previous Sunday's services and looked forward to the coming Sunday. I shared the themes I intended to preach and we considered how the services could be structured to be most effective. This was especially helpful to the minister of music in planning the selection of hymns, choruses, and special music that would best complement the service. It also provided an opportunity to intelligently focus our prayers for Sunday.

The remainder of Wednesday morning and afternoon was directed to preparing the Wednesday evening Bible study. I generally preached through books of the Bible in this service. Late afternoon I tried to take an exercise break and then return to the office to prepare my heart for the evening service.

Thursday morning (following prayer and Bible reading) I prepared my Sunday morning message. Lunch was devoted to the local Rotary Club meeting. The afternoon was given to normal pastoral duties (administration, appointments, visitation, etc.). Thursday evening was my visitation night.

Friday morning was my day to open the church. The board members who were able joined me to pray. Then I studied for my Sunday evening message. The afternoon was the same as Thursday. Friday evening was a family night. On Saturdays I concentrated on seeking God for Sunday's services, polishing my messages, and calling absentees.

Organizing the Pastor's Office

Most people who have effective work habits have found tools and procedures that help them stay organized.

A TIME-MANAGEMENT SYSTEM

On the market today are a number of good time-management systems that include a calendar (yearly and monthly), a daily "to do" list, a place for daily notes, a telephone number-address book, and other key information for ready reference. These systems include *The Franklin Day Planner, The Daytimer,* and *The Christian Service Planner.*[5]

Discipline yourself to learn and follow one of these systematic planners.

A LIBRARY

Preaching the Word is a primary responsibility of the pastor. Everything you can do to sharpen your skills is vitally important. Developing a well-rounded library and reading good books are essential. It is extremely helpful if early in your ministry you will organize your books by a simple system like the Dewey Decimal System. It is frustrating to spend valuable time searching for a book you know you have in your library.

A FILING SYSTEM

Another essential tool is a good, easy-to-use filing system. I am indebted to Rev. Robert Strand for sharing his plan with me. It is simple, easy to use, and effective, proving to be the best method I have tried. It places immediately at your fingertips articles, illustrations, sermons, as well as sections of books that you have noted for future use.

The system begins with small notebooks that hold sheets of paper 8 ½ by 5 ½ inches. At the top of each page is a place to record the subject reference, along with any notes on possible cross-references. The left-hand side of the page allows space to record where the information is filed. The remainder of the line permits you to note the title or other pertinent information.

Subject Reference	Headings Cross-Reference
File, Book, Magazine, etc.	Title, General Contents, Quotes, Possible Use
SF	Sermon File
GF	General File
LD	*Leadership Magazine* (issue and page numbers)
EN	*Enrichment*
HER	*Heritage*
EV	*Pentecostal Evangel*

These pages are arranged in alphabetical order by the subject or reference heading. The subject or reference is the topic you are filing the information under, such as missions, evangelism, etc. A key component of any filing system is cross-referencing. In this plan you can record the location of the information under every subject it could possibly pertain to. For example, an article may have ideas you can use for missions, evangelism, stewardship, giving, soul winning, witnessing, etc. It becomes a simple matter of turning to each of those pages and recording the location and title of the article, sermon, book chapter, or appropriate pages of the book.

A significant portion of my pastoral preaching was done in series. Those sermons are filed in hanging file folders under the series title. Other messages are filed by topic. Some messages that didn't fit those categories are filed by year, for example "1995 Sermon File." In addition, I keep a sermon log of what I preached for every service of the year. This log notes any information about that service (number of people saved, baptized in the Holy Spirit, etc.) that I want to remember, along with where the message is filed.

An important component of this program is the section of files entitled "General Files." It comprises hanging file folders that hold twenty-five pieces of information (articles, stories, illustrations, etc.). These folders are marked with the designation G.F. 1–25, G.F. 26–50, G.F. 51–75, and so on. An article I want to file under missions, stewardship, and evangelism might carry the designation G.F. 502. That designation is written on the top, right-hand corner of the article and placed in that order in the "General File Folder" 501–525.

Jesus was a master communicator. He had the ability to proclaim profound truth in simple terms that His hearers could understand and identify with. One of His favorite methods was to tell stories that illustrated truth. We call them parables. Approximately one-third of our Lord's recorded public teaching was done in parables.

Illustrations have been compared to windows. Stories let in light. Be on the lookout for good illustrations. When you go to a conference and hear a great story, buy the tape, transcribe the illustration, and file it in your general files. It will help you become a more effective communicator.

Declaring War on Clutter

"A cluttered desk is the result of a cluttered mind." I'm not sure the cliché is always true; Dianna Booher, in *Clean Up Your Act,* puts a different spin on it: "A cluttered desk means cluttered time."[6] Clutter probably does add tension to a pastor's life. I would find it demoralizing to walk into my office and find an avalanche of paper.

However, the old dictum "Learn to handle paperwork only once" is probably not entirely practical. Richard Winwood recommends stacking paperwork in four piles:

1 = Must be done—critical
2 = Should be done—important
3 = Could be done—low value
4 = Waste of time—no value

The fourth pile should immediately find its way into the wastebasket. Place each of the remaining piles in folders and allow on your workspace only the paperwork you are currently handling.[7] This plan will help you to keep your priorities in view and be the most productive with the limited time you have to devote to the administration of your ministry.

Developing Leaders

A principle called the 80/20 rule seems to hold true: Twenty percent of church activity produces 80 percent of its results. Eighty percent of the church's activity delivers only 20 percent of its results. It would be prudent to determine those activities that God is blessing and concentrate a greater percentage of energy in those areas. By the same token, 20 percent of the people in a church accomplish 80 percent of the ministry. Yet, often a pastor spends 80 percent of his time with the 20 percent of the people who are the least involved and only 20 percent of his time with leaders and workers.

As a church grows, it is essential that the pastor devote more of his time to developing leaders and equipping them to carry out the ministries of the church. After all, the church is people. They will make the ministries of the church effective or ineffective. People are the lifeblood. This is true of the several, then scores, and finally hundreds of volunteer layleaders, along with the professional program staff, that will be needed on a full- or part-time basis.

The first paid position after the senior pastor should be a competent secretary who can help the pastor establish an efficient and professional office. Next, the church should provide for the cleaning and the maintenance of the church. This will permit the pastor to devote his time to prayer, study, and developing leaders for ministry.

After these needs are satisfied, the pastor can begin adding professional program staff. Often the first position filled is minister of music or minister of youth. Of course, these are not the only options. A careful evaluation should be made of the strengths and weaknesses of the current ministries of the church in the areas of worship, discipleship, fellowship, and evangelism (Acts 2:42–47). Next, staffing to seize opportunities for an exciting balance in each area will give the church new potential to grow. Perhaps the greatest need and opportunity would be to add a minister gifted in training people in evangelism, or a pastor of administration, or someone anointed to reach children. The philosophy should be "staff to grow." Eventually, as the church grows, ministry to children, youth, young families, singles, senior adults, men's and women's ministries, Christian education, music, and evangelism become bridges to reach more and more people with the love of Christ.

> **" The first position after senior pastor: a paid, competent secretary. "**

Of course, the growth of staff makes it incumbent on the pastor to learn to manage himself and others effectively. A study by the U.S. Labor Department shows that 50 percent of new hires last only six months in their new jobs.[8] Some of them are so successful they are promoted to new positions during this time. But unfortunately many of these people are not a good fit for the position they are called to fill. Calling the right person at the right time for the right ministry is critical.

Martin John Yates, author of *Hiring the Best,* suggests that three important questions be asked when looking for staff: (1) Is this person able to do the job? (2) Is he or she willing to do the job? (3) Is he or she manageable once on the job?[9] If you can find the person who fits these criteria, you are well on your way to developing a team that will impact your city for Christ.

God has paid us a wonderful compliment in calling us to be the undershepherds of His flock. The way we use our time is supremely important. Let us develop good habits that will encourage growth, blessing, and success.

The Pastor's Study

Bill Wilson

The church I attended as a teenager was a vibrant and visionary fellowship. The people were dedicated and hardworking, leaving a deep impression on my life to this day. In the late 1950s, the rural congregation had displayed tremendous faith by constructing an impressive and attractive church complex in the center of our small community. The sanctuary seated about four hundred people and attracted several hundred each Sunday to participate in dynamic and inspirational services. It was here that I had many formative experiences with the Lord, including my own Pentecostal Baptism. I have always been grateful to the energetic and supportive pastor who consistently came to the pulpit with a fresh word from the Lord.

The special sanctuary was modestly designed, and to the left of the platform, in view of all, was a door clearly marked "Pastor's Study." All acknowledged this was a special place designed for our pastor. Understand that this special place did not contain any high-tech equipment, except an electric typewriter and a phone. However, it was understood that this room was one of the most important in the entire building. The pastor's study was the place where our pastor enriched his personal life and prepared for public ministry.

I am convinced that the pastor's study is still necessary. Today's pastor and spiritual leader unfortunately is pressured to exchange the study for the chief executive office. The demand for counseling, committee meetings, and calendar planning can easily turn the pastor's study into the administrator's professional office. No matter how small or large a church, every pastor needs to establish a place of study. This is the only way spiritual leadership can properly deal with the common press and stress of pastoral leadership.

The apostle Paul was used of God to mentor young Timothy. His inspired insights are invaluable, worthy of careful reading. First and 2 Timothy contain vital instruction the veteran preacher gives the rookie pastor. It is in the second letter that Paul addresses the importance of study: "Do your best to present yourself to God as one approved, a workman who does not need to be ashamed and who correctly handles the word of truth" (2 Timothy 2:15). I am sure Paul was not envisioning a specially equipped room in a modern-day church building. He was laying the foundation for a very important exercise requiring the servant of God, the proclaimer of the good news, to get alone in a place set aside for study. We call it the pastor's study.

This admonition to quality workmanship would refine and refocus Timothy. It would be in study that the newly appointed pastor would find insight and inspiration. It would be in study that the servant of the Lord would experience the personal presence and power of the Lord himself.

Imagine for a moment if the apostle gave you a call today and asked to have lunch with you next Tuesday. What do you think he would say to you? What insights would he pass on to you about effective spiritual leadership? I think it would be safe to assume that this seasoned preacher would carefully articulate much of what we read in the two letters to Timothy. No doubt he would talk to you about having a place where you can get alone with the Lord, a place every pastor needs, a place of study. Richard E. Orchard writes, "As with men in all professions, it is important that the pastor have a study or workshop. Some prefer a separate room in the parsonage, while others prefer one in the church building. It should be kept as private as possible even though its uses may be many."[1] Allow me to suggest several important benefits of establishing a private place of study.

A Place of Devotion

The study is to be a place of devotion. In such a place one can set aside distractions and give the Word of God undivided attention. Eyes can be opened to see who God really is. In the study one can have ears open to hear what God is saying. One can have a heart open to experience who God really is. Every spiritual leader entering the twenty-first century must find this place of devotion, or be devoured by the demands and pressures of leadership.

When Moses was attempting to lead over two million people to the Promised Land, he found it absolutely necessary to get alone with the Lord. No one had ever had such an assignment. The weight of the responsibility and duty became heavy, and soon discouragement set in. Moses realized that without direction from the Lord the task was impossible. Moses found a reprieve by getting alone with the Lord in times of intense prayer and conversation. Although he had no office in a local church building, he had a tent he could get away to. "Moses used to take a tent and pitch it outside the camp some distance away, calling it the 'tent of meeting.' Anyone inquiring of the Lord would go to the tent of meeting outside the camp" (Exodus 33:7). The tent of meeting became the place where God revealed himself to Moses. It was a place of devotion. It was there that he learned the presence of God, the power of God, the plan of God, the purpose of God, as well as the peace of God. There Moses was reminded, refined, renewed, and re-established.

Every pastor has felt the drain and pain of leading the children of God. Every pastor has come to face disappointment with people. The pastor who hopes to be an effective leader in the twenty-first-century church must institute a study, a place of devotion.

A Place of Discipline

The study is a place of discipline. In my nearly twenty-five years of pastoring, I have discovered that a formal place of study puts worthy demands on me. More than a place to display a fine library or a top-of-the-line computer hooked up to the Internet, the study is where the pastor can develop the habit of investigating and enriching himself in the Word of God. When Paul was mentoring young Timothy, he instilled in his student the significance of taking time for study: "Physical training is of some value, but godliness has value for all things, holding promise for both the present life and the life to come" (1 Timothy 4:8). The discipline of the study brings great gain to all pastors.

Robert G. Lee, the faithful preacher of a generation ago, once observed that a pastor cannot live on skim milk during the week and preach cream on Sunday. The pastor's study can help you implement a regular schedule of research, filing, preparing, and sharpening your understanding of the greatest book in all the world, the Bible.

As pastor, arrange a consistent weekly schedule for yourself. Make it known that certain times of the week are set aside for study. You will discover that the people you shepherd will respect that time and also pray for you on those days, knowing that you are seeking the Lord for a word. For example, you might designate Friday as your day to prepare for Sunday morning services. On several occasions I have been blessed by people in our local fellowship who have said, "I was praying for you, pastor, on your study day." Such actions build positive relationships and positive responses to ministry.

The discipline of the study, when used effectively, equips you for expositing the inspired Scriptures and applying them to the daily life of the Church. Thus, you must not only maintain a high level of scholarship, but also be alert to the needs of those God has given you oversight of.

A Place of Destiny

The pastor's study is a place that will determine your destiny. Every pastor faces the challenge of recognizing what needs to be done and then finding out how to go about it. It is in the pastor's office that strategic planning is done and the course of one's ministry set. There one can become quiet before the Lord, reflecting on the divine assignment.

I began my ministry in 1972. I had been asked to serve as a youth pastor. At the time I was still attending college and looking forward to becoming involved in ministry. When I arrived the first day, I was shown my office, a small room off one of the Sunday school rooms. I remember sitting at my desk, with a pad of paper, my Bible, and a library of three books, asking myself, *Now what do I do?* I soon discovered that the small office would become a place to meet God and discover His will and plan for the work He had so graciously allowed me to be part of.

It was in my study that the words of the Psalmist came alive to me. "If my people would but listen to me, if Israel would follow my ways, how quickly would I subdue their enemies and turn my hand against their foes! Those who hate the Lord would cringe before him, and their punishment would last forever. But you would be fed with the finest of wheat; with honey from the rock I would satisfy you" (Psalm 81:13–16).

Today's pastor faces many demanding questions. What areas of Scripture should I be presenting to the church? How should I lead the church in the years ahead? What is God's long-term plan for this local body? What should we be doing for our children, youth, singles, young families, middle-aged members, and seasoned saints? Answers to all these questions are found in those times of seeking the Lord in the study.

Solomon said, "Where there is no vision, the people perish: but he that keepeth the law, happy is he" (Proverbs 29:18, KJV). A pastor entering the twenty-first century without a vision will never lead effectively or enthusiastically. In fact, one's ministry will quickly dry up and die without time in the study to receive direction. Such redirection may come in rethinking the service schedule, reconsidering your approach to preaching, reevaluating your conduct of church board meetings or annual business meetings. It may be in the study that the Lord sparks an idea on how to reach youth more effectively or begin an "impossible" building program. These kinds of things can happen when a pastor allows time in the study to discover God's destiny for ministry. Anything less leads to stale and fruitless efforts.

For a number of years now I have taken time in my study to outline the direction of my Sunday morning message. I seek the Lord for the direction I should take, then begin preparing the text, title, and theme. This has helped maintain an expanding and edifying preaching and teaching ministry and helped me avoid the Saturday night uncertainty of *What should I speak on tomorrow?*

A Place of Discovery

In the pastor's study one can discover the mighty works of God. The pastor who establishes quality time in his study will also be the pastor who continues to make meaningful and life changing discoveries. For example, when preparing a series in 1 Corinthians, I discovered that for years I had missed the main point of a key verse. First Corinthians 2:9 says, "No eye has seen, no ear has heard, no mind has conceived what God has prepared for those who love him." When I quoted that verse I generally made reference to heaven. However, a closer look at the text revealed that the true message concerned the unbeliever's blindness to the works and wonders of God. Although this is a more elementary discovery, such findings come only when a pastor spends adequate time in his study.

In the pastor's study the ways of God are discerned and the gems of eternal truth are unearthed. God's people deserve a pastor who has taken time to observe the deeper things of God revealed by the Holy Spirit.

A Place of Defense

The pastor's study serves as a place to prepare for spiritual battle. The letter to the Ephesians gives us these insightful words: "Be strong in the

Lord and in his mighty power. Put on the full armor of God so that you can take your stand against the devil's schemes. For our struggle is not against flesh and blood, but against the rulers, against the authorities, against the powers of this dark world and against the spiritual forces of evil in the heavenly realms. Therefore put on the full armor of God" (Ephesians 6:10–13).

These words should guide the prayer life of the serious and sincere pastor. I have found tremendous help in this text by praying to be armed just as it describes. I have asked that I would be truthful in conversation and in the presentation of myself, that my conduct would be righteous, that I would be a peacemaker rather than be a peace taker. I have appealed to the Lord for great faith to believe that the impossible can become possible, that my mind be clear of clutter and distractions, that I would think on those things that will assist in effective and wise leadership. Finally I have prayed to be a pastor of the Word.

In the pastor's study one finds a powerful defense against the three most common areas of temptation: motives, morals, and money. Throughout one's ministry, the allure of these areas is present. The only way one can keep a check on them is to spend time with the Lord in the pastor's study.

A Place of Delight

It is not uncommon for pastors and other spiritual leaders to find themselves empty spiritually, emotionally, and physically. They begin to bend under the press and demand of long hours and extended assignments.

I will never forget the Sunday I told my wife I wanted to give up my pastoral ministry. At the time, we were in one of the leading churches in our movement, with a full schedule. Although I was not one given to depression, on this Sunday I felt empty and depleted. I had worked hard preparing a teaching I thought was profound. It was. In fact, it was too deep for the audience and had little relevance to what they faced from day to day. This came home to me during the delivery of this "masterpiece." Not only did I realize that my congregation was not with me, they seemed not even to care. I was sinking and sinking fast. Cutting the message short, I went home defeated, discouraged, and depressed.

Something happened to me in the next twenty-four hours. The Holy Spirit used my wife to challenge me to set aside my agenda and seek the Lord. On Monday I went to my study, got alone with the Lord, and He unfolded an entirely new direction, which in the weeks that followed touched the hearts of many people.

King David wrote, "You have made known to me the path of life; you will fill me with joy in your presence, with eternal pleasures at your right hand" (Psalm 16:11). The pastor's study can be a place of great joy and delight.

Finally, it is with enthusiasm that I recommend the following practical steps for the place every pastor needs.

1. Stake out your own pastor's study.
2. Draw up a consistent schedule of weekly preparation.
3. Organize the room to be efficient and inviting.

4. Prepare a workable filing system according to subject.
5. Form a plan to add quality and helpful resources regularly.
6. Inform the church of the one day a week given to study.
7. Expect tremendous times of reward and revelation.

For six years Jonathan Edwards worked in a four- by eight-foot nook he called his study. Although the place seems small by our standards, it was from this limited space that he became one of the great writers and preachers of all time. Experience tells us that every pastor needs a place to be alone with God, a place to hear God speak, giving a word for His people that will ignite their hearts with passion for Him and His work. As the pastor waits on the Lord, there will come a new compassion for people. The study is a place every pastor needs!

Expository Preaching

George O. Wood

I grew up as an MK, PK, and EK (missionary's, pastor's, and evangelist's kid) in the Assemblies of God. My parents moved often. I don't want to count the number of different schools I attended. The longest my family stayed in any one place was about two and a half years. Most of the other stops were shorter. Although called to the ministry myself, I did not want an itinerant lifestyle. My goal was to find roots, locate one place, and remain in it.

I went to seminary and one day in the library I picked up the current issue of *Christianity Today*. The lead article focused on W. A. Criswell and his twenty-fifth anniversary as pastor of First Baptist Church in Dallas. In the article, Criswell was asked the reason for his longevity in one pastorate. He replied, "Expository preaching." He went on to recount that upon arriving at First Baptist, he began preaching from Genesis 1:1, and throughout those twenty-five years he had journeyed straight through the Bible and had finally come to the end of the Book of Revelation.[1]

I was amazed and intrigued. Criswell said the Bible was inexhaustible, and if you preached it, you wouldn't run out of things to say. I thought to myself, *If that's how I can stay in one church for a long time, then I'm going to be an expository preacher also.*

That was a poor motive for getting into expository preaching. I soon found many other good reasons. And, I didn't try to copy Criswell in journeying through the Bible from cover to cover. I took a Bible book at a time, in a nonsequential order, as I felt the Spirit lead me. But I did stay seventeen years in my one and only pastorate.

My First Sermon

I had an interesting beginning. There were maybe sixty people at my try-out sermon. I had my best sermon all polished and ready to go, but as I sat on the platform through the early part of the service, I felt the Holy Spirit telling me to lay it aside (a rare event for me) and simply step to the pulpit and quote Scripture. I had committed to memory about forty-five minutes of the Gospel narratives on the life, death, and resurrection of Christ. I argued with this impulse: (1) I hadn't reviewed my memorized passages in a couple of weeks. What if my mind blanked out? The congregation would think me a fool. (2) Or, if I did successfully remember and deliver my memorized life of Jesus, they would think I was showing off.

The moment came when I was introduced. I had to make a decision as I stepped behind the pulpit. I opened my mouth and out came John 1:1: "In the beginning was the Word, and the Word was with God, and the Word was God." And, I continued quoting the entire prologue of John's Gospel. People opened their Bibles, expecting me to begin preaching from that text, but I was quickly out of John into Luke 2, the birth narrative. From there, on to Jesus' baptism and temptation, the wedding at Cana, and so on. After about ten minutes, a holy hush began to descend on us. People put away their Bibles and began to listen. The power of the spoken Word—just the Word itself without explication or explanation—rivets hearts. Many minutes later I finished the sermon with Isaiah 53, the interpretative overlay for the mission of Christ, and sat down. In that entire forty-five minutes, I had never said one word of my own. I had not greeted the people. I had not introduced my family. I had spoken only God's Word.

Throughout my years as pastor of that wonderful church, I looked back on that try-out sermon as a prophetic tip-off to what the Lord wanted of me as a pastor to those people. He wanted me to take His Word and break it as the bread for life.

My first expository series as pastor lasted about six months—from John's Gospel. I was straight out of a college classroom context, and those dear people had to suffer greatly from my bookish approach to Scripture. I had 100 percent good exegesis, hermenutical aptitude, and almost no practical relevance. Thank the Lord for good, gentle laypeople who encourage young ministers just out of school—bold, confident preachers who have all the answers without knowing any of the questions!

Preaching through Leviticus

My series in John did not draw crowds. But Criswell's article remained to me as north on the compass, a fixed guideline for assuring pastoral longevity. As I drew near the end of John, I prayed about the next series and felt the Holy Spirit impressing me to next preach through Leviticus. I must say, at the time, I wasn't sure this prompting was from the Spirit or from craziness. I protested: "Lord, this is a boring book. When people make New Year's resolutions to read the Bible through, their wagons of intention break down in the wilderness of Leviticus." I am not an allegorical preacher, and I wasn't about to get into fanciful interpretations of the color of threads in the tabernacle. How could Leviticus be relevant?

Still, the impression remained, *Preach through Leviticus.* My trump card was Leviticus 15. I said, "Lord, I can't even read that chapter in public [it deals with bodily emissions], let alone preach from it." I felt the Lord say to me, *Start with chapter 1, and when you get to chapter 15, I'll show you what to do with it.*

Reluctantly, I began. My opening comment to the congregation, in introducing the series, was, "We are going to find out practically if 2 Timothy 3:16 is actually true, '*All* Scripture is God-breathed and is *useful* for teaching, rebuking, correcting and training in righteousness.'" Please don't fault me here. My theological conviction is firm that 2 Timothy 3:16 is true regardless of my experience. However, our unwillingness to preach from whole segments of the Bible speaks louder about our confidence in Scripture than our mental affirmation of doctrine.

> **One reason for longevity: 'Expository preaching.'**

The five offerings of Leviticus 1 through 7 opened powerfully before me week after week as they addressed human need and God's answers. Incredibly, the congregation began to grow. I guess word must have gotten around that a young preacher was in this hard-to-find A-frame church, preaching from, of all things, the Book of Leviticus, and it was making sense! Months later, when I finished Leviticus, I was preaching to three hundred people rather than the one hundred who were in the pews when the series began.

My weekly sermon preparation followed this pattern: Monday, day of study and exegesis for the sermons to be preached that week; Tuesday morning, more study; Wednesday morning, putting the outline together and finding supporting illustrations, plus finishing Wednesday night's message; Thursday, all day completing preparation for Sunday's sermons. In short, about twenty-four hours of every workweek was given over to sermon preparation. The balance of the time went to pastoral leadership, administration, visitation, or whatever. This pattern almost never varied over my seventeen years in pastoring, except for the weeks I had guest speakers.

If you do not spend a significant amount of your time in preparation, you will not feed your flock. And if the flock is not fed, they will start eating you and their fellow church members.

Scholar Richard Israel of Yale University told a proverbial story about the elders of a little Eastern European community: Approaching their rabbi, they told him how concerned they were about his health. Studying the sacred texts twenty hours a day was just too much for him, they protested.

The rabbi responded, "I really have no alternative. If I study twenty hours a day, you will study fourteen hours a day. If you study fourteen hours a day, the students in the academy will study twelve hours a day. If they do that, then the householders of the village will come to the synagogue three times a day to say their prayers. If our simple householders pray three times a day, then the merchants who pass through our village will be embarrassed not to go to the synagogue on the Sabbath; and if the merchants go to the synagogue every Sabbath, then I know that Rothschild will be in the synagogue for the Day of Atonement!" This rabbi had wisely understood the power of personal example impacting the behavior of those he ministered to.

My fundamental duty as a pastor is to preach the Word. My secondary duties may include administration, promotion, overseeing development of physical facilities, visitation, etc. But unless I give the preaching of the Word my first priority, the heart of the church has collapsed. The heart is a pump. God has ordained that through the preaching of the Word a constant supply of spiritual life and power be pumped into the church, His people.

> **"Find out if 2 Timothy 3:16 is true."**

Churches die when the pastor has nothing from God to say to the people. The congregation may be in a beautiful building; the educational, social, and organizational emphases may be superb; but unless the pulpit rings with a vibrant word from God, that church has a terminal illness. The illness may be short or long, but eventually death results. The study of God's Word must be at the top of my personal priorities if I expect members of my congregation to have it as one of theirs.

Oh, Leviticus 15! What happened?

I came to my office at eight o'clock that Monday morning, sat down at my desk, and opened my Bible to Leviticus 15. Before ever cracking the commentaries, I always take time to look at the Scripture without any aids. Just the Bible and me. That morning I said, "Lord, it's the week of Leviticus 15. You told me You would show me what to do when I got here. Well, I'm here." Instantly, as I read the text, the Holy Spirit dropped this sermon title into my heart, "A Very Personal God." Titles for sermons are invariably difficult for me, and usually they never come until the end of the sermon preparation process. But here it was, the title even before I had done the exegesis, sermon structure, or illustrations!

That Sunday I read Leviticus 15 to a very quiet audience. I can assure you that if you read that chapter publicly your audience will also be quiet. I then began, "Many of you think God is remote. He's called the Man Upstairs. You may think He is far removed from your personal world, and your cares. You may feel He doesn't even know you exist. Well, this chapter tells you that God knows you rather well. He designed your plumbing system. If He knows even those details about you, you can be assured He knows the rest of your life also."

Why do I relate these personal experiences? Because the best definition of preaching I ever heard was "Preaching is you." It's the divine communication of truth through your human personality. None of us will preach exactly the same way from any given text, but those who preach the Word will find the Lord at work in their own life and the lives of the people they pastor.

What Is Expository Preaching?

Expository preaching involves taking a block of Scripture (a verse, a paragraph, a chapter, a book) and answering two questions: (1) What *did* it say? and (2) What *does* it say? In answering those two questions, the proposition, main points and subpoints of the message are all controlled by the text itself. In topical preaching, the preacher can choose his or her own outline. In textual preaching, the main points are controlled by the text, and the preacher can fill in whatever he or she feels led. However, in expository preaching, the text totally controls the content of the message: one is not free to hunt or pick what one wants to emphasize or ignore. Let's consider the two questions above. To preach expositorily, I must answer both.

The first question, "What *did* it say?" involves exegesis and hermeneutics. I want to understand as best I can what each word or phrase meant to the biblical writer, to the people of God to whom this word first came. Thus, I hit the Bible dictionaries, lexicons, concordance, commentaries— anything I can get my hands on to better understand this text. Too often we want to skip the hard task of really understanding Scripture in order to get immediately to the application. This is one reason why difficult parts in Scripture are often skipped (such as Leviticus).

No sermon is complete, however, if we have answered only the first question. We must also consider, "What *does* it say?" In other words, I must move past exegesis to application. How does this ancient living Word relate to the contemporary needs of persons to whom I will preach? Preaching must always involve one foot planted firmly in exegesis and the other in application. Sermons will be dry as chips if only exegetic. Exegesis tells what the Scripture *said;* application, what it *says.*

Many a congregation has been put to sleep by a sermon that never made it into the here and now of experience. It becomes a very dry, dull history lesson. However, sermons that neglect exegesis for the sake of application will eventually produce a biblically illiterate congregation, prey to false winds of doctrine and the gales of Satanic adversity. Generally, if a sermon fails to interest, inspire, or challenge, it is because one or both of these questions were not answered by the preacher. Phillips Brooks, the great American preacher of another generation, so aptly said, "No exhortation to a good life that does not put behind it some truth as deep as eternity can seize and hold the conscience."

> **Two questions: What did it say? What does it say?**

Paul told Timothy to keep "the . . . pattern of sound teaching" (2 Timothy 1:13). Essentially Paul was saying that he followed a system of teaching, that his own preaching-teaching methods had not consisted of isolated pieces of information and scattered spiritual exhortations. One has only to read Paul to detect how orderly he is. In Bible study a person is not well-advised to try a hop-and-skip method. If a person reads a chapter in Romans one day, switches to a part of Revelation the next, and goes back to Exodus the following day, continuing this random procedure for long periods of time, he is not really going to profit. Just imagine trying to study a foreign language, history, or science textbook in that unsystematic fashion! Study of the Bible is not exempt from the same principles that apply to study in other areas.

If the above comments are true about personal study, they also apply to preaching. Does my preaching carry on the systematic exposition of truth? Am I giving forth a *pattern* of sound words? What would happen if a construction worker tried to build a house by putting the bricks down in unconnected places rather than fitly joining them together? Too often our sermons, from week to week, are unrelated bricks. Should there not be a relationship between last week's sermons and this week's? Or last month's and this month's? Or even last year's and this year's?

Some feel that following a sermon plan wherein the preacher takes weeks or months to sequentially walk the flock through a book in the Bible actually inhibits the Holy Spirit. "Aren't you ruling out the leading of the Spirit?" they ask. Not at all—unless your view of the Spirit means that everything He does must be instantaneously spontaneous. I believe the Spirit can give me direction for a whole series just as easily as He can for one message. But I must never get inflexible. If while in the midst of a series, the Holy Spirit puts upon my heart some special word, I have no hesitation to interrupt the series.

Expository Preaching Builds the Church

Over the years, I have found in expository preaching great advantages for both myself and the church. Here is how expository preaching helps the church.

Over a period of time, the congregation is exposed to the totality of God's Word. If I just preach "how to do it" messages ("how to" make a marriage work, raise children, be financially secure, become a success, defeat stress—all the popular topics of the day), I will completely omit essential truths upon God's heart. On the other hand, if I faithfully preach the Word, I will address all the felt needs of people, since God's Word is fantastically relevant.

By preaching through major blocks of Scripture I am forced to preach on subjects I would not normally choose, but God has ordained they be given consideration. Such exposure of the people to God's Word will ground their faith, not in the opinions of men nor in hobbyhorse doctrines nor latest wave fads, but God's written revelation. If you get your people into the Word, you will get the Word into your people.

Spiritual maturity is built. The Pentecostal/charismatic world has been through waves of fads in the past twenty years: extremes in discipleship emphasis, fascination with coughing up demons, health-and-wealth gospel, dominion theology—you name it. All during this time, I simply kept systematically preaching the Bible to our people. We lost almost no one to these elements of "charis-mania." Why? Our people had been grounded in the Word. They had become accustomed to having Scripture dealt with in context, line by line, word by word. They could tell a Scripture-twister a mile off. They knew when someone was lifting a text out of context and distorting it.

In our emphasis on revival, we must never forget that the first hallmark of an apostolic church is commitment to the apostles' doctrine (Acts 2:42). How can people become grounded in the teaching of the apostles if all they get is someone's latest revelation? Expository preaching helps our people not become prey to every wind of doctrine.

All the issues God wants dealt with are dealt with in God's time. I am always amazed at how God would apply a sermon within a series at just the right time of need, either for the congregation or an individual in it.

I think of the runaway girl who found herself in our church one Sunday evening. I "so happened" to be in a series on the Ten Commandments. Which one do you think I preached from the night that girl wandered into our midst and was saved? "Honor your father and mother. . . ."

I think of the second series I did on Leviticus, ten years after the first one. My text that Sunday was from chapters 13 and 14, a lengthy passage on leprosy. I explained to the congregation that the Biblical word "leprosy" embraced many skin conditions, including psoriasis. I didn't know that a local community college professor and his wife were visiting the church that morning, that he had a long-standing and painful condition of psoriasis which was untreatable and inoperable. This couple comes in, and hears a minister preaching on the theme, "What Your Skin Is Telling You About God." How odd, but peculiarly relevant!

If I were simply selecting what I wanted to preach on week by week, I would have never chosen Leviticus 13 and 14. But the Lord knew this couple would be there that Sunday. They were so intrigued, they came back the next Sunday. At the close of the service, they responded to the altar call and God healed him instantly.

Preaching expositorily gave me great liberty to deal with sensitive matters. The congregation knew I wasn't personally picking on them when I came to a text that was uncomfortable for them. This wasn't the opinion of a preacher, it was God's. The preacher hadn't singled them out; the passage simply fell open to them that day because that's where the pastor was in his journey through that book in the Bible.

Preaching expositorily builds a sense of reliability. Persons in our congregation knew they could bring unsaved family and friends to the service and they would not be surprised by an unprepared, rambling sermon. Often in Pentecostal circles, we almost venerate unpredictability. I think we need to place more emphasis on predictability. Our people knew where to open their Bibles when it came time for the sermon. In fact, as our church grew, people often identified their entry into the church by the text I was in that Sunday. "Oh, pastor I came to church first when you were in Romans 8," or, "1 Samuel 17," "Revelation 3," "Nehemiah 1," etc.

Expository Preaching Helps the Pastor

If there are advantages for the church in the pastor's preaching expositorily, they are even greater for the preacher himself.

There is no fumbling for direction each week. I don't know how many hours I would have wasted over seventeen years if every week I had started from scratch trying to figure out what I was going to preach on that week. I always knew. The next chapter. Or the next paragraph. This meant I was able to avoid the Saturday night panic. In seventeen years of pastoring, I believe there were only two times when Sunday's sermons were not ready for delivery by the end of the workday on Friday.

Each Monday, I came to my office early in the morning, opened my Bible, and started with God's Word for my life and our church that week. Never once did I sense God failing to speak to me from His Word. God is not silent when we approach His Word. God always spoke to me even though I was not always a good conduit for His message. Yes, even expository preachers lay an egg from time to time!

Expository preaching provides ample opportunity to develop sermon resources. As I entered into a new series, I visited Christian bookstores and libraries to cull out what tools I needed to purchase for the new series. I bought those commentaries or helps that assisted me in answering well either of my two foundational questions: What *did* it say? and What *does* it say? Over the course of years, I was able to develop a good library as well as a rich resource of illustrations and applicational materials.

Nothing fosters personal spiritual growth in a pastor more than expository preaching. Why? One is forced to study systematically, to inculcate God's Word personally. I always had more material than I could ever use in the preaching event. I was the beneficiary of the overflow. Expository preaching enables you to minister from the overflow rather than a half-full or empty cup.

Expository preaching promotes longevity in the pastorate. I lasted seventeen years and never felt that I had run out of things to preach on. Why do so many pastors leave the ministry? Surely one reason is burnout.

> **"No fumbling for direction each week."**

There is a depletion of the minister's energy physically, mentally, emotionally, and spiritually. I found the systematic study and personal spiritual preparation required for expository preaching an irreplaceable source of renewal. The congregation never grew tired of God's Word, and I didn't either.

As a pastor, you cannot be all things to all people. Early on, I determined my major concentration would be upon the ministry of the Word, and that I would allocate the time necessary to do that well. After all, each minister is called upon to be "a workman who does not need to be ashamed and who correctly handles the word of truth" (2 Timothy 2:15). This meant I had to give lesser priority to counseling, administration, visitation, and all other sundry aspects of the ministry. This did not mean, however, that these other ministries were neglected. As pastor, I could delegate many things, and I did. But the one thing I for sure could not delegate was my preaching ministry. The apostles came to this conclusion for spiritual leadership long before me: "[We] will give our attention to prayer and the ministry of the word" (Acts 6:4). Keep your priorities straight, and God will build His church through you!

You don't have to be an expository preacher to faithfully proclaim God's Word. There are all kinds of preaching styles and methods the Holy Spirit blesses. But expository preaching will certainly enrich your own life and that of the people God has called you to.

How Do You Preach Expository Sermons?

Now comes the critical question. You want to preach expository sermons. How do you go about that? Let me walk you through the process by taking one of the most familiar passages of the Bible, Matthew 28:18–20. In fact, this text is so familiar that many never preach from it at all.

Topical preachers might use this text as a jumping off point for a sermon on the need for evangelism or missions, and simply take the one word "Go." Textual preachers might take one phrase, such as "Go into all the world"; link it with another, for example, Acts 1:8; and speak, in this instance, of the three realms we are to go into: home, the place nearby, and the utmost parts of the world.

But expository preachers are required to include every single word of the text in their sermons. Matthew 28:18–20 focuses on matters more inclusive than that of "going" or where we are to go.

Remember the first question in preparing an expository message? What *did* the text say? To answer this question we must do good exegesis. Do not, however, begin your exegesis by flying to the commentaries. An expository preacher should first simply study with nothing but the Bible in hand; no commentaries or helps of any kind.

It is important that you begin sizing up the text. What is it saying? How can the Holy Spirit help you to understand it afresh? What parts seem to jump out at you? What do you not understand? Where are the nouns? The verbs? The adjectives? The adverbs? What's the main thought of the passage? What are the subthemes? It never hurts to write out your own paraphrase of the text. Imagine you are going to preach this text to a mixed audience of eight-year-olds and college professors. How would you phrase what is being said so both groups would clearly understand?

Why is it important to first wrestle with the text before consulting outside helps? Because this passage must begin to get into your own spirit. You can never successfully preach expositorily if your messages sound like book reports. And that's what they will be if all you do is fashion your sermon after studying the commentaries. God's Word must speak to you first if it is to pass through you and speak to anyone else. During this initial, direct encounter between you and the text, begin to ask yourself, *How would I outline these verses? What title seems appropriate?*

Spend at least an hour on your own with the text before you consult your Bible study resources. If you know Greek or Hebrew, of course, spend time in the original text gaining the nuances from the biblical language. You should not begin to look at the commentaries until the text itself has gotten imbedded in your spirit.

Then pull out the helps: Bible dictionaries, concordance, interlinear translation, paraphrases and other versions, word-studies, commentaries. Don't be sparse in your repertoire of commentaries. Some make the mistake of relying almost exclusively on one or two commentaries, and their sermons become simply a restatement, a rehash, of what that learned individual said. I try never to use fewer than about eight commentaries on any given passage. This ensures I am drawing from multiple viewpoints, some of which I will not agree with or be helped by, but I need the multiplicity of input to properly understand the text. I must resist the impulse to jump into the application of the text without first engaging in the thorough process of examining it.

As you carefully mine the text of Matthew 28:18–20, you begin to notice the major themes. They stand out. In verse 18, Jesus makes a very striking claim. In verses 19 and 20a, He gives an order. And in the last phrase of verse 20, He issues a promise.

An expository sermon will, therefore, build upon this skeletal structure within the text itself. Always, the text itself must control your outline. Expository preaching does not give you license to force your own ideas onto the text. The text must be allowed to speak for itself. As you focus on the exegetical aspects of the text, begin to notice some things that stand out, for example, the word *all*. In the King James text, the word *all* occurs three times: "all power," "all nations," "all things." In the New International Version, *all* occurs only twice: "all authority [or "power"]," "all nations." But in the underlying Greek text, *all* [Greek root *pas*] actually occurs four times: "all power," "all nations," "all things," "all days." As I note that, I say to myself, *That's an important repetition. That needs to be included in the message. How shall I use that?*

> ## First, simply study with nothing but the Bible.

My exegesis also makes me focus on connectives. First, Jesus claims authority. Then, He issues orders. Finally, He makes a promise. Aren't these connected? Doesn't His authority serve as the underpinning for the orders? Would Jesus send us out on a mission that had no hope of success? Isn't our responsibility therefore linked to the success of His own mission? Unless He has authority, we have no responsibility. But are we sent forth to do His work on our own? No! With the commission comes also an assurance: He will be with us.

Do you see what we are doing here? We are working on the *connectives*. Sometimes a sermon contains simply a bare-bones outline: points one, two, and three. Yet, the preacher never connects the points. If we have point one, how does it relate to point two? Point three? You can almost always tell whether you are connecting your points if you will silently insert the word *therefore* or *because* between them. For example, in this text: Jesus has authority. Therefore, we have responsibility to that authority. Because we have responsibility, we need His presence if we are to accomplish what He has asked.

Seek to follow the logical flow of the text itself. When God speaks, as in the Bible, He does not stutter. Words are not given in random order, but in proper sequence. There is a purpose and method within God's revelation. Seek to see it, and proclaim it!

We're still working on the exegesis, "What did the text say?" I began to notice in my own time of study that four verbs dominate the middle of Matthew 28:18–20. In the English, two of the verbs are imperatives, or commands: "Go" and "Make disciples." Two of the verbs are participles: "baptizing" and "teaching." At first, that means nothing to my sermon development; I simply take note of it. As I consult the Greek text, I discover only one verb in the imperative: "Make disciples." The other verbs are all participles: "going" (or "as you go" or "having gone"), "baptizing," and "teaching." I have no ideas as to what I plan to do with this discovery. I'll have to think on it awhile, and do further work in the commentaries. You will often experience this same phenomenon in preparation. Something will strike your attention, but you initially will be clueless as to how you can develop the observation.

All the while I am studying, I am making notes. By now, I have pages of notes. My exegetical study ends. I think I have a fairly accurate understanding of the meaning of the words. Now it's time to build the sermon and begin to answer the second question, "What *does* the text say?" How do I take these verses and have them leap off the page into the hearts of people I minister to? That's the work of the Holy Spirit, and it is also my work. Such effort cannot be successful without prayer. Thus, underlying all study is the act and attitude of praying, "Lord, teach me first what this passage is saying to me, and then open it to the hearts of my people."

As Pentecostals, we do far more than preach to inform. We preach to persuade. We want people to do something after we preach. We are looking for a response. Dry, cold sermons produce dry, cold people. We want our sermon to be a live coal from God's altar. It cannot light a fire in our congregations if first a spark is not lit in our own hearts. My goal, therefore, in building the sermon is to apply the text to the people I preach to, beginning with myself.

Pictorially, I see the sermon like a house with a front porch, main rooms, and a back porch. Let the front porch be a welcome center for the sermon; don't keep your guest forever on that front porch by a long, rambling introduction. Keep it to the point, and let it be a setting for welcoming the guest to the main rooms of the house, the major themes of the message. When the sermon is done, I think of exiting my guest through the back porch. That porch also is smaller than the main house, even as the conclusion to the sermon should not be greater than its body. The end should be to the point and provide opportunity for decision or response. Endlessly extending the conclusion is like never releasing people off the back porch to get back into the landscape of the everyday.

> **There is a purpose and method within God's revelation. Seek to see it, and proclaim it!**

The three things, therefore, that require most work in sermon preparation—after exegesis—are (1) the title and introduction to the message (front porch), (2) the proposition (main rooms), and (3) the conclusion (back porch).

Expository preachers differ on which of the above will concern them first in the preparation process. Some prefer to begin, like a lawyer, with crafting their summation or conclusion. Others give first attention to the introduction, treating it as the headwaters for the flow of the sermon—believing that the rest of the message will follow the channel begun in the opening words. Almost always, I concentrate first on building the proposition and outline.

Of course, the congregation never hears me say, "Now, the proposition of my message is . . ." The proposition is for my benefit, and if I build it well, the congregation will retain what is preached. Simply put, the proposition is a one-sentence summary of your entire message. It will include your main points. If you cannot reduce your sermon to a one-sentence, clearly-articulated summary, it is not ready to preach. Simultaneous to building my proposition, I am constructing the outline of the message, since the two go together.

> " I see the sermon like a house: front porch, main rooms, back porch. "

Within that process, or at the conclusion of it, I seek to crystallize the message with an appropriate title. For example, it's hard to title Matthew 28: 18–20 as anything other than "The Great Commission." That's the name given it over the course of Christian history. Perhaps, for effect, you might try a variation, "The Great Co-Mission." You might choose a more creative or contemporary title. However, avoid titles that promise more then they can deliver, or mislead, or misrepresent the content of the text.

Employing the historical title, I asked myself, *What's so great about the Great Commission?* In other words, why has the word "great" been inserted? "Great" does not appear within the text itself. The more I reflected on this question (and good sermon preparation requires that you do considerable prayer, meditation, and reflection) I realized the text itself answered the question. The great commission is great because it contains a great claim, a great responsibility, and a great assurance! And there it is—both my proposition and outline in one sentence. I can employ it throughout the sermon!

In the introduction, I can ask, "Why do we call these words of Jesus 'The Great Commission'?" Then, the main body of the sermon answers that question. Because, first, it makes a great claim: "All authority in heaven and on earth has been given to me." Second, it carries a great responsibility: "Make disciples." And, third, it conveys a great assurance, "Surely I am with you always to the very end of the age." In the conclusion, I return to those themes. Have you accepted the claim of Jesus? Have you acted on the responsibility given? Are you filled with the assurance He has promised?

For me, the title, proposition, and conclusion serve somewhat like the design on a coloring book. I can't begin to color unless I know what I am filling in. Carefully and methodically, I begin to craft my notes for the message. At the top of the page I write the title, "The Great Commission."

Then comes a paragraph called "Introduction." In expository preaching, the simple goal for all introductions is to get the text into the people and the people into the text. A simple way to sum up an introduction to the Great Commission is to note that these are Jesus' last words, in the Gospel of Matthew, to His disciples—and they're also His last words for us. It was their commissioning message, but it is also ours. If the last words of a dying loved one are important, how much more so the last words of the risen Christ!

From there, the first main emphasis unfolds: "The great claim." If you have done your exegetical homework in the greater context of Matthew's gospel, you will be instantly drawn to Matthew 4:8–10 where Jesus, at the beginning of His ministry, turned down the devil's offer of "all the kingdoms of the world and their splendor." You will want to drive home the application that Jesus could not have made the claim at the end if He had fallen to the temptation in the beginning—and it's the same way in our own lives. Power with God comes through the pathway of obedience, resisting the enemy's temptations.

You will also want to emphasize the universal claim of Jesus. His authority extends to heaven (something the devil could not offer since he is not in heaven and has no authority there) and earth. Jesus is telling us that in that day we will not answer to Mohammed, Buddha, Confucius, or any other person. We will answer to Him.

I could not have reached the above insight without connecting the immediate text to the whole text. Expository preaching requires you to develop a passage within its context: immediate (chapter and book of the Bible) and general (the whole of Scriptures). Only as I did concordance work on the word *all* in the Gospel of Matthew did the observation come to me that I should connect Matthew 4:8–9 with Matthew 28:18–20. Continually, stay with the work of relating Scripture to Scripture.

Search Out Appropriate Illustrations

Within each point of your sermon, you will want to employ an apt illustration, if at all possible. A sermon without illustrations is like a house without windows. In declaring Jesus' great claim, I reflect to myself that some in my audience may have problems with that statement: If He has all authority, as the preacher says, then why do we see so much that is out of control? Why does evil win so frequently? Why am I having difficulty? It's important, therefore, to note that what Jesus is talking about is final authority: the decisions that relate to heaven or hell, forgiveness of sins, eternal life, ultimate realities.

The illustration I used to anticipate and overcome this silent objection is one from my own experience. I had a friend who, as a young man, had an opportunity to buy Sony stock when it was only ten cents a share. Had he known what would happen with Sony, he would have sold everything he had to buy as much stock as he could. In the same way, Jesus' words let us know final outcomes. How is my behavior today affected by what I know about the future He holds securely? If I am persuaded that He is victor, I will invest everything I am in His cause today!

After focusing on the great claim, a moment of transition comes. Every expository sermon needs to navigate carefully the transitions. What connection does point one have to point two? In this case, the great responsibility (point two) flows out of the great claim (point one). Jesus' connective word is "therefore." Thus, our responsibility flows out of the power claimed by Christ. He would never send us on a mission which had little or no hope of success.

Quickly, the transition comments flow into the development of the core of our responsibility. Remember, in exegesis we discovered that three of the verbs are participles and one is imperative? That now controls the development of this second point.

Our main responsibility is "to make disciples." Jesus is not content that we just get people to say the "sinner's prayer." He is not primarily interested in head counts of decisions made. So often our focus on evangelism is go get people ready for heaven, but discipleship impels us also to focus on getting heaven into people. A Christian is a follower of Jesus, one who lives as His disciple.

The participles define the process of making disciples. First, there is going. Unless believers go to others, no one can become a disciple. In the English text, our exclusive focus sometimes is on the word "go." But that's not the focus of Jesus. The Greek text has no explicit command to "go." What Jesus says is, "As you go" or "having gone." In other words, He assumes we will go. Going is not the end of it, however; going is just the start. "Going" is to result in "making disciples." Today, a lot of people are "taking trips," assuming that is a fulfillment of the Great Commission. But, Jesus says, the evangelism or missionary trip must have a purpose: make disciples.

Baptizing is the second element in making disciples. Baptism is important enough that Jesus included it in the great commission. But Jesus' focus is not upon the outward ritual but the inward surrender. Jesus desires public and visible identification with Him through water baptism. The illustration I found helpful here was the post-apostolic description of baptism in *The Didache* ("The Teaching"), written in the late first century or early second century. These early believers required baptism to be in running, cold water. Why running? To symbolize the carrying away of sins. Why cold? To illustrate that the Christian life was one of rigor, a "real shock to the system." Living the gospel is not a matter of convenience, but commitment. The focus of Jesus is not on self-fulfillment, but self-denial; not on cross-avoidance, but cross-bearing.

> **A sermon without illustrations is like a house without windows.**

A challenge of expository preaching is that it requires you to develop every word or phrase of the text before you, yet you must at the same time not get bogged down by over-developing a particular point. For example, commentaries devote page after page to the words "baptizing them in the name of the Father and of the Son and of the Holy Spirit." You will see long treatises on infant baptism versus believer baptism, the mode of baptism as immersion, pouring, or sprinkling. Further, some would focus main attention on how this text refutes "Jesus Only" teaching.

If I were preaching a sermon on water baptism, I would want to deal with all these issues. But I am not preaching a water baptism sermon; I am preaching from a text on the Great Commission. So I must not get lost in the forest of baptismal topics. You must make similar judgment calls as you work with the text before you. Your exegesis may tempt you to spend more time than you should on developing a subtheme within the text. Don't get distracted by making details into themes.

I simply note that if one is a disciple of Jesus, one will be baptized. The baptism is more than into water, it is into the very person of God. "Name" is a singular noun—we are therefore baptized into the One God who has revealed Himself as Father, Son, and Holy Spirit. In being baptized into that name, I not only get wet, I am placed into a relationship with Him.

The third component within the text for making disciples is "teaching them to obey everything I have commanded you." There is a curriculum in the lifelong course of discipleship. It's everything Jesus has commanded— by personal example, discourses, parables, precious sayings, promises, warnings, lessons on hypocrisy, prayer, humility, trust, forgiveness, obedience, marriage, discipleship, cross-bearing, etc. Our Lord never foresees a time or circumstance when any part of His teaching will become antiquated or untrue, inappropriate or needless. How easy, as ministers, to preach some things and not others, to preach "our things" rather than "everything" He has ordered. How frequently we are tempted to ride themes Jesus said absolutely nothing about!

Steps in Preparing Expository Sermons

1. Take time to thoroughly read, meditate upon, and pray over the Scripture passage you will be preaching from. Do this without the aid of any outside studies—just you and the Bible. Take notes of the thoughts and questions that come to you.

2. Consult the commentaries. Use a wide selection of study aids. Take copious notes.

3. Develop your title, proposition, and outline. Can you express the entire message within a single declarative sentence? Is your title true to the text and does it elicit interest?

4. Think through your introduction (get the people into the text and the text into the people). Does it grab attention?

5. Think through your conclusion. What appeal are you making, what response are you seeking? What do you want people to do with the message you have preached?

6. Does your sermon have windows? Do your illustrations fit, or are they forced or far-fetched? Tell a story to make a point, not just to tell a story.

7. Have you paid attention to your connectives? Will the people be able to clearly follow your train of thought? Are your points connected to each other? Do they flow out of your proposition? Have you kept your main points succinct and memorable?

8. Is your message soaked in prayer? Do you feel it is "fire within your bones"? Do you have a sense that you fill a prophetic role as you preach—that what you proclaim is indeed God's Word to your people for that occasion?

For illustration here, I find a quote from Hugh Thomson Kerr most helpful: "We are sent not to preach sociology but salvation; not economics but evangelism; not reform but redemption; not culture but conversion; not progress but pardon; not a new social order but a new birth; not revolution but regeneration; not a new organization but a new creation; not democracy but the Gospel; not civilization but Christ . . ."[2] For application, here is an excellent opportunity to underscore the importance of personal Bible study, prayer, stewardship of time and talents, obedience to Jesus, and a host of other issues that concern learning to be a disciple.

At this point in the sermon, I am still working my proposition. For transition, I review where I am. The Great Commission is great because (1) it contains a great claim, (2) it gives a great responsibility, and finally, (3) it conveys a great assurance. Once more, exegesis helps builds the emphasis. In the Greek, the literal translation is "I *myself* am with you." Jesus, in employing the reflexive pronoun, underscores the surety of His own personal presence. Thus, subpoint "a" is easily stated. The great assurance is (a) personal. "I myself am with you." But it is also (b) an abiding assurance: "always."

If you have done the exegesis carefully on this text, you are now ready to point out a very exciting truth. The word *all* in the Greek text occurs four times in Matthew 28:18–20. "All authority"—there is no power that is left out, over which Christ does not have control. "All nations"—there is no person that is left out, of any color, ethnicity, or background. "All things"—there is no precept vital to our relationship with God that Jesus failed to teach us. "All times" [literally, "all the days"]—there is no period in our life as a disciple of Jesus when He is not personally with us! "All the days" includes days of strength and weakness, of success and failure, joy and worry, youth and age, life and death. All the days! Finally, the great assurance is not only (a) personal and (b) abiding, it is (c) a victorious assurance: "to the very end of the age."

For illustration on the great assurance, I found the story of David Livingstone pertinent. He once said, "For would you like me to tell you what supported me through all the years of exile among people whose language I could not understand, and whose attitude towards me was always uncertain and often hostile? It was this, *'Lo, I am with you alway, even unto the end of the world.'* On those words I staked everything, and they never failed!" Livingstone said of this phrase, "It is the word of a gentleman of the most strict and sacred honour . . ."[3]

> **The conclusion must touch not only the mind but also the heart.**

As you near the conclusion of your message, you realize that it must not only touch the mind of your audience, but also their hearts. Jesus understood this, and that's why He so often told stories. You will never be effective as an expository preacher, nor any other kind of preacher, unless you incorporate material that moves your own heart and the hearts of persons you preach to.

The sermon quickly draws to a conclusion. Relying upon the Holy Spirit, you seek to bring people to a response. Have they accepted the claim of Jesus? Have they accepted the responsibility He himself gave? Do they live in the assurance He has made? It is now time for the altar— a moment when people can respond to the preached Word, making a personal commitment to it.

My purpose in walking you through preaching from Matthew 28:18–20 is simply to give you a working model for how to preach expositorily. The principles and insights given will apply to any text in Scripture. Don't be surprised, when you begin to preach expositorily, if you struggle at first. Some of my earliest expository sermons I would not want to repreach today. Like all disciplines, expository preaching comes more readily as you practice it. But the dividends are worth it!

There is nothing that will more dramatically affect your own spiritual growth than constant absorption in expository preaching. You will take in far more than you ever give out. And the people you preach to will readily mature spiritually, for you will be putting God's word, rather than your own ideas, into their lives.

Back to the Word in Our Preaching

Thomas E. Trask and Wayde I. Goodall

There is no question but what the Early Church lived within the realm of the supernatural.[1] Signs and wonders were not out of the ordinary; miracles were normal and in fact expected. "They were continually devoting themselves to the apostles teaching and to fellowship, to the breaking of bread and to prayer. And everyone kept feeling a sense of awe; and many wonders and signs were taking place through the apostles" (Acts 2:42–43[2]).

Many in the Early Church had seen the miraculous ministry of Jesus Christ himself. This is attested to in Peter's sermon on the Day of Pentecost. Peter said, "'Men of Israel, listen to these words: Jesus the Nazarene [was] a man attested to you by God with miracles and wonders and signs which God performed through Him in your midst, just as you yourselves know'" (Acts 2:22).

The results of Peter's sermon were miraculous as well: "So then, those who had received his word were baptized; and there were added that day about three thousand souls" (Acts 2:41). Over and over in the Book of

Acts we discover that miraculous signs and wonders happened when the Word of God was preached.

A Pentecostal Message

The Pentecostal church known as the Assemblies of God is a fellowship that began supernaturally as a result of a mighty outpouring of the Holy Spirit. God has blessed this fellowship from its inception because of its dependence on Him, coupled with an uncompromising devotion to being led by the Holy Spirit, taught by the Word of God, and used to reach this needy world for Jesus Christ. From our beginning we have been blessed with mighty signs and wonders. We humbly thank God for that.

We have tried to model the Assemblies of God after the Early Church as described in the New Testament. The reason is obvious: We want to be like the original Christians and be used of God in the same ways they were. We want the growth, passion, and compassion that they had, and we desperately want the same results. We are Pentecostal because they were Pentecostal. We pray for signs, wonders, and miracles because they experienced them. We are not perfect and do not claim to be, but this was also the testimony of the Early Church.

I have little patience with those who want us to deny or diminish the message of Pentecost and the work of the Holy Spirit. I pray that God will spare us from ever coming to that condition, for if that day arrives, we will cease to be what God raised us up to be in the beginning. There is no question that God desires us to be a fellowship that uses the Early Church as its example.

The first Christians were persecuted because of their message and because of who they were. We will be persecuted, too. They were misunderstood by the society in which they lived. We will be misunderstood, too. Other religious groups rejected them because of their dogmatic stand that Jesus Christ is the risen Lord and is actively involved in the affairs of the church. We will be rejected, too.

The first Christians were threatened, beaten, rejected, and warned to stop what they were doing. Rather than slowing down, they fell on their knees and prayed, "'Lord, take note of their threats, and grant that Thy bond-servants may speak Thy word with all confidence, while Thou dost extend Thy hand to heal, and signs and wonders take place through the name of Thy holy servant Jesus.' And when they had prayed, the place where they had gathered together was shaken, and they were all filled with the Holy Spirit, and began to speak the word of God with boldness" (Acts 4:29–31).

Please note that they were all filled with the Holy Spirit and began to speak the Word of God with boldness. The Early Church preached the Word, and it was through this act that God caused the Church to grow. We must do the same.

A Proclaimed Message

God will bless a church or ministry when the ministers consistently preach the Word and live godly lives. The apostle Paul made this point clear when he said, "In Christ Jesus I have found reason for boasting in things pertaining to God. For I will not presume to speak of anything except what Christ has accomplished through me, resulting in the obedience of the Gentiles by word and deed, in the power of signs and wonders, in the power of the Spirit; so that from Jerusalem and round about as far as Illyricum I have fully preached the gospel of Christ" (Romans 15:17–19). Paul's testimony was that he preached the Word and lived accordingly, and God honored his ministry with supernatural results. Our word becomes of little effect if it isn't supported by righteous living. Let's look at each of these aspects of the proclaimed message.

WE MUST PROCLAIM THE WORD

Why does God bless the preaching of the Word? He does so because the Word is spirit, and when it is preached it speaks to a person's spirit. Jesus said, "'It is the Spirit who gives life; the flesh profits nothing. The words that I speak to you are spirit, and they are life'" (John 6:63, NKJV).

God gave us His Word to help us with all we go through in life, but it especially nourishes our spirit. The Word is the bread of life, and the Spirit is the breath of life. We need both. That is why we grow in faith when we hear the Word. "Faith comes from hearing, and hearing by the word of Christ" (Romans 10:17).

God is supernatural. When His supernatural Word is preached, supernatural events are the result. This is an incredible truth to understand. Biblical preaching brings about the life of Jesus Christ in a church. I can tell you for a fact that if you take the Word out of the church, the life of the church will go, too. No matter how well orchestrated the church is, how many fine programs it has, or how superb the organizational structure, the life will be gone.

Please understand that I am supportive of organization, structure, and needful programs. However, if we do not get our direction from God's Word, then all of these creative ideas will fail.

Worship is a wonderful experience, and I pray that we may worship God continually. God has given to the Church around the world a new desire to worship Him. Yet we must not misunderstand what the Lord is doing. He does not want us to worship the act of worship. Worship should express our love and adoration to our Lord and help open our hearts to hear His Word. Worship should not divert the church from hearing the preaching and teaching of the Bible but should make us more hungry and open to the precious Word of God. The preaching of the Word must take the central place.

When God's Word is preached we can expect supernatural results. Observe this example from our Lord's life:

> When He had entered Capernaum, a centurion came to Him, entreating Him, and saying, "Sir, my servant is lying paralyzed at home suffering great pain." And He said to him, "I will come and heal him." But the centurion answered and said, "Lord, I am not qualified for You to come under my roof, but just say the word, and my servant will be healed. For I too am a man under authority, with soldiers under me; and I say to this one 'Go!'

and he goes, and to another, 'Come!' and he comes, and to my slave, 'Do this!' and he does it" (Matthew 8:5–9).

The centurion recognized that Jesus was a man of authority. He knew that if Jesus said the word then his servant would be healed. We need to understand that Sunday after Sunday, service after service, the miraculous can happen. In this marvelous Book are life, miracles, and the supernatural power of God. Jesus said His words are "spirit and life" (John 6:63).

When people hear or read the Bible, faith comes alive (Romans 10:17). The Word is living seed. It has germinating power to bring forth life. However, receptive soil is needed to receive it. People are soil. The Spirit of God accompanies the Word as it is preached and taught, and the seed is transferred to the soil of a person's heart. When the seed hits receptive soil something dynamic, powerful, and supernatural happens. Faith comes alive. It doesn't necessarily happen at an altar in a particular church, but wherever this seed finds lodging within the heart.

If a person's heart is not open to the Word, then the seed will not come to life. The writer of Hebrews explains, "The word they heard did not profit them, because it was not united by faith in those who heard" (Hebrews 4:2). But if a person's heart is receptive, then faith springs up.

This truth ought to bring great encouragement to every believer and preacher. If we are faithful in our witness and in preaching God's Word, the Word will have tremendous supernatural effects on people's lives. "He sent His word and healed them" (Psalm 107:20, NKJV).

We do not have to work something up. God's Word will come alive and take root when it hits receptive soil. When that soil has been touched by the Holy Spirit something dynamic will happen, and signs and wonders will occur supernaturally.

You may say, "I didn't know it was that easy." When God gets involved the results will follow. We cannot take the glory; it belongs only to Him. We should never take the credit for what God does through our witness or ministry. To do so is to greatly misunderstand what has occurred. Our responsibility is to be faithful to His Word and leave the results up to Him.

The apostle Paul said, "Our gospel did not come to you in word only, but also in power, and in the Holy Spirit and in much assurance" (1 Thessalonians 1:5). We should rest in the fact that God blesses His supernatural Word when it is communicated. It is not our responsibility to confirm the Word; that is His responsibility.

God stands guard over His Word to perform it on behalf of those who will dare to believe in its power. "While Peter was still speaking these words, the Holy Spirit fell upon all those who were listening to the message" (Acts 10:44).

WE MUST PROCLAIM THE MESSAGE BY OUR DEEDS

"I write so that you may know how one ought to conduct himself in the household of God, which is the church of the living God, the pillar and support of the truth" (1 Timothy 3:15).

The church is where God's written truth is communicated, where truth is proclaimed and lived out. The way the world lives is not the way God intended, for the world does not live according to Kingdom truth. The church introduces reality to the world; it is the conscience of society.

The church displays the truth so people can see and understand it. It displays Jesus. Although the world tries to shut the truth of Jesus off, the Holy Spirit convicts the world of sin, righteousness, and judgment (John 16:18).

Paul also explains that the church is the support, or foundation, where truth is found. God's people hear the truth spoken in the church and then take it to the lost and dying world. People today are hungry and begging for truth. They are looking to material gain, drugs, alcohol, other people, education, and a multitude of other illusionary solutions for answers to life. The church gives the world the solutions it is looking for by preaching and teaching God's Word. "The Bible is God's chart for your ship to steer by, to keep you from the bottom of the sea, and to show you where the harbor is, and how to reach it without running on rocks or bars."[3]

The church is to display Jesus in all that it does. The Lord Jesus is found from cover to cover throughout the Bible. He is seen throughout the Old Testament and is the central figure in the New Testament.

The Bible tells us, "In the beginning was the Word, and the Word was with God, and the Word was God. He was in the beginning with God. All things came into being by Him, and apart from Him nothing came into being that has come into being. In Him was life, and the life was the light of men. . . . And the Word became flesh, and dwelt among us, and we beheld His glory, glory as of the only begotten from the Father, full of grace and truth" (John 1:1–4,14). John tells us that Jesus is the "Word of Life" (1 John 1:1). This precious truth is once again given to us in Revelation 19:13: "He is clothed with a robe dipped in blood; and His name is called the Word of God."

> **The church introduces reality to the world; it is the conscience of society.**

Jesus is so closely identified with the Word of God that He is actually called the Word. When the Word is preached, taught, or studied we can expect the miraculous to happen in our hearts and lives because in this Word is life everlasting.

A Productive Message

If any church ought to understand the source of signs and wonders, the Pentecostal church should. Our dependence upon the Spirit results in signs and wonders. Peter tells us, "No prophecy of Scripture is a matter of one's own interpretation, for no prophecy was ever made by an act of human will, but men moved by the Holy Spirit spoke from God" (2 Peter 1:20–21).

Holy men of God wrote the Bible as they were empowered by the Holy Spirit, and holy men of God quickened by the power of the Spirit are needed to bring revelation to the church today. God is holy, and He expects His children to live holy lives.

THE HOLY SPIRIT IS THE SOURCE

Jesus said, "'It is the Spirit who gives life; the flesh profits nothing; the words that I have spoken to you are spirit and are life'" (John 6:63). This is a powerful truth to understand. It is not my responsibility to give life. As a pastor, I do not need to make something happen in a service. As a Christian, I do not need to be under the pressure of having to perform to get spiritual results. Magic is not involved in God's signs and wonders. The Holy Spirit moves when God's Word is preached and we depend on Him for the results. The church does not need fleshly demonstrations; it needs a Holy Spirit demonstration. People are turned off when the flesh is involved in our churches.

There is something powerful, dynamic, wonderful, and glorious when people come into the presence of Jesus Christ. The Spirit makes the room alive and fills it with the power and anticipation of what God is doing. When we have the privilege of being in such a place, the Holy Spirit is the quickening agent. "The very same Holy Spirit who led [the Bible's writers also] longs to lead us *today* so we can understand. Without the Holy Spirit, the Bible is like an ocean which cannot be sounded, heavens which cannot be surveyed, mines which cannot be explored, and mysteries beyond unraveling. We must—we must—yield to the leadership of the Holy Spirit."[4]

Paul said, "Not that we are adequate in ourselves to consider anything as coming from ourselves, but our adequacy is from God, who also made us adequate as servants of a new covenant, not of the letter, but of the Spirit; for the letter kills, but the Spirit gives life" (2 Corinthians 3:5–6).

As ministers of the new covenant, we should not be under pressure to perform. God has given us our adequacy. When we preach the Lord of the new covenant from His Word, God will act. We do not need to worry about our own human adequacy; we can depend on God's ability and His enablement. That ought to excite any Christian!

I often have the opportunity to hear wonderful reports from people whom God is mightily using. One young pastor in Texas went to serve in a church of about fifty people. When he arrived he thought that he would be satisfied with a staid, formal, and proper church that would be well accepted in the community.

One day he read the book *Back to the Altar: A Call to Spiritual Awakening.*[5] When he finished it, he read it again. The Holy Spirit convicted him, and he stood before his congregation and apologized and repented. He said he had not given place to the work of the Holy Spirit in his ministry. He determined in his heart that he would be a different kind of pastor and let the Holy Spirit have His way.

Since that day the church has grown to an average of 189 in Sunday school and is preparing to go to two Sunday night services. While many churches are closed on Sunday nights, this church is packed. The congregation already has enlarged the church. The pastor says the growth is due to allowing the Holy Spirit to have His way and allowing the operation of the gifts of the Spirit in the services. Jesus is in that place! People are being saved, healed, and filled with the Holy Spirit. Miracles are taking place. What is that pastor doing differently than before? He is giving the Holy

Spirit His proper place and letting Him take control.

The Spirit seals, sanctifies, strengthens, convicts, convinces, confirms, reveals, restores, and revives. That is only a portion of what He does if the believer will just stand back and say, "Jesus, have Your way. I yield to the leadership of the Holy Spirit." Paul said, "My message and my preaching were not in persuasive words of wisdom, but in demonstration of the Spirit and of power" (1 Corinthians 2:4). Each of us needs to pray, asking God to give us preaching that operates in the demonstration of the Spirit and of power.

Often I hear from believers or ministers who are spiritually bound. Sometimes they are bound up in tradition. I am not against traditions; the Word tells us to "stand firm and hold to" some of them (2 Thessalonians 2:15). The problem is when traditions become bondage.

Bondage results in the inability to freely deliver the Word of God. Bondage prevents the anointing and disallows the power of the Spirit of God to move in and through your being. This need not be the case because "if . . . the Son shall make you free, you shall be free indeed" (John 8:36).

People are also often bound by the opinions of others. Bondage can result from fear and intimidation. People sometimes are afraid to step out by faith for fear they will be rejected. Paul's answer to this bondage is in his explanation that "where the Spirit of the Lord is, there is liberty" (2 Corinthians 3:17).

> **We do not need to worry about our own human adequacy; we can depend on God's ability and His enablement.**

Some Christians wonder what people will think if they step out by faith. It doesn't matter. We must be released from the worry of what others will think. The enemy of our souls would like to keep us so bound up that God cannot accomplish His purpose in our lives.

Jesus Christ can set us free! We need to surrender ourselves to Him so that we can experience the freedom of the Spirit. The Holy Spirit is eager to move in our lives and in our churches. When we preach and teach God's Word and depend on the Holy Spirit for results, He will honor our faith.

SIGNS AND WONDERS ARE THE RESULT

When the Holy Spirit moves and the Word is preached to hungry hearts, there are incredible results. The Early Church knew that God would demonstrate His presence with signs, wonders, and miracles when they met. They anticipated the supernatural.

Jesus set the expectations of the disciples when He proclaimed, "'Go into all the world and preach the gospel to all creation. He who has believed and has been baptized shall be saved; but he who has disbelieved shall be condemned. And these signs will accompany those who have believed: in My name they will cast out demons, they will speak with new tongues; they will pick up serpents, and if they drink any deadly poison, it shall not hurt them; they will lay hands on the sick, and they will recover'" (Mark 16:15–18).

The early disciples did what their Lord commanded, and God performed mighty miracles and the church grew dramatically.

When the Holy Spirit moves with signs and wonders, people respond to Christ. The Early Church proved this to be true.

Signs and Wonders Growth Report

Signs and Wonders	Church Growth
Acts 2:1–4	Acts 2:41–43
Acts 3:1–8	Acts 3:10; 4:3–4
Acts 5:1–13	Acts 5:14–15
Acts 6:1–8	Acts 6:7
Acts 8:6–7	Acts 8:12
Acts 9:17	Acts 9:31
Acts 9:32–34	Acts 9:35
Acts 9:36–41	Acts 9:42
Acts 11:15	Acts 11:21
Acts 12:20–23	Acts 12:24
Acts 13:8–11	Acts 13:12
Acts 14:3	Acts 14:21–23
Acts 16:25–26	Acts 16:31–34
Acts 19:11	Acts 19:20

The same God who was active in the Early Church is active today. God continues to honor His Word through spiritual results.

Some time ago I was preaching on a Saturday night at an area-wide rally in Mobile, Alabama. The power of God was present, and people had been invited to the altar. There was a marvelous move of the Spirit.

One of the pastors had brought to the service a man with a brace around the middle of his back. The man was seated just a short distance from my wife, Shirley. I was on one side of the altar ministering and was unaware of what was happening on the other side. Shirley later told me how this man responded after God miraculously healed him. "I watched him as the Spirit of God came on him. He opened his coat, took off his big brace, and threw it on the front pew of the church. He then began to run back and forth across the aisle."

The Spirit and the power of God working in the church when the Word is preached set the captive free. "They will lay hands on the sick and they will recover. . . . And they went out and preached everywhere, while the Lord worked with them, and confirmed the word by the signs that followed" (Mark 16:18,20). He will do it!

Our responsibility is to faithfully proclaim God's Word. If we are obedient in our preaching, God will confirm His Word "with signs following" (Mark 16:20, KJV).

Unit

2

The Pastor's Personal Life

Introduction:
The Pastor's Personal Life

James K. Bridges

No volume discussing the role of the Pentecostal pastor would be complete without addressing the pastor's personal life. The beginning minister, as well as the seasoned pastor, will do well to pay close attention to these truths if he is genuinely concerned about attaining and sustaining an effective ministry.

The Call to Personal Integrity

The pastor's public and private lives must be in agreement. In *Lectures to My Students,* Charles Spurgeon urged the minister to take care that his personal character agreed in all respects with his ministry. He told the story of the man who preached so well and lived so badly that when he was in the pulpit everybody said he ought never to come out; when he was out of it, they all declared he never ought to enter it again. Then Spurgeon challenged the minister with this analogy: "May we never be priests of God at the altar, and sons of Belial outside the tabernacle door."[1] Reportedly, Voltaire said of Louis XIV, "He was not one of the greatest men, but certainly one of the greatest kings that ever lived."[2] The men of this world may get away with such hypocritical living, but a man of God, never! One who would be among the greatest pastors must be among the greatest men.

It seems today that people enter politics, business, and other professions and succeed publicly without regard to their private lives. However, such success is not so with the ministry, at least not for any length of time. The quickest way to end a pastor's ministry is for the congregation to discern that personal conduct is not measuring up to public image. Hypocrisy may be condoned in the White House, but not in the church house. Far better never to enter upon such a high and holy calling if one's personal life does not measure up to the ethical and moral standards set by Holy Scripture for the pastoral ministry.

To Timothy, the apostle Paul wrote: "Take heed to yourself and to the doctrine. Continue in them, for in doing this you will save both yourself and those who hear you" (1 Timothy 4:16[3]). Here Paul established a priority not only for Timothy but for all those who would follow him in ministry, first to keep oneself in line and then to examine one's preaching and teaching. Richard Baxter said it well: "Take heed to yourselves, lest your example contradict your doctrine . . . lest you unsay with your lives, what you say with your tongues; and be the greatest hinderers of the success of your own labors."[4]

As Spurgeon pointed out in his lectures, "True and genuine piety is necessary as the first indispensable requisite; whatever call a man may pretend to have, if he has not been called to holiness, he certainly has not been called to the ministry. . . . Holiness in a minister is at once his chief necessity and his goodliest ornament. A holy minister is an awful weapon in the hand of God."[5]

Let us follow the example of the apostle Paul, who reminded the church at Thessalonica of "how devoutly and justly and blamelessly" he and his coworkers had lived among them (1 Thessalonians 2:10). Later he added, "God did not call us to be impure, but to live a holy life" (1 Thessalonians 4:7, NIV). Let the minister's public and private life be holy unto the Lord.

Biblical Qualifications

The Lord Jesus Christ, as Head of the Church, never left the standard for membership or the qualifications for its leaders to be determined by the church itself. Rather, He reserved to Himself the responsibility of calling His ministers and qualifying them to preach the gospel. Consequently, He has set forth in Holy Scripture clearly established guidelines that govern the public and private conduct of ministerial and lay leaders of the church.

Some refer to 1 and 2 Timothy and Titus as the "Shepherd's Manual" because of the valuable instructions and qualifications given for the ministry and the church. First Timothy 3 has very specific guidance for any minister who desires the office of the pastorate. (For clarification, the titles "Bishop," "Elder," and "Pastor" or "Shepherd" are used interchangeably in Scripture and refer to the same office but express different responsibilities, such as administrative oversight, spiritual leadership and ministry, as well as feeding and tending the flock of God. In Acts 20 all three concepts of bishop, elder, and shepherd are used in reference to the leaders of the church at Ephesus.[6])

To desire the office of a bishop (pastor) is to aspire to a "good work" (1 Timothy 3:1), or a "noble task" (NIV). However, such a desire brings a person immediately to the point of needing to qualify for such a ministry. Just having a desire is not enough. It is essential that we hear the Holy Scriptures say in an unequivocal tone, "A bishop [pastor] must. . . ." What follows are essential requirements for every candidate. These qualifications cover personal conduct and public behavior, which the church has no authority whatsoever to alter or ignore. To allow for a lesser qualification would be to tamper with the Word of God and to show disrespect to the direct authority of the Head of the Church, our Lord Jesus Christ.

AN IRREPROACHABLE LIFE

The first qualification of a pastor is to live "blameless" (1 Timothy 3:2), not just living so as to not deserve blame, but actually being without blame. To be irreproachable means that there is nothing in your life that Satan or anyone else could take hold upon to attack you or bring criticism against you. This doesn't mean perfection, but it means living in a manner so that reputation is untarnished. It is living a life "fitting for saints" (Ephesians 5:3), not allowing the sins of the world to be *named among* or *identified with* you. As Don Stamps wrote, "The proven character of those who seek leadership in the church is more important than personality, preaching gifts, administrative abilities, or academic accomplishments. The focal point of the qualifications falls on behavior that has persevered in godly wisdom and right choices [personal holiness]."[7]

EXEMPLARY MARRIAGE AND FAMILY

When the apostle Paul wrote that the pastor was to be "the husband of one wife" (1 Timothy 3:2), the Roman Empire was morally at an all-time low, with flagrant disrespect for the institutions of marriage and family. The leadership of the church, both pastors and deacons, were to provide the profligate society with an example of marriage and family as the Lord intended. Church leaders were not to have been divorced and remarried. As our society continues its moral decline, the need for exemplary marriages and families will be even greater.

Also needed will be the pastor's ability to manage his home well, giving his family the care and guidance that will in turn bring the respect and submission needed to truly preside as head of the home. It is no easy task to develop a godly family, but with the help of the Holy Spirit and Holy Scripture as the foundation, the pastor can order both home and marriage in the light of God's Word, not the social mores of a degenerate society.

VIRTUOUS CONDUCT

A pastor must exhibit several positive virtues: vigilant, sober, good behavior, given to hospitality, and patient. *Vigilant* means watchful and alert. Keeping your head in difficult situations and making sensible decisions is the mark of a balanced person. *Sober* means to be discreet, prudent, serious-minded, earnest about one's work. Some people never get past the fun and games. Getting down to business and working for God is a powerful trait. *Good behavior* means to be disciplined, organized in thinking and living, orderly, and modest. Having things together mentally, emotionally, physically, and spiritually is the sign of a well-behaved person. *Given to hospitality* means being a people person. If you prefer books to people you may not qualify as hospitable, i.e., "loving the stranger." When we use our home, vehicle, finances, and time to reach out to people we qualify as "given to hospitality." *Patient* means to be gentle. Paul wrote to Timothy: "A servant of the Lord must not quarrel but be gentle to all, able to teach, patient" (2 Timothy 2:24). These essential traits qualify a pastor for the office.

NEGATIVE TRAITS

The Word of God makes clear statements about what a minister should avoid: "not given to wine, no striker, not greedy of filthy lucre;. . . not a brawler, not covetous;. . . not a novice" (1 Timothy 3:3,6, KJV). When all Scripture is considered, it is unthinkable that churchmen use *not given to wine* to teach social drinking. There is no sane connection between wine used in the Bible and the damnable alcohol industry of today. Given the documented physical diseases and moral problems associated with drinking alcoholic beverages, there is not one reason for a believer, especially a preacher, to ever drink one drop, but there are millions of reasons (alcoholics, damaged pregnancies, broken homes) why a believer should never drink.

No striker means not contentious, not violent. In view of our Lord's earthly example, it seems strange to think of a pastor looking for a fight. Yet, a pastor came to me once and confessed he had been involved in a literal fight with a member of his church for saying something negative about the pastor's family. My comment to him, "You may have won the fight, but you have lost any future opportunity to minister to these people." As for spouse abuse, to quote Paul from another context, "Let it not be named once among you, as becometh saints" (Ephesians 5:3, KJV). There is no place in the ministry for a person with such a lack of control.

Not a brawler means not to quarrel. The striker fights with his hands, but the brawler fights with his mouth. He's the troublemaker instead of the peacemaker. As someone said, "Short tempers do not make for long ministries."[8] A controversialist will make a bad pastor.

Not covetous means not being avaricious or money-grabbing. However, coveting applies to more than money. Scripture teaches that covetousness is idolatry (Colossians 3:5). Paul warns also that covetousness should not even be named among believers (Ephesians 5:3).

Not a novice means a new convert should never be put into a pastorate lest his pride cause him to fall like it did Satan. We should protect our young Christians while they are growing up in the Lord. This is true for the office of deacon as well.

Not greedy of filthy lucre. Paul taught, "The love of money is a root of all kinds of evil" (1 Timothy 6:10). The way money is used determines if it is "filthy lucre." A pastor who seeks "dishonest gain" (1 Peter 5:2) corrupts the office and the calling. A pastor will face plenty of occasions for mishandling, commingling, and getting his hands dirty with filthy lucre. Many a good pastor, board, and church have been sacrificed at the altar of mammon. There is no amount of money worth a pastor selling out his ministry and his soul.

Positive Traits to Be Nurtured

ABILITY TO TEACH

Handling the Word of God in teaching and preaching is one of the main ministries of the church. Church members will forgive a pastor for not knowing more about business than they do, but they will not forgive the pastor for not knowing more about the Word of God than they do. The pastor's ability in the Word will determine the length of tenure with the church. Also, a pastor's ability in the Word will be determined by the private time spent in study.

GOOD TESTIMONY OUTSIDE THE CHURCH

The pastor must have a good reputation for paying bills, for being a good citizen, for sharing in community projects. Most important, the pastor must be respected as God's servant, a spiritual leader for the entire community. A pastor's lifestyle affects not only personal reputation, but the reputation of the church. When Paul told Titus, "Let no one despise [depreciate] you" (Titus 2:15), he was concerned with leaders' influence both in the church and outside the church. The servant of God must not be set aside as unnecessary, uninfluential, and unwanted. A pastor whose personal life is in order will avoid being a castaway. "Be ye clean, that bear the vessels of the Lord" (Isaiah 52:11, KJV).

The Character of the Lord's Servant

Zenas J. Bicket

Until a generation ago, character was of primary importance. Professionals and laypersons alike were expected to meet minimum standards of integrity and morality. But in the years following World War II, character was mentioned less and less, in religious as well as in secular circles. In its place, personality and personal effectiveness came to be valued more highly. The personal life, or character, of a politician was considered of secondary importance to the success he had in accomplishing community and social goals. The business tycoon was declared a success on the basis of his ability to turn a profit, no matter whose feet he had to step on to accomplish it.

The public today, however, is becoming concerned about the character and integrity of its political, business, and professional leaders. The character failures of religious leaders and media figures, blazoned across television and printed news reports, have prompted great skepticism about all leadership. If the ones who teach and preach integrity cannot be trusted to be what they proclaim, who then can be trusted? There is today a crisis of credibility for all who accept leadership roles.

Character is no longer a single-definition, commonly understood idea.

To some, character is tolerance for all opinions and lifestyles, for all behaviors and beliefs; these persons place great value on standing up for minorities and causes regardless of the right or wrong involved. For others, character is independence or individualism, the courage to stand up against traditional values and ideas. An entire generation rose in opposition to all forms of established organization, whether the established creeds and practices were right or wrong. The fallout from this is still seen in overt opposition to authority, whether civil, religious, or organizational. There may be times when institutions must be opposed, but true character does not denounce authority just because it is authority. There must be character standards for individuals and for organizations. Arbitrary opposition to authority, without any ethical or moral basis, leads only to anarchy and chaos. Society today seems not too far removed from that state. The minister, of all persons, must have a clear definition of character and model it with clarity.

Character and Action

Character is never proved by a written or oral statement of beliefs. It is demonstrated by the way one lives, by behavior, by choices and decisions. Character is virtue lived.

A Double Standard of Ethics

When a brother takes a long time to do something, he is slow. When I take a long time, I'm thorough.

When a brother doesn't do what should be done, he is lazy. When I don't do it, I'm too busy.

When a brother does something without being told, he is overstepping his bounds. When I do it, that's initiative.

When a brother strongly argues his position, he's bullheaded. When I argue strongly, I'm being firm.

When a brother ignores a few rules of etiquette, he's rude. When I overlook a few rules, I'm original and independent.

When a brother performs well and pleases the boss, he is polishing the brass. When I do it, I'm a team player.

When a brother succeeds, he certainly had lucky breaks. When I manage to get ahead, hard work did it.

Bad character or unethical behavior has been compared to body odor: We are offended when we detect it in others, but we seldom detect our own. Spiritual leaders must always be sensitive to the fact that their actions speak a much louder sermon than their words from the pulpit. Because one's own actions are seldom perceived as evidence of defective character, introspection and self-evaluation are essential, not because one wishes to please or avoid offending others, but because the minister's reputation and character must both be above reproach (1 Timothy 3:2,7). Our words and thoughts should be acceptable in God's sight (Psalm 19:14), but our actions reveal our character to others.

The character traits God requires of those who want to dwell in His presence are actions rather than a passive state of being. "Who may dwell in your sanctuary? Who may live on your holy hill? He whose walk is blameless and who does what is righteous, who speaks the truth from his heart and has no slander on his tongue, who does his neighbor no wrong and casts no slur on his fellowman, who despises a vile man but honors those who fear the Lord, who keeps his oath even when it hurts, who lends his money without usury and does not accept a bribe against the innocent. He who does these things will never be shaken" (Psalm 15).

Secular and Biblical Components of Character

Historically, character has been of primary concern for Christians and non-Christians alike. The Greeks spoke of *virtues,* a word that has almost disappeared from our vocabulary. Psychologists talk about *behaviors.* Politicians talk about *values.* To speak of behaviors and values avoids the strong moral and spiritual emphasis associated with the word *virtues.* Everyone has values, but values vary from person to person. "Family values" means biblical values for the Christian, but something entirely different for homosexuals who "marry" and become a "family." The use of *behavior* to describe human actions reduces human beings, created in God's image, to animal life, which can also be described in behavioral terms. Only humans can demonstrate moral virtues, the foundation of human character.

Classical Greeks identified four cardinal virtues: *wisdom* (or *prudence*), *courage, temperance,* and *justice.* Prudence is practical wisdom that makes wise choices and decisions. Courage, according to classical thinking, is the ability to do the right or necessary thing even when faced by adversity. Temperance, or self-control, is the ability to control one's impulses, to delay immediate gratification for a long-term gain. Justice is the fair and honest application of prudence, courage, and temperance to all human relationships.

> ## Character was once a concern of everyone.

These four virtues are noble traits of character. They have been called the cardinal virtues of natural law because they are found in many systems of ethics and moral behavior. They are obviously to be found in Scripture:

- Prudence (or prudent)—15 references in Proverbs
- Courage—Deuteronomy 31 and Joshua 1
- Temperance or Self-control—1 Corinthians 9:25, Galatians 5:23, Titus 1:8; 2:2, 2 Peter 1:6
- Justice—Psalm 82:3, Proverbs 21:3, Isaiah 56:1, Micah 6:8

But Christian virtues as advocated in sacred Scripture go far beyond these natural virtues recognized even by unregenerate people.

The Biblical Mandate of Christian Character

While the classical virtues were essential traits for successful living, they had little to do with interpersonal relationships in the community. Courage called on community members to stand strong against an outside enemy. Prudence and self-control were emphasized as means of achieving personal success in a competitive community. Justice was an abstraction that applied more to the establishment than to the individual. The Bible, however, is extremely practical when it describes the ideal character of the Christlike believer. Conversion is only the beginning of a life-long process of character formation.

Every reading or hearing of Scripture should be an opportunity for an in-depth character check. The Lord's servant, with the help of the Holy Spirit, should continually grow stronger in interpersonal character virtues. Psalm 15 forms an outline for the practical character traits God desires. The New Testament commentary on Psalm 15 is the Book of James and the Book of 1 John.

SPEAK TRUTH FROM THE HEART

We do not define a person of character as one who keeps the Ten Commandments, one who does not murder, steal, or commit adultery. These basic moral commitments are assumed. Instead, character involves integrity, forthrightness, and utter truthfulness in relationships with all humans of God's creation. "To speak in [from] the heart" is a Hebrew idiom for "to think." Christian character begins with honesty and openness before God. When Nathanael met Jesus, the first words he heard from his soon-to-be Master were "'Here is a true Israelite, in whom there is nothing false'" (John 1:47). Jesus, who could supernaturally discern character, recognized that Nathanael was already a man without guile, pretense, deceit, or hypocrisy. His tongue and his hand were in complete unity with his heart. May all spiritual leaders who represent the Lord have the same testimony!

What is in the heart toward God is reflected toward others. Our human relationships are not simply a matter of keeping rules. Absolute perfection in dealing rightly with others is impossible. We all fail at some point. But if there is a sincere intention and desire to obey and please God every moment, there is also a sincere desire to edify and bless others.

Pilate asked Jesus the question, "'What is truth?'" (John 18:38). Pilate, of course, didn't really want a technical definition. He wouldn't have understood if Jesus had responded, "I am the truth" (cf. John 14:6). But many today, like Pilate, are uncertain about the nature of truth. One contemporary philosophy emphasizes the subjective nature of truth—something personal that varies from individual to individual. "Truth for me," it says, "is not necessarily truth for you." But biblical truth is objective. It is true even if no one believes it. In a society that believes in pluralism and relativism, the objective definition is not readily accepted. Christians must not be swayed by a subjective attitude toward truth. We must cling to objective truth in spite of the current cultural tide, but we must do it in love (Ephesians 4:15).

Truth can be used destructively as well as constructively. Love is the ingredient that makes truthfulness a blessing rather than a curse. "We will no longer be infants, tossed back and forth by the waves, and blown here and there by every wind of teaching and by the cunning and craftiness of men in their deceitful scheming. Instead, speaking the truth in love, we will in all things grow up into him who is the Head, that is, Christ" (Ephesians 4:14–15). Repeating a true fact is no justification for a malicious attack on character or reputation.

SPEAK NO SLANDER OR GOSSIP

The person of character never speaks evil of anyone. The perceived mistakes and faults of others are not chosen topics of conversation. He or she seeks to disprove a negative story about another Christian. If that is not possible, the story goes no further; the person of character does not spread a negative report, even if it is true. Not only does the person of character guard his or her own tongue, but also the tongues of others to avoid propagating slander.

If a person of character does not spread a negative report, one may ask, "Is sin then to be condoned in the body of Christ?" Certainly not! But there is biblical principle for handling such a problem without gossiping to ever-eager ears. Sin against Christ and His Body can be dealt with in a manner similar to the Matthew 18 pattern for sin or offense between two Christians. "'If your brother sins against you, go and show him his fault, just between the two of you. If he listens to you, you have won your brother over. But if he will not listen, take one or two others along, so that "every matter may be established by the testimony of two or three witnesses." If he refuses to listen to them, tell it to the church; and if he refuses to listen even to the church, treat him as you would a pagan'" (Matthew 18:15–17).

The underlying principle is clear. Problems in the Body are best resolved by dealing with the situation through as small a number of persons as possible, not by capricious talking or gossiping. First, if it is not appropriate to confront the offending brother directly, the matter should be referred to the proper religious or spiritual authority for investigation and action. These leaders have responsibility for the spiritual health of the body. (This course of action, however, does not apply to differences of opinion that do not constitute obvious sin in the Body.)

WRONG NO ONE

To move through life without wronging a single person would seem to be an impossibility, especially apart from the supernatural work of the Holy Spirit. A spiritual leader, much like a circuit court judge, must settle disagreements in which one party is the winner and the other is the loser. But there is no intent to harm either party. It is simply an effort to achieve fairness. Self-interest is the major problem in determining true motives. Secular psychology maintains that all behavior is motivated by self-interest, or the personal advantage that comes from a decision or action. Biblical truth, however, advocates looking out for the interests of others: "Each of you should look not only to your own interests, but also to the interests of others" (Philippians 2:4). Knowing that self-interest is a natural motivation, we sometimes judge wrongly the motivation prompting the decisions and actions of others. Yet we can never be completely sure of our own motivation, to say nothing of the motivation of others.

The character of spiritual leaders must have a strong component of fairness if one is to avoid being charged with mistreating others. James admonishes: "Suppose a man comes into your meeting wearing a gold ring and fine clothes, and a poor man in shabby clothes also comes in. If you show special attention to the man wearing fine clothes and say, 'Here's a good seat for you,' but say to the poor man, 'You stand there,' or 'Sit on the floor by my feet,' have you not discriminated among yourselves and become judges with evil thoughts?" (James 2:2–4).

> **"**
>
> # Favoring the rich is not the only prejudice.
>
> **"**

But discrimination in favor of the rich is not the only prejudice we must confront. The Israelites were warned, "'Do not pervert justice; do not show partiality to the poor or favoritism to the great, but judge your neighbor fairly'" (Leviticus 19:15). Fairness is essential in all circumstances, whether related to economics, race, age, education, position, or occupation. Christian character shows proper respect for all persons.

Doing the Lord's work is never an excuse for cutting corners. God expects His work to be done with openness and integrity. Sometimes overlooked by local church leaders is the wrongful treatment of music composers and publishers. Music directors who would never think of stealing a neighbor's hard earned money do just that when printed music is duplicated or lyrics projected on a screen for choir or congregational singing. The composer whose livelihood depends on royalties from what he or she has created is cheated out of income that is rightly earned.[1] To say that a wealthy publisher or composer doesn't need the extra royalty is showing the character flaw of favoring the poor over the rich, in violation of Leviticus 19:15. Christian character is mindful of laws that appropriately request public compliance, rendering to the government and business entities their proper due (cf. Mark 12:17). The only circumstance under which a Christian can refuse such "voluntary" cooperative support is when the state asks for compliance with a law that conflicts with obligations God requires.

HATE EVIL AND HONOR RIGHTEOUSNESS

Scripture never instructs believers to hate people, no matter how evil or threatening they may be. But the evil such people work in violation of God's laws is a proper object for our hatred. Not only is it a proper object of our hatred, we are commanded to hate evil (Psalm 97:10, Amos 5:15).

Christians living in a secular culture face a difficult conflict when government leaders support or push legislation and executive actions in direct conflict with biblical teaching. At such times they readily identify with the apostles in Acts: "'We must obey God rather than men!'" (Acts 5:29). The admonition to obey secular authorities is clear, "Everyone must submit himself to the governing authorities, for there is no authority except that which God has established. The authorities that exist have been established by God" (Romans 13:1). But when that authority by edict restricts the preaching of the gospel or legitimizes sin, we must obey God rather than men. Of course, civil disobedience cannot use violence in resisting the evil designs of secular leaders. In a democracy, a Christian has a God-given responsibility to vote according to conscience for those candidates and issues agreeing with biblical principles.

KEEP PROMISES WITH HONESTY AND INTEGRITY

Paul's instruction to the Colossians seems straightforward: "Do not lie to each other, since you have taken off your old self with its practices and have put on the new self" (Colossians 3:9–10). But human nature finds other ways to conceal the truth than direct statement. People sometimes speak truth with their lips, but with a different meaning in their heart. Personal transparency is honesty about oneself, about one's emotions, desires, and preferences. It is not necessary to lay bare one's innermost feelings and thoughts to everyone we meet, but it is necessary to avoid pretense and deception. Discussions of honesty often deal with dilemmas in which some great evil will happen if one does not tell a lie. If heathen enemies were coming after a spouse, could one lie to spare a life? If one needed a special medication to save the life of the spouse, but lacked the funds to pay for the drugs, could one steal or lie in order to get the needed medication? Such academic contortions serve little purpose. The emphasis of Scripture is clear. It is never right to plan to tell a lie, under any circumstance. If we spent more time resisting the temptation to use mental reservation, white lies, and lies of etiquette to extricate ourselves from awkward situations, we would become men and women of true character.

Christian character requires moral integrity. Unfaithfulness to marriage vows is not just a forgotten promise to a spouse. It is a loss of integrity for the Christian community that has invested its trust in the minister. Failure to keep other promises destroys character and trust. Leaving unpaid bills in a community devastates the character of the church and creates genuine credibility problems for a successor. Anything borrowed, whether money, books, or a neighbor's tool, is received with a moral obligation to repay or return. A minister's promise, expressed or implied, should be as good as a binding written contract. Character is at stake.

We hear little today of the humanistic philosophy of "situation ethics." But the practice is all around us and has crept stealthily into the church. To teach that there are circumstances or situations in which it is desirable to lie, steal, cheat, or kill leaves society without universal moral principles. There are complex situations in which a person must choose the

> **Human nature finds other ways to conceal the truth than direct statement.**

lesser of two evils, but that choice must never be looked on as proof that the choice was morally positive. Scripture passages relating to just war, self-defense, and capital punishment can bring confusion to the simple text "Thou shalt not kill" (Exodus 20:13, KJV). The Christian soldier who takes the life of an enemy can never delight in having done a morally exemplary deed. Although war can be justified as a necessary evil, it is nevertheless still evil. One's conscience must be a guide in such impossible circumstances. But that conscience must be founded in divine love and strong desire to please God. Situation ethics, based on the whims of each individual, is no substitute for the Christlike character God seeks to instill in each of His children.

HANDLE MATERIAL POSSESSIONS WITH INTEGRITY

The concern in Bible times was the charging of usury or interest on loans to the poor, who lacked the financial resources to provide for their essential needs. Today, the pursuit and mishandling of money by servant shepherds is the equivalent. More ministerial character and reputation has been shattered by the misuse of money and material possession than practically any other temptation. Few have learned to replicate the example of the apostle Paul. True, it was Paul who noted that elders (pastors) are worthy of double honor (possibly, but not necessarily money). He also noted, "'The worker deserves his wages'" (1 Timothy 5:17–18). But the same Paul refused to accept wages from the Corinthian church, choosing rather to support himself by other means rather than to be interpreted as seeking to gain personal wealth from those he wanted to win for Christ.

> If others have this right of support from you, shouldn't we have it all the more? But we did not use this right. On the contrary, we put up with anything rather than hinder the gospel of Christ. . . . I have not used any of these rights. And I am not writing this in the hope that you will do such things for me. I would rather die than have anyone deprive me of this boast. . . . What then is my reward? Just this: that in preaching the gospel I may offer it free of charge, and so not make use of my rights in preaching it (1 Corinthians 9:12,15,18).

Financial accountability by spiritual leaders is extremely desirable to avoid unnecessary speculation about their remuneration and lifestyle. One public television minister has invited true accountability to a properly chosen and commissioned board of directors so that his ministry's income from all sources is properly monitored. Accountability is not intended to restrict personal income, but to let the public know that a guard has been instituted to prevent the possibility of abuse. Though the Old Testament prohibited Levites from owning personal real estate, the restriction is not so stated in the New Testament. Yet spiritual leadership should always guard against the greed of accumulating earthly possessions, which dull the impact of servant ministry.[2]

The Role of the Holy Spirit in Developing Character

Character does not just happen. The conversion experience alone does not put fully developed character into a new convert. Though a new creature in Christ, the convert still must "grow in the grace and knowledge of our Lord and Savior Jesus Christ" (2 Peter 3:18).

The Pentecostal pastor, evangelist, or teacher is often identified by the message and exercise of the supernatural manifestation of the Holy Spirit. But the real character of any Christian leader or layperson is seen in the "manifestation" of the fruit produced by that same Spirit.

The fruit of the Spirit are beautiful character essentials: love, joy, peace, patience, kindness, goodness, faithfulness, gentleness, and self-control (Galatians 5:22–23). Five out of nine is not good enough. Christlike character must be moving toward fulfillment and demonstration in all of the fruit. The indwelling Spirit that produces this fruit is a holy Spirit; holiness is the bedrock of Christian character. The life that consistently displays the nine fruit of the Spirit will speak truth from the heart, speak no slander or gossip, do a neighbor no wrong, hate evil and honor righteousness, keep promises, and handle material possessions with integrity.

The development of personal character requires our cooperation with the indwelling work of the Spirit. In an early book on pastoring, demonstrating the wisdom that would ultimately propel its author into the office of General Superintendent of the Assemblies of God, Ralph Riggs offered a timeless challenge: "Day by day let us pore over the sacred pages; let us meditate therein day and night (Psalm 1:2). Let the word of Christ dwell in you richly (Colossians 3:16), remembering that if His words abide in us, we shall ask what we will and it shall be done unto us (John 15:7). Our Bible reading should not be merely in preparation for sermons or Bible studies, but there should be the daily devotional reading of the Word solely for our own spiritual strengthening and edification."[3]

Christlike Character—A Treasure in Earthen Vessels

There is today a crisis of character in all professions. Unfortunately, the ministry—which is a calling more than a profession—is no exception. On Judgment Day the yardstick of character will have more pain for clergy. Having preached, taught, and supposedly modeled the Christian character spelled out so powerfully in God's inspired, authoritative, and inerrant Word, the Teaching Manual on which their ministry has been based, they will also be judged by it. "Not many of you should presume to be teachers, my brothers, because you know that we who teach will be judged more strictly" (James 3:1).

God's Holy Spirit dwells in our vessels of clay. And one unmistakable evidence of that indwelling presence is the Christlike character He produces in us.

The Unique Struggles of Today's Pastor

Dennis A. Davis

After being in the ministry for forty years and experiencing and observing the unique struggles of the minister, it is a pleasure to share some thoughts born out of personal experience and observations. I had the privilege of being the son of a pioneer preacher who entered the ministry when I was four years old. From the very inception of his ministry he involved me in what he was doing. I grew up with a great love for the church and respect for the ministry.

I avoided some of its struggles by the positive training and attitudes I received in my early years. I was taught by my father's example to have respect for leadership and those who were "over us in the Lord." (See Heb. 13:17.) There was never a time that our family did not start the day with prayer and "family altar." I know the Bible condemns vain, repetitious prayers. However, my father had a repetitious prayer that I heard every day of my life: "God, be with those today who have the rule over us in the Lord. And especially bless my district superintendent." Then he would call him by name. When I was sixteen years old, the district superintendent came to our home. When he walked in I thought God had come to our house, for I had heard my father pray for him every day of my life. After I became a district superintendent I realized it was not God who came to visit us; it was a man who was highly respected by my praying father. So our struggles become less when we recognize those whom God has placed in our lives to provide leadership and accountability.

The Call

Yet we often struggle with our call. I suppose my greatest fear is that individuals are motivated to go into the ministry by a desire to help people rather than as a response to a call from God. There are a lot of social agencies that can satisfy one's desire to be in the people-helping business without responding to a divine mandate to preach the gospel. I am a firm believer in the call of God. The most difficult dimension of that call, however, is finding the place where one exercises that call. Some suggest that I have been too sensitive and that any place you serve is a proper response to God's call on your life.

As a church leader, I am distressed with the increasing number of résumés sent out to churches searching for a pastor. When a rather small and insignificant church receives one hundred résumés (as reported to me recently by a district superintendent), what is the impact on the ninety-nine who are not selected? It certainly puts the selected pastor under some pressure when he is told that the church had ninety-nine others standing in line for his job.

There will be difficulties and struggles in every place of ministry. If you know you have been called to that place, you can endure a lot of pain, crucifixion. In my early ministry I accepted the call from a church that had experienced some real internal difficulties and divisions. The pressure on me as a young pastor became intense. At times I thought I was going to cave in and even questioned my sanity. During the most difficult part of this period, a large church called me to serve on their pastoral staff. I wanted to run, but I had the distinct sense I was in the will of God. The larger church called later and said, "We know why you could not respond. We didn't offer you a large enough salary." So they offered more money. I informed them that it was not the money, but that I knew I was where God had placed me. The situation in my pastorate turned around and we experienced significant growth and impact in the community, ultimately proving to be one of the happiest times in my life.

> **Every place of ministry will have its difficulties.**

The eighth year of my twenty-year tenure as pastor of The People's Church in Salem, Oregon, was one of the darkest times of my life. The congregation had voted with a strong majority to relocate. We were in a nearly new building at that time, close to the downtown core. It was determined that if we were to impact our city we needed to relocate because we had very limited off-street parking. The faith of the congregation was expressed in their vote to move forward even after having made great sacrifice to get where they were. The vote was taken, the new acreage on the edge of the city was purchased, architectural drawings were completed, pictures of the finished facility were displayed—and nothing happened. I felt it was imperative that we sell our present facility before we undertook a multimillion-dollar expansion. Months went by. In the middle of this time a church called me. They presented an exciting opportunity. I told them later that if I ever wrote a book on how to get a pastor I would give them an entire chapter. They were impressive in all they did: sending their daily newspaper to my home for a month, a different person calling me every day for a week, putting my wife and me in a penthouse on the top floor of a hotel during a visit.

While this was going on, Dr. Robert Schuller came to our city to speak. The sponsoring group asked if I would introduce him, since I had had previous contact with him through his Institute for Successful Church

Leadership. He arrived just in time to speak, and we had very little time to visit. On the way to the stage I told him my dilemma: how I could not get this project off the ground and the wonderful opportunity that had been presented to me to move.

"How long have you been here?" he asked.

"Eight years," I replied.

"Do you mean you are going to throw away an eight-year investment and start over again?" he asked. I had told him that the Chamber of Commerce of the other city had informed me that their city was going to quadruple in ten years. He added, "If that town quadruples, this town will double in the same period of time."

> **'Do you mean you are going to throw away an eight-year investment and start over again?'**

He then reached into his pocket, pulled out a coin, and thrust it into my hand. "Take this and build that church for God. If you don't, nobody else will." By then we were walking on the stage.

After the meeting I pulled the coin out of my pocket and read three verses of Scripture on one side: "Be still, and know that I am God" (Psalm 46:10). "If God is for us, who can be against us?" (Romans 8:31). "I will not die but live" (Psalm 118:17).

On the other side was this prayer: "Thank you, God for solving so many of my problems in the past. Please God, help me today. I need you and I trust you. Amen."[1] That evening was a turning point for me. Dr. Schuller became God's voice to me to remain faithful to the place He had put me.

A few days later I went home in the evening and found an unlighted house. I looked through the house and found Nancy, my wife, in the back bathroom, crying. I asked her, "What is the matter?"

She answered, "You have a wonderful opportunity to get out of here, and I say let's go."

"Nancy, I can't," I replied. "If I leave now I will spend the rest of my life wondering what would have happened if I had stayed. I am going to stay and prove that it can't be done, if that is the case."

Through her tears she said, "I knew you would say that. I don't think you're committed, you're just stubborn."

We have laughed many times about that night and our hour of deep discouragement.

I will not go into the details of how God solved our problem. And not ours only, for He took care of some big problems for several other groups in our city at the same time that we sold our downtown property and made the move. On the day we moved into that multimillion-dollar facility, I spoke on "The Coin That Built a Two-Million-Dollar Church!" referring to that divine encounter I had with Robert Schuller. I realized God had called me to that city. I felt as if it was my city to reach for God and that the entire responsibility rested on our church, which leads me to my next observation.

Cooperation

In the ministry we struggle to be cooperative and not competitive. We must have a wholesome respect for everyone involved in advancing God's kingdom. I sought to develop friendships by faithful attendance and involvement with the ministerial associations. I purposed that if anyone was working to reach people for Christ that I would help on a united basis. However, when we begin to think that someone else is responsible for reaching a portion of the populace, the temptation is to reduce our efforts to that degree.

I was asked to speak to the ministerial association at a luncheon meeting on the subject of church growth. I presented some principles that any of us could use. I concluded by saying, "I love all of you in this room. I have a great respect for what you are doing in this city, but when we walk out of this room today I want you to act like Denny Davis does not exist and that the responsibility of reaching this city for Christ rests solely upon you. I am going to do the same. As much as I love and respect you, I am assuming that the responsibility of reaching this city is mine and mine alone." No matter what we experience in the growth of the local church, we can never let a feeling of success grip us until every person in our community comes to know Christ.

FIND OUT WHAT IS NOT BEING DONE, THEN DO THAT

DUPLICATING SAME WORK, EFFORT, TASK

Balance

A third struggle is the balancing act between work, family, and recreation. Over the years I have received some wonderful counsel that has changed my life. When my son was newborn, one of my pastor heroes, who had influenced me through his relationship and friendship with my parents, came to conduct meetings in the church I was pastoring. I told him of my desire to be a good father to my new son. He said, "If you will plan your home time like you do your work time, you will have nothing to worry about." Thereafter, I always tried to make my time at home meaningful. Many fathers spend time at home, but they are doing nothing to contribute to family life while they are there. Home time is more than just being a carcass in the house. My wife and I included our son in our activities.

I have always recognized the value of pastoral visitation. It is easy to include children in this activity (and much easier if they are well-behaved). Rest homes are a wonderful place to take children. When my son came home from college for a holiday, he would spend one day with me doing nothing more than visiting in rest homes. We would spend six hours, driving over one hundred miles around the city and surrounding areas, visiting these elderly people. It was a joy to visit my son one Christmas season where he was serving on a church staff. He came home rather late on Christmas Eve and I inquired where he had been. He said he had been to the rest homes. Since this was not part of his pastoral duties, I asked why. He replied, "It's Christmas and nobody else was going." That made this father proud.

I took a life-changing thought home from a luncheon featuring Dr. Elton Trueblood. His topic was "If I Was Starting Over in the Ministry."

Although I forgot most of what he said, this statement changed my life: "I would have a fuller date book." I knew that Fuller made brushes, but had not heard about his date book. He went on to explain, as he showed us his date book, that we needed to fill our date books. He showed us the date of his wife's birthday recorded in his date book. He said that he would be taking no speaking engagements that day; he was going to spend it with her. He showed us three weeks blocked out for writing and nothing else. Shortly after that I scheduled dinner with a young attorney friend of mine for a social evening with our wives, which had taken weeks to arrange for both of us. Sometime later, before our scheduled dinner, a church called and asked if I could speak at a banquet. I looked at my "fuller date book" and said I was already committed for that evening, the same night as my dinner engagement. I told them I could come the following week. They called back the next day and said that the next week would work fine for them. I would not have done that without my commitment to my "fuller date book."

We know the value of planning our time. There are seminars constantly advertised on the subject. One of the best investments of any day is to take a few minutes at the beginning to plan your activities. Not just to make your "to do" list, but to then prioritize the list as well as put your activities in geographical order. Why run to the same area of the city twice in one day when, with a little planning, you could do both things in one trip? Thoughtful, creative planning can lead to a productive life both at work, with family, and with our broader interests and activities.

Many pastors are seemingly afraid to get close to people, feeling that if they do, people will take advantage of them. I am sorry, but I have little tolerance for the minister who is so important that people cannot touch him personally, or by telephone. That's real isolation!

I was visiting in the home of a friend who gave me an extremely helpful hint. He had been one of several doctors in a clinic. One of the doctors asked him, "Why am I called out every night and you never are called out?"

My doctor friend replied, "Because you play too hard to get. You always give the impression how busy you are and that you are not available. I tell all of my patients, 'I am your doctor twenty-four hours a day. You can call me anytime, day or night.' My patients wake up in the middle of the night with a pain, but they know they can call me if it gets worse. They may wake up again and the pain is worse, but they know I am still there and determine that they can wait until seven o'clock in the morning when I will be in my office. Your patients wake up with a little pain and immediately call because they don't know if they can get you and the pain may get worse while they are trying." The doctor then said to me, "Pastor, if you will do that with your people you will find that your phone will ring less."

I took that to heart. On a regular basis I would say, "I am in this city for only one purpose and that is to be a help and blessing to you. I am

> **'I would have a fuller date book,' he said.**

your pastor whenever you need me, day or night. You can call me anytime." The people knew I kept regular office hours. They sensed I was a busy person. They knew that I cared about them. My phone hardly ever rang at home except for a real emergency because my congregation knew I was always there when they genuinely needed me.

Finances

A fourth area of struggle in the pastor's life is finances. Most, if not all, of our financial struggles are self-inflicted through lack of discipline and unscriptural behavior. In serving as a college president, I became greatly concerned over the amount of student debt being accumulated. I see this as a great deterrent in responding to the call of God in one's life. Some of that particular debt is due to lack of planning by parents for their children's education. Some is caused by the lack of a good work ethic in many of today's youth.

Debt accumulated through credit for expendable goods is a great evil. The desire to have now and pay later is destroying a lot of people. I have plastic in my pocket too, but have never paid any interest on them. Credit cards are fine if they are used only as a substitute for not carrying cash. This particular discipline has allowed me to respond to some interesting opportunities. Personal financial accountability begins in our relationship to stewardship. Thankfully, my father taught me the joys of tithing and giving as a small child. There has never been a time in my life that the tithing principle was not practiced. My wife and I have enjoyed for many years giving a second tithe to missions causes. If we are faithful to God I firmly believe that God in His kindness will meet our needs. The Psalmist testified, "I was young and now I am old, yet I have never seen the righteous forsaken or their children begging bread" (Psalm 37:25).

Jay Kesler tells of a time when he was a young student pastor and went to a little church to speak in their revival meeting. After arriving early and checking the church out, he was approached by the old janitor, doing some clean-up. "Are you the young fellow who is preaching here tonight?" he asked.

Jay replied he was, and then related the old janitor's comments. "Well, I want to tell you something," he said, "I was pastor of this church for thirty years, and I'm retired now, but they let me be the sexton." He paused. "Maybe after church tonight you'd like to come down and have a little pie with my wife and myself." He pointed down the street two or three doors to a white house with flowers in front. It was a modest home right up against the sidewalk.

"We never thought we'd have a house of our own because we always lived in a parsonage," he said. "But look how well the Lord has taken care of me. I have pastored in this church and in other churches, too. I've got this job, so I can continue to serve. And now I've got this nice house. I just felt the Holy Spirit telling me to tell you that a servant of God will never have to beg bread."

Jay wrote, "I couldn't help but see that this janitor's spirit was full of the goodness of God. I went away thinking, *I've just met a saint. I hope I can live up to his example. If I can end up my career as a janitor with good health, a nice little house, and a piece of pie to share with a visiting minister, I'll be a happy man. God will have taken good care of me.*"[2]

That's the God I know and have confidence in for all of my tomorrows.

Spiritual Gifts

A fifth obstacle as I perceive it is not understanding our own gifting and the gifting of those we are called to minister to. One of the most liberating experiences of my life was attending a conference that featured an in-depth study of the gifts as recorded in Romans 12. I left knowing for the first time why I act as I do and why people respond to me as they do. It also helped me to understand my people and how to deal with them.

One Wednesday shortly after, I received a call that a parishioner had died. I spent time that day with the family, helping them make some difficult decisions. By the time I got to church for our Wednesday evening activities I had arranged for the organist, the soloist, the pallbearers, and all the details for the funeral service. On my way to the pulpit that evening one of the women in the church asked, "Are we going to have a dinner for the family following the funeral service?" That had not entered my mind that day.

I responded, "I don't know." She sweetly asked, "Would you like me to take care of that?" I assured her it would be nice. She picked up the responsibility, arranged for food to be brought in, got the dinner place decorated, and did all the work. She had exercised her gift of serving. We need every gift functioning in the body of Christ. This woman did not criticize me for my lack of attention to the meal. I had used my organizational gifts to make funeral arrangements. I had exercised the gift of mercy with the family earlier.

"God whispers His call for ministry to people who possess many diverse gifts. Like snowflakes or aspen leaves, no two pastors are alike. Therefore, the issue is: 'How can I honor my call with my dedicated best in education and in personal spiritual development?'"[3]

When we recognize who we are, it will eliminate a competitive spirit among colleagues and staff. It keeps us from comparing ourselves with someone else. Calvin Miller says, "As a leader, your work, like your life, must bear the scrutiny of your own tough evaluation. You will do God no favor if you charge out into the world with no real understanding of who you are. Ignorance about yourself is a self-imposed limitation that will keep your full leadership potential from developing."[4]

> **Recognizing who we are eliminates a competitive spirit.**

W. A. Criswell writes, "When a statistic was reported that one out of ten men who enter the ministry quit the work somewhere along the way, a survey was made to find the reasons why. The replies in order of reasons given were these: inadequate salary, excessively heavy workload, fishbowl living, opposition to pastoral leadership. Other reasons given were discouragement because of unconcerned church membership, family problems, loss of faith, lack of personal satisfaction, lack of security." He goes on to say, "Truly, the problems in the ministry are legion: social isolation, excessive demands on the part of the people, financial strains, administrative pressures, professional competition, psychological tensions, feelings of inadequacy, anxiety, anger, and ten thousand other demonic devices to destroy the effective work of the pastor."[5]

You can see by that litany of struggles that the list is endless. Elsewhere in this book, detailed treatment is given to the common struggles with our sexuality, with temptations, with sermon preparation, and with moving on. In concluding this chapter I want to discuss what I feel is probably the greatest obstacle we face, the struggle to communicate in understandable terms to our culture. If it is our desire to reach our culture with the claims of Christ, this has to be a deep frustration.

Communication

I was touring the state of Oregon, acquainting myself with our pastors in area meetings. Traveling with me was a young missionary. The second night of our tour he made the statement, "Before a person can go as a missionary to another country there are two things that must occur. The person must know the language and must understand the culture." He then said, "I think it is time that the American church took language studies and cultural studies to identify with those we wish to minister to."

We must face the fact that we as Christians are no longer part of mainstream America. We are part of a subculture. I listen to the language we use. We speak a language foreign to our culture. We use acronyms, phrases, terms, words that only we understand. Remember, Jesus told only one person to be "born again." He used that terminology to arrest his attention and get a response. That person immediately asked what it meant to be "born again." Jesus had the opportunity to explain what he meant. (See John 3.)

We are often guilty of asking someone a question from a biblical or spiritual context they have no understanding of. We leave them confused by our language.

The following exaggerated but still typical illustration speaks to our problem.[6]

Ed asked his friend, Bob, "Have you ever been saved?" "Yes," Bob replied, "once when I was nine years old. I was swimming at Jones Beach on Long Island. A strong undertow began dragging me out to sea and my uncle saved me."

"No, not that kind of saved," responded Ed. "Have you ever been redeemed? Reborn! Washed in the Blood!" Bob wondered what in the world Ed was talking about.

Ed told Bob he needed to be convicted. Bob responded by saying that he had never been in any trouble with the law.

The next time they met, Ed was a little late, explaining that he had been having some "quiet time." Bob did not know what that meant, so Ed explained that he had been praying in his prayer closet. "You pray in a closet?" Bob asked. "No," replied Ed, "in my car." Bob had a real problem with a closet in a car.

Ultimately Bob received Christ as his Savior. When Ed heard about it he hurried to tell Bob he needed to find a good body. Bob started calling the health clubs and at one he met Denise, who had a good body. Denise became a believer, so Ed told them that they now needed to be planted so they could grow together.

Bob missed church one Sunday; Ed told him later he should have been there because God had really moved. Bob was disturbed because he had just found God and wanted to know where He was now.

> **'Old friends no longer understand me . . . that I follow the Lamb.'**

Ed told Bob further that the gifts were really flowing. Bob wanted to know why they were giving gifts to one another. Ed then told Bob that Denise had been there and she was on fire. Bob was afraid she had been burned.

The story ended with Ed saying, "Well, I've been plugged in for two years since I was saved and delivered. I've been planted and committed to a good body. God has been moving and I've been stepping out in the gifts. I've developed a new problem, it seems. My old friends don't understand me anymore. When I share about redemption, they don't understand that I've been washed white as snow and that I desire to follow the Lamb. They just seem to tune me out. I guess they're just convicted because I'm on fire."

This exaggerated story has an important point. We talk this way and wonder why an unbelieving world does not respond to our message. We are talking a "foreign language" to a non-Christian culture.

Martin Luther said, "Sermons should be addressed to the . . . [common people]. If in my discourses I were to be thinking about Melancthon and the other doctors I should not do good at all: but I preach in plain language to the plain, unlearned people, and that pleases all parties. If I know the Greek, Hebrew, and Latin languages, I reserve them for our learned meetings, where they are of use, for at these we deal in such subtleties and such profundities, that God Himself, I wot, must sometimes marvel at us."[7]

Someone has well said, "Remember, you are feeding sheep, not giraffes. Keep the feed down where they can eat it."

* * * * *

We have touched only a few of the unique challenges facing the pastor. But we have good resources for achieving success in our ministry. God expects us to use the common sense He has given us as we struggle with our call, with our urge to compete, with demands that push our lives out of balance, with our shortage of finances, and with the absolute necessity of reaching the lost with a clear and convincing message. But common sense is inadequate in and of itself to win the victory. The wisdom and quickening of the Holy Spirit provides the edge that makes us "more than conquerors" (Romans 8:37) as we face the unique struggles of being called by God.

The Minister's Wife

Nancie Carmichael

A s hard and as ill-defined a role as it is, one of the best-kept secrets is the privilege of being a minister's wife.[1] There's nothing else quite like it. I've worn a lot of different "hats" in my lifetime, but there's something very special about being the pastor's wife. Here you're at the heart of people's lives: marriages, births, deaths, life-conversions, etc. It's a life centered around teaching the treasures of God's Word, helping people grow, empowering them in their own ministries, and seeing individuals make decisions to follow Christ.

It can be discouraging and heartbreaking, too, as you see up close the pain in many people's lives. Your wife needs your sensitivity, understanding, and support as she supports *you* and the call God has placed on you. It will help her to have energy, a sturdy sense of self, a strong faith in God—and I might add, a sense of humor! One day when I was down on my knees in the men's restroom cleaning the toilets, I began to wonder if this was really part of the job description of being the pastor's wife. This was not what I'd envisioned when as a young person I had come to the altar on the third verse of "I'll go where You want me to go, dear Lord" as I consecrated myself to serving God. But following Christ means a great adventure, and half the battle of successful pastoring is not taking one's self too seriously, instead, taking God very seriously. There is no substitute for one's own personal, authentic walk with God.

What Is the Role of a Minister's Wife?

Years ago when we were pastoring a church without many staff members, I soon took on more than I should have, picking up all the loose ends that no one else seemed to see—occasional janitorial chores, nursery duty more than my share, playing the piano, visiting the elderly and sick with my husband, not to mention being a mother to three active little boys. The previous pastor's wife, a gifted woman who was older than I, had developed an effective outreach for women in the community. Not waiting on God to see if this was for me, I added that to the list of things I was doing, trying to maintain what she had started. To my dismay, the outreaches under my direction fizzled, flopped. Devastated, I felt like a failure and wondered what went wrong.

My husband gently but firmly encouraged me to be myself. "You don't have to do all this stuff," he told me as I agonized over my role in the church. Later, I had to admit that taking on my predecessor's ministry in addition to everything else I was doing had felt forced and artificial to me. It wasn't "me"—it wasn't my gift. I did it because it was a good idea, because it worked for her, and I thought others expected it of me. Together, my husband and I discussed my involvement in the church. I was needed most in the music department, so I helped by playing the piano. And my heart was really in Bible study, so I let go of my other obligations and began a low-key, simple Bible study with two other women. To my surprise, it thrived and grew and became a successful ministry of the church.

> **" It takes courage and strength to be 'real.' "**

Chalk it up to my youth or shaky self-esteem. Either way, I learned a valuable lesson. It's exhausting and impossible to have unrealistic expectations of ourselves, not to mention accepting them from others. I wanted so much to please, to help my husband succeed, for things to go well for him. But I learned that God is the One I walk before—I can have no other gods before Him, including the church. My husband and family is my next priority, and out of these priorities, I learned to serve.

As I simply sought God to meet me where I was, I began to understand that a "role" is something one puts on, such as assuming a part for a production or a play. A role is artificial and forced. One must practice to pull it off successfully. Pity the churches if we wives of ministers take our "role" seriously and try to be someone we're not! Give us instead the woman who can laugh at herself, who dares to have friends, who doesn't mind running to the grocery store in her blue jeans, who stays interested in life and is a learner, and who takes seriously the declaration of Christ that we are all joint-heirs with Him. It takes courage and strength to be "real," and the husband can play an important part in encouraging his wife to be true to who she is in Christ. The times call for us to be authentic. The needs are great; God's mercy and grace are sufficient, and we can do no less than cling to Him.

The minute your wife is dubbed *minister's wife,* there are a myriad of unspoken expectations thrust upon her as she faces a curious combination of esteem and criticism. Some people in the church think the wife of the minister should: (a) play the piano, (b) organize a church dinner on a two-day notice, (c) entertain with the greatest of ease and serve nutritious, delicious meals, (d) be a Bible scholar, but be willing to teach the beginner's class, (e) have the perfect marriage and family with weekends and evenings full, (f) look attractive, stylish, *and* modest on a minimal salary, (g) be a balanced and sane person even though she's not supposed to have friends in the church, (h) head up women's ministries, whatever *that* may be, and (i) ad infinitum. And we all know a few pastor's wives who seem actually to be able to do all of these things, which makes it harder for the rest of us! I am told by a younger friend in ministry that things really are changing, that people are being less demanding of the minister's wife. I hope that's true, because no one in her right mind would agree that one person can be all things to all people. And yet I confess when my husband was pastoring, I felt enormous pressure, both from myself and from others in the church.

Ministry couples face the same challenges that plague other couples in our society, only it can be more difficult for the pastor's wife. After all, who can she turn to? Her husband has his hands full with pastoring, and she is told by some "experts" that the minister's wife should not have friends within the congregation. But when one moves frequently, as many pastors do, it is difficult to keep a support base of friends and extended family that is so helpful in maintaining a balanced perspective of life. Friends help keep you sane, help you laugh at some of the things that happen to you as a pastor's wife. One wife told me that shortly after assuming their pastorate, a long-standing Sunday school teacher in the church pulled her children aside and quizzed them to see if they knew the Ten Commandments. When the children didn't answer to the woman's satisfaction, she made a big deal over it. The pastor's wife was embarrassed and angry at the intrusion. The hurts can be deep and personal, and wounds of rejection from God's people can be hard to heal.

Invest in Your Wife

Perhaps one of the most important callings of your ministry is investing in your wife. Remember, "If Mama ain't happy, ain't *nobody* happy!" God has created us to be "one flesh," and we are stronger united than divided. Share your dreams, your vision with her. Share your fears, too— not "dumping" on her all the negative things that are going on, but being personally vulnerable, telling her how she can pray for you. This makes a wife feel needed and an integral part of your ministry, that you really are a team.

You can invest yourself in your wife by taking the time to listen to her, to discover her as a unique person, not just someone there to take care of your needs. Listening says that you care about the things she cares about: the children, the leaky faucet, what to fix for that Board dinner. And there's a big difference between *hearing* and *listening*. Listening does not necessarily mean offering solutions or advice. It may mean just being there for her. One of my favorite "theologians," Winnie the Pooh, was walking down the road one day when Piglet sidled up to Pooh from behind. "Pooh!" he whispered. "Yes, Piglet?" "Nothing," said Piglet, taking Pooh's paw. "I just wanted to be sure of you."

Listening is a powerful, eloquent way to say, "I love you, I am committed to you. Tell me—what are your dreams? Your fears? I will be here for you." No judgments, no glib solutions, just listening. Listening to your wife is one of the greatest gifts you can ever give her. There is a part of us in our deepest of bondings that is made whole when we feel we are listened to, especially from our husbands and wives. Nothing else is so affirming. Listening involves depth and discernment, learning to ask the good questions or knowing when just to be silent and wait. Being heard is closely related to feeling loved. Being heard gives me a sense that someone cares, someone sees and hears me. When we are listened to, we feel whole, we feel visible, we feel real.

Walter Wangerin writes poignantly in *As For Me and My House* about a crisis he and his wife faced. One day his wife confronted him, accusing him of not paying attention to her. Walter responded:

> "You decide my whole life for me, but you hardly pay mind to the decisions. You do it with your left hand, carelessly. You run me with your left hand. Everyone else gets the right hand of kindness. Everyone else can talk to you. Not me."
>
> "Thanne! I'm not a bad person. I do everything as well as I can. What have I done to you? I try to please God. I'm a good pastor—"
>
> "A good pastor!" she spat the words. "You *are* a good pastor, Wally. God knows, I wanted you to be a good pastor. But sometimes I wish you were a bad pastor, a lazy pastor, a careless pastor. Then I'd have the right to complain. Or maybe I'd have you here sometimes. A good pastor! Wally, how can I argue with God and take you from Him? Wally, Wally, your ministry runs me, but you leave me alone exactly when I need you. *Where are you all the time?*"
>
> I didn't answer . . . For counseling and for sermons, my words, she said, were beautiful: a poet of the pulpit. But for our bedroom conversations my words were bitter, complaining, and unconsidered. We talked of my duties. We talked of my pastoral disappointments. Or we hardly talked at all.
>
> "How often I wanted to tell you of the troubles here at home," she said, "of my mistakes with the children." But I was doing the Lord's work—the Lord, Thanne wailed, whom she loved dearly. So what could she say to me through all of this? How could she find fault with a divine command?
>
> I was ministering. I was a whole human, active in an honorable job, receiving the love of a grateful congregation, charging out the door in the mornings, collapsing in bed at night. I was healthy in society; she was dying in a little house—and accusing herself for the evil of wanting more time from me, stealing the time from God. I laughed happily at potlucks. She cried in secret. And sometimes she would simply hold one of the children, would hold and hold him, pleading some little love from him until he grew frightened by her intensity, unable in his babyhood to redeem her terrible sins. In those days the smile died in her face. The high laughter turned dusty in her throat. Privately the woman withered—and I did not see it.[2]

Walter and Thanne Wangerin restored and forgave one another, but it was a process of time and healing. He determined to come home from the office an hour earlier every evening, sit in the kitchen with her, and simply listen to her. At first it seemed awkward, and yet over time she grew to believe that he really did love her as he listened to her.

Invest in Your Own Marriage

A lot is at stake here, not only for you and your family's happiness, but for Kingdom business as well. Great ministries have crumbled when the marriage at the top floundered. Healthy marriages don't just happen, and some people are more compatible in their marriages than others. There are different temperaments, different "histories" we all bring to our marriages. They take work. Deal with your issues, acknowledge the baggage you bring to the marriage. Colossians 3:12–14 says: "As the elect of God, holy and beloved, put on tender mercies, kindness, humbleness of mind, meekness, longsuffering; bearing with one another, and forgiving one another, if anyone has a complaint against another; even as Christ forgave you, so you also must do. But above all these things put on love, which is the bond of perfection. And let the peace of God rule in your hearts, to which also you were called in one body; and be thankful."[3]

Your relationship has a subtle but pervasive influence on your congregation, not to mention your wife and your family.

Celebrate your relationship. Somehow take the time to build family traditions, couple-traditions. No, you can't afford to, you don't have time; yet you can't afford *not* to, and you take the time. This includes making sex and romance a priority; it includes minivacations, taking walks together, little things that count. Every once in awhile, just as you celebrate the 4th of July, you need to have fireworks go off in your relationship, to have a special memory or two between the two of you. If your marriage only consists of pressure and people-problems, you are vulnerable to burnout. *Celebration* is important to a marriage—to celebrate one another, to celebrate the relationship. Go rent a red convertible, put the top down, and go park somewhere! Do something really unforgettable and wonderful—something that is yours alone, a place of escape and renewal. Sometimes you just need to take matters in your hands and take your love away. It will do wonders. Solomon wrote: "Rise up, my love, my fair one, And come away! 'O my dove, in the clefts of the rock, In the secret places of the cliff, Let me see your countenance, Let me hear your voice; For your voice is sweet, and your countenance is lovely.' Catch us the foxes, The little foxes that spoil the vines" (Song of Solomon 2:13–15).

Years ago when we were pastoring, I was pregnant with my fourth child; I was nauseated and exhausted. Times had been difficult in our church. We were not seeing the growth we thought we would; instead, unexpected conflicts seemed to prevail and we were both discouraged and worn out. Then just before Christmas, Bill did something completely crazy and illogical. He sold his prized Datsun pickup, bought two tickets to Hawaii, wrapped them up and put them under the tree as a Christmas present for me. I was astounded. We hardly had any money, so we charged the rest of the trip on our credit card. It took us a while to pay it off, and I'm not advocating going into debt, but that trip became an absolutely unforgettable, special memory for us as a couple. Did our circumstances change? No, but when we came home and back to reality, we were refreshed and ready to go again. We were reminded that if we had the Lord and each other, everything would be fine. And it was.

Invest in Your Wife Spiritually

It is essential now and then to get away to connect not only romantically, but spiritually. Whether a day or several days, or even an afternoon or evening, share personal, spiritual goals, and pray for one another. Invest in each other spiritually by listening together to an inspiring tape or reading material that is provocative and insightful. Share the Word with one another—not for sermon material, but for your own personal growth with God, for wonderful deep nuggets that inspire you to go on.

In our almost thirty years of marriage, life has continually handed us surprises and changes. We went from youth-pastoring to pastoring to Christian publishing. Now we are doing more writing and speaking. We find that we never outgrow the need as a couple to get away from the routine to evaluate where we are as a couple. Where are we individually, and how is God leading us? Where do we need to grow? It is easy to start seeing each other as "commodities" to be used rather than the wonderful, fragile gifts that we are to each other, needing care and forgiveness daily as we strive to minister.

I confess I tend to be more driven by the urgent, and my husband takes the lead in making sure we get away at least once a year to go over our calendars in-depth, to think and talk and pray about direction, and then meet monthly to update and plan. The calendar and deadlines tend to dictate our lives if we are not proactive in planning for the really important issues of our life—where we are with God.

Invest in Your Wife As a Person

When we let go of our "death grip" on each other in our marriages and allow God to develop our unique ministries as we seek Him, surprisingly wonderful things can happen. There are many inspiring examples of unique personalities throughout the history of Christendom. "In domestic affairs I defer to Katie. Otherwise I am led by the Holy Ghost."[4] So said Martin Luther, renowned leader of the Reformation, about his wife. Both of them came out of the Roman Catholic Church in the sixteenth century. They had no marriage manuals to refer to, no previous tradition of how to forge their marriage; Katie had been a nun, Martin, a priest. They only knew a growing, vibrant quest in wanting to follow Christ in a faith-walk.

"There's a lot to get used to in the first year of marriage," Luther once admitted. "One wakes up in the morning and finds a pair of pigtails on the pillow which were not there before. . . . Of course the Christian should love his wife. He is supposed to love his neighbor, and since his wife is his nearest neighbor, she should be his deepest love. And she should also be his dearest friend." Luther went on to say, "Nothing is more sweet than harmony in marriage, and nothing more distressing than dissension. Next to it is the loss of a child. I know how that hurts."

Katie was one of nine nuns that Martin Luther smuggled out of a convent. Times were perilous, and there were death threats on them. He commented about these nuns: "They were a wretched bunch. All they knew was how to sing and pray." Eventually they were married off to different ex-priests, Katie being the last, so Martin married her. He wrote, "Before I married, no one had made up my bed for a whole year. The straw was rotting from my sweat. I wore myself out with work during the day, so that I fell into bed oblivious." Talk about adjustments! In the monastery, he had been accustomed to being secluded, but Katie would not stand for that. According to one story, he once locked himself in his study for three days until Katie had the door removed. Innocently, Martin asked as he saw Katie standing in the doorless doorway, "Why did you do that? I wasn't doing any harm."

If Katie Luther were to apply for the "role" of pastor's wife today, she would probably be denied. And yet she was a woman for her times, and God used her in wonderful ways as she pioneered the role of a minister's wife. Nothing had ever prepared her for such a role; she simply followed Christ where she was, using what was available to her at the time. Katie, with her strong entreprenurial and organizational skills, ran a brewery, bought and managed a farm some distance away, and oversaw Martin's home and meals, which literally grew into a seminary within their very home as Martin's "table talks" expanded, and many people came to learn and grow in the things of God.

Another interesting couple is Calvin Stowe, a congregational minister and teacher at a seminary during the Civil War, and his wife, Harriet Beecher Stowe. Calvin realized that Harriet was gifted in her writing. Although they had a young family (including a set of twins), he encouraged her to persevere in her writing, and she authored *Uncle Tom's Cabin*. The book about slavery became an overnight sensation and the catalyst for the Civil War (according to Abraham Lincoln). History records that although Calvin was at times grumpy about basking in Harriet's limelight as she received accolades from around the world, he was proud of her accomplishments. She in turn encouraged him to write a theological book, which he eventually did, and the book was well received.[5]

How to Handle Friendships

One of the more successful pastor-wife teams that I know lives in the community where I live. She has a small business, and they have a busy, active family. Their church is growing and vital. What the two of them do that is so refreshing—yet ordinary—is simply be part of the community. They are often found at the local schools, working the concession booths, or sitting in the bleachers watching a ball game. They are approachable, down-to-earth, yet with a heart to reach their community for Christ. She told me her friends are very important to her but she's careful not to exploit them, or tell them things that should be held confidential, especially church matters. She is careful not to flaunt her friends in the church to the point others feel excluded. I believe friendship in the church can happen; it just takes discretion and wisdom.

Years ago when we were very young in the ministry, I had a young woman in our church offer me her friendship. We had a lot in common, both being young wives and mothers. "If you ever need a friend," she told me, "I would love to just have coffee with you sometime." "Thanks very much," I smiled, and inside thinking, *Are you kidding? Never! Pastor's wives can't have friends.* As it turned out, I desperately needed a friend. As wonderful and supportive as my husband was to me then, I needed women friends. He couldn't understand completely what it's like to be a woman, a mother, a wife. Besides, as my "provider-protector," when sometimes I needed just to "vent," he thought he had to solve all the problems I was venting. Another woman could say, "Yeah, I know what you mean," and I would feel a whole lot better, and we could get on with living life.

Pastors and pastor's wives are just people—all of us unique, with different strengths and weaknesses. Churches, like people, can have very different personalities. Bible school and seminaries often don't train us for the issues that surprise us in the daily life of the church. Sometimes we deserve the criticism we receive. Sometimes we allow ourselves to be placed on a pedestal, then we wonder why we fall off with a thud. We are real people with real needs.

Dealing with Criticism

Dealing with criticism just seems to be part of the minister's job description. Not much has changed through the centuries. In the pre-Revolutionary days of the mid-1700s Jonathan and Sarah Edwards received unrelenting criticism from people in their Massachusetts church: Why should Jonathan have wigs, when one did very well for most? It made no difference that he wrote some of the most eloquent sermons ever. "Sinners In the Hands of an Angry God" was so powerful that it sparked a revival. Sarah Edwards dressed too well to suit some of the people in the church, and their family ate off pewter plates rather than wooden planks as some of the people did.

But the real problems in the church began when Jonathan decided not to accept the "non-committed" into church membership. Sarah reported that Jonathan "told me that he would not dare ever to admit another person without a profession of real saving religion and spake much of the great difficulties that he expected would come upon him by reason of his opinion." Sure enough, it did. Eventually a petition was circulated and they were let go from their church and forced to take a mission on the far-reaches of civilization, preaching to Indians through an interpreter. There is no evidence in their writing and correspondence that they were bitter, however, and God used them even there.[6]

In the mid-1800's, William Booth, cofounder with his wife Catherine of the Salvation Army in England, faced criticism from people in the church and officials for his lack of education and polish. Worried about not being able to provide for his new bride, he toyed with the idea of getting out of the ministry. Catherine wrote to him in a letter, "Never mind who frowns, if God smiles. . . . Don't give way to such feelings for a moment. God loves you. He will sustain you." The two of them went on to establish a worldwide ministry that is still highly respected and vital today.[7]

When it comes right down to it, we in ministry must realize that our "significant audience" is God, not people. As we wait on Him, He shows us how to be servant-leaders, and helps us deal with unrealistic expectations from ourselves as well as from others.

Respect the 'Holy Ground' between You

We recently went back to Southern California College and watched another of our sons graduate. As I watched him walk across the platform, I remembered being on that same campus almost thirty years ago, in love with life, and with Bill Carmichael, a warm, wonderful guy with dreams and plans of his own. And I thought, *Oh, if I could talk to this young girl with an un-lined face that was me so long ago, I would say: "Nancie, you can't know what's ahead. You are grabbing the hand of that wonderful man, running down the road to marriage, to ministry, to raising a family, and somehow in your mind it's all set to grand, glorious music. You have no idea how hard marriage can be! The times when you are completely misunderstood, or the times you cannot comprehend him (or want to), and he infuriates you so.*

But you also have no idea how wonderful marriage can be—sharing dreams, being best friends, the incomparable joy of having children, the warmth of having a Significant Other who loves you. You say your number one desire is to follow God whole-heartedly. That's good. But there is no way to describe the conflicts that are ahead. The challenge of making life choices, career choices, spiritual choices. You can't know the giants in the Promised Land you are so eagerly embracing. To you now, the giants are opportunity and finances. But the real ones you will deal with are less obvious—the ones inside of you: low self-esteem, insecurity, fear, unbelief, lack of discipline. These are the real giants you must overcome on your way to the Promised Land, of being all you can be for God."

When we married, Bill gave me a beautiful little pendant on a gold chain. It is two leaves with a pearl in the middle. To me, the pearl between those two gold leaves symbolizes respect. Henri Nouwen wrote, "Can real intimacy be reached without a deep respect for that holy place within and between us, that space that should remain untouched by human hands? Can human intimacy really be fulfilling when every space within and between us is being filled up?"[8] He went on to say that in our mobile, transient society with so many fractured families there is a temptation to expect our husband or wife to fill up all the holes, to meet all our needs. I see in this gold-and-pearl pendant the holy ground between us, the God-shaped vacuum that only He can fill. Intimacy asks respect, first of all, for that place.

Bill and I have learned painful lessons about mutual respect. Of course, *it starts with self-respect,* something that would seem obvious. Bill has a weight problem that I keep trying to solve (in vain). Bill has tried for years to make me more organized, to think like he thinks and plan ahead (in vain). None of our efforts to change each other ever really work, they only cause anger and frustration. We have come to realize that the more secure each of us is in our individual walk with God, and the more we comprehend His love, the more we can really love each other and let go of our need to "fix" each other. We cannot be God or Holy Spirit to each other. And we must forgive each other for our humanity and differences. We have found that respect for our differences enhances intimacy.

Henri Nouwen described intimacy as "the two cherubs whose out-

> **Low self-esteem, insecurity, fear . . . These are the real giants on the way to being all you can be for God.**

stretched wings sheltered the Ark of the Covenant and created a space where Yahweh could be present. Marriage is a relationship in which a man and a woman protect and nurture the inner sanctum within and between them and witness to that by the way they love each other. . . . Marriage . . . is an intimacy based on the common participation in a love greater than the love two people can offer each other. . . . They are brought together, indeed, as two prayerful hands extended toward God and forming in this way a home for God in this world."[9]

That is what we want—to be a place where God is at home. And I believe it's a longing that all of us who feel called to minister have. We want God to be so at home in us, and among us, that the fire of His Holy Spirit will burn within us and be a light for others to see the good news of Christ's love and redemption.

I have written this chapter toward husbands and wives who want to be in the ministry. I know there are many pastor's wives who do not want to be involved at all, who for various reasons dislike and fear being a pastor's wife. My heart aches for these women because I know being "the minister's wife" can be a lonely and difficult path. And yet we serve the All-Sufficient One! *He* is our significant audience; when we keep our eyes on Jesus, "the author and finisher of our faith," walking humbly before Him in our weakness and inadequacy, He will show Himself strong.

Coping with Financial Pressures in the Family

G. Raymond Carlson

How important is money? Money can be a master or a servant. Money as "the root of all evil" is an incorrect quote of Scripture. The Bible declares, "The love of money is a root of all kinds of evil" (1 Timothy 6:10).

The love of money caused Judas to betray the Lord Jesus Christ (Matthew 26). Ananias and Saphira were struck dead because they lied about their money (Acts 5). Achan was destroyed, along with his family, because of his love of money (Joshua 7). Self-interest was the dominating motive as Gehazi, in his covetous heart, sought to peddle the gracious act of God for material gain (2 Kings 5). The lust for possession brings deterioration of character.

Wealth is not wrong. To be rich is not wrong. But wrong occurs when we place our trust in riches. People allow greed to possess them, to consume them. In His Parable of the Sower, Jesus stated that the deceitfulness of wealth choked the Word, making it unfruitful (Matthew 13:22). Monetary deception comes because of greed. "The more I have, the more I want" syndrome robs a person of spiritual life. Pressures increase and contentment flees.

Contentment eliminates monetary deception. In writing to Timothy, Paul said that some think that "godliness is a means to financial gain" (1 Timothy 6:5). Further on he stated, "Godliness with contentment is great gain. . . . [and] People who want to get rich fall into temptation and a trap and into many foolish and harmful desires that plunge men into ruin and destruction. For the love of money is a root of all kinds of evil"(1 Timothy 6:6,9–10).

Wealth Is Not Wrong

From a quick review of the subject of wealth in Scripture, we learn that riches are not wrong. It is what wealth can do to us that is wrong. Again and again the Bible cites examples of the tragedy of greed and ill-gotten gain. We have the mistaken notion that if we own things, we have prosperity. We own cars, boats, motorcycles, homes, cabins, and all of the latest in technology. The general attitude is that if we have these things we have it made. But things are not the answer. There are riches far greater than material prosperity. The obsession with success and pleasures does not satisfy. Solomon points that out graphically in Ecclesiastes 1 and 2, stating that all was without meaning and purpose apart from God's will.

We live in a day when values seem to be askew. Athletic heroes and entertainers are paid millions. The salaries of other professionals, such as teachers, cannot compare. And then there are the salaries of ministers of the gospel. Some are given adequate salaries, but hundreds live with constant financial pressure because their income is limited. The star athlete, the successful CEO, have incomes far above the salaries offered to preachers.

My hat is off and my heart reaches out to those great souls who have responded to the call of God and labored long and hard to reach the lost and build the Lord's Church. They have enriched thousands, making them ready for the final audit. Many of them have given themselves at great financial sacrifice.

A dear fellow minister shared his heart with me regarding his family. Every part of the ministry was extremely rewarding to him. God blessed him and his wife with three sons and three daughters. The greatest sacrifice made by him and his wife affected their daughters; because of his limited income, they did not have many of the nice things their peers in the church enjoyed. He regretted that his financial income did not permit much beyond the necessities. The children are now grown. Obviously, the financial pressures they lived under were handled well. All but one of the children are in the ministry; two are missionaries and the others are either pastors or pastor's wives. In turn, several of the grandchildren are either in pastoral or evangelistic work or in Bible college preparing to answer God's call to the harvest field.

Enjoying Growth and God's Blessing

After many years of close observation I have concluded that if a church is to enjoy growth and God's blessing, it must deal properly with two financial matters. First, the church must care for the financial needs of its pastor, then it must maintain a strong missionary program. Jesus said, "'The worker deserves his wages'" (Luke 10:7). Paul declares the same truth in 1 Timothy 5:18. God's blessing will not rest upon a church that does not support its pastor or a missionary program.

Financial pressure is an ever-present problem unless steps are taken to put the financial load in proper order. This is a matter of vital concern. Every minister must chart a course of financial integrity, beginning in one's personal life. A Christian must not "rob God." How can we rob Him? The answer: "'In tithes and offerings'" (Malachi 3:8). To disobey this command is to bring a curse upon oneself.

Financial integrity means that bills are paid. We must not buy without regard to payday. Paul admonishes us, "Be careful to do what is right in the eyes of everybody" (Romans 12:17). Unwise buying or spending creates unnecessary problems. Usually these actions are in the realm of the nonessentials. We are to be people who practice faith, but faith does not pay bills. Cash is required.

Learning to live within one's income need not be difficult. To do so may require denying oneself not only luxuries, but also some necessities. A bad financial record can damage a person's life and follow him for years to come. It is important to maintain an honorable financial standing in the community. Build a good financial record in fair weather, so that you may borrow in foul weather. Rainy days come to all of us. How helpful to have a record that has invited trust and confidence!

Commenting on the minister who must supplement his income with another job, Adolph Bedsole states, "Under such circumstances it is honorable for a minister to dig ditches on Monday (if it must be, which it shouldn't) in order that he may face his people with a clear conscience on Sunday."[1] Far too many ministers are poor managers of their own funds. In recent years clergy credit has improved. At one time credit officers listed them in the "three Ps" of poor credit—painters, paperhangers, and preachers. I don't know that the first two named should have such a rating tacked on them, and I hope that preachers would make that charge untrue.

Handle Credit with Care

The unending pressures of "more month than money" is enough to tear families apart. But in some cases more money is not the cure. We must begin to properly manage what we have. Husband and wife must work together (and there may be the time and place to involve the children). Look beyond monthly payments. Get the picture of total debt in focus. We thank God that a credit rating will permit us to borrow money, but don't be fooled. Interest is costly. Credit cards have been the ruination of many homes. Better to stop buying on credit unless you can discipline yourself to limit spending. Quit using credit cards for purchases when you know there will be no money to pay for them. Pay your bills when they come due. When payments can't be made, communicate with your creditor.

One pastor told me that he and his wife were so saddled with monthly payments, they were unable to tithe. To remove yourself from tithing is to remove yourself from blessing ground. God does not honor bad management. We are to be good stewards. We are to "Honor the Lord with [our] wealth" (Proverbs 3:9–10). Wealth reaches beyond the tithe. The tithe belongs to God. We are called upon to honor Him with what we have left over after the tithe. This is clearly set forth in our Lord's Parable of the Talents (Matthew 25:24–30). The servant who hid his one talent in the ground was strongly censured by the Lord.

Further, some men who are capable in the pulpit have weakened their ministry because they are slow to pay their debts. Others have left a trail of debts wherever they have lived. Such financial irresponsibility has left a blotch on the cause of Christ, on their churches, and on the ministers themselves. With justifiable pride, I received the compliments of the lending institutions in the city where I pastored. They told me, "Your people have integrity. They pay their bills on time and if they have a problem, they come to us." Can you know how I, as the pastor, appreciated these commendations. The members were not only believing the gospel we preached, but were also behaving it. The same experience was shared with me by numerous lending institutions when I was a district superintendent. In many cities, Assemblies of God churches and their pastors ranked number one in credit rating. Sadly, not every pastor and church had this rating.

The Bible Teaches Ministerial Support

The principle of a salaried ministry is clearly outlined by Paul in 1 Corinthians 9. The passage sets forth the truth that a minister has the right to be supported so that he can devote all his efforts to the ministry. However, Paul, though an apostle, chose to seek other ways to support himself at Corinth to meet the need of a particular situation. Nevertheless, the surrender of his privilege of support by the local church did not lessen the normal obligation of a church. He waived that right, but at some length went on to assure that those rights were acknowledged.

Paul used the example of the other apostles, including our Lord's brothers and Peter. Not only were they provided for, but their wives as well. Paul went further to show that reward for labor is a common practice: The soldier receives his salary; the farmer and the shepherd expect to be adequately recompensed. In each of these cases, the remuneration was sufficient so that recipients would not need to look elsewhere. The plowman and the thresher should rightfully expect to share in the harvest. Paul then turns to the Law of Moses for further support, pointing out that the examples he drew from experience were outlined in God's Word. The oxen when threshing the grain were not to be hindered from eating the corn. If God outlined this principle for a beast, He surely makes the same provision for those who sow spiritual seed to reap a material harvest.

The apostle proceeds further to defend the principle of ministerial support by calling attention to the divine provision that those who labored in the temple were supported by temple offerings. He raises a logical question: "If others have this right of support from you, shouldn't we have it all the more?" (1 Corinthians 9:12). Paul summarizes the argument by stating, "In the same way, the Lord has commanded that those who preach the gospel should receive their living from the gospel" (9:14). Here Paul was only reiterating what Jesus told the Seventy as He sent them forth: "'The worker deserves his wages'" (Luke 10:7).

Note that Paul uses a strong word in the Corinthian passage: "The Lord has *commanded*" (9:14). God has given orders that those who preach the gospel should be supported by those who accept it. There are people who believe that ministers should live by faith, having no set remuneration from the church. Living by faith has great rewards, but we must balance that principle with the clear instructions about ministerial support outlined by Paul. It is not right that a pastor should be kept praying without ceasing for his bare necessities when those he ministers to are well able to supply his need. A minister should receive enough to provide himself and his family relief from financial anxiety.

> **"Those who preach the gospel should be supported by those who accept it."**

The Holy Spirit dealt with my wife and me early in our ministry. We had excellent jobs and salaries before we began our pastoral work. In fact our monthly salary was the same as that of our first year in the pastorate. Feeling that we could provide for ourselves, we found it difficult to accept support that came sacrificially from the congregation.

God blessed the work. Revival swept many into the Kingdom and into the Pentecostal experience. Then came the great need to enlarge the facilities. This was done in due time. I was anxious to retire the debt and led the church in making sizable monthly payments. New members on the board agreed that this was not right. The pastor and his family should not pay for the building by not being properly supported by the church. At that point, the Lord showed me that I had not been training the people properly. God "commanded" that the shepherd should be given adequate support. Adjustments were made and the debt was retired even at a more rapid pace. I had to learn not only is it blessed to give, but it is also blessed to receive, and I must not rob the people of their reward for faithful financial support. The emphasis of the Bible is not on material wealth, but on spiritual development. When financial prosperity follows spiritual prosperity, greed will not find fertile soil to grow in.

Practice Frugal Living

The ministry was never intended to provide a comfortable living for preachers. The road will be strewn with sharp stones and often covered with mud, ice, or snow. One of the great struggles that ministers face may be in financial matters. Bills multiply and debt overwhelms. What shall the minister do? Husband and wife need to take time together to review their financial situation. If debt has brought them to an impasse, they need to look at the cause and then proceed to find the remedy. Getting out of debt is a family project. Children who are old enough, especially teenagers, need to be brought into the project. An awareness on their part will help the entire family attack the difficult decisions that must be faced.

In some instances, the family may be the major problem. Possibly the pastor does not discipline himself. The wife may refuse to share the responsibility. But if husband and wife prayerfully deal with the problem, taking steps to get out of the difficulty, the children will do their best to cooperate. When the parents have to say no, the children can see the logic for they have seen the family budget.

All of us face emergencies—illness, hospital and medical bills, and death. They come like a flood. Money is not available to meet the avalanche of expenses. Few ministers have laid aside sufficient funds to meet emergencies. How shall the need be met? First, we must go to the Lord. Our Master is pleased to answer our prayers. I could testify to many of God's marvelous provisions for our family, some of them in the realm of the miraculous. In all of our planning, we must never forget that the God we serve will meet our need. The cattle on a thousand hills are His, as are the silver and gold in those hills.

I am a strong believer in building a savings account; some money, be it ever so little, should be laid aside regularly toward retirement. My wife and I began with one dollar per month when the Ministers Benefit Association was founded in 1944. Little by little we increased that amount as the years rolled by. After fifty years, that amount has accumulated to the point where we can, in turn, contribute much of it to the Lord's work.

The Bible is very explicit in teaching us to help those who are impoverished. We must never turn our backs on those who are in need. Whenever and however we can assist those who are coping with financial pressures, we are doing right.

An old proverb says:

What I hoard I lose.
What I try to keep will be left and fought over by others.
What I give will continue to return . . . forever.

And another says:

Earn all you can.
Save all you can,
So you can *give* all you can.

Devotion to Christ is often demonstrated in generosity.

Staying Healthy in the Ministry

Richard D. Dobbins

For some time, the ministry in modern America has been a profession of increasing health risks and decreasing commitment. Allen C. Reuter stated several years ago: "The rates of suicide, divorce, alcoholism, depression, heart attack, and other stress-related maladies are all significantly higher today among clergy. The dropout and early retirement rates are also up."[1]

Dr. Woodrow Kroll also addresses the subject of decreasing commitment and offers as a partial explanation that "the cleanliness of theory" taught in Bible colleges and seminaries is no match for "the mess of reality" the minister finds upon entering the field.[2] The young seminarian comes out of the classroom ready to set the world on fire for Christ—only to discover that clean, precise theories so carefully studied in the classroom must now be applied in the messy and often-chaotic laboratory of life in the institutional church.

Remembering from their earliest Sunday school days that Jesus promised an easy yoke and a light burden (Matthew 11:30), many parsonage families are surprised and perplexed by the physical and emotional toll the institutional ministry exacts from them. However, there is a big difference between following Jesus and serving the demands of the institutional church. The work of the institutional ministry *is* stress-producing. Look at some of the sources of this stress.

Sources of Stress

Today's nuclear age. We are the first generation required to live under the threat of global nuclear destruction. Although the intensity of this threat waxes and wanes with international politics, it is always there. One cannot help wondering if these were the days Jesus had in mind when He said: "There shall be signs in the sun, and in the moon, and in the stars; and upon the earth distress of nations, with perplexity; the sea and the waves roaring; men's hearts failing them for fear, and for looking after those things which are coming on the earth: for the powers of heaven shall be shaken" (Luke 21:25–26[3]).

Information overload and rapid change. Modern transportation and communication methods are shrinking our world into the proverbial "global village." The first airmail sent from Chicago to New York took just over ten hours in 1918.[4] Passengers now routinely fly from America to cities all over Europe in the same time or less.

News of our involvement in World War I (back in 1917) took several weeks to reach many rural Americans, who got their news from weekly papers delivered on horseback. When the Persian Gulf War began in January 1991, news teams from around the world were broadcasting live coverage as the first few planes took off on their bombing runs.

This present era is being called variously the information age and the information society. Much of the reason is certainly due to the computer, specifically the Internet, which boasted fifteen million users in 1995. How one is to manage the flood of information this represents has yet to be determined.

Sex, violence, and moral compromise. The American entertainment media's preoccupation with sex and violence both reflects and stimulates our cultural propensities in those directions. According to a recent report by researchers Patterson and Kim, at least one-third of all married Americans have had, or are currently having, an affair. Over 20 percent of our children lose their virginity by the time they are thirteen years of age. One in every seven Americans is sexually abused as a child.

> **'The cleanliness of theory' is no match for 'the mess of reality.'**

We are also a violent nation. Americans are among the most heavily armed people in the world. At a minimum, every seventh person you pass on the street in America is carrying some kind of weapon. Wife abuse is at an all-time high. Sixty percent of Americans have been victimized by crime at least once. America has the highest homicide rate of all industrialized nations.

Further, our national character is eroding at an alarming rate, according to these same researchers. Unethical activities among business executives are cited as the number one cause of business decline in the United States. Both employers and employees are untruthful in business situations. They steal both time and material goods from their businesses. College students freely admit cheating on exams. Depending on the statistics one reads, it would seem that very few make it to graduation any other way.

In the area of marriage and the family, Patterson and Kim credit the baby boomers with separating sexual expression from marriage in the '60s and '70s. "Free love," as it was called then, became an all-too-common rite of passage. The children of the baby boomers, often called the "baby busters," are now credited with separating parenthood from marriage. It is socially acceptable in America to have children without providing for them the security of parents committed to each other or to them through the God-ordained institutions of marriage and the family.[5]

Stresses in our children's world. Children have their own unique stresses. Over half of America's children must contend with the divorce of their parents. Others are lost in the shuffle of a two-career family. Our young people's peers—the only circle where many feel accepted or cared for—are putting increased pressure on them to conform to the ways of the world. Alcohol abuse, pregnancy, abortion, and suicide are at record levels for teens, and still climbing. Schools are trying to narrow the gap between where students are and where they should be academically, adding still more pressures. Make no mistake: all young people are affected by the desperate social climate they live in.

When the family car heads for church, it carries not only the family members, but all of their stresses as well. The minister is found at the focal point of family stress more often than any other professional person in our society. Over two decades ago, Edgar Mills and John Koval conducted a landmark study with over 5,000 ministers representing twenty-one denominations in the United States.[6] These two researchers discovered job-related stress to be the most common source of discomfort among ministers. What was the specific source of this job-related stress? Demands made on them by members of their local congregations.

Although stressed-out people may make unrealistic or thoughtless demands on church leadership, a predictable amount of the minister's stress also originates in his or her own life and marriage. This personal stress is simply aggravated by the demands of congregants.

The Typical Work Pattern of a Pastor

Gary Kuhne and Joe Donaldson studied the actual characteristics of the work activity of five experienced, evangelical, Protestant pastors with a Master of Divinity (or equivalent) degree. They found these pastors' workdays to be "taxing, fast-paced, and unrelenting . . . patterns of activities [that] were marked by brevity, fragmentation, and variety."[7] Nearly 50 percent of the time the pastor's task changed within five minutes or less. This pace alone is stress-producing because so many things are left half-finished. It is like opening a book to read a passage and having to stop halfway through, opening another book on top of it and starting to read it, having to open another book on top of that one and starting to read it—over and over again. At the end of the day, all of the books either have to be put back on the shelf with the salient passages unread or left stacked there for a try again the next day. Either way, it is a stressful situation because nothing gets finished.

Now add to this the researchers' observation that the pastor must change moods with almost every telephone call as he or she goes from celebrating good news with a parishioner, to presiding over a difficult committee meeting, to receiving a heartbreaking telephone call that a beloved child or some saintly man or woman of God in the church family has just been struck dead by a hit-and-run driver. Calls like this can take the pastor from the mountaintop to the valley floor in sixty seconds or less. Such are the normal demands made on ministers in one way or another by their parishioners. These are the kinds of demands ministers expect; they have dedicated their lives to meeting them. Nonetheless, they are stressful and validate the observations of Mills and Koval.

Kuhne and Donaldson also cite earlier research indicating that the minister is highly prone to "polychronic" activity, doing two or more tasks simultaneously: signing correspondence or filling out routine forms while on the telephone, dictating correspondence while driving to visit a parishioner in the hospital, making telephone calls or conducting meetings while eating lunch, etc.[8] This, too, is stressful since it demands attention—which saps energy—on at least two fronts at a time.

Stress Inherent in the Pastor's Personal Life

Mills and Koval found that ministers identified several specific times when stress was greatest: during the first five years after ordination, eight to twelve years after ordination, and twenty years after ordination. Are these times when the congregation goes through changes en masse? No, they are times when the pastor's family is experiencing predictable stresses. The good news is that because these stressful times are somewhat predictable, they are also somewhat manageable. To be forewarned is to be forearmed.

Five years after ordination, around twenty-five to thirty years of age, the minister is usually completing the acquisition of pastoral skills and adjusting to being married. Both of these experiences can be stress-producing. Trying to satisfy a mate's needs for intimacy and to live up to one's own ambitions to build a great church are often in conflict with each other—and create stress for the young pastor.

Eight to twelve years after ordination, the pastoral family is coming to terms with the stresses of parenthood. Finding time for the children among the flurry of parsonage activities can be difficult. The pastor and his spouse must at this point determine how many of the church activities, which consume so much of their time, are absolutely necessary. This is a highly subjective matter and calls for careful assessment.

However, someone has to care for the children's needs. Since the ministry is still a predominantly male profession, it is generally the wife who must take "a leave of absence" from church activities while the couple's children are young. Many pastors are insensitive to this need and see it as an indication that their wife's commitment to ministry is waning. Such an attitude leaves her feeling abandoned in parenthood and resenting either the ministry in general or her spouse in particular. Neither of these feelings is healthy for the couple's love life.

Twenty years after ordination, we find the ministry couple dealing with midlife issues. There is no mystery why these are among the most stressful years of the minister's life. Ministry couples are like most other couples here. The children are growing up, finding mates, and leaving home. The couple's parents are showing signs of aging and are perhaps in poor health. The minister's career has often "peaked" at a lower altitude than he or she had hoped. One spouse or the other has probably been faced with a major health problem. In addition, the minister begins to realize that congregations' frequent preferences for younger pastors are limiting his future opportunities.

Against this professional and personal backdrop, the minister must stay healthy in order to fulfill his calling. Staying healthy in the ministry is a challenge that requires the minister to expend both preventive and protective energies to stay spiritually, emotionally, and physically healthy.

Staying Spiritually Healthy in the Ministry

The minister's spiritual health is the most vital resource of his life and vocation. He faces no greater challenge to health and wholeness than that of establishing and maintaining personal spiritual discipline. One of the ways the pastor can do this is to deliberately separate *his walk with God* from *his work for God.* In his work, he reads the Bible in search of material for sermons and other teaching opportunities. His work also requires him to spend time in prayer, both publicly during worship services and privately when he prays with or about people and/or situations in the church.

It is easy for the minister to deceive himself into believing that these should be adequate for his personal spiritual health. However, time spent studying the Bible for sermons and praying in his role as minister should not be considered part of his devotions. These are functions of his profession: They are part of the work God has called him to and people are paying him for.

There is no necessary correlation between a minister's walk with God and his work for God. His ministerial work may be statistically successful, but that doesn't mean his relationship with God is healthy. It simply means he is talented and skilled in the work he does; he is good at the work of the ministry. However, the minister can be a personal failure at the same time he is a professional success. The shock of such a discovery is a blessing in disguise when it forces the minister to focus more on his walk than his work. Nothing pleases the Lord more, for *He is much more interested in our walk than He is in our work.*

Nevertheless, one of the minister's biggest temptations is to focus on the work rather than the walk. After all, it is one's work that others notice. Like everyone else, the minister's walk with the Lord is cared for almost entirely in private moments, alone with Him. Only the Lord sees our walk. And His rewards are mostly delayed until His coming. But remember, in the long run it is the minister's walk with God that brings credibility to his work for God. Success in your walk with the Lord will keep you humble in the face of your successes and encourage you when you fail in your work.

PERSONAL DISCIPLINES AND SPIRITUAL HEALTH

First, the minister must develop the habit of devotional Bible reading. One way to do this is to read through the Bible from Genesis to Revelation. For the serious reader, every reading of the Bible produces new insights and becomes an exciting adventure.

Bible characters and Bible families make particularly interesting studies as certain traits are traced from generation to generation. For example, Rebekah and her family were deceivers. She deceived her husband and taught their son to do the same. When Jacob's deceit put his life in jeopardy, he fled to Rebekah's brother, Laban. Laban deceived Jacob on his wedding night by giving him Leah instead of Rachel.

Later, sometime after Jacob had finally married Rachel, he deceived Laban and had to run for his life again. Rachel deceived her own father by hiding his special gods under her dress, preventing their discovery by pretending to be menstruating. This is just one of scores of interesting character studies in Scripture. Studies like this broaden one's understanding of the way certain issues are dealt with over time in Scripture.

Another exciting way to approach Scripture is to trace the great doctrines of the Church through the Word. Although this is done for one's own devotional benefit, it will inevitably enrich preaching and teaching by providing a greater knowledge of, and love for, God's Word.

Greek and Hebrew word studies enrich the pastor's appreciation for sound exegetical interpretation of the Word. For example, it was enlightening for me to discover the difference between the Greek words *soma* and *sarx*. *Soma* always refers to the body and *sarx* usually refers to the fallen nature of man. The first is to be nourished and cherished; the other to be hated and crucified. At times, both are translated by the English word *flesh* (Ephesians 5:28–29; Romans 7:18). Knowing this one bit of information helps the pastor understand why some people mistakenly believe the Bible teaches that the body is evil.

Second, the pastor needs to take time for personal prayer. Prayer is far more than the stereotypical list of requests sandwiched between two thank-yous. It includes a great many forms of expression. *Petitionary* prayer is probably the most common form of prayer. It is recommended by Paul in Philippians 4:6. It consists of one's petitions to God—a list of things that God can do for the suppliant or others. While this is an important form of prayer, it should not be a person's only method of praying.

Paul refers to *intercessory* prayer in Romans 8:26–28. These are the moments when we don't even know what we should pray for, or how to pray, but we know we need to communicate with God. In these times, the Holy Spirit makes intercession through us and expresses our petitions to Him. He helps us pray "as we ought." We don't have to understand how this wonderful process works to take advantage of what God has so beautifully provided. We just need to participate and thank Him for caring that much about our spiritual health.

Meditation is another form of prayer. In the early days of Christianity, this was a much more popular form of prayer than it is for us today. However, there is a wonderful sense of spiritual refreshing to be found in prayerfully meditating on biblical words such as *faith, hope, love, peace,* and *joy,* or focusing on a Bible scene that is reassuring and consistent with our spiritual and emotional needs. More and more people are learning the spiritual benefits of meditating on uplifting scenes from the Word. In fact, an interesting devotional study might be to note the occurrences of various forms of the word *meditate* in Scripture.

If you wish to try this form of prayer, choose a quiet time and place. Get comfortable. Bring your thoughts "into captivity" to Christ (2 Co-

> **Refreshing comes from meditating on biblical words.**

rinthians 10:5). Then allow yourself to get caught up in a refreshing Bible scene. If you are focusing on Jesus calming the storm on Galilee, fix the visual image of the storm. Picture in your mind the boat being tossed around and the fright of the disciples. Imagine what noise the wind would make. Try to feel the water spray on your face. Imagine you can hear Jesus saying, "Peace, be still!" Imagine that you can see the waves subside and the sea become like glass (Mark 4:35–41). Notice the calming effect this experience has on your own inner world.

Years ago a friend loaned me a copy of a small paperback, *The Practice of the Presence of God,* written by a seventeenth-century French Carmelite monk named Brother Lawrence.[9] He was a lay brother in a Paris monastery and was the cook for over thirty years, until he finally went blind from age.[10] His message was about living in the presence of God everywhere, every day, through constant conversation with the Christ he adored. One of the prayers I recall from his book said simply, "Lord, make me a saint by getting meals and washing up the pots and pans and plates."

> **We should see our whole life as a prayer to God.**

Everywhere he went—the kitchen, the vegetable garden, the root cellar—Brother Lawrence worked at being in the presence of God. His example could be that of *praying without ceasing,* another kind of prayer we need to practice at times. We should see our whole life as a prayer offered to God as a "living sacrifice"—which is part of what Paul was addressing in Romans 12:1. We'll have less trouble acting and reacting like a saint when confronting the big issues of life if we practice prayer without ceasing and acting and reacting like a saint when confronting the "pots and pans" of life—the little things. It is, after all, when the prayer of your life and the prayer of your lips become one and the same that you are truly "walking in the Spirit."

"Singing and making melody in your heart to the Lord" is another form of prayer Paul mentions (Ephesians 5:19). For many years I have been enjoying this form of spiritual expression. Sometimes I am surprised by the choruses and hymns the Holy Spirit brings to my mind. I have found that keeping a song in my heart has helped me get through many difficult days.

Speaking in other tongues, our Pentecostal distinctive, is spiritually and mentally healthy in several ways. First of all, speaking in tongues requires us to get beyond pride, bypassing intellect to cry out to God simply from our spirit to His Spirit. At times, I may not even know what I'm saying to Him. I just know I need to commune with Him on an intensely deep and personal level. At that point, my pride and intellect are irrelevant. My need for this kind of close communion supersedes anything else. At other times, "I will pray with the understanding also" (1 Corinthians 14:15).

Remember, "He that speaketh in an unknown tongue edifieth himself" (1 Corinthians 14:4). There are times when soul and spirit need the kind of edification nothing else can provide. I often come out of my office at the end of the workday just loaded with the pain and sorrows people have deposited in me. And though I know I am called of God to this task, many times it wearies my spirit. I get "weary in well doing" (Galatians 6:9) and need God to refresh me. Praying in the Spirit is always a mentally healthy practice. How do I know? It is always integrative in my life rather than disintegrative. It enables me to function more effectively in my life roles. Rather than diminishing and fragmenting my energies, it consolidates and strengthens them. It edifies and refreshes and restores my spirit for the immediate as well as the long-term tasks God has given me.

A *personal journal* is also a good tool for maintaining spiritual and emotional health. This is different from a diary in that you write only as you feel inspired. However, try to write at least once a month and be as honest as possible. A journal is a safe place to deposit your feelings, and it will be a tremendous source of reassurance during hard times in the future as you look back at the "many dangers, toils, and snares" through which you have already come.

Incidentally, the story behind that marvelous old hymn "Amazing Grace" makes for *great* inspirational reading! The author, Englishman John Newton, wrote it as a testimony to God's marvelous power in delivering him from a life of vulgarity and wayward living as a seaman-adventurer.[11]

Third, the pastor should pray with his spouse and children. Your spiritual discipline will have a greater effect on the spiritual health of your marriage and family than any other thing you do. Be sure to lead your wife in brief moments of prayer each day. The absence of prayer together is the greatest weakness in parsonage marriages. Your prayer times as a couple do not have to be long, but they should be regular. Begin with just a few minutes of sentence prayers. You will be amazed at the effect this has on your wife's respect for your spiritual leadership in the family as well as in the church.

> **" Praying in the Spirit is a mentally healthy practice. "**

Have appropriate times of prayer with your children—as their loving father, not as their pastor. They need to hear you pray for them and with them. In most instances, these prayers should be brief. Pray about your hopes and concerns for them. This is a part of you God wants your children to see. And listening to them say their prayers will give you insight into parts of their lives that you would never otherwise have.

Fourth, the pastor should utilize meaningful rituals for pleasant family memories. Institute some meaningful religious rituals in your family life, apart from the traditional seasonal activities and those of your Christian Education Department. For instance, in your family celebration of Easter, you may want to serve your family Communion and find an appropriate time to read the Easter story from the Bible. The Cross and Resurrection are at the very heart of the gospel and should be at the heart of a Christian family's celebration of the Easter season.

Read a passage from Psalms before Thanksgiving dinner. Briefly remind your family of some special things you are thankful for, and let them voice their own thankfulness for something special before you ask God's blessing on your family feast. Again, participate as the head of your family rather than as their pastor.

Read a New Testament account of the Christmas story to your family on Christmas Eve or Christmas Day, before you open your packages or before you eat Christmas dinner. Find a prominent place for a manger scene as part of your Christmas decorations. Share the stories behind some of your family's favorite Christmas hymns.

Staying Emotionally Healthy in the Ministry

My definition of an emotionally healthy human being is one who is able to love, work, play, and worship in balance. This is true for the minister as well. Additionally, in the institutional ministry you must become a good steward of your attitudes toward life. A positive mental attitude is a must. Your reading habits are a major factor in keeping this kind of healthy perspective, or worldview.

If you are not careful, you will find yourself reading only those materials directly related to your work: sermon preparation and teaching assignments. Broaden your focus; determine to read at least six books a year that are not directly related to your work. Read biographies of people you admire. This vicarious sharing in the lives of others helps one see one's own life more realistically. Read books about people of other cultures and other times. Read about the marvels of our world and universe.

At least once during each year, read a reputable book about relating your faith to the emotional needs of your life. This will help you with your own (and others') inevitable recurring battles with such issues as fear, anger, guilt, and/or depression.[12]

Management of personal feelings is especially important for the minister, since his feelings affect not only his own marriage and family but a much wider circle among the family of God. And the healthier his own soul and spirit are, the healthier his teaching and preaching will be.

Think again about Jesus' words in Matthew 11:30, where we read, "My yoke is easy, and my burden is light." No one has ever had a nervous breakdown from following Jesus. No one has ever gone to pieces doing the will of God. However, a minister can kill himself working for the institutional church. That is why it is so important to know the difference between serving the institutional church and serving the body of Christ.

The institutional church measures success by an endless list of comparative statistics. How large is your Sunday school? How many missionaries do you support? What is your average Sunday morning attendance? How many ministers are on your staff? What is your church's annual income? The Lord measures success in terms of faithfulness. Even if we have only a little, a "few things," but are faithful in caring for what we have been given, we have His Word that our reward will be great *because we have been faithful* (Matthew 25:14–30). Others may make heavier demands on us; however, the Lord requires us only to be faithful. That is all it takes to hear His "Well done."

The pastor gets out from under the heavy burden and the galling yoke of his driving ambition in the institutional church by shifting to a new focus. Numbers are not the most important thing about his work. His primary task is to serve the Lord and further His kingdom. He may have to develop skill in dealing with church boards and committees, but he doesn't work for them. He works for the Lord. What does it mean to work for the Lord? He is an employer who invites His laborers to come to Him when they are tired and hungry and thirsty. When you are in need of spiritual refreshing and reassurance, He urges you to come, "Casting all your care upon him; for he careth for you" (1 Peter 5:7).

FORMING REALISTIC EXPECTATIONS

Many couples enter the ministry with unrealistic expectations of church people and themselves. In our youthful zeal and idealism, we set ourselves up for needless frustration. For example, we expect the Christians we pastor to be "spiritual." Even a casual reading of the Epistles reveals the majority of Christians pastored by the elders of the Early Church were certainly not spiritual. They were carnal. Expecting today's church people to be more spiritual than first-century believers is bound to set you up for frustration. If you assume most of the people you pastor will be carnal, you probably won't be so disappointed. Then, when some are spiritual, you can be pleasantly surprised. Require yourself to be spiritual, but be patient with the carnality of others.

While keeping your vision keen and fervent, be modest in the growth you anticipate. Goals are important. There is truth in the old saying, "It's better to aim at something and miss it than to aim at nothing and hit it." Set your goals far enough from your present accomplishments to challenge you, yet close enough to be reached. This will spare you the stress of feeling like a failure and give you a greater sense of accomplishment.

CASTING YOUR CARES ON JESUS

Remember to practice the message of 1 Peter 5:7, "Casting all your care upon him; for he careth for you." When I pastored, it occurred to me one day that in my sermons I seldom told people *how* to do what I'd said they *ought* to do. And that's where so many people need help—with the "how-to" of the Christian life. They pretty much know the "ought to," but they often have trouble figuring out how. So let's look at how to cast your cares upon the Lord. I have found it helpful to honestly respond to a series of questions I ask myself when I am overloaded with care in some area.

First, *can anything be done about what concerns me?* It is easy to become greatly agitated and concerned over matters about which little or nothing can be done by anyone. We get so focused on these issues that other matters—which we *could* do something about—escape our attention. When you find yourself becoming unduly focused on something about which nothing can be done, acknowledge that fact and thus "cast" that care upon the Lord. It's beyond any personal intervention or control.

On the other hand, if something can be done about it, ask a second question: *Can I do anything about it?* We tend to become greatly involved and concerned in areas where we can personally do very little. If you know you cannot personally do anything about the matter, then again you must simply "cast" it on the Lord. Wisdom would dictate that a person never extend his or her sense of responsibility beyond the limits of personal control. If you don't control it, God doesn't hold you accountable for it.

Finally, if you honestly believe you can do something about the matter, the next step is to *define what you believe you can do and when you can do it.* If you can do something immediately, then go ahead and do it. If not, write it down in your planning calendar so you won't have to feel guilty later for forgetting to do what you could have done. When you have done what you can, or when you have recorded a note for action at a later date, then "cast" this care as well into the Lord's keeping, at least for the present.

MAINTAINING A POSITIVE ATTITUDE TOWARD LIFE

We have already addressed, briefly, the mental health implications of a pastor's positive attitude toward life. Let's revisit that area, looking at how it is formed and what is involved in changing it.

First of all, it is important to realize that attitudes are a major part of a person's identity—deeply held and second in importance only to one's core Christian values. If the home you were raised in provided you with more pleasure than pain, then you already have a positive attitude toward life. You tend to see the glass half full instead of half empty. However, if you experienced more pain than pleasure, especially in the early years before you started to school, then you have perhaps learned a rather negative view of life. You tend to see the glass half empty. When your father's attitudes, or worldview, joined with your mother's, the two of them created a family climate which produced a fairly predictable worldview in their children.[13] They more or less taught you whether to focus on the "full" or "empty" quality of that figurative glass of water.

A person's worldview is virtually immune to outside attempts at change. It has, after all, been reinforced by years of memories and imaginations. Change comes only from within, with deliberate, sustained effort and a miracle of spiritual warfare fought in God's strength. In 2 Corinthians 10:3–5, Paul describes the effort necessary to win this battle, which is the first step in making this kind of change: "Though we walk in the flesh, we do not war after the flesh: (for the weapons of our warfare are not carnal, but mighty through God to the pulling down of strongholds;) casting down imaginations, and every high thing that exalteth itself against the knowledge of God, and bringing into captivity every thought to the obedience of Christ."

Here are more elements of the battle that need your attention if you want to improve your general attitude toward life:

Become aware of the difference between the events of your life and your interpretation of those events. This is a new insight for many. Some people believe the way they have chosen to view the facts of their personal history is the only honest way those facts can be seen. As "the accuser of [the] brethren" (Revelation 12:10), Satan knows how to persuade many believers to buy into damaging interpretations of the things that have happened to them in life. However, the Lord can help you put together a more creative, less painful way of remembering any given event.

Realize you live with the memory of your life events, not with the events themselves. What are your memories of events? They are the interpretations, or stories, you tell yourself about them. And these stories can be changed. They can be edited by the destructive power of the enemy or by the redemptive grace of God.

If you don't think that is possible, consider the story of Joseph's brothers selling him into slavery in Egypt and his classic line to them after he had saved them from famine and revealed his identity: "Ye thought evil against me; but God meant it unto good, to bring to pass, as it is this day, to save much people alive" (Genesis 50:20). Joseph could have spent those years in Egypt feeling sorry for himself, forsaken by God, becoming incredibly bitter toward his brothers. No doubt Satan presented these options to him. But Joseph chose to tell himself a different story. He chose to stay focused on God and His purpose in all that was happening.

Your feelings about the events of your life flow from your interpretation of those events. Satan will provoke you to believe the most destructive possible story about the painful parts of your past. If he gets his way, you will be so crippled by the pain of your past that your personal and professional productivity will be greatly reduced.

Just as God helped Joseph deal creatively with his brothers' envy and hatred, He helped me find a redemptive way to view the fact that my birth was the cause of my mother's death. Through most of my teen years, I accused myself of murdering my mother, just as much as if I had put a gun to her head and pulled the trigger. But then the Lord helped me to see her death as adding to the value of my life. He suggested to me, *Not only did Jesus die for you, but your mother also died for you. How valuable your life must be. Be sure you make it count for something!*

Through the years, I have also seen Him bring this kind of inner healing to many others. If you are carrying this kind of hurt, He can heal you, too. You may need someone to help you in your search for a creative, redemptive interpretation, a new story. Be willing to set aside your sense of self-sufficiency or personal pride in order to find relief. Just as you urge others to accept your help and guidance, give someone the opportunity to minister to you in this way when you need it.

> **Memories are the interpretations, or stories, you have told yourself about events.**

Practice various ways of interpreting the events of your life. Notice the different feelings each interpretation evokes. This exercise allows you to experience what spiritual warfare is all about. And you'll discover that the way you choose to view the events of your life makes a big difference in how you feel about those events. Victory or defeat in life's spiritual warfare is not determined by what happens to us, but by how we choose to think and feel about what happens to us.

Place the most constructive interpretation on the daily events of your life by keeping your thought life healthy. In Philippians 4:8, Paul tells us how to evaluate and repair our thought life: "Whatsoever things are true, whatsoever things are honest, whatsoever things are just, whatsoever things are pure, whatsoever things are lovely, whatsoever things are of good report; if there be any virtue, and if there be any praise, think on these things."

This passage provides a tremendous thought filter. Notice, Paul assumes that among those things that are "honest," some things are not "just." We can put an unjust twist on an honest statement. From among those things that are just, some things are not pure. From among those things that are pure, some things are not lovely. Eventually, the believer is left with only those thoughts that have passed through the filters and come out as honest, just, pure, lovely, virtuous, and praiseworthy. What a tremendously creative mental environment that would be!

I have worked at this filter for years. I'm a long way from perfecting it, but it has made a valuable contribution to my own mental health and I heartily recommend it.

PROTECTING CLERGY MARRIAGES

Exercise good stewardship over your marriage and family. More American clergy marriages are ending in divorce today than at any other time in this century. Many other clergy marriages are being held together primarily to assure continued credentials for ministry or to avoid the stigma of a parsonage divorce and the guilt from a tarnished ministry.

What follows next is a sample of the most common causes of clergy divorce among the ministry couples seen at EMERGE Ministries—and we have worked with several hundred. Most of the time, if they are willing to invest sufficient time and energy, we are able to help them salvage their marriage and usually even their public ministry. However, the sad fact is that some clergy marriages are beyond saving by the time we see them. Neither husband nor wife is sufficiently committed to each other or the Lord's work to invest the time and emotional energy necessary to save their marriage.

Marital infidelity is the most frequent cause of clergy divorces. The Hartford Connecticut Seminary's Center for Social and Religious Research conducted a 1993–1994 survey of ten thousand Protestant clergy on divorce and other topics. Of the nearly 50 percent who responded (4,544 total, i.e., 2,458 women and 2,086 men), 25 percent of the women and 20 percent of the men indicated they had been divorced *at least once.* Divorced clergy by denomination included 47 percent of the women and 44 percent of the men in the most liberal group surveyed; 4 percent of the men and 17 percent of the women in the most conservative group surveyed. The researcher (Adair Lummis of Hartford Seminary) noted, in discussing the project, that the Assemblies of God do not permit divorced persons to be pastors except in very rare cases, although no statistics were given for Assemblies of God clergy. Only God knows how many former Assemblies of God clergy have been divorced.

In most of the denominations surveyed, more clergywomen than clergymen had been divorced. There was no indication how many of the respondents were senior pastors or how many were in other associate pastoral positions.[14] While these statistics are below the nonclergy rate of divorce, they are still far too high for a profession where the biblical standard is marriage to one spouse until death separates them (1 Timothy 3:1–2).

Most often, when marital infidelity is involved, the male minister has become involved with another woman. In many of these cases, he has unwittingly set himself up as an easy target for this kind of attack by the enemy. If he spends twelve to fourteen hours a day at his work (and this is typical for far too many ministers), he doesn't have much energy left for loving his wife (or his children) when he gets home. The most energetic hours of his day have been spent with other people. In a sense, the minister is defrauding his wife in such situations by avoiding her for the ministry. As Paul warned, that kind of behavior sets up both partners for temptation (1 Corinthians 7:5). It is just a question of who the enemy will get to first.

Ministers who find it difficult to put their marriage and family before the interests of the institutional church would do well to remember Paul's admonition in 1 Timothy 3:1–5. In this passage, he makes it clear that the pastor is to model the Christian life he wants others to follow. By being a loving and sensitive husband to his wife, he shows other men in the parish how they should treat their wives. By building a loving relationship with his children and disciplining them within that love, he shows other fathers how to raise their children. If a pastor organizes his work well (and this obviously is not always the case, according to Kuhne and Donaldson), those times when his work conflicts with his family life should be the exception rather than the rule.

> **"14-hour workdays leave little energy for loving."**

There are going to be some evening and weekend demands on his time. And there will be times when parishioners' emergencies mean his family plans must be interrupted or postponed. However, if nonemergency interruptions of family times are happening on a regular basis, one of two things needs to occur. Either the pastor needs to be more sensitive to his family and plan his time more carefully, or the parishioners need to be discreetly educated about the parsonage family's need for time-out and time together. If the former situation is draining his energies from family activities, then his wife needs to lovingly confront this behavior and ask him to plan more carefully. If nonemergency calls and interruptions from parishioners are the culprit, the pastor needs to begin gently encouraging people to place routine calls during office hours. He can do this publicly from the pulpit by commending them for their consideration in making their routine calls during his office hours and reassuring them that he will always be available day or night for emergencies.

Eugene Peterson has written an informative and entertaining article on the importance of keeping one's own Sabbath each week and what this practice meant to him and his wife when they were in parish ministry.[15]

He addresses the importance of time for both "praying" and "playing" on a regularly scheduled day of Sabbath, a day set aside for "being" rather than "doing." This is a wonderful prescription for good spiritual and mental health.

The wise pastor sees the benefit of spending more time with his wife. After all, she is the person who will be there when the people in the church—or the parsonage couple themselves—have moved on. She is the person with whom he is to have his longest-lasting personal relationship on earth. It is to his benefit, and hers, to make sure they have sufficient time alone as a couple; it is to the children's benefit to make sure they have sufficient time as a family, so they learn to love the ministry rather than resent it. Hopefully, they will follow in their parents' footsteps rather than, like so many, abandon any interest in the ministry.

> **" Plan two-night getaways for you and your spouse. "**

Plan two-night getaways for you and your spouse three or four times a year. Put them in your calendar the same way you note a special speaking engagement. Guard and protect these dates. Plan to leave your children with family or responsible friends. Take your wife to a nice hotel or motel within easy driving distance. Devote these getaways to nurturing your marriage. See them as islands of escape in an ocean of responsibility. If one feels he has to swim across an ocean, he becomes easily discouraged. But if land is in sight, he can usually muster the strength to make it to shore. In the same way, if your wife knows that in a few more days or weeks she will have you all to herself for two days and nights, it will give her the endurance she needs to keep her head above water between islands.

Remember, you have two energy-producing relationships in your life. They are your relationship with God (Isaiah 40:31) and your relationship with your wife. Every other relationship you have is energy-demanding. The enemy wants to use the urgency of your energy-demanding responsibilities to cause you to neglect your energy-creating opportunities. Don't be so driven as to play into his plan. Stay close to God and close to your spouse.

Kroll indicates that many parsonage dads go so far as to discourage their children from following them in the ministry by encouraging them to attend other schools than the one dad attended; to enter a profession where they will have more in this life than their parents have had, rather than encouraging them to prepare for a vocation where the rewards are measured in eternal returns.[16] One cannot help wondering how many of these fathers have become this discouraged simply because they did not take some basic steps to assure their own spiritual, emotional, and physical health in the ministry.

Financial problems are the second largest cause of clergy marital breakups. In eliminating this threat, the minister and his wife must work closely together. Some churches expect—because they are used to getting—two full-time workers for one salary. This is unfair, however, and no healthy congregation expects it. This is one of the elements of marital satisfaction among clergy couples studied by researchers Brent Benda and Frederick DiBlasio.[17] They cite earlier research which dubbed this phenomenon of two workers for the price of one as a "two-person single career."

If the minister's spouse is working part-time or full-time in a staff position for the church, that should be a paid position. If not, and the minister's salary is not sufficient to meet the family's average and ordinary needs, then the couple should discuss the possibility of exchanging that unpaid job for paid part-time or full-time work. Some churches realize their financial limitations and will permit the minister to work another job on a part-time basis to provide adequately for his family's needs. However, this route should be taken only with extreme care and in unusual circumstances.

Benda and DiBlasio also note that when the pastor and spouse have separate careers, the "spouses' refusal to assist in the performance of the clerical role . . . can be tantamount to clergy being unable to successfully fulfill their professional role."[18] They also indicate that the pastor's spouse working for money either inside or outside the church office is a relatively new phenomenon which can fuel fires of marital discontent among those clergy spouses who work alongside their pastor-spouse without pay.

However the problem of single-earner versus dual-earner marriage is managed, the ministry couple must be in agreement on their approach to it. If they decide together to get by with less, their marriage should not suffer. If they agree together that it would be best for the wife to take on at least a part-time job outside the home, their marriage should survive it well. The difficulty comes when one partner feels such a decision has been forced on him or her: when the wife feels forced to work in the church with inadequate or no pay, or the husband feels that his wife's taking a job has been forced on him.[19]

Job pressures compose the third largest threat to the minister's marriage and have been discussed earlier in this chapter. However, let me reiterate the importance of time management in keeping the work of the institutional church from taking time from the minister's marriage and family. Work can become an excuse for staying away from an unpleasant marriage or avoiding the often overwhelming responsibilities of parenthood. However, these problems can't be avoided indefinitely. Sooner or later they must be faced—and the sooner, the better.

Staying Physically Healthy in the Ministry

Staying healthy in the ministry also requires us to stay physically healthy. The greatest threat to the minister's physical health is, once again, stress. Before we consider what stress *is*, let's look at what it *is not:* Stress is not nervous tension. It is not simply the aftereffect of a bad experience. Drawing on the work of Hans Selye (acknowledged expert on stress research), Philip Goldberg defines it as "the body's nonspecific response to any demand placed upon it, whether that demand is pleasant or unpleasant."[20] Selye considers an appropriate, or optimal, stress level to be that which keeps one motivated, energized, alert, calm under pressure, and realistic. Without this healthy level of stress, it would be impossible to function productively, in the ministry or elsewhere. On the other hand, an overload of stress produces the opposite of these qualities in one's life: apathy, indecisiveness, irritability, and poor judgment.

Gordon MacDonald identifies as a stressor the feeling of being *driven* rather than *called*.[21] He defines driven people as those who are usually abnormally busy, have limited or undeveloped people skills, are highly competitive, are primarily gratified only by measurable accomplishments, and are preoccupied with symbols of those accomplishments. Are you driven or called in the ministry? God calls. The institutional church often drives. Be careful not to exchange that very healthy call for a very unhealthy drive.

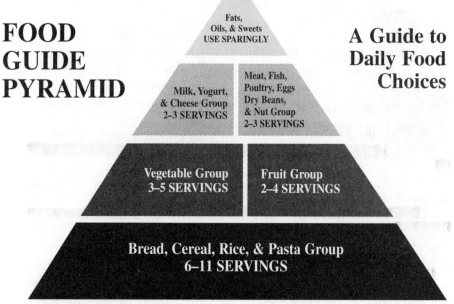

FOOD GUIDE PYRAMID

A Guide to Daily Food Choices

Fats,
Oils, & Sweets
USE SPARINGLY

Milk, Yogurt,
& Cheese Group
2–3 SERVINGS

Meat, Fish,
Poultry, Eggs
Dry Beans,
& Nut Group
2–3 SERVINGS

Vegetable Group
3–5 SERVINGS

Fruit Group
2–4 SERVINGS

Bread, Cereal, Rice, & Pasta Group
6–11 SERVINGS

SOURCE: US Department of Agriculture/US Department of Health and Human Services

There are also some physical considerations to managing a stressful life. Stress can be alleviated by relaxation techniques, adequate exercise, and a proper diet. Twenty minutes each day in deep relaxation is one effective means of coping with stress. Christian meditation, which we've already addressed, is a very effective form of relaxation.

Some ministers think physical exercise is a waste of time. This may be related to the way some people view the body: as an evil whose only good is found in being sacrificed to God's service (remember our brief word study on *sarx* and *soma*). However, in 1 Corinthians 6:19–20, Paul reminds us that our bodies are temples of the Holy Spirit. Good stewardship of them is our sacred responsibility. Adequate exercise doesn't require a great amount of time. Aerobic (cardiovascular) benefits from exercise are typically linked with twenty-minute periods of strenuous exercise performed at least three times per week. However, if you feel you cannot currently take time for three workouts per week that include a warm-up period, twenty minutes of sustained aerobic activity, and a cool-down time, try to get at least five minutes of strenuous exercise at least three times a week. Check with your doctor before you begin any strenuous exercise, of course, and make sure that what you attempt is consistent with your age and general health.

Excess weight is a hazard to your physical health and in many ways affects your whole sense of well-being. What you eat—and how much— are matters of lifestyle. Therefore, a brief crash-dieting program will not alleviate the problem. Lifestyle changes must occur, and this will not happen overnight. It takes several weeks, if not months, to make this kind of lasting dietary—and thus lifestyle—change. Begin by eating less of what you do eat. Take smaller portions. Break yourself of the habit of cleaning your plate; leave some food on your plate after every meal. These simple steps will help you lose a pound a week, which is a reasonable goal.

Remember, the basic food groups are not coffee, cheeseburgers, fries, and desserts. Have you noticed the Food Guide Pyramid, the USDA's replacement for the older basic food groups chart? The chart only identified the food groups, without recommending proportions. The pyramid, on the other hand, immediately suggests proportions. The foundation and bulk of a healthy daily diet consists of grain products: cereal, rice, pasta, and bread (six to eight servings). The next largest category, in about equal proportions to each other but in lesser amounts than grain foods, is a wide assortment of fruits (two to four servings) and vegetables (three to five servings). This is followed, again in about equal proportion to each other but smaller amounts yet than fruits or vegetables, by dairy (milk, yogurt, cheese; two to three servings) and other protein items (beef, pork, poultry, fish, dry beans, eggs, nuts; two to three servings). At the top of the pyramid, representing a very small percentage of one's diet, are things like fats, oils, and sweets (sugars) to be used sparingly.[22]

If you are not on a special dietary program ordered by your doctor and have no dietary health problems, you may wish to consider adapting your diet to fit the guidelines of the food pyramid. Don't expect overnight results. Healthy weight loss occurs over a period of time as you learn new lifestyle and eating habits. Losing weight over a longer period of time is also easier on your body than rapid weight loss. You will look and feel better, and experience more lasting results.

*　*　*　*　*

Don't expect more of yourself than God expects of you. Realize that although God can be all things to all people at all times, *you* cannot. And He doesn't require that of you.

In an interesting study by Allen Nauss, ten specific tasks relevant to the institutional ministry and the skills necessary to perform them were evaluated by congregants and clergy in over four hundred Lutheran Church–Missouri Synod congregations.[23] High skill-levels in some tasks were found to be uniformly necessary for the senior pastor; however, many other skills were not as critical. Nauss referenced researchers H. Newton Malony and Richard Hunt, who have done similar studies, and came to the conclusion that "no minister can do all these tasks exceptionally well—if only because a pastor does not have adequate time to develop proficiency in each one. More importantly, although parish clergy are 'generalists' and churches expect them to function [at some level of proficiency] in each of these roles, it is a very rare minister who enjoys them all or can perform equally well in all of them."[24]

Realize that you will be more skilled at some parts of the ministry than others, and fill your paid or volunteer staff positions with people whose skills are strongest in the areas you do not personally have to fill. God gifts each of us differently. Use your gifts, and encourage others to use theirs.

A healthy ministry should be complemented by a healthy minister. Good stewardship of yourself is not selfish, it is a service God requires of all of His children. As a minister, your stewardship is a service rendered in your own interests as well as in the interests of those you are called to serve. Carelessness with your spiritual, emotional, or physical health minimizes and shortens what you can do for others in the name of the Lord. Take good care of yourself. God not only needs you in the ministry, He needs you to be a healthy minister rendering healthy ministry to Him and others.

Handling Stress and Avoiding Burnout

Wayde I. Goodall

Without question, pastoral ministry involves unique stresses. There is the feeling of living in a fishbowl, loneliness, moving frequently, too many expectations (from others as well as yourself), always being on call, marriage and family tensions, financial pressures, conflict or power struggles within the church, and the feeling of carrying the entire responsibility of the church—just to name a few. The cumulative weight can be burdensome. Missionary Charles Greenaway once reminded me that wherever God calls us, He will give us the ability to do what He has called us to do. Unfortunately, many pastors simply take on more than God ever expected them to, or their unorganized schedules restrict their productivity, or they carry the burden themselves rather than sharing it with Jesus. Jesus said, "'My load is light'" (Matthew 11:30[1]). Somehow, every pastor needs to find a balance of hard work, delegation, "equipping the saints for the work of the ministry" (Ephesians 4:12), and letting Jesus Christ bear the pressure that can come with the divine assignment.

The term *stress,* a relatively new term, was originally a physics or engineering term. It referred to a severe force put on a building or a bridge; the goal was to build a structure strong enough to withstand maximum stress. For people, stress is the nonspecific response of the body to any demand made upon it. The minister needs adequate structure for the pressures of ministry; otherwise, he or she will buckle or fold. Moses' father-in-law spoke to Moses about his very demanding ministry. "'You will surely wear out, both yourself and these people who are with you, for the task is too heavy for you; you cannot do it alone'" (Exodus 18:18). Paul spoke to the Corinthian church about the great pressure he went through while ministering in Asia. "We were burdened excessively, beyond our strength, so that we despaired even of life" (2 Corinthians 1:8). Both Moses and Paul found a way to handle their stress. Moses found spiritual leaders he could delegate some of his responsibilities to. Paul found reliance on the God "who raises the dead," the only answer to "the sentence of death" he felt (see 2 Corinthians 1:9–10).

> ## Ministry
>
> An incredible call to an inadequate person to do an impossible task for an indefinite time.

Stress is a force weighing on us or an unresolved conflict within us. Everyone has stress. From the time we are born until the day of our departure, we will have stress. Some stress is positive. We have stress when we drive our cars, shop for groceries, take a test, get involved in conflict, prepare to preach, and preach the Word from the pulpit. There is stress in marriage, in raising children, in getting older, and even in dying.

Though we all have stress, everyone handles it differently. Our ability to handle stress is partly dependent on how we have been taught to handle it. We may have learned wonderful skills while growing up; on the other hand, we may have observed bad examples of adults dealing with the pressures of life. Those who through research and study have learned techniques to deal with stress effectively can teach us some basic skills for handling the unique stresses of ministry.

There are two major categories of stress: *intense* and *prolonged.* Intense stress results when an emergency arises and we react immediately. Our bodies many times react to the emergency without our consciously even thinking about it. Prolonged stress is, of course, drawn out: an ongoing financial pressure, a conflict that is not brought to closure, a continuing marital or family difficulty, or pastoring a difficult church. Intense stress usually ends quite quickly. On the other hand, prolonged stress can cause burnout, emotional pain, marital difficulty, and even physiological problems. The head of Menninger Institute has stated that up to 70 percent of minor ailments, such as colds and fatigue, are psychosomatic reactions to day-to-day stress, and that they can lead to more serious problems.

Stress is not new. Scripture records many examples of men and women of God who experienced various kinds of stress. Moses and Paul have already been noted (Exodus 18:18 and 2 Corinthians 1:8). After seeing tremendous miracles from God, Elijah "was afraid and arose and ran for his life" (1 Kings 19:3). He became so despondent that "he requested for himself that he might die" (1 Kings 19:4). Throughout history we have examples of godly men and women who have experienced both intense and prolonged stress.

Understanding Ministry Stress

It is helpful to understand where our stress is coming from and, if possible, to do something about it. Asking "What is happening and what can I do?" is helpful. There are several things we should understand when evaluating our stress in ministry and life.

Life itself is stressful. When we serve people in the ministry, we not only deal with our personal stresses but we help others with theirs. Many of us live in high-pressure communities where life rushes by. Just living a normal life—raising a family and doing what we need to get by—can bring a great deal of pressure. As we minister, people naturally bring their life struggles and concerns to us. This is normal, and we are to be there as an example pointing each person in the right direction. We teach the people we serve how to pray, rely on Jesus, and walk by faith. In doing this, we often feel the burdens our people are feeling.

Spiritual forces can cause stress. Demonic forces can be the cause of stress. Peter alerts us: "Be sober, be vigilant; because your adversary the devil, as a roaring lion, walketh about, seeking whom he may devour: whom resist steadfast in the faith, knowing that the same afflictions are accomplished in your brethren that are in the world" (1 Peter 5:8–9, KJV). Paul exhorts us, "Do not give the devil an opportunity" (Ephesians 4:27) and "Put on the full armor of God, that you may be able to stand firm against the schemes of the devil" (Ephesians 6:11). Paul also informs Timothy about "the snare of the devil" (2 Timothy 2:26) that can come into some lives. Jesus taught His disciples to pray "Do not lead us into temptation, but deliver us from evil" (Matthew 6:13). Numerous examples in Scripture demonstrate that the devil and his demonic forces can be the cause of temptations, trials, problems, barriers, and stress. The spiritual attack of the enemy can be dealt with only on spiritual ground. The minister must be a person of prayer, committed to the constant study of God's Word, and determined to live according to God's truths. This personal discipline, along with the prayers of those in the body of Christ, will protect the servant of God from overwhelming demonic stress.

Personal sin can cause stress. When we are not right with God, we go through unique pressures and stress. The Holy Spirit that lives in the believer brings conviction and allows difficulty when we have grieved Him. When David decided to follow the ways of his flesh instead of the ways of God his life radically changed for the worse (see 2 Samuel 11 through 17). The Bible clearly describes David's sins and the tragic consequences that came to him and his family. In fact, all of Israel was affected because of the sins of their leader. God has shown us examples of people who have failed, because He wants us to learn from their failure. Paul points out, "These things happened to them as an example, and they were written for our instruction, upon whom the ends of the ages have come" (1 Corinthians 10:11). David's life became a confused, unhappy life of compromise because of his sin. And it took years for the ripple effect of his sin to stop. The writer of Proverbs asks rhetorically, "Can a man take fire in his bosom, And his clothes not be burned?" (Proverbs 6:27). So it is with sin. When we choose to disobey God there will be a corresponding judgment and discipline that will come from our loving heavenly Father.

Ministerial stress can result in someone else's growth. This is an upside to stress from leadership. Moses spent forty years in the desert preparing to lead the complaining Israelites. The lessons Moses needed to learn before he could do all that God was calling him to do had to come from a "desert" experience. I am sure he thought many times about the mistakes of his past and had feelings of isolation and loneliness. Though he did not know it, God was preparing him for a great task.

Our Lord Jesus suffered for the sins of humanity. He paid the price and endured the cross for our sin. He lived a life of sacrifice because of His love for us. Paul tells us: "Although He existed in the form of God, [He] did not regard equality with God a thing to be grasped, but emptied Himself, taking the form of a bond-servant, and being made in the likeness of men. And being found in appearance as a man, He humbled Himself by becoming obedient to the point of death, even death on a cross" (Philippians 2:6–8). Jesus gave us an example of sacrificial living for the benefit of those being served.

Ministers often suffer offense and difficulty for the sake of the church. Sometimes we need to speak up, correct, rebuke, or even remove a person from the fellowship; more often we simply decide to be quiet and pray for an individual or situation. All ministers enjoy seeing a new convert come to Christ; their sometimes radical commitment to change and zeal to influence others for Jesus are very refreshing. Along with all of the wonderful attributes that come with their new life in Christ, many still have a lot of bad habits. They might be brash, unwise, inappropriately dressed, or have some behaviors that we know should be eliminated. Most of the time the best way to work with new converts is to pray for them. We simply must give them time to grow.

> **It took years for the ripple effect of David's sin to stop.**

Working with all different types of people is stressful at times. As leaders we do it because it is what the ministry is all about. At the same time, we need to ensure that our own walk with Jesus is growing and maturing. That is the secret to keeping a good attitude while serving a diverse group of people.

Ministerial stress is necessary for our own growth. Character is not learned, it is developed. Aristotle said, "People become house builders through building houses, harp players through playing the harp. We grow to be just by doing things which are just."[2] Robert Freeman said, "Character is not made in a crisis—it is only exhibited."[3]

Discipline can be stressful, and God permits stressful situations to come to our lives so we can grow in Christian character. The Bible tells us, "It is for discipline that you endure; God deals with you as with sons;

for what son is there whom his father does not discipline. . . . All discipline for the moment seems not to be joyful, but sorrowful; yet to those who have been trained by it, afterwards it yields the peaceful fruit of righteousness" (Hebrews 12:7,11). James counsels us, "Consider it all joy, my brethren, when you encounter various trials, knowing that the testing of your faith produces endurance. And let endurance have its perfect result, that you may be perfect and complete, lacking in nothing" (James 1:2–4). This "endurance" is a capacity to bear up under difficult circumstances.[4]

Peter had this to say to those undergoing affliction: "In this [inheritance incorruptible] you greatly rejoice, even though now for a little while, if necessary, you have been distressed by various trials, that the proof of your faith, being more precious than gold which is perishable, even though tested by fire, may be found to result in praise and glory and honor at the revelation of Jesus Christ" (1 Peter 1:6–7). If we can look at the stress, difficulties, and trials that come to our lives as opportunities to grow in Christ instead of as hazards in life to be avoided, we will rejoice over what we learn through the experience.

Stress keeps us in proper relationship with God. Stress can help us remain humble. Paul was given a "thorn in the flesh" (2 Corinthians 12:7) to counter the "surpassing greatness of the revelations" he received from God. Paul again speaks of an affliction that came to him while he was ministering in Asia. This difficulty helped him trust in God (2 Corinthians 1:8–9). Pressure in life can force us to pray and look to God for our help. Again Paul tells us he had "learned to be content in whatever circumstances" (Philippians 4:11) he faced. He learned the secret, "I can do all things through Him who strengthens me" (4:13). The key is understanding that our strength to minister in difficult situations comes from Christ. We can rely and depend on Him. Whether it be a problem in our ministry or in our personal lives, we can know a place of rest and dependence on God. Paul learned this contentment because he knew how to take all of his concerns to Christ in prayer. Paul said, "Be anxious for nothing, but in everything by prayer and supplication with thanksgiving let your requests be made known to God. And the peace of God, which surpasses all comprehension, shall guard your hearts and your minds in Christ Jesus" (Philippians 4:6–7).

Dealing with Stress

Several steps will help you deal with stress:

Use your spiritual resources. Ask the question, "Am I praying and studying the Word—is my devotional life doing well?" Your spiritual life and disciplines are your spiritual resources.

Write down the stressful situations in your life. These might include personal conflicts, obligations, and other issues pressuring you. Look at all of them together and ask God to help you prioritize them. Take time to pray through this list and give the anxiety to Christ.

Talk confidentially to a close minister friend. Great assistance comes from speaking to one of our peers about how they handle the unique ministerial pressures. Often we learn wisdom that will last a lifetime. Paul was giving very specific instruction about ministry when he wrote to Timothy such things as "God has not given us a spirit of timidity, but of power and love and discipline" (2 Timothy 1:7). Seek a "Paul" for your life.

Reexamine your priorities. The priorities in our lives should be (1) our relationship with God, (2) our relationship with our spouse and children, and (3) our ministry. We become overwhelmed when our priorities are out of order. We suffer from guilt, knowing that we need to adjust.

Work on one stressor at a time. Ministers often worry about how much needs to be done in their church and community. Thinking about all the needs can be overwhelming, and the only way we can handle it is by doing one thing at a time. We can work on many projects and be in prayer about all we want to accomplish for God's glory, but we can write only one letter, do only one project, prepare only one sermon, at a time. In the spring of 1871, a young man picked up a book and read twenty-one words that had a profound effect on his future. A medical student at the Montreal General Hospital, he was worried about passing his final examination, about what to do, where to go, how to build up a practice, how to make a living. The twenty-one words this student read in 1871 helped him to become the most famous physician of his generation. He organized the world-famous Johns Hopkins School of Medicine. He became Regius Professor of Medicine at Oxford—the highest honor bestowed upon any medical man in the British Empire. He was knighted by the King of England. When he died, two huge volumes containing 1,466 pages were required to tell his life story. His name was Sir William Osler. The twenty-one words, written by Thomas Carlyle, helped him lead a life free from worry: "Our main business is not to see what lies dimly at a distance, but to do what lies clearly at hand."[5]

> **Twenty-one words written by Thomas Carlyle helped him lead a life free from worry.**

Build skills. If you are concerned about your preaching ability, attend a public speaking or preaching class or read a good book on the subject. If you are anxious about how to deal with crises in the church, then meet with an expert in crisis management. Skills do not come overnight, but we can learn them from people who not only have the know-how we seek but are able to pass it on.

Make changes. As we examine all our responsibilities and the demands on our time, it is often necessary to make some changes. Some responsibilities can be delegated to another competent person. Some can be postponed or even dropped. If you are overwhelmed by the busyness of your calendar, begin to analyze what commitments can be changed. This is what Jethro observed about his son-in-law, Moses. "'You will surely wear out, both yourself and these people who are with you, for the task is too heavy for you; you cannot do it alone'" (Exodus 18:18).

Change your environment. If the pressure is still overwhelming after we have done the things listed above, then it could be that a new ministry situation would be advisable. This decision must come after much prayer and counsel. We should never change or move from our ministry positions too quickly. Ask trusted friends to pray with you about this possibility, then try to sense if God has released you from the present ministry position. If He has, then look for the open door that He, in His time, will provide.

Recognizing Burnout

Burnout is exhaustion due to excessive demands on energy, strength, or resources. Burnout is typically characterized by a cluster of physical, emotional, and mental exhaustion reactions. Typical responses of burned-out individuals include:

Physical Exhaustion: low energy, chronic fatigue, weakness, weariness, becoming accident-prone, increased susceptibility to illness, frequent headaches, nausea, muscle tension, and overall changes in eating and sleeping habits.

Emotional Exhaustion: feelings of depression, hopelessness, helplessness; loss of coping and control mechanisms; magnifying; feeling emotionally depleted, irritable, nervous.

Mental Exhaustion: development of negative attitudes toward ministry, life, and oneself; lowered self-esteem; feelings of inadequacy, inferiority, and incompetence; development of negative and derogatory attitudes toward parishioners.

CHARACTERISTICS OF BURNED-OUT MINISTERS

Feelings of apathy, anger, resentment	Vulnerable to illness
Feeling let down	Avoidance of office and daily work
Feelings of cynicism	Changing churches (job change)
Blaming parishioners for personal problems	Increased marital and family conflicts
Rigid resistance to change	Inappropriate humor at others' expense
Avoidance of involvement with parishioners	Derogatory, impersonal references to members
Aloofness from others (withdrawal into self)	Loss of concern and sympathy
Boredom, frustration, loss of enthusiasm	Avoidance of social times with parishioners

Coping with Burnout

Feelings of exhaustion are often God's warning that we are either too committed or have unrealistic expectations. When an experience or relationship leaves one feeling angry, anxious, or depressed, this may be an indication of faulty goals.[6]

Anger can sometimes come from a blocked goal. Any goal whose success can be blocked by outside forces (other than God) is not a healthy goal, because success in that arena is out of your hands. A pastor may say, "My goal in ministry is to reach this community for Christ." Good goal? It may be a wonderful desire, but if one's worth is dependent on that desire being fulfilled, he or she will experience tremendous emotional turmoil.[7] Every person in the community can potentially block the goal. The church can block the goal. Board members can block the goal. Success in ministry should not be dependent on others.

Factors that Contribute to Burnout

- Lack of awareness of one's personal need for recreation and leisure
- Unrealistic expectations about the nature of ministry
- Limited opportunities for promotion, inadequate remuneration
- Excessive commitment to work (workaholism)
- Excessive need to be liked and accepted by others
- Overinvolvement in rescuing or helping others
- Accepting too much responsibility for parishioners' successes or failures
- Equating parishioners' rejections of help with personal rejection
- Inadequate professional training in intervention skills
- Parishioners who criticize one's ministry
- Constantly focusing on parishioners' weaknesses and problems
- Lack of opportunity to talk about personal attitudes, feelings, and trials
- Long working hours
- Inability to delegate (not enough help)
- Frequent focus on the problems and negative aspects of ministry
- Not being able to say no
- Unrealistic blaming of self for lack of church growth
- Feeling that one has to be at every church event
- Feeling overwhelmed because of the great need
- Not finding balance between ministry (work), family, rest, and play
- Not maintaining a consistent prayer and devotional life
- Being a loner in the ministry
- Unresolved family and personal problems

Anxiety can be caused by an uncertain goal. When you feel anxious in a task or a relationship, your anxiety may be signaling the uncertainty of a goal you have chosen. You are hoping something will happen, but you have no guarantee it will. You can control some of the factors, but not all of them.

Depression can signal an impossible goal. When future success is based on something that can never happen, you have an impossible, hopeless goal. Depression is a signal that your goal, no matter how spiritual or noble, may never be reached. Place your hope in the Lord, who always does right, not in people who can fail you.

We can respond inappropriately to those who frustrate our goals. When our self-worth or success hinges on the achievement of a goal that can be blocked or is uncertain or impossible, we often attempt to control or manipulate the people or circumstances that stand between us and our success. This behavior is not Christlike, however. People desperate to reach their goals will unfortunately resort to attempts to control and manipulate.

Turning Bad Goals into Good Goals

Examine your goals realistically. Depression often signals that you are desperately clinging to a goal you have little or no chance of achieving, and that's not healthy. Ministers often set for themselves goals that are not realistic. We need to pray about our goals and let God give us vision. He always gives the ability to do what He has asked us to do. Ministers often compare their personal lives and ministries to those of other ministers. They set their goals based on what they have seen someone else do. It is helpful to learn from others; our goals, however, need to be realistic in keeping with our gifts and abilities.

Learn to distinguish a godly goal from a godly desire. A godly goal reflects God's purposes for one's life without depending on people or circumstances beyond one's ability or right to control. Who do we have the right to control? No one but ourselves.

We cannot base self-worth or personal success on our desires, no matter how godly they may seem. We cannot control their fulfillment; the fulfillment of desires can be blocked. Some desires are uncertain; some are impossible.

When a desire is wrongly elevated to a goal and that goal is frustrated, one must deal with the anger, anxiety, and depression accompanying that failure. However, when a desire isn't fulfilled, one faces disappointment. Learn to distinguish goals from desires. When you begin to align your goals with God's goals and your desires with God's desires, you will rid your life of a lot of anger, anxiety, and depression.[8] The pastor whose self-worth is based on his goal to win the city for Christ, to have the best youth ministry in the country, or to increase missions giving by 100 percent is headed for frustration, anger, and depression.

To handle stress and avoid burnout, learn to make God's goals your goals. When you seek goals in line with things of interest and value to God, success is inevitable. For example, God is interested in

- Character development. "I'm going to be the pastor God wants me to be" is a great goal because no one can block it except you.
- Demonstration of the fruit of the Spirit. Walk in the Spirit one day at a time.
- Our communicating with Him. Be in the proper attitude where you can pray anytime.

- Our witness to a lost and dying world. The Father draws people to Jesus (John 6:44).
- Our obedience to His will.
- Our attitude. We cannot control people, but we can control our attitude.
- The development of our faith. Place your faith in Jesus Christ, not in anything else.
- Our seriousness in shepherding His sheep. We are not responsible for other's behavior; we are responsible only to do our best.
- Our growing relationship with Him.
- Our growing knowledge of His Word.

So do your best and trust God with the rest!

The Pastor's Person, Possessions, Habits, Moods, and Leisure

Robert J. Strand

We are all well aware of the biblical admonition not to look on the outward appearance. What is inside is more important than what can be seen by others, according to God. However, we do live in a culture different from that of biblical times. It is possible to turn listeners or followers off or on by such "outward" things before we even begin ministry. People today are conscious about appearance. In fact, entire industries thrive because of such concerns. So then, how should clergy look and position themselves in regard to such issues? Little things are important, and if not properly handled, they can become big things that hinder ministry. So let's attempt to deal with some of these issues.

The apostle who wrote the "constitution and bylaws" for the emerging first-century Church has also given us some personal guidelines for life and ministry. Love must permeate everything. Perhaps we should remind ourselves that none of us live or die to ourselves. The record is written in the letter to the church in Rome, "Love must be sincere . . . live in harmony with one another . . . If it is possible, as far as it depends on you, live at peace with everyone" (Romans 12:9,16,18). The Christian's "handbook" for personal behavior is then amplified further in Romans 14:1–23. We are to "stop passing judgment on one another. Instead, make up your mind not to put any stumbling block or obstacle in your brother's way" (14:13). And "let us therefore make every effort to do what leads to peace and to mutual edification. Do not destroy the work of God for the sake of *cars, clothes, material possessions, habits, dispositions, moods, or leisure pursuits.* All *such things may be acceptable* but it is wrong for a *pastor to do anything* that causes someone else to stumble" (14:19–20, italics and paraphrase mine).

With all of this in mind, it is time to set or correct your course on such issues. The story is told of former President Reagan and a shoemaker in his hometown. The cobbler was making a pair of shoes for the boy Reagan and asked if the young Ronald wanted a round or square toe. Ronald was unsure, so the shoemaker told him to return in a day or so to let him know. A few days later the shoemaker saw the young Ronald on the street and asked what he had decided. Reagan was still undecided. The shoemaker said the shoes would be ready tomorrow. When Reagan picked up the shoes, one had a round toe and the other had a square toe. Says Reagan, "Looking at those shoes taught me a lesson. If you don't make your own decisions, somebody else makes them for you." Let's start first with the pastor's emotions.

The Pastor's Disposition and Moods

Disposition and moods is just another way of talking about attitude, mental constitution, tendency, inclination, or frame of mind. And according to philosopher William James, this is something we have control of and can change: The greatest discovery of the twentieth century is that one can change one's world by changing one's thoughts. There is probably nothing else that will influence your ministry and life quite as much as this subject.

According to Paul, "Your attitude should be the same as that of Christ Jesus" (Philippians 2:5). So what kind of a mind-set or attitude did Jesus exhibit?

- Everything Jesus said about Himself was positive, yet not prideful (John 7:29; 10:36; 11:42).
- He kept in close touch with the Heavenly Father (John 11:41–42).
- He articulated His mission, lived with a mission, stuck to that mission (Matthew 16:21; John 4:4; 7:6).
- He believed in Himself.[1]
- He lived with internal control rather than being governed by outside forces (John 12:42–43).
- He tackled and did the difficult things (Isaiah 50:7, John 18:11).
- Gratitude was a key element of His leadership style (John 17:6–7).
- He was constantly in an attitude of celebration.
- He didn't waste time or energy judging others.
- He expressed Himself so others could see His attitude in action (Mark 9:17–27).
- He was passionately committed to His cause (John 2:17; 4:34).
- He asked for noble things (Isaiah 32:8).
- He did not despise small things or small people (Matthew 12:20; 19:14).
- He saw people as persons packed with possibilities (John 1:42).
- He was a man of action; He had a plan (Matthew 15:32–35).

- He saw things differently from those around Him (Matthew 9:24–25).
- He lived boldly (Luke 15:2).
- He lived one step, one day, at a time.
- He was open to people and to their ideas (Matthew 16:13; 17:27).
- He wanted the best for everyone; He wanted to lift up others, to take others with Him.

What an exciting place to begin working on letting our attitude be the same as that of Christ Jesus! There simply is no place in the ministry for people who have lousy attitudes or who are given to moods, mood swings, or just plain being moody. In the ministry, perhaps more than in any other vocation, altitude will be determined by attitude. High premiums are placed on people who are consistently uplifting, who are builders of others, who will bring out the best in others, and who are not easily defeated.

The major key to an attitudinal change is in one's thought life. "Finally, brothers [and sisters], whatever is true, whatever is noble, whatever is right, whatever is pure, whatever is lovely, whatever is admirable—if anything is excellent or praiseworthy—*think about such things*" (Philippians 4:8, italics mine). This personal aspect of living—attitude, mood, and disposition—will probably affect your future ministry as much as or more than anything else. Why? Think about the bottom line in ministry. What is it? *People skills!* How you get along with people, how you deal with people, how you lead people, how you care for people, will probably account for about 80 to 90 percent of the reason a given ministry succeeds or fails. You might be able to preach like Peter or pray like Paul, but if you can't get along with people, life in ministry will be tough. If you can't solve your own attitude or mood challenges, how can you help anybody else? Or lead anybody else? What you are shouts louder than what you say every time.

Just one short word about depression: If it is chronic in your life, please go and get some professional help. Such things can be helped. If you need work on your attitude, find a mentor who will help you. And don't be like the preacher in a small town who regularly dropped in at a local restaurant for coffee. On this particular day, the friendly waitress couldn't get a smile out of him. He was dour, sour, depressed, and dejected all through the coffee break. And the homemade roll was delicious. As the preacher paid the bill and was turning to leave, the waitress called out, "Have a wonderful day!" To which the preacher replied, with a frown, "I'm sorry, but I've made other plans."

The Pastor and Possessions

How much is enough? How much is too much? Would Jesus wear a Rolex watch or drive a Rolls Royce? Or lay up treasures here on this earth? One Christian confessed, "Dear Lord, I have been rereading the record of the 'rich young ruler' and his obviously wrong choice. But it has set me to thinking. No matter how much wealth he had, he could not . . . ride in a car, have any surgery, turn on a light, buy penicillin, hear a pipe organ, watch TV, wash dishes in running water, type a letter, mow a lawn, fly in an airplane, sleep on an innerspring mattress, or talk on the phone. If he was rich . . . *then what am I?*"

We are probably the only generation of clergy that has had to wrestle with this issue. Some denominations solve this dilemma by requiring their clergy to take vows of poverty or set everybody up on a subsistence pay scale. There is a lot of guilt we have to deal with in these areas because of some of the hard sayings of Jesus. Did He really mean we must sell everything in order to follow Him? Did He have to say the rich have an almost impossible task of attempting to get into heaven? Is Jesus aware that we are Americans and we live in America—which can be very expensive? How would Jesus live if He came to our town? Does He know how hard it is to save for retirement? Surely He didn't mean that I must give all my goods to feed the poor! How can I preach the total Word with conviction when I make allowances for my desires to have nice material things? Where is the line? How do we find a balance? Are we to be content only with food and raiment? Would He allow us to enjoy some of the finer things of life? Help!

> **"How would Jesus live if He came to our town?"**

Let's add another factor or two such as a country parish or urban church, large or small salary, how the community expectations are met or not met. Also our day has been bombarded by lots of "kings kids" and "name-it-and-claim-it" philosophies, which have encouraged a materialistic lifestyle, because God wants all of His children to prosper; pastors have not been immune to such teachings. But the easiest way to deal with each of the issues in this chapter might be to simply say, Be moderate, be modest, be conservative, and be frugal. But that doesn't really deal with such issues head-on.

Back in Bible college days, one of my professors, Dr. T. J. Jones, had a saying that brought some sort of priority to the heads of single young men. He'd thunder: "Books, Buick, and bride!" And it was always in that order! We can successfully parade a host of Scripture proof texts and argue both sides of the "How much is enough" question. But taking precedence over all of this is the admonishment, "If anyone does not provide for his relatives, and especially for his immediate family, he has denied the faith and is worse than an unbeliever" (1 Timothy 5:8). Strong language! Just what does "provide" mean in this context?

Further complicating this issue are the people we minister to. There will always be someone who is willing to offer criticism of your lifestyle. At the same time, you have those who *commend* and those who *condemn* the choices you make. You can't run and hide from the issue either, because you will have to deal with it on an ongoing basis. And in our world and society "enough" has become a moving target.

Perhaps more than any other biblical writer, Paul seems to have discovered the answer to these issues: "I have learned to be content whatever the circumstances. I know what it is to be in need, and I know what it is to have plenty. I have learned the secret of being content in any and every situation, whether well fed or hungry, whether living in plenty or in want." Listen carefully to this next verse, for in it Paul shares the secret of being content—it is in our relationship with Christ. "I can do everything through him who gives me strength!" (Philippians 4:11–13).

Yet to some that's still not an answer, or at least not the answer they have been looking for. There is no one right answer, but there is a principle. Success in terms of material possessions is the fruit of natural laws, not supernatural interventions. Success is also a multiplier, not a divider, in that it makes more for everybody. The condemnation Jesus heaped upon those who were rich was because of the way in which they accumulated their riches or the way they hoarded or improperly used their riches. "Bible readers have created more wealth than any other people on earth," says Richard Gaylord Briley. "And [they] have generated more happiness and hope than any people in history. Now the new generation must prepare to lead the rebuilding of America."[2] Jesus told us not to be obsessed with collecting riches but also not to be obsessed with collecting trivia in the forms of worries about this life, either. Neither of these two attitudes should stand in the way of our being fruitful for God in ministry.

Perhaps the philosophy of John Wesley (expressed in, among other places, the conclusion of his sermon "Causes of the Inefficacy of Christianity") will help us:

"I fear, wherever riches have increased (exceeding few are the exceptions), the essence of religion, the mind that was in Christ has decreased in the same proportion. Therefore I do not see how it is possible, in the nature of things, for any revival of true religion to continue long. For religion must necessarily produce both industry and frugality; and these cannot but produce riches. But as riches increase, so will pride, anger, and love of the world in all its branches."

Then recognizing the problem suggested by his observation, Wesley went on to propose a solution: "What way then can we take that our money may not sink us to the nether most hell? There is one way, and there is no other under heaven. If those who gain all they can, and save all they can will likewise give all they can, then the more they gain, the more they will grow in grace and the more treasure they will lay up in heaven."

The Pastor's Appearance and Dress

The pastor's appearance is another subject of dilemma. It represents choice and preference, fashion and culture. And it's also a moving target. Are you serving people in the Midwest or on the West Coast? Geographic location is a factor. And then there is today's cultural movement that advocates, Be yourself. Express it in what you wear and how you wear it. Our culture tells us to make our statement by what we wear.

To further complicate this subject, there are no biblical mandates about clergy dress code, other than for the Levitical order of priests in Old Testament worship (see Exodus 39). But how would you wear the "urim and thummim" or how would you attach the "bell and pomegranates" around the hem of the robe, especially when we don't generally preach in robes? Perhaps the female clergy will have an easier job adapting to this ancient dress code. Then again, how do you construct or wear an "ephod"? And then there were the "turbans" and "headbands" and "undergarments of finely twisted linen." Also "they made the plate, the sacred diadem" attached to a blue cord. Yes, it might certainly draw a crowd, but where would you get the pure gold and the rows of precious stones? And how would you insure this outfit? Where would you store it so it wouldn't get stolen? Okay, okay! Point well taken.

It's not fair or just that a minister's success or failure can depend on how he or she dresses! But we also must acknowledge that the way we dress has a remarkable impact on the people we minister to professionally or socially and to some extent affects how they respond to us. This is especially so when assuming the role of pastor in public. Dressing in a manner that enhances your ministry is really nothing more nor less than achieving good taste and a look that reflects what people perceive as acceptable for leadership and ministry.

How to determine that look may be a bit tricky. Observation is a beginning point. Take some time to notice how the bankers, morticians, lawyers, and company executives dress in your area. Drop in on a weekly meeting of the local Rotary Club and you'll have a fairly good idea of the appearance expected of people whom others trust with important aspects of their lives.[3]

Dressing appropriately need not be expensive. Buy your clothes cheaply. Note that I didn't suggest that you buy cheap clothes. Buy good clothing cheaply by planning wisely. For example, buy on sale. You will find fall and winter merchandise usually on sale after January 1; spring and summer clothing after the July 4th weekend. Factory outlets can also be an excellent source of good clothing buys. But be careful, learn how to distinguish the good merchandise from the shoddy. Buy fewer items but buy quality. You can further save if you buy conservative, traditional styles; they will last a whole lot longer in your wardrobe than contemporary styles. You can also purchase multifunctional pieces.

> **You must dress to fit your audience's expectations.**

Let's talk about the business suit, because it is the central garment that will most likely influence any viewer's judgment of the wearer. The suit establishes authority, credibility, and likability—qualities important to any public ministry. The darker the suit, the more authority it tends to convey. A black suit is the most authoritative but should be worn only by funeral directors or preachers. The most authoritative pattern is the pinstripe. Suits that give you the most credibility with middle-class people are dark blue and dark gray solids and pinstripes of both colors. The most accepted suit is solid navy, which should be in every person's wardrobe. If you are weak on projecting authority, it is excellent.

Remember, the first and most important message a speaker delivers to an audience is a nonverbal one. You must dress to fit your audience's expectations. Even in today's casual, dress-down culture, audiences expect their ministers to look like ministers. Suits, white shirts, and ties for men still hold. For women clergy, business suits and crisp, clean, white blouses are meeting most of today's expectations. If you dress well and are put together well, you look like you are disciplined and have a personal lifestyle that is purposeful.

The Pastor and the Clergy Car

Another problem for the minister is the kind of transportation. This choice is filled with all kinds of subtle meanings. Some psychological research seems to indicate that with a car selection we tell on ourselves, we reveal some deep, inner secrets. Unfortunately, the clergy car is more than simply transportation. It sends a message—good, bad, subtle, or strong.

You can probably drive a car on par with the choices that five of your seven deacons have made. If you have a board that drives Lincolns and Cadillacs, at least two out of three, you might get by driving a black, used one, with one hundred thousand or more miles on it. If the majority of your board drives import cars, you might pull it off, too, but not in Detroit. It used to be so simple, back in the '50s or '60s, just select a basic black Ford, Chevrolet, or Plymouth with a column shift and push-button radio (but no whitewall tires). Today's choices are infinitely more varied. There are hundreds of choices, both domestic and foreign. The absolute no-no for a minister would be to drive a bright red convertible. A real problem might be how to appear properly pious driving a Lexus 400 or a BMW 725!

The best solution would be to have the church provide you with a car (carefully selected by the board members, some might add with a wink). The next best solution is to carefully weigh all your options and make a choice, not too extreme in any direction, then enjoy!

Whatever car you drive, please keep it clean, especially on Sundays! Do the regular maintenance recommended—grease jobs, oil changes, check-ups, summer and winter tune-ups—so your car will last longer. Don't overbuy, and don't put yourself into bondage with car payments. Remember, a car is a depreciating item. A car won't make you money; it will cost you dearly.

The Pastor and Habits

A habit is a practice, behavior pattern, routine, tendency, habitual action, fixed practice, or confirmed way of doing things. Habits can be servants, tools, helpers, or they can be ruts that take us toward oblivion. Habits can be good or bad. It's incumbent upon clergy to cultivate habits that enhance ministry and character. Let's just take a look at the following bits of advice on habits accumulated from a lifetime of ministry and from many sources.

1. Start every day with God—Bible reading, prayer, meditation. Commit the day to God.

2. Make a plan for each day. Set some immediate daily goals, short-range goals, and long-range plans. Plan your work and work your plan.

3. Keep your priorities in mind: God, yourself, family, and ministry.

Why *yourself?* In setting priorities, ask yourself, "With whom will I be spending the longest amount of time in my life?" The longest relationships demand the greater priorities.

4. Cultivate a habit of being punctual.

5. Determine to become a living example of what you preach.

6. Live within your means. Pay your bills on time. Set aside a little for a rainy day.

7. Set aside time in every day for family needs. Plan special times with your spouse and children away from the demands of day-to-day ministry. Cultivate good family life.

8. Never step into the pulpit unprepared physically, mentally, spiritually, or psychologically. Keep yourself fit in all these areas.

DRESS RULES THAT WILL PAY BIG DIVIDENDS

- If you have the choice, dress well.
- Always, always be clean, neatly pressed and coordinated.
- Remember, men, the tie is the single most important indicator of who you are. Buy the best tie you can.
- Wear a moderate hairstyle (not too long, or too greasy, or too kooky), and always make sure your hair is well-combed.
- Never, never wear a short-sleeve shirt for any ministry or business purposes, particularly under a suit coat!
- Always dress as well as the people to whom you will be ministering.
- Never wear sunglasses or glasses that change tint as the light changes when you are indoors because people must see your eyes if they are to believe you.
- Never wear nonfunctional jewelry.
- Always carry a good pen and pencil.
- Never take off your suit jacket unless you absolutely must; it weakens your message.
- Remember that neatness counts.
- Always check yourself in a mirror before stepping to the platform.
- Make sure you don't fade into the background. If your background is blue, don't wear a blue suit.
- Don't have anything in your pockets or wear anything that jingles, jangles, clangs, crackles, or pops. Cufflinks that hit the podium near a mike sound like firecrackers.
- Never appear on a platform without your shoes in good condition and highly polished.
- If you have a protruding tummy, never wear your slacks or suit pants under it.
- Never, never, never wear white socks with your suit.
- Dress appropriately for the occasion. There are lots of times to leave the suit at home and be casual.
- Build a good basic wardrobe: navy blue suit, dark gray suit, and black suit. Supplement that with a navy blue blazer with gray slacks and a camel blazer with navy blue slacks. Have a sufficient supply of shirts and matching ties.
- Remember, you're not really well-dressed until you wear a pleasant smile, so smile, smile, and smile some more!

9. Do a brave thing—schedule an annual physical.

10. Cultivate a positive mental attitude. Don't allow yourself to become angry, defensive, defeated, caustic, or negative.

11. Become a student of the Word, of good literature, of people.

12. Read, read, and read some more. How about setting a goal to read a book a week or even two books a week? Subscribe to good periodicals.

13. Build your library diligently.

14. Learn to say nice and positive things.

15. Be consistent, dependable, a person to be counted on.

16. Deliver on your promises or don't make foolish promises.

17. Never speak ill of anybody publicly.

18. Be an enthusiastic person.

19. Be flexible.

20. Take a day off each week; take your annual vacations.

21. Never counsel anybody of the opposite sex alone or behind closed doors.

22. Be a tither and giver of offerings; be generous with everything you have.

23. Be loyal to your church, your church board, your family, your God, your denomination. If you can't be loyal, get out; do something else.

24. Be a person of integrity, be honest.

25. Don't be a plagiarist. If you use other people's materials, give them credit. Don't be a taker only; put something into the pipeline of ideas and concepts for others to use, too.

26. Don't allow others to set the priorities for your life and ministry.

27. Always carry some kind of breath freshener with you and use it, especially after you have finished speaking. Although halitosis is better than no breath at all, it is still inexcusable.

28. Be a good neighbor, become a part of the community you serve in, be a contributor and not just a taker.

29. Be approachable by everybody, including little people.

30. Remember to be human.

31. Don't slouch while on the platform.

32. Don't lean on the pulpit when you speak.

33. Don't become known as a long-winded preacher. Stand up, speak up, shut up!

34. Cultivate a sense of humor. A preacher without a sense of humor is like a car without a bumper.

35. Treat everybody alike, from CEOs to little children.

36. Keep working on your ministry skills, your sermon preparation, your sermon delivery, your people skills. Become a lifelong learner. Continually upgrade yourself.

37. Get in the habit of never taking yourself too seriously—your ministry, yes; yourself, no! Be willing to apologize and admit wrong. "If you mess up, 'fess up."

38. Remember, your board members are not the enemy, neither is your neighboring pastor or church.

39. Develop a hobby and leisure activities, but don't let any of them

control or dominate you. If you golf, don't do it so much you become a par golfer.

40. Just be nice! Remember who it is you are serving.

41. Like the sampler says, "Live Each Day With Eternity In View."

In an age when time seems to be more and more limited and valuable, why do millions of people return to our churches week after week to listen to preachers preach sermons? There are many reasons. The bottom line is that people still have a desire to hear an authentic word from God, through an authentic servant of God. Being a pastor is an awesome responsibility because the people who come are filled with anxiety about life and the future. They come to you as God's messenger, hoping you will remind them that their lives matter, that God cares, that there is hope, and that preparation for life after this life must be made here and now. They, with hope, come much like the Greeks came to Philip, asking, "Sir, we would see Jesus." Therefore it is important that we do not hinder their coming by placing any kind of barrier in their way—barriers of possessions, habits, moods, cars, or dispositions, marring the life or message of the messenger. A large order, but with Paul affirm, "I can do everything through him who gives me strength" (Philippians 4:13).

Continuing Education to Meet Changing Needs

Del Tarr

The mind is a lot like an umbrella; it works best when it is open." Some people believe that if a little knowledge is a dangerous thing, a lot of knowledge is lethal! That, however, must not be the attitude of today's pastor regardless of educational background. He or she must make the effort to stay current or lose the keen edge of effectiveness. God is not limited by a person's knowledge, but He seldom uses less.

I agree with John Gardner, founder of Common Cause, when he speaks about current educational trends (we in Assemblies of God higher education should show similar concerns): "Much education today is monumentally ineffective. All too often we are giving young people cut flowers when we should be teaching them to grow their own plants."[1] In like manner, we should be teaching mature credential-holders in ministry better ways of *how* to think—not just *what* to think. After all, one doesn't expect anything original from an echo! More and more, our churches are expecting scriptural content to accompany inspired oration from the pulpit and the church classroom.

The Need for Continuing Education

There was a day in traditional Pentecostal circles when the pursuit of education was largely discouraged. That day is generally past. Pentecostals for the most part have given up the older idea that it was not possible to be both educated and spiritual. We finally realized that the most anointed writers of both the Old and New Testaments were also the most powerful spiritual models available. Moses and Paul were not only responsible for the greatest number of books in each Testament, but were the best educated men of their day. They were also singularly approved of God (one might say selected). In speaking of our Pentecostal history, David Womack states: "Many of the first wave of Spirit-filled preachers were well-educated pastors who left or were rejected by other denominations. By the late 1920s, however, a lesser-educated clergy was being trained in short-term institutes."[2]

When I was growing up in the Midwest in the 1950s, it was popular to attack education. With few exceptions, camp meeting speakers, General Council speakers, and preachers in national conventions could always bring the house down with a sharp attack on "higher learning." They were right to reject the liberalism and intellectualism of the folks who threw out the Pentecostal pioneers, but these critics overgeneralized when they labeled education as antithetical to spirituality. Now, years later, and writing as the CEO of the only seminary of one of the nation's largest Pentecostal denominations, I need to be clearly understood on this matter.

Pentecostals have reason to fear those who would seek advanced degrees only to advance themselves, their private egos, or to substitute a title for courage and humble servanthood in ministry. On the other hand, I'm thankful to have lived to see the day when Spirit-filled pastors and teachers, well educated and possessing the balance of *heat* and *light,* can demonstrate *knowledge on fire.* Thank God, the old oxymoron "Pentecostal scholar" is no longer an oxymoron. We don't have to worry about degrees as long as there is temperature!

The Explosion of Knowledge

In older, traditional society, it was assumed that learning came to an end with adolescence. What one had learned by age twenty-one would apply, unchanged, the rest of one's life. Traditional apprenticeship was based on these assumptions. Today, however, is the age of the entrepreneur, not the apprentice. Individuals now should expect to continue learning well into adulthood. What one has learned by age twenty-one today may well be obsolete in five to ten years and will either have to be replaced or updated with new skills and knowledge. Scientific papers published daily number in the hundreds. The result: education has a shorter shelf life. While the content of biblical knowledge is stable, one's personal understanding of the Word of God should always be growing.

Besides the skills required for staying relevant in the age of exploding knowledge, perhaps communication and people skills for transmitting knowledge about God represent the greatest need among today's ministers. This means today's pastor must constantly grow, intellectually as well as spiritually. Information is not necessarily knowledge, but the information explosion is overwhelming. David Linowes, professor of political economy at the University of Illinois, states that more new information has been produced in the last thirty years than in the previous five thousand.[3] The bright note is that there have never been as many varied ways of assimilating information as exist today. The electronic age is here in full bloom. We should use it to gain interpersonal skills as well as theological knowledge.

When the first edition of *And He Gave Pastors* was printed, one could more easily advance in ministry just by seniority, by "progress in grade" (as in the military). That's changing. Now, even more, mature pastors need to find, determine, and develop a number of professional upgrades during their working life to stay abreast of the congregation's expectations.[4]

Vertical versus Lateral Thinking

Recently I have started becoming a techie—at age sixty-one! I didn't think this possible only a few months ago. Having learned to type in high school (the only subject for which I received a C), I have long believed I had a slight form of dyslexia: it has always been very easy for me to transpose letters on a keyboard. Even as I key in the words for this chapter— if you gave me a speed test, I'd go in the hole and end up with a negative score! Determined, however, not to be left totally behind in this fast-paced, technological world, I ordered a laptop computer a few months ago and forced myself to stop relying exclusively on the typing skills of my wife, Dolly. I have resisted, up until now, the computer age because of my age *and* a conviction that computers are perhaps the most logical result of a predisposition to the limitations of vertical thinking (I'll explain below). In spite of all this, I realized my own need to grow in an area of technology and personal skill that I had been neglecting. This is the age of the computer, and we rely on it to perform remarkable functions, which often replace people. (But don't forget, a computer cannot generate a single new idea.)

The following story illustrates how only the human mind, under the pressure of a real-life circumstance, can find a creative solution. It tells me that as a minister, I must be constantly growing and never stop learning, reading, and waiting on God so as not to stagnate. This describes what I was doing with current technology and how I was skipping the computer age. Edward De Bono challenges the reader of his little paperback *New Think* to expand thinking power by learning to think not only *vertically or analytically* (as the Western world has learned from Aristotle's Greco-Roman model) but also to think *laterally*.[5] Lateral thinking is concerned not only with problem solving, but specifically with new ways of perception that lead to creative ideas and discovery. Because of our cultural bias to think only vertically, most of us have to practice intentionally, or make a conscious effort to learn, the lateral mode of thought. This personal conviction about the need to learn and practice wisdom, as did Solomon, leads me to this story illustrating lateral thinking:

Many years ago when a person who owed money could be thrown into jail, a merchant in London had the misfortune to owe a huge sum to a money-lender. The money-lender, who was old and ugly, fancied the merchant's beautiful teenage daughter. He proposed a bargain. He said he would cancel the merchant's debt if he could have the girl instead. Both the merchant and his daughter were horrified at the proposal. So the cunning money-lender proposed that they let Providence decide the matter. He told them that he would put a black pebble and a white pebble into an empty money-bag and then the girl would have to pick out one of the pebbles. If she chose the black pebble she would become his wife and her father's debt would be canceled. If she chose the white pebble she would stay with her father and the debt would be canceled. But if she refused to pick out a pebble her father would be thrown into jail and she would starve.

Reluctantly the merchant agreed. They were standing on a pebble-strewn path in the merchant's garden as they talked and the money-lender stooped down to pick up the two pebbles. As he picked up the pebbles, the girl, sharp-eyed with fright, noticed that he picked up two black pebbles and put them into the money-bag. He then asked the girl to pick out the pebble that was to decide her fate and that of her father.[6]

Now, imagine, that you were asked to give advice to the daughter at that moment. What kind of logic would you use to advise her? Vertical thinkers are usually not much help in this situation. Analytically, the girl doesn't have many choices. (1) She could point out, up front, the two black pebbles and the cheating merchant, but an embarrassed merchant wouldn't solve her father's problem. (2) She could refuse to take a pebble with still no solution for her father. (3) She might even take a pebble and conceal it in her palm, asking the merchant to identify the color of the remaining pebble. This, however, would cause the merchant to again openly lose face with certain dire consequences for her and her father. (4) She could meekly accept the inevitable and sacrifice herself for her father. What would you advise her? Are there other options? (Before you read on, imagine what you would give as counsel.)

The girl in the story put her hand into the money-bag and drew out a pebble. Without looking at it she fumbled and let it fall to the path where it was immediately lost among all the others. "Oh how clumsy of me," she said, "but never mind—if you look into the bag you will be able to tell which pebble I took by the color of the one that is left." Since the color of the pebble is of course black, it must be assumed that she has taken the white pebble, since the money-lender dare not admit his dishonesty![7]

Just the fact of continuing your education, by formal or informal means, does not promise that you can transform your mode of thinking by adding lateral thinking to your options. But one thing is certain. *You will expand your potential for options in the face of real-life problems.*

A minister of the gospel makes a mistake when he or she believes that because the gospel message never changes, ways of presenting the gospel are also unchangeable, or never need to be updated. Isn't it true that the best pastors never stop learning and growing both mentally and spiritually? One of the ways many ministers keep growing is through formal continuing education programs. The disciplined route to mental growth is best accomplished, for most of us, by enrolling in some formal, structured class that facilitates our resolve to reach goals. There are many forms: (1) completing an undergraduate degree by correspondence or independent study; (2) taking an advanced degree in residence at a seminary or university; (3) studying on a modular system of intense one- or two-week seminars (like the Extension Department of the Assemblies of God Theological Seminary [AGTS] operating at seven locations in the U.S.), so one need not be displaced from ministry. AGTS now offers a number of graduate-level courses totally by independent study. Soon, both Berean University and AGTS will offer courses on the Internet. The potential is large and getting larger every day.

Of course, an informal method is simply personal enrichment, with no tie to a school or classroom of any kind. One can keep the mind and spirit alive with persistent discipline.

What should you study? There are many valid suggestions that could be made here about continuing education for ministers and the areas of study so profitable in that growth. I mention only one of those possibilities because of the constraints of space: *cultural sensitivity* in a North American society that is very diverse and getting more complex with every passing year. I have chosen to highlight only one because most texts omit or neglect this one.[8] Other obvious areas of study we do not have space to discuss here could be the Bible, sociology, psychology, preaching, management and leadership, conflict resolution, organizational methods, counseling, cultural anthropology, communications, and media. The list could go on and on. Allow me to speak to the one so needed but so neglected, cross-cultural learning and sensitivity.

I have in mind not only so called Anglos who have little interest in learning about African-American, Hispanic, or Native American issues, but also minority pastors who, while they must live in a basic White (Anglo) American majority environment, do not try to narrow the gap of their own misunderstanding of the very culture they are dominated by. If better understanding could be accomplished through dialogue and a serious study of each other's values, why, one may ask, do we not do this? Why must all parties "go to school" on this issue? *Because each subculture has a distinct prism through which it views the world.*

Statistics of the "Browning" of America

In 1981 Isidro Lucas wrote a book titled *The Browning of America.*[9] The author noted that at the book's writing, 25 percent of his church's population was Hispanic, yet the church was greatly insensitive to this segment of the population or to its needs. The Assemblies of God is facing similar growth of this minority. Do we see the need for sensitivity to this segment of our church? There are now nearly seventeen hundred Assemblies of God Hispanic congregations, and the latest reports from the Home Missions Department show that over 40 percent of Assemblies of God growth in the U.S. in the last decade took place in that branch of the church. Hispanics are the new immigrants to America. The keen observer will note the vast differences that exist among these people themselves. They are called Latinos, Latin Americans, Mexicans,

Chicanos, Puerto Ricans, Cubans, Hispanos. Their histories, their traditions, even their spoken accents, differ. Nevertheless they do have many things in common, especially the Spanish language.

To know Hispanics better, to learn to communicate with them, to begin to learn from them the special qualities of their culture, is a major challenge for all Americans.[10] This is especially true of Pentecostals who have, it seems, a privileged inroad to Hispanic hearts and allegiance. Thankfully, at the 1995 General Council in St. Louis, Missouri, the Assemblies of God made provision for an ethnic presence (in this instance Hispanic) on its highest administrative body, the Executive Presbytery. This was very timely, the first step leading the majority Anglo presence to understand how better to include and influence the evangelization of African-American, Native American, and Asian-American populations (as well as others).

Where is the growth in the U.S. church? Where is the greatest need for evangelism? Of what significance are those facts to the issue of *cultural sensitivity* and effectiveness in evangelization? Consider the inspired commitment by the Division of Home Missions of the Assemblies of God, called "Invasion 39," to reach the inhabitants of the thirty-nine U.S. cities of one million or more, where 50 percent of the population of this land resides. Let us not believe this effort can be successful without the participation of us all. Most of us are as unprepared to skillfully minister in the inner city as the owner of a snowblower would have been ready to fight if sent to the recent Desert Storm war! The Division of Home Missions recognizes that this challenge calls for new strategies in the form of no-nonsense, long-term commitments to unconventional evangelism. This means the training of specialists, or the utilization of Spirit-filled individuals who are already street-smart.

"Majority" American Values

Americans are like people everywhere else in that they don't think of themselves as having unique values. We believe, as do others, that the qualities we hold are universally shared. This is also true of the subcultures and regionalisms inside our own country. Minnesotans (I grew up as one) are surprised that the esteemed food called "barbecue" means only pork in South Carolina. South Carolinians haven't even heard of the lutefisk eaten in Minnesota (in my opinion it's just as well!). Food is indeed a symbol of our regional differences, just like the gumbo of Mobile is uniquely different from the refried beans of Albuquerque! As I have attempted to train Americans, Africans, Chinese, Indians, Europeans, and Latin Americans to be more effective as cross-cultural witnesses, I'm always saddened at their unawareness of the significance of cultural differences.

What should an Anglo pastor learn about a Hispanic or African-American fellow pastor or layperson? Aren't we all Americans, some ask? Don't we share the same values? While these diverse people may all value their citizenship equally, they hold many variations on the same stated values. An understanding of these variations will go far in effective human relationships in ministry. Here are only two of twenty that might profitably be considered:

1. *Time.* The northern European influences on the majority, or dominating, culture in the U.S. (and Canada) teach children in the home and school that "time is money." Efficiency is almost a fetish for Anglos. If anything warms their heart it is the speed of operations, from bank lines to grocery lines. They are not the place for chit-chat. If you neglect to fill out your deposit slip until you are in front of the bank teller, you will feel their eyes of disfavor on your back as you complete the task. Edward T. Hall calls us a "monochronic culture," where a schedule drives all activity.[11] That schedule is more important than any human interruption to it. Thus, the "polychronic" roots of both Black and Hispanic cultures have influenced its members to more readily make room for the *personal* dimension of life and relationships. Being late for an appointment is less severe for someone not so driven by an all-important schedule. For them, people rate higher than precise schedules. (There are, of course, exceptions to both of these generalizations.) There are schedule-driven folks in all American ethnics, just as there are Anglos whose priority for personableness make them a constant irritation to their fellow Anglos by always being late.

Think, pastor of an Anglo church, what is your attitude towards those who don't operate on your time clock? Consider, ethnic pastor, have you sought to know why you are so irritated with people who are willing to stop any activity when the bell rings, no matter how interesting or intense the meeting? Should not all of our "continuing education," whether formal or informal, give some attention to "the little foxes that spoil the vine"?

2. *Relationships.* Esther Wanning reminds us that real western cowboys were never very numerous in American history and are certainly scarce now.[12] But they hold great symbolism by characterizing the American ideal of a self-reliant, tough, risk-taking, and masculine personality. The most numerous first settlers to North America were from northern European stock. With few exceptions, they became the cowboys who have been so mythologized by Hollywood. Other major immigrant populations were not as predisposed to hyper-individualism as our Anglo cowboys. Southeast Asians (and Koreans, Japanese, Chinese, and the more recent Vietnamese, Thais, Hmongs) are wonderful additions to the great diversity of America. They bring a commitment to family little understood by any northern Europeans or their American cousins. Add to this the family/community orientation of southern Europeans (the Latin stock, especially the Italians) who, though different again on this matter than the Asians, are not much better understood by the British and other Germanic peoples of northern Europe.

> **An understanding of variations in values will go far.**

"In many countries, people cannot conceive of themselves apart from the family or group they belong to. Their loyalty is to the group and their achievements are for the group. In America, self-reliance is the fundamental virtue. Each person is a solo operation, and independence is considered the birthright of every child . . . Many decisions that would be made by the group in other cultures are made by the individual here."[13]

Faced with these differences, the Korean pastor in the U.S., for example, will be scandalized by the average Caucasian's lack of community commitment and be shocked at that individual's willingness to make independent decisions without consultation with or approval from those in higher authority (the Caucasian's perception). How much better to see the southeast Asian's predisposition to authority as a tool, a growth potential, for respecting God's authority. Equally disrupting is the Anglo's disgust at the "indecisiveness" of the Asian communicant who must discuss with the family any major decision before committing to a yes or no. Why are such things important? Why would a pastor born and reared in Great Falls, Montana (with less than 2 percent of any ethnic population), need to learn about Blacks if he or she finds ministry in Detroit, Michigan? Three reasons: (1) simply to better know how to evangelize the lost in that subculture; (2) to better know how to interact socially and spiritually with members who may already be in that congregation; (3) to discover true Christian kinship (relationally) with the many Black Pentecostal pastors already in Detroit. This same exercise in understanding could, of course, be duplicated for all other minorities.

Practical Issues

Do you, Caucasian brother or sister, know the significance of the "Black walk," which shows both acceptance and submission as well as defiance and rejection? Are you aware that White American expectations about certain kinds of eye contact (holding a person's gaze in normal conversation) can be totally misunderstood cross-culturally? Anglos are generally raised to show both respect and integrity in a two-way conversation (such as an employer-employee interview) by looking directly at the person being talked to. In a job-seeking interview, many white employers expect the same eye contact that they demand of their children ("Look at me when I talk to you!"). Most Black Americans are taught from childhood to show *deference and respect* by generally keeping the gaze downward and only occasionally looking a perceived superior in the eyes.[14] Can you imagine how this opposite expectation could lead to gross misunderstandings and a perpetuation of misconceptions?

Not every African-American exhibits every feature in his nonverbal behavior. However, these features occur with such frequency in the Black population that they can be considered patterned behavior: There is the "eye roll" that shows impudence and disapproval. Rolling the eyes is probably the reason many African-Americans, when conversing with each other, will often say: "Don't look at me in that tone of voice." Most Anglos and many Hispanics won't even pick it up! Non-Blacks would do well to study about "Signing," "Styling," and the "Rap stance," windows on this culture, rich in significance for achieving mutual understanding.[15] Research done by Mary Jane Collier on communication competence suggests that African-Americans place more weight on sincerity and respect for the individual than do their Anglo American counterparts who stress honesty and confidentiality in relationships.[16]

Do you, Anglo and African-American brother or sister, understand the power of the Hispanic family in North America today? For the less well-educated Mexican/Puerto Rican/Dominican Republic citizen, whose family lives in cramped quarters and seems to you to be overly dependent on family for everything, you may have forgotten your recent past. The hyperindependent mode of living espoused by the TV models on the multiple sets at your house teach you that having all the gadgets and means of locomotion is the norm. In a thousand subtle ways Anglos teach their children to be independent of them (and then decry being left alone in a rest home at old age!). Financially challenged Hispanics generally still consult each other for major decisions about employment and marriage partners and even long journeys. What difference does this make for an Anglo pastor who has Hispanics in the congregation? Don't expect your Hispanic brother or sister to make on-the-spot decisions on major issues; they often must first consult the larger family circle. Knowing this will remind you not to think of them as being indecisive or worse. Latinos are described as looking for respect and support for a relationship when interacting with the Anglo population. Collier proposed a theme of bondedness to describe communication among Mexican-American families, which requires a new level of relationships Anglos don't often seek.

The constraints of the gospel insist that today's pastor give the same attention to these elements as a foreign missionary who seeks to relate to a target audience overseas. If your prevailing attitude about people different from you is let *them* conform to *us,* then I promise, you'll have very few in your congregation. Yet, they may be the very ones the Lord considers your primary target audience. Cultural insensitivity is really not a Christian option.

Sexual Ethics in the Ministry

Wayde I. Goodall

King David had an ethical decision to make during an evening walk on the roof of his palace. That night he saw a woman bathing. His decision could have been to turn his head and walk away, but he chose to stare, think sinful thoughts about her, and plan how to sexually take advantage of her (2 Samuel 11). David's sin caused him untold heartache, set back the nation he ruled, and left a devastating message about weakness of personal character.[1]

Professional ethics are the rules or standards governing the conduct of the members of a profession. "Evangelical faith without Christian ethics is a travesty to the gospel."[2] We know the incredible damage that comes to a minister's life, family, congregation, and community when he violates sexual ethics. We also must continually remind ourselves that we have an obligation to hold the ethical standard high so as to protect our Christian testimony and the precious body of believers we serve.

Questions Ministers Need to Ask

Paul admonished the Corinthian believers: "Examine yourselves to see whether you are in the faith; test yourselves" (2 Corinthians 13:5). We should do no less.

1. Do you know your risk areas?

A 1988 *Leadership* magazine poll surveyed nearly one thousand pastors and an equivalent number of non-pastor subscribers to *Christianity Today* magazine.[3] The findings from a 30 percent response rate revealed a pervasive and painful problem in Christian ministry. One pastor confided that the survey questions covered "the greatest agonies of my life." Twelve percent of pastors and 23 percent of the subscribers admitted to extramarital intercourse. Nearly a quarter (23 percent) of the pastors acknowledged some form of "sexually inappropriate" behavior while in local church ministry. Of those persons pastors were involved with sexually, 69 percent came from within their own congregations, including 17 percent who were counselees. Physical and emotional attraction was noted as the major reason for the misconduct by 78 percent of the responding pastors, while marital dissatisfaction was noted by 41 percent.

2. Do you consciously or subconsciously engage in nonerotic contact (hugs, pats, putting your arm around a shoulder) with opposite-sex parishioners only?

Such action among counselors is not only sex-biased but a practice hazarding later sexual indiscretion.[4] As ministers we must be careful of this kind of behavior. The *Leadership* "Family and Ministry Survey" found that the ministers who completed the survey fantasized about sex with someone other than their spouse on an average of 23 times a year.[5] This activity leads only to pain and damage for all involved. James tells us, "When lust has conceived, it gives birth to sin; and when sin is accomplished, it brings forth death" (James 1:15[6]). Do you allow yourself to engage in sexual fantasies about your parishioners? The writer of Proverbs reminds us, "As [a man] thinks within himself, so he is" (Proverbs 23:7).

3. Do you ask unnecessary questions or details about a client/parishioner's sex life?

Do you initiate conversation about sexual problems, preferences, or fantasies for the purposes of sexual gratification? Do you share details about your own sex life? Do you make comments on sexual or physical characteristics or imagined sexual performance? Such behavior is considered sexual exploitation by counselor licensing boards and may be punishable as a felony. Ministers must use extreme caution when discussing anything sexual, especially with a person of the opposite sex. Remember the counsel from Jesus in Matthew 15:18: "'The things that proceed out of the mouth come from the heart, and those defile the man.'"

4. Do you misuse the advantage of authority and expertise that you have over the parishioner?

You must continually remind yourself that the people you minister to put you on a pedestal. When you use your power as a minister to take advantage of a parishioner, you are courting trouble. Our standard should be the Golden Rule, "Treat other people exactly as you would like to be treated by them" (Matthew 7:12, Phillips).

5. Are you aware that victims of past sexual abuse may be more vulnerable to successive victimization?[7]

Ministers must carefully avoid sexually questionable behavior with people who have suffered such abuse. The pain these people have gone through is something only the Lord can thoroughly heal. Should a minister take advantage of such a person, the damage done is not only tragic but also sinful.

Christian counselor Gary Collins notes in his book *Excellence and Ethics in Counseling:*

> Significant personal, marital, vocational and financial harm is suffered by the great majority of people who become involved sexually with another person in a ministry related relationship. A study of California psychologists who worked with clients who had been involved sexually with former therapists reported that 90 percent of these victims had suffered adverse effects. Eleven percent required hospitalization and 1 percent had committed suicide. Direct assessment of therapeutic abuse victims also reveals significant and pervasive levels of personal impaired social adjustment, increased drug and alcohol abuse, divorce and marital conflict and inability to use subsequent therapy effectively are the common harms reported.[8]

He later notes:

> After reviewing the limited evidence on the harm that existed fifteen years ago, Masters and Johnson asserted that it [sexual abuse] should be viewed and prosecuted as a form of rape. The charge of a "conspiracy of silence" that works to deny, minimize, and ultimately protect male-dominated professions and ministry cannot, and should not, be dismissed by the church in view of the manifold evidence regarding this epidemic. Again, as in all other areas of ministerial and professional misconduct, failure of the professions and the church to control its harmful members invites the legal control it detests.[9]

If you have reasonable cause to suspect a client has been a victim of sexual misconduct by a mental health services provider, even by clergy, most states require that you report it to the proper authorities.

6. Do you consider yourself to be above or beyond temptation?

If you feel this way, you stand on dangerous ground. Even the Lord, in His human state, was tempted (Hebrews 4:15). We know that Jesus used Scripture as His defense when He was tempted (Luke 4:1–13). The *Leadership* survey found that 10 percent of the ministers surveyed avoided sexually tempting situations weekly, while 25 percent did so monthly. The question was also asked, "How often in the past year have you looked at sexually explicit media or pornography (in print, video, or movies)?" Two percent said regularly, 11 percent said sometimes, 17 percent said seldom (yearly), 32 percent said rarely, and 38 percent said never.[10] Temptation is a reality in the minister's life just as it is in anyone else's life. We must constantly guard against anything that would give entrance to sinful temptation. What people consume through their eyes, ears, or conversations becomes part of their lives.

7. Do you maintain a daily time of prayer and study of God's Word?

A consistent personal devotional life is a defense against Satan's attacks. It is critical that we maintain a life of prayer and study of God's Word. Most of the ministers who have failed morally did not have a consistent devotional life.

8. Do you have an accountability group of other ministers you meet with regularly?

The *Leadership* survey found that 55 percent of ministers do not have an accountability group or even a close friend with whom they would be able to discuss sexual temptations.[11] James 5:16 states, "Confess your sins to one another, and pray for one another, so that you may be healed."

9. Have you confronted past sexual abuse, exploitation, or harassment in your life?

If a minister has had such a traumatic experience in his or her life, it would be good to discuss it with a qualified Christian counselor. We need to bring the pain, loss, anger, and damaged self-esteem to Christ for healing so we will not pass the same agony on to others. A godly pastor-counselor can help us do that.

10. If you have experienced sexual temptation with a parishioner that is not quickly and easily corrected, have you referred that person to another Christian counselor and sought help for yourself?

A minister should immediately refer people or cases which trigger sexual temptation in his or her own life. A Christian counselor may also help the struggling minister discover why he or she has a weakness in this area. God instructs us to flee immorality (2 Corinthians 6:12–20, 1 Thessalonians 4:3–7; 5:22).

11. Have you devoted time and energy to your spouse as a way of strengthening your own Christian marriage, thus reducing the temptation of sexual sin?

Seldom does a person yield to sexual temptation when he or she has a physically and emotionally fulfilling marriage. Paul gives married couples instruction about this truth in 1 Corinthians 7:1–5. A partner's disobedience to Paul's instruction, however, is no justification for having an adulterous affair. The entire weight of Scripture demands faithfulness and moral purity, no matter how much a mate may feel neglected.

12. Do you recognize boundary violations, and are you aware of manipulation by, or dependence needs of, people with borderline personality disorders?

Ministers must be aware of the learned subtle seduction, conscious or subconscious, coming from victims of sexual abuse: Parishioners who have experienced sexual abuse may not be able to distinguish between erotic and nonerotic hugs; any touch at all might cause them fear, pain, sexual arousal, and flashbacks. Cocounseling can alleviate the temptation to succumb to boundary stretching, dependency, manipulation, and seduction by borderline personalities.[12] "Patients with borderline personality disorders apparently constitute the majority of those patients who falsely accuse therapists of sexual involvement."[13]

13. Are you on guard for "transference," with its power to produce flattering attitudes in the counselee, and of countertransference, with its potential to trigger in the pastor the feeling that only he or she can save the client?[14]

The technique of cocounseling can also help guard against the transference potential. "Psychodynamically oriented therapists believe that the use of cotherapists reduces the intensity of the transference by dispersing it among the two, thereby facilitating the treatment of severely disturbed patients."[15] As much as possible a minister should cocounsel, with his spouse, board member, or staff member.

14. Are you on guard against deviating from your standard of moral ethics?

Danger signs include rationalizations such as, "I don't usually do this with others, but for you . . . ," "Although I really didn't think I'd be doing this . . . ," or "I can't believe the feelings I am beginning to have toward you. . . ." One of the blessings of the Holy Spirit is the conviction He brings when we get into a questionable situation or have a sinful thought. God has given us the ability to discern good from evil (Hebrews 5:14).

15. If you counsel people of the opposite sex, do you avoid secluded offices or areas?

I have decided not to counsel women unless it is during daytime hours, when my secretary is outside my office door, my door is partially open, or (whenever possible) my wife is present. I do not meet women in restaurants or other types of establishments for counseling. We ministers should have a window in the office door so people can see in (without hearing the conversation, of course), always sit where we can be seen, and refer a client to another Christian counselor if we anticipate a problem with sexual temptation for either the client or ourselves.

16. Do you have a plan of escape should you ever be in a questionable situation?

Count on God to provide a way of escape should you find yourself in a possibly compromising situation (1 Corinthians 10:13). Before such a situation occurs, rehearse how you will get out of the danger. Planning and forethought is a good policy. Secular counselors who are unable to resist sexual temptation in the counseling relationship are advised to practice their profession in areas having no client contact, such as research, consultation, publishing, lecturing, or other careers within the legal and educational fields.[16] Ministers should be even more concerned about being circumspect, because of the sacred trust that has been given them. Those who dishonor God by betraying the trust of their parishioners through sexual misconduct must remove themselves from the role of pastor immediately. They desperately need help and the counselee now desperately needs healing.

17. Do you take precautions to avoid any circumstance that could be misinterpreted as an improper relationship with a child or with a person of your own gender?

Church workers and leaders are not immune to charges of homosexuality and child sexual abuse. The media are filled with accounts of religious organizations personnel using church settings as opportunities for improper and immoral conduct with younger parishioners. Youth pastors and male children's workers should avoid being alone with children or youth of either sex for any period of time. Spending inordinate amounts of time with a member of the same sex can encourage gossip and destroy the effectiveness of one's ministry.

* * * * *

Sexual ethics in the ministry is not a congenial topic. I wish we did not have to focus on such problems. But the increasing frequency of problems in this area demands that we speak forthrightly. If you can answer affirmatively each of the questions above, you have a foundation for providing physical, emotional, and spiritual help for your parishioners. But even if you can answer all questions positively, there is still a word of caution. Stay close to the Master Counselor. Let the Holy Spirit do His work through you as you are available to meet the critical emotional needs in your congregation. Men with academic degrees in psychology and counseling, possessing the best natural preparation humans can provide, have still failed morally in their profession. A desire to help others is not sufficient. That desire must be prompted by the Holy Spirit. The ministry of counseling or helps must be empowered by that same Spirit. You can do all things through Christ who strengthens you, but you must always be dependent on His supply, not on your own (Philippians 4:13,19). He provides power!

When the Pastor Needs Professional Help

Richard D. Dobbins

The pastor and his family are people, too. This means there may be times when the pastor will need to reach out to someone else for help just as the people of the church need to reach out to him. Unfortunately, ministers usually are quicker to give help to other hurting people than they are to reach out for help when they, or members of their families, are hurting.

The Difficulty in Reaching Out for Help

Our culturally ingrained admiration for those who are self-sufficient and our self-imposed need to be that way too make it difficult for ministers to reach out for help. Most people, and men in particular, do not like to admit they need help from anyone. The vulnerability involved in exposing personal pain to another is extremely threatening to one's sense of selfhood. This is why it is so difficult for hurting people, believers and unbelievers alike, to reach out for help.

Christians often have a harder time than unbelievers in seeking help with their problems. They can understand why people without Christ may need to reach out for help from others during the hard times of life, but believers tend to feel that since they have a personal relationship with Christ, they should be "more than conquerors" (Romans 8:37) in every situation. All of this is especially true for ministers. After all, we reason, people can't have confidence in our ability to help them with the painful circumstances of *their* lives if we don't know how to manage *our own* problems. (We are blind to the fact this projects a proud "spiritual elitism"—something we find very distasteful in others.)

Second, the pastor fears what his peers and the people in his congregation will think. Those parishioners who believe they should be able to handle any situation with what they describe as "just the Lord's help" will probably find it difficult to understand why the pastor or someone in his family who's hurting needs help from any other source. These people believe the pastor and his family should "set a better example for the congregation."

The pastor fears that reaching out for help when he or members of his family are suffering would hurt his reputation with the people of his congregation. And his reputation is both his greatest current asset and his future insurance in the ministry. Any threat to this paralyzes him. Protecting his pastoral image becomes a major factor in creating the pretense that makes the life of the minister and his family so artificial, isolated, lonely, and painful. Although believers are admonished to live transparently (1 John 1:7–9), the sad reality is that the church is better known for pretense. When believers gather, no one wants anyone to know that embarrassing or unpleasant things may be going on in his or her life.

When someone at church inquires about how things are going in the pastor's life, his predictable and automatic answer is "Fine. Fine. Everything is fine." Now, in addition to the pain of his circumstances, he experiences fear and agony over what people in the church would think if they knew. This happens with congregants, too; however, these fears are much greater for the minister and his family than for other members of the church.

Granted, there is wisdom in the pastor and his wife not becoming intimate friends with members of their congregation, maintaining enough distance to accommodate the pastor's position as the group's spiritual leader. However, the minister and his spouse are often afraid to trust *anyone*—even a fellow minister or ministry couple—with unfavorable information about themselves or any member of their family. This isolates them from the very people who understand what they're experiencing and could at least offer supportive friendship.

The intensity of this fear has often been demonstrated in the apprehension of ministers calling the telephone help line at EMERGE Ministries, our Christian mental health center in Akron, Ohio. Those who call are never asked to identify themselves. However, to provide a competent referral, the ministers staffing the phones ask the part of the country the caller is from. But some callers are reluctant to reveal even that—for fear their identity might be learned; providing even the most limited identifying information is too threatening.

Spiritual leaders in sectional, district, and national offices suffer even greater intimidation than those in local ministry. Years ago a dear friend of mine, and a leader in his denomination, shared his fear of trusting fellow ministers with confidential matters of his heart. After sharing some tragic stories about broken confidences and the grapevine in the ministry (which we are all too familiar with), he told me what he did when he needed to share the burdens of his life with someone else in the ministry.

"There's a little Catholic church down in the southern part of my district," he said. "And when I'm in that part of the state, I park my car where I'm sure it won't be identified. Then, I walk back to this little church and go into the confessional booth where I can pour out my heart to a person I know will never tell anyone what I confide in him. When I leave, I always feel much better." What a tragic commentary on our inability to help our own! When someone trusts us with personal and confidential information, we must realize how important it is to treat it the same way we would want them to treat our shared confidence. By doing this, we can create a safe climate for practicing James 5:16, "Confess your faults one to another, and pray one for another, that ye may be healed" (KJV).

When to Reach Out for Help

Ministers often experience crippling stress from fear, anxiety, anger, hostility, and guilt. These are the major stress producers in the minister's life. Many Americans (ministers included) are so out of touch with their feelings they cannot recognize what any of these emotions feel like—or distinguish among them. They may be able to describe symptoms or problem behaviors, but they have no idea of the underlying emotions that have produced them.

Our public education is largely devoted to helping us learn how to think and reason. Very little attention is given to our feelings. And in most families, parents are unable to help their children identify their feelings and learn how to deal with them because years earlier, when *they* were children, no one attended to these matters in preparing *them* for life. Generation after generation, we have very few opportunities to identify feelings and talk about them in the course of growing up. Consequently, specific emotions are often difficult to sort out in adult life. This is especially true when they merge in varied proportions and are experienced as depression or a generalized anxiety for which no specific cause can be identified.

Our society almost exclusively associates pain with the body—physical pain. In a society as frightened by death as we are, we become experts at identifying sources of physical pain. However, people can be suffering from exaggerated levels of painful emotions and not have any idea what is wrong. So how *can* a person tell when he or she is dealing with truly overwhelming emotional situations?

When the normal physiological functions of life are disturbed for a week or more, emotions are announcing your need for some kind of help. Changes in your sleep patterns, appetite, elimination habits, or sex drive are ways your body tries to focus your attention on your emotional pain. As a rule, the sooner you heed these signals and reach out for help, the briefer your recovery time will be.

The severity of your emotional problems is usually indicated by the number of physiological functions affected, the extent to which they are affected, and the length of time involved. The greater number of natural functions that are disturbed, the greater the degree of such disturbance. The longer such disturbances continue, the less likely you are dealing with problems that can be cured simply by the passing of time.

In the early stages of stress, confiding in friends and taking some time off may be all that is needed to bring recovery. This is why it is so important to (1) develop one or two friendships you can trust, and (2) stay in touch with the way your body is responding to your feelings. The earlier you address uncomfortable levels of stress in your life, the less likely you are to be incapacitated by them. Unfortunately, many people would rather deny their problems than deal with them. However, major problems only grow more complicated, involve more people, and become more difficult to resolve when denied or ignored.

Sources of the Minister's Stress

From our work with over eleven hundred ministers and missionaries, we have learned that stress in the minister's life largely comes from one or a combination of three sources: from himself, from his marriage, and/or from his work or ministry.[1]

THE MINISTER AS A SOURCE OF STRESS

When the source of stress is the minister himself, it is likely to be rooted in his personality. The minister is usually blind to this, but his spouse and children are going to be very aware of it. Some ministers tend to be more driven than led. Differentiating their personal ambitions from the zeal of the Lord is very difficult—until they begin to suffer severe disturbances in their mental health, marriage, or family. Until the minister himself is affected, he tends to blame his spouse and children for not sharing his burden and vision. This may be true in some instances; however, it is more likely that the minister has grown insensitive to the needs of his marriage and family. If one is doing the work of the Lord *as Christ intended it to be done,* it will seldom, if ever, be overwhelming. After all, Jesus did *not* say, "'Come unto me, all ye that labor and are heavy laden, and I will give you *a nervous breakdown.*'" His yoke is always easy. His burden is always light (Matthew 11:28–30).

A minister may also be suffering from an emotional disturbance or mental illness. As ministers, we are no more immune to these than we are to any other kind of sickness. To complicate matters, there is still an enormous stigma connected with these forms of sickness. Thankfully, it is less of an issue now than it was in earlier decades. However, Christians in general and ministers in particular have great difficulty acknowledging even the possibility of ever being so affected.

A pastor's wife once called me to report that her husband had been severely depressed for several weeks. On more than one occasion, he had carried a loaded revolver from room to room, seated himself before a window, and raised the revolver to his head. When he would get in the car and drive away with the gun on his person, she would be frantic until he returned. With her help, we admitted her husband to our inpatient psychiatric program. Putting him in a locked ward for his own safety so troubled her that she had to call me back for help in dealing with it.

That pastor had his own preconceived ideas of what it would be like. He had heard many stories about godless psychiatrists—but not all psychiatrists are godless. The first night of his hospitalization, this pastor was listening through the wall of his hospital room to try to find out what was happening to the teenage patient he'd seen in the room next door. *He overheard a Christian psychiatrist leading that young man to Jesus Christ.* Needless to say, this pastor's view of mental illness and its treatment was changed by his experience. The Word of God and Bible study were part of his daily treatment. In group therapy, he was confronted with the theological issues that were part of his problems. While hospitalized, he learned the wisdom of accepting treatment for this kind of pain and agony—and God brought a marvelous healing to his life.

Now he understands something about mental illness and its treatment that would never have made sense to him before his own experience. He knows it could happen to him, because it did. And now, through his role as a spiritual leader, he has the unique opportunity to be a major social force in removing the undeserved stigma attached to these forms of human suffering. His suffering and subsequent healing gave this pastor a different and more compassionate view of mental illness and its treatment.

MENTAL ILLNESS VERSUS EMOTIONAL DISTURBANCES

The difference between mental illness and an emotional disturbance is not as difficult to determine as one might think. In most cases, mental illness is of genetic origin. As with physical diseases, one inherits a predisposition to mental illness rather than the illness itself. Mental illness involves neurotransmitters in the brain. These substances, which transmit electrical impulses between and among brain cells, affect the way a person thinks and feels. A disturbance that affects the neurotransmitters can result in thought disorders (such as schizophrenia) or mood disorders (including major depression and bipolar/manic-depressive disorders).

The good news is that with proper medication, the vast majority of people with mental illness can lead a normal life. Remind people of this. And if you or members of your family should be stricken with mental illness, remember this for yourself. I have had to break this kind of news to a number of ministers who have sought my help for mental health problems over the years. To bring a little levity to such heavy times, I have often reminded them, "You don't have to have perfect mental health in order to be used of God." Since no one is mentally healthy in every moment of life, this observation should bring comfort and encouragement to us all.

Some Signs of Mental Illness

Hallucinations and delusions are involved in mental illnesses. Typically, they are visual or auditory experiences not shared with or validated by others. The afflicted person sees or hears things other people do not see or hear. Hallucinations may involve one or any combination of the five senses: sight, hearing, touch, taste, and smell.

There is a difference between these kinds of experiences and a healthy faith. Many Christians believe that people can see visions and hear voices from God. These experiences are a cherished part of our spiritual heritage. God has provided biblical guidelines to help us discern whether such experiences are indeed from Him or are symptoms of mental illness. For example, we know that Jesus will not appear to anyone in a vision and tell that one to commit murder or suicide or to perform *any* destructive act. Obviously, this is not a vision from God. It is a hallucination and a symptom of mental illness. No voice from God will ever tell a minister that the world can be reached only through his particular ministry. This is a delusion of grandiosity and a serious symptom of mental illness.

Since delusions often deal with matters of persecution and grandiosity, they are more difficult to discern than others of a bizarre nature. However, if the guidelines of Scripture are carefully followed, the distinction between what God would say to a person and the delusional thinking of the mentally ill can be easily distinguished. Even though delusions resulting from mental illness may be disguised as revelations from God, they are not. If the minister or someone in his family can recognize that fact and help him seek treatment, his ministry can be saved and the body of Christ can be spared needless confusion and division. Let me give an example.

Several years ago, a highly gifted young man was referred to me by his district officials for psychological evaluation. He believed God was opening doors of ministry to him in remarkable ways. On more than one occasion, he had accepted two different speaking engagements in two different parts of the country—for the same night. Furthermore, he had bought round-trip airplane tickets for both destinations. Some of his elders accused him of lying and judged his character to be bad. However, if he were lying, it is highly unlikely that he would use his own money to purchase two airplane tickets for two different destinations from the same airport on the same day. We found the young man was suffering from bipolar disorder, a form of mental illness that often results in this kind of incredibly bizarre behavior. When he was properly medicated, there were no more grandiose delusions.

People suffering from a bipolar disorder have a tendency to take themselves off medication when they are "on a high," in a manic phase of their manic-depressive illness. This phase of the illness gives patients an exaggerated sense of well-being, which they enjoy. They feel good, so they take themselves off their medication. Since during this time they are likely to make incredibly foolish decisions that can affect the lives of many others, this is the time when patients, their families, and health care professionals must work together to prevent such decision-making from happening.

Until God gives victims of mental illness a more perfect form of healing, they will need to be on medication and monitored by the prescribing physician. Medical science has made tremendous strides in combating mental illnesses. In most cases, even those people suffering from schizophrenia (the most dreaded form of mental illness) can lead productive lives with the help of medication. Of course, there is still a powerful stigma attached to taking medication for mental illness. The minister has an important role to play in removing this stigma for parishioners who seek his help. However, until the church takes a more compassionate view toward members of the body of Christ who need this kind of treatment, it is probably best for a minister who is on some form of psychotropic medication to keep it confidential. He may not even want to share this information with his closest friend. Only his wife and doctor need to know.

Some believers entertain the mistaken notion that doctors may simply substitute medication for exorcism or deliverance—thereby masking the role demon spirits may play in mental illness. However, where demon possession or oppression is involved, prayer and fasting are essential parts of the exorcism, or deliverance, needed to bring desired relief. Nevertheless, from Scripture we may assume that demon spirits, being supernatural beings, are immune to the remedies of this world such as shots and pills. If mental illness is responsible for the person's symptoms, medication generally brings great relief. Therefore, why should we deny patients the relief that medication *can* provide simply from the fear that we are masking greater spiritual problems?

In all my years of experience, I have seen many people who were bound or oppressed by the devil, but only four clearly discernible cases of demon possession. Three of these situations were dealt with in public services; the other one involved someone who was hospitalized in our inpatient psychiatric program. All of these people responded to exorcism and were able to resume a normal life.

The Signs of Emotional Disturbances

Unlike mental illness, emotional disturbance does not permanently affect the neurotransmitters. It results from a distorted way of looking at life, usually originating in one's early years. Paul says no one sees life as it really is. Each individual looks at life through a dark glass, or distorted lens (1 Corinthians 13:12). However, some adopt a view of life *so distorted* that it results in unhealthy fear, anxiety, anger, hostility, guilt, and/or depression.

Of course, everyone experiences one or more of these emotions from time to time. Does this mean that everyone is emotionally disturbed? No. Remember, emotional disturbance is recognized by emotionally extreme behavior—outbursts of anger, paralyzing fear and anxiety, crippling guilt, and/or depression. Emotional disturbance is determined by the degree and duration of the emotional extreme(s). When the degree and duration of the disturbance interferes with one's ability to behave appropriately and productively in his or her life roles, we say the person is emotionally disturbed.

The Causes of Emotional Disturbances

Emotional disturbances often have their roots in traumata from one's past. Wartime experiences, sexual molestation, physical abuse, parental death or divorce, verbal abuse, betrayals, rejections, personal and business failures, tragic illnesses, and accidents—these are the kinds of experiences behind many emotional disturbances. The enemy takes advantage of the shock and/or shame involved in such experiences to invoke silence about them. In this way, these events from one's past become dark and closely held personal or family secrets. They tend to become distorted and even more tragically exaggerated with time.

Satan builds his strongholds in these secrets of the past. He enforces that secrecy through silence. If victims are to be free, the silence must be broken and the secrets brought to the confidential attention of someone who cares and is able to help. At times, this can be a friend, a minister, or a Christian mental health professional. Denial and repression will never disarm these strongholds. Such cover-ups only magnify their power to cripple or destroy one's ability to celebrate Kingdom peace and joy. To "put away childish things" (1 Corinthians 13:11) and forget "those things which are behind" (Philippians 3:13), these secrets of the past must be exposed to God's healing grace.

Treatment for "Sores of the Soul"

Sometimes these hurtful sores are healed by "praying through." There are four steps in this process. First, I encourage people to talk to God honestly about what hurts them. This involves getting alone in God's presence and rehearsing everything they can recall about their source of pain. It's like taking the lid off their bottled-up feelings and just pouring them out into a safe container. Writing a "letter" to God or the person responsible for one's pain can be an effective tool in this first step toward praying through. While praying, one can read the letter out loud to God. If such a letter is addressed to a living person, then it is often best to symbolically destroy the letter rather than mail it. One should seek the counsel of a wise friend or a competent professional person before mailing such a letter.

Second, the person may rather unexpectedly express to God some long-hidden emotions related to this pain. This kind of prayer can be upsetting to others, especially children, because it so often results in loud and tearful praying. That is why it is best for people to pray through when they are alone. However, these emotions need to be experienced and voiced as part of the healing process.

Third, when a person has rehearsed the hurt in prayer and is emotionally spent, he or she is to meditate on what God would present: "Wait on the Lord" (Psalm 27:14) for a more healing and redemptive way of viewing this part of one's history. Just as God helped Joseph discover a redemptive way of dealing with his brothers' betrayal, God can help us see the pain of the past in a way that makes us *better* rather than *bitter*.

This is the time when believers legitimately experience the "voice" of God. It may come through a verse of Scripture or the wisdom of a friend. It may be a powerful "burning bush" or a "still, small voice." It may be the words of a half-forgotten hymn or a totally new revelation. However, it will always be integrative rather than disintegrative for the individual and for the Kingdom.

Fourth, persons in the healing process are encouraged to spend time praising and thanking God for new, healing ways of looking at their old hurt. Expressing gratitude and praise for this new and redemptive view of their trauma helps to erase the old views and embed the new one deeply in their memory. If the love and prayers of friends and this kind of self-help do not bring relief, then the person should seek the aid of a competent Christian mental health professional who can help them reclaim that peace and joy the Lord Jesus died to provide.

STRESSES OF THE MINISTER'S MARRIAGE

Perhaps no other profession places as much stress upon a marriage as the ministry. Several aspects of the ministry contribute to this. The minister's family comes under more public scrutiny than that of any other professional. Everyone in the congregation knows the minister's spouse and children, but it is doubtful that they could identify the spouse and children of any other professional person in their community. The kind of public display the minister's marriage and family are subjected to results in what is often referred to as the "fishbowl complex."

Living under this kind of continual inspection creates its own unique stress. The minister's wife may already feel that in her husband's priorities, everyone else's needs come before hers or the children's. Congregational demands on the minister's time and energy leave him little of either to give his family. This may leave his wife feeling like she is competing with a mistress. When she also feels constantly "on display," the stress is multiplied many times over. The resentment this breeds tends to grow over the years until it takes a tragic toll on her love for her husband—and the ministry.

Each minister's wife will have her own way of dealing with such a situation. She may grow to resent the church for stealing time and energy from her and the children. When this happens, her husband often finds his work environment more pleasant than his home environment and unconsciously begins to spend even more time in church work. Gradually, over the years, the crisis in this marriage reaches disastrous proportions. By the time a couple realizes what has happened, professional intervention will be required to save the marriage because the level of hostility and resentment generated in both of them has become so great.

At other times, the wife will compensate for the lack of her husband's time and attention by over-investing in the lives of the children. In this situation, the pastor figuratively marries the church and his wife marries the children and her role as their mother. This appears to be a peaceful accommodation to the situation until the children begin to leave the family to lead their own lives. Then, the couple tragically discover that instead of *growing together* through the years, they have *grown apart*. This creates a different kind of crisis, but also one that will require professional help if the couple are to salvage their marriage.

Another source of marital stress for the minister happens when he and his wife come from very different family backgrounds. Often, ministry couples have grown up in different parts of the country, met in Bible college or seminary, fallen in love, and decided to marry before they have learned much (if anything) about each other's family. Regardless of what they discover when they visit each other's home, their relationship has usually progressed too far to reconsider their approaching marriage.

When families are too disagreeable, the couple experiences unbelievable stress in attempting to reconcile differences. Areas that create particularly difficult adjustments include shared devotions and prayer, expressions of affection, sexual openness, recreational activities, family finances, and how children should be disciplined. When such differences exist, they should be dealt with early in the marriage. However, few couples see the wisdom of this. Consequently, when a minister's marriage fails, at least one of these areas is usually involved.

Ministers' wives most commonly complain about the lack of time and romantic attention given them by their husbands. Often, they also resent his lack of involvement with their children. Ministers themselves most often complain about being severely criticized by their wives and the infrequency of her physical desire for intimacy. When an affair breaks out in the parsonage family, the roots are likely to be found in one of these areas. Such problems are usually not self-correcting, but they are highly treatable. However, prevention is always better than cure. If couples really understood the pain and loss that occur in the wake of an affair, they would seek treatment early in their marriage, at the first sign of trouble, to spare themselves this excruciating experience.

There are few places in the country so remote that a parsonage couple cannot find competent, Christian, professional help for their marriage. In many instances, however, they are wiser to locate help far enough from their community to keep their treatment totally confidential. Sometimes help can be found close enough to the minister's home to commute for each session. At other times, the distance may be so great they would be wiser to stay over two or three nights and be seen for several appointments in a few days' time. Regardless, the wise ministry couple will take whatever steps are necessary to get the help they need.

THE STRESS OF THE MINISTER'S WORK

Unfortunately, ministers get very little education or training in the management of stress and conflict. More and more of my time is being spent consulting with pastors and boards locked in uncomfortable levels of stress and conflict. Sometimes this is related to alleged child sexual abuse by a member of the staff or a lay leader. At other times, some prominent member of the church or ministerial staff is involved in some kind of sexual misbehavior. Then, there are times when sharp differences exist over how some aspect of church business should be conducted. Frequently, a crisis develops during the time when the church is in pastoral transition. A building program may also threaten to divide a church.

Today, when pastors' schools are so accessible, a pastor may too quickly attempt to adopt many of the appealing ideas he has learned. Changes in worship style, departmental organization or programs, and evangelism all take time. Diligent education of your staff and congregation, thorough training, and patience are essential to a smooth transition. Even then, some prime feathers may be at least temporarily ruffled.

In addition to praying for God's guidance during times like these, the wise pastor will seek out godly counsel from those whose life, training, and experience he respects. Often, humbling himself to get this kind of input from others can spare him, his family, and the Kingdom needless pain and frustration.

We have identified specific circumstances in which the pastor may benefit from professional help. Whether the discomfort is found in him, his marriage, or his work situation, the wise minister will get the help he needs to preserve his sanity, protect his marriage and family, and perpetuate the effectiveness of his ministry.

Finding the Best Source of Help

Competent Christian, professional mental health care is available in most communities. Take the time to think through exactly what kind of help you need . . . and then ask God to help you find the right provider.

When and if you feel a need to consult with someone for personal or professional situations that seem unmanageable, first of all, determine the nature of the problem. If the problem is not too sensitive, you may find help in your local area. This would include problem-solving skills, decision-making, some career situations, and most parenting issues. For highly personal and confidential matters where exposure might threaten your marriage and/or future ministry, you may wish to seek help outside your community in order to maintain total confidentiality. A good first step is to call the confidential Enrichment Office help line, which is answered at EMERGE Ministries in Akron, Ohio. All calls are confidential. Callers are welcome either to share their needs with a Helpline counselor or simply ask for referrals in a general geographic area—or both.

Your choices of where to go for help depend first of all on the options available under your insurance program's mental health provisions. From those options, you will want to select the provider who is most competent and whose religious views most closely match your own, in an appropriate proximity to where you live. (Ideally, your health care program would allow you to seek help from providers whose religious beliefs are compatible with your own.)

How do you know if someone is competent and if his or her practice is consistent with evangelical Christian beliefs? There are many levels of training among mental health professionals. The most highly trained is a *psychiatrist*. This is a medical doctor who has also had extensive training in psychology. Because he is also a physician, the psychiatrist is the only mental health professional who may legally dispense medication. Next is the *psychologist,* a person licensed by the state to practice psychology without the supervision of someone more highly trained. The psychologist has an earned Ph.D. degree and has passed a state licensing exam. Most states require all professional counselors to have at least a master's degree in psychology or a related behavioral science field and pass a licensing exam to legally provide counseling services. Depending on local laws, counselors may or may not require supervision by a psychologist or psychiatrist.

Reputable Christian counselors are also generally affiliated with at least one professional organization. Look for someone who is accredited with one or more of the following:

- The American Association of Christian Counselors (AACC)
- Christian Association for Psychological Studies (CAPS)
- The American Association of Marriage and Family Therapists (AAMFT)
- The American Psychological Association (APA) and/or your state Psychological Association, e.g., Ohio Psychological Association (OPA).

Second, look at the compatibility of your religious beliefs and the counseling process. Many people, often with good reason, are suspicious of help from the behavioral sciences. They fear that science and faith are like oil and water—they simply do not mix. And in all honesty, this *was* the case for many years. However, many people from both disciplines now understand the benefits of an interdisciplinary approach to managing life's problems. Psychologists and psychiatrists are helping the minister better understand emotional issues involved in a person's religious life. Ministers are helping the behavioral scientists better understand the spiritual issues involved in a person's emotional life. The result is better quality mental health care for believers.

>
> **" A good first step: the Enrichment office help line. "**

At the same time, many Christian mental health professionals have been much more thoroughly trained in the behavioral sciences than they have been in Scripture. Their philosophies and methods have not been subjected to a biblical test; thus, their science and their faith are not fully integrated in their own minds. Believers are likely to leave such a counselor's office more confused or shocked than helped, even though the person is a "Christian psychologist" or practices "Christian psychology."

There is a major difference between a Christian who merely practices psychology and the practice of a psychology which is truly Christian or biblical. The latter professional is one whose study of human behavior is pursued under the discipline of Scripture. He or she is a believer who is thoroughly grounded in Scripture *and* well trained in the behavioral sciences. This person's approach to counseling will at the very least not be contradictory to Scripture. And at best, it will be highly supportive of and supported by Scripture. There is much that is healthful and helpful in the behavioral sciences.

For too many couples (clergy and laypeople alike), serious marital problems and other highly personal matters, such as sexual dysfunction, go untreated until they have a long, painful history—which only further complicates the treatment process. Those experiencing these kinds of problems need to locate a counselor who is trained to manage these specific situations in a manner consistent with their faith.

Whether his problems be of a personal, ministerial, marital, or family nature, the best advice I can offer to any minister of the gospel is to prayerfully seek God and be willing to accept professional help without delay when circumstances warrant it. Why is this so important? When you are spiritually, physically, mentally, and socially healthy, you will find it much easier to attract people to the Christian way of life because they will be eager to discover what you have found. The kingdom of God needs you to not only be on your way to heaven, but also enjoying the trip!

The Pastor As Shepherd

Wayne Kraiss

A shepherd is a most appropriate metaphor for the biblical concept of pastor. Society looks upon the pastor as a professional—and appropriately so. However, something fresh and simple is recovered when pastors view themselves as shepherds of God's flock placed under their care. The flock belongs to God. Each shepherd will give an account to Him for their oversight of the flock. The apostle Peter cautions against lording authority over the flock or accepting leadership for monetary reasons (1 Peter 5:2). It is significant that Christ chose the example of a shepherd to describe His relationship with us (John 10:11,14): The shepherd protects, comforts, and feeds the flock.

A Humble Call

When Jesus referred to Himself as a shepherd, He spoke of a humble and lowly position. When He told Peter to feed His sheep, He was asking Peter to accept a role viewed with disdain and derision in first-century culture. This was not a call to public prominence or luxury. It was not a call to prestige and respect. It was a call to live with sheep and goats. Peter did not forget the significance of that call and referred to it in 1 Peter 5. He knew the implications of that role required that one serve willingly, "not greedy for money, but eager to serve; not lording it over those entrusted to you, but being examples to the flock" (1 Peter 5:2–3).

After the exile, Pharisaic rabbis caused a great devaluation of the role of shepherd. They forbade pious Jews to purchase wool, milk, or meat from shepherds. Because shepherds had little income, many were suspected of stealing and dishonesty. Civic privileges were taken from them. The literature of the day stated, "No position in the world is as despised as that of the shepherd" (Midrash on Psalm 23).[1] Shepherds, like tax collectors, were treated with contempt by the public.

Jesus referred to Himself as the good Shepherd, distinguishing good shepherds from the bad. There will always be bad shepherds. There will always be pastors who fail to live up to the high and holy calling of the ministry. Those who are good and faithful in their stewardship as a pastor must not be disheartened by the bad. Instead they must stand in sharp contrast to those who are not faithful.

Just as Christ "made Himself of no reputation" (Philippians 2:7, KJV), the pastor must not make decisions or prepare messages in an attempt simply to enhance his reputation. Pastors must be faithful to the Word and obedient to the humble call the Lord has given them. Trust cannot be demanded from a congregation. Shepherds earned the trust of their flocks as the sheep learned they were safe when the shepherd was present. Through faithful obedience to their calling, pastors will gain the trust of the congregation. Christ did not demand the comforts or respect He was rightfully due. He willingly picked up a towel to serve the very disciples who should have served Him. It was not accidental that His birth was announced to shepherds and occurred in a stable. Those who serve as undershepherds must not demand more than the Chief Shepherd left as an example.

Meeting the Needs

David's opening comment in Psalm 23 is noteworthy: "The Lord is my shepherd, I shall not be in want" (v. 1). The role of the shepherd was to care for the needs of the flock. Sheep are quite helpless, dependent on the shepherd. He must recognize their needs, whether it be for water, pasture, rest, protection, rescue, a healing balm, or assistance in giving birth. The fastest-growing churches have pastors who are driven to meet the needs of the congregation.[2] The people in our communities have much less loyalty to denominational affiliation or programs launched for growth. Many surveys indicate people are choosing a church based on whether their needs and the needs of their family can be met in that congregation.

This is not a new principle in growth. It is as basic as understanding that sheep with needs will not be content and will not bear young. The effective pastor understands that the needs of his community may vary widely from those of a neighboring community. Simply copying the format of worship and outreach at another growing church may not be effective. Communities with diverse ethnic populations represent unique needs. Churches adjacent to large college and university campuses with many single young people have needs much different from those located in agriculturally dominant rural settings. A church located near large manufacturing and industrial plants will present different needs than the suburban community populated by commuters. A church with many young couples will need children's facilities and activities.

The needs of sheep change with the seasons. The heat of summer brings parasites and the need for shade and water. The winter and rainy seasons bring the need for shelter. Birthing seasons limit the distances the flock can travel with the young. The wise pastor will carefully plan for the changing needs of the congregation. People tend to be restless when they are in need. Stability is one of the results of a satisfied congregation.

Making the Sheep Lie Down

"He makes me lie down in green pastures" (Psalm 23:2). The shepherd does not beat the sheep into submission until they lie down. He understands what the flock needs in order to be content, to relax and lie down. He then creates the environment in which the sheep will lie down. Four requirements must be met before sheep will lie down. They will not lie down if they are afraid for their safety. They will not lie down if there is friction or turmoil within the flock. They will not lie down if they are hungry. They will not lie down if they are tormented by flies or parasites.[3]

The pastor must know and understand both the needs and limitations of his flock. He must recognize the strategies of the enemy and provide a defense for his congregation. He is responsible to maintain harmony within the congregation. He must provide an adequate diet of teaching to keep the congregation healthy and strong. When Jesus saw the crowds, "he had compassion on them, because they were harassed and helpless, like sheep without a shepherd" (Matthew 9:36). The helpless and harassed members of the congregation must find compassion from their pastor. Their plight must not be met with indifference or lack of concern.

The pastor of a large growing congregation notes, "It is important to provide hope and comfort for the congregation on Sunday. Many of them come to church badly bruised from the turmoil of the week. Unless they find healing and strength in the house of God, why would they want to return?"[4] It is not surprising that the congregation he served was a growing congregation.

Implicit in Jesus' teaching about the good shepherd is the presumption that the shepherd is near his sheep. He has not distanced himself from them or their needs. He knows them well. He is close enough to notice the wolf circling the frightened flock. His voice calms the sheep. The contemporary pastor must maintain a delicate balance between spending enough time with the members of the congregation to know their needs and spending enough time in the Word and prayer to have the resources to meet those needs. Such balance helps create circumstances inviting the sheep to lie down.

Protecting the Sheep

Protecting the sheep can be costly for the shepherd. What separates good shepherds from unreliable shepherds is their response when the flock is threatened. The good shepherd is unselfish and will protect and defend his flock at great personal risk, even to the point of laying down his life. Such bravery results from a unique relationship between the shepherd and the sheep. It is much more than an employee-employer relationship. After spending much time with the members of the congregation, the pastor values each person. He has an investment in each one, an investment of prayer, teaching, preaching, counseling, and support. It causes him to rejoice with their victories and weep over their defeats.

This extraordinary value of the individual sheep is illustrated in Jesus' account of the shepherd leaving the ninety-nine to seek the one lost sheep (Matthew 18:12). For a lost sheep to find its way back to the fold is rare; standing and bleating for help is more likely. Such a lamb would be easy prey for a predator. Many people who drop out of church are like that lost lamb. They rarely find their way back to the congregation by themselves. They are vulnerable, frightened, and alone. Their salvation often depends on the value the pastor places on them and the length to which he is willing to go to rescue them.

As shepherds, some pastors behave like hired hands. They have no personal stake in the welfare of the flock. They serve for the salary and personal gain. The protection, growth, and comfort of the flock are incidental concerns for them. They do whatever is required and necessary to be paid, unless the personal cost is too great. They flee when responsibility becomes too costly. They will sacrifice one or more lambs to save themselves.

Pastors are in the best position to protect the flock. In the analogy of the shepherd (John 10:1–18), Jesus reminds us that the enemy will attack the sheep. It is of interest that Christ said the shepherd can see the attacker approaching. At that point, the sheep are often unaware of the danger. By the time they are aware, it is often too late to save them. These are times when the choice to leave the flock and not make the personal commitment necessary to defend it may be a tempting option. The pastor who loves the congregation not only remains to defend it in times of peril, he does not make it the subject of derision and contempt in conversation. The good shepherd takes personal delight in the success and growth of the flock. He sees the potential good in each lamb.

Finding Water

It is said that thirsty sheep will stampede in the direction of water. But putrid or contaminated water can be fatal for the sheep. Sometimes the shepherd will lead a thirsty flock on an extended detour rather than risk having it stampede to a polluted pond and quench its thirst with poisons that could be fatal. Thirsty congregations are susceptible to the lure of polluted water. The latest doctrinal fad is not as appealing to the well-fed congregation as it is to the thirsty ones. It is the responsibility of the shepherd to know the condition of the water in the vicinity of the flock. The pastor must know the doctrinal pitfalls surrounding his congregation; he must lead the flock away from them. This is tedious work. It requires study, a firm commitment to Scripture, and a solid grasp on theology.

In ancient times, shepherds would often dig wells in arid areas or in places where clean water was not available. They did this in anticipation of the needs their flocks. It was something sheep could not do for themselves. The tedious work of sermon preparation is similar. The pastor anticipates the needs of the congregation and does what they cannot do for themselves. He digs into the truth of God's Word and makes fresh water available for the sheep.

David used an interesting illustration in Psalm 27 as he described the care given in the "day of trouble." In verse 5 he refers to being set "high upon a rock." This no doubt is a reference to a shepherd's action when he observes a snake moving toward a defenseless lamb. Knowing the lamb is unable to overpower the snake, the shepherd picks the lamb up and places it high on a nearby rock, out of reach of the snake. The shepherd then turns to battle the snake. As the lamb watches from the safety of its perch on the rock, the shepherd kills the snake. The battle that was to be the lamb's becomes the shepherd's; the victory that was to be the shepherd's becomes the lamb's. The result for the lamb is described in verse 6: "Then my head will be exalted above the enemies who surround me." The pastor often functions in this role. He takes the initiative and battles the enemy of the members of his congregation. It is not because he is personally under attack or threatened. It is because those who have been entrusted to his care are threatened.

Herding Is Not Leading

David observed that as a shepherd, the Lord leads and guides (Psalm 23:2–3). The pastor is more than the corporate leader of the congregation. Like a shepherd, he determines the direction and pace of the journey. It must be focused on some objective. The pastor must know where the congregation is and the direction it should take. He must know where the danger is and lead the congregation away from it. He must know where green pastures are and lead the congregation to them. He must know where fresh water is and plan an itinerary that will bring the flock to places of refreshing. He must know the ability and maturity of the congregation and carefully plan their spiritual journey. More than any person in the congregation, the pastor is responsible to set the agenda, describe the goals, and present a vision for the congregation to follow.

Sheep are followers. They take comfort in knowing the shepherd has preceded them on the path and knows where he is going: The dangers have been discovered. The snakes have been cleared out. The path is safe. Clean water is within reach. Adequate pasture is near. A good shepherd does not drive or herd the sheep from the rear of the flock. When driven, the flock may exhibit frustration and bewilderment. The driven flock responds from fear of retaliation. They are required to go in a certain direction or suffer unpleasant consequences. Consensus is good, but it is best when it results from suggestions and options presented by a leader under the direction of the Holy Spirit. Few boards or congregations are able to take a problem and design a solution in the absence of someone who leads them toward consensus and helps them weigh the options. The sermon that upbraids and belittles the congregation for its failure resembles herding more than leading.

Through the Valleys

Every shepherd knows the path will not always be easy. Some days are filled with sunshine and green pastures. Others are filled with shadows and trails that wind through rough terrain. It is no different for the pastor. There are weeks filled with the joys of births, weddings, conversions, healings, and baptisms. The compliments for the sermon seem to never end as the congregation leaves the sanctuary. The offerings are above budget and visitors are plentiful. Growth seems endless. Other weeks are filled with incidents of death, birth defects, marital problems, spousal abuse, and addictive behavior. It seems offerings are the smallest when needs are the greatest. The pastor cannot during the next Sunday morning sermon unload the burdens that have been dumped on him. He must take them to the Lord and be comforted in knowing that He was there in the times of need and people trusted Him with their valley experiences. Jesus reminded His disciples that it is not the healthy who need the physician, but the sick (Matthew 9:12). We have all heard of the minister who confessed he loved souls but could not stand people.

People in our congregations will often journey into the valley of death, for death is not always physical: Hope dies; faith dies; marital fidelity dies; trust and confidences die. In each case the pastor must come alongside and walk through these valleys with those who are hurting. It is a great privilege. It is a time when ministry can be very fruitful. Hearts are open and hungry for comfort. The pastor can bring hope where sorrow is plentiful. Fortunately, we pass through these valleys; we do not remain there. Joy returns in the morning. The pastor is in a privileged position to observe the faithfulness of the Lord in comfort and deliverance.

The pastor who has a long tenure with a congregation has a rich heritage of journeys with them through the valleys. Such experiences build their trust and confidence in his leadership. When a couple grips the hand of the pastor at the close of the year and says, "Thank you for walking through the valley with us this year," it makes the journey worth the effort. Even though no one else in the congregation may know what that journey was all about, that couple know they were valued and loved by a caring pastor. For the pastor, it may have been like leaving the ninety-nine and rescuing one troubled lamb.

A Rod and Staff

To the sheep, the rod and staff are symbols of comfort. Why? How do they relate to the role of the contemporary pastor? The rod was a short club, often with a knob on the end. It was used in a variety of ways. Ancient shepherds would rarely be seen without a rod in their hand or attached to their waist. At times it would be thrown with extreme accuracy to scare off a predator. Sometimes it was even thrown in the direction of a wayward lamb, an attempt to stop it from wandering farther from the main flock or too near a poisonous plant. In these uses, the rod was an extension of the authority of the shepherd. It was like an extension of his outstretched arm. The authority of the shepherd and his ability to control the flock with the rod was a source of comfort. The pastor must use the rod of authority with great care but never hesitate to defend the congregation or alert members to approaching danger.

The rod was also used by the shepherd as he stood at the gate of the fold at night to stop each sheep long enough to count it and quickly examine it for any injuries sustained during the day. This is a custom referred to as "passing under the rod" (see Jeremiah 33:13; Ezekiel 20:37). Flocks in Palestine could number from twenty to five hundred. Some shepherds actually recognized their sheep sufficiently to name them. Often as the sheep were stopped at the gate, the shepherd would run his hand over their bodies to feel for hidden thorns or parasites. This would have been the logical time to anoint the sheep and dress their wounds. Today's congregation is comforted by the pastor who takes the time to learn about the needs of those under his care. His personal attention is reassuring. Different methods are used to provide personal attention, depending on the size of the congregation. Although visits are recognized as impractical in a large congregation, a phone call from the pastor is still possible. Sometimes a personal note can be an unexpected reminder that you are mindful of a trial a member is facing.

> **Pastoring involves so much more than just preaching on Sunday.**

The shepherd's staff had a much different function and appearance from that of the rod. It was much longer and often had a large crook at the end. The shepherd would use the staff in a variety of ways to reassure the sheep: to stir the high grass in front of the advancing flock to frighten away any snakes, to nudge a sheep back to the trail and out of harm's way, to draw the timid sheep closer to himself. Some shepherds could be seen walking for miles with the tip of the staff just touching the side of a lamb, bringing reassurance by maintaining contact. During times when lambs were being born, the staff was used to lift them onto their feet and place them alongside the mother. This avoided the scent of the shepherd's hands on the newborn, a possible cause of rejection by the mother.[5] People in our congregations need the reassurance of the "shepherd's staff." Some need to be gently nudged, others need constant reassurance and affirmation. The timid need to be drawn toward the shepherd and reminded of their value, and the newborn in the faith must be lifted and helped to stand on their own.

Each shepherd's staff was carefully crafted by the shepherd. Each carried some aspect of the shepherd's personality, making each staff unique. Pastors will differ in the way they go about their shepherding functions in the congregations they serve. What works well for one pastor may not be comfortable for another. But common to all pastors is the understanding that pastoring involves so much more than just preaching on Sunday. The needs of the people under the pastor's care vary widely. His resources must be extensive. As he demonstrates his concern and competence, the flock will be comforted. The ancient shepherds recognized they could not rely on their strength and skill alone but needed both a rod and staff to care for the sheep. The contemporary pastor quickly discovers that all of his skill, education, and natural gifts will never be adequate to accomplish the work he or she has been called to do. The Word and gifts of the Spirit often become a rod and staff in the hands of the anointed pastor. He understands the power of the Word and the Spirit.

Protecting the Protector

The pastor who accepts the role of shepherd over the flock will become the target of the enemy's attack. "'Strike the shepherd, and the sheep will be scattered'" (Zechariah 13:7). Satan knows this principle and often focuses his attack directly on the pastor. The pastor's family are likewise the target of Satan's attacks. The moral or ethical failures of a pastor produce more than a public relations scandal. When the pastor fails, the protector is removed from the flock, leaving it vulnerable to the enemy's attack. Congregations are at great risk during periods of pastoral transition because the protector is absent. For the flock to be protected, the shepherd must be protected.

The pastor must be alert to the personal dangers and temptations not only for his own sake, but for the sake of the flock. It is foolish for the pastor to believe the sheep under his care are vulnerable but he is not. Very few church boards comprehend the value of a shepherd who is strong and capable of defending the flock of God. The attempts of the pastor to inform the board of the personal threats to his own welfare are frequently misunderstood and appear to be self-serving. The need to protect the pastor can become the source of tension between the needs of the flock and the welfare of the shepherd. This tension must be carefully managed or the pastor will either be consumed with self preservation and neglect the flock, or be consumed with protecting the flock and neglect his own defenses.

> **The pastor must be alert to personal temptations for the sake of the flock as well as for himself.**

One of the responsibilities of the shepherd is to keep the flock together. With every transition, sheep are at risk. Congregational harmony is often at risk during pastoral transitions; when a congregation is without a pastor, it tends to scatter. The church with a history of short pastoral tenures seldom manifests the strength or growth of a healthy congregation. This sobering fact should cause the pastor to consider carefully the consequences of the decision to resign and relocate. If the resignation is primarily to save the pastor's skin, it is similar to the hireling's actions, who is not a good shepherd because he flees when he sees the wolf coming (John 10:12–13). Congregations should carefully consider the serious implications of a pastoral change before asking for the pastor's resignation.

Pastoral transitions almost always result in a negative impact on the flock regardless of its size. A very effective pastor who has completed twenty-five years of ministry at one church said, "I get frequent invitations to consider relocating to another church. But if I left this church, it would take time to learn the needs of the new congregation and what does and does not work there. I already know what works here. The pastor who would follow me may not know what is effective here. There would be a period of adjustment that might not be good for either the congregation or the new pastor. I think it is best to stay where I am and continue to work with people whose needs I know."

Ending Well

Psalm 23 ends, "Goodness and love will follow me all the days of my life, and I will dwell in the house of the Lord forever" (v. 6). That is the end for those who have come under the care of a good shepherd. They have survived the temptations and trials of life. The weak have been strengthened. The broken have been healed. The lost have been found. It is a good end.

What about the end for the shepherd? At the journey's close, how is he or she ending? In his work on mentoring, Dr. J. Robert Clinton has observed that Christian leaders must end well. He observes that the primary causes for the failure to end well are the abuse of power, the abuse of money, pride, sexual temptations, and family issues.[6] Dr. Clinton also lists several characteristics of those who end well. Among them are having good mentors, maintaining a learning posture throughout life, and continuing to grow spiritually.

Shepherds spend long periods out of sight of those they are accountable to. They might be away for weeks with their flock. At such times there is no one to notice whether they are protecting the sheep or not. Similarly, pastors have extraordinary opportunities to abuse their position. This is particularly true of the schedule maintained by pastors of smaller congregations. Few, if anyone, will notice how much time is spent in study and prayer. Who is to know what calls are being made and why? Who is to know what funds handed privately to the pastor are being reported? What other occupation gives as much power to one person with as little accountability? "Men ought to regard us as servants of Christ and as those entrusted with the secret things of God. Now it is required that those who have been given a trust must prove faithful" (1 Corinthians 4:1–2).

Recently, one of my board members invited me to lunch while I was experiencing a rather stressful month. I had no idea what was on his mind, but since he chaired a prominent committee of the board, I thought it probably was related to the business of that committee. Shortly after we were seated at the table and had ordered our lunches, he looked me straight in the eye and asked, "How are you doing?" I immediately launched into a report about finances, progress on various projects, and personnel issues. He stopped me and said, "I am not asking about your work, I am asking about you. How are things between you and the Lord? Between you and your family? You and your wife? You and the bank? How are you feeling physically?" I was stunned. He looked at me and continued, "I care about you. Your welfare is part of my responsibility. This luncheon is not about business. It's about you. If you are not healthy, the ministry you represent will not be healthy." I struggled to hold back the tears. I had been under a lot of pressure but never anticipated what a load would come off my shoulders as this layman continued to ask probing questions about me, my family, and my walk with the Lord.

The conversation could never have taken place without a foundation of trust and confidence. He had carefully built that foundation for years. I knew at that moment he was being used by the Holy Spirit to minister to me. He wanted me to end well. It is useful to ask yourself what the profile of the pastor of the church you serve would look like if you ended well. It might help provide new direction in your role as shepherd.

Unit

3

Preparing for Revival

Introduction:
Revival Is . . .

Charles T. Crabtree

B elieve it or not, I received the greatest insight into the true meaning of revival in an airport terminal. I was rushing to catch a connecting flight but had to pause for a moment to see a drama unfolding. A large man was lying on his back on the floor. He had been stripped to the waist, and paramedics were frantically fighting for his life. I did not have the time to see the final results. I do not know for sure if the man lived or died. What happened to the man on the terminal floor and how others reacted to him need to be understood by spiritual minds and put into practice by people of faith, especially people of Pentecostal persuasion.

True Revival Is the Reviving of Spiritual Life

It was obvious to everyone in the airport that day that a body must have the breath of life. A body without signs of life is a tragedy, a precursor to death. In the physical world, this crisis is immediately apparent because men and women are physically alive and physically aware through physical senses. The moment death makes a bid, everyone who cares does everything possible within their responsibility and expertise. The wife begins to cry for help. The alarm goes out as 9-1-1 is called. Paramedics speed to the scene and use every tool and method at their disposal. Why this frantic activity? They know they have a very brief opportunity to revive the body and bring the man back to life.

What a tragedy if people who passed by the man in the airport were not aware of his physical condition. Worse yet, would it not be bizarre if we began to regard senseless bodies as normal and acceptable? How pitiful to visit third-world countries where death is so common that corpses are routinely removed from the streets once a day.

What would be tragic and bizarre in the physical world has become almost normative in the Christian community. Just as there is a clear reality and demarcation of physical life and death, the same holds true of spiritual life and death. However, the tragedy of a spiritual crisis and threat of death has far greater consequences because of its eternal dimension.

Revival means "to bring back to life," "consciousness." Of course, there is the entire world of the unsaved never yet born of God. A sinner cannot be revived spiritually. There is nothing to revive. A person who has never known God must have a new birth, a creative miracle. Revival is a miracle of spiritual resuscitation.

> **"Revival is a miracle of spiritual resuscitation."**

Revival does not begin with the unconscious or the spiritually dead. It begins with spiritual caretakers. It begins with those who are spiritually alert, know the truth, and are not ashamed to call on God and people to help. They are not concerned about themselves. Their whole focus is on the desperate condition of the person they are responsible for.

My experience in the airport terminal underscores this truth. Nice, proper, and perhaps bashful people suddenly are dramatically changed by the truth. Their actions say, "My husband, my friend, this valuable human being is in danger of being lost to me. I don't care what people think or where we are. I'll do or say anything to bring him back to life." Revival will begin in America when a few spiritually alert people recognize the true spiritual condition about them and begin to call on God in desperate faith.

There are no limitations on the ability of God Almighty to revive His people and His church. He is able to revive a drowsy, apathetic, tired believer. He has power to resuscitate a church that is dead. He has the supernatural ability to reconnect a bunch of dry, disconnected bones, breathe life into them, and make them into a mighty army. God has always chosen to use human instrumentality. Revival will begin when someone becomes aware of the true spiritual condition of the people and has the faith to believe an unconscious, dysfunctional, or even disjointed part of the body of Christ can not only be revived but also become a mighty force for the cause of Christ.

My greatest concern as I travel this country is the passiveness of individuals and churches; they show no signs of spiritual life—no new births, no sense of God's presence, no fruit of the Spirit, no manifestations of the gifts of the Spirit, and clearly no evidence of spiritual productivity. Even more tragic is the lack of concern in parents and family members.

Some time ago, I asked a Pentecostal lady about her family. Her answer was startling: "Oh, they are doing very well. Joe has moved up the corporate ladder, we have a wonderful daughter-in-law, and the grandchildren are absolutely darling. Leonard and I are a bit disappointed they are not going to church right now, but other than that, they are terrific." I was so stunned I experienced a total loss of words (a bit rare). I believe that Pentecostal mother and grandmother articulated nearly everything spiritually wrong in our culture. That woman's family is not doing well at all. They are in imminent danger of losing their souls. Her grandchildren are being robbed of spiritual life. How would she have responded if she discovered her grandchildren were doing very well except the parents were no longer feeding them?

It is time to sound the alarm. Spiritual dysfunction and death can no longer be accepted by moms and dads, pastors and church leaders. The condition is desperate but not hopeless. The diagnosis is grim, but thank God there is a remedy. The message of revival is at once a message of spiritual crisis and supernatural faith.

Do not turn away in despair from spiritual unconsciousness and death. Call on God. Believe God. Pray until life returns. Can you imagine the unspeakable joy if the man in the airport would have revived, opened his eyes, and begun to speak! "Wilt thou not revive us again: that thy people may rejoice in thee?" (Psalm 85:6¹). There is life from heaven, and when it comes, there will be rejoicing.

True Revival Brings Spiritual Wholeness

There is more to life than consciousness or mere existence. Revival is more than an event; it must include a restoration to full health. If the man in the airport lived but was plagued by permanent disabilities, the joy growing out of the initial reviving would be short-lived. His family would be grateful for life but burdened with the responsibility of maintaining life.

The insightful question posed to the man at the pool of Bethesda is critical to a revival of spiritual life and health. "Wilt thou be made whole?" Jesus asked (John 5:6). In other words, "Do you want to continue living in a state of dependence upon others, or do you want to be revived and restored to a state of wholeness?" Jesus wanted the man to decide between the luxury of being served because of his helplessness or whether he was ready to be healthy, take care of himself, and be a contributor to the community. The revival we need today must go beyond signs of life to a spiritual quality of life that creates strong and powerful Christians. Otherwise, we will eventually see the day when there will be more people "poolside" than in the harvest field.

Wholeness is soundness. It means every part of the body is functioning properly. When someone has been sick and is restored to health, that one will invariably say, "I feel like a new person." A true revival will have the same effect upon the spiritual body. How we need spiritually sound people who have anointed their eyes with "eyesalve" (cf. Rev. 3:18) and need not be led by others. Oh, how we need people whose spiritual ears are attuned to the voice of God instead of having to receive truth by hearsay and human interpretation. Oh, how we need people with strong hearts beating with compassion, strong minds to discern truth and impact life, strong limbs and muscle tone so they can "run and not be weary, . . . walk and not faint" (Isaiah 40:31, NKJV).

The body of Christ needs to be sound in order to fend off disease and defend itself from the destroyer. This ingredient of revival is too often ignored to the detriment of God's people. Our prayer should be "Restore Your Church, oh Lord, to wholeness." The proof of spiritual wholeness is in the lifestyle of the believer. He or she will be revived and restored not only to *wholeness* but also to *wholesomeness,* a product of holiness. The strong, healthy believer will have wholesome appetites and relationships.

Every true revival in history has been marked by a wholesome spiritual appetite. Suddenly the things once loved are hated, and the things once hated are loved. Holy desires are born in a Holy Ghost revival. There is a hunger to be in the presence of God.

From time to time, I have had the privilege of ministering in a great church known for its Pentecostal fervor and revival atmosphere. The prayer meeting is the largest, best-attended meeting of the week. The services are quite long by American standards—always over two hours and many times close to three. The pastor made a statement that has stayed with me. He said, "When there is true revival, there will be a desire to linger in the presence of God with the people of God. That is the atmosphere and culture of heaven." Then he added these words, "I cannot understand why people who want to go to heaven are anxious to leave the atmosphere of heaven, where God's people are praising and worshiping, to be involved in things and activities that will not be in heaven."

True revival will result in a wholesome relationship with God. There has never been a genuine revival without fervent prayer and obvious communion with the Lord. People are again in right standing with God. When people have a good relationship with others, it is a delight to be in constant communication with them. When I disobeyed my father, I did not want to see him or talk to him; but when I was right with my dad, he was great to be with and I had no problem in expressing my needs and desires to him. The same is true of my Heavenly Father. If the truth were known, many believers need to have their relationship with God revived and restored.

Genuine revival will result in wholesome relationships with others. Time and again the Bible commands us to make certain our relationship with others is right from heaven's point of view. In recent days, we have been hearing of a sovereign move of God on college campuses across America. Many of these colleges are non-Pentecostal, but God's visitation has been marked by students being broken in repentance and asking forgiveness of one another. There is no revival where unwholesome relationships exist, but God is pleased when His children put away impurities and evil communications.

Another mark of genuine revival is a wholesome relationship or attitude toward the world and the things of the world. Greed, avarice, worldly amusements that contaminate the soul, and unholy alliances and friendships are put away—not because of an external force but because of an internal love for God, which makes the world and the things of the world insignificant in comparison to God's kingdom.

It would be difficult to overemphasize the important part revival plays in restoring the believer to a *normal* quality of spiritual life. The American church must be strong and healthy in every cell to fulfill its divine purpose and meet the challenge of a spiritually hostile culture.

True Revival Is a Revival of Spiritual Power

It is not enough to simply exist, nor is it enough to be strong and healthy. If the believer and the Church are to fulfill their destiny, they must become a resource for God's power to flow into this world to change the world.

Our man on the airport floor must not only be revived to consciousness and health, he must also be revived to productivity if the joy of the household is to be complete. What good would it be for the revived man to be satisfied just to build a strong body, eat well, work out at the gym, but never go back to work, never contribute to the family, and never make a living again?

I fear greatly that we are satisfied in a spiritual sense with body building. The ultimate use of a body and a brain is to accomplish something. It would be a terrible waste for a person with a fine mind to go through medical school, earn an M.D., and then just hang it on the wall and never practice medicine. What a waste to build a beautiful body and then stand in front of mirrors and admire it. We are in this world to do something, not just be something. True revival is a revival of power—God's power—for God's purpose: to destroy the works of the devil and to make disciples of those whom those devilish works were destroying.

Power without purpose is a waste. It simply dissipates and is lost. Hydroelectric power has a purpose, but if that purpose is not connected to the need it was created to meet, the water just keeps flowing over the dam, the generators keep roaring—but the lights do not come on, the heat dies in the furnace, and all electronic communication ceases.

> " **Power without purpose is a waste. It dissipates.** "

Pentecostal power has a purpose, but when that power is not flowing through the channels of divine purpose, the power is misused, misapplied, and misunderstood. True revival reconnects the power of Pentecost to divine purpose. That purpose is to bring the living Christ into the world through a witness so powerful and indisputable, with signs and wonders, that it will bring life out of death. We will receive power after the Holy Ghost is come upon us, and we will be effective witnesses (Acts 1:8).

First, you will have power in *Jerusalem*. We will be witnesses for Christ in our present locale. It will be a powerful witness replacing religion gone formal, gone bad. Can you imagine the cynicism of people in Jerusalem? It was a city full of religion and tradition. I am certain there had been scandals in the clergy, a crass use of money in religious practices to line the pockets of the priests. Without doubt, the temple services were a farce, dead in performance and meaning. Into this dead, religious, corrupt church came the people of God with a new message, endued with a new spirit: Jesus is alive again, and we are His witnesses. With that power came a tremendous change. Jerusalem was turned upside-down for God. A powerful, new faith became an option for a dead, formal tradition.

You will have power in *Judea*, the suburbs, the place of wealth and materialism. You will have power where the Church had nearly died and where even the cold, religious ceremonies were no longer attended by the great percentage. Into this self-satisfied, nominal Church population came the power of God.

You will have power in *Samaria*, where racial hatred simmers on the front burner. Where once you would not even think of going, you are now sent in the power of the Holy Ghost to ride roughshod over prejudice and bring the message of peace and reconciliation.

You will have power *throughout the whole world.* There is no place so remote, no tribe so bound by Satan's power, no witchcraft so supernatural, no false religion so demonic, that it can withstand the power of God coursing from a Church full of the Holy Spirit.

The time has come to face the truth. We are not making an impact upon our world because we are at fault. We who know the Lord and have grown up in Pentecost have settled for what is and not for what can be through an obedient, powerful Church. The devil has had his way in the world, in our families, and in our churches long enough. We need a revival, a revival fueled by Pentecostal power, but it will begin only as we acknowledge our true spiritual need, repent of our own pride and self-will, to rise up in the name of God, with the Word of God, in the Spirit of God, to lift Jesus Christ before the human soul and the human condition.

Implanting Mission and Vision in Others

Tommy Barnett

In my many years of ministry, beginning when I was young and preaching to empty pews in my father's church, I have learned some in-house imperatives that have revolutionized my life and churches. In retrospect, I have heeded the message Albert Einstein brought when lecturing his erudite contemporaries. Everything must be simple and no simpler.

Pastors tend to complicate their mission and vision. Everything needed for a minister and the ministry is presented in the Word of God. The simplicity is revealed through the Holy Spirit, our resident truth teacher who graciously unfolds the hidden meaning of the Bible.

Great works do not just happen, they are caused. Vision, likewise, is caught, as well as taught. Proverbs relates, "Where there is no vision, the people perish" (Proverbs 29:18[1]). I am convinced that where there are no people the vision perishes. Why? Because in the New Testament, people were added to the church daily. Such a challenge has become my mandate.

Building a Growing Church

Crisscrossing our great country and traveling around the world scores of times, I have been asked familiar questions: How do you build a growing church? Where do you find dedicated staff? How do you prepare? Where do you discover your mission or cultivate your dreams and vision?

Visionaries act. Academics study. As pastors we are to interface the two. My personal vision has been clear. It is a combination of my spiritual destiny and an intensive library that includes classics—tapes and volumes and study books. I believe in visions, dreams, and goals, as long as they are God's goals, and the dreams and vision of His heart. If they are in the plan of God, I write them on the tablet of my heart, and then test to be sure they will glorify God. If convinced, I go for them with zeal, conviction, and the confidence that "He who has begun a good work in you will complete it until the day of Jesus Christ" (Philippians 1:6, NKJV).

> **" Everything for building a church is in your house. "**

I often talk of visions and dreams because I am aware of how important they are. Jacob dreamed, "and behold a ladder set up on the earth, and the top of it reached to heaven" (Genesis 28:12). Joseph interpreted dreams while he was imprisoned. On another occasion the psalmist said, "When the Lord turned again the captivity of Zion, we were like them that dream" (Psalm 126:1). Daniel had dreams. Throughout history we see dreamers. Columbus had a dream of a new world where he hoped to establish a church and a nation dedicated to God.

Dreams often precede mission and vision. Of course, obstacles may be encountered, but Paul imparted some good advice: "We do not lose heart, but though our outer man is decaying, yet our inner man is being renewed day by day" (2 Corinthians 4:16, NASB). When the inner man is renewed, the character is strengthened and the spirit becomes vibrant and alive. I have learned that when God meets us in our imagination, He will not only show us things that are not yet seen by natural eyes, He will also call the things that are not as though they are. It is better defined as revelation. Henry David Thoreau wrote some inspiring words. "If one advances confidently in the direction of his dreams, and endeavors to live the life which he has imagined, he will meet with a success unexpected in common hours. He will put some things behind, will pass an invisible boundary; new, universal, and more liberal laws will begin to establish themselves around and within him; . . . and he will live with the license of a higher order of beings."[2]

Our Lord enables those whom He calls. Never despise the day of small things, but never let small things impede your vision of greatness for God. The principle of daily adding people to the church is proven. How? I have found that everything you need to build a church is in your house. The key to implanting that vision is not complicated. Tell the dream. Make it clear. Get people to write it down. Believe in people. Make them want to do it. Convince them they can do it. Get excited. Enthusiasm is half the battle.

A Miracle in Every House

Let me assure you, there is a miracle in every house. Early accept the vision that everything you need to build your great church may be found within your church house, seated in your congregation, no matter how small. This truth is liberating and it works. Pastors tend to look everywhere except among their own people to find the human resources needed to accomplish great exploits for God. From the time I started growing churches, I learned the lesson of looking within the congregation.

Come with me to Scripture and a simple, life-changing vignette in 2 Kings 4. The story revolves around a destitute widow with two sons. She was not unlike homeless women on the street today who have no place to turn. She was penniless, her husband died leaving her no means of support, and there was famine in the land. Her situation was made more desperate by the practice in those days of taking children as payment for debt. There was no welfare system to meet her need and no bureaucracy to provide food stamps. She epitomized a problem, wrapped in a dilemma.

> **To accomplish great exploits for God I learned the lesson of looking in the congregation.**

From this narrative I have formulated ten great principles, which some have called the ten commandments for making a miracle. As you study them, never forget that God is the source of miracles. We are His currency; He uses our resourcefulness. Romans 11:36 spells it out: "Of Him, and through Him, and to Him, are all things." He is our source, resource, and goal. Consider these principles in defining your vision and building your mission.

1. *Know where to go when you don't know what to do.* This widow's husband was described as a "son of the prophets." He had obviously worked in the temple, and she was aware there was a poor box. After exhausting her own cupboards she set out to find the man of God, Elisha. She knew what to do. In the past Elisha had been part of a miracle that supplied a whole army. He had subdued a takeover attempt by the rebellious people of Moab, yet he found time to help meet the needs and heal the hurts of this mother. To Elisha, she and her children were not just disposable people of the street, but individuals loved by God. Never forget, the ground is level at the foot of the cross.

Knowing where to turn when you do not know what to do should be the simplest equation of our ministry. "Behold, I lay in Zion a chief corner stone, elect, precious: and he that believeth on him shall not be confounded" (1 Peter 2:6). God delights in showing himself strong on our behalf. As we go to Him in prayer, believing, He answers because He is touched by the feeling of our infirmities and needs. Thus, we need not be confounded.

2. *Do not seek an earthly messiah.* How wise Elisha was when he encouraged the widow to look about her house for in-house resources. Paltry as those resources may have been, his wisdom directed her not to rely on the poor box in the temple, nor beg on the streets, nor accept the charity of a few coins that would soon be spent. No, he pointed her to the source of her needed miracle. It was God, the multiplier. Elisha had experienced that little is much when God is in it. He was well versed in godly counsel.

3. *Find out what is in the house.* Human nature tends to look at a glass as half empty rather than half full. The man of God discovered the destitute woman still possessed a small jar of oil. She had been focusing so much on what she did not have that she automatically answered "nothing" when he questioned what she had in her house. Then she remembered something, although she thought it insignificant. In spite of her almost barren pantry God could take her nothing and make it something for His glory and her good. He specializes in taking nothingness and linking it with His almightiness. The divine connection causes great things to transpire.

Within every church is the seed of a miracle. People on the surface may appear to have little to offer. But they may be deeply rooted in just what you need to birth another ministry. Someone may be able to drive people who have handicaps or who lack transportation to church, or they may lend their support to outreach and evangelism.

4. *Do not be blinded by negativism, but move on to the positive.* When viewing that half-empty glass, I prefer to believe I am pouring into the container rather than drinking from it. Therefore the glass will be refilled. That is what God wants to do with us and our vision for ministry. He is in the business of opening the windows of heaven and pouring out His Word, His Spirit, and His love until we so overflow that the excess finds new channels of blessing.

It is often natural for us, like the widow, to say, "I have nothing" (cf. John 6:9), but then the supernatural reminds us, "nothing . . . but a small jar of oil." Everything great starts with small things. Faith does not deny present reality. It acknowledges that all things are possible with God. Faith changes perspective.

Miracles begin with faith. It takes faith, an action based on belief, to break through the nothing and see the seed of something and begin cultivating it. Discover the Elishas in your congregation and the faithful members who have varying degrees of skill for multiplying your oil. You will be surprised and enriched.

5. *Faith is not faith until you do something—action is required.* Faith without works is dormant. Diagnosis is no cure although it is a step toward health. The widow was told to send out her sons to find empty vessels and not just "a few." It was an act of faith and most likely an ironic, inane confusion to the neighbors who supplied the empty jars.

I am often reminded that two-thirds of the letters in *God* spell "go." The first two letters of *gospel* are "go." A verb of action always starts an avalanche of activity. Every supernatural victory won by Israel when they finally entered the Promised Land under Joshua's leadership was accompanied by some corresponding action on their part. They modeled faith that offered their own resources. Then God multiplied and blessed.

6. *Do not put limitations on God's ability to provide.* God instructed David in shepherding His people; so God feeds us according to the

> " **Our nothingness linked with His almightiness causes great things to transpire.** "

integrity of His heart and leads us by the skillfulness of His hands (cf. Psalm 78:72). I often wonder if the woman had any intuition about those borrowed jars. Had she and her sons been presented with the God of Abraham, Isaac, and Jacob by her husband? As husband and father had he been faithful to teach those entrusted to him in his house?

Each of our homes is a place to build faith and bring to reality the biblical principle that "one generation shall praise [the Lord's] works to another" (Psalm 145:4). You cannot do great things for God if you do not attempt great things for Him in your home or in your church. God reveals himself to us according to our expectations or, conversely, our lack of them. Never neglect your family.

At the Phoenix church when we were preparing to build, the board of elders wanted the church to seat ten thousand. I felt more comfortable with three thousand. They had more faith to fill the empty pews. Then I watched with one of my deacons Pat Robertson's *700 Club* program. Pat's words were piercing: "You pastors are building your churches too small." He went on to say, "There's a pastor listening just now who is planning far too small." The deacon's elbow was planted firmly in my side. We built for sixty-five hundred. A few years later it proved too small. Ten thousand was the right size. We are still growing!

7. *Shut the door on doubt.* How revealing that the widow was instructed, "'Go in and shut the door behind you and your sons'" (2 Kings 4:4, NASB). Elisha had been through the scenarios before. He insisted she shut out the skeptics and be deaf to doubt. Faith is to be in God alone, not faith in the fear of failing. I know many pastors who have been discouraged and had their expectations crushed because of dream-killers in their lives. Never forget, "'Your Father who sees in secret will Himself reward you openly'" (Matthew 6:4, NKJV). Here was an opportunity for the widow to put her past need behind her. God was about to do a new thing. In a quiet place, distractions are minimized and the doubting Thomases are disallowed. God can do everything . . . but fail.

8. *Pour until there is no more.* With empty pots stacked as high as expectations, the widow, heeding the instructions of the man of God, began to pour. Faith was the substance of the pouring, an evidence previously unseen. When she tipped her meager vessel of oil, the miracle began and the pouring indicated "God and I are one in this together." What blessed confidence.

Pastors, pour into your people God's love and great provision. In return they will pour into your church until it overflows. Work with them side by side. Believe in them, encourage them, and they will not fail. Let your enthusiasm be a great motivator. I am convinced Elisha exemplified the faithful God, becoming a model of Father God to that little family of three. It is impossible to "out-pour" God. "He who supplies seed to the sower and bread for food, will supply and multiply your seed for sowing and increase the harvest of your righteousness" (2 Corinthians 9:10, NASB).

9. *Move beyond the miracle.* "The earth is the Lord's, and all its fullness" (Psalm 24:1, NKJV). As His heirs and children we are offered every good and perfect gift. The widow, having seen what God accomplished,

was able to pay her bills and have funds to live on. Surely her boys grew strong having experienced the faithfulness of God. I believe her witness would have been extended to those who gave the empty jars, and their skeptical kindness was repaid by observing their neighbor back on her financial feet.

Miracles are for God's glory, not for our boasting or entertainment. If it were not for God alone, I would have fallen on my face many times. That is why He is the sole recipient of all glory, honor, and praise. He has done great things, and I, as a grateful bystander, remain in awe of who He is and what He has accomplished through this humble pastor. Thus, I move ahead undaunted to outreaches that exceed my ability and resources, knowing that hitherto the Lord has led me and will continue to do so as long as I am faithful to the mission and vision He implanted within me.

10. *Remember that there will always be enough.* One of the profound principles in this gripping story is the line spoken by Elisha to the widow: "'You and your sons can live on what is left'" (2 Kings 4:7). Yes, little signs have great significance. I have often experienced the reality of that statement throughout the years that I have served the Lord. Recently the principle has been reaffirmed with regularity.

Since a young man, I have been burdened for the great cities: New York, Los Angeles, Miami, Philadelphia, and many others. I early envisioned a church that resembled the United Nations: a place where all cultures and races could meet at the feet of Jesus, and where translation of the Word was available; a place where homeless and helpless, the disenfranchised and gang members, could come and find the true meaning of life. I have preached "What's in Your House?" and commensurately challenged the body of Christ to enlarge their circle of love. We can no longer ignore the inner cities. We must proclaim Jesus to them.

In late 1994 God opened the door to that dream and vision in Los Angeles. Through the mission assistance of the Assemblies of God, the congregation at our first location consisted of forty-eight dear Filipinos. I had searched for a famous man of God or great preacher to network with me in this challenge, but God had someone in my own house. My youngest son, Matthew, was

> **If it were not for God, I would have fallen on my face many times. I am a grateful bystander.**

called to copastor with me—a miracle and joy to this father's heart. In late 1995 we were averaging five thousand for the glory of God.

The in-house philosophy has never been more operative. Existing inner-city ministries have partnered with us, bringing the skill and people in their houses to help in this multiculture mission. Churches, districts, and individuals continue to provide support and encouragement.

After purchasing the historic Queen of Angels Hospital, a Los Angeles landmark abandoned for five years, we discovered among our first five hundred residents the talent and resources we needed to help bring this vision to reality. Within the Los Angeles International Church ("Dream

Center" to almost everyone), a bridge of grace is crossed by uncommon people who have chosen to move among the bikers, low-riders, and untold numbers of empty vessels who seek to be lifted above circumstances and themselves by the power-driven finger of God. We are in miracle territory, experiencing miracle after miracle. We are lifting Christ amid the crossfire of a great city and discovering new converts who are expressing a desire to prepare and become equipped to reach out to other cities of the world. The vision extends as the mission enlarges. It took years for this vision and mission to be fulfilled, but I never lost heart. I encourage you never to waiver, for though your vision tarries, wait for it with expectation from heaven.

I continue to be impressed at the value and mission of the house church as recorded in the New Testament. In early days people met in their own homes around the Lord, in simple worship and praise, reading the scrolls and parchments of God's Word. In isolated places today, there is in-house worship where no church exists and God is sending out giants of faith to proclaim His name to the ends of the earth from those little flocks.

The Great Cities of the World

The setting of the following story was in a first-century, Mediterranean home. It revolves around Onesimus, a slave and property of Philemon. As a model, it challenges me when I consider the great cities of the world. In the early days of the faith, Christians treated their slaves with kindness, according to the instruction given regarding slaves in the Epistles. "Masters, do the same things unto them [the slaves], forbearing threatening: knowing that your Master also is in heaven; neither is there respect of persons with him. . . . Masters, give unto your servants that which is just and equal" (Ephesians 6:9; Colossians 4:1).

Onesimus, the slave in Philemon's house, had been well treated by his owner, yet he had taken advantage of it. When he found he could steal from Philemon, he did just that and then fled to Rome.

There is some supposition as to what happened to this slave in Rome, but historians relate that most likely he became destitute and homeless. In the mercy of God, someone who was an early Christian saw his need and invited him to hear a noted prisoner of Rome. Hearing that the prisoner was named Paul, Onesimus recalled his former master had often talked of Paul and held him in high esteem. He was amazed that Paul was located in the needy city of Rome.

We will not know the whole story of Onesimus until glory, but we do know he found the Lord. He heard the gospel and responded. At some point, he encountered Paul and recounted his past as an unworthy slave of Philemon, confessed his theft, and repented. He told Paul he desired to return to Philemon and serve him as a Christian slave.

Paul wrote a magnificent letter to his friend on behalf of Onesimus, speaking of the runaway slave as "my son" (Philemon 10). Paul offered to put the charges of Onesimus' wrongdoing on his personal account. A marvelous explanation and expression of grace, notice that Paul's letter was addressed to several individuals, including the church in the house of Philemon.

What a day it must have been when Onesimus returned and was restored. A slave became a brother. And such is the vision and mission we have for Los Angeles and the cities of the world. There are a multitude of slaves to sin. Some have had a Christian background. Some have been influenced in the past in their own homes, but made wrong choices. During His life on earth, Jesus chose to identify with poor and destitute people. He lived as one who was homeless, and His ministry was marked by compassion for those in need. Thus, our church in Los Angeles has become a center and spiritual hospital where restoration is a priority—a place where we operate in-house just like churches and missions—winning souls, healing hurts, and meeting needs. Diligently, we daily pour into empty vessels the life-changing message of Jesus Christ. The inner city church has also become a place where mended, broken vessels can serve God with all their hearts.

I have no intention of retiring. I am not sure Christians are given that luxury. My Father works unceasingly, and so must I. My motivating joys are my family, seeing souls saved, listening to my sons preach, and living vicariously through pastors who tell me they are dreaming new dreams, staking their claims, and witnessing multiplied miracles to accompany their vision and mission. I rejoice and identify with them as they discover miracles in their houses, miracles that have transformed their work for God.

A Miracle in Your House

Discover first the miracle inside you, then help others develop their miracles and continue enlarging your circles of love in your city and inner city. Let biblical faith spring up in you as a spiritual activator, a lifted latch that allows God's blessing to come pouring down in such abundance that you can pour your excess into others. Faithfully and diligently take note of what is in your house, your congregation, and when you discover those individuals, work with them, side by side, for the glory of God. Your mission and vision will increase. It will become fruitful and multiply. Then, in return, seek to implant vision and mission in the lives of others. Freely receive and freely give.

"Whatever is born of God overcomes the world. And this is the victory that has overcome the world—our faith" (1 John 5:4, NKJV).

Seven Steps to a Pentecostal Revival

David A. Womack

F ew words in our Pentecostal vocabulary carry the emotional impact of *revival*. At its mention, many of us feel an uncomfortable tension between longing for what the church should be and laboring over its present reality. As a result, we refer to it broadly in terms of the greater Church, redefine it narrowly to allow for temporary self-gratification, or relegate it to short spans of evangelistic emphasis. Yet we are left vaguely dissatisfied and yearning for a fresh spiritual awakening.

A Definition of Revival

One encyclopedia calls revival "a predominantly North American Protestant phenomenon in which itinerant preachers exhort their hearers to accept forgiveness of personal sins through faith in Jesus Christ and to commit themselves to spiritual self-discipline and religious exercises."[1] By this definition, a revival is a scheduled church event with a special speaker.

This definition, however, fails to describe the real significance of the spiritual awakening we are praying for. The object of our prayer is not a fleeting condition but an enduring relationship with God. The fact that we have been baptized in the Holy Spirit heightens that inner desire to "know him, and the power of his resurrection" (Philippians 3:10[2]). Here is a better definition of what we mean by revival: "Revival is a spiritual state in which believers draw nearer to God, repent and purify themselves according to biblical standards of holiness, are filled with the Holy Spirit, expect and experience supernatural manifestations, and cooperate together to glorify God, edify one another, and evangelize the lost for Jesus Christ."[3]

The New Testament presents much the same idea in James 4:8–10: "Draw nigh to God, and he will draw nigh to you. Cleanse your hands, ye sinners; and purify your hearts, ye double minded. Be afflicted, and mourn, and weep: let your laughter be turned to mourning, and your joy to heaviness. Humble yourselves in the sight of the Lord, and he shall lift you up." This is a call to church people because James wrote these words to believers—"my brethren" (1:2).

The Old Testament gives a similar appeal in 2 Chronicles 7:14. "If my people, which are called by my name, shall humble themselves, and pray, and seek my face, and turn from their wicked ways; then will I hear from heaven, and will forgive their sin, and will heal their land." Thus, revival is a restoration of biblical relationship with God. It should not be an occasional phenomenon but the normal spiritual state of a church that identifies itself with New Testament Christianity.

Three Types of Revival

We may distinguish three types of revival, which we may compare to three kinds of ocean waves: ripples, swells, and tidal waves. We may further recognize cycles, returning like the tides.

The Local-Event Revival. The first type of revival is a scheduled event such as a local evangelistic campaign, usually with an itinerant evangelist. Such ripples of revival have been a vital part of the Pentecostal Movement because we place so much emphasis on personal experience. In the past, such meetings would continue for a week or more, but today they seldom last more than three or four days. Many such events are not true revivals but a series of meetings on a theme intended to educate, entertain, or refresh the congregation. Seminars on Christian living or family financial planning have their place, but they do not replace old-fashioned revival services with enthusiastic singing, anointed preaching, and tear-stained altars.

The Spiritual-Surge Revival. The second type of revival is more like an ocean swell, which begins far out at sea and builds until it breaks on the shore in a sensational display of surf and spray. Such a revival is a local or regional surge of spirituality that generally has a life span of about three years. Examples in the Pentecostal Movement would be the 1901 outpouring of the Holy Spirit in Topeka or the 1906 Azusa Street Revival in Los Angeles. People tend to see such times of spiritual blessing as spontaneous and sovereign acts of God, but the truth is that God always desires our enthusiastic response and is ready to bless us whenever we loosen our grip on the world and open our hearts to Him. "I am the Lord," God says, "I change not" (Malachi 3:6). If God is constant in His desire for our revived state, then we must be the variable. Indeed, the short life span of most revivals may be attributed entirely to human factors. These spiritual surges result from a growing hunger for more of God until a strong desire breaks forth in fervent worship and evangelization.

Several phenomena contribute to the short-term nature of such revivals. First, we cannot maintain a highly emotional atmosphere indefinitely. People become emotionally sated, and as the level of intensity wanes we try to regain by human means the atmosphere of excitement that first came from spontaneous responses. Second, we are apt to major on the joy of revival rather than admitting that God works through a wide variety of human reactions. Revivals often begin with weeping rather than rejoicing. Third, not everyone in a congregation will make an equal commitment, so with time some will tire of the intensity and call for a return to what they consider normal Christian behavior. Fourth, revivals draw new people into the church. As their needs are met, their very satisfaction with the church will diminish the hunger that first caused the revival. Once it begins to wane, the revival atmosphere dissipates quickly, and the church must go into a new phase of training and assimilation of the results. This type of revival will have a beginning, a middle, and an end. In times of general revival these surges will happen often and in many locations, but in spiritual drought their occurrences are rare.

> ## "
> The spiritual needs of our times cry out for more than local surges of religious intensity. We need a tidal wave . . .
> "

The Reformational Revival. The spiritual needs of our times cry out for more than local surges of religious intensity. We need a tidal wave of revitalized spirituality that will fill our horizon and come crashing onto the shore with such force that it will change the whole religious landscape, carry away the silt and sand of our sinfulness, and restore the solid foundations of biblical Christianity.

We need more than another outburst of American revivalism; the times call for a move of God on a grand scale such as occurred in the Reformation. There could be many evangelistic events and powerful surges of spirituality, but they would happen so often that we would experience deep and lasting changes in believers, churches, and church movements. Best of all, such a revival would bring people by the millions into the kingdom of God. The sixteenth-century Reformation was "a movement within Western Christendom to purge the church of medieval abuses and to restore the doctrines and practices that the reformers believed conformed with the Bible and the New Testament model of the church."[4] It may be argued that church history since the early sixteenth century has been a step-by-step return to the foundation of original Christianity.

The Pentecostal Revival, which with its companion Charismatic Renewal, has become the dominant church movement of the twentiethth century. There were many local and regional manifestations of the revival, but it was not dependent on any single group or culture. Quite apart from any human planning or opposition, it continued to break out anew in different areas and among different people. It was truly a tidal wave that struck the shore with such power that it forever changed the spiritual landscape of the world.

In addition to the three kinds of revival waves—ripples, swells, and tidal waves—some scholars believe that revivals come in recurrent cycles like the tides. Since God always "will have all men to be saved, and to come unto the knowledge of the truth" (1 Timothy 2:4), we must conclude that the cyclical nature of revivals springs more from human inconsistency than from any ebb and flow on God's part.

James Burns said in *The Laws of Revival,* "Times of awakening in the individual mostly occur at times of transition, especially from one stage of development to another. Spiritual awakenings coincide with profound change in the social or political life of the people."[5] The Great Awakening of the eighteenth century swept the country before and during the Revolutionary War era through the ministries of such preachers as Jonathan Edwards and George Whitefield. The Second Great Awakening came at the turn of the nineteeth century, gathering large crowds in frontier America. Tom Phillips said of that revival, "By its very name, The Second Great Awakening proved that revival could happen again. If evangelism was an ongoing command, revival was a periodic movement meant to bring a nation back into a right relationship with God."[6] Another awakening was the Great Prayer Revival of 1857–1859, and the greatest revival in numbers of people saved was the twentieth-century Pentecostal Movement.

Although revivals may seem to come in cycles, what we may be seeing is a long pattern of return to New Testament Christianity. Martin Luther rediscovered that "the just shall live by faith."[7] John and Charles Wesley became aware that salvation is a personal experience. American revivalism restored anointed evangelistic preaching. And the Pentecostal Movement called for a full return to New Testament spiritual experiences, including salvation, the baptism in the Holy Spirit, divine healing, and the second coming of Christ (sometimes called the Four Cardinal Doctrines but really four experiences available to every believer). Revivals may recur like the tides, but there is no fixed cycle of years. An awakening comes when spiritual and social conditions are so bad and people so desperate that Christians cry out to God for a fresh moving of His Spirit.

What Must Be Revived

The word *revival* does not appear in the Bible. The verb *revive* occurs eight times in seven verses in the King James Version, five times in four verses in the New International Version, and a few more times in the New American Standard Bible.[8] Revivals occurred in the Old Testament, but throughout most of the New Testament period believers were still in their primary experiences with no need for revival. The Day of Pentecost was not a revival but the very birth of the Church. Some sixty-five years later, however, John had to write to the church in Ephesus that it had forsaken its first love (Revelation 2:1–5). After complimenting the Ephesus church on its many good qualities, the Lord said through John, "Nevertheless I have somewhat against thee, because thou hast left thy first love" (Revelation 2:4). The Greek verb translated *left* meant "to go away or forsake."

In its beginning, the Ephesian church was fanatically aflame for Christ. When Paul laid hands on its first believers, "the Holy Ghost came on them; and they spake with tongues, and prophesied" (Acts 19:6). So powerful was the move of God that within two years "all they which dwelt in Asia heard the word of the Lord Jesus, both Jews and Greeks. And God wrought special miracles by the hands of Paul" (Acts 19:10–11). In just two years they evangelized the entire province of Asia Minor: demographically ("all they which dwelt"), geographically ("in Asia"), and ethnically ("both Jews and Greeks"). This pervasive evangelism was accompanied by "special miracles by the hands of Paul." So strong was the work of God that the silversmiths who made heathen images started a riot and a period of persecution against the apostles. That was the church at Ephesus when it did its "first works." As years went by, the Ephesians forsook their earlier fervor in favor of a more moderate and less confrontational style, until they were unable to pass on their passion to the next generation.

A Threefold Solution

The Lord prescribed a threefold solution to the fallen church: "Remember therefore from whence thou art fallen, and repent, and do the first works; or else I will come unto thee quickly, and will remove thy candlestick out of his place, except thou repent" (Revelation 2:5). They were to *remember, repent,* and *repeat.*

Remember. The answer to the spiritual need of the fallen Ephesians was not in some new trend or innovation but in returning to their original experiences in Christ. They had to admit their condition and remember their first state. Yet, they were having a generational problem. The people who had spoke in tongues, prophesied, and witnessed signs and wonders were either old or dead, and the younger people had not experienced what their fathers had known. We must remember! And that backward look will place upon us new demands for personal experience with God.

Repent. The act of repentance is the hardest part of revival. We expect a spiritual awakening to come as an outburst of joy, while in fact it first manifests itself through tears of repentance. Are we ready to admit that our lack of revival is sin? Can we acknowledge that an unrevived church is a fallen church? Until we deal with these issues and ask forgiveness for our sins, we will not see revival.

Repeat. As if remembering and repenting were not enough, the Lord added, "And do the first works." It was not enough to recall the good old days or even to ask forgiveness for having fallen. The Ephesians had to return to what they used to be, to do what they used to do. Once more, they were to speak in other tongues and prophesy. They were to return to the fiery-eyed intensity of faith, practice what once took the gospel to their whole region, and experience again the signs and wonders of divine healing, deliverance, and other miracles. These biblical characteristics will return again to a church that remembers, repents, and repeats its first works.

The Lord added an "or else" clause to these commands: "Or else I will come unto thee quickly [suddenly], and will remove thy candlestick out of its place, except thou repent." This passage refers to the Menorah, the seven-branched golden Lampstand in the Tabernacle and Temple. There were three pieces of sacred furniture in the Holy Place: the Lampstand, the Table of Shewbread, and the Altar of Incense. Symbolically, they represent the three main elements of the inner spiritual life: the baptism in the Holy Spirit, the nourishing of the Word, and the life of perpetual prayer. All three had to be replenished regularly. If the Ephesian church would not remember, repent, and repeat its first works, the Lord would come suddenly and remove His anointing!

The Next Seven Steps

No single key unlocks the door to revival. The need takes something like a combination lock, for which a series of factors or steps must be done in correct sequence. Let us consider the following seven steps to revival.

Step 1: Desire. Some claim that prayer is the first step to revival, but such is not the case. The kind of prayer that brings a spiritual awakening is a strongly motivated and sharply focused crying out to God. The first step must be a strong desire to be revived. Psalm 10:17 says, "Lord, thou hast heard the desire of the humble: thou wilt prepare their heart, thou wilt cause thine ear to hear."

In one of the most beautiful passages on spiritual desire, the Psalmist says, "As the hart panteth after the water brooks, so panteth my soul after thee, O God. My soul thirsteth for God, for the living God" (Psalm 42:1–2). Revival does not come until we want it more than anything else in the world. Pentecostals sang, "Take this whole world, but give me Jesus." Our Lord said, "Blessed are they which do hunger and thirst after righteousness: for they shall be filled" (Matthew 5:6). Then in Mark 11:24 He made it clear that desire precedes answered prayer: "What things soever ye desire, when ye pray, believe that ye receive them, and ye shall have them" (Mark 11:24). We are to desire, pray, believe, and receive. Desire must be the driving force behind our prayers for revival.

> **Unlocking the door to revival is like working a combination lock.**

Step 2: Prayer. It takes a combination of different kinds of prayer to bring revival. Paul wrote of "supplications, prayers, intercessions, and giving of thanks" (1 Timothy 2:1). Supplications are a nonverbal crying out to God from the depths of our soul, often "with groanings which cannot be uttered" (Romans 8:26) or by praying in other tongues. Prayers are verbal requests and other expressions to God. Intercessions are earnest prayers for the needs of other people, often involving both verbal and nonverbal pouring out of the soul. And thanksgiving is praise to God for who He is and what He has done. Desire-driven prayers are fervent expressions of faith. If "faith is the substance of things hoped for, the evidence of things not seen" (Hebrews 11:1), then such prayers must express honest belief that the revival indeed will come despite any apparent evidence to the contrary. Psalm 85:6–7 gives us an example of such prayer: "Wilt thou not revive us again: that thy people may rejoice in thee? Show us thy mercy, O Lord, and grant us thy salvation."

Step 3: Repentance. An ironic truth about revival is that the quest for it can go awry at any of the steps required to reach it. For example, the desire for revival can be turned from a hunger for God to a seeking of physical or emotional manifestations for their own sake. Prayer can easily turn to an excessive introspection and produce a withdrawal from the very world we are called to reach. After a stage of honest self-examination before God, our prayers, to be effective, must result in repentance to God and confession of faults to one another. There must follow a deeper commitment to Jesus Christ in preparation for creative worship, miracle-working, and soul-winning. Paul said, "Confess your faults one to another, and pray one for another, that ye may be healed. The effectual fervent prayer of a righteous man availeth much" (James 5:16).

Many believe Isaiah already had written five chapters of his book when he saw the Lord high and lifted up. Yet, when he experienced the pure presence of God, he repented of his sinfulness. "Woe is me! for I am undone; because I am a man of unclean lips, and I dwell in the midst of a people of unclean lips: for mine eyes have seen the King, the Lord of hosts" (Isaiah 6:5).

> **"Holiness and righteousness differ sharply."**

Prayer driven by an intense desire to know God intimately will lead to a personal awareness of the power and presence of God. This in turn will lead to repentance, by which we receive forgiveness of sins. We come face to face with the cross of Jesus Christ and His sacrifice for our sins, for "to him that knoweth to do good, and doeth it not, to him it is sin" (James 4:17). Repentance can go amiss by a failure to change the behavior we have asked forgiveness for. The New Testament word for repentance means a change of heart, or mind. An insincere repentance is not repentance at all, nor will it achieve its intended results.

Step 4: Holiness and Righteousness. Out of our desires, prayers, and repentance will come a change to a more godly lifestyle. James 4:4 asks, "Know ye not that the friendship of the world is enmity with God?" Paul wrote, "Come out from among them, and be ye separate, saith the Lord, and touch not the unclean thing; and I will receive you" (2 Corinthians 6:17). Of course, revived believers will not commit such outright sins as those listed in the Ten Commandments, though they will agree less on certain behaviors not specifically mentioned in the Bible. Nevertheless, the closer we get to God the more we will release our hold on the world. There are some things that spiritually sensitized Christians will not do, places they will not go, and things they will not say because of their heightened reverence for God and His Word.

There is a sharp difference between holiness and righteousness. The first, also called sanctification, is a separation to God and from the world. The furnishings and utensils of the Tabernacle were separated from common use and dedicated solely to God and His service. That is holiness, the committed knowledge that we belong to God alone. Righteousness is toward people. God is righteous because He treats us justly. The revived Christian will demonstrate both holiness toward God and righteousness toward people. Jesus said, "Thou shalt love the Lord thy God with all thy heart, and with all thy soul, and with all thy mind, and with all thy strength: this is the first commandment. And the second is like, namely this, Thou shalt love thy neighbor as thyself" (Mark 12:30–31). The first commandment speaks of holiness and the second, of righteousness.

Jesus Christ will return for "a glorious church, not having spot, or wrinkle, or any such thing; but that it should be holy and without blemish" (Ephesians 5:27). This does not mean that revival can come only to a perfect church. The revived church will continually repeat all the steps of desire, prayer, repentance, holiness/righteousness, and those steps to come.

Step 5: Evangelization. A repentant church whose sins have been forgiven and its people sanctified (i.e., made holy in God's sight) will be a convert-making church. Neither a lack of love nor hypocrisy will be present to repulse or turn away new people. If the backslidden Ephesians forsook their first love, then the restoration of love must be at the core of the revived state. There will be a love for the Lord, for His church, and for the lost. Marginal or non-Pentecostals often fear that open praise and spiritual manifestations will drive away prospective converts, but exactly the opposite is the case—the largest and fastest-growing churches in the world are those that most emphasize praise and response to God.

The salvation of souls is the ultimate purpose of revival. Any so-called revival that does not reach out in love to the lost and bring them into the kingdom of God is a revival gone wrong. How easily a revival can turn from its divine mission of soul-winning to an egocentric celebration of self-gratification! It feels good to be revived, but every revival service is a preparation of the believers to carry the gospel to the world. The most common way for evangelization to go awry is to fail to assimilate converts into the church. We cannot really say we have saved a lost soul until we have the person safely in the security of the family of God.

Step 6: Signs and Wonders. In the last verses of the Gospel of Mark, Jesus told His followers, "Go ye into all the world, and preach the gospel to every creature" (Mark 16:15). Those who would believe would be saved, and those who would not would be lost (verse 16). He then said in verses 17 and 18, "These signs shall follow them that believe; In my name shall they cast out devils; they shall speak with new tongues; they shall take up serpents; and if they drink any deadly thing, it shall not hurt them; they shall lay hands on the sick, and they shall recover."[9] In His name they would speak in tongues, cast out devils, receive divine protection from dangers in nature (such as snakebites) and mankind (such as poisonings), and lay their hands on the sick and have them recover.

> **A repentant church will be a convert-making church.**

Jack Deere, in *Surprised by the Power of the Spirit,* said, "There is a distinction between signs and wonders and the gift of healing. Signs and wonders are an outpouring of miracles specifically connected with revival and the proclamation of the gospel. The gift of healing is given to the church for its edification (1 Corinthians 12:7) and is not necessarily connected with revival or an abundance of miracles."[10] A revived church is characterized by all the gifts of the Spirit: the word of wisdom, the word of knowledge, faith, gifts of healing, working of miracles, prophecy, discernment of spirits, different kinds of tongues, and interpretation of tongues (1 Corinthians 12:8–10). We Pentecostals avoid overcategorizing supernatural events, for God may use any of the gifts to bring people to himself. The difference between signs and wonders and gifts of healing may be only in the quantity of miracles performed during any time or event.

A revived church will see an increase of supernatural healings, deliverances, miracles, and other gifts; and sometimes there may occur a spectacular outburst of miracles to bring people to Christ. Jesus tested the nobleman's faith, saying, "Except ye see signs and wonders, ye will not believe" (John 4:48). But many people do believe when they see miracles. The main problem with signs and wonders is that some people will use them to put on a show rather than bring glory to Christ, thus causing the unsaved to doubt and fail to accept the gospel. A ministry of healing or other miracles requires a deep dedication to Christ and a humility of spirit.

Step 7: Celebration. A true revival develops into a veritable explosion of joy! Upon feeling their own liberation from sin, witnessing the salvation of the lost, and seeing miracles of healing and deliverance before their very eyes, believers often break forth in shouts of praise, joyful singing, and enthusiastic talking about Jesus. They arrive at church early and leave late. And they require a little more room in the pew than the average churchgoer as they clap their hands, reach around to shake hands, or lift up their hands to the Lord in praise. The Bible abounds with appeals to worship the Lord wholeheartedly and out loud. One favorite example is Psalm 98:4—"Make a joyful noise unto the Lord, all the earth: make a loud noise, and rejoice, and sing praise." Such worship may bother unrevived Christians, but it is biblical.

Some pastors are afraid to allow spontaneous outbreaks of praise in their churches and will quote Paul's words, "Let all things be done decently and in order" (1 Corinthians 14:40). Let us not forget that this was said to a church that was having *more* than three messages in tongues and interpretation, or prophecy, in a single service! A revived church must have a revived pastor who is in the Spirit and knows what is of God, the flesh, or the devil. Attempts to limit the spontaneous responses of the people for fear that things might get out of control are like pouring water on a fire. The wise, Spirit-led pastor will know when to encourage a behavior, when to discourage it, and when to gently lead his congregation in true uninhibited worship. The worst thing that can happen to a celebration-style church is that the people may turn from evangelization to self-gratification. We should not worship to please ourselves but to please and glorify God.

Keeping Revival Alive

We must learn to keep alive the spirit of revival. Each church and the whole Pentecostal Movement will go through phases of growth and the assimilation of converts. Human emotions will rise and fall like the tides. But the sense of being in God's presence, remaining holy in His sight, and doing His will must not diminish. There will be times of joy in our salvation and times of weeping over the lost, but the revival must go on.

"Wilt thou not revive us again: that thy people may rejoice in thee? Show us thy mercy, O Lord, and grant us thy salvation" (Psalm 85:6–7).

Developing a Prayer Ministry in the Local Church

Dick Eastman

The late Dr. Paul E. Billheimer, one of the great prayer strategists of our time, said in his classic book *Destined for the Throne,* "Prayer is not begging God to do something which He is loath to do. It is not overcoming reluctance in God. It is enforcing Christ's victory over Satan."[1] The author adds, "It is implementing upon earth heaven's decisions concerning the affairs of men. Calvary legally destroyed Satan, and canceled all his claims. God placed the enforcement of Calvary's victory in the hands of the church (Matthew 18:18 and Luke 10:17–19)."

Billheimer elaborates, "He has given to her [the church] 'power of attorney.' She is His 'deputy.' But this delegated authority is wholly inoperative apart from the prayers of a believing church. Therefore, prayer is where the action is. Any church without a well-organized and systematic prayer program is simply operating a religious treadmill."[2]

Prayer, indeed, is foundational to the establishing and sustaining of a healthy, growing congregation. Yet it is unfortunate that many churches lack a truly significant prayer program, especially one that involves members of the congregation on a regular and systematic basis.

Concerning this deficiency, Paul Billheimer further expressed:

The average local church provides an intelligent educational program through the Sunday school and such auxiliaries as the Vacation Bible School. It may provide well-directed youth programs, including social activities and recreational Bible camps. It may sponsor teacher training and personal evangelism classes. Many churches launch great evangelistic campaigns, featuring big-name evangelistic parties with a high potential of religious entertainment. Many have an efficient, well-structured, and highly-successful stewardship and financial program. All of these may be working smoothly, and in high gear. This is not to discount any of these programs per se. They may be good. But if they are substitutes for an effective prayer program they may be useless so far as damaging Satan's kingdom is concerned.[3]

A generation earlier Dr. R. A. Torrey, founder of the Bible Institute of Los Angeles (today Biola University), said bluntly, "The devil is perfectly willing that the Church should multiply its organizations and its deftly contrived machinery for the conquest of the world for Christ, if it will only give up praying."[4] The evangelist continues, "He [Satan] laughs softly, as he looks at the church of today, and says under his breath: 'You can have your Sunday schools, and your Y.M.C.A.'s and your Y.W.C.A.'s . . . and your Boys' Brigades, and your Institutional Churches, and your Men's Clubs, and your grand choirs, and your fine organs, and your brilliant preachers, and your revival efforts even, if you do not bring into them the power of Almighty God, sought and obtained by earnest, persistent, believing, mighty prayer.'"[5]

A Praying Church

But where do we begin in developing a truly praying church? The answer almost certainly begins with three simple words: a praying leader. I well recall the earliest years of my ministry when serving as youth pastor of First Assembly of God in Kenosha, Wisconsin. On one uniquely blessed Sunday morning during a missions convention, First Assembly hosted a young Korean pastor on his very first visit to America (according to what I was later told). In fact, it was his first speaking assignment of his very first visit. As the years would pass, this unusual preacher would visit the country many times, and become one of the best-known Christian leaders and church growth strategists of the twentieth century.

The short, thin visitor decided he would not speak through an interpreter, but rather struggle through his message in broken English. I was glad he did. It became quickly evident that this brother from the Orient was uniquely anointed by the Holy Spirit. He described how their church had begun in a relatively small tent in central Seoul, Korea, some six years earlier. He spoke of how less than a hundred gathered at the outset, but how on a weekly basis they began to cry out to God for multitudes to come to a knowledge of His love. Before long they were boldly asking God, by faith, to give them a thousand new members each year. I recall the young pastor smiling as he spoke of how God had not answered their prayers the way they prayed them. After all, he said, the church was now six years old and if God had answered their prayers exactly as they had prayed them they should have six thousand members. "But," he said, "we now have seven thousand members. So we've been asking God why He gave us one thousand too many."

I remember driving this young leader, whom we know today as Dr. David (Paul) Yongi Cho, to the Chicago O'Hare airport after that Sunday morning encounter. I was deeply impressed by the simplicity of this pastor's faith and conviction that nothing was beyond God's capacity to provide and perform—if only we sought Him fervently. It was clearly evident in our conversation, as well as from his morning message, that the secret to what God had done in the Full Gospel Church of Seoul, Korea, was prayer. Further, the secret of the prayer life of the Full Gospel Church in Seoul was the prayer life of its pastor.

Almost two decades later I would have the privilege of participating in an International Prayer Assembly in Seoul, Korea, during which my wife and I and several thousand delegates from around the world would experience, firsthand, the dynamics of this remarkable assembly. It was now nineteen years after Dr. Cho had visited our church in Kenosha, and twenty-five years after he had founded what now is known as Yoido Full Gospel Church on Yoido Island in Seoul, Korea. If, indeed, the church had continued to grow by an amazing one thousand a year, by then it would have reached some twenty-five thousand in number. But the fact was, the congregation now numbered far in excess of five hundred thousand worshipers, and at that stage in its growth was increasing by approximately ten thousand new members per month.

A decade after that International Prayer Assembly, we would again visit the Yoido church only to discover it now numbered in excess of seven hundred thousand members and had considerably extended its influence throughout the globe. It was during that last visit, while speaking with one of its senior staff, that we discovered prayer was still as much a fact of its spiritual life as ever. In fact, we were told *all* of the pastoral leadership spent a minimum of three hours personally in prayer daily. Dr. Cho, himself, as our guide explained, often spends five hours in prayer. And although it is impossible to fix a specific amount of time in prayer as guaranteeing some level of success, we can be certain that such leadership in prayer will significantly impact a congregation.

Called To Mobilize

More than a century ago the noted Dutch missionary to South Africa, Andrew Murray, said on the subject of prayer mobilization, "The man who mobilizes the Christian church to pray will make the greatest contribution in history to world evangelization."[6] I believe all spiritual leaders, no matter the size of their congregations, nor the scope of their influence beyond the walls of their church, ought to purpose in their hearts to become just such mobilizers of prayer. As Leonard Ravenhill declared, "The man who can get believers to praying would, under God, usher in the greatest revival that the world has ever known."[7]

Years ago while developing the multihour seminar called *Change the World School of Prayer,* my heart was quickened by an interesting passage of Scripture from the life-experience of Ezra the scribe. Ezra, I discovered, had a unique grasp of what was required to be an effective mobilizer of God's people. In describing Ezra, whom God used to help lead His people from their Babylonian captivity back to Jerusalem, Scripture says, "Ezra had prepared his heart to seek the Law of the Lord, and to do it, and to teach statutes and ordinances in Israel" (Ezra 7:10[8]).

In this single verse of Scripture a significant threefold plan for the mobilization of God's people is set forth in simplicity. We're applying these words specifically to the mobilization of prayer because Ezra's desire was to mobilize Israel to live in and apply God's law, which in Ezra's day was God's communication to man.

To Seek It

We first discover that Ezra was committed to "seek" an understanding of God's law, or His communication to His people. This suggests that before the scribe had any intention of attempting to communicate the principles of God's ways to others, he was determined to understand these principles himself. Of course, because an understanding of God's laws, or His ways, is really at the heart of prayer, it is easy to see why we might readily apply these concepts to mobilizing the Church to pray. Like Ezra, who determined first "to seek" an understanding of God's ways, God wants leaders today to pursue an understanding of what His Word says about prayer and how it works.

We should begin this pursuit by searching the Scriptures for insights into the subject of prayer itself. We will soon discover that the Bible is really a book of answered prayer. Its main theme is human communication with God and God's plan for the reconciliation of humanity to Himself through Jesus Christ.

Then, we might continue this pursuit by reading good biographies of respected spiritual leaders who demonstrate the importance of prayer in their lives. For example, books such as *Rees Howells: Intercessor,* by Norman Grubb (Christian Literature Crusade), and other similar biographies include a richness of illustrations from the lives of those who passionately sought God's ways and were mightily used of Him as a result.

Books on Prayer by Dick Eastman

A Celebration of Praise. Grand Rapids, Mich.: Baker Book House, 1984.
Change the World School of Prayer Manual. Colorado Springs: Every Home for Christ, 1992.
The Hour That Changes the World. Grand Rapids, Mich.: Baker Book House, 1978.
The Jericho Hour. Orlando, Fla.: Creation House, 1994.
Living and Praying in Jesus' Name, with Jack Hayford. Wheaton, Ill.: Tyndale House Publishers, 1988.
Love on Its Knees. Grand Rapids, Mich.: Chosen Books, 1988.
No Easy Road: Inspirational Thoughts on Prayer. Grand Rapids, Mich.: Baker Book House, 1971.

For information on the author's books and study materials on prayer write: Dick Eastman, Every Home for Christ, P.O. Box 35930, Colorado Springs, CO 80935-3593.

There are also many devotional books on prayer available that can help a spiritual leader develop insight into the importance of prayer, as well as describe how to ultimately transfer these insights to others. I have written several books on prayer for a number of reasons. For one, the Lord impressed on me early on that we must understand prayer and apply it in our own walk with God; only then will we see the release of His power and potential in our lives, as well as in the lives of those we might touch through our prayers.

To Do It

As Ezra's three-part plan unfolds we next discover the scribe intends to apply what he has learned during the seeking process. He says not only will he "seek" the law (or ways) of the Lord but he will "do it." He is thus suggesting that before he would attempt to transfer these principles to anyone else, he would first "do" what he had learned in that searching process. John R. Mott described it thus, "The plea and purpose of the Apostles was to put the Church to praying. I used to lay down a great many points on how to get people to pray, but I made up my mind that the only way to get them to do it is to do it myself."[9]

Obviously, to be effective in our ability to mobilize others, we must understand, by application, what it is that we intend to transfer to them. This is especially essential in prayer. We cannot teach what we do not know. Further, if we lack the wise application of prayer in our own lives, our ministries will be clearly lacking in God's spiritual energy. A great prayer warrior of a previous generation, E. M. Bounds, said, "Every preacher who does not make prayer a mighty factor in his own life and ministry is weak as a factor in God's work and is powerless to project God's cause in this world."[10]

> **We cannot teach what we do not know.**

As leaders we need to pray for wisdom in both applying prayer in our own lives as well as in transferring this prayer mantle to others. The Bible speaks often of the significance of wisdom and how it is foundational to all of our understanding of God's ways. The author of Proverbs wrote, "Wisdom is the principal thing; Therefore get wisdom. And in all your getting, get understanding" (Proverbs 4:7). Wisdom, simply stated, is the application and right use of knowledge—especially essential in the study of prayer. Years ago I heard a Bible teacher from England suggest that wisdom is to know where you're going and to know how to get there. It is one thing to have a certain degree of "head knowledge" about God's ways regarding prayer (and even how prayer may work), but it's an entirely different matter to apply what we know on a regular basis.

It is therefore absolutely essential, if we as pastors are to mobilize our congregations to pray, that we make prayer the main business of our own spiritual walk. We must respond obediently to the injunction of Paul who commanded believers at Rome, "Be . . . faithful in prayer" (Romans 12:12, NIV).

We also note that one of the first administrative decisions of the apostolic leadership of the Early Church (Acts 6:1–4) was to appoint deacons to assist them administratively so they might give themselves "'continually to prayer and to the ministry of the word'" (Acts 6:4). The apostles recognized that being consumed with a multitude of details would draw them away from their primary focus. And even when we note the order of the listing of their twofold priority, we discover prayer is listed first. Only with a proper emphasis on prayer will the ministry and proclamation of the Word achieve its intended impact.

To Teach It

Finally, Ezra realized that what he had come to understand and apply needed to be transferred to others. His was a call to mobilize. The scribe not only purposed to "seek the law of the Lord" and "do it" but he declared his intention to "teach statutes and ordinances in Israel" (Ezra 7:10). Ezra wanted to transfer to others what he had proven and applied in his own life.

Generations after Ezra's experience in ancient Israel, Paul would say to his beloved Timothy, "You then, my son, be strong in the grace that is in Christ Jesus. And the things you have heard me say in the presence of many witnesses entrust to reliable men who will also be qualified to teach others" (2 Timothy 2:1–2; NIV).

To what degree have we as leaders sought to carry out this mandate of Paul—specifically as it relates to mobilizing the Church to pray? A century ago, E. M. Bounds offered this passionate question: "Is prayer a fixed course in the schools of the church? In the Sunday school, the home, the colleges, have we any graduates in the school of prayer? Is the Church producing those who have diplomas from the great University of Prayer?"[11]

What are some of the specific ways we might make prayer a priority in the church? The following directives may be a good place to begin.

A Prayer Program

First, we need to develop an actual church prayer program. The word *actual* in this first directive is especially significant. Many churches assume they have a prayer emphasis but most do not have a systematic, well-planned program of prayer such as they would for youth and music.

A Prayer Strategy

Thus, an actual church prayer program needs to begin with a carefully developed *prayer strategy.* Before Job approached the Lord's presence he declared, "I have prepared my case. I know I shall be vindicated" (Job 13:18). When Job spoke of being "prepared," he used the Hebrew word *arak,* which means to arrange something. It is a word used throughout the Old Testament to speak of setting something in order or of having an ordered strategy. In Judges 20:20 we find eleven tribes of Israel preparing for a key battle against the rebellious tribe of Benjamin by "put[ting] themselves in battle array." Here *arak* is translated "array," describing a well-ordered strategy for attack. Pastors need to put on paper exactly what their battle plan is for calling the church to prayer. And at the heart of this strategy ought to be a twofold focus for our praying.

First, our prayer should focus on *spiritual awakening,* or true revival in the church. Indeed, a dead church will never evangelize a lost world.

Thus, even before we pray for the evangelization of lost souls in our community (or the world) we need to focus much prayer on a local church awakening.

Second, our strategy should focus much prayer on *world evangelization.* We need a well-ordered plan to help members of our congregations focus regular intercession on our global missionaries and national workers, who are seeking to fulfill the Great Commission. This should be done in a systematic way, perhaps including a seven-day calendar in each Sunday's church bulletin that provides a prayer list of specific nations and missions.[12]

A PRAYER CONCERT

A further way to develop a true prayer program in the church is to develop a *prayer concert.* What specifically is a concert of prayer? The term *concert of prayer* has emerged in the last decade to describe gatherings of prayer that usually involve believers from various congregations coming together for focused and directed prayer.

Of course, the same principles that are used in these kinds of united, interchurch prayer gatherings easily can apply to organized times of prayer for a local congregation. It involves planning periodic united prayer meetings when most of the congregation will be present. In other words, avoid planning prayer concerts on off nights, such as a Monday or Friday, and rather seek to incorporate concert elements into those services attended by most of the congregation—such as during a Sunday morning worship gathering.

Jesus told His disciples, "'If two of you agree on earth concerning anything that they ask, it will be done for them by My Father in heaven'" (Matthew 18:19). When Jesus used the word *agree* He used the Greek word *symphoneo,* from which we obviously derive our word *symphony.* The Lord was suggesting that when any gathering of believers (even with only two present) agree in prayer they become a glorious sound—a symphony.

One specific way to introduce a mini-concert of prayer in a local church is to follow a unique suggestion offered by David Bryant, founder of Concerts of Prayer International. He suggests that pastors shorten their Sunday morning messages by five to ten minutes (whether regularly or at least occasionally), and allow people of the congregation to pray together in small clusters, focusing specifically on elements of the message. For example, if the pastor has preached a four-point sermon on spiritual growth, he might encourage people in small prayer groups to ask God to help them apply these four points during a brief time of prayer. Clusters should be no larger than three or four persons (to give each person a chance to pray); on some occasions the pastor may encourage two-person groups. Interestingly, when such a plan is developed on a regular basis, people not only learn how to pray, but they also pay much more attention to the outline that the pastor has preached.

If a pastor feels that doing this every Sunday would lose its full impact, it might be desirable to select one Sunday a month as Concert of Prayer Sunday and design the entire service around a prayer focus. In this case the message may be only fifteen to twenty minutes with the rest of the meeting being devoted to *directed* prayer. Be sure to explain to guests that you want them to join a group but that they should feel comfortable to let the others of the group know they are visitors and that they can merely observe if they wish. Often this is an excellent way for regular church members who know what is happening to ask guests if there is something they might pray about concerning them. This can have a very positive effect on newcomers, who usually come because of some need.

A Prayer Fellowship

A third way to develop an actual local church prayer ministry is to organize a *prayer fellowship*. Take the concept of small clusters of prayer described in the preceding section and encourage such prayer clusters (based on where people live) to meet on a regular basis throughout the community. In recent years many churches, and even youth organizations, have sought to mobilize believers to form clusters for prayer consisting of at least three participants in each group (called "prayer triplets") that meet either weekly or monthly to focus prayer on specific issues of the day. In the ministry I direct, Every Home for Christ, we call these groups "Jericho Chapters" because the primary focus of each group is to strategically and prayerfully confront those Jericho-type strongholds of a community, nation, and even the world that oppose the spread of the gospel.

For years many churches also have found significance in organizing cell groups of believers to meet regularly (usually in homes of church members) not only for prayer but also for encouragement and discipleship training. Where this is the case it would be relatively easy to strengthen the prayer emphasis of these gatherings by encouraging them to conclude with a twenty to thirty minute concert of prayer.

A Prayer and Fasting Chain

Another way to develop an actual local church prayer program is to organize *a prayer and fasting chain.* On some occasions pastors may wish to develop such a chain over a relatively short period, such as a week or month, during which prayer is specifically focused on a project or some key issue. Others have sought to have a "chain of prayer" (that may also include fasting) for the purpose of continuously covering not only the needs of their church but other serious issues that arise locally, nationally, and globally.

To organize a prayer chain, all that is needed is some type of a large clock, drawn on poster board and covered with transparent plastic, giving people the opportunity to sign up for various time slots throughout the week. Usually a prayer coordinator (or someone at an information table) using a water soluble marking pen can sign people up at appointed times. Naturally, the larger the congregation the more likely there will be enough participants to sustain such a chain.

To organize a plan for continuous fasting, simply develop a large, thirty-one-day calendar, cover it with transparent plastic, and allow people to sign up for at least one day a month when they will fast a minimum of one meal during that day. The pastor might encourage participants to select the day number of their birth, and when that specific day comes during the month, they will fast at least one meal on the day. For example, a person born on the 10th of a month might fast at least one meal on the 10th of each month. Participants should be encouraged to try spending the normal time they would eat a meal in prayer. Commitments for either the prayer or fasting chain could be renewed every three to six months, and the plastic that is covering either the clock or the calendar could be fully cleaned at that time and a new call to prayer and fasting be delivered from the pulpit for several Sundays. Another way to have people sign up for the prayer or fasting chain is to distribute a simple prayer and fasting response card in the Sunday bulletin that would allow members to register their commitments for either of these focuses. Then, a prayer coordinator could compile a list of both the prayer and fasting chains.

How's to

A PULPIT PRAYER EMPHASIS

Another key to developing and sustaining a call to prayer in the local church is to *preach periodic messages on prayer.* This is also a good time to promote and encourage sustaining the prayer and fasting chain. The pastor might want to consider devoting at least one message per month to some aspect of prayer, spiritual warfare, or intercession. Further, you might want to plan at least one or two annual series on the subject of prayer, consisting of at least two to four messages. This will keep the importance of prayer before the congregation.

A PRAYER LAY LEADERSHIP

Also essential for developing an actual prayer program in the local church is to *appoint a prayer lay leadership.* As pastor you cannot do all of this on your own. However, with the help of committed intercessors in the church it is possible to implement many of these suggestions at minimal expense. It is said that Charles Spurgeon had a band of at least thirty men who prayed for him each time he preached. The prayer room was said to have been immediately below the pulpit of the church. When Spurgeon felt that his sermon wasn't getting through, or it didn't appear to be as anointed as he would like, he would stamp his foot on the platform, signaling the intercessors below that they needed to pray harder.

In recent years some churches are actually seeking to employ either full-time directors of prayer or are assigning the prayer focus of the local assembly to an assistant pastor as a major portfolio. This individual then works with the pastor to develop many aspects of the prayer program such as those shared in this chapter.

A PASTOR'S PRAYER SHIELD

Yet another way to develop a praying church is to organize a *pastor's prayer shield.* This is accomplished when various members of the congregation sign up for a particular day of the week to help provide a special prayer covering for the pastor and his family and for various other key issues regarding the life and growth of the church. As few as seven people can form a weekly prayer shield, with each participant agreeing to set aside a certain portion of his or her assigned day during the week to pray specifically for needs provided by the prayer shield coordinator. This does not necessarily need to be a twenty-four-hour prayer covering, but it assures that the pastor and his family are covered significantly throughout the week with prayer. The pastor should have his secretary or other appointed coordinator compile a brief list of certain prayer requests that could be available each Sunday in the church foyer for members of the prayer shield.

A PLAN FOR TRAINING

Finally, at the heart of an actual prayer program in the local church is *ongoing prayer training.* Training, by definition, is a systematic plan of teaching that embodies substance and structure. Sermons often are inspirational and challenging and do have an impact in exhorting people to recognize the importance of such qualities of discipleship as prayer. However, a well-rounded and balanced prayer program in the local church must also include well-prepared, ongoing training. This emphasis seeks to go beyond what might be presented through sermons in Sunday morning messages and consists of more practical and substantive training regarding prayer. In some cases it will actually allow the participant to practice certain aspects of prayer right in the session.

Other kinds of already existing prayer training programs also might be helpful. For example, Every Home for Christ makes available a multihour *Change the World School of Prayer* that God has used to impact the lives of nearly one million believers in more than one hundred countries. This training seeks to give concentrated attention to key issues concerning prayer, including practical ways to develop both devotional as well as corporate prayer. Further tools have been developed to provide thirteen-week training courses (covering a quarter of the year if used weekly) that might be used in either Sunday school classes or midweek Bible training sessions. Other similar resources may be available from other sources to accomplish a similar purpose and could be very helpful in sustaining the prayer focus of the church.

Of course, the key in all of this is to get people doing it! It is in praying that we learn to pray. As Leonard Ravenhill reminds believers, "Books on prayer are good, but not good enough. As books on cooking are good but hopeless unless there is food to work on, so with prayer. One can read a library of prayer books and not be one whit more powerful in prayer. We must learn to pray, and we must pray to learn to pray."[13]

A Fresh Anointing

It is obvious as the spiritual warfare of this present age continues and increases that our congregations will need a fresh anointing of God's Holy Spirit to stand in opposition to the growing assaults of the enemy. And for that to happen, we as pastors will need to retreat far more often to our personal closets of prayer. E. M. Bounds said of the church and its leadership, "What the church needs today is not more machinery or better, not new organizations or more and novel methods, but men whom the Holy Ghost can use—men of prayer, men mighty in prayer. The Holy Ghost does not flow through methods, but through men. He does not come on machinery, but on men. He does not anoint plans, but men—men of prayer."[14]

Indeed, it will not be our myriad plans or methods that will ultimately bring about awakening in our churches with the resulting evangelization of our communities and the world. It will be the pouring forth of God's power and presence, through His Holy Spirit, that finally will fulfill Christ's great commission and bring His kingdom fully and forever to this planet (see Revelation 11:15).

As Paul Billheimer reminds us: "From heaven's standpoint all spiritual victories are won, not primarily in the pulpit, not primarily in the bright light of publicity, nor yet through the ostentatious blaring of trumpets, but in the secret place of prayer. The only power that overcomes Satan and releases souls from his stranglehold is the power of the Holy Spirit, and the only power that releases the energy of the Holy Spirit is the power of believing prayer."[15]

Beloved leader, I encourage you to make prayer the main business in all of your planning and strategizing for your local assembly—not only for its own growth and development, but for its potential to impact your community (and world) with the good news of Jesus Christ. So give yourself to prayer, and give yourself to teach others to pray. Prayer, after all, is at the heart of the harvest!

Revival through Prayer and Fasting

Robert W. Rodgers

On the Day of Pentecost, Peter quoted the prophet Joel, "It shall come to pass afterward, that I will pour out my Spirit upon all flesh; and your sons and your daughters shall prophesy, your old men shall dream dreams, your young men shall see visions" (Joel 2:28[1]).

Jerusalem was filled with Jews from all over the world. They had come for their national holiday. The gathered multitudes were amazed because they heard local Spirit-filled believers speaking in the various languages of the visitors. The 120 spoke at least sixteen languages. As we trace the different nations represented, we find that a subsequent revival spread the gospel of Christ in each of these countries.

One of the languages spoken was that of the Mesopotamians, or Assyrians. The Assyrians invaded Israel and took many Jews back to their country (2 Kings 17:6). After the Day of Pentecost, the Assyrian Jews returned to Mesopotamia with the Holy Ghost and told about the resurrection of Christ. Then later the apostle Thomas came and began to preach to the Assyrians. He continued with his apostolic mission until A.D. 45, twelve years after the Ascension. He proceeded to India to begin his pioneering and Christian teaching there. The results of his work still exist in Malibar, India, under the present Assyrian Archbishop Martemateuss.

Assyrian missionaries took the message of Christ into the remote corners of the world: Tibet, Mongolia, China, Japan, Indonesia, and Ethiopia. The Assyrian church, or, as it is now known, the Ancient Apostolic Church of the East, was one of the strongest Christian churches in the world. Today there are three million Assyrian Christians.

This was the first and only worldwide revival that has touched the inhabited earth. John Wesley's revival affected only England and the United States. George Whitefield came to America and preached across this country, shaking our nation for Christ. The revival, however, did not even cross the English Channel to France. It was a regional outpouring of the Holy Spirit. The Welsh revival under Evan Roberts was also a regional move of God that affected only a seventy-mile radius. When Evan Roberts died, only fifteen people attended his funeral.

Fasting in the Upper Room

I personally believe that on the Day of Pentecost the church was fasting in the Upper Room. I base this conclusion on three observations. First is the statement of Mark 2:19–20: "Can the children of the bridegroom fast, while the bridegroom is with them? as long as they have the bridegroom with them, they cannot fast. But the days will come, when the bridegroom shall be taken away from them, and then shall they fast in those days." Jesus declared that His disciples (the children of the bride chamber) could not fast as long as He was with them. However, when the Bridegroom (Jesus) ascended to heaven, then His disciples would fast. So we know that Jesus expected his disciples to fast. When did they begin to fast? I believe they began immediately. They fasted. They sought God for direction and guidance. Thus began a systematic time of fasting for the church.

The second reason I believe they were fasting on the Day of Pentecost is because of what preceded Joel's prophecy. Peter quoted this prophecy, "It shall come to pass afterward" (2:28). After what? Joel 2:15 says, "Blow the trumpet in Zion, sanctify a fast, call a solemn assembly." Then a time of repentance and restored relation with God was to follow. After that came the familiar prophecy of a future Pentecost. Peter's listeners would have been familiar with the entire context of the quotation from Joel. So the parallel suggests very strongly that they had been fasting. The outpouring of the Holy Spirit came after fasting.

The third reason I believe they were fasting relates to Peter's declaration to the multitude, "These are not drunken, as ye suppose, seeing it is but the third hour of the day" (Acts 2:15). The church up through the sixth and even seventh centuries fasted on the days they would partake of Communion. Believers would fast until 3:00 P.M. to cleanse and purify themselves for the holy Communion to be taken that evening in church. They learned this practice from the orthodox Jews, who would set aside a half fast: not eating until after 3:00 P.M. on their special Jewish holidays. The orthodox Jews would say their prayers, read the Torah, and then after 3:00 P.M. join in the feast days. This is how John Wesley conducted his fast in the Methodist church. His followers fasted on Wednesdays and Fridays of each week until 3:00 P.M. After 3:00 they would eat. This was called a half fast. Peter was simply saying, "It is only 9:00 A.M. and we, being Jews, fast until 3:00 in the afternoon."

A Fasting Church

The Early Church was a fasting church. In Acts 13, while the believers were fasting and praying, the Holy Ghost called for the separation of Paul and Barnabas for the work of an apostle and missionary (verse 2). In Acts 14, every church that was established fasted and prayed. "When they had ordained them elders in every church, and had prayed with fasting, they commended them to the Lord, on whom they believed" (Acts 14:23). Fasting was expected and practiced by the Early Church.

The earliest existing book published on the subject of fasting is *The Holy Exercise Of A True Fast,* written in 1580 by Thomas Cartwright.[2] This Puritan minister felt that fasting was a commandment of God. He based his belief on Leviticus 16:29–31 which uses the words "a statute for ever." Cartwright concluded that the Jewish annual fast on the Day of Atonement should be observed by Christians. He disregarded the coming of Christ and the promises of the gospel, insisting that Christians are still required to have an annual day of personal humbling.

A Spiritual Discipline for All Believers

We do not agree with Cartright's conclusions. However, we do believe that fasting is a duty of Christians. Not only did Jesus say, "Then shall they fast in those days" (Mark 2:20), which means Christians are to fast today, but in Matthew 6:1–18 Jesus taught fasting as a duty of Christians. Fasting is to be a natural outcome of discipleship. We are to fast for the same reason we pray.

Jesus addressed fasting in association with both prayer and almsgiving. Matthew 6 declares "when you [give]," "when you pray," and "when you fast." Fasting is a duty for all disciples of Jesus Christ. God's Word does not say how often we are to fast, but we should certainly do it. Just as prayer is a duty, fasting is a duty. Just as God expects us to give to His work and to the needy, God also expects us to fast.

In 1988 I became the pastor of Evangel Christian Life Center in Louisville, Kentucky. Our church was millions of dollars in debt. Seemingly there was no way we could meet the mortgage payments. During that time attendance had dropped, and now I was the new pastor facing a very difficult situation. I asked the people to join with me in fasting for twenty-one days. They were asked to fast one meal a day for twenty-one days. I fasted the first week totally. I reasoned that three meals a day times seven equaled my twenty-one days. However, at the end of that time

I felt impressed to go a second week, and then a third week. I fasted the whole twenty-one days on liquids only. At that point our church began a miraculous recovery. Our income increased, our attendance began to grow, and by midsummer we began to have the whole church fast for the first three days of each month.

We set aside the first Monday, Tuesday, and Wednesday of each month and fasted three days. Then we held a miracle service. There were so many people gathered for the service, I could barely get into the building. Two people were healed of cancer. Then a woman with a large growth on the calf of her leg, a growth the size of a grapefruit, was miraculously healed. Visiting from a Baptist church, she had come for prayer. When she got home she discovered the tumor had disappeared. She came back and showed us her leg. It looked as if there had been surgery: There was an indentation where the tumor had been. That year thirty-seven people in our church were healed of cancer. The church began to experience enormous growth.

The next year I again asked the church to fast the whole twenty-one days, and as many as could to fast just on liquids. Fourteen completed the twenty-one-day fast on liquids only. Many others fasted for lesser periods. The next year 50 fasted for twenty-one days. The following year 79 fasted twenty-one days on liquids only. This past year 263 completed a twenty-one-day fast on liquids only.

The results have been miraculous. We have seen our congregation almost triple in attendance. Our finances have tripled. I believe the victory came because our church has given, prayed, and fasted. Fasting is the greatest church growth tool one can use. It draws people together. It unifies a church. It releases an anointing of the Holy Spirit that nothing else will do. Of course, it is not the ritual of fasting that brings the victory. It is the intensity and seriousness of prayer as demonstrated by our setting aside all hindrances and distractions through fasting.

Corporate Fasting

As I study Matthew 6, I become convinced that our primary fasting should be corporate fasting. Secondary fasting is fasting by oneself. In the clause, "when thou doest alms" (v. 2), *thou* is a singular pronoun. "When thou prayest" (v. 6), *thou* again is singular; but in verse 7, "when ye pray," notice that *ye* is a plural pronoun. There is praying by oneself, as well as praying with other people. Jesus placed emphasis on praying alone more than on praying with other people. Some things—things so personal you don't want others to know—you would not express aloud when others are around.

Jesus put emphasis on corporate fasting. "When *ye* fast" (v. 6, italics mine). The reason is that it is easier to fast when you are fasting with other people. Furthermore, there is an increase in anointing and consciousness of God's presence when fasting with a group of people. One may be fasting for healing, another for financial breakthrough, another for the salvation of some family members. You may be blessed financially because someone else was praying for that need and experienced a breakthrough. You received a part of their blessing.

I also believe it is better to fast as a group because it greatly unifies a church. This creates bonding and togetherness that nothing else can. You will be surprised at the people who will participate in a churchwide fast.

The testimonies of fasting people are proof of what God does when people fast and pray. One of the women in our church had four of her grown children come to Christ during the fast. There have been healings of sugar diabetes, heart disease, cancer, deafness, and even blindness. Marriages have been restored. Many have received outstanding financial breakthroughs. Our church is seeing more people saved each month than we used to see in a year. This is true revival.

We are living just before the Lord is to come back. We are beginning to see a worldwide revival for the first time since the Day of Pentecost. It is time for your church to fast and claim your city for God. Fasting will bring breakthroughs that nothing else will bring.

Reaching and Discipling Ethnics

Jesse Miranda

The ABC television announcer for a recent Summer Olympics surprised some of us when he observed that every nation participating in the games was also represented among the residents of Los Angeles. God is internationalizing the cities in North America in our generation.

A few years ago I addressed a missionary convention in an Assemblies of God congregation in Sandy, Oregon, by saying, "This morning I woke up in a motel owned by a businessman from Pakistan. I was picked up by a Cuban pastor (from the Hispanic congregation) in a German Volkswagen bus on its way to a Japanese strawberry farm to bring Mexican workers to an Anglo-American congregation, pastored by an Italian minister, to hear me, a Mexican-American, speak." The United States is truly "a nation of nations."

The church is ordered by the Lord to "'Go into all the world and preach the good news to all creation'" (Mark 16:15). But the world is now at our doorsteps. This does not negate our responsibility to go the world. It does, however, say to us that the mission field has come to us in the form of ethnic groups residing within the United States. There is great need for a massive church planting and missionary effort in our nation.

Some General Considerations

Jesus was standing in the midst of an ethnic harvest when He exhorted His disciples in Samaria: "'Open your eyes and look at the fields! They are ripe for harvest!'" (John 4:35). Jesus must have taken His disciples to Samaria intentionally for this lesson. They needed to see that the harvest did not lie only within their culture, race, and socioeconomic group. God's plan of salvation for the world could not be defined in their terms. The "whosoever" of John 3:16 (KJV) is the crucial word for the church today. Over one hundred ethnic groups live in America, each speaking a different language. The increasing number of ethnics should cause us to rethink our attitude toward them. A major shift must take place in our mission philosophy. No longer can we think solely in terms of a macrovision of a few major groups; we must now adopt a microvision, focusing on the many subgroups within our nation.

> **" We must now focus on the subgroups in our nation. "**

Moreover, there is a rise in ethnic pride among these groups. Some would even say an ethnic revival is taking place. What this means is that cultural groups are wanting to feel a part of the whole—to be accepted as equal, not as a foreign element. They are not asking for separation or "Balkanization" from the American way of life. They are not asking for a corner in which they can exist separate from the main body. They do desire, however, a chance to pursue the freedom of their own cultural values and heritage within both the church and the country.

Immigrant groups coming to America in the past expected to be assimilated and acculturated. In 1909 Israel Zangwill said "America is God's crucible, the great melting pot where all races are melting and reforming." But one hundred years later, immigrant groups are more resistant to change, preferring to keep their cultural distinctives. The so-called global village is a reality in the minds of new immigrants as time and distances have been shrinking. Today's immigrants are not severed from their roots by distance and time as were the first immigrants to this country. Today's modern transportation and communication allow people to stay in touch with their homeland and loved ones.

What does this imply for the Christian church? It represents a challenge to have a greater understanding of ethnic groups and to fine-tune our ministry to reach them. Myths must be replaced with proper teaching. Cross-cultural barriers such as language, values, and class must be overcome. Unity does not mean uniformity. Unity means accepting others just as they are. It means allowing for differences, adjusting to those that may be at variance with our culture and loving each other amid the diversity.

The ethnic challenge is greater and more complex than it has ever been. Historically, mainstream America has ignored distinct ethnic groups. While such groups have always made efforts to belong, they have been turned away repeatedly. At first it was the Irish, the Italians, and the Jews. Today it is the African-Americans, Native Americans, Hispanics, and Asians. Ethnic groups reacted to the ensuing marginalization in a variety of ways, adopting a variety of reactions and positions. For instance, African American groups prefer *integration,* Hispanics and Asian groups *insulation,* and Native Americans *isolation.* This oversimplification allows a glimpse into the problems of diversity, marginalization, and level of involvement exhibited among ethnic groups. As one might guess, every ethnic group stands at a different distance because of its unique historical position, language, and culture.

If the church is to reach modern-day ethnics, it needs to consider the level of involvement it will pursue with these communities. The strategy for reaching the unchurched has traditionally been the three P's: *Presence, Proclamation and Persuasion.*

Proclamation of the gospel to non-Christians with the intention and hope that they will repent, accept Christ, and join His new kingdom community is central to evangelism. This does not preclude the visible demonstration (social actions) of the gospel, since Jesus' announcement of the Kingdom was in word and deed. Evangelism and social action are not identical, yet Christians are called to do both. This is particularly true in relationships with ethnics. The incarnational gospel of Christ requires the physical presence of believers in the community of lost souls.

Distant and impersonal methods of outreach—radio, television, and other similar means—do have results, but the best results are those where the church has been personally involved. Many of the methods used today to reach ethnics have proved unsuccessful. "Guerrilla warfare" approaches, evangelistic blitzes, one- or two-day excursion trips, etc., have yielded little fruit. The benefits have been greater (as has the cost) for those participating in the events than for those such efforts have been intended for. This is especially true because ethnics do not readily rush into a relationship with strangers in a strange land.

Nonethnic persons are often fearful of reaching into an ethnic group with the gospel. Much of this is due to their ignorance of a particular community. A better understanding of what is fact and what is fiction about the group being evangelized is very important. Equally important is an understanding of the basic differences of the particular ethnic group one wishes to reach. History has helped shape the identity of groups.

A Land of Immigrants

There is no group indigenous to the continental United States. Native Americans are said to have come across the Bering Strait of Alaska, thus becoming the first inhabitants of this land. Since then, there have been three major waves of immigration to this land. All these human movements have been either in the quest for freedom or for the conquest of poverty. This is a common human experience for all groups. All groups are the result of one immigration wave or another.

The first wave consisted of Northern and Southern European immigrants. Christopher Columbus was sent by Spain to the new world. The immigrants coming from England seeking religious freedom are well known from American history. Less well-known is a second major wave of immigration consisting of several migrations from Mexico beginning in the early 1900s and continuing for fifty years. Whether impelled by revolution in their home country or attracted by job opportunities in the U.S., the flow has not ceased since. The third and latest major wave of immigration has taken place in the last two decades. Immigration from Latin America, Asia, and the Carribean has brought a million or more aliens (documented and undocumented) each year since the 1980s.

This explains in part the diversity even within the many ethnic groups now residing in this country. The extent of assimilation and the membership of each group varies greatly. The spectrum extends from the newly arrived immigrants to those who have been in this land for generations. Such is the case for Hispanics: There are those who arrived last night or last week and then there are those who are descendants of the Spanish explorers, who preceded the Mayflower and were residents of the Mexican territory that became the southwestern United States. Each experience and perspective of life varies a great deal.

Older immigrants have much more in common than do the more recent immigrants from the two latest immigration waves. These more recent arrivals fall into the following categories: *fellow travelers,* who have just arrived in this country; *the marginal group,* which fits neither in the old country nor in the new land; *the saddened ones,* who resent their social predicament; *the fleeing ones,* who wish to leave the cultural traits of their homeland and strive to adopt the ways of the new country; and finally, there are *those who have been thoroughly assimilated* into the ways of the new land.

Ministry Considerations

What are the implications of these ethnic realities for our ministry opportunites? First, the primary causes of failure in ministry to ethnic groups are lack of knowledge and vision. Historically, the church has been diligent in studying and engaging people on the foreign field, but its interest and intensity wane once these same people are on American soil. In this chapter I seek to shed some light on the similarities and uniquenesses of ethnic groups in America in order to dispel the fear and ignorance that may exist. It should be no mystery that all racial and ethnic groups now residing in America had a similar beginning. We were all strangers at one time. On the other hand, every group and subgroup is unique. When, how, and why a particular group came to this land and its experience since arriving make it unique. The question of English being a first or second language is also unique to many groups residing in America today and may constitute a challenge for the first generation or two. But it is not insurmountable.

Another key to success in ministry to ethnics is a positive sense of direction. Congregations afflicted with complacency or lethargy need a redefinition of the role of the church, a soundly based philosophy of ministry. Most efforts to reach ethnics fail because they are solely event driven. But the following imperatives can help a ministry succeed: (1) biblical priorities must be established, (2) the ministry context must be investigated, (3) the target group or groups must be identified, (4) denominational distinctives must be contextualized (i.e., related to each ethnic culture), and (5) God-given ministry resources within the congregation must be activated.

A philosophy of ministry statement is more than a human product. It is the fruit of corporately seeking the will of God and emerging with a clearer sense of self-identity and purpose. These are both essential prerequisites for serving as fellow workers with God (2 Corinthians 6:1). In addition, this philosophy of ministry must be culturally relevant to the group one seeks to reach.

When the members of a congregation set out to minister within an ethnic community, they are using their gifts and serving as fellow workers with God. But for what purpose? Are they seeking *decisions* within the ethnic community, or are they seeking *disciples?* Do they intend to evangelize individuals and leave them unattached, or do they incorporate them into, and serve them as part of, the sponsoring congregation? Is language or culture as limitation taken into consideration? Or is the intent merely to build an ethnic church in that community?

Growth Considerations

The local church is God's design for developing believers to the full measure of Christ. Anything short of this is not the will of God. Many ethnic people are being evangelized but not discipled. Planting churches that can win and disciple converts should be the goal of the church today. Underdeveloped church members weaken the body of Christ in the world. It is through the local church that discipleship takes place. Not only should there be the planting of churches in every nation, but in every community.

Christianity has grown by the birthing of new churches. The Book of Acts records how the Christian faith was extended to the farthest regions of the world through the establishment of new congregations. Even to this day, each generation repeats the model. You and I have this faith today thanks to those who came before us faithfully reproducing the church by establishing new churches!

The growing population of the world demands the multiplication of new congregations. In the United States, 70 percent of the population does not belong to a church. The percentage is higher among ethnic groups. So church planting is critical among ethnic groups if the new converts are to be discipled. As my professor in seminary, Dr. Peter Wagner, stated frequently, "Church planting is the most effective evangelistic tool we have." Churches are indispensable for the discipling of ethnic believers.

Some, however, object to planting churches among ethnic groups based on the following:

1. *The Utopic Objection.* Some hold a very idealistic view of all believers under one roof as one happy family. But their own congregation is immature and unable to service all people.
2. *The Economic Objection.* Some want to add others because of their potential financial contribution. They speak of the cost effectiveness of sharing one facility.
3. *The Romantic Objection.* Some enjoy the emotional warmth felt in seeing different nationalities in the congregation. But their concern is superficial rather than a concern for souls.
4. *The Exotic Objection.* Some see the cultural diversity and the col-

orful array of ethnics but fail to interact with ethnics in fellowship and service.

5. *The Myopic Objection.* Some have a defective and nearsighted vision, focusing only on those persons and issues closest to them.

Such attitudes have served to departmentalize and eventually alienate the ethnic peoples attending these congregations.

A word about ethnic departments in congregations having a racial majority membership: Only in exceptional cases have ethnic departments successfully discipled the ethnic membership of the congregation. Departments or programs that focus on ethnics may function successfully in their initial stages, but they reach a plateau after two or three years, eventually becoming stagnant and then declining. This happens because these departments (by accident or by design) are for evangelistic and not discipling purposes. Eventually they are unable to hold the interest of those believers seeking solid food and the full counsel of God. This results in constant turnover or stagnation of ethnic believers.

An ethnic department should not be an end in itself. It should not be a permanent structure of the church unless it is to serve as a point of entry. Having a department is a good evangelistic strategy, but a discipleship program must also be in place, to provide the necessary service for all its members to "prepare God's people for works of service, so that the body of Christ may be built up . . . [and] become mature, attaining to the whole measure of the fullness of Christ" (Ephesians 4:12–13). The unity that most congregations seek with ethnic persons is physical and programmatic, but this unity is incomplete "until we all reach unity in the faith and knowledge of the Son of God" (Ephesians 4:13). The church is weakened by the uneven growth and development of any of its members.

> **An ethnic program should not be an end in itself.**

The Lord desires that all the members of His body, including ethnic members, be developed by means of the gifts he has provided for the church. Christ has given the mandate in Matthew 28:19 to "make disciples" (not just decisions). He desires that all the gifts be in operation in His church, not just the gift of the evangelist. There are two possible places where an ethnic believer may be fully discipled as ordained by the Lord. One is in the congregation that has an ethnic department, with full provision for growth and development "to the whole measure." The other is in an indigenous ethnic church, freestanding and homogeneous in focus. In both cases the goal should be to reach and disciple every member by providing access to all the gifts Christ has given to the church. To this end the challenge of language, culture, and conceptual styles must be met at every level of the church structure, from the Sunday school to the boardroom, from participation in revival campaigns to business sessions of the church, from having access to Christian literature to the church bylaws. Anything short of this will not produce the "unity in the faith and knowledge of the Son of God" that Paul talks about. Occupying the same building space and talking to each other in the church parking lot does not guarantee unity in the faith.

The ethnic church follows the indigenous principle, which the Assemblies of God has successfully utilized for many years. Over time, ethnic churches have proven to promote faster growth and development among ethnic believers because of several factors:

1. *Understanding*—Language and culture help the communication and contextualization of the gospel, which in turn produces opportunity for growth and development;
2. *Involvement*—More people are utilized and become an integral part of the congregation, rather than mere spectators, because there are fewer obstacles to overcome;
3. *Responsibility*—Ethnic churches develop pride of ownership, of programs and property, rather than a mentality of dependency or welfare;
4. *Bridge Building*—Well-churched ethnics reach out to unchurched ethnics because of their proximity to the unchurched community;
5. *Advocacy*—A clearer and stronger voice is heard in the community.

Why would one wish to plant an ethnic church? There are a number of reasons for planting a church in an ethnic community. The most important is that one must answer the call to reach the lost. Out of this assurance of a great commission come positive motivations such as (1) compassion for the lost, (2) consciousness of a need for more churches in specific ethnic communities, (3) desire to expand the kingdom of God, (4) a spiritual burden for a specific group, and (5) the call of God to a specific ministry.

What kind of ethnic church should be planted? A church that reaches the lost and disciples believers "so that the body of Christ may be built up until we all reach the unity in the faith and in the knowledge of the Son of God and become mature, attaining to the whole measure of the fullness of Christ." Assuming that God has ordered the planting and a sound philosophy of ministry is in place, the new church should be built on (1) faith, vision, and prayer; (2) worship, service, and evangelism; (3) spiritually focused and culturally relevant programs; (4) effective pastoral leadership; (5) mobilization of the laity; (6) biblical stewardship; and (7) ability to reproduce itself.

How are ethnic churches planted? Ethnic churches are to be planned and planted. They should not be the result of divisions or accidents. Ethnic churches have been planted by various methods and bodies: (1) district sponsored, (2) sectional sponsored, (3) mother-church sponsored, and (4) individually sponsored. In each case the resources needed to initiate and continue the effort are these:

1. A dependable leader (pastor) who has the calling to pioneer the church;
2. A small core of capable leaders, with the same vision as the

founding pastor, to serve as (a) an evangelism coordinator, (b) a worship leader; (c) a children and youth leader, (d) a secretary-treasurer;

3. A place to hold meetings;

4. Musical instruments such as an electric piano and/or an electric guitar; and

5. A budget to meet the initial expenses and a reserve for emergency expenses.

The strong denominations of tomorrow are planting ethnic churches today. May we never lose sight of the call to reach every creature (every man, woman, boy, and girl) no matter what the ethnic background, economic condition, or geographic location.

Planting a New Congregation

Charles Hackett and David Moore

One of the best means of evangelizing and nurturing new converts is through the planting of indigenous churches. According to C. Peter Wagner, professor of church growth at Fuller Theological Seminary School of World Mission in California, planting a church is the most effective form of church growth.

A new church provides opportunities for the lost to be saved and for believers to be taught. Prayers of the people in a new church stand as a beacon for those on the pathway to death and as a testimony to the community. A new church promotes evangelism. People invite their neighbors to services and share the gospel. Increasing our efforts to open churches will preserve what pioneer church planters have labored to gain. These churches can be planted across America, from the countryside to the city.

Janie Bourlware-Wead, a nationally appointed home missionary, is fulfilling the church-planting challenge in northwest Arkansas. In 1991 she planted the first Hispanic church in Siloam Springs. Eventually the need for its own building became the principle focus of the ministry's missions outreach plan. Many other cities in Arkansas needed a Spanish-language church as well. If Hispanic Arkansas, which includes thousands of Hispanic families, is to be reached, an aggressive church-planting paradigm equal to the challenge had to be employed. One of the most successful types of church planting is the mother church concept, in which existing churches catch the vision and commission workers to start a new congregation.

Hispanic Project . . . 2000 has assembled an aggressive team of some of the finest Hispanic pastors to open new works and build the facilities necessary to house new congregations. Together with supportive local pastors who open their buildings to house the new congregations in the initial stages, a great church-planting body has pooled their resources to meet the challenge.

Hispanic Project . . . 2000 has planted five churches. Three have achieved significant strength: (1) El Centro Cristiano Hispano in Siloam Springs became a fully indigenous work, self-governing, self-propagating, and self-supporting, in 1995. (2) El Centro Cristiano Hispano in Van Buren began as a Sunday school class at First Assembly of God; today the class is a congregation that has constructed a building with the help of MAPS RV volunteers on a main thoroughfare in the city. (3) El Centro Cristiano Hispano in Rogers began through ministry outreaches, invading the city two nights a week; today it consists of a thriving congregation with its own facility. Other churches planted by *Hispanic Project . . . 2000* are leading aggressive campaigns to reach Hispanic Arkansas, a virgin mission field that must be evangelized if we are to fulfill the Great Commission.

Qualities of a Church Planter

The qualities listed below are helpful for planting a self-sustaining church. The goal must go beyond establishing another gospel meeting place. The contemporary church planter must have the goal of impacting neighborhoods with the gospel to change a godless culture. If every pastor had this goal, Christians would make more progress in taking their city for Christ.

1. *Has the capacity for vision*
   - projects future results
   - develops a mission statement
   - sells the vision to others
   - approaches problems as opportunities
   - does not erect artificial ministry limits
   - establishes a clear church identity based on mission
   - believes in God's willingness to do great things
2. *Is motivated*
   - commits to excellence
   - shows perseverance
   - shows aggressiveness without being pushy
   - is willing to work long and hard
   - is a self-starter able to build from nothing
   - has physical stamina

3. *Creates ownership of ministry*
   - helps people feel responsible for ministry success
   - helps people commit to the vision
   - establishes a congregational identity
   - avoids imposing unrealistic goals on congregation
4. *Relates to the unchurched*
   - communicates well with the unchurched
   - understands the mentality of the unchurched
   - interacts with the unchurched without fear
   - gets acquainted with the unchurched on a personal level
   - breaks through barriers erected by the unchurched
   - handles crises faced by the unchurched

5. *Has spouse's cooperation*
   - agrees on spouse's role in ministry
   - accepts rules regarding use of home as an office
   - evaluates effects of ministry upon their children
   - models wholesome family life to the community
   - plans family life and protects privacy
6. *Builds relationships*
   - responds quickly to the expressed needs of people
   - displays godly compassion toward people
   - gets to know people on a personal basis
   - makes people feel comfortable in his or her presence
   - does not respond prejudicially to new people
7. *Commits to church growth*
   - believes in church growth as a biblical principle
   - appreciates consistent growth
   - is not preoccupied with quick success
   - commits to numerical growth as part of spiritual growth
   - sees status quo as threatening and self-defeating
   - holds the goal of a financially self-supporting church
   - does not fall into maintenance ministry
8. *Responds to the community*
   - understands the culture of the community
   - assesses community needs
   - attaches priorities to community needs
   - respects community efforts of other religious groups
   - does not confuse community needs with what the church offers
   - learns community's character
9. *Utilizes the gifts of others*
   - equips and releases people to do ministry
   - discerns spiritual gifts in others
   - matches the gifts of people with ministry needs
   - delegates effectively
   - avoids personal overload
   - does not assign ministry before people are equipped
   - places no unwarranted restrictions on others' gifts
10. *Shows flexibility*
    - copes with ambiguity
    - copes with frequent and abrupt change
    - uses methods consistent with the uniqueness of the new church
    - adjusts priorities during various stages of growth
11. *Builds group cohesiveness*
    - develops and trains core group(s) as a foundation
    - incorporates newcomers into a relational network
    - engages others in meaningful church activity
    - monitors the morale of people
    - utilizes groups effectively
    - deals with conflict assertively, constructively, tactfully
12. *Shows resilience*
    - experiences setbacks without defeat
    - rides attendance ups and downs
    - expects the unexpected
    - rebounds quickly from loss and disappointment
13. *Exercises faith*
    - possesses assurance of his or her call to church planting
    - believes in God's action
    - has expectation and hope
    - waits for answers to specific prayer
14. *Shows cultural relevance*
    - at ease with ethnicity represented in the target area
    - at ease with the socioeconomics of the target area
15. *Embraces Pentecostal distinctives*
    - places high value on personal prayer life
    - favors church altar services
    - expresses appreciation for the gifts of the Spirit
    - emphasizes the baptism of the Holy Spirit

16. Demonstrates strong personal integrity
- embraces a moderate lifestyle
- is wisely cautious in practical affairs
- has a good reputation in secular and religious community
- demonstrates high ethics in business affairs

17. Relates well to denominational leadership
- understands responsibility to the district
- knows what resources are available through the district and national offices
- shows loyalty toward leadership
- shows loyalty toward those in supervisory roles

Planting a New Congregation

The success of a person's ministry coincides with the call God gives. If a person believes God has led to a certain place for a certain time, he or she will show a greater diligence for the work. Anyone who is sent to start another assembly must fulfill the requirements of 1 Timothy 3:1–7 and Titus 1:6–9.

Those responsible for approving church planters must of necessity assess the candidate's character, family relationships, doctrine, maturity, abilities, preparedness, philosophy of ministry, spiritual habits, faithfulness, money matters, and motives. Verification of God's call is based on these findings.

SELECT A TARGET AREA

We are often too vague in declaring the mission of the church. Above all other activities, the church must be engaged in evangelism and discipleship. Hopes are seldom actualized without strategies. The performance of the church is a paradox. It is good at dreaming, but very poor at planning and implementing. Notice the cautionary statement of James who encouraged us to say, "'If it is the Lord's will, we will live and do this or that'" (James 4:15). James is encouraging us to make plans—but plans subject to God's ratification.

In setting priorities for target area selection, we must focus on unchurched areas, responsive areas, and the urban or inner-city setting. Targeting urban areas for evangelization was the method of the apostle Paul. Fifty percent of America's population, nearly one hundred twenty-five million people, live in just forty-one metropolitan centers.

SOLICIT "SENDING CHURCHES"

It has been said that everyone's task is no one's task. Someone must take the lead if anything is to be accomplished.

David J. Hesselgrave, in *Planting Churches Cross-culturally,* states, "If local churches are to be truly missionary churches, denominational leaders and local pastors and officers must furnish the required information, inspiration, and example."[1]

Local churches must be acquainted with missions opportunities on the home front. Pastors should encourage involvement in missions. Fear of losing revenue and people should be replaced with a vision for equipping people to participate in the harvest. Many laypeople have come to life when their talents were used in missions ministry. Any gift can be used for the glory of God—carpentry, drama, sewing, electronics, transportation, puppetry, welding, and hospitality. The Mission America Placement Service (MAPS) Department in the Division of Home Missions (DHM) was created to fill such a need. The same MAPS principle can be used on a smaller scale by a district, section, or urban area. People in local churches are a great source of help for the church-planting team endeavor.

A local church may decide to make a financial commitment to a new church for one to two years. This might be their annual missions convention project. A "sending church" will materialize when the need is presented.

PLANT ETHNIC CHURCHES

When God lays a burden on people's hearts, they will most naturally inquire of the district or the church-planting leadership about potential open doors. The inquirer is always encouraged when church-planting supervisors know where the need is the greatest in their areas. Familiarity with ethnic concentrations in the urban areas is absolutely essential because this often represents the greatest opportunity as well as the greatest need.

Bible schools. District officers or pastors may visit Bible colleges and plant seeds for future ministers. Some who feel called to ministry among foreign cultures will not get to the foreign field. However, they can find fulfilling ministry among ethnics in America. Furthermore, working with Bible college placement services could direct workers into an enterprising district or area of ministry.

Local churches. The idea of ethnic church planting should be addressed when church-planting leaders minister in local churches. One never knows when he is addressing a minister in transition, waiting for a word from the Lord. Another reason for sharing the vision of planting ethnic churches is that God may lay the burden on a church to support this endeavor. Support in prayer, finance, and workers is essential to getting the new work launched. Scattering visionary seed often brings results.

Prayer. We must not forget the biblical admonition to pray for workers. One of the only recorded prayer requests Jesus left with us was "Ask the Lord of the harvest . . . to send out workers into his harvest field" (Matthew 9:38).

UTILIZE DISTRICT AND NATIONAL PROGRAMS

Programs like Boys and Girls Missionary Crusade (BGMC) and Light-for-the-Lost (LFTL) are valuable to the new church. BGMC offers a $400, onetime benefit to new churches for items such as a Communion set and church hymnals, and a 50 percent discount on Sunday school literature for one year. LFTL gives grants for literature conveying the plan of salvation. More information on how to qualify for these benefits is available from the BGMC or LFTL office at the Assemblies of God Headquarters in Springfield, Missouri.

Division of Home Missions Opportunities

DHM Executive Director Charles E. Hackett has said, "The vision and philosophy of DHM is found in our self-imposed job description. We are not church planters or fund-raisers. We are facilitators and helpers, organizers and teachers. We are servants, foot washers, equippers. We are ready to share the knowledge gleaned from around the country on reaching inner cities. We also know something about reaching ethnic minorities."

Those who feel called of God to reach the inner city or to evangelize ethnic minorities should seek district or national home missions appointment. National appointment opens the door for developing a prayer- and financial-support team.

Visibility. National appointment gives missionaries national visibility within the Assemblies of God. Publications such as the *Pentecostal Evangel* and *American Horizon* track the missionaries' progress, giving valuable exposure.

Fund-raising and Accountability. National appointment gives credibility to the ministry's finances. Churches and individuals may sponsor a ministry by pledging prayer and financial support. Accounting services such as filing Form 1099s, establishing an annual housing allowance, automatic deductions for retirement and health insurance, as well as consulting services, are available.

Promotional Help. Help in developing tools for ministry promotion (e.g., press releases, promotional photos, free literature for distribution to churches and supporters, pledge forms) are available.

Deputational Help. Deputational training and advice for writing news and prayer letters are a provided service.

Networking. Networking with other home missionaries is helpful. The DHM team encompasses six departments and several subgroups. The departments are Chaplaincy, Intercultural Ministries, Teen Challenge, New Church Evangelism, MAPS (Mission America Placement Service), and Chi Alpha Campus Ministries.

> **We are not church planters but facilitators.**

Credibility. Being a member of a national ministry enhances the missionary's credibility. It tells the supporting church that the appointed missionary is abiding by a system of checks and balances. He or she is accountable to a trusted national organization.

The Department Secretary. Having a department head available to serve you when difficult questions come up can be a valuable benefit. It is encouraging to call a person who has walked the same road, carries a similar burden, and has the national vision in mind. This is a good person to know when advice, encouragement, and prayer are needed.

Facilitation. The goal of the Division of Home Missions is one of facilitation and support. DHM exists to equip and facilitate the front-line men and women called to specific ministries.

* * * * *

America's cities and ethnic neighborhoods are whitened fields ready for harvest. Planting new congregations in areas as yet untouched by the Pentecostal message of salvation, the Spirit-filled life, healing for the body and mind, and the promise of Christ's soon return must have top priority in our efforts to fulfill the Great Commission. The night is coming when we will no longer be able to work.

Acts: The Church Planter's Blueprint

Scott Hagan

No one has difficulty recognizing the red of the Bible—the shade of forgiveness. But can you also spot the blue? You must look closely—especially if you have been called to a ministry of church planting. The blue I'm speaking of is the *blue*print for Kingdom life as revealed through God's Word.

If anyone owns the patent on "beginnings," it is King Jesus. "All things have been created through Him and for Him" (Colossians 1:16, NASB). And this includes the drafting and inauguration of a local church. The Church was conceived, formed, birthed, nurtured, and is replicated by God himself; it belongs to Him. And the church planter must decide early on if he is going to trust the biblical prescription for church planting with the same faith and tenacity that he trusts the other miracle-systems of God.

The Book of Acts provides the flawless blueprint of the church. It is tempting, because of our information age, to bypass the biblical blueprint and follow the modish and novel—to settle for a fresh idea rather than a fresh baptism of biblical understanding. But the Early Church must remain the model for every church. God may sanction "new information" to refine eternal footings, but never to lay new foundations. The kingdom of God is constructed from immutable patterns, which are not bettered by inventive dimensions of culture and commerce. It takes the ragged and spent peasant woman the same nine months to incubate an infant in her womb as it does the groomed and opulent princess. When it comes to birthing life, spiritual or physical, greater resources are often immaterial. That is why a thorough grasp of the Acts blueprint is a must for the church planter. He has nowhere else to turn.

The aim of all ministry is to duplicate the biblical experience, much in the same way Stephen duplicated the words of the crucified Christ during his martyrdom: "'Lord, do not hold this sin against them!'" (Acts 7:60,

NASB). Reproducing the biblical adventure distinguishes a ministry as effective and lasting. The successful church planter is someone convinced that the Bible is the sole authority for message and method. The Acts pilgrimage began with a rushing mighty wind, which has grown more deafening with the passing of two millenniums. Acts is no musty set of antique lecture notes, to be respected but dismissed as irrelevant, as some claim. Others say there is too much expression of the Holy Spirit for the sophisticated seekers of the twenty-first century. Both objections miss the intent of Acts, which is to reveal the pattern of operative ministry and then to establish the Holy Spirit as the everyday agent for everyday people. This divine Agent came to anoint people first and organizations second.

The first church was not identified as Baptist, Lutheran, Charismatic, or Fundamentalist. Instead, it was known as the church of Peter, James, and John. The Holy Spirit's favorite address is still the human heart. No elitist would dare mistake the Upper Room for a penthouse suite or a Carnegie Hall for the hypergifted. Routine folk met there. And the common clay vessels of Acts had one clear link: none had their *act* together without Jesus. They were a cultural patchwork quilt sewn together by threads of grace.

During our church planter's journey through Acts, I would like to point out two guideposts to successful church planting. These guideposts should encourage those seeking God's will concerning church planting. For anyone facing a new venture in church planting, they could mean the difference between the life or death of one's vision. Please pray through them carefully.

The transition from the four Gospels to the Acts account does not mean a shift from the centrality of Jesus. Even after the Early Church achieved viability, Jesus' words and presence remained pivotal. Whether He was enlightening the disciples just before His ascension (see Acts 1) or encouraging the apostle Paul during a stormy sea (see Acts 27), Jesus was there to uniquely touch those He had chosen. That touch enabled the disciples to reach a new level of ministry. The church planter must experience this same touch.

The first question I ask the prospective church planter, long before one word about strategy or budgets is uttered, is this: "Has Jesus touched you for this assignment?" How God touches, when God touches, where God touches—that is a sovereignty issue. But clearly, no man can seed a church without the commissioning of God.

Such a commissioning will pass through two stages: the subjective realm and the objective realm. When a person receives a vision for a new or changing ministry, it is often accented by oddities that are difficult for outsiders to understand. For Peter (see Acts 10), it was an unkosher sheet dropping from the atmosphere. For Paul (see Acts 9), it was a Son-stroke on an isolated Damascus off-ramp. For aging John the Beloved on the Island of Patmos (see Revelation 1), it was the thundering voice and the

> " **Guidepost 1: What role should the touch and whisper of Jesus have in your decision to birth a church?** "

personification of Glory. When I hear prospective church planters testify of their new vision, they usually accompany it with a look that says *I doubt anyone is taking me seriously.*

But in every case, for the vision to prove legitimate, the subjective moved into the objective. The church planter's vision must become real to others before they can be expected to lend their support. Peter needed to rehearse carefully the events at Cornelius' house before he was assured of the apostles' support for the new move of the Spirit to the Gentile world (see Acts 11). Peter did not arrogantly report, "Hey, I saw a big sheet falling out of a pure blue sky. So there! Now support my ministry." The subjective experience of the sheet-vision, though captivating Peter, was not enough to persuade the apostles to support the vision. They needed proof. They supported Peter only after he presented the estimable facts of his fruitfulness. History proves that the outpouring of the Spirit at Cornelius' house wasn't the full measure of God's plan for the Gentiles, but it was adequate enough to give credibility to Peter and his message.

There will always be a period in the church planter's journey between the receiving of the vision and the sharing of it so others will contribute to it. If the man or woman of God spiritually misunderstands this time delay, it could spell the end to God's great possibilities. It is crucial to remember that no cross or calling comes with a guarantee of time frames and deadlines. Between the call and the birth will be God's time for arranging a substantive support base for the new ministry; God always combines the necessary components when He calls.

If no one else is recognizing in your life the kind and measure of fruit for the task ahead, then stop pushing. Ask yourself, *Do my nearest ministry companions believe I have the abilities to nurture and lead a new church-planting venture? Is God confirming this project by speaking to others on my behalf about supporting this ministry?*

> # Guidepost 2: What breed of man or woman is God going to use to birth a church?

If these supportive components cannot be identified in the early stages, then hold your course and continue to seek God's direction. The timing is not right. Your vision could still be Throne-room initiated, but God needs a further interval during your foundational phase for bringing together the proper fittings.

The church planter travels on two paths. One path is characterized by planning, flowcharts, marketing, sound systems, letterhead, fund raising, and computers. The other path, by prayer life, study, fasting, holiness, long suffering, integrity, brokenness, and family life. The success of the second course determines the success of everything.

The dynamic that draws people to the servant of God is divine *radiance.* Radiance is the reality of God's friendship and favor that shimmers from the soul and lips of God's instrument. God longs for His ministers to possess radiance. But the prerequisite of radiance is fire. Moses met that radiance at the end of a mountainous marathon. The burning bush became the burning countenance (see Exodus 34). Stephen also met that radiance while being stoned on behalf of the Rock of Ages. The most difficult decision a church planter faces is not the obedient step through the doorway of opportunity, but the obedient step into the refining furnace of divine radiance.

For many church planters, this will be their first senior pastorate. While an excited cadre of new workers nurture the embryonic church, the new pastor suddenly finds himself in unaccustomed dimensions of spiritual tension. The private weight of leading a flock, the anxiety of weekly preaching, the strain of being a rookie CEO—all these factors and more represent new degrees of purgation for the soul. I've spoken to many church-planting pastors who find this time spiritually unnerving. The joy of responding to God's call seems ground away by millstones that can come with a fresh harvest.

> **God is not obligated to reveal the refiner's fire.**

When God gives a person a dramatic glimpse of tomorrow, He is not obligated to reveal the refiners fire that awaits—fire that produces radiance, fire that forges readiness into effectiveness. Peter was burned by this holy and purposeful fire. It illuminated his weakness and exposed the emptiness of his verbal pledges. But strangely, Peter's fire came on the heels of an affirmation by Jesus, affirmation for the revelation, "Thou art the Christ, the Son of the living God" (Matthew 16:16, KJV). Peter idolized the prospect of associating with Kingdom eminence. Anyone would. But when he then heard Jesus speak of His dying at the hands of the religious establishment, Peter became unstrung. He knew *his* death could not be far behind. What Peter failed to comprehend was that authority for being a Kingdom mouthpiece came from the willingness of the mouthpiece to become a martyr. And God still needs the spirit of the martyr—total commitment—in His church planters.

It takes two types of people to successfully plant a church: one humble enough to receive the vision and another ready to die under any assignment. They can be the same person. The church planter should anticipate a series of perplexities, quandaries, and sharply fashioned Satanic arrows to come when he or she faithfully accepts the journey of church planting. God's blueprint never changes.

Be encouraged! God ultimately carried out His dream through Peter. With the help of a raucous rooster announcing a betrayal more than a sunrise and an illustrated sermon featuring fish, Peter finally grasped with his heart, not just his head, the Kingdom equation for *radiance* in leadership. Any man or woman who will likewise grasp what Peter grasped can experience the same fulfillment. Successful church planting is impossible without it.

Evangelizing a Community

Randy Hurst

The apostle Paul told his young disciple and friend Timothy, "Do the work of an evangelist" (2 Timothy 4:51). It is evident that Timothy was called and gifted for a pastoral ministry. Yet his model and mentor exhorted him to do the work "of an evangelist."

While God assigns His servants to certain roles, no two ministers are alike. Not everyone in itinerant ministry is primarily an evangelist. On the other hand, many pastors minister in their communities as gifted evangelists. Unfortunately, some have taught designations concerning spiritual gifts that can become too rigid and categorical. Stereotypes of ministry can be very limiting and can even cause us to fall short of our calling.

The apostle Paul himself is an example of a blend of spiritual gifts. He functioned first as an apostle, but also as an evangelist, a prophet, and a pastor-teacher. From the perspective of having ministered in a variety of roles, he exhorted Timothy to do the work of an evangelist.

The Pastor As Model

Evangelizing a community begins with the pastor. Before a pastor can motivate his congregation to do outreach, he must first model doing outreach himself. I have ministered many years in itinerant ministry and have observed hundreds of Pentecostal pastors and churches. I have never seen a praying church that does not have a praying pastor. I have never seen a giving church that does not have a giving pastor. A worshiping church has a worshiping pastor. A missions church has a missions pastor. What the pastor is, in time, the congregation largely becomes.

Luke opens the Book of Acts with an instructive phrase about our Lord: "Jesus began both to do and teach" (Acts 1:1, KJV). The order is significant. The tendency of modern education is to try to teach first and then expect students to do what they have been taught. Jesus did first—then He taught. Our Maker became our Model. The apostle Paul understood this: "Be imitators of me, just as I also am of Christ" (1 Corinthians 11:1) and "Those things, which ye have both learned, and received, and heard, and seen in me, do" (Philippians 4:9, KJV).

Children do what their parents do much more often than they do what their parents say. The greatest leaders in history have all led by example more than by command. Almost all of us can look back through life at the people who influenced us most and see this principle. The old adage is true: "The most important lessons are caught rather than taught"—especially in evangelism.

This modeling principle can be seen throughout Scripture: in relationships such as those of Moses and Joshua, Elijah and Elisha, and Jesus and His disciples. It continued in the New Testament Church with Barnabas and Paul, Paul and Silas, and then Paul and Timothy. Where does a pastor today model the ministry of evangelism?

1. *In the pastor's family.* PKs who are committed to the Lord are representative of a home that has given them a good taste for the life in Christ. (At the same time, it must be noted that a child from such a home, having a will of his or her own, can turn away from God in spite of the good parental modeling.) Modeling a lifestyle of evangelism must begin in, of all places, the home. Evangelizing and discipling our children is a major part of the ministry God has given us.

2. *Before the congregation.* One of the most important ways a pastor can model evangelism in his church is by giving regular public invitations to salvation. Even when no one responds to a salvation invitation, an important thing is happening. People in the congregation are witnessing their pastor's concern, passion, and commitment to reaching the lost. If evangelistic efforts are only done perfunctorily, the congregation observes not only what the pastor does, but how he does it. Invitations to commitment and any other evangelism effort in the church service should be done with conviction, faith, and earnestness. The pastor's attitude about reaching the lost will be apparent to the people in his congregation.

3. *In the community.* The most effective evangelistic pastors I have known have all made a direct personal impact on people outside the church. Building relationships with the unchurched in the community and being genuinely interested in them as people will provide opportunities later on, when one of them is in spiritual need, to invite them to church or deal with them personally. When a pastor encounters people in his everyday activities and learns they do not regularly attend a church, it should be natural for him to invite them to visit his church. Pastors should acquire the same nickname as the Chief Shepherd, who became known as "a friend of sinners."

> "**'The most important lessons are caught rather than taught' —especially in evangelism.**"

One of the most powerful aspects of evangelism, to be dealt with in greater detail later, is simply praying with someone for a need or for the need of a member of that person's family. This practice is especially effective when done by pastors. Pentecostal people believe that God answers prayer. We should practice our belief by praying with and for people in the community. Just hearing a born-again believer pray has a significant effect on an unbeliever. And when God answers prayer, it can be the means of opening hearts to the gospel.

4. *In the pastor's world.* There is a direct correlation between a pastor's heart for the lost in his own community and his vision for the lost of the world. When a congregation can observe that their pastor's heart is burdened for the lost of the world, it affects how the congregation views the lost around them in their community. An expansive vision and burden for the lost everywhere will bear fruit in the local church.

Jesus said, "You shall receive power when the Holy Spirit has come upon you; and you shall be My witnesses both in Jerusalem, and in all Judea and Samaria, and even to the remotest part of the earth" (Acts 1:8). Some have mistakenly interpreted Acts 1:8 to imply that we must first reach our Jerusalem and then reach Judea, Samaria, and the remotest parts of the earth. That is not the wording of Scripture. Jesus did not say, "first . . . then" but "both . . . and." Our commitment to reaching the lost must be not only far-reaching but simultaneous. Generally, a church that commits to supporting missionaries and praying for the lost around the world will have an increased vision for reaching the lost in their own immediate world.

The Pastor As Motivator

We must always remember that the motivating power for evangelism comes from the Holy Spirit himself. What believers in a local congregation need as much as anything is just a little encouragement and training. In motivating believers for outreach, we are cooperating with the work of the Holy Spirit.

Pastoral motivation to evangelize comes basically in two ways: in personal exhortation and in public preaching. A pastor normally gets what he preaches. To motivate a congregation to evangelism, a pastor must strategically and regularly preach the Word that motivates people to do evangelism. Merely preaching a sermon concerning evangelism once or twice a year is not enough to keep a congregation focused on outreach.

Another effective way of motivating is personal testimonies, both from the pastor and the people in the congregation. If the pastor is modeling evangelism in his everyday life, he will have testimonies to share publicly. (It is best not to publicly name people to whom the pastor has witnessed, but testimonies discreetly shared will encourage a congregation to follow their pastor's example.)

Testimonies by other congregational members are most effective when they are selected and directed by the pastor. I was in a service in which the pastor invited evangelism testimonies from the congregation. Only one testimony out of six was appropriate. If church people are encouraged to tell their pastor about their witnessing experiences, he can occasionally ask certain ones to share a testimony with the congregation. Testimonies are most effective if they are used selectively and sparingly.

It is not emotional or sensational things that most effectively motivate believers to practice evangelism. I have found the two most powerful motivational factors are these:

A response to Christ's sacrifice. To effectively evangelize, we need a genuine realization that Christ died for us. Our Christian service is a logical and "reasonable" response to the sacrifice of our Lord (Romans 12:1, KJV). The apostle Paul took the Lord's sacrifice personally, and that was the secret to the powerful motivation he had to reach the unreached (Galatians 2:20). Paul reveals that his personal motivation came from the logical conclusion that "One died for all . . . and He died for all, that they who live should no longer live for themselves, but for Him who died and rose again on their behalf" (2 Corinthians 5:14–15).

The Work of the Spirit. We need an understanding that evangelism is primarily a work of the Holy Spirit. Convicting unbelievers of their sin is not our work, but the Holy Spirit's. We are the witnesses for Christ, but the Spirit is the One who wins people to Christ. He is the One who convinces unbelievers of sin and leads them to confession and repentance. It is also the Spirit who empowers believers to express effectively, through both word and action, the truth and reality of Jesus in their lives. The pastor who keeps his congregation focused on both the Lord's sacrifice and the power of the Holy Spirit, who enables us to obey our Lord's commands, will be providing the two most powerful motivators for evangelism.

The Pastor As Manager

The importance of regular public salvation invitations must be emphasized again. Whether or not someone responds to an invitation is not an indication that a particular sermon or service was a success. If no one comes forward, this is not an indication that the pastor's message was ineffective. On the other hand, the fact that someone responds to a salvation invitation is not an evidence that the pastor's sermon *was* a success. A person coming to Christ is a work of the Holy Spirit. We proclaim the message of the gospel and give the invitation, but only God can open a heart (Acts 16:14). Paul said about his apostolic ministry, "I planted, Apollos watered, but God was causing the growth" (1 Corinthians 3:6).

When a pastor commits himself to giving regular salvation invitations, God will send unbelievers to that church to respond to the invitation. It is not we who are building the Church, but Jesus Christ himself!

A young man who had just accepted a pastorate came to me for advice. One of the things I exhorted him to do was to give a salvation invitation at the conclusion of every Sunday service, even if no one came for an entire year. When I ministered in the young man's church about a year later, it had grown from a little more than one hundred to more than seven hundred. He said that one of the major reasons for the growth was salvation invitations every Sunday, and God had blessed them by sending unbelievers and backsliders to the church to respond.

Minnesota District Superintendent Clarence St. John pastored for twenty-one years in Hibbing, Minnesota. He faithfully gave salvation invitations every Sunday for *seven years* before seeing a breakthrough. Then 50 came forward for salvation in one year. Two years later, even after erecting a new building, they still had to go to two morning services. They had 377 come forward for salvation that year, more than one for each day of the year.

TRAINING FOR EVANGELISM

Christ gave pastors to the Church "for the equipping of the saints for the work of service, to the building up of the body of Christ" (Ephesians 4:12). Training members of the congregation for personal evangelism is one of a pastor's most important biblical responsibilities. Many people in our congregations are regularly being stirred by the Spirit to share their faith and experience with unbelievers. What they need from the pastor is a little encouragement and a little training. I emphasize the words *a little*.

> **" When the Spirit is moving, a little training will do. "**

When the Spirit is moving in people's lives, they do not need to be pushed to do what God is leading them to do, but simply exhorted and encouraged.

Again we emphasize the importance of teaching a critical principle for motivating outreach: God is the One who saves people. The Holy Spirit is the One who convinces of sin. It is Jesus who is building His Church. We simply take part in the miracles that God is working in this world.

When it comes to training, there are many approaches to personal evangelism. However, the volume of content sometimes taught can be overwhelming, intimidating. This is one of the reasons so many Christians do not get involved in evangelism training courses. People certainly need encouragement to know the Word and to be prepared for certain common situations they may encounter. But the most effective witness people can give is not about *what* they know but *Who* they know.

Many Christians have been given the false impression that they must memorize great amounts of Scripture to share with unbelievers. Although Jesus quoted Scripture frequently, it is interesting to note that He did not quote Scripture to the Samaritan woman or to Nicodemus. We must always remember that we are not just imparting knowledge or convincing people of the truth of our religion. We are giving testimony to a relationship.

Having done churchwide training sessions for personal evangelism in many churches, both in the United States and in foreign countries, I have found that the following suggestions are most helpful in leading Christians to become effective personal witnesses:

1. Share from your own experience how you knew your sins had been forgiven, that you are a new creation in Christ and have an eternal home in heaven. The apostle Peter said that you should always be "ready to make a defense to every one who asks you to give an account for the hope that is in you, yet with gentleness and reverence" (1 Peter 3:15).

2. Learn to avoid religious argument and controversy in encounters with people. Focus instead on a person's relationship with God, on whether or not that one has found the peace of knowing God's forgiveness and is assured of eternal life.

3. Find opportune ways to invite people to come to church where they can experience God's presence and receive the ministry of the Word from the pastor.

4. Pray with unbelievers. One of your most powerful means of witness is simply praying in the presence of an unbeliever. Unbelievers almost always sense immediately the reality of our experience with the Lord when they hear us speak to Him. As born-again believers, we can sometimes take for granted the living relationship we have with our Lord. Even though unbelievers may pray at times, praying is an awkward and uncomfortable practice for them. Public prayers offered at events can also be an example of the difference between the impersonal formal prayer of a nominal Christian and that of a born-again believer. Even unbelievers can tell the difference!

PROVIDING OPPORTUNITY FOR EVANGELISM

Another major aspect of managing evangelism is providing opportunity for church members to participate in evangelism. The Holy Spirit is continually dealing with people in the congregation, moving them to be witnesses. If given leadership, these people will reach out to unbelievers. Sometimes motivation in itself is not enough. People need to be challenged with achievable and specific projects they can participate in. Space will not allow discussion of the many ways we can provide opportunity for church members to witness, but I have found the following to be especially effective:

1. *Prayer triplets.* This approach to prayer offers an opportunity to put Matthew 18:19–20 into practice. Church members join two others in regular prayer for specific friends and family members who do not know Christ. On a particular Sunday, church members gather in groups of three and write down on a Prayer Triplet card (which is a Bible marker) the names of between one and three friends and family members who do not know Christ; the group agrees in prayer for them. Participants try to join in prayer with one or both of their prayer triplet partners by phone a couple of times during the week and possibly for a few moments together at church before or after services. Prayer can then be put into action by giving an evangelism gift book and later an invitation to each unsaved person to attend special church services. Prayer triplets can be utilized either on an ongoing basis or for a specific period of time, especially leading up to special evangelism services or Easter and Christmas services.

2. *Special sermon series.* A productive approach to evangelism that I utilized when I pastored was preaching a special sermon series. These were mostly expository messages, but I tried to choose titles that were both representative of the biblical content and had the appeal to stimulate interest among the general public. Some of these series had titles such as "Testing Your Mental Health," "Divine Guidance," "Spiritual Warfare," and "Last Days Lifestyles." Printing fliers or brochures for congregation members to distribute to their friends worked very effectively, as did advertising the sermon series in the newspaper.

3. *Friend Day.* For many churches, "Friend Day" has been especially effective for attracting unbelievers to church services. Friend Day gives a good reason for church members to invite their friends and also gives their friends a good reason to come. The bond of friendship creates a wonder-

ful opportunity for a Christian to invite a non-Christian friend to church.

4. *Christmas and Easter evangelism.* Christmas and Easter offer two of the most opportune times for an evangelism focus in a church. Encouraging congregation members to invite unbelievers to Christmas and Easter services can be the two most productive times of the year for outreach. Two activities that can enhance this are: (1) getting people in the congregation into organized prayer groups, such as prayer triplets, in the weeks leading up to Christmas or Easter, and (2) involving the church families in Bible-reading disciplines for the same time period. I have seen hundreds of churches have great evangelistic results in the process. Numbers of pastors have testified that they have seen more unbelievers come to Christ and become a part of the church as a result of this kind of program than any other organized evangelistic outreach they have used. The pastor and the church must be prepared to make the most of these evangelistic opportunities through both invitation and follow-up.

5. *Evangelism gift books.* Having evangelism gift books on hand for opportune encounters with unbelievers is a very effective way to facilitate outreach. Congregational members can be encouraged always to have two or three copies of a readable translation of the Gospel of Mark, the Gospel of John, or an evangelistic book that can be given to an unbeliever the Holy Spirit is dealing with. I recommend the Gospel of Mark more than the Gospel of John because it is a simpler, shorter, more direct presentation of the life of Christ than the Gospel of John. Other books I have found very helpful to share with unbelievers are narrative testimonies like *The Cross and the Switchblade* by David Wilkerson and *Born Again* by Chuck Colson. For some people, a book like *Mere Christianity* by C. S. Lewis is very helpful. A harmonized life of Christ, utilizing passages from all four Gospels, is especially appropriate for unbelievers.

6. *Ministries to meet specific spiritual needs.* Developing ministries in a local church that focus on the unique spiritual needs of groups, such as the single parent, the divorced, or the unemployed, can reach people with the gospel in their time of greatest need.

7. *Community prayer ministry.* A pastor-friend of mine saw great evangelistic response by taking specific prayer needs of the community. Groups of two from the church walked through neighborhoods praying for the residents house by house as they walked. After doing this for three weeks, they visited the homes and told the residents that they were from the Assemblies of God church, that they believe God answers prayer, and then asked if there were any prayer requests to share with the church. Many people freely shared prayer requests. The congregation began praying for those requests and a few weeks later the prayer teams returned to the houses. They asked people if the Lord had been answering their prayers and invited them to attend church services. The first Sunday, 52 people received Christ as Savior.

Effective Evangelism

Although this chapter has suggested ways of leading a church in evangelism, nothing is more important than a pastor seeking the Spirit's creative direction for his life, his church, and his community. The Holy Spirit knows how to reach each community, and He knows the spiritual gifts and resources of every pastor and local church. A pastor who will seek the Holy Spirit's creative direction will find it! I have found three characteristics that can make a church especially effective in evangelism:

1. *A church of the Word.* Strategies for attracting people to the church will ultimately fail if the Word of God is not presented in power when those people come. The "seed" for planting the harvest is always the message of the gospel. If a local church has a reputation in the community as a place where the Word of God is preached with power and effectiveness, people will come to hear it, and their lives will be changed.

2. *A church of the manifest presence of the Holy Spirit.* The Spirit's presence empowers a church as nothing else can. Even unbelievers can sense that something is different about a Pentecostal church. The pastor and congregation should continually pray for the moving of the Holy Spirit in church services.

3. *A church on a mission.* We are led by the Spirit, live in the Spirit, and minister in the Spirit in order to reach our world before Christ returns (Acts 1:6–8). Pentecostal believers who anticipate having the Spirit lead them into divine encounters with people will be prepared to be used by God in evangelism in many ways beyond those planned by the pastor and the church.

The pastor can model evangelism, motivate for evangelism, and manage evangelism. But we as Pentecostal ministers and believers must never forget that evangelism is first and foremost a work of the Holy Spirit and that Spirit-filled believers are privileged to have a part in the miracles that God is working in people's lives to bring them "out of darkness into His marvelous light" (1 Peter 2:9).

Mobilizing Men and Women for Outreach

Dale Lane

Reaching the lost of America has not been one of the church's great successes. Many missionaries have been sent to foreign fields, while few have stayed to reach the American heathen. The church has put great resources into missions, which is necessary; but at the same time we need to reach our "Jerusalem." Here at Phoenix First Assembly we have decided we must go to the streets of our valley to win a lost and dying world. We need people all over America to stand and say, "This city is ours in the name of Jesus."

Mobilizing people was the spark that brought this great revival in Phoenix. Jesus said, "Go ye into all the world, and preach the gospel to every creature" (Mark 16:15[1]). We have assumed this command is fulfilled from behind the pulpit. But this false assumption is stripping laypeople of a God-given assignment. It wrongfully restricts to the clergy a ministry that belongs to all of God's children.

In mobilizing people for ministry, we must follow the New Testament church plan, "They, continuing daily with one accord in the temple, and breaking bread from house to house, did eat their meat with gladness and singleness of heart, praising God, and having favor with all the people. And the Lord added to the church daily such as should be saved" (Acts 2:46–47). A New Testament church is one whose members come to be strengthened, edified, equipped, and then sent out to fulfill God's purpose for their lives. "He gave some, apostles; and some, prophets; and some, evangelists; and some, pastors and teachers; for the perfecting of the saints, for the work of the ministry, for the edifying of the body of Christ" (Ephesians 4:11–12). Paul here records the leadership offices God has given to the church. For what purpose were they given? "For the perfecting of the saints," that they (the saints) may do "the work of the ministry." The layperson has an assigned ministry, the winning of the lost and the healing of the hurting. At Phoenix First Assembly, approximately 60 percent of the congregation is involved in such ministry.

Faithfulness year after year after year is the mark of a great church and pastor. The pastor reproduces himself in the lives of the people. The people are not customers, not spectators, nor do they stand in the arena and gaze—they are participants. Members of the New Testament church were participants. "They that were scattered abroad went every where preaching the word" (Acts 8:4). The Greek word translated *went everywhere* means literally "passed through," that is, they went from place to place announcing the good news, the Word. Every child of God has a calling. All have been called to be obedient to their Lord and Savior, Jesus Christ. The people are the ministers. Mobilizing the people of God to obedience in witnessing is our job as leaders in the church.

What is motivation? One dictionary defines the act of motivating this way: "To provide with an incentive or a reason, to impel, incite, invoke or inspire." Another dictionary says, "The inciting of an individual to action based on internal force." Jesus said, "Whosoever will save his life shall lose it: and whosoever will lose his life for my sake, the same shall save it" (Luke 9:24).

How Do We Start?

Today's church is too often always on the verge, always just about to do something. The pews are filled with unrealized potential, untapped energy. We end up having a church of "pew potatoes." We must rouse pew potatoes to become the warriors God wants them to be. In reality, tradition often stops new and creative ideas. Attempted change is met with the claim, "We do not do that here; we have never done that before." Tradition is tremendously important in the right setting, but it too often hampers church growth. The church must always be on the cutting edge in reaching people with the gospel.

How do we start? Pastoral and layleaders must learn to train, equip, and delegate. To delegate means working oneself out of a job, releasing people to minister. Trusting the disciple to do the job assigned comes next. About 50 percent of the time, the volunteer will get the job done differently than the pastor would. That does not make it wrong. Here is the secret. If the result of the volunteer's plan is to build and extend the kingdom of God and win souls, then we should flow with the plan. Our goal is the same although our methods may be different.

Leaders Enable and Mobilize

As leaders, we must be enablers. Leaders meet goals and encourage volunteers to meet goals. Enablers support and train the volunteers. The focus must be on the volunteer and not on the program or ministry. There are four basic factors that mobilize people: conviction, needs, goals, and perspective.

CONVICTION

Conviction is what a person really believes deep within. Paul said, "'I consider my life worth nothing to me, if only I may finish the race and complete the task the Lord Jesus has given me—the task of testifying to the gospel of God's grace'" (Acts 20:24, NIV). If we are to devote a major part of our life to a cause, we must be firmly convinced as to why we should do it. Are we fully convinced there is a heaven to gain and a hell to shun? Do we know why we serve God? Do we know why we work for God? Knowing how is tremendous, but when you know why, it drives you to action. Mobilizing people should become part of the fiber of our doing and being. It is simply obeying Christ's command to make disciples.

Why should volunteers be committed to the task? (1) *The brevity of life.* David prayed, "When I am old and grayheaded, O God, forsake me not; until I have showed thy strength unto this generation, and thy power to every one that is to come" (Psalm 71:18). (2) *A sense of stewardship.* We have a responsibility for the life God has given us. We are bought with a price—He has made an investment in us. "Let everyone bless God and sing his praises, for he holds our lives in his hands. And he holds our feet to the path" (Psalm 66:8–9, TLB). (3) *Desire for my life to count for God.* I would hate to reach the end of the road and have it said I had never lived at all. I want to pass on abundant life in Christ to many others. I can do it through spiritual multiplication, reproducing myself.

NEEDS

Each person has needs. As leaders, we must let our people know the needs of others in our cities and around the world. The mission statement of Phoenix First Assembly describes a soul-winning church as having a pattern of good works that might inspire other churches around the world to imitate. "Go ye therefore, and teach all nations, baptizing them in the name of the Father, and of the Son, and of the Holy Ghost: teaching them to observe all things whatsoever I have commanded you: and, lo, I am with you alway, even unto the end of the world" (Matthew 28:19–20). To achieve this goal, with excellence in every area, it is necessary to establish and maintain strong, integrated ministries of education, discipleship, and prayer that will undergird hundreds of outreach ministries designed to meet needs and heal hurts. Our motto is "A Church with a Heart." We encourage our people to find a need and fill it, to find a hurt and heal it.

"I have compassion on the multitude, because they continue with me now three days, and have nothing to eat: and I will not send them away fasting, lest they faint in the way" (Matthew 15:32). Jesus' compassion when he saw the needs of the people always brought action. This fundamental truth that mobilized Jesus should be the underlying principle for all outreach ministries.

GOALS

First, our life goal should be, like Paul's, to know Jesus.

[For my determined purpose is] that I may know Him—that I may progressively become more deeply and intimately acquainted with Him, perceiving and recognizing and understanding [the wonders of His person] more strongly and more clearly. And that I may in that same way come to know the power outflowing from His resurrection [which it exerts over believers]; and that I may so share His suffering as to be continually transformed [in spirit into His likeness even] to His death (Philippians 3:10, TAB).

Second, people must also have intermediate goals. Philippians 3:14 says, "I press toward the mark for the prize of the high calling of God in Christ Jesus." Every individual in the church has a high calling (a dream) to fulfill. As leaders, we often fail to release volunteers to fulfill that dream due to our own fears and insecurities. However, if we are effectively communicating the vision God has given us, their dreams will be *our* dreams. When Pastor Barnett and I came to Phoenix First Assembly, we prayed that God would send people to us who had the same vision as we have. Not only did God bring new people to the church, he began to change those who were already there to embrace this vision as well. When your vision, your dream, is clear, it will be reproduced in the lives of your people.

Third, people must also have short-term goals. These goals can be yearly, monthly, weekly, daily, whatever is fitting. For example, we set goals in bus ministry for each route for the week. These should be goals that are attainable, but challenging, so that volunteers will feel a level of success. This will in turn motivate them to set new goals at a higher level. These goals will also include leadership positions, giving people a sense of fulfilling their calling (intermediate goals). As the short-term goals are accomplished, so are the intermediate and life goals.

PERSPECTIVE

Perspective, the way a person sees things, determines the extent and direction of motivation. "Ever since we first heard about you we have kept on praying and asking God to help you understand what he wants you to do; asking him to make you wise about spiritual things; and asking that the way you live will always please the Lord and honor him, so that you will always be doing good, kind things for others, while all the time you are learning to know God better and better" (TLB).

When we begin to see things from God's point of view, we will be properly motivated to operate in His perspective of love. Love means action! Love will compel you to reach out to the lost. It will make you go where the sinners are, outside the four walls of the church. Love will make you run down to the valley of the shadow of death to get someone and bring that one to the mountaintop of God.

Good Models Make Good Lay Workers

If we are to effectively mobilize men and women for outreach, we pastors and leaders must be living what we preach and teach. Our people should be able to imitate us, to follow us as we follow Christ. Our lives must reflect the following:

Right motives. Motives must be true and consistent with the Word of God. The foundation must be winning people to Christ and developing praiseworthy disciples. People must always have a sense that their work is building the kingdom of God, not a badge of prestige for the pastor.

Right attitudes. As leaders, we do not have the privilege of staying discouraged or remaining depressed. We need to be self-starters, excited, motivated, and positive. Attitude is a reflection of character. Character is more important than talent. God commits to character.

Love of people. We must be marked by love for God and humanity, willing to serve. John Wesley's number one requirement in selecting leaders was that they must be truly alive to God, with love for God and mankind. If you truly love people, they will love you back. They will follow your example. They will not voluntarily follow leadership unless they know that you love both God and them. Ed Cole, founder of Christian Men's Network, recently said, "No one cares what you know until they know you care." If you reach out to people, your people will reach out to others in need.

Vision and plans. After God has given you the vision, you must develop a plan for fulfilling it. Workers become disillusioned when the vision is only talked about. Outreach ministries should be systematic and started one by one. Instruct and inspire the congregation in the ministry you are beginning. Let them know what to expect. My suggestion would be to start with a soul-winning program and bus ministry. From these two, other outreach ministries will evolve.

A consistent example. You as the pastor need to set a pattern of good works. Remember, no one can follow a dead horse. If you do not work, your people will not work. Start your meetings on time, be organized, and have a plan. While you are trying to mobilize people, you may face deficiencies in your relationship with your congregation which hinder your leadership of them, for example, inattention to their problems, staying aloof from them, failing to listen, being disorganized, not praying for them. Good models, free from besetting hindrances, will mobilize people for effective service.

Leaders Communicate the Vision

A leader is someone who dreams dreams and has visions and can communicate them to others in such a way that they say yes. The great illusion of leadership is thinking that people can be led out of the desert by someone who has not been there. The leader must consider people more important than programs. We must be aware of the tremendous impact we have on those we lead. Whether we enable or disable, encourage or discourage the volunteer, our personal feelings must never be allowed to hinder the work of God. It is our responsibility to lead, but it is the volunteer's responsibility to be led. We need to be transparent, but always show the answer, not the problem. Leaders are ordinary people who just do not quit.

The mandate is clear. As the people of God, we are to be about the Father's business. We are to be doing great exploits for Him. The church is not to be served, but it is a work force to be released to greatness. I challenge you to go to your "Jerusalem" and turn your city upside down for the glory of God.

Training and Commissioning Elders and Deacons

Richard L. Dresselhaus

Leadership under God is the key. Build a strong team of leaders, and the church will prosper. Surrender leadership, and the entire enterprise will ultimately collapse. The key is leadership.

And, Pastor, the focal point of this essential leadership is the board of elders and deacons. Collectively, under your anointed oversight, they will set both tone and direction for the work God has given you charge of. If you succeed here, your church cannot help but prosper. But if you fail here, you can anticipate dismal and disastrous failure. Again, the key is leadership. And the focus of your leadership energies must center in the official boards given you by God to help shoulder and lead the church you pastor.

Participatory Leadership

The pattern for participatory leadership is dynamically modeled by Jesus himself. Faced with the task of world evangelization, Jesus called to himself twelve common men He could impart himself to. To these men He ultimately entrusted the work of carrying the gospel to the ends of the earth. Consistent with this strategy, Jesus dedicated three years to the equipping of them so they might fulfill this universal mandate.

Reflect on this incredible strategy for a moment. If you had but three years to launch a global mission, how might you spend your time? In addition, if you also faced the pressing demands of the masses, how might you expend the resources available to you?

Added to this, what if those recruited to serve with you in this incredibly demanding task were uninitiated, unlearned, and ill-prepared? It is just this sense of demanding complexity that brings credibility to Jesus' strategy. He simply lived and served with His disciples. In this way they participated in His life, so then when He was gone, they represented Him to the world. The evidence is in. The method worked. In three years Jesus departed. But His disciples, now empowered by His Holy Spirit, led the most world-changing spiritual revolution ever known. So much so that commentators described these disciples as having turned the world upside down.

A wise pastor will learn well from the master Teacher. Faced with the same mandate, to carry the gospel to the ends of the earth, this pastor will pour his life into a team of leaders in such a way that by his example and spirit, they will be well-equipped to carry on the Lord's work. This paradigm of multiplication in ministry is imperative. Work alone, and you will achieve what one person can achieve. Train and commission others to serve at your side, and you will multiply the work in incredible ways.

Sadly, some pastors have been diverted from participatory and relational ministry because of the pressing demands of ministry. Visitation, funerals, administration, counseling, and preaching preparation have been relentless; little time seems left for investment in team ministry.

This is a mistake of the first order and a radical violation of the principles of leadership modeled by Jesus. Violation here can mean short-term pastorates, ineffective ministry, a deeply frustrated and hurt family, and, frequently, depleted strength and ruined health. Wise pastors will embrace the leadership style and strategy of Jesus. It alone really works.

The Contemporary Crisis

Pastoring is not like it once was. The radical shift from rural to urban, from service to information, from general to special, from intimacy to isolation, and from spiritual to secular have put a pressure on pastors unknown in earlier years. Never before has a pastor been called upon to be so much to so many. The task seems overwhelming!

The threat of litigation, prequalifying children's workers, mandatory reporting—these are matters rarely faced in the past. Now the pastor lives daily with their possibility. The expectations of excellence, the high demands for effective communication, and the ever-present indifference of a secular society—these test the depth of dedication in every pastor. Couple to all of this the crush of the principalities, powers, and the darkness of this age, and any honest minister of the gospel will cry out, "Who is equal to such a task?"

It is against this complex and compelling backdrop that we speak here about training and commissioning elders and deacons. The day is past, and maybe never was, when one person can carry the load and discharge the ministry mandate under which the church serves. The call here is for a well-trained leadership team, serving side by side with the pastor, to carry on the multifaceted ministry characteristic of today's church.

New Testament Patterns

Participatory leadership is not only exemplified by Jesus but is widely demonstrated in the Early Church. Although every detail of church government may not be required of the church in our day, those early patterns of church government offer a great deal of instruction. Their lessons are many.

DEFINITIONS

We begin by defining the leadership offices in the Early Church. *Elders*—When churches were set in order in the first century, elders *(presbuteroi)* were appointed to conduct the offices of the local church. Literally, the word meant "older men." *Bishop*—The term *bishop (episkopos)* was used interchangeably with the term *elder* (Acts 20:17,28). Literally, the word meant "overseer." Perhaps *elder* designated the person and *bishop* defined his office. *Deacon*—The term *deacon (diakonos)* designated one who was chosen to serve, a servant to the body of Christ.

How does this work out in a local church? Typically, one of three models is followed: (1) The pastor and his associates function in the role of elders, and the elected board fulfills the role of deacons or trustees. The pastor and his staff provide overall direction for the church, and the board of deacons or trustees come alongside to assist in facilitating the vision and direction of the church as defined by the pastor and his staff. (2) Qualified laypersons are recognized as elders to serve with the pastoral team in all spiritual matters, while the board of deacons or trustees deal with matters of administration and accountability. (3) A board of elders, including the pastors, gives overall direction to the church in all matters, and the board of deacons or trustees become the facilitators of that established direction and vision.[1]

Since New Testament patterns of church government appear to be more descriptive than prescriptive, it is right that each local church determine what leadership model will best serve its particular needs. Following are some questions that need to be asked in making such a determination: (1) Is the pastor granted enough authority to assure dynamic and effective leadership? (2) Are safeguards for assuring the highest levels of accountability set in place? (3) Is the will of the congregation allowed full expression and authority? (4) Does the structure facilitate the best kind of participatory leadership?

Again, although the patterns of church government in the New Testament may not be incumbent on the church in every generation, their principles are indeed applicable. That is, whether administrative leadership is assigned to elders or deacons/trustees may well be somewhat incidental, but the principle of servanthood and integrity remain always a requirement. While laypersons may serve as elders alongside the pastor, that in no way strips away his prophetic role.

QUALIFICATIONS

Gene A. Getz, in *The Measure of a Man,* lays down the general qualifications for spiritual leaders.[2] These requirements are applicable to pastors, elders, and deacons or trustees.

1. *Above reproach* (1 Timothy 3:2). The emphasis here, as well as in Titus 1:6–7 and Acts 6:3, is on a man's reputation. Spiritual leaders are to be well spoken of and highly regarded by both the community within and without.

2. *Husband of one wife* (1 Timothy 3:2). The Roman culture of Paul's day was infected with moral looseness much as our culture. In some cases, this influence had gotten into the church in ways incomprehensible even to the pagans of the day. Against this background Paul calls for the highest level of fidelity and single-hearted devotion to the institution of marriage. A spiritual leader is to be the husband of but one wife and, we might add, be living with her in tranquillity, peace, and honor.

3. *Temperate* (1 Timothy 3:2). The word here speaks of balance and self-control, free of indulgent behavior. This quality, exhibited gracefully, will enhance the impact of a spiritual leader in every exercise of his spiritual leadership.

4. *Prudent* (1 Timothy 3:2; Titus 1:8). The apostle Paul uses the same word in Romans 12:3: a believer is "not to think of himself more highly than he ought to think; but to think soberly . . ." (KJV). To "think soberly" is to practice "prudence." In other words, spiritual leaders are called upon both to live and to serve with a sense of intentionality and deliberateness. Careless conduct and thoughtless decision-making are here prohibited.

5. *Respectable* (1 Timothy 3:2). The word here refers to a life that is well-ordered, proper. It speaks to the practical matters of cleanliness, tidiness, and appearance. The point is clear: How we look and how we act give credibility to the leadership we exhibit. Here is one way to love and care for people in a way they cannot ignore.

6. *Hospitable* (1 Timothy 3:2; Titus 1:8). Graciously serving the practical needs of the body of Christ is part of what spiritual leadership is all about. This may involve opening your home to others, providing meals, or simply providing transportation when needed. While spiritual leaders may not always be available for such acts of kindness, the responsibility to provide such care rests there in any event.

> **Integrity always remains a requirement.**

7. *Able to teach* (1 Timothy 3:2; Titus 1:9). The word used here *(didaktikon)* is also used by Paul in 2 Timothy 2:24, where the force of the word extends to the quality and manner of life. The meaning is powerful. Spiritual leaders teach as much by example as by precept. Ability to teach speaks to all of life. It has to do with industry, integrity, and attitude. Put most simply it means "to practice what you preach."

8. *Not addicted to wine* (1 Timothy 3:3; Titus 1:7). The word translated here is *paroinon,* which means to "overdrink," or to "drink to excess." Modern society is plagued with alcoholism. It accounts for thousands of

deaths, either by accident or illness. This says nothing about the violent behavior it produces in the home. Spiritual leaders must avoid any behavior or practice that might contribute to this affliction on modern society.

9. *Not self-willed* (Titus 1:7). Here Paul warns against appointing any individual who is absorbed in himself, whose world revolves around himself, and who seeks his own cause rather than the welfare of others. He is determined to speak his own mind, advance his own cause, and promote himself whenever possible. Such a person is unworthy of spiritual leadership.

10. *Not quick-tempered* (Titus 1:7). Unchecked anger has the power to destroy the work of God. Acts of rage, cutting words, sharp criticism, bad moods, and every form of hostility rise out of the spirit of anger. Sadly, like feathers scattered by the wind, it is virtually impossible to mend the damage caused by expressions of anger. Rightly, a quick temper disqualifies any person from serving as a spiritual leader.

11. *Not pugnacious* (Titus 1:7). The King James translation has captured the meaning of the Greek word used here by translating it "striker," one who physically lashes out against another. The reference is to an expression of anger that moves beyond verbalization to action. When Cain killed his brother, when Moses murdered the Egyptian, or when Peter cut off the ear of the high priest's servant, it was "pugnacious" behavior.

12. *Uncontentious* (1 Timothy 3:2,3). The Greek word translated uncontentious is *amachon,* which might best be translated "peaceable." All of us have met individuals who are contentious. They argue on almost every point, push hard to get their own way, and can still find fault when others offer only praise. That nasty spirit of agitation—that restless and disquieting attitude—undermines the work of God.

13. *Gentle* (1 Timothy 3:2,3). The word used here is *epieike,* which describes that coveted attribute of kindness and forbearance. It has the force of a kind and gentle response to confrontive harshness. Jesus is the supreme model of this much-needed attribute. In the heat of controversy, this is the kind of leader who will apply the oil of kindness and inspire an attitude of reasonability and righteousness.

14. *Free from the love of money* (1 Timothy 3:3). The word translated here, *aphilarguron,* is a three-part composition word: *a*—not; *phil*—love; and *arguron*—silver, money. Jesus warned about the danger of a wrong regard for wealth. Rightly, spiritual leaders are to seek first the work of the Kingdom and then trust that God will add all else that is needed. Misplaced affection at this point will neutralize the impact of a spiritual leader.

15. *One who manages his own household well* (1 Timothy 3:4). The most powerful sermons preached by any spiritual leader are delivered by the members of his own family. It was precisely here that Eli the prophet and David the king both failed. The one did not restrain his wanton sons, and the other neglected his sons for the work of the kingdom. The consequences in both cases were disastrous. God charges spiritual leaders to devote themselves fully to the nurture and care of their families. This is the first charge of ministry to the people of God.

16. *A good reputation with those outside* (1 Timothy 3:7). The church

is called to be the showcase to the world of the redemptive love of God in Jesus Christ. How can this become a reality if spiritual leaders have a blighted reputation in the very community the church is located in? It might be well if nominating committees for elders and deacons/trustees would speak first with a man's neighbors and those he works with. Their report will become a final kind of judgment on the acceptability of a candidate being considered for spiritual leadership.

17. *Loving what is good* (Titus 1:8). Some have an eye for the wholesome, positive, constructive, and good. Others have an eye for the unwholesome, negative, destructive, and bad. Obviously, the eye will see only the object of its focus. Spiritual leaders are to have a trained inner eye on all that is good.

18. *Just* (Titus 1:8). The word *just (dikaios)* picks up on both the vertical and the horizontal aspects of living and serving in a "just" way. That is, the just man is in right relationship with God and with his fellowman. Fairness and equity become indispensable attributes for effective leaders in the body of Christ.

19. *Devout* (Titus 1:8). This essential quality for effective leadership places the accent on a person's being set apart from the world and given unto the Lord. To be devout *(hosios)* means to be consecrated for sacred service much as was the furniture of the temple used in Israel's worship. However, this kind of separation in no way suggests an isolation from the world. Rather, it is a call away from what is immediate and of this earth in order to return to the world and bring it to Christ.

20. *Not a new convert* (1 Timothy 3:6). The emphasis here is on depth of maturity as demonstrated by quality of life. Thus the new convert *(neophutos)* might be "chronologically new" but well advanced in spiritual growth and development. Of course, one might be "chronologically old" but behind in a corresponding spirituality. Paul's warning is clear. It is folly to place into leadership anyone who lacks the understanding and maturity to deal with the complex and demanding work of the church.

Rightly, the Scriptures hold a high standard for spiritual leaders. There is no work so important in either time or eternity as the work of the Kingdom. A wise pastor will insist that those chosen to serve as spiritual leaders will meet the qualifications set forth by the apostle Paul.

The Selection Process

In a sense, the selection process is where the work begins. Who in the church should be chosen to provide leadership? Who possesses the essential qualifications for leadership as set forth in Scripture? By what mechanisms of selection might these individuals be chosen? Several matters must be considered.

Selection procedure. It is impossible here to discuss all of the varieties in board selection processes found in our churches. A brief summary will be helpful: (1) The board of deacons/trustees is elected for a specific term by the membership. The term of office is typically three years. (2) The board of deacons/trustees is elected by the membership but the term of office is indefinite. That is, the members of the board, once elected, will serve until resignation, removal, or death. (3) The board of elders is "recognized" as having attained already a place of spiritual influence and leadership. The term here is also indefinite. The board of elders is "non-administrative" in function and serves to complement the work of the pastoral team. In cases where the board of elders serves as the primary policy-setting and accountability board, it is wise that they be in some way selected by the membership.

Nomination. Here again, the procedural variety found in our churches is great. In smaller churches the entire membership is frequently involved in the nominating process. Where individuals are well known, this procedure can work rather well. In larger churches a committee is usually appointed by the board to place in nomination a list of candidates who in the judgment of the committee meet the qualifications for these offices. While it is still possible to entertain nominations from the floor, to do so tends to invalidate the work of the committee.

What is the function and purpose of the nominating committee? (1) Its members must be fully aware of all the qualifications necessary for those offices nominations are being made for. Both scriptural and bylaw requirements must be followed. (2) Nominating committee members must devise whatever means necessary to determine whether or not a prospective nominee meets all requirements. It might be well, especially in larger churches, to devise and send a questionnaire to all those persons under consideration to determine if indeed those requirements would be met. Conversion, baptism in the Spirit, marital status, faithfulness, tithing, giftedness—these are just a few of the areas a questionnaire might cover. Personal interviews can also prove very effective. One thing is clear: this committee must be well informed if it is to make the proper choices in the nominating process.

Presentation. It is the responsibility of the nominating committee (assuming its existence) to place in nomination those who have been selected. Again, in larger churches especially, it will be helpful to post the list of nominees well in advance of the meeting. That listing could include pictures, vocation, length of membership, offices held, ministry involvement, family, and giftedness. Members will be grateful for this information as they prayerfully consider their choice. Also it is very important that each nominee be properly presented at the membership meeting. Typically an alphabetical introduction will be sufficient. It is generally unwise to ask each nominee to speak. Previous notification will have given people opportunity to make inquiry on their own in a private and more appropriate context.

Leadership Principles

The point has already been made that Jesus exemplified participatory leadership; that is, He poured His life into His disciples over a period of three years. He then dispersed them into the world to fulfill the great commission He had entrusted to them. But how might a pastor apply that fundamental principle in working with his own boards? Here are a few suggestions: (1) Give time at each board meeting to train and equip. (2) Schedule regular retreats to facilitate planning, equipping, and personal enrichment. (3) Provide reading materials for board members to help them fulfill their position of leadership. (4) Spend personal time with each board member—a lunch, a visit, a golf game, or some other occasion that will foster relationship. (5) Send board members to leadership seminars where they can be exposed to good principles of leadership. Often district councils provide such opportunities.

What are some of the essential principles of ministry leadership that in one way or another must be communicated to board members?

1. *Ministry is by relationship.* It was true with Jesus, and it must be true with us: The impact of spiritual leadership is measured in terms of relational health. If a leader has a dynamic and authentic relationship with God and people, the impact will be profound. If not, the results are dreadful. A richly gifted individual may squander all those resources simply because relational wholeness in personal interaction is lacking. The truth is this: people will not follow one they cannot respect. And relational immaturity will cause just that. A wise pastor will both model and communicate this essential principle of leadership: Ministry flows out of Christ-centered relationships.

> " **People will not follow one they cannot respect.** "

2. *Ministry is by inner resource.* The inner flow must always be commensurate with the outward demands. It was just this that called Jesus away from the crowds into the solitude of the hills where He was refreshed through prayer and communion. It is no less true with us: The inner man must be nourished and the spirit refreshed. Only then can the heart speak and serve out of its abundance. This is why busyness is one of the leader's greatest enemies. It dries up the very wellsprings of effective ministry.

3. *Ministry is by way of incarnation.* Jesus "became." That is the heartbeat of the gospel and the essence of Christ's mission. He was incarnated (became a man) by His heavenly Father. It was through this becoming that He has reconciled us back to God. Here is both the model and enablement for authentic ministry today. Spiritual leaders, and all other believers for that matter, are called to become Christ to a lost and dying world. That is, we "stand in for Jesus" by loving and serving in His name. When spiritual leaders grasp experientially this principle, their lives will bear much fruit.

4. *Ministry is by example.* Most people are not conceptually oriented. They prefer to *see* rather than just *hear.* "Show me" is the cry of needy people all around us. They hope to catch a glimpse of an authentic faith, a faith lived out in life. How do leaders teach love? By being loving. How do they teach forgiveness? By being forgiving. How do they teach tithing? By being tithers. How do they teach faithfulness? By being faithful. How do they teach forbearance? By being forbearing. How do they teach holiness? By being holy. Here is a principle of ministry leadership that if practiced will bear much fruit.

Accountability in Action

5. *Ministry is by intentionality.* Good leaders pray, think, plan, execute, and follow through. They work and serve by design. They reject the haphazard and lock in on the intentional. This is leadership that does not

ignore details, gives logical and thorough responses to inquiries, and is careful never to forfeit leadership by being lax. I have often said "The ticket to the pulpit is bought with management dollars—you fail to manage, and soon you will fail to preach." True! Failure to manage time, conflict, people, resources, and spirituality will nullify the efforts of any leader. The same principle is true with all leadership. Effective board members will be well trained in execution. They will lead by intentionality.

6. *Ministry is by Spirit empowerment.* Authentic and effective ministry is exclusively by the enablement of the Holy Spirit. "'Not by might nor by power, but by my Spirit,' says the Lord Almighty" (Zechariah 4:6, NIV). Be it praying, preaching, teaching, counseling, helping, planning, or visiting, all must be done in the name of Jesus and in the power of the Holy Spirit. A wise pastor will be sure that the leadership team he directs understands both in concept and in practice the indispensability of this principle. What may appear to be the work of the Kingdom may in fact be only the expression of human ingenuity. Only that ministry empowered by the Holy Spirit will count as the true work of the Kingdom.

These are leadership principles essential to the effective work of pastors, elders, board members, and any others who partner together in the work and ministry of the church.

Operational Guidelines

It is time now to consider some of the guidelines which must be followed if the operation and function of the church is to proceed effectively and efficiently. While the guidelines given here may apply differently to different boards, in principle they will still find a significant and helpful application. Obviously, space limitation requires a measure of selectivity.

1. *Agendas.* Boards do not work well in an informational vacuum. It is the responsibility of the pastor to be certain that essential information is made available in a timely fashion. Following are typical items that might be included in church board agendas: (a) Time and place of meeting, (b) the minutes of the previous meeting, (c) financial reports, (d) specific items to be discussed, along with all supporting information, and (e) any items that may be added by members of the board at the beginning of the meeting.

Provide the agenda well ahead of the announced meeting. A rule of thumb might be that board members should have the agenda in hand prior to the weekend preceding the meeting. In this way board members will be able conveniently to make any inquiries that may be useful in the decision-making process.

The minutes should be taken carefully, accurately reflecting the collective decisions of the board. While brevity is desirable, it should never be at the expense of truth and openness. Minutes should be carefully filed for future reference. Carelessness in these matters can result in unnecessary church division and unrest. Congregations appreciate knowing that the church is thorough in its administrative work.

Financial reports should be both accurate and simple. The membership need to feel confident that all moneys are meticulously accounted for. Policy setters cannot be expected to make decisions without knowing fully the financial impact of those decisions. Financial reports need to be clear and accurately reflective of the overall financial condition of the church. With a quick review of the report, board members should have income and expense comparisons, the balance in all accounts, the relationship between cash positions and budget, and a summary of assets and liabilities. It is wise to consult a qualified accountant to be sure that all of the financial records are in proper form. Also wise is a periodic audit of all financial reports.

Each item in the agenda should include a full description, along with any recommendations which may be appropriate. Board members need to know history, financial impact, possible alternatives, and finally the recommendation deemed most appropriate by the pastor and staff. Much time will be saved if an agenda includes all supporting documentation and recommendations. Typically, church boards are policy setters and the pastoral team the administrators. If this distinction is preserved, it will result in greater efficiency of operation and harmony in relationships.

It is recommended practice that board members consult ahead of time with the pastor before requesting that items be placed on the agenda. With his direction, those items can be processed in a more orderly fashion. Ideally, such items can be included in the formal agenda, along with any supporting documentation. The relationship between process and unity is absolute—do things properly, and people will be encouraged to give their support.

2. *Task designations.* In some cases, it may be helpful for the pastor to assign a portfolio to each board member. While each church would have different needs, I suggest the following assigned portfolios: (1) children, (2) youth, (3) adults, (4) music, (5) facilities, (6) missions, and (7) outreach. Obviously there will be great diversity here because of the unique ministry of each church.

Several cautions are in order here. An assigned portfolio does not carry with it the authority to act unilaterally. All decisions of significance must necessarily flow through the pastor in order to avoid confusion and to facilitate decision making. Also, board members do not give equal effort to their assigned areas. Departments may feel that they are being weakly represented and secretly wish that the assignments had been made in a different way. The only way to avoid some of these potential problems is for the pastor to provide strong but sensitive leadership.

3. *Operational manual.* Every church should have a comprehensive list of operational guidelines. In larger churches this might be rather lengthy, for smaller churches much more brief. However, the necessity is the same for both. This manual should include appropriate job descriptions, employment procedures, vacations, conference leave, continuing education, financial policies, work hours, accounting flowcharts, department structures, and any other procedural guidelines that may be dictated by specific needs.

Carefully stated guidelines yield positive results. Unless these guidelines are formalized and written, they will soon be forgotten and ignored.

Pastors are usually surprised how frequently they will need to refer to this manual for guidelines on vacation time, holidays, expense forms, benefits, etc. Again, these policies and procedures must be formalized and written.

Division in church life is typically the result of mismanagement. Spiritual leadership should not settle for less than the very best in policy and procedure. It is well worth the effort.

Commissioning

Church leaders will serve best if those they lead regard them with godly respect and honor. It is the pastor's duty and privilege to establish that kind of regard for those who comprise the leadership team. Typically a congregation will regard as important and valuable what is so established by the pastor. If the pastor places a high premium on participatory leadership, the congregation will know that and hold in high regard those who serve as a part of the leadership team.

It is recommended here that the pastor set aside a specific time when the boards of the church are presented to the membership and formally commissioned to the task they have been chosen for. Although this might be done in any number of ways, what is important is that the leaders of the church are consecrated before the Lord and His people for the task they have been called to. It will be this service that will set the pace for anointed and empowered leadership.

What greater privilege could anyone have than to be a chosen leader set aside to serve the body of Christ, which is His church?

The Gift of the Evangelist: A Pastor's Perspective

Glen D. Cole

The New Testament makes it obvious that evangelists are one of God's gifts to the church (Ephesians 4:11). Paul told Timothy, "Do the work of an evangelist" (2 Timothy 4:5[1]). Very likely at that time evangelists carried the gospel to new regions as missionaries. The biblical relationship of the evangelist to the local church pastor could well be described as "partners in reaching our world for Christ."

A report to the 1987 General Presbytery from the Total Church Evangelism Strategy Committee contains a paragraph that clearly establishes what the Assemblies of God has always believed:

The vitality and growth of the Church of Jesus Christ is directly related to its commitment and participation in the winning of the lost. We must do it. It is important to consider the context of evangelism. Jesus commanded his disciples to make disciples of all nations. As we seek to set our course for the coming decade, we need to recognize that evangelism includes (1) bringing people into a personal relationship with Jesus Christ, and (2) discipling each person until he is ready to win another person to Christ.[2]

As we consider, therefore, a pastor's perspective on the gift of the evangelist, we need to state that some who carry the title of evangelist are really teachers with specialty ministries. Their ministry is, appropriately, to the saints.

As the church moves to a new millennium, perhaps the emphasis needs to be that spoken by Jesus:

"The Spirit of the Lord is upon Me,
Because He has anointed Me to preach the gospel to the poor.
He has sent Me to heal the brokenhearted,
To preach deliverance to the captives
And recovery of sight to the blind,
To set at liberty those who are oppressed,
To preach the acceptable year of the Lord" (Luke 4:18–19).

In these end times the local church and the evangelist are harvest partners. The great need is for apostolic credentials. Then will follow what I sense most of us are looking for—a Book of Acts demonstration!

As a pastor working for over forty years with evangelists to help reach our world for Christ, I have chosen a key word for our focus: *partners.* Let me suggest four areas that will assist us in accomplishing the statement from the Total Church Evangelism Strategy Committee report.

Partners in Prayer

First of all, the pastor and the evangelist must be *partners in prayer.* The church should be led by the pastor in prerevival prayer; at the same time, the evangelist must be preparing his heart and life through prerevival prayer.

It has been my privilege to participate in no less than four Billy Graham crusades through the years. I have been a vice-chairman in two of those crusades. A reporter put a microphone in my face as people streamed to the altar at the invitation of Rev. Graham following a simple gospel message. His question was "Can you explain this?" There is at least one explanation for the multiplied hundreds who have come in every crusade service through the years. That is the investment of prayer. Months before a crusade ever happens, a multiplicity of prayer opportunities are set in motion: Pastor's prayer meetings. Women's prayer meetings. Youth prayer meetings. Men's prayer meetings. City-wide prayer meetings. A prayer card giving a prayer topic for every day helps congregational members who need a focus of prayer. The community of faith becomes partners in prayer with the evangelist long before he arrives on the scene.

As a guest speaker in an Assemblies of God church recently, I noticed the Communion table covered with pictures of individuals. I learned from the pastor that he had encouraged his people to bring photographs of unsaved family members so that prayer could be offered for them regularly. It was no surprise when he reported to the congregation the miracle conversion of a member's daughter whose picture had been placed there for prayer.

I do not wish to be negative, but I must point out the importance of the pastor and evangelist praying together when the time of revival emphasis has arrived. I have been disappointed in certain cases where the evangelist did not heed my invitation to attend the Saturday night prayer meeting prior to the Sunday beginning of a crusade. Others, of course, responded with eagerness. Prayer sets the table for what will follow!

Partners in Stewardship

The pastor and the evangelist become *partners in stewardship.* Stewardship is the investment made in any given effort. The church makes an investment and the evangelist makes an investment.

PUBLICIZING THE REVIVAL

The pastor leads the way by preparing appropriate advertising materials to get the word out that a special emphasis is coming. These could include newspaper advertising, radio spots, television clips, bulletin inserts, and handouts for congregational members to leave with family and friends. The word must get out!

How can the evangelist help in this? By sending ahead captivating message titles that will appeal to the nonchurched and unsaved. The interest factor must be developed ahead of time if a meeting is to be successful. Both the pastor and the evangelist contribute to this preparation. As the evangelist crisscrosses the country in meetings, he might come upon samples of advertising that have brought significant results and forward those to the pastors he will be working with in the future.

Banners and posters will help announce the coming of an evangelist. The church calendar should be completely cleared for the emphasis so that conflicts will be at a minimum. Let the focus be on winning the lost and reviving the saints.

THE EVANGELIST'S REMUNERATION

Another part of *stewardship* has to do with the way an evangelist is compensated for his ministry. There are three areas to consider.

1. *Travel expenses.* It will help the evangelist greatly if preparation can be made ahead of the crusade for payment of travel expenses. For example, if an evangelist flies to the crusade city, that ticket must be secured well in advance for the best rate possible. The evangelist should feel free to report that cost to the local church for reimbursement as soon as the cost is known. Other expenses relating to travel could include car rental and food. These should always be the responsibility of the inviter, not the invited. A pastor blesses the ministry of the evangelist when these items

are handled with loving care and foresight.

2. *Lodging.* An evangelist (including wife and/or family) needs as commodious a place as possible for effective ministry. Quiet time is essential to prepare one's heart and mind for ministry. Access to appropriate meals is another consideration associated with lodging. Specific needs of the evangelist should be made known in ample time for local arrangements. The evangelist makes an investment of time, family, and giftedness to help a pastor reach his community for Christ. May the local investment in the time the guest evangelist is in the city be thought through and carried out in a Christlike manner.

3. *Honoraria.* What is the policy of the local church in giving to the evangelist? This should be clearly understood prior to the time of the crusade. I believe that people should be given the opportunity to bless the evangelist with offerings, just as they are blessed by the ministry. A church should never begrudge giving generously to the gifted ministers that grace the platforms of our fellowship. These servants of God cannot have meetings fifty-two weeks a year. Their income must be sufficient to cover those times when there is no income. The time of remuneration is the time to remember these words: "'It is more blessed to give than to receive'" (Acts 20:35).

When done properly, a special evangelistic emphasis does not cost, it pays! God's Spirit at work in the hearts of the people will more than take care of the financial need. It is the responsibility of the local leaders to give the Spirit that opportunity to work.

Partners in Dedication

The pastor and evangelist become *partners in dedication.* I would like to suggest how you as a pastor may spell "evangelist."

Servant—The evangelist comes with the spirit of servanthood.

Enthusiastic—There is a sense of life in the ministry of the evangelist. Jesus came that they might have life. We don't need "dead" evangelists!

Resourceful—He is alert to every opportunity to bless the local church, bringing every power of his office to combat the forces of darkness in any given community.

Valuable—This is a God-appointed office. It is therefore not something we put up with, but rather part of God's effort to reach lost humanity.

Available—If called, he doesn't quit! He doesn't let discouragement turn him aside. The greatest victory of his ministry may be just ahead.

Necessary—The church cannot get along without the evangelist. If "God has put in the church . . ." let us never consider the calling unnecessary.

Triumphant—May there be the sound of victory in the voice of the pastor and of the evangelist as they press the claims of Christ on the hearts of people. "I serve a risen Savior, He's in the world today."

Let the evangelist, the pastor, and the church do their very best as *partners in dedication.*

I was watching a sports special recently on television. Heroes of the past were being highlighted. The face of Tom Dempsey came on the screen, the former kicker for the New Orleans Saints football team. Tom was born with only half a right foot and a deformed right arm and hand. Although he played outstanding football in high school and college, he was turned down by the pros. They were saying to him, "You are not professional material." Tom refused to accept that view of his abilities. *He was dedicated to being an achiever.*

Tom Dempsey set the record for length of a field goal kicked in a professional game. That record came in a game with the Detroit Lions. The New Orleans team had victory in their grasp when with 11 seconds left, the Lions' kicker booted a field goal from 18 yards out and put them ahead 17 to 16. It looked like the game was over. However, in two plays the Saints took the kickoff back to their own 45-yard-line. With two seconds on the clock, the coach sent Tom into the game to attempt the longest field goal ever made. It would take a 63-yard kick to send the ball through the uprights. Tom was so far from the goalposts that he wasn't sure it had crossed the bar until the official underneath raised his arms to signal a score.

The sports world is still saying, "Unbelievable!" But it happened. A man dedicated to his sport and to his ability to perform did the impossible. I believe the same kind of conviction and dedication will bring the blessing of God upon the efforts of the pastor and evangelist who determine that their combined commitment can make a big difference in these sensual, seductive, and skeptical times.

Partners in the Harvest

Finally, I go back to an earlier statement on becoming *partners in the harvest.* In the September 7, 1969, issue of *The Pentecostal Evangel* (p. 13) was a brief account by Vance Havner titled "Saints In Circulation." This took place during the 1600s.

> During the reign of Oliver Cromwell the government ran out of silver coins. Cromwell sent his men to a cathedral to see if they could locate any silver.
>
> They reported, "The only silver we could find is in the statues of the saints standing in the corners."
>
> "Good!" he replied, "we'll melt down the saints and put them into circulation!"
>
> Certainly the need of the hour is that the saints be melted down in revival fires and put into circulation winning the lost.

The thrill of partnering in the harvest as pastors and evangelists is to see the saints turned on to Jesus so that winning the lost becomes second nature. It can happen! It is happening where this team concept is understood. May God bless our pastors and our evangelists in the great effort. "The gates of hell shall not prevail." (Matthew 16:18).

The work of the evangelist, from a pastor's perspective, also includes the altar. May our altars be filled with seeking souls. The pastor and the evangelist work together in ministry at that sacred place. I was ministering as a guest in a church on a Sunday night. The altars were filled with seekers, and my wife and I diligently sought to pray with each one and assist them in any way possible. When the last person had left the altar, the custodian came to inform me that the pastor had gone home earlier with his family. The pastor had left his thanks for our coming with the custodian. A partnership? Not that night!

The pastor's perspective is summed up in the words of Paul: "We then, as workers together with Him" (2 Corinthians 6:1). The pastor and the evangelist are vitally linked with God in reaching the world and nurturing the flock.

The Gift of the Evangelist: An Evangelist's Perspective

Jimmy Davis

H ave your evangelism goals become root-bound like redwood trees stuffed into flowerpots? Are you failing to reach the evangelism potential in your local church due to limited horizons? Are you willing to develop up-to-date, creative approaches to evangelism? The life of the local church must center around a biblical orientation to winning the lost. Pentecostalism is evangelism. When the heartbeat of evangelism slows or dies in the local church, there will be fewer revival emphases for the saints and less evangelistic campaigns for the lost. Evangelism and Pentecostalism are inseparable in the life of the church.

The ministry gift of the evangelist has immeasurable spiritual influence in the church. For example, five hundred evangelists preaching only forty weeks per year to an average of one hundred people per week equals two million hearers annually. God is raising up a new generation of evangelists who are prepared both intellectually and spiritually to equip the church and to evangelize the lost in this highly technological and global community. The gift of the evangelist is crucial for continued vitality in the church.

The gift of the evangelist is just as valid today as it was in the early decades of the Christian Church. For the local Pentecostal pastor to fully utilize the gift of the evangelist, he must not only understand the biblical *position, purpose,* and *portrayal* of the first-century evangelist, but also comprehend the *priorities* and *preparations* of the twenty-first-century evangelist. Foundation precedes function. The first-century evangelist is our biblical example for the ministry of the twenty-first-century evangelist in the life of the local church.

The Position of the Evangelist

In the New Testament, there was not much difference between an apostle and an evangelist since all apostles were evangelists. However, not all evangelists were apostles, since a direct call by the Lord was essential.[1] The term *evangelist* appears only three times in the New Testament (Acts 21:8; Ephesians 4:11; 2 Timothy 4:5). *Evangelist* in Ephesians 4:11 seems to denote an order of workers between apostles and prophets on the one hand, and pastors and teachers on the other. Is it coincidental that the evangelist is located in the middle of the five ministry gifts in Ephesians 4:11? Or is this a further indication that evangelism is to be in the central function of the church?

The twenty-first-century evangelist should have an evangelistic ministry as well as an "equipping" ministry. The position of the evangelist should build a bridge between prophetic and pastoral ministries in the church. The evangelist has an essential role in *repentance* and *revival* today.

The Purpose of the Evangelist

The evangelist's purpose is clearly defined in the Ephesian letter. The aim of all five ministry gifts is to equip God's people for "works of service" (Ephesians 4:12, NIV). For the evangelist, the works of service are evangelism. The message and ministry of the evangelist challenge the Christian to abandon spiritual infantilism and become a perfect and full-grown person.

This maturing process depends on an interrelationship of the various ministries in Ephesians 4:11. The whole is continually being fit together and held together by each separate ligament (Ephesians 4:16). It is only when each part is working properly that the body of Christ receives the full support it needs to do the "works of service." To recapture the spirit of evangelism in the church, the biblical role of the evangelist must be reestablished.

In the years ahead, ecclesiastical discussions should not center around categorizing a person as an evangelist or a revivalist. Rather, those with itinerant ministries should be encouraged to fulfill their New Testament position and purpose as evangelists. *In the final analysis, however, the church determines the kind of ministry the evangelist will have within the body of Christ.* The evangelist can have a soulwinning ministry only when he is preaching in a soulwinning church or is given the opportunity to proclaim the gospel to unchurched people.

Portrayal of the Evangelist

Although examples of itinerant preachers, or evangelists, abound in the New Testament (John the Baptist, Jesus Christ, the apostles, the Seventy, Philip, Paul, and others), three distinct pictures clarify the function of an evangelist in the church. Below are three New Testament functions of the Pentecostal evangelist essential to the energized life of the twenty-first-century church. Regardless of our ministry gift in the twenty-first century (apostle, prophet, evangelist, pastor, teacher), our central purpose is evangelism. Evangelists can be effective in local church crusades, in the pioneering of new churches, as part-time or full-time ministers of evangelism in a multistaff church, on the mission field, and in national evangelistic ministries.

Preacher-Evangelist	Pioneer Evangelist	Pastor-Evangelist
(Luke 10:1–19)	(Acts 8)	(2 Timothy 4:5)
Dignified Mission (v. 1)	Supernatural Wonders (vv. 5–8)	Thoughtful Evaluation (v. 5a)
Difficult Mission (vv. 2–3)	Scriptural Work (vv. 9–12)	Tremendous Endurance (v. 5b)
Disciplined Mission (vv. 5–8)	Submissive Will (vv. 13–24)	Tireless Evangelism (v. 5c)
Deliverance Mission (vv. 9,17–19)	Spirit-led Witness (vv. 25–40)	Total Effort (v. 5d)
Preaching Christ	**Reaching the City**	**Teaching the Church**

The Priorities of the Evangelist

Unless a person has traveled for an extended period of time, it is virtually impossible to understand the lifestyle of an itinerant minister. The following priorities are intended to crystallize for pastors the behind-the-scenes life of the evangelist. The first priority of the evangelist is his *faith in God.* Dr. Billy Graham has said, "Evangelists are activists. Traveling, meeting new people, organizing, and preaching keeps us busy. But we need to remember that it is not so much our activity for Christ as our captivity for Him which is most important."[2]

As the influence of an evangelist expands, greater physical and spiritual demands are made upon him. He must constantly guard private time with God. An evangelist needs godly wisdom and spiritual discipline to maintain the balance of study, prayer, personal growth, health, and administration while traveling full-time today. A changeless core is essential to handling a changing environment week after week. Normal community life does not exist for the full-time itinerant preacher.

It is most appropriate for the pastor to help the evangelist guard his or her spiritual life during the church crusade. For example, the pastor should not send a member of the opposite sex to pick up the evangelist, whether at the airport or the hotel. The pastor should permit the evangelist flexibility during the week to study and pray for the nightly services and nourish his own devotional life with Christ. The evangelist needs to be accountable to the pastor during the week of crusade services. He should insulate himself from the world, but not isolate himself from his fellow laborers in the harvest field.[3] There needs to be a well-balanced association between the evangelist and the pastor.

The second priority of the evangelist is *family.* If the evangelist travels alone, his family is without a father/husband most of the year. They have sacrificed along with the evangelist to seek and save the lost. A burden for those without Christ, invitations to preach the gospel, and the financial concerns in the ministry make it difficult for the itinerant preacher to remain home for extended periods of time.[4]

Checklist for Selecting an Evangelist

To help pastors select evangelists for particular congregations, the following checklist is a compilation of the New Testament purposes and patterns of the evangelist in the Early Church:

1. What is the purpose of the upcoming ministry event (Ephesians 4:11–16)?
2. Will the evangelist fit the purposes of this crusade?
3. Is the evangelist known as a solid Bible preacher (Ephesians 4:12–13)?
4. Will the evangelist equip the saints for evangelizing the lost (Ephesians 4:11–16)?
5. Does the evangelist conduct himself as a Christian ambassador for the Lord (Luke 10:1)?
6. Does the evangelist live by faith for his finances in the local church (Luke 10:4-8)?
7. Do supernatural signs follow the evangelist's message (Luke 10:9, 17–19)?
8. Is the evangelist accountable to fellow ministers (Acts 8:14–24)?
9. Does the evangelist refrain from engaging in sensationalism to attract crowds (Acts 8:9–12)?
10. Is the evangelist submissive to authority (Luke 10:18–19)?
11. Is the evangelist willing to go to a church when the timing is best for the local assembly?
12. Is the evangelist ethical in all areas of ministry?
13. Does the evangelist do the full "work of the evangelist" (2 Timothy 4: 5)?
14. Does the evangelist focus on exalting the name of Jesus Christ (Acts 8:12)?
15. Is the evangelist a personal soul winner (Acts 8:25–40)?

If possible, the local church should pay for the evangelist to make a daily phone call home during the crusade. This would be an additional blessing to the spiritual, emotional, and financial well-being of the evangelist's family. Another possibility would be for the pastor to receive a love offering for the evangelist's spouse, who in effect has labored along with the evangelist in the ministry. The church must consciously be aware of the constant stress on the family that an itinerant minister endures on a regular basis.

The third priority of the evangelist is *physical fitness* under difficult circumstances and demands. The evangelist lives with changing locations featuring different surroundings, unfamiliar sleeping conditions, a new schedule (with a new pastor), and a changing menu nearly every week. It is difficult to maintain an exercise routine, much less other normal patterns of life. Nevertheless, one must work diligently to maintain physical fitness. The evangelist has to be flexible in order to meet the unique demands of ministry. This is a crucial concern to the evangelist and the longevity of his or her ministry.

The fourth priority of the evangelist is *staying current.* In our culture the combination of traveling and staying in hotels is synonymous with vacation. However, while traveling, the twenty-first-century evangelist will maintain a fully functional office on the road, in the air, or in the hotel. Correspondence will be maintained with a portable notebook computer and laser printer. Future, cost-effective cell phone networks and electronic mail will make the evangelist accessible anywhere in the world. Sending and receiving faxes in the setting of a hotel room, without even going to the registration desk, will be normal. Computer desktop publishing will make it possible to design and print newsletters out of town, and financial programs with on-line banking will permit up-to-the-minute bookkeeping while on the road. The Bible and sermon software of the twenty-first century will make it possible to prepare sermons with full access to theological libraries throughout the world via the Internet. The pastor should understand that just as the local church has an ongoing office during the crusade, the average evangelist will have a full functional office in the motel room. For maximum results, pastor and evangelist together will need to decide how to put "first things first" individually and jointly during the evangelistic crusade.

The fifth priority of the evangelist is *finance.* Even though the evangelist may not speak freely about personal finances, it is of great concern. The pastor should approach the evangelist with a willingness to comprehend the evangelist's financial needs. Without such information, we may be operating on erroneous assumptions.

Even though often on the road, an evangelist must maintain a home residence with the expenses of mortgage, lawn care, taxes, utilities, and a ministry office. The pastor should ask himself what a week or two costs to own and maintain the residence he lives in. Evangelists must maintain an automobile. Due to the long distances evangelists travel, they need a large, roadworthy vehicle. If the evangelist comes by air, the church should cover this expense in advance, since tickets were probably purchased several weeks or months in advance. If the evangelist has two or three days free time between meetings, motel and food costs will be an additional financial burden.

The evangelist has medical, car, and house insurance premiums. Yet there are many weeks without income due to certain holidays when churches have their own special activities. Many churches do not schedule evangelists from Thanksgiving to New Year's, on holiday weekends, or in the summer. The evangelist does not receive a Christmas bonus from the church, paid expenses to ministerial functions, vacation and sick pay, or reimbursement for office expenses. These are some of the financial realities of the evangelist's ministry. To relieve some of these financial burdens, today more churches are providing monthly financial support to help the evangelist stay in the harvest field.

In the final analysis, it is the evangelist's responsibility to behave and minister as an ambassador for Christ. It is the local church's responsibility to provide financially for the evangelist's travels and ministry. Woe to the evangelist who places high financial demands on the local church. Woe to the local church that robs or takes advantage of Christ's ambassador (Luke 10:4–8,10–11,16).

Preparation for an Evangelist

In today's world, publicity requires more than prayer, a poster, a pulpit, a program, a preacher, and a place to meet both the saved and the unsaved. Evangelist and pastor should work together, according to proven principles of evangelism. The following principles will assist the evangelist, the pastor, and the entire congregation toward evangelism and revival.

PLAN TO BE PRODUCTIVE

Expect more effort and energy to go into the creative phase than into the crusade phase. Preparation comes before proclamation. Every goal requires a plan. Planning in advance coordinates the work of many people to ensure a successful crusade. Ninety percent of an iceberg is below the surface of the water; only 10 percent of it is above the water line. The larger the 90 percent portion, the larger the more visible 10 percent area. The more foundational work done prior to the crusade, the more visible will be the results of the event.

Do not allow tradition to stifle an upcoming crusade. Just because the local church has always had a "spring crusade" does not mean that a couple with school-age children, for example, will come every night of the crusade. If possible, the evangelist and the pastor should schedule around events in the community that may conflict.

PRIORITIZE WITH PURPOSE

What is the purpose of the future crusade? Is it evangelism? Is it revival? The purpose of the crusade determines our priorities, and our priorities determine our procedures. In the natural realm, a farmer spends 80 to 90 percent of his time preparing for the harvest. Only some 10 percent of his time is actually spent in harvesting. The simple point is that quality sowing time will produce reaping results in the local church. Preparation for an evangelistic crusade must not be treated as a last-minute, all-night cram session for a final exam. The pastor should answer the following two questions: What procedures need to be practiced to attract lost people to the crusade? What will involve the whole congregation in the evangelistic event or revival crusade?

PROMOTE FOR PARTICIPATION

The pastor and the evangelist must do more than merely inform the congregation of an upcoming evangelistic event. They must instruct them regarding their participation in the crusade. The pastor should consult the evangelist about what has worked in other churches in order to attract the unconverted to the crusade as well as to increase the involvement of the saints.

Every believer can be involved in some way to prepare for the gift of the evangelist to be exercised in the local church. Dr. Sterling Huston, Director of the North American Crusades for the Billy Graham Association, writes:

> Management experts tell us that involvement plus participation equals commitment. . . . Involvement in the process, and participation in the decisions, yields commitment toward the goals of any project. . . . The larger the number of people in some meaningful role in the preparations, the larger the number of people who will be influenced by these involved people. Each Christian has a web of relationships about his life involving family, friends, neighbors, and acquaintances where he works, shops, or goes to school.[5]

It is extremely important to plan, organize, and recruit within the local church to assure maximum involvement in the evangelistic event. Effective evangelism is the result of organizing people and executing procedures based on the priorities of the Bible.

The evangelist and the pastor should promote for full participation of the body of Christ in evangelization of the unchurched. There should be responsible individuals over music, counselors, finances, advertising, children's ministry, the nursery, ushers, prayer, discipleship, prospective converts, etc. Dr. W. E. Biederwolf said, "The devil comes along with something the natural man wants, and he paints the town red to let them know he is coming. The church comes along with something the natural man doesn't want, and thousands of pastors seem to think a mere announcement of the project from the pulpit is quite enough."[6]

PRAY FOR POWER

Although people, procedures, and programs are important in preparing for the evangelist, prayer is the greatest priority. We cannot organize prayer, but we can organize opportunities for prayer. Be creative in arranging as many people as possible to pray specifically for the evangelistic event. The pastor and the evangelist must be the pacesetters for the church in prayer.

Prayer is foundational to success in crusade evangelism. Prayer will release the power of God and will motivate church members to be involved in other areas of the crusade as well. We must pray as though the outcome of the crusade depended on God and plan, prepare, and promote as though it depended on us.

PROVIDE FOR PRESERVATION

The final invitation of the crusade is not the conclusion of the event. It is only the beginning of the discipleship process. Just as every believer needs to be involved in preparing for the evangelist and the actual crusade, so must every Christian fulfill a part in "disciple-making." The follow-up of newcomers is just as important as their response to the evangelist's invitation. The ultimate purpose for ministry is not to make decisions but to "make disciples" (Matthew 28:18–20).

Drawing In the Net

Jesus Christ is chairman of a great worldwide fishing enterprise and desires us to be His partners in catching people alive for Him (Luke 5:1–11). It is time to stop having lifeguard meetings while people are drowning in sin. The Church must launch out into the deep waters of our culture and evangelize, believing God for bountiful results. This will require teamwork among all the various ministry gifts in the church.

God has called the entire Church to evangelism and has chosen particular people to be the gift of the evangelist to the body of Christ. God has historically used evangelists to begin spiritual movements that shake entire nations. John the Baptist, Jesus Christ, the apostles, the Seventy, Paul, and others in the New Testament were itinerant preachers. They left us most of the New Testament. They impacted their communities, cities, and countries for Christ. They were imprisoned, crucified, and even beheaded for proclaiming the gospel.

A great chasm separates the churched and the unchurched today. The various ministry gifts of the church must again make evangelism the heartbeat of saints. While people talk about their culture, let the church talk about Calvary. While Americans discuss the problems of education, let the church proclaim the power of salvation. We need to be willing to turn pulpits into fishing boats, our automobiles into ambulances, our homes into shelters, our bodies into the temples of the Holy Spirit, and our churches into hospitals where the souls of men and women can be healed by the grace of God.

The tide is going out. People are calling for someone to save them as they are about to sink under the surf for the last time. Adjourn the lifeguard meeting and reach them before it is eternally too late!

Bibliography

Armstrong, Richard. *The Pastor as Evangelist in the Parish.* Philadelphia: Westminster Press, 1990.

Davis, James O. "Equipping for Effective Evangelism." *Enrichment,* winter 1996, 1.

_____. "Evangelism in the Church." *Advance,* March 1995, 31.

_____. "The Evangelist's Biblical Role in the Church." *Advance,* April 1995, 31.

_____. "Revitalizing the Revival." *Advance,* January 1994, 30.

_____. "The Zip Code Revival." *Pentecostal Evangel,* 30 April 1995, 82.

Douglas, J. D., ed. *The Calling of an Evangelist: The Second International Congress for Itinerant Evangelists.* Minneapolis: World Wide Publications, 1987.

Graham, Billy. *A Biblical Standard for Evangelists.* Minneapolis:World Wide Publications, 1984.

Sweeting, George. *The Evangelistic Camp.* Chicago: Moody Press, 1955.

Signs and Wonders

Gordon L. Anderson

Pentecostals believe in miracles. Jesus said that the Spirit was on Him so He could preach the gospel to the poor, proclaim release to the captives and recovery of sight to the blind, to set free the downtrodden, and to proclaim the acceptable year of the Lord (Luke 4:18–19). For Pentecostals, the power given at the baptism of the Holy Spirit allows the believer to minister as Jesus did, and the gifts of the Spirit outlined in 1 Corinthians 12 include miracles. Still, there is a great deal of confusion about signs and wonders and just how and when they occur.

This confusion has increased as new movements have come along in the past number of years with various claims about faith and God's provision for believers to be both healthy and rich. Others claim that various activities such as falling and laughing are manifestations of the power of God. But is this so? Is "falling under the power" a miracle, a sign, or something else?

In this chapter I will attempt to clear up some of the confusion by defining a few key terms *(sign, wonder, miracle, manifestation, human response)* and answering a number of questions, including Do miracles occur today? What is their purpose? Do signs and wonders produce faith? Are there any dangers involved in miracles? What about revival movements and miracles? And what kind of miraculous activity should we expect in normal church life?

Definition of Terms

Part of the reason for the confusion about signs and wonders is that people often mean quite different things when they address the issue. Clarification here will help. I take a sign, wonder, and miracle to mean that God has done something that cannot be accomplished in the natural realm using natural powers and abilities. These are supernatural acts. For example, there are both natural and supernatural healings. A broken leg will mend in approximately six to eight weeks. The body has natural healing powers. This mending is a natural healing. But if the leg heals instantly, then something supernatural has occurred. Broken legs do not mend themselves instantly. With this in view I use the words *sign, wonder,* and *miracle* interchangeably to indicate a supernatural act.

I contrast this with the term *manifestation* of the Spirit. While this is also a supernatural work, it is of a different kind and has a different function and purpose. The Bible lists these manifestations in 1 Corinthians 12. These are supernatural, spiritual ministries given to the church.

Finally, there are *human responses* to the Spirit. When people sense the presence of God they respond in a variety of ways, including weeping, being silent, running, falling, shouting, laughing. Are these signs, wonders, or miracles? Are these manifestations of the Spirit? No. They are simply the ways some people react to an awareness of the presence of God. None are supernatural. God does not *cause* any of it. And no one of these things is more spiritual than another. They are simply human responses conditioned by personality, culture, and the community. God does not make people respond in any particular way, neither does He cause any particular revival to take on certain of these activities.

Distinguishing between signs (including wonders and miracles), manifestations of the Spirit, and human responses will help in understanding the whole issue of signs and wonders.

Signs and Wonders Today

Although signs and wonders occur today, throughout church history opinions about them have differed. John Calvin, the Reformation theologian, believed that the supernatural work of the Spirit, the *sign* gifts, ceased after the first century. This "cessasionist" position holds that there are no signs and wonders today; they occurred only in the apostolic period to establish the Church. Modern dispensationalists follow Calvin and likewise assert that signs and wonders do not take place today.

The Calvinistic and Dispensational argument seems to rest, first, on the contention that miracles have not been seen since the first century and, second, on a treatment of Scripture to explain that contention. For example, Leon Morris says, "The early Church knew quite well what all these gifts were. They exulted in the exercise of them. But, in view of the fact that they disappeared so speedily and so completely that we do not even know for certain exactly what they were, we must regard them as a gift of God for the time of the Church's infancy. They did not last very long, and in the providence of God evidently they were not expected to last very long."[1]

To justify this view Calvinists and Dispensationalists argue that Paul had this in mind when he wrote 1 Corinthians 13:8–10. They claim that Paul is here contending that the gifts of the Spirit would cease when "that which is perfect is come." They take "that which is perfect" to mean the Scriptures, meaning that when the Scriptures were completed at the end of the first century, the gifts were no longer needed and ceased to function. They are, however, wrong on two counts. First, miracles have continued to occur, as ample evidence through the centuries proves. Second, they argue that prophecy, tongues, and knowledge would all cease when that which is perfect is come. Has knowledge ceased? No. So then, why should prophecy and tongues cease and not knowledge? Unless it can be proved from Scripture and confirmed by evidence in history that the gifts ceased to function at the end of the first century, we should assume that they should still occur today.

A better position is that God provided for supernatural ministry by giving His Son, the Spirit, and supernatural power, and that this has not changed. When Jesus sent out His disciples He commanded them to heal the sick and cast out demons (Mark 6:7–13; Luke 10:9,17). The apostles went out performing miracles (Acts 6:8; 8:6; 19:11). Paul performed miracles as part of his ministry and as proof of his apostolic calling (2 Corinthians 12:12). First Corinthians clearly asserts that supernatural gifts are given to the Church, and there is no indication that this would cease. Beyond this there is the evidence of history. Many documented miracles have occurred throughout the history of the church. Signs, wonders, and miracles do take place today.

The Purpose of Signs and Wonders

There seem to be two main purposes in signs and wonders. First, they demonstrate the power and divinity of Christ; second, they meet the needs of people. Jesus indicated that people should believe in Him because the works He did were a testimony to His divinity (John 5:36; 10:25,37–38). And Paul claimed that his ministry was grounded not in words but in signs and wonders, which were themselves conclusive proof of the power of God behind his message (1 Corinthians 2:4–5; 2 Corinthians 12:12). Signs and wonders are a testimony. They are evidence of the power of God.

We should not, however, forget that miracles also meet the needs of people. They are not only a testimony to God. Jesus was moved with compassion and ministered to the needs of those who came to Him. In quoting Isaiah 61:1 (Luke 4:18) He makes it clear that the power of the Spirit is given to meet human need. When Paul outlines the gifts of the Spirit in 1 Corinthians 12, it is obvious that these gifts are to minister to the needs of people.

Bearing this in mind we have some guidance when assessing ministries that purport to specialize in the miraculous. Do they testify to the power of God and bring people to faith in Christ, and do they really meet the needs of people?

Faith and Knowledge

Signs, wonders, faith, and knowledge constitute difficult subject matter, but understanding them will help us resolve the issue of signs and wonders. We have seen that Jesus claimed signs were a testimony to His divinity and that they helped people come to faith. It is a common assumption that if there were more miracles, more people would come to faith in Christ. But there is more to it. What is faith? How do people come to faith? What about miracles, the inner work of the Spirit, and the power of the Word in bringing people to faith in Christ? And what effect do knowledge and evidence have on faith? These questions must be explored.

First, what is faith? Is it the same as knowledge? If not, how do these two differ? How does a person come to faith and come to knowledge? The Bible says, "Now faith is the substance of things hoped for, the evidence of things not seen" (Hebrews 11:1²). From this we see that faith is radically different from knowledge. It is a work of the Spirit in the realm of those things which cannot be seen, producing a sense of absolute certainty. In fact, this work of the Spirit is so powerful that even when the observable evidence is contrary, the sense of certainty is not diminished. Abraham experienced this when he journeyed to a land he was unfamiliar with and when he was commanded to kill the son of promise. Job experienced this when he claimed that he would continue to believe in God even if God killed him. Habakkuk had this kind of faith when he testified that he would continue to believe in God even if the flocks and fields were barren. Paul made it clear that believers rest on that which cannot be seen rather than on that which can be seen (2 Corinthians 4:17 through 5:1). This kind of certainty is a spiritual work and cannot be produced or diminished by evidence in the observable realm. It must be noted that some kinds of mental illness are characterized by an inability or unwillingness to adjust to observable facts. Is faith, then, mental illness? Of course not! I mention this only to point out how unlike ordinary knowledge faith really is. It is a kind of certainty produced only by the Spirit and by the Word of God (Romans 10:17).

> **Though observable evidence is contrary, faith's certainty is not diminished.**

Scientific knowledge, on the other hand, is produced by observation. Knowledge is a mental affirmation that something is true. This sense of certainty (or ability to affirm intellectually that something is true) is the product of human reason and the ability to see the extent to which observations are regular and consistent and the extent to which statements accurately represent those observations. For example, dropping a pen on a table a number of times will lead a person to believe that there is some power pulling the pen downward. Every time we drop the pen it falls. Our knowledge of the law of gravity, and every other scientific fact, is produced this way. If the observations are consistent and the statements about those observations are accurate, then we claim that we have arrived at the truth and can have mental, or intellectual, certainty. This is the way people come to knowledge.

It should be obvious that faith and knowledge are quite different, and recognizing this difference is vitally important. It is true that signs can help people come to faith, but, ultimately, faith cannot result only from signs. It must be a product of the working of the Spirit. Here's why. A normal, intelligent person will continue to believe that something is true only so long as the observations that opinion is based on continue. If pens stop falling to the floor when dropped, people will develop serious doubts about the law of gravity, and they will do so quickly. As pointed out above, faith is not susceptible to this kind of doubt. The certainty is a product of the Spirit, not of observations.

An example of this principle is seen in the dialogue between the rich man and Abraham. The rich man asks Abraham to send Lazarus to his brothers to warn them about the horrors of hell. The rich man says that if someone comes to them from the dead they will repent. Listen to Abraham's response: "They have Moses and the prophets; let them hear them. And he said, Nay, father Abraham: but if one went unto them from the dead, they will repent. And he said unto him, If they hear not Moses and the prophets, neither will they be persuaded, though one rose from the dead" (Luke 16:29–31).

This is an important passage. The rich man expresses the common notion that seeing something supernatural will produce faith and repentance in his brothers, but this is not so. Abraham articulates the true nature of faith when he asserts that if the brothers will not believe based on the testimony of Scripture, then observations of the supernatural will not be convincing. It is hard, however, for people to accept this.

Accepting this is so difficult because people confuse knowledge based on observation with faith based on the work of the Spirit. In one sense it is true that "seeing is believing." But it is also true that not seeing is not believing. When it comes to knowledge, that is the way it should be; people should not claim they "know" something when the evidence is contrary. But faith is different. It remains even when the observable evidence is contrary. It is a product of the Spirit, not of observation. Specifically, the Bible says that "faith comes from hearing the message, and the message is heard through the word of Christ" (Romans 10:17, NIV). Bearing this in mind is helpful in understanding the relationship between signs and wonders and faith.

Signs and Faith

We have seen that Jesus used signs as evidence of His divinity. Paul, likewise, claimed that his ministry was authenticated by signs. Signs do have an important role, but we must understand that God wants to produce faith in people, not knowledge based on observation. God would have no trouble in bringing people to knowledge of His power. He could easily create the kinds of spectacles that would convince people that He is God. And, in fact, He will do that someday. But that does not produce faith. Faith is a spiritual work, a response to the Word and Spirit of God. It is part of the spiritual union of a person with God and the presence of God in a person's life. This explains Abraham's response to the rich man. Even if the brothers might momentarily be impressed with the reappearance of a dead man, they would not come to faith. It is amazing how resistant the nonbelieving heart is to all manner of evidence. Doubters can readily explain away everything. Jesus met this attitude regularly in His dealings with the Pharisees. More important, confidence based on evidence goes away as soon as the evidence is gone. How can it be otherwise? It is not faith at all, but empirical knowledge, knowledge based on sensory perception. God does more. He creates faith through His Word.

A principle can be extracted from these remarks. So-called faith, based on an abundance of miracles, is not faith at all, but empirical knowledge, and God wants much more than that. For this reason He does not do so many miracles as to compel intellectual assent. He could easily overpower the human mind through supernatural activity, but this is not faith and is not the way He works. He calls people to faith by speaking to the spirit within them. This is more than enough and creates a faith that is much more substantial than the easily eroded confidence based on observation.

Signs, Wonders, and Demonic Deception

With all the recent attention given to signs and wonders too little has been said about the dangers of getting caught up in signs. The Bible is abundantly clear that the devil will use miracles as a means to deceive people and lead them into apostasy and rejection of God. Please give attention to the following list of Scriptures.

- Matthew 7:21–23; 24:24
- John 4:48
- 1 Corinthians 1:22–23
- 2 Thessalonians 2:2–12
- 1 Timothy 4:1
- 2 Timothy 4:2–4
- 2 Peter 2:1–2
- Revelation 13:13–14

The pattern set out in these verses is unmistakable. Satan desires to deceive people and destroy their relationship with God. He will use miracles to accomplish this. People who are inadequately grounded in sound doctrine and the Word will be led astray by miracle workers who have false doctrine. Miracles alone are not proof that the power comes from God. It may come from the devil. Miraculous ministries must be accompanied by sound doctrine. When this is not the case, they should be examined carefully and rigorously. The ability to do miracles does not exempt a person from doctrinal evaluation. False prophets and teachers resist this, insisting that the miracles they perform authenticate their ministries. This is not so. False prophets and the beast in Revelation will be able to do miracles. In fact, one way to identify a false prophet is to see if he or she is willing to undergo doctrinal scrutiny. If not, beware.

Signs, Wonders, and Human Responses

What is going on when someone falls down during prayer, or breaks out laughing hysterically? Is this a sign? A wonder? Usually not. It is a human response to an awareness of the presence of God.

During periods of renewal or revival, meetings are often characterized by unusual behavior. People may run, leap, shout, cry, sit in silence, fall down, laugh, or respond with other such demonstrations. Noting these activities people sometimes say that "God is doing a new thing" in a certain place. Is God doing this? That is, does God make people act a certain way? Does He make people laugh or cry, run or jump? There is a strong tendency to try to establish the spiritual authenticity of these behaviors by asserting that God is making people act in a certain way, that God "made me do it." This is usually not the case, nor is proof of divine initiative necessary to affirm the spiritual authenticity of these experiences. In the vast majority of cases people are simply responding to a new awareness of the presence of God, doing so in a way that suits their personality, culture, and the group expectations at the time. People may claim that their behavior is totally out of character for them, and, therefore, God is responsible. While it may be true that people act in ways during revival that are new to them, this does not mean that God makes them do whatever they are doing. It is more readily explained by demonstrating that during periods of spiritual slumber (or death—revival brings things back to life) people are not aware of God's presence and consequently don't do much. When they wake up to God they may act in unusual ways. When David saw the ark coming he danced before the Lord. When you see what David saw, you may do what David did, but God will not make you do it.

Now, it must be noted that occasionally God does interrupt people and make them do unusual things. God made Zacharias mute (Luke 1:20–22). This was a divine interruption, not a human response. In Acts 9 we see God interrupting Paul: He sent a bright light, Paul fell to the ground and got up blind. This was not a human response. However, these kinds of experiences, as real as they are, are not the norm. Occasionally God makes things like this happen, but this is not usually the reason people fall down, run, leap, shout, cry, or laugh. The better explanation of these experiences is that people are simply responding to the presence of God in ways that suit them when they feel His awesome presence.

Consider this: If God really does make people fall down or laugh, etc., then it is reasonable to conclude that when He "makes" a person do something, they do it. But surprisingly, it is not uncommon for those who have these experiences to become judgmental of those who do not, hinting that people who do not act in a certain way are not as spiritual or cooperative with the move of the Spirit as they. This is inconsistent and unfair. Either God makes people do certain things without their cooperation, or they are somehow involved. The better answer is to see that people are personally involved in these human responses. God did not make David dance. David simply got involved.

Does human involvement mean that the experiences are not genuinely spiritual? No, and by distinguishing between miracles and human responses to God, we help keep the issue clear.

Church Life

What is the proper role of signs, wonders, miracles, manifestations of the spirit, and human responses to God in the ongoing life of the church? *Signs, wonders, and miracles:* There is no reason to believe that God's plan for these ministries is any different now than it was at the beginning of the Church. And it is probably true that we would see more miracles than we currently do if people would pray, fast, wait on God, and exercise faith. Even so, God will never do so many miracles that He coerces mental agreement apart from faith, and faith is produced by the Word and the Spirit, not by observation. God still does miracles in the lives of believers because the supernatural is a way that He can bless and help His people, but we should be careful to keep things in perspective. God's plan does not end with human life as we know it. There is a future, with the further unfolding of God's plan to heal the universe. There are sufferings in this present time (Romans 8:18–25), and it is not God's plan to miraculously rectify all these ills during this dispensation. It is not lack of faith to have a biblically sound appraisal of what God has provided for the Church Age. God's plan is to bring people to faith and salvation through the proclamation of the Word and the working of the Spirit. There will be a number of miracles, but they will remain unusual and extraordinary events. People will continue to age and die. The ultimate healing for the human condition lies in the next life, not this one.

> **"Gifts are given to provide miraculous help in those cases where God's will allows for it."**

Manifestations of the Spirit: Paul makes it clear that the Spirit is given to the Church for the purpose of supernatural ministry. This will continue. However, as outlined above, we must understand that these gifts are given to provide miraculous help in those cases where God's will allows for supernatural intervention. This will not occur in all cases and failure to see as much as we might like in this realm is not due to lack of faith. It is simply God's design of things in this age.

Human responses to the presence of God: One of the greatest challenges any traditional church faces is to keep the members spiritually awake and alive. The more people are aware of the presence of God, the more they will respond to Him. And when this happens, we should expect to see demonstrations of His presence. This could take any number of forms, and all of them can be authentic spiritual experiences. Exuberant singing and worship, energetic prayer, profound reverence, powerful preaching, and lively altar services, including a full range of human emotions, should be expected.

Pentecostals believe in miracles because God is a miracle-working God. Even though there has been confusion about this aspect of New Testament church life, we continue to affirm that signs and wonders are part of God's plan and will, and they continue to occur today. We must avoid the extremes of claiming too much (the error of Kingdom Now theology) or too little (the error of the dispensational school) for the present dispensation; rather, we must find a proper understanding of how God works today and how people should appropriately respond to Him.

The Priority of Revival

Charles T. Crabtree

To say we need an old-fashioned, Holy Ghost revival would be met with an enthusiastic amen in most Pentecostal settings. It would also be safe to say that one would get as many different definitions of *Pentecostal revival* as there are people asked.

It is critical to define the word *revival* and even more important to define the term *Pentecostal revival.* We define these terms to remove confusion and inadequate expectations so we can agree together in faith for the revival God desires to bring to the Pentecostal world as well as to the entire church world.

One of the reasons the word *revival* is difficult to define with clear biblical focus is that the New Testament does not use the term revival in relation to the Church; rather, it addresses spiritual life with all its meaning and manifestations. It is my strong conviction that revival is the full restoration and development of spiritual life.

In the minds of many, revival is an event. A person with this mind-set will inevitably focus on the effects of revival and ignore the causes. This approach sees revival as an end in itself. We must not allow ourselves to fall into the trap of missing what God *wants* to do because we are concentrating too much on what we think God *ought* to do. Revival is not an end in itself. While revival begins with an event, true revival is sustained spiritual health, a daily renewal of the inmost being.

To add the word *Pentecostal* to the word *revival* is to add the dimension of the supernatural to spiritual life. In a sense, all spiritual life is supernatural, but there are unique supernatural dimensions that set a Pentecostal revival apart from a spiritual renewal or a revival of religious devotion and commitment. Pentecost interjects the miraculous into the spiritual life of the believer and the Church.

When I hear, "We need an old-fashioned Pentecostal revival," I say a qualified amen. It would be better to leave out the term *old-fashioned* because that terminology suggests a desire to recapture a historical era. Those who want an "old-fashioned Pentecostal revival" are really saying, "We want the same Pentecostal manifestation and/or phenomena we experienced as kids." Others mean, "We want to return to a Puritan standard of holiness or to the lifestyle of Pentecostals in the early part of the twentieth century." Still others mean, "I want to see a revival of Pentecost as expressed in the Azusa Street revival in 1903–1906 or as experienced in the revivals of the late '30s or early '40s." Some want to recapture the Charismatic renewal of the late '60s and early '70s.

God is not interested in renewing a historical era. He is not about to do an old thing. He is more creative than that. He will retain the foundation of faith, which is not just old—it is eternal. Upon that Rock He will build His Church. He will build it with new life, new methodologies, and new demonstrations. He is not the God of a single generation. He is the God of the generations—plural. God is not bound by or to history. He is bound only by His Word.

The Pentecostal Minister and Revival

The Pentecostal minister must see revival from a true Pentecostal perspective. Pentecostal revival is the Church in a state of such robust spiritual health that God can constantly and consistently channel through it His prophetic Word and miraculous works. The role of the minister in Pentecostal revival is at once a glorious challenge and an awesome responsibility. As in all divine assignments, the task is impossible without an ever-present dependence upon an ever-present God.

By its nature, Pentecostal revival is primarily promoted and guided through the office of the pastor. There is, of course, room for all other ministry gifts. As a matter of fact, all the ministry gifts should operate in an atmosphere of the Pentecostal dynamic. The apostolic, prophetic, and evangelistic ministry gifts operate primarily in demonstrations, events, and emphases. The ministry gift of the teacher lends the strength of systematic truth and fundamental doctrines to revival, but it is the pastor who under God must orchestrate all of the ministry gifts, exercise spiritual authority, and insist upon balance in order to maintain a state of Pentecostal revival in the local church.

Two vast areas of spiritual ministry and responsibility confront the Pentecostal minister in a true Pentecostal revival. They are the responsibility of perfecting the saints to do effective ministry (Ephesians 4:12[1]) and the responsibility of ministering to, in, and through the church in the supernatural (1 Corinthians 12 and 14). It is not a matter of either-or; it is both-and. Without spiritual perfection, the supernatural will be misunderstood and misused, resulting in the destruction of the church. Without the supernatural, the church will develop a form of godliness and deny the power, resulting in the spiritual death of the church.

The pattern for perfecting the saints in Pentecostal revival is clearly set forth in the New Testament. The "shortened version" is given in Acts 2: 41–47. Here we discover the necessary ingredients for initiating and, more important, sustaining a Pentecostal revival. The minister has a choice to make. It is the choice between a short-term sensation resulting in impressed people or a long-term strategy resulting in impressive people God can use. It is a choice between a church being built solely from what happens on the platform or being built by what happens in the people in the pew.

Some years ago, a great Pentecostal church experienced an unusual phenomenon. An evangelist came to the church and conducted a series of meetings that went on for weeks and weeks. Everyone was excited about the crowds and the ministry of the evangelist. When the evangelist left, the crowds left. Unbeknown to everyone, the church had been replaced by a crowd. The platform became a focus of spiritual life. The evangelist flourished, but the church suffered such irreparable damage it no longer exists as the same church. What happened? The event impressed a crowd but did not build the church. The crowd seeks an impression; the true church seeks perfection.

The Ingredients of Pentecostal Revival

The New Testament Church had demonstrations of the Holy Spirit which were indeed impressive, but the demonstrations operated from and in conjunction with a strong, healthy church, a church that refused to neglect the eternal underpinnings and spiritual infrastructure of an enduring Pentecostal Church. Acts 2:41–47, our "shortened version" of the Pentecostal agenda for sustained revival, sets forth the following ingredients:

Pentecostal preaching was followed by a commitment. Those who had come as part of a crowd became a part of the church by following the Lord in baptism. By doing so, they were identifying themselves as disciples and followers of Jesus Christ. A true revival results in discipline and obedience after the event as well as immediate commitment to a church body.

They continued steadfastly in doctrinal studies. It is instructive to study what the New Testament Church continued to do day by day or on a regular basis. Any revival that is not built on solid Bible doctrine is doomed to a short life.

They continued in the apostles' fellowship. Strong Christian relationships are vital to the stability of an enduring revival movement. Their fellowship included praying together and eating from house to house. Sensational revivals focus on a personality; enduring revivals focus upon wholesome relationships.

They continued in prayer. The New Testament revival was fueled by prayer. Believers daily set time aside for prayer (Acts 3:1). They prayed when they were confronted with unusual situations and needs (Acts 4:24). The New Testament is filled with accounts of a Pentecostal Church in prayer. Sensational revivals are marked by public prayer; enduring revivals are marked by private prayer and fasting as well as public prayer.

They continued in financial and material generosity. Pentecostal revival will produce a church that gives and sacrifices in order to meet the needs of one another. In sensational revivals centering upon a personality, the man or woman is invariably given inordinate amounts of money. In a sustained revival, everyone is blessed by generosity. The ministries are well provided for, the poor have their needs met, world missions is funded.

They continued in evangelism. The ultimate proof of a sustained Pentecostal revival is the regular, effective witnessing of Spirit-filled believers. In a short-lived, sensational revival, there will be conversions and additions because of signs and wonders, but the strength of the revived church over the long haul will be daily ministry and evangelism in the marketplace.

The powerful Pentecostal revivals in Korea and South America, which have gone on for many years, have been fueled by a Spirit-filled laity perfected by leadership to the point that they have become an effective force for God day by day.

Priorities for Pentecostal Revival

The Pentecostal minister in Pentecostal revival must set spiritual health and ministry development as an absolute priority for the Church. This is especially important in America, where the unchurched have become cynical toward "professional ministry." The next great revival in America will be initiated and sustained by leaders who train the laity in Pentecostal disciplines and then loose them in Pentecostal ministry.

In addition to perfecting the saints for Pentecostal ministry, *the minister must become an authority on the supernatural* in order to expose the church to the miraculous and give leadership to the proper operation of the gifts of the Spirit. Many churches have lived far below their potential because those with ministry gifts have been ignorant or afraid of the supernatural. A true Pentecostal revival can be experienced and sustained if Pentecostal pastors and leaders will view the supernatural as spiritual normalcy and not as some isolated or unique event. The promises of God to His Church include all the ministries of the Holy Spirit which, of course, include the fruit, operations, administrations, and gifts of the Spirit.

The fruit of the Spirit should be constantly preached and taught, especially in times of revival. The fruit of the Spirit is the supernatural character of Jesus Christ lived out spontaneously through the believer who is abiding in the Vine. The fruit must be viewed as the ultimate test of spirituality, for "by their fruits, ye shall know them" (Matthew 7:20). It must be coveted as much as we covet the gifts of the Spirit. It will determine the quality of Pentecostal revival. Modeling the fruit is more important than demonstrating the gifts because character determines the value of the gifts. Supernatural power must flow through supernatural character, or supernatural gifts will be dissipated by carnal minds and wills.

The Pentecostal minister must have divine insight and authority in the administration and operations of the gifts of the Spirit. Of course, it is incumbent upon the minister to "covet . . . the best gifts" personally (1 Corinthians 12:31). There is a crying need in the Pentecostal world for leaders who operate in the gifts as role models for younger ministers and laypersons. God has given pastors, as spiritual leaders, scriptural authority to encourage those He has placed in their care, to instruct them in the gifts of the Spirit. The Lord has provided the gifts to enrich the Church and edify the body of Christ. Any Pentecostal minister who does not make the gifts a priority is derelict because the Church is robbed of divine enablements.

It is my strong conviction that in the coming Pentecostal revival there will be a cry for and a new receptivity to all the gifts. For years

Pentecostal churches witnessed primarily speaking in tongues and interpretation. I am heartened by the new desire I hear articulated over and over for faith that the Church will experience again the gifts of prophecy, miracles, the word of knowledge, etc.

Another earmark of the coming revival, in my opinion, will be *an emphasis on tongues as a prayer language*—an agent for daily renewal. If Pentecostal people are taught the difference between congregational tongues and personal tongues, they will enter a dimension of spiritual life they have not known. Many have not grown in the Spirit-filled life because they believe that after receiving the initial physical evidence of speaking with other tongues only a privileged few are given the gift of tongues; they have not understood that Paul's comment that tongues is the least of the gifts is a reference only to public tongues without interpretation. The same man who said tongues is the least of the gifts is the same man who said, "I thank my God, I speak with tongues more than ye all" (1 Corinthians 14:18).

> ## The church has suffered because pastors would not deal with people moving in the flesh, not in the Spirit.

The Pentecostal minister should pray for confidence in judging the spirits in those who are operating in the gifts. The church has suffered in some situations because a pastor would not deal with people who, though sincere, were moving in the flesh and not in the Holy Spirit. It has been my responsibility from time to time to take people aside and request they not give a public utterance in tongues again until I was certain they had received proper counsel concerning the gift and were willing to come under spiritual authority. In rare instances, I have had to ask a person publicly to stop speaking in tongues because they were obviously out of order. We are not to quench the Spirit, but as Pentecostal leaders we must take responsibility—with tact and wisdom—to quench the flesh.

The final challenge to Pentecostal leaders is in the area of supernatural demonstrations and/or phenomena. It is in this forum where the minister, especially the pastor, must *seek for special discernment.* From time to time, God chooses to demonstrate His power in such a way that our faith will not stand in the wisdom of the flesh. We are not to be fearful of the supernatural—we are to be discerning.

Throughout Pentecostal history, God has used unusual demonstrations to bring a needed emphasis to the body of Christ or to speak directly to the unsaved. When we move in the realm of the supernatural, we must move with a spiritual mind and a sensitive ear. We must not assume something unusual is not of God. On the other hand, we must be ready to put a stop to deception, spurious philosophies, and demonic influence robed in religious practices.

Paul said, "I determined not to know anything among you except Jesus Christ and Him crucified" (1 Corinthians 2:2, NKJV). Paul's determination is a great pattern for the Pentecostal minister to follow. This spiritual giant was insisting on Jesus Christ as the preeminent priority. Without

Him, everything else counted for nothing. When a ministry or a church is known primarily for something or someone other than Christ, it will not endure. All the fruit, gifts, and demonstrations of the Spirit must exalt Christ and edify Christ's Church. In all things, the Pentecostal minister must insist upon everything in and through the church bringing glory to Christ. After all, that is the stated purpose for the work and ministry of the Holy Spirit.

Let us contend for the faith and covet earnestly the best gifts in such a way as to lead the Church to a new revelation of Jesus Christ so He will become all in all.

Unit

4

Effective
Accountability

Introduction:
Accountability to the Fellowship

Charles Kelly

Ministers of the gospel have received a treasure above all treasures: "the call of God" (Ephesians 4:1–16[1]). The Designer and Architect of redemption has uniquely selected them to participate in that plan of salvation conceived before time began. They are chosen not because of personal merit, but because of His grace. They have become laborers together with Him in the ministry of reconciliation, encompassing the whole earth and every creature for all time. That same enabling grace places within them certain gifts, talents, and abilities, which, when properly tended and cultivated, fulfill the assignment to the highest possible potential. What an awesome responsibility for which we are accountable to God!

We approach our personal accountability before God fully aware that "we shall all stand before the judgment seat of Christ" (Romans 14:10). The call must never be taken lightly.

All life is attuned to responsibility and accountability. The words are sometimes used interchangeably. But for our purposes, we make a distinction. *Responsibility* means that certain tasks and relationships have been assigned, requiring one's undivided attention to fulfill. *Accountability* simply means one is required to give answers or explanations to someone for designated relationships, actions, beliefs, and practices.

The broader subject of accountability is discussed in other chapters; therefore, the focus of our concern will be the minister's accountability to the Fellowship and to other ministers.

Accountability to the Fellowship

There are two kinds of accountability: *professional* (organizational and mandatory) and *personal* (voluntary). Professional (organizational) accountability defines how one should act in relation to the organization and to associations within that organization; certain accountability attaches to each person belonging to the organization or fellowship. Personal accountability includes how one should act in relation to oneself.

Accountability is essential for establishing and maintaining wholesome relationships. It is important at every level of society (e.g., there is political accountability, employment accountability, social accountability, and business accountability). Actually, we are all accountable to someone or something. Everyone needs the values and benefits of accountability. It helps keep people honest and credible; it preserves and protects one's integrity; it prevents one from becoming complacent and negligent in personal relationships and professional responsibilities. At the same time, it challenges one to become all that one has the potential of becoming. Accountability helps sharpen our focus.

It was out of the great spiritual revival at the turn of the twentieth century that the Assemblies of God fellowship was birthed. The organizational meeting in Hot Springs, Arkansas, in the spring of 1914, marked the beginning of a powerful Pentecostal fellowship, which has enjoyed phenomenal growth and blessing. Since 1914, the Assemblies of God has become a worldwide ministry organization.

Statements in the General Council Constitution define the purpose, scope, and focus of the Fellowship as follows:

ARTICLE II. NATURE. The General Council of the Assemblies of God is a cooperative fellowship based upon mutual agreements voluntarily entered into by its membership.

ARTICLE III. PREROGATIVES. The prerogatives of The General Council of the Assemblies of God shall be:

a. To encourage and promote the evangelization of the world.

b. To encourage and promote the worship of God.

c. To encourage and promote the edification of believers.

d. To provide a basis of fellowship among Christians of like precious faith.

e. To establish and maintain such departments and institutions as may be necessary for the propagation of the gospel and the work of this Pentecostal fellowship.

f. To approve all scriptural teachings, methods, and conduct; and to disapprove unscriptural teachings, methods, and conduct.

g. To have the right to own, hold in trust, use, sell, convey, mortgage, lease, or otherwise dispose of such property, real or chattel, as may be needed for the prosecution of its work.

ARTICLE IV. PRINCIPLES FOR FELLOWSHIP. The Assemblies of God shall represent, as nearly as possible in detail, the Body of Christ as described in the New Testament Scriptures. It shall recognize the principles inherent in the Body as also inherent in this Fellowship, particularly the principles of unity, cooperation, and equality. It recognizes that these principles will enable it to achieve its priority reason-for-being as an agency of God for evangelizing the world, as a corporate body in which man may worship God, and as a channel of God's purpose to build a body of saints being perfected in the image of His Son.

The Fellowship is built and strengthened as each member becomes aware of and protects the nature, prerogatives, purposes, and principles of the Fellowship and holds each other accountable personally and professionally.

The principle of voluntary cooperation that the General Council of the Assemblies of God is based on involves the following:

By "voluntary" it is meant that, upon learning the principles, doctrines, and practices of the Assemblies of God and by seeing the benefits one can derive from being associated with such an organization, a person of his own free choice decides to become a member, thus subscribing to all that for which the organization stands.

By "cooperation" it is meant that, to the best of his ability, one will comply with all decisions setting forth and defining duties and responsibilities incumbent upon members of the organization and will respect the will of the majority, expressed through democratic processes, as long as he remains a member.

Hence "voluntary cooperation" means that one, of one's own free will, decides to become a cooperating member of the Assemblies of God, this cooperation being obligatory and not optional.[2]

Within a voluntary, cooperative fellowship, there are standards, requirements, and expectations necessary for quality relationships at both personal and professional levels. Every person receiving credential recognition subscribes to the governing principles of the voluntary, cooperative Fellowship of the Assemblies of God. Each one also indicates a willingness to "be faithful to the sacred trust of the ministry by diligence, by uprightness in business matters, by ministerial ethics and courtesy, by self-sacrifice, by purity, by avoiding the very appearance of evil, by cherishing the anointing of the Holy Spirit, even unto death."

Certain expectations, responsibilities, and accountabilities are shared by every minister belonging to this Fellowship. There is a well-established system of accountability. That system is not intended to be restrictive but rather protective. It is not possible to belong to a denomination, a ministry organization, or a fellowship without incurring corresponding obligations and requirements. The Architect and founders of the Fellowship believed that fact and provided for a consistent means of quality accountability. Denominational leaders, since those early days, have continued to define and refine these principles of accountability. Certain principles and requirements have been adopted by the General Council, General Presbytery, district council, and district presbytery and are set forth in the Constitution and Bylaws (General Council and district councils), in policy and procedure manuals, and in position papers.

Credentialing—Doorway to Accountability

The first level of accountability for Assemblies of God ministers begins with the credentialing procedure. Completing the standardized credential application, written exam, and reference forms brings an awareness of the principles of a voluntary, cooperative fellowship and a corresponding commitment from the credential applicant. The credential application, the interview of the applicant by a sectional credentials committee, an interview by a district credentials committee, the applicant's approval by the district presbytery, and final approval by the General Council Credentials Committee usher one into accountability to the Fellowship. There are certain standard requirements for ministerial accountability within the Fellowship.

Since one will be identified with the Assemblies of God, several resources should be of major interest: (1) the history of the Assemblies of God, (2) Assemblies of God doctrine, (3) position papers adopted by the General Presbytery, (4) the General Council Constitution and Bylaws, (5) one's district council constitution and bylaws, and (6) organizational and governmental structures.[3]

A study of the history of the Assemblies of God will reveal the divine mandate and mission adopted by the Fellowship and how that mission has prospered in the intervening years. One will also discover how the Fellowship was formed and the path it has walked since its inception. Knowing what the Assemblies of God has become and how it became what it is will instruct and enrich one's ministry. Every credentialed minister is responsible for knowing our denominational history.

A careful study should be made of the Constitution and Bylaws (both General Council and district council) and the General Council position papers scripturally defining critical subjects and the denominational stand on them, including theological positions and social concerns. The General Council Constitution contains the Statement of Fundamental Truths, which should be carefully studied. This study will help one learn the doctrinal and organizational structure of the Assemblies of God and how that structure and its governance have evolved and forged a strong Fellowship that proclaims the timeless message of Christ in a world of continuous change and challenge.

Every minister is responsible for knowing both the doctrine and the governing documents of the Assemblies of God. The credentials renewal procedure of the Assemblies of God provides for annual accountability of every minister. This accountability comes through a well-established system of reporting.

Accountability through Credential Renewal

Each year after ministerial credentials have been granted, the minister must renew that certification and reaffirm his or her personal level of participation with the Fellowship regarding fundamental doctrinal beliefs, financial support to the General Council and the minister's local district council, the extent of one's preaching, and a recommitment to the principles of the Fellowship.

The general secretary's office provides the necessary forms for credential renewal. This process providing annual accountability for each Assemblies of God minister should be completed in a timely manner and sent to the district office according to detailed instructions. Failure to renew before the credential renewal deadline could result in a late fee or the lapse of one's credentials. If credentials have been listed as "lapsed" for failure to renew, the minister must follow a prescribed procedure for credential reinstatement.

OTHER ACCOUNTABILITY VEHICLES

The Annual Church Ministries Report (ACMR) serves as an information gathering system and reflects church ministry on a local level. It supplies vital information for the General Council and district council offices. Completion of the ACMR provides for accountability on a different level. Pastors submit this information on an annual basis using the appropriate form from the general secretary's office. The General Council of the Assemblies of God convenes biannually to conduct business affecting the broad concerns of the Fellowship. Special time is also set aside for worship, fellowship, and ministry. Other meetings sponsored by the General Council are designed to enhance, strengthen, and refocus the Fellowship. District councils convene annually to conduct business on the district level. Districts also offer ministers retreats. Although attendance at these meetings is not mandatory for ministers, attendance and participation are very important and should be included in personal accountability. The information, inspiration, fellowship, worship, and ministry tend to renew, enlighten, and strengthen the individual participant. At these meetings vision is articulated, amendments to the Constitution and Bylaws are adopted, the election of officers is conducted, and other important decisions are made. Every minister should attend these meetings and become actively involved in shaping and reshaping this Fellowship while continuing to build and strengthen ministry, evangelism, organizational focus, and fellowship.

Tithing is widely accepted and practiced within this Fellowship. Each minister agrees to give financial support to the General Council and one's local district council in accordance with the respective bylaw requirements. Failure to comply could result in the loss of credentials or appropriate disciplinary action. Because of the financial structure and ministry support base of the Assemblies of God, it is tremendously important for each minister to fulfill financial responsibilities to the Fellowship.

Accountability to Other Ministers

Accountability to other ministers within the Fellowship is a vital part of a healthy ministerial fellowship. Both General Council and district council constitutions and bylaws impose responsibilities that regulate relationships between ministers and ministries. These responsibilities are spelled out in the respective bylaws.

Upon receiving credentials, each minister agrees to be governed by the principles of this voluntary, cooperative Fellowship, until such time that those documents are amended through proper procedures. The fulfillment of this pledge of commitment is *accountability.*

However, there are responsibility and accountability on a personal level. Relationships between ministers are determined by the values and principles that regulate one's life. These standards are not imposed by the organization, but are self-imposed. The quality of those values determines the quality of relationships.

In *Ministerial Ethics and Etiquette,* Nolan Harmon observes:

> Relationships with professional ministers present problems in ethics and etiquette. In fact, in the codes of ministerial ethics that have been developed, the nucleus has been an attempt to clarify the relationship between members of the profession. "Ministerial ethics" to most ministers means the way they feel they should treat other ministers and, even more, the way they feel other persons in the ministry should treat them.
>
> Henry Ward Beecher once asserted that it was not good for ministers to associate too much with one another, nor to develop a "class consciousness." Another clergy person decried the way the professions, including the ministry, "flock together and see things in their own light." While this might indeed be dangerous if carried too far, the growth of a great conscious fellowship is a magnificent thing, especially when this fellowship is composed of men and women who are ministers of God. Why should not this fellowship be able to make rules for its own members? If lawyers are the sole judges of who may be disbarred from the practice of law, and if physicians have a code governing their relations with one another, why should not ministers recognize that they, too, have a fellowship that may well look to each of them for conformity to its ideals?
>
> Ministers, of course, will not and should not yield on that principle that is at the heart of Protestantism: Every person must find in his or her own conscience the ultimate guide. A ministerial fellowship able to prescribe and enforce rules on all its members would destroy the very freedom in which each member of that group ought to stand. Nevertheless there is a suggestive value, a guiding value, in the attitudes and pronouncements of the ministerial fellowship itself, and nowhere is this stronger than at those points where ministers measure and evaluate the propriety of their conduct toward one another.[4]

The Golden Rule is a good principle for regulating relationships and accountability between ministers.

Leadership's Role in Teaching Accountability

Leaders lead first by example then by position and proclamation; therefore, the following values and principles will help define positive relationships:

1. *Ethics* is a predetermined set of moral principles and values. To be viewed as ethical, we must conform to accepted professional and personal standards of conduct. Being ethical says that one can be trusted not to violate or defraud another in any way. One's ethics must have a strong biblical base, providing nonnegotiable values that guide conduct in all relationships.

2. *Sensitivity* is being aware of the feelings and needs of others and act-

ing accordingly. This personal quality is the basis of good ministerial relationships. Being sensitive enables one to "rejoice with them that . . . rejoice, and weep with them that weep" (Romans 12:15). The person without problems exists only in the imagination of other people. Taking time to understand where our fellow ministers are in their life struggles will better prepare us for ministry to them. We are our brothers' keepers.

3. Where *credibility* gaps exist, there is little chance for quality relationships with fellow ministers. Building credibility requires character consistency and the avoidance of contradictory conduct and speech. To be believable is a quantum step in building positive relationships.

4. To be *honest* is to be free from fraud and deception. It implies being legitimate, truthful, respectful, reputable, credible, good, worthy, and marked by integrity. Whenever honesty has been violated, every effort should be made to correct that violation in order to protect one's reputation and relationships.

5. *Consistency* is a trait of great people. The degree of consistency in personal virtues and values will determine the strength of relationships. To be consistent means showing steady conformity to high principles in one's character, profession, beliefs, and conduct. Such people are the same wherever you see them.

6. *Mutual respect* means having a special regard for one another. The esteem one has for another determines the quality and longevity of a relationship. Maintaining mutual respect is a form of accountability and is essential for a quality working relationship.

7. *Trust* is a requirement for good relationships. While personal characteristics differ between individuals, if mutual trust is maintained, lasting and productive relationships can be enjoyed.

8. A person of *integrity* is above reproach. He or she lives by a code of high moral values. One must never compromise integrity for gain or advantage. Commitment to integrity demonstrates that self-worth is of greater value than reputed worth (or reputation). When ministers are accountable and responsible to each other, integrity is more readily maintained.

> **Leaders lead first by example, then by position.**

9. *Loyalty* is fulfilling one's lawful organizational and relational responsibilities. It is being faithful to those to whom fidelity is due. Loyalty implies being faithful to commitments, to organizational and Fellowship commitments. To be loyal and faithful is to be accountable.

10. *Love* communicates! The apostle Paul enumerates the virtues and values of love in 1 Corinthians 13. Where there is genuine love, there will be quality accountability. One cannot love without accountability. Love is our protection in a ministerial association based on the principles of a voluntary, cooperative fellowship.

Life is made up of relationships. The quality of those relationships is important to our happiness and well-being. Some ministers have had great heartaches and difficulties because they never learned to relate to others in a positive way. May we as fellow ministers in this great

Assemblies of God fellowship build relationships and accountabilities that are wholesome, affirming, and productive.

The words of Paul to Titus provide closure for this chapter, "This is a faithful saying, and these things I will that thou affirm constantly, that they which have believed in God might be careful to maintain good works. These things are good and profitable unto men" (Titus 3:8).

Every Timothy Needs a Paul . . .

Wayde I. Goodall

How can I learn to get along with this guy—he's so set in his ways?"

"I never have freedom to minister the way I think God wants me to. The pastor just ties my hands and has me do all his busy stuff."

"I wish I had more opportunity to preach. How does he expect me to learn? Besides, I think I'm a good preacher."

"You know, there are a few people who are complaining about him . . . . I'm beginning to wonder if they could be right."

Comments like these are not uncommon among younger staff members in our churches. Frustration often describes the relationship between the associate and senior pastor.

In my opinion, one of the greatest contributing factors to the short tenure of associate pastors (youth, Christian education, music, etc.) is strained staff relationships. We need to look out for each other. Those who walk alone in life and ministry can become isolated, absorbed in their emotional or other struggles, and the enemy can attack easier. Perhaps all of us have watched documentaries about how African lions hunt. They try to separate an animal from the herd—usually one that is young, wounded, or confused by the herd's movement. When the lion gets the animal away from its companions, he comes in for the kill. The devil has similar strategies.

What are some things we can do to facilitate better staff relationships and understanding?

Jesus had several associates during His 3-year ministry. How did they relate to each other? What did they do together? What kind of leader was Jesus?

Be An Example

Jesus was a constant example to His traveling companions—not just in ministering to people but in attitude as well. His gentle acceptance of little children, His understanding with the woman caught in adultery, His love toward so-called insignificant people, and His constant patience with His disciples. When all is added up, we come to the conclusion that Jesus was the example of all He taught.

If we look at the lives of Paul, Peter, Timothy, and other followers and leaders of that time, we find a similar situation. All tried to be what they preached. They lived what they thought. They were indeed examples to those over whom God had placed them.

The same should be true of leaders today. Pastors and associates should be examples to their parishioners.

Work In Unity

I wonder if there can be unity within the Body if there is not unity among the staff. I will not say it's impossible but do feel it would be difficult.

I've known assistant pastors who intensely disliked the senior pastor, and the same goes the other way too. How can we think this escapes the eyes of the people? They know our feelings toward each other; they sense our love or lack of it. There's no way we can preach unity within our churches when we do not love and respect the guy we are working with.

Our Lord prayed for His disciples "that they may be one as we are one" and that "they be brought to complete unity" (John 17:22,23). Unity is near to the heart of God. It's the key to evangelism (John 13:34,35). It's the key to health in the body of Christ (1 Corinthians 12). We as leaders should let nothing get in the way of unity with our staff members. If we want unity in our churches, let's have it among the staff.

Spend Time Together

Perhaps the staff members have never spent significant time together, or when they are together, they talk shop. Are a busy schedule, a lack of time, or the belief that such times are unimportant among the reasons for not spending time together? Then consider the many scriptural examples of ease of ministry, peace, joy, power, and great friendships of those who strove to befriend and love the ones they worked with.

When Jesus was first approached by John the Baptist's disciples Andrew and John, Jesus asked them what they wanted. When they said they wanted to know where He was staying, He said, "'Come...and you will see." John says they "spent that day with Him" (John 1:39). A great introduction! Later in His ministry, Jesus told His disciples, "I no longer call you servants, because a servant does not know his master's business. Instead, I have called you friends, for everything that I learned from my Father I have made known to you" (John 15:15). Should we regard our staff any differently than the Master regarded His?

> **"Are a busy schedule, lack of time, or the feeling it is unimportant the reasons for not spending time together?"**

I wonder where Paul would have been without his friend and associate Barnabas. I wonder where Timothy would have been without his friend and associate Paul. These men truly loved one another, and the church knew it.

Submit To One Another

The attitude of submitting to one another should be part of our lifestyle. Often a feeling of competition develops among staff members. Seniority due to one's length of stay, age, or position can cause younger staff members to feel insecure and unimportant and may even dim their vision. This should not be the case.

As I see it in the Scripture, respect is given to all involved in a shepherding, or pastoring, ministry, no matter what their ages, positions, or size of the church. One staff member may have certain gifts, while other gifts are present in different staff members. When each is making use of the other's gifts, balance can be created, greatly benefiting the church.

The apostle Peter, indeed an elder among elders, when writing to the Christians throughout Pontus, Galatia, Cappadocia, Asia, and Bithynia, addressed each of the elders as a "fellow elder" (1 Peter 5:1) serving under the "Chief Shepherd" Jesus (verse 4). Peter did not have the attitude of being the head elder but recognized himself as a "fellow elder" who was being used in this office as were so many others.

Show Respect

Even though the attitude of submission needs to be present among all staff members, younger members should show a deep respect for their seniors. Many of senior pastors have years of experience and wisdom from seeing God direct in many different situations. They are indeed wiser, more mature, and more knowledgeable than most of us. There is much we can learn from them.

I feel God has not only called us to work with certain people but also to learn from them. We position ourselves to do so by showing respect, by acknowledging that, generally speaking, the young learn from the old, the inexperienced from the experienced. Proverbs teaches that a son should listen to his father, that "wisdom is found in those who take advice" (Proverbs 13:10), that "the wise in heart accept commands" (Proverbs 10:8). I believe our attitude as associates should be "How can I serve this senior pastor more effectively?" (that's the Christlike attitude) and "How can I learn from this pastor?"

Encourage One Another

Many times the ministry is a lonely occupation. Counseling, preaching, teaching, encouraging—a story of giving and often not receiving. Hours of study and preparation can go into a Sunday morning message, and even though many people receive from God through the message, seldom does appreciation come back to the messenger.

If God has given us men and women to work with in the ministry, we have a blessing that many others do not have. We can give and receive encouragement and affirmation. Again I wonder where Paul would have been without the encouragement of Barnabas? Timothy without the affirmation of Paul? The Scripture talks many times about encouraging one another and affirming one another. But due to a busy schedule or possibly thinking that other staff members really do not need encouragement, we neglect this needed touch from God.

On one occasion my pastor said to me in a brief moment of conversation, "You're an achiever." Little did he know that inside I was looking for anything to hold onto that day. I was feeling discouraged, wondering if I really was doing the job, having kind of a pity party. That one word encouraged me to go on and indeed achieve. Other times little notes have been left on my desk, affirming notes, like "Good job!" "I need you; hang around."

It goes the other way, too. When is the last time you encouraged your pastor and fellow worker? They are human, just as you are.

Bring Correction

Along with encouraging one another, we need occasionally to go to one another with possible correction, discipline, or guidance. We are going to make mistakes, and we need each other to keep us in balance.

I think of the time when Peter came to Antioch, and Paul "opposed him to his face because he was clearly in the wrong" (Galatians 2:11).

The Scripture also tells us to bring correction with a spirit of love and gentleness. The Word points out that God disciplines only those He loves (Hebrews 12), so we could deduce that we also should discipline those we love.

Ministers are in a unique profession where they can often avoid accountability. Even though they spend much time with people, deep and transparent relationships with thei peers are rare. It has been estimated that 70 percent of ministers do not have a close friend. The same percentage has a lower self-image now than when they started in the ministry. Ministers can pastor large churches and have numerous acquaintances but remain isolated and lonely. This is tragic. Peer friendships are important. Caring for one another is biblical. Having people we are accountable to is critical.

If at any time our lifestyle is in question, other staff members should be the first to feel free to bring correction. There needs to be health among the staff, and sometimes to have health we need to be confronted about possible error in our lives.

Please understand that this should be flooded with an attitude of love and acceptance, or it could bring a quick division among the staff. We are a model to the church. If we can go to each other, members of our congregation will do the same.

Most of us have had the experience of a staff person coming to us with a problem involving another staff member. It could be about an associate pastor or a younger staff member. This is not uncommon on a multistaff.

What do we do? Extreme care is needed in such a situation. We need to listen to the person but at the same time be careful always to protect and support the others we are ministering with.

On one occasion I had a person come to me about another staff member. His complaint was that he didn't agree with something this person had said in a

> **"There needs to be health among the staff, and sometimes to have health we need to be confronted about possible error in our lives."**

message. He also noted he was doing his best not to tell too many people but was having a difficult time.

I listened to the complaint but had no response. This person wondered why I could not respond. In turn, I pointed to Matthew 18:15: "If your brother sins against you, go and show him his fault, just between the two of you." I then said, "Can I schedule an appointment with him for you?"

The person felt the problem was not important enough to go personally to this minister—but it was important enough to complain about.

Now, this person could have been right in his judgment. Even so, as Matthew 18 states, the offender and the offended need to discuss it personally. We as staff members should covenant to support and protect one another.

It could be that God has called you to work in your present situation for many years, or even for a lifetime. If God has called you to a specialized ministry, such as youth, counseling, Christian education, or music, this is not a lower calling than that of the senior pastor. We are all pastors sent as a gift to the particular church where we are ministering. Our calling is a high calling, and we need to consider it as such.

It also could be that the Lord is preparing you for future ministry as a pastor—or to move from pastor to a specialized (associate) ministry.

You should not be in a hurry to get to that role you believe is down the road. Do a complete job now: Learn all you can. Be thorough. Get involved in all the various aspects of ministry you can. Fill your mind with wisdom learned from experience.

Every Timothy needs a Paul.

Every Paul needs a Barnabas.

A Long-Range Plan for the Church

Glen D. Cole

When I became acquainted with the girl who was to become my wife, I found myself visiting her home church as a student in Bible college. I was rather shocked to discover the long list of pastors that church could display. It appeared to me that no pastor had been there more than two years, some considerably less than that. That trend continued until just a few years ago when the church relocated and seemed to develop a vision for the area. For over forty years that church was on a survival mode.

The Three Stages of a Church

Churches go through stages. I have heard those stages characterized in the following way:

1. *The risk-taking stage.* This characterizes the new church in its first years of existence. The members are willing to take risks. They are willing to pray for the direction of the Holy Spirit, step out in faith, and wait for God to bless their efforts.
2. *The caretaking stage.* A church usually enters this stage after its buildings are built and its bills are paid. The theme song of the care-taker church is "I Shall Not Be Moved," and its major goal is to maintain the status quo.
3. *The undertaking stage.* If a church remains caretaker long enough, it soon will be ready for the undertaker. The undertaker church is in a rut, which has been defined as "a grave with both ends knocked out." The last words of an undertaker church are "But we have never done it that way before."

That well describes the natural process of what was intended to be a dynamic organism. I stepped into a church in Oregon while on vacation years ago for Sunday worship. The pastor was introducing a building pro-gram to his people. I was impressed to hear him say, "We are not inter-ested in using the people to build a great church. We are interested in using the church to build a great people!" That is critical to long-range planning. It would be well for everyone reading these lines to memorize the pastor's statement. It touched me deeply at a time in my ministry when church growth and planning for the future was to become a driving force in my life.

After almost forty years of pastoring in the Assemblies of God, I wrote the following to share with my congregation on "What I've Learned Pastoring Churches That Grow." I have learned that

1. God is good.
2. People are basically kind and loving.
3. You can get into trouble doing your job and obeying God.
4. Not everybody tithes!
5. I am blessed by a great staff.
6. I am blessed by a great board.
7. Not everybody tithes!
8. We have had a minimum of trouble, discord, and complaint.
9. It is good to be missions minded.
10. A church can be blessed even during major capital improvement programs.
11. Not everybody tithes!
12. Witnessing growth and the discipling of converts is a delight.
13. I can't do it alone.
14. Not everybody tithes!
15. It is better to try and fail than not to try at all.
16. God is faithful.
17. Keeping busy is no problem.
18. My wife is very patient and long-suffering.
19. Not everybody tithes!
20. Not everybody likes me.
21. I have a great family.

22. God loves me.
23. Not everybody tithes!
24. The future excites me.

What the above hopefully points out is the foundation stone for a long-range plan: The pastor must be settled in his call. Dr. Robert Schuller used to say, "Plan to stay forty years. If something goes wrong after the second year, so what! You still have thirty-eight years to work it out." The "greener grass" syndrome has curtailed the development of our church over the years. Let's be in it for the long haul. There is a settledness in the pulpit and in the pew when this attitude prevails.

It would be well to consider the importance of making the ministry our primary objective as well. Too many are finding other avenues of income and interest while trying to lead Christ's church. I believe leadership in the church must be the driving force of our lives. Some do have to have secular employment when churches are struggling and growing, but our goal should be that of a full-time leader. Let us not be sidetracked by lesser things. Jesus encouraged His newly called disciples to leave the fishing nets and the tax booths in order to fully follow Him.

Now that we have established a foundation for long-range planning, the following seven principles are vital to a good long-range plan.

Visibility

The first is *visibility.* Note these Scripture verses from Acts that underline this important development in the church.[1]

- "There was great joy in that city" (Acts 8:8).
- "It became known throughout all Joppa, and many believed on the Lord" (Acts 9:42).
- "A great number believed and turned to the Lord" (Acts 11:21).
- "The word of the Lord was being spread throughout all the region" (Acts 13:49).
- "'These who have turned the world upside down have come here too'" (Acts 17:6).
- "The word of the Lord grew mightily and prevailed" (Acts 19:20).

Even the negative statement in Acts 28:22 reveals the great visibility the church had achieved early in its existence: "'Concerning this sect, we know that it is spoken against everywhere.'" Long-range planning for any church must include visibility, that which can be seen! If we are to impact our communities, we have to do a much better job of getting the ministry before the people. Very few impact churches exist. Why is that? In our planning sessions four areas need to be examined.

1. *Location.* How long can the site you now occupy really meet the needs of not just your church but your community as well? We had thirteen acres in Sacramento when I arrived in 1978. A fine facility existed, but there was no elbow room, no adjacent property that could be secured for future expansion. I began to pray for a miracle piece of property. That prayer was answered through a sixty-three-acre gift on a major freeway. I have said so many times, "A congregation cannot vote down a miracle!"

It was brought to my attention that 144,000 cars a day pass by that piece of property. *That* is visibility. You may get a good deal on the other side of the tracks, but will it be a long-range solution?

2. *Advertising.* As I travel about this nation, I see very little of the church in cities and towns. By that I mean, as the weekend draws near, they are too often not listed in the newspapers or in hotels and motels where I stay or on billboards that hover over freeways and highways. We need to do a better job of getting the ministry of the church out on Front Street. What do people really know about us?

I recently moved into a new community twenty miles from our church. I thought everyone would know of The Singing Christmas Tree—a holiday tradition for forty years in Sacramento. To my amazement, my new neighbors did not know what I was talking about when I invited them to attend. We often take too much for granted. There are many means to advertise the work and outreach of the church. Some are free, others cost. Develop a plan. Put it into the budget. Let the people know something good is happening where you are.

3. *Media.* Radio and television can be your friend. With the new cable systems that dot the landscape come opportunities for visibility. Check out what is available through media for the declaration of who you are, where you are, and what you present. Just as with advertising, some opportunities can be secured for no cost; others will need to be written into the budget. But let us be as wise as "the children of the world." They have swayed this generation with their constant barrage of information.

4. *Program.* What does the church offer? Henry Kaiser used to say, "If you want to be a success, find a need and fill it." What needs are there in your community that no one else is meeting? Program to meet those needs.

I took a poll on Sunday morning to get a profile of who was listening to me each week. To my amazement, I learned that one-third of the congregation was single. We had a very weak ministry to this growing segment of our community. A full-time singles pastor was secured. In a very short time there were six hundred singles gathered on a Monday evening to worship, to grow, to learn. This was their night! It was a powerful new thrust in the development of the local church.

Viability

The second *V* principle in long-range planning is *viability.* The meaning of the word is "able to stay alive"! Three areas in planning need to be evaluated.

Are the morning, evening, and midweek services of the church alive, or are they so predictable that they put people to sleep? Are the services of the church able to stay alive? How many people sleep through our services because they can predict the next thing that is going to happen. Some creativity and a new anointing is often the answer to sagging attendance and waning interest. Make sure that there has been plenty of prayer preparation, that the musicians are ready, that the song leader is prepared, and that you as pastor are "on fire" as you await the moment of truth.

A walk through the facility can tell you a lot about the education arm of the church. What kind of atmosphere exists for the training of children, youth, and adults? The drop in attendance throughout our nation's Sunday schools demands that we look at the following:

- Preparation of workers.
- Adequate space for training.
- Adequate equipment in a day of mass media.
- Proper lighting, ventilation, etc.
- The best material possible for presentation (Radiant Life).
- A renewal of commitment to the teaching arm of the church. This cannot be considered an extra, but rather one of the vital streams of life in the assembly.

Our buildings are the most costly in town if used only one or two hours a week. Our long-range plan must encompass a full use of what God has provided for ministry. Our viability as an institution demands good stewardship of property and facilities. Many churches are building with a Christian school in mind or build multipurpose buildings where the community can discover ministry outlets for themselves and their family.

Remember our definition of *viability:* "able to stay alive." Your long-range plan will always have this in view.

Veracity

The third *V* principle is *veracity*—truthfulness, correctness, accuracy. One of the weaknesses in certain church circles today is going with fads rather than concentrating on developing a ministry of veracity.

We must back up our preaching and teaching with godly living. Series preaching will bring people back to the pews Sunday after Sunday. The long-range plan includes a pastor who knows where he is going with the Word.

Over a thirteen-year period we journeyed chapter by chapter through the New Testament on Wednesday evenings. Teaching grows people. It builds interest. The Word becomes the focus. It is a long-range investment in the lives of your people.

We must back up the preaching and the teaching with godly living. There is no substitute for the long-range commitment to excellence of life. There are no compromises. There is no reason for the community to say, "See, I told you so!" If God should lead you to another ministry, the next leader will not have to implement a long-range plan of fence mending and rebuilding the church's reputation in the community.

Vitality of the Spirit

The fourth principle in our long-range look is *vitality of the Spirit.* There is a good deal being written and spoken about "seeker sensitive" services and programs. I believe the Assemblies of God has been basically a seeker sensitive movement through the years. We have been a people of the altar and of the prayer room. We have trusted the Holy Spirit to use our witness to bring the lost to Christ. The question arises, Where does the human end and the Spirit begin? I'm not sure I can answer that question, but it is fair to say that without the Spirit, our efforts are futile and without substance.

For the vitality of the Spirit described above to be present and working, leadership must be dedicated to seeking God for continued blessing. Do you have a weekly leader's prayer meeting—a time when you do not talk business but wait on God for the needs of the fellowship? If not, the ministry is not working on a long-range plan. Only the Spirit can generate life and keep that life active and glowing.

Valued Importance

We come to the fifth characteristic of a good long-range plan. It must be *valuable;* it must be worth something!

Paul speaks to Timothy on this issue in his second letter to his son in the faith: "Be diligent to present yourself approved to God, a worker who does not need to be ashamed, rightly dividing the word of truth" (2 Timothy 2:15). It would not be difficult to leave off the last two letters of the word *worker* and simply apply this to the "work" God has called us to lead. It is valuable in God's eyes, and it should be valuable in ours. It is almost as if Paul is saying, "Timothy, do it well!"

I love the story of Joseph. When he had been given his dreams by God, his brothers did not look kindly toward him. As they were out in the fields, they looked and saw Joseph coming. "'Look, this dreamer is coming!'" they said (Genesis 37:19). But Joseph had this sense of value about his dreams. He was dragged through the pit to the palace, to the prison, and back to the palace to take leadership and make Egypt into the greatest nation of its day.

What is your vision of the church? No matter what the size of responsibility, we can do it well. The church was bought with blood! It is indeed valuable.

Venturesomeness

Our sixth word is *venturesomeness*—inclined to take risks! There is a lot of play-it-safe leadership in the church. In our long-range planning, there must be of necessity the element of risk. Theologically we call it faith, but translated it implies that we do not just do what we can afford. God has no lack!

One of the churches I pastored in the '60s had a leaky mimeograph machine, a worn-out vacuum cleaner, and no folding machine for the bulletins—in general, the equipment was ready for the dump. My venturesome spirit told me that if we were to develop long-range goals and a ministry that would revitalize a community, the people would need to learn how God provides when we apply ourselves.

One of the things I learned in that church after arriving was that they took no offering on Wednesday night. I understood why. They met in a small room at the front of the sanctuary so they wouldn't have to turn the heat on in the larger room (there was a wall heater in the meeting room). This seemed practical, but it was killing any plan for the future. I moved the service immediately to the sanctuary, implying that I expected a greater attendance than that small room in front would hold. It worked! Instead of ten people, there were twenty, then forty, then eighty, and soon over one hundred people were attending on Wednesday night. I was excited!

Then I took on the big challenge. I had a brand new mimeograph machine on loan from the office supply store in front on Wednesday night. I had the stencil cut for the Bible study outline and on the drum of the machine. I turned it on and showed the people what a beautiful job this machine could do. The notes were distributed with delight. Then I showed them how we could pay for that machine in one month. How? I held up a dollar bill. I informed the folk that it would take only 345 of those dollar bills to purchase this piece of equipment. In less than a month it was all paid off. And it was fun!

Then I brought in a folding machine. Then I blessed the custodian with a new vacuum and cleaning equipment. On and on it went—all purchased with money the church would have never received! What happened from that small beginning was a move to a beautiful acreage, the construction of a wonderful facility, the growth of the church into 5 percent of the local population attending churches, and the blessing of leading the Assemblies of God in foreign missions giving two years in a row. You have to start somewhere! Get that venturesome spirit!

Vulnerability

Our final principle is *vulnerability*—capable of being wounded or injured. Scars showed the commitment of Jesus to His mission! You will never develop a long-range plan without the spirit of vulnerability. As I pointed out in the list at the beginning of this chapter, not everybody will like you. You will have to keep perspective during criticism. Choose to be a happy person. Convey that happiness to your fellow leaders, as well as to the congregation.

In the annual leaders' retreat we had for years, one of our sessions was always devoted to writing down what we thought the church should be in five, ten, and twenty years. We talked about it. We laid out strategy that would bring us to those goals. I will never forget the first such planning session. The list that was developed looked monumental. However, instead of it being accomplished in twenty years, the entire outline had been successfully completed in six years! I was astounded, and I'm still astounded as I look back on those days.

As you recruit, train, and deploy workers in the vineyard and follow through on the seven *V*s of this chapter, your long-range plan will need to be revised again and again. It just works that way. And may the communities we labor in see us coming and say as Joseph's brothers, "Look, this dreamer is coming!"

Working with Church Boards

T. Ray Rachels

Max DePree, author of *Leadership Is an Art,* tells a story about his brother-in-law, Jim Kaat, who for twenty-five years was a great major league baseball pitcher.

In the mid-'60s, Kaat had the memorable opportunity of pitching against the famous Sandy Koufax in the World Series. When asked about Koufax's talent, Kaat explained that he was beautifully disciplined and trained. "In fact," he said, "Koufax was the only major league pitcher whose fast ball could be heard to hum. Opposing batters, instead of being noisily active in their dugout, would sit silently and listen for that fast ball to hum. They would then take their turn at the plate already intimidated."

DePree advised Kaat how opponents could have solved this problem. It would have been "a simple solution," he said. "You could have made me his catcher."[1]

What he meant, of course, was that every great pitcher needs an outstanding catcher, and that his own talent as a catcher was so unskilled that Koufax would have had to slow down his most powerful pitch, thus depriving himself of his greatest weapon.

Every great pastor needs an outstanding board if his ministry is to succeed at its highest level. Otherwise, the pastor's pitch will fall into the hands of those unready and unable to help produce winning scores. A pastor, no matter how excellent, will find his best efforts frustrated unless church board members have a clear understanding of their role, have developed a positive attitude for partnership with the pastor, and are willing to provide the spiritual complement for effective ministry.

In a study of Church of Christ pastors who left the ministry, 60 percent said that unsatisfactory relationships with the [church board] was the chief problem.[2] Another study of a large focus group pushed that percentage to 85. If unsatisfactory relationships are indeed a ministry-denying element eating away the heart and soul of people called by God to do the work of ministry, then surely some hope must be available to neutralize it. Expectations today are growing more exacting and causing widening ministerial grief, so a wise leader must proceed with caution, recognizing the culture's climate for criticism and impatience.

While pastor of a Florida church, Thom Raines asked his deacons to write down the number of hours they thought he should spend on various pastoral duties. When he tabulated the results, here's what their expectations were:

Sermon Preparation	18 hours
Administration	18 hours
Hospital/Home Visitation	15 hours
Prayer	14 hours
Worship/Preaching	10 hours
Outreach Visitation	10 hours
Counseling	10 hours
Community Activities	5 hours
Denominational Tasks	5 hours
Church Meetings	5 hours
Miscellaneous	4 hours

That's a total of 114 hours (out of 168 hours in a week).[3] Expectation overload? I think so. Even the deacons thought so. But unless there is mutual respect and understanding, our best work will be lost among the thistles of unrealistic expectations held by those we are called to serve and lead. Serving and leading are two terrible tension points for people in ministry. These tension points, if misunderstood, will cancel each other and chaos will prevail. On the other hand, if these tensions are embraced and understood, they will lead you, your board, and your ministry into the promised land of God's will. Serving and leading are part of the same biblical fabric. One serves by leading and leads by serving.

Jesus solved a conversational tug-of-war between his disciples about who is greatest when He said: "Whoever wants to become great among you must be your servant, and whoever wants to be first must be slave of all. For even the Son of Man did not come to be served, but to serve" (Mark 10:43–45).

What are the elements of successful pastor-board relationships?

Begin Well

You need to begin well when first coming into a local pastorate. When U.S. troops were first sent to Bosnia as part of the NATO peacekeeping force, they were told to watch out for mines, which could be almost anywhere, ready to explode. A wisecracker suggested that the best way to cross a mine field was to follow someone else.

Every local church has its minefields and (no matter how sweet the smiling faces) its content will detonate if not crossed with care. Those local-church mines, traditions and peculiarities, are all locked away in its board members—who are the wonderful custodians of the map by which you can negotiate your way through the first years of ministry among the people without getting blown to bits. But we do have Someone out front, leading the way. Our job is to stay behind Him and in His tracks.

Before you are ever selected as a pastoral candidate, the interview with the church board is critical. It won't be too hard to tell if you are classical music in a country-western church or community, or vice versa. It matters. Think and pray carefully before you embark on a major confrontation with those whose basic style differs too dramatically from your own.

When you come to be their pastor, use your first meetings with the board to instill confidence that you love them, love their church, appreciate and respect their history and traditions, and will give them the honor and respect they thought you would when they called you.

You will also begin to discover expectations that may not have been clearly communicated during the interview. Have patience. Listen. Trust comes slowly and is often built through subtle ways. Do more listening and absorbing than posturing and trying to convince them that you are the person in charge.

Go slow with changes. That isn't a hard and fast rule that must always take precedence over your own initiative and personal vision, but in most cases it is wise. This board will be your right arm, eyes, ears, and muscle. Their confidence in you has a price: You must lead them carefully; you must take their agenda seriously; you must not be a spendthrift but use a businessman's approach to money matters; you must know the difference between faith and presumption; you must be a person of your word; you must demonstrate, in ways they can see, your commitment to God and His Word and to your family and theirs.

Begin to lay out carefully your pastoral style, allowing it to gently bump against the issues and ways of their church's history as it needs to. As your style of leadership succeeds with the board, more confidence will be given you. As more confidence is given, you will be able to extend your arms further toward the vision God gave you when He called you to the church, without fear of tripping more mines. Building confidence takes time.

> **Do more listening and absorbing than posturing.**

Find out who the real leaders are on the board and make them your friends. Ask their advice when you have questions. Give them problems to solve and accept their solutions, unless to do so would violate your conscience. If they are the real leaders on the board, it is most likely so because they are known for having good judgment.

Get organized. Bring to your first meeting a printed agenda of items you want to discuss. Don't bring more than can be reasonably discussed in an hour and a half. If you have a long-range vision, put it down in the "spiritual dreams for our church" category and ask them to pray with you about its advisability, wisdom, and future possibility. They are already seeing into your pastoral heart; the time will come later when your vision and dream items can more easily appear on the regular agenda for their more thoughtful counsel. Have patience!

Remember the story of the snail and the cherry tree. One raw, windy day a snail started to climb a cherry tree. Some birds in a neighboring tree chattered their ridicule. "Hey, you dumb snail, where do you think you're going?" said one of them. "Why are you climbing that tree? There are no cherries on it!"

"There will be when I get there," said the snail.

Start on time. Board members have jobs where the clock is important and they know the power of the second hand. End on time and you'll win friends. If you aren't finished with the agenda when time runs out, carry over the rest until next month, unless it can't wait. If you think it can't wait but they think it can, take their advice and let it wait. If it's a toss-up, vote on it quickly, then move on. The law of the harvest is on your side. You'll reap benefits with incremental abundance as they take your measure as a person of wisdom who cares about their feelings.

While I was pastor of Christian Life Church in Long Beach, California, with thirteen board members, our young women's ministries group met on the same night each month as our board meeting. It became traditional for the women to bring in to our meetings, after about an hour, carts filled with coffee and freshly made pies and cakes. We always broke our agenda to enjoy fellowship and treats. We laughed, salivated, and thanked God for their consideration. We all grew in Christian fellowship.

Take the last five or ten minutes of the meeting to end well. Give the best and most encouraging words you have at this time. Did you get a great letter from a missionary who is supported by the church? Read it (or at least excerpts). Is there a testimony of God's grace at work in the life of a person who attends the church? Tell it. Are there birthdays on the board? Sing "Happy Birthday" and give a token of appreciation. Are there any anniversaries? Did one of their kids do something worth mentioning? Mention it. End the meeting on a high, positive note. Pray for one another and then let them lay their hands on you in final prayer. It is important that you begin well in your pastoral leadership with the board.

Serve with God's Power

Leading and serving a church board requires a personal spirituality that accepts one's giftedness and allows it to be connected to the power of God. Madeleine L'Engle, a wonderful Christian writer, tells in her book *Walking on Water* about the choices we make in life: "If the work comes to the artist and says, 'Here I am, serve me,' then the job of the artist, great or small, is to serve. The amount of the artist's talent is not what it is about. Jean Rhys said to an interviewer in the *Paris Review:* 'Listen to me. All of writing is a huge lake. There are great rivers that feed the lake, like Tolstoy and Dostoyevsky. And there are mere trickles, like Jean Rhys. All that matters is feeding the lake. I don't matter. The lake matters. You must keep feeding the lake.'"[4]

To serve should be a privilege, and it is to our shame that we tend to think of it as a burden, something we do if we are not fit for anything better or higher. "I have never served a work as it ought to be served," adds L'Engle. "My little trickle adds hardly a drop of water to the lake, and yet it doesn't matter; there is no trickle too small."[5]

What an eloquent witness to the life-giving purposes of God in the world, and to us, whose ministry of servanthood flows equally and generously into God's reservoir, "the lake." Few testimonies could outweigh the deep spirituality seen in a pastor simply adding his own unselfish work, or "trickle," to the mainstream of gospel work. Its very flow has on it the kiss of the Spirit and is a winsome quality for the board to see.

Keeping one's spirituality includes turning over to God all the excuses and reasons you may have for being the person you are. In board meetings, the clearest sounds we make can be our attempts to be someone other than ourselves. God has made us as we are, gifted us as He has, and called us into the place where we are. It is comforting to people who serve on boards to hear their pastor express satisfaction with God and with himself as he enfolds himself with his own unyielding commitment to God's gracious will. The pastor's tiniest trickle can be made a roaring, white water of spiritual hydrodynamics by the hand of God, as He channels the trickle toward "the lake."

On the other side is something we need to face as well. L'Engle says that a deeply committed Christian who wants to write stories or paint pictures or compose music to the glory of God simply may not have been given the talent, the gift, which a non-Christian or even an atheist may have in abundance. God is no respecter of persons, and this is something we are reluctant to face.

"We would like God's ways to be like our ways," says L'Engle, "His judgments to be like our judgments."

> It is hard for us to understand that He lavishly gives enormous talents to people we would consider unworthy, that He chooses his artists with a calm disregard of surface moral qualifications as He chooses His saints.

> Often we forget that He has a special gift for each one of us, because we tend to weigh and measure such gifts with the coin of the world's market place. The widow's mite was worth more than all the rich men's gold because it represented the focus of her life. Her poverty was rich because everything she had belonged to the living Lord. Some unheard-of Elizabethan woman who led a life of selfless love may well be brought before the throne of God ahead of Shakespeare, for such a person may be a greater force for good than someone on whom God's blessings seem to have been dropped more generously. As Emmanuel Cardinal Suhard says, "To be a witness does not consist in engaging in propaganda, nor even in stirring people up, but in being a living mystery. It means to live in such a way that one's life would not make sense if God did not exist."[6]

Our quest for spiritual success must lead us away from worrying about living (i.e., leading) in another person's shadow. We live and lead in our Lord's shadow. Church boards pick up that attitude from their pastor and support it with a wholeheartedness that spills over into the sanctuary. Every layperson longs for a godly pastor who is transparent, secure, selfless, and who models righteousness. The size of your talent has a diminishing importance when the fruit of the Spirit is obvious: "Love, joy, peace, patience, kindness, goodness, faithfulness, gentleness and self-control. Against such things there is no law" (Galatians 5:22–23). Those qualities win every time.

A board needs to ask really only one basic question before every decision: "What will please God most and honor His church best in the matter before us?" I remember meeting with a church board who had lost their pastor and were acting as a pulpit committee, interviewing candidates, searching for the right person to fill the vacancy. They showed me a list of questions they had prepared and were using as guidelines for their interviews. One area of questioning centered on the candidate's devotional life: "Tell us about your spiritual life. How do you hear from God? When you do hear from God, what do you do about it? What about your prayer life?"

One of the board members grimaced and said, "This has been one of the most enlightening experiences of my time on this board. Doesn't the Assemblies of God have pastors who can express their spiritual life to us? We have talked with three candidates, and all of them trip up on these questions about their spiritual life. They seem unable to give us a clear witness about their prayer life. One of them even said he didn't have time to pray each day because the work of the church kept him so busy, so he tries to just let all his daily activities be a prayer to the Lord."

The deacon looked sadly toward me, then at the others, and finished: "If we on this board need to be men of prayer and to lead our families in prayer, shouldn't our pastor also be a person who makes prayer a major part of his work?"

I asked a group of board members recently who were looking for a pastor, "What is the most important quality you look for in your pastor?" Almost in unison they shot back, "We want a pastor who has a spiritual heart!" They went on to tell me that the pastor who comes to them may lack in many of the leadership traits often noted as essential for success, but if he is Christlike and has a growing spirituality they would more easily forgive his other inadequacies.

Move Forward with Organization

Leading and serving a church board requires intelligent organization that will effectively move the church forward. I believe it was Philip Rise who said, "All houses have a junk drawer. Anything wanted from the junk drawer will be found at the bottom. Once any item is removed from the junk drawer—no matter how large or small—the junk drawer will not close." Some churches operate out of organizational "junk drawers" like that.

Peter Drucker, one of the world's foremost management gurus, makes a subtle but huge distinction between efficiency and effectiveness: "Efficiency is doing things right. Effectiveness is doing right things." The difference between a leader and a manager, says Drucker, is that a manager does things right while a leader does right things.[7]

An effective pastor, working carefully with his board, seeks to do right things. Right things aren't always obvious; they must be *found*. That's why it is wise for a pastor and board to be in partnership and have a close relationship. Finding right things to do is a joyful and fulfilling discovery, as well as cementing confidence. The pastor applauds the board for their part in leadership, and the board embraces their pastor for his remarkable leadership. Win-Win.

Putting structure into your leadership reminds me of a bulletin board I once saw in my daughter's fourth grade classroom. It was parents' night and my wife and I were visiting Heather's room. It was science fair time, and I saw on the bulletin board the words "How to Be a Scientist," with these steps underneath:

1. Hypothesize
2. Collect data
3. Experiment
4. Observe
5. Make conclusions

For a pastor, that process works too. In searching for right things to do, the first step for the pastor and board is to *hypothesize,* or make assumptions. Say, for example, the church is growing, your facility is crowded, and it appears you'll need more space, possibly requiring a move.

As you *collect data,* or begin to investigate the idea of moving, you try to figure its overall financial impact. Will you lose people? Are there alternatives to moving? What ideas are better?

Then you *experiment* by getting reports on all your questions and testing the answers against your current income and experience. Can you live with what you find?

As you *observe* over a period of months the congregation's positive and/or negative dynamics and the board's solidarity around answers that are now coming in, do those observations lead you to *make conclusions* for moving your congregation from one facility to another? If so, then do it! If not, don't! Mostly, however, the board and pastor's organizational work takes what all institutions who seek excellence require: planning and hard work.

Building the monthly board agenda needs an artful touch. Don't underestimate the power of well-laid plans on the agenda. Print it and pass it out. Think about what needs to be put on it and what needs to be left off. If you want to buy something, be sure you need it, and have the facts to support the need. Honor the budget. Don't ask the board to approve expenditures for things you can't afford or can do without. It's a good thing for a pastor to say no occasionally, if the item is either unreasonable to buy at the time or can be delayed until later. Let the board overrule you if necessary. Ultimate responsibility for all decisions will fall to you, and the people will usually hold you accountable for all things spent or misspent.

> **Avoid secrets, which is different from confidentiality, and confidence will soar.**

Stay away from secrets, which is different from confidentiality. If people know you and the board keep no secrets, confidence will soar, and they will more easily understand and appreciate confidentiality. Secrets promote paranoia. People suspect sinister motives when hushed tones and tiptoeing always come from board meetings. "What are they doing in there?" Disclosure is a pastor and board's mightiest tool for making friends and building appreciation. Confidence is built through disclosure. Confidentiality protects a person or issue from unwise focus. Secrecy pulls down the shades and locks the doors. Nobody gets in—except discontent and suspicion.

Always have a financial report, and let the treasurer give it. Don't hide bad news; rush it to the front. If expenses are overtaking income, be the first to recommend ways to even up the balance sheet. Tighten your belt during lean times. The day will come when the board will remember your good sense and reward your wise leadership. Make a budget every year to guide the board's financial decisions. Make sure the board studies and approves the budget. Few things can weaken a pastor more quickly than a board's belief that their pastor is financially irresponsible. Trust is hard won, and when lost, almost impossible to win back. And a pastor's major currency with his board is confidence and trust.

> **A pastor's major currency with his board is confidence and trust.**

Give away meaningful responsibility to each board member. One way is to assign portfolios, special areas of church life and work among the people and/or facilities. Part of a board's agenda should include reports from portfolio holders who have things to report from their month's work. A portfolio system gives the board opportunity to delegate work that may be too big or complicated to handle at their meeting. Another group or person can spend time in a more thorough exploration of an issue and can report their findings back to the board, unless, of course, the board gives the authority to make the decision. This also prevents a board from bogging down in things that can be worked through by others.

My friend, Buddy Ashurst, is a beekeeper and board member in El Centro. He tells me that on a warm day about half the bees in a hive stay inside beating their wings while the other half go out to gather pollen and nectar. Because of the beating wings, the temperature inside the hive is about ten degrees cooler than outside. The bees rotate duties and the bees that cool the hive one day are honey gatherers the next. Wise bees!

Timing is important in presenting issues to the board. One board member said to me once concerning his pastor, "He wants to bring everything to a head. Every issue we talk about is major. There are no minor issues to him, and he fights for every one. I wish he would give us some breathing room in our meetings. We've begun lately to fight him back, but I don't like the feel of it. I go home emotionally exhausted." If reaction to an item is strongly negative, you may need to move it off the table quietly and wait for another time to bring it back. In the meantime, you'll be able to explore reasons for reticence and to give your reasons privately for its benefits.

Seek Good Personal Relationships

Leading and serving a church board requires skill in personal relationships. The essence of working together effectively as a board rests on seeing and understanding each other's point of view—flexibility—not insisting on being right.

J. Robert Clinton, in *The Making of a Leader,* tells of a time when he served on a board that met often for prayer, sharing, and problem solving.

During one extended period when a question was being processed by the board, he took a strong position, pressing it forcefully and with unyielding passion. Other board members, he said, were still trying to find their way through the question (which involved a spiritual direction for one of the brothers), but "I had felt that the Holy Spirit had led us to a conclusion. . . . I pushed hard and my style of pushing on the issue probably lacked finesse." He was confronted strongly about his brusque style by other board members, informed that over the years it had always been offensive to them, and was ultimately removed from the board. He was asked not to come to the office anymore and put distance between himself and the board.

Hurt by the action and embarrassed before his friends, Clinton decided to not fight back but rather take the banishment as an act of spiritual authority delegated from God. He submitted. His pastor preached during one of those Sundays from Romans 6 about "counting yourselves dead to sin, but alive to God in Christ Jesus." After the message, the pastor passed out small pieces of paper shaped like tombstones. On them were the words:

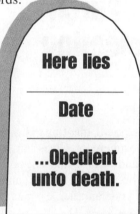

Here lies

———————
Date

———————
...Obedient
unto death.

Clinton explained, "Each of us was supposed to fill in his or her name and then list what we felt God was pointing out in our lives to which we needed to die. We were told to write on the back if we needed more room. . . . It was an emotional moment for me. I knew it was more than just an ordinary Sunday morning.

"I sensed that God was pulling together what had happened to me and focusing it to teach me something important. I had been brought through the conflict and discipline. I had been forced to reevaluate my ministry and my past relationships.

"On the front I wrote in my name and the words 'evaluation of life and ministry.' As I was turning it over to write on the back, it came to me in a flash: *I was inflexible.* It was as if the Lord spoke to me himself. I wrote on the back, *'Die to the right to be right.'*

"I have that tombstone in my Bible today. Occasionally, I get it out to remind myself. Every now and then my wife reminds me too, 'Don't you have a tombstone somewhere that says you don't have to be right?'"[8] Moments like those are pivotal in one's leadership development.

Legendary Alabama football coach Paul "Bear" Bryant once told an audience: "I'm just a plowhand from Arkansas, but I have learned how to hold a team together. How to lift some men up, how to calm down others, until finally they've got one heartbeat together, a team. There's just three things I'd ever say: (1) If anything goes bad, I did it; (2) If anything goes semigood, then we did it; (3) If anything goes real good, then you did it. That's all it takes to get people to win football games for you."

The greatest privilege in ministry is to work with a church board whose goal at every meeting is to deepen relationships, cry a little, laugh a lot, and find God's will for that moment.

Reading List

Dresselhaus, Richard L. *The Deacon and His Ministry.* Springfield, Mo.: Gospel Publishing House, 1977.

George, Carl F., and Robert E. Logan. *Leading and Managing Your Church.* Tarrytown, N.Y.: Fleming H. Revell Co., 1987.

Greenleaf, Robert K. *Servant Leadership.* Mahwah, N.J.: Paulist Press, 1977.

Malphurs, Aubrey. *Planting Growing Churches for the 21st Century.* Grand Rapids: Baker Book House, 1992.

Osborne, Larry W. *The Unity Factor.* Irving, Tex.: Word Books, 1989.

Thompson, Robert R., and Gerald R. Thompson. *Organizing for Accountability.* Wheaton, Ill.: Harold Shaw Publishing, 1991.

Conducting the Church Board/Business Meeting

Fulton W. Buntain

A successful church business meeting (or board meeting) is one in which business is conducted in an atmosphere of Christian love, respect, and order. "Let all bitterness, and wrath, and anger, and clamor, and evil speaking, be put away from you, with all malice: and be ye kind one to another, tender-hearted, forgiving one another, even as God for Christ's sake hath forgiven you" (Ephesians 4:31–32[1]).

The key to the proper atmosphere is found in one word: *preparation.*

Spiritual Preparation

Church leadership must pray! It is essential for the pastor to meet with members of the church board for a time of focused prayer on behalf of the business of the church—both board and church business meetings. In these times of prayer the Holy Spirit is given the opportunity to creatively move His church ahead for God's honor and glory. This time of prayer will build unity in the leadership. A church business meeting will surely be filled with tension and stress if church leadership is not in unity. After these times of prayer, open dialogue should be encouraged. Recognize that the personalities of church leaders vary. A willingness to accept those differences, and at the same time flow together as the body of Christ doing His work effectively, is of utmost importance.

I have found that areas of disagreement can often be resolved by postponing a decision until more thought and prayer are brought to bear on the issue. Occasionally time itself will melt away resistance and ill feeling. After all, the key to success in all areas of the Lord's work is unity.

As the body is one, and hath many members and all the members of that one body, being many, are one body: so also is Christ (1 Corinthians 12:12).

The body is not one member, but many (1 Corinthians 12:14).

There should be no schism in the body; but that the members should have the same care one for another. And whether one member suffer, all the members suffer with it; or one member be honored, all the members rejoice with it. Now ye are the body of Christ, and members in particular (1 Corinthians 12:25–27).

It is certain that the church body cannot fulfill its true mission without a high level of unity of mind and spirit. Only eternity will reveal the agony suffered in churches when the proper spiritual preparation did not precede the church's annual business or board meeting.

Proper Documentation Preparation

The second key to a successful church annual business meeting or board meeting is *proper documentation preparation.* The meeting should go forward under the accepted rules of *Robert's Rules of Order (Revised).*[2] These are the basic, established rules of most formal business meetings. Reference to these rules allows the structure in which business can proceed. A parliamentarian who is well versed in the procedures of a business meeting might assist the pastor or chairman on points of order.

Types of motions and their treatment include (1) *the main question*— the item under immediate consideration; (2) *the subsidiary motion*—an item that relates to the main question and seeks to affect the main question by amendment, substitution, delay, committing, or referring; (3) *the privileged motion*—an item that takes precedence over all other motions because it concerns the welfare and comfort of the assembly (e.g., adjournment, call for a division on a motion, appeal on a declared action); (4) and *the incidental motion*—an item of order subject only to limited debate (e.g., raising a point of order, limiting speeches, closing debate, calling for the question, and procedure of consideration).[3]

The essential part of a business meeting is an agenda clearly defining what is going to be discussed in the meeting. An agenda committee is most helpful in keeping the meeting on track. This official committee should meet prior to all official church meetings, possibly in an informal setting, to lay out the agenda. If the full body agrees at the outset of a meeting to abide by a previously prepared agenda, the possibility for a smooth meeting is greatly improved. Many problems in church meetings come when the floor is opened to any discussion on any subject, without proper investigation, prayer, and documentation.

Here is one suggested order of business, and another follows.

1. Call to order by the pastor/chairman
2. Devotional (may include congregational singing and rejoicing in what God is doing in the church or in individual lives)
3. Determination of quorum by roll call or visual check
4. Approval of the minutes of the previous meeting and agenda for current meeting

5. Reports
6. Unfinished business
7. Elections
8. New business
9. Special items such as announcements
10. Adjournment

The pastor/chairman of the business or board meeting must guide the meeting in an orderly manner and maintain an efficient schedule by observing parliamentary rules. The chairman does not dominate the meeting but simply leads the board or congregation through the items of business in a spirit that will bring honor to God's kingdom. We must remember that even though we do all we can to be organized and operate within proper guidelines, we are serving the Lord and His work. Paul told

An Issue Is Not Ready for a Vote . . .

When there are very few comments. If the chairman brings up a topic and there is an uncomfortable silence, the time is not right for a vote. Once in a board meeting I brought up the need for a new van for the church. Because of the financial concerns that particular month, there was hesitation from several about making a decision. I sensed their concern and said simply, "Let's study this need a little further and bring the item up again next month." We assigned two or three people to look into the need and give a report the next month. When they finished I again brought up the subject of purchasing a van. The difference this month was that the finances were stable and a well thought out "need-study report" was given by the committee. It was unanimously voted on that we should purchase the van.

When a private dissenter remains silent. If a board member has shared misgivings about a proposal with you one-on-one but keeps quiet about it during a meeting, don't force a vote. If you think you can slide it by while he's being compliant, think again. He will probably undermine the decision later. Move on from the topic but contact him later and ask why he was unwilling to express his concerns. Encour-

age him to share them at the next meeting. If he doesn't, let the group know of his objections and his reluctance to share them; then discuss them.

When you get bland or questioning looks. When you see bland looks, it usually means ideas haven't been communicated clearly enough. Go back and explain the topic again until you are sure everyone is "on the same page."

When some members are in deep contemplation. Sometimes people need time to process and digest information, especially if it contains bad or surprising news. Everyone processes issues at different speeds. Encourage board members to take time at home thinking about it. Then address the issue in the future when everyone is ready.

When key issues are not being discussed. Sometimes when you are brainstorming an idea, you know there are key objections, but they are not brought up. Avoid the temptation to move for a vote. Any negative issues not discussed will not simply disappear; they will fester and get worse. Encourage board members to discuss their concerns. And if they won't bring them up, do so yourself.[4]

Timothy, "I write so that you may know how you ought to conduct yourself in the house of God, which is the church of the living God, the pillar and ground of the truth" (1 Timothy 3:15, NKJV). The meeting that conducts the business of the church is a spiritual meeting just as a Bible study or Sunday service is a spiritual meeting. The focus may be somewhat different, but the conduct of church business is essential to the health and proper functioning of the local church.

John Maxwell states: "Two common problems in board meetings are (1) each person has his own agenda, and (2) the pastor has a difficult time maintaining control of the meeting." Maxwell is right. He recommends avoiding digressions by sticking to an agenda prepared before the meeting. He has a further helpful suggestion of dividing the agenda into three categories: *information, study,* and *action* items.[5]

> **The meeting that conducts the business of the church is spiritual.**

1. *Informational items:* Every meeting should start off on a positive note, and the informational section of the agenda makes this possible. Include five or six positive reports on the ministry of the church. Report how many people attended membership class last week or the exciting ministry of the Holy Spirit at the women's event the day before. Give news of upcoming events, meetings, or special services. Use this time to inform and remind of the reason for the meeting. This part of the agenda differs from the "old business/new business" plan, which is sometimes fruitless, boring, and negative.

In traditional meetings, more often than not, finance is the first topic addressed, and many meetings never move forward from there. Informational items, on the other hand, are chosen specifically because they are positive, exciting, and set the tone for the rest of the meeting. Spend no more than five minutes in this area—just enough time to inspire hearts and prepare them for the most productive segment of the meeting.

2. *Study items:* This part of the agenda always contains the most items. Ninety-five percent of meeting time should be spent studying or discussing these issues and items of interest. Your goal during this part of the meeting is to brainstorm ideas. Work to get every possible suggestion—and objection—on the table.

Never vote on any item that you have listed as a study item. The pressure of a vote causes people to take sides and discourages free and creative thought. Never vote on a study item before the next meeting.

You may keep some study items for months, allowing every option and objection to be put on the table and explored. Other subjects may be study items for only one meeting and then moved on in the next session. Keeping items in the study section of the agenda allows people to process information without feeling threatened, and eventually a consensus is reached. Only then is an item ready to be put before the body for action.

3. *Action items:* The final section of the agenda contains action items, which have already been in the study section for at least one meeting, have already been discussed, and are ready for a vote. Never spend more than five minutes in this area. If your board has been candid and the dis-

cussion and study have been thorough, there is no reason to spend a lot of time in this section.

If you are currently frustrated by board meetings, you are not alone. Every pastor has been there, and most of us have dreamed of a world without committees. But the truth is we need our board members. They give us perspective, experience, and strength that we don't have alone. A well-managed board actually multiplies the efforts of the pastor and staff in accomplishing the ministry.

The official minutes of a meeting should include (1) the name of the organization, (2) the nature of the meeting—regular or special, (3) time and place, (4) name of the chairman, (5) the devotional title or topic, (6) correction and approval of previous minutes, (7) business transacted (8), adjournment, and (9) signature of secretary and date of approval. The pastor may take some liberty in arranging identifying information at the beginning or end of the minutes.

* * * * *

It is evident from the Book of Acts that even in the Early Church, division and disunity were a problem (e.g., Paul and Barnabas disagreed regarding John Mark's involvement in an upcoming missionary journey). Wherever humans gather, disagreement will be part of the group dynamics. However, the believers' practice should demonstrate to the world that love and understanding prevail when Jesus is brought into the center of all church business meetings.

Appointment Process: Board Member/Elder Selection

1. **Suggestion Period**
   Names can be suggested to the board selection committee.

2. **Consideration Period**
   The appropriate leadership talks to the nominee with an explanation of doctrinal issues, constitution and bylaws, frequency of board meetings, time and ministry commitments, etc.

3. **Investigation Period**
   This step needs to be thorough. Issues are addressed, such as, Do you have a consistent devotional life? What is your prayer life like? Do you have a strong marriage? Are you a tither? Are you involved in personal evangelism? Are you a church member? Are you aware of time commitments for this responsibility?

4. **Interview Period**
   How do they control temper, lust, passions, etc. Are they walking a consistent Christian life?

5. **Approval Period**
   During this time members of the church can give a signed note of disapproval to the board selection committee.

6. **Evaluation Period**
   Informal or formal evaluation meetings are helpful to both the pastor and the board member.

7. **Dismissal Procedure**
   In case of moral failure or divisive issues (Titus 3:10), it is good to have a dismissal procedure approved by the board.

Biblical Accountability in the Church

Bob Schmidgall

James had been active in a local church for a number of years. But subtly his marriage began to deteriorate. Its stresses were further amplified by his wife's sickness, as it placed great limitations on her. Later, in spite of cautions, he divorced her and, after some time, began to see another woman. When the senior pastor became aware of what was happening, he called James into his office and severely warned him of possible consequences. But James ignored the warnings and soon married the woman. The pastor again asked James to come in and told him that because he had ignored the counsel given him, his membership was being placed on probation by the official board of the church; furthermore, he was not to be a part of any ministry in the church. Later, James returned to the pastor deeply repentant for his actions and attitude. Because of the severity of what had happened, he was given a five-year probation. James submitted to the discipline and after four years was returned to ministry in the congregation. Accountability is a desperately needed quality in the body of Christ today. Had James not been called into account, he might never have been restored to integrity and would have continued in ministry with an unresolved issue in his life.

Glenn and Sarah were leaders of a children's church ministry. They became frustrated with what they considered the senior pastor's lack of support as well as with peripheral issues. Their attitude became negative, and they began to speak to others about their displeasure. Meetings between them and the pastor did not seem to resolve the conflict. Eventually, the pastor suggested that they step down from leadership, since their attitude was beginning to affect the church. They unhappily did so. Eventually, they left the church without totally resolving the situation. Accountability in the church is so important that even if exercising it results in a loss of someone, it will still accomplish its desired purpose. In this case a cancer was excised, restoring the body to harmony.

Ralph was a member of the pastoral staff. When approached by the pastor about rumors of immorality in his life, Ralph vehemently denied them. Later, a person in the congregation confessed immoral activity with Ralph, who then admitted to it. He was broken and had a repentant attitude. In this case, the pastor and official board of the church felt led to invite Ralph to find reconciliation and restoration within the context of the congregation. With the permission of the district, he was assigned to serve his rehabilitation at the church, with no ministry for two years. A membership meeting was called following the next Sunday night service. The pastor presented the general facts and then invited Ralph and his wife to enter the room. Ralph spoke to the congregation about his deep sorrow and asked them to forgive him. At the conclusion of the meeting, people lined up to greet him and share their support and love. Ralph found a secular job in the area and attended the church for two years. He later found a productive ministry in another congregation, having been affirmed by the church where he had been and released by the district in which he was located. Accountability demands that those who are in positions of authority exercise compassion and concern, with firmness, for the healing of the persons who have failed their responsibilities.

In this chapter, we want to speak to two critical issues: First, how can we realize our biblical expectations in our people in the church. Second, how can we as leaders model accountability before the church.

Developing Accountability within the Church

Several concerns relate to developing accountability within the church: (1) How can we establish expectations and accountability for leaders, members, and persons participating in ministry (i.e., *standards*)? (2) How can we develop new believers spiritually and continue to hold a goal of spiritual growth before all believers (i.e., *growth*)? And (3) how can we administer corrective measures to restore people after moral, attitudinal, and spiritual failure (i.e., *discipline*)?

We need an understanding of biblical accountability. Accountability implies that one reports or informs an individual or a group about one's actions, thoughts, and attitudes. It requires giving a reason. Peter said believers should be ready to give an answer for the hope that lies within them (1 Peter 3:15). When we are accountable, we willingly give insight into our motives to the ones we are accountable to. Accountability also carries with it the idea of submission. To be accountable is to be responsible. Hebrews 13:17 (cf. v. 7) instructs us to obey those who have the rule over us.

The Bible indicates that God expects accountability on a regular basis. He confronted Adam and Eve with the fact that they had hidden themselves. He did not let them off the hook, but waited as they gave an explanation for their actions. He followed up with discipline. There are many other examples of accountability in Scripture: Cain, who murdered his brother, Abel, was required to face the Lord. Moses, who in a fit of rage did not follow God's instructions carefully, was by God forbidden to enter the Promised Land. David, who committed immorality, was confronted by the prophet of God. Ananias and Sapphira, who lied to the Holy Spirit and to Peter, were not only asked a reason for their actions, but were judged for them. The Corinthian man who committed immorality with his stepmother was ostracized from the church. It is clear from Scripture that accountability is part of the divine plan. It is a key to keeping on course or correcting one's course, being put on the right path again. In Matthew 18, Jesus taught how individual believers can require accountability from other believers or from leaders. Definitive steps for dealing with issues like this are clearly outlined in His words. Paul gave clear instruction to the Corinthians concerning the handling of the young man who had fallen into immorality; they were to confront him, and if he rebelled, they were to ostracize him.

GOALS FOR ACCOUNTABILITY

The goals for accountability in the church are as follows:

Prevention. By requiring people to report on their actions, explain the reasons for what they have done, and submit to authority, we will set a standard that will help prevent them from falling into wrong actions or attitudes. The old saying "An ounce of prevention is worth a pound of cure" is very true in this case. Though some dispute the value of capital punishment, recent studies have shown that where major crimes are punished severely, including capital punishment, there has been a noticeable decline in criminal actions.

Correction. Through accountability, we can assist people in catching wrong actions or attitudes before they become full blown. This will help them rediscover their first love and stay on course spiritually. In the process, we will also find that the actions of others will be corrected through example. Once when we dealt with someone who had committed immorality in the church, another man went to his office the next day and told the secretaries who had been flirtatious that they should never try that again. The correction of someone who had fallen into error provoked another person to also make corrections.

Restoration. The purpose of accountability is to help restore people to usefulness and truthfulness. Accountability is not to give us leverage or lordship but to aid us in helping people rediscover fruitfulness in their lives. The intent is not to control or depress, but to release and revive.

Purification. Accountability will help purify the church. It allows for cutting off destructive and divisive influences in the body. A pure church will be a more powerful church.

MEANS OF ACCOUNTABILITY

Accountability in a church may be cultivated through several channels:

Peers. The writer of Hebrews said we should provoke one another to good works (Hebrews 10:24). People voluntarily submitting themselves to one another is one of the most powerful ways to develop accountability in the congregation. In recent years, fellowship groups and accountability groups have been used very effectively. Getting men to commit themselves to meet with other men and open their hearts to one another can be a very effective tool for developing accountability among men.

Authority. God has placed certain persons in authority in the church to design and develop accountability systems for the people in the congregation. Pastors, deacons, and elders are charged with the responsibility of creating that accountability. Part of the problem is that many times people in authority do not want to pay the price of requiring accountability from others. However, without accountability there cannot be effective leadership.

Mentoring. Paul told Timothy to gather around himself faithful men he could teach and charge with responsibilities of ministry (2 Timothy 2:2). To mentor is to influence other people's lives by a godly example, allowing them to watch the mentor function as a believer. They can then follow the model set before them.

Certain forces drive the accountability process. To have true accountability, there must be a relationship. Persons who are required to explain themselves or report about their lives can feel secure. More focus needs to be placed on relationship, because it is the oil that makes accountability run smoothly. For a number of years I have enjoyed the wonderful experience of working with deacons in leadership. As a board, we meet monthly to conduct business. We have an agenda and follow it. However, each Wednesday night we meet together to share a meal where we fellowship and pray together. We spend four times a month working on our relationship and one time a month conducting business. In the context of relationship, accountability comes much more easily.

Accountability also includes the factor of organization. Where good organization is lacking, accountability is very difficult. Through good organization we can communicate our expectations to people, either through job descriptions, flowcharts, or other means. When people know what is expected, they more easily measure up to it. Good organization will help to explain their task as well as provide a procedure for decision making and reporting the results.

A third factor in accountability is divine revelation. When we communicate to people God's expectations and His standard, they will respond. It is also important to seek to lead people into a fresh relationship with the Lord. When people are walking in fellowship with God, they find it easier to walk in fellowship with one another and with those over them.

Implementing Accountability in the Church

One practical way to implement accountability in your church is by establishing standards. We can clearly define standards for those who become members. We should not be ashamed or apologetic about establishing standards that require proper attitudes and actions from persons who become members. We should seek to back those standards with Scripture. In our congregation, three times a year I teach a membership class. Those who attend the class learn the following:

- The philosophical commitments of Calvary Church and the Assemblies of God
- The philosophy of ministry of Calvary Church
- Our doctrinal statement (Statement of Fundamental Truths)

- Understanding your gifts
- God's financial plan for the church (tithes and offerings)
- A proper lifestyle—staying pure in spirit (motives), in our soul (attitudes), and in our body (actions)
- Review of the Constitution and Bylaws
- Explanation of the membership application

Through this class we are able to set a standard of accountability we can hold people to after they become members. In addition, we have written expectations for persons in leadership. As an example, we have a list of expectations for deacons, which a person signs upon accepting the nomination to the office of deacon.

We can encourage accountability through spiritual growth. It is not possible in a few weeks to change a new believer into everything we want him or her to be. It takes time to work with that new believer and help him get to a place where God wants him to be. It is imperative that we not lead people to Christ and then leave them to fend for themselves. As someone has suggested, we would never bring a new baby home, set him in the kitchen, and say, "Now there is milk in the refrigerator, water in the faucet, and food in the refrigerator and the cabinet. Eat every day and take good care of yourself." What we do is take that baby home and treat him like a baby. As he grows and develops, we give him more and more independence. If we treat a physical baby so carefully, should the church not treat new believers with the same care and concern?

We can fulfill this responsibility of spiritual growth by providing new believers' classes, counselors who will help lead people to Christ and then follow them up, mentors who can meet with people and help disciple them, and other means of leading people into spiritual growth. Another critical area of spiritual growth involves challenging people who have been serving the Lord for many years. Growth comes through involvement in *service* and *fellowship*. People must understand that if they are going to grow, they must engage in those two activities. We need also to keep in touch with people, to ask them to report and explain to us what they are doing in these areas.

> **We should not be apologetic about standards.**

Accountability is enhanced by proper biblical discipline. Dealing with moral, attitudinal, and spiritual failure is critical to the health of the church. Healthy churches have new babies, unhealthy ones don't. Tolerating and ignoring sin in this area only cripples us. Three critical factors relate to discipline in the church:

Communication. We must help people understand what God expects of them and the consequences of failing to follow His expectations. When someone begins to slip, instead of ignoring it, we should seek to touch them through fellowship and communication.

Confrontation. When something becomes more serious, it is time to confront. We need to let people know that they are going down a wrong path and that if they don't make a course correction, they are headed for disaster. We must let them know we care about their possible failure.

Compassion. Accountability is made palatable for people when it is administered with genuine love. When people know that they are loved, they are willing to accept responsibility. Leaders need to exercise compassion in their dealings with people. This will mean that we will do our best not to embarrass people, that we will seek to be gentle with them, and that we will not give up on them.

Modeling Biblical Accountability for the Church

One of the greatest keys to accountability in the church is leadership that models accountability. If we as leaders do not practice it, our people will not catch on. One of the things in the body of Christ that mystifies me is the number of times I see leaders who do not themselves want to be accountable but want their people to be accountable. This doesn't make sense. Paul said, "Follow my example, as I follow the example of Christ" (1 Corinthians 11:1). Leaders today should be able to say that to their people, or they cannot ask the people to follow them.

Spiritual leaders and pastors need to be accountable to the fellowship they have joined. The Assemblies of God has a wonderful structure for accountability, which if followed, will lead to productiveness and fruitfulness in a minister's life. We need to support all our leaders. As we accept their influence, leadership, and authority in our lives and ministries, we will be blessed.

We also need peer group accountability. Part of this is realized through attending fellowship meetings. As a pastor of a small home mission church in earlier years, I observed that the pastors of the large churches did not seem to ever have time for fellowship meetings. It made me feel like they considered me an inferior. I made a vow to God that if I ever had the privilege of pastoring a larger church, I would not forget my other brothers. It is a habit of mine to regularly attend fellowship meetings. Often, I will delay departure for a ministry trip to make it possible to be at the fellowship meeting. I believe that this provides a vehicle of accountability for my life and ministry that I cannot do without. We can also practice accountability through mentoring. One of the greatest benefits I have enjoyed in my life has been older men who have loved me and set a godly example before me. I can think of a number of men who filled that role in my life. Their model provided a goal to strive toward.

I believe that every minister should be accountable in some way. In fact, it is my opinion that every evangelist should have a home church and a pastor to whom he can report, give an explanation for his actions, and be in submission. I believe that itinerant ministries would be much more powerful if they would practice this.

* * * * *

In conclusion, I would like to comment on a couple of attitudes I feel people in authority should seek to develop. The first is that it is God's church. It is not our church, but His. Therefore, we should trust the ultimate responsibility of the well-being of the church to Him. If we develop a possessiveness about the church we pastor or the ministry we have, we will inhibit its growth and development. Releasing it to the Lord will free us from a lot of anxieties.

Second, leaders should seek to be nondefensive. We don't have to defend ourselves, because the Lord will defend us. If we do defend ourselves, then we are taking that responsibility away from God and limiting His ability to defend us. One of the greatest compliments I have ever received came from a brother who said to me, "Pastor, one thing I've noticed about you is that you do not defend yourself. You are patient and ride out the storm. The result is that over the years, I have seen the Lord preserve and protect your life and ministry."

There is nothing that any of us desire more than to be considered faithful in our ministry. Each of us anticipates the Lord saying, "Well done, . . . good and faithful servant" (Matthew 25:21). Part of the key to hearing the Lord say that is a commitment to accountability, both in ourselves and in those we serve.

Knowing and Using the Legal System

Richard R. Hammar

A s the number of lawsuits filed in this country continues to escalate, churches and pastors are finding themselves involved in the legal system more than ever before. Many are being sued. Some are suing. And many pastors are asked to testify in court proceedings involving church members. This involvement will continue for the foreseeable future, since the number of lawsuits is projected to double over the next few years. It also raises a number of questions. How does the legal system work? When should an attorney be retained? How does a church or pastor find an attorney? What about the clergy-penitent privilege? Do pastors have to serve on juries? Let's look at each of these questions.

How does the legal system work?

Remembering a few basic principles will help:

Federal and state—First, there are two systems of courts in this country: federal and state. Federal courts hear only certain cases (they have limited jurisdiction). State courts can decide almost every kind of lawsuit (they have general jurisdiction). The vast majority of lawsuits, including those involving churches, are brought in state courts.

Different levels of courts—Both the federal and state court systems have different levels of courts. At the bottom level are trial courts where lawsuits are filed and then argued before a jury or judge. Above the trial level there normally are two levels of appellate courts. Parties that lose at the trial court ordinarily can appeal to the first level of appellate court. An appeal to the highest court (usually called the supreme court) generally is possible only if the court agrees to hear the case. The United States Supreme Court accepts fewer than 3 percent of cases that are appealed to it.

Civil and criminal—Trial courts hear both civil and criminal cases. Civil cases include such claims as breach of contract, personal injuries, and property damage. When churches are sued, it is almost always a civil lawsuit. Criminal cases are brought against persons who violate certain laws. The government, through a prosecuting attorney, brings the suit against the "defendant" who is accused of violating the law.

Procedure—Civil lawsuits begin when one party files a summons and complaint (or petition) against another. The party filing the lawsuit is called the "plaintiff," and the party being sued is the "defendant." The defendant must file an "answer" to the lawsuit within a specified time (usually twenty or thirty days). After this first round of pleadings, the lawsuit enters the "discovery" stage. This is when the whole process slows down, and months or even years can go by with little if anything happening. During the discovery stage the attorneys seek information from the other side or from witnesses. This is done through interrogatories (questions calling for written answers), depositions (giving sworn testimony before the attorneys and a court reporter), and requests for the production of documents and records. Lawsuits that are not settled out of court proceed to trial. As noted above, the outcome of a civil trial can be appealed.

Settlement of cases—The vast majority of civil cases (in some states, as many as 95 percent) are settled before or during trial.

When should an attorney be retained?

Whenever a church is sued it is important for the pastor to immediately deliver the lawsuit (summons and complaint) to the church's liability insurance company. The insurance company will determine whether or not the lawsuit is covered under the church's insurance policy. If it is, the insurance company will retain an attorney to represent the church. It is important for pastors to understand that lawsuits must be answered within a short period of time (usually twenty or thirty days). Any delay in transferring the lawsuit to the church's insurance company will make it more difficult for the insurance company to retain an attorney who can respond properly to the lawsuit in a timely way. If the lawsuit is not submitted to the insurance company until after the deadline for filing an answer has expired, a court may award a "default judgment" in favor of the plaintiff.

In some cases it is advisable for churches to inform their insurance company about *potential* lawsuits. For example, assume that a pastor learns that a child has been molested during a church activity. The pastor should immediately inform the church insurance company of this incident even though no lawsuit has been filed. If the church has its own attorney, this person should be contacted as well.

Churches of course should consult with an attorney when preparing legal documents such as contracts, deeds, and employment manuals and forms. Do not make the mistake of thinking you can save a few dollars by preparing these documents without the assistance of an attorney. This can lead to disaster.

How does a church find an attorney?

Many pastors when confronted with legal issues do not know where to turn for legal advice. Unfortunately, there are very few attorneys who specialize in church legal matters. Many legal issues are routine and do not require a specialist in church law. An example would be a church that needs an attorney to assist with the purchase or sale of property. However, when the issue involves religious considerations, such as the discipline or dismissal of a member or employee, it is preferable to deal with an attorney with experience in church law. How do you find one? Call other churches in your area for references, or your district office. In addition, there are associations of Christian attorneys that may be able to provide you with a referral. These include the Christian Legal Society and the Rutherford Institute.

What about the clergy-penitent privilege?

Every state has a law making certain communications to ministers "privileged." This means that neither the minister nor the "penitent" can be forced to testify in court (or in a deposition or certain other legal proceedings) about the contents of the communication. Not every communication made to a minister is privileged. The typical statute applies only to (1) communications (2) confidentially made (3) to a minister (4) acting in his or her professional capacity as a spiritual adviser.[1]

The privilege does not excuse a minister or the person making the communication from appearing in court. It merely excuses one from disclosing the communication in court against his or her will. When the person who made the communication or the minister to whom it was made is asked about the communication in court (or in a deposition), then is the proper time to assert the privilege. Before a person answers, the question must be objected to on the ground that it seeks to elicit privileged information. If one makes no such objection, the privilege is waived—even if the question is later challenged. If the person being questioned objects at the appropriate time and is overruled, that will serve as a basis for appeal.

A number of state clergy-penitent laws specifically nullify the privilege in the context of child abuse reporting, meaning that a minister cannot rely on the privilege in explaining a refusal to report. Further, the concept of *privilege* generally applies only to courtroom testimony (or depositions) and not to contacts with state officials. On the other hand, some states preserve the clergy-penitent privilege in the context of child abuse reporting.

Do pastors have to serve on juries?

Every citizen has a duty to serve as a juror when called upon to do so, unless specifically exempted or excused. In some states ministers are exempted from the duty of jury service. The exemption may be automatic, or it may be available only upon timely application. If the exemption is available only upon the filing of a timely application, a court is under no duty to inform a minister of the availability of the exemption—the burden is on the minister to claim it. Of course, ministers who are exempt may waive the exemption and have their names placed on the list of eligible jurors.

In those states that do not exempt ministers from jury service, a minister often may be excused from service by showing undue hardship or extreme inconvenience. Such a decision is entirely within the discretion of the court. Obviously, a minister who is not exempted from jury service should be excused if there is a funeral to perform, several church members are in the hospital and in need of visitation, the church is engaged in the construction of a new facility, or there are urgent counseling needs.

A minister who is not exempt from jury service may be excused if challenged. A prospective juror may be challenged on the grounds of prejudice, direct interest in the litigation, previous knowledge of the facts, acquaintance with a party to the lawsuit, prior jury service in the same or a related case, or preconceived opinions about the lawsuit.

* * * * *

Understanding the answers to the above five questions will provide the minister with a basic knowledge of the legal system so that he or she can confidently discuss with an attorney the possible courses of action that should be followed in any matter having potential legal consequences.

Basic Legal Issues

Richard R. Hammar

Churches exist in an increasingly litigious and regulated society, which makes an awareness of legal obligations essential. The need for such awareness will only increase in the future. Consider the following:

- According to the most recent statistics released by the National Center for State Courts, more than one hundred million new cases were filed in state courts in a recent year! These included nearly twenty million civil lawsuits, and this number is expected to double over the next few years. This ominous trend will directly impact churches, since the litigation experience of churches will reflect the general trends in society at large.

- As all levels of government (local, state, and federal) become more regulatory, there will be more and more "points of intersection" between government regulation and the autonomy of the local church.

• Being uninformed about legal obligations can be costly, resulting in fines, penalties, and jury verdicts. And while such costs were in the past borne by the church, in the years ahead the focus will increasingly be on the personal liability of church leaders.

What are the most important legal and tax concerns for church leaders? Consider the following:

Incorporation

There are many reasons why churches should incorporate. By far the most important is to protect members from personal liability for the actions of fellow members. In many states, the members of an unincorporated church may be personally liable for the actions of fellow members in the course of church activities. For example, members may be personally liable for the sexual molestation of children by another member in the course of a church-sponsored youth activity. This potential liability should be a concern to any member of an unincorporated church. Churches can simply and easily protect their members from personal liability for the conduct of other members by incorporating the church. While incorporation will not protect a member from liability for his or her own actions, it will protect other members who did not participate in the member's actions.

Incorporation is a simple and relatively inexpensive process. Of course, it requires the assistance of an attorney. Unfortunately, many church leaders do not know if their church is incorporated. Others assume that it is. This can be a very dangerous assumption, since it may mean that members are personally responsible for the liabilities of the church. Even if a church has incorporated in the past, the incorporation may no longer be in effect. This can occur in a couple of ways. First, many churches have incorporated for a limited term instead of an indefinite (or perpetual) term. For example, a church might have been incorporated for a term of twenty-five years in 1950. Such a corporation expires automatically at the end of the term. For this reason we urge you to check your church's articles of incorporation to see if your church was incorporated for a specific term. If so, has it expired? If it has, you will need to file a new application for incorporation. If your church was incorporated for a limited term that has not expired, you should consider amending your articles of incorporation to reflect a perpetual term. Second, churches can lose their corporate status in some states by failing to submit an annual corporate report to the office of secretary of state. It is a good practice to check periodically to see if your church is a corporation in good standing. You can do this in most states by contacting the office of secretary of state in your state capital. However, in a few states churches are permitted to incorporate by applying to a local court—a type of incorporation that may not be communicated to the secretary of state. As a result, your church may be incorporated even though the secretary of state has no record of it. Fortunately, this is not a common occurrence. In most cases if the secretary of state has no record of incorporation, it's probable that your church is not incorporated.

Some church leaders are opposed to incorporation on the basis of theological considerations. Note that theological opposition to incorporation will not be a defense to the personal liability of church members. Church leaders who are opposed to incorporation on theological grounds should share their position with the church membership. After all, it is entirely possible that church members will not share this theological position when they are apprised of the potential consequences. They should not be exposed to personal liability without their knowledge and consent.

Child Abuse

The problem of child abuse on church premises and during church activities continues to plague churches. Fortunately, more churches are beginning to take this risk seriously. Many incidents have been avoided through preventive maintenance. If your church has implemented a screening program, it is essential that you maintain a continuing commitment to it. Resist complacency. If you have not implemented a screening program, do so at once. Remember, you are not just protecting your church from a lawsuit and negative publicity. Far more importantly, you are protecting your children!

Child Abuse Reporting

Child abuse is of epidemic proportion in our country. Ministers often learn of incidents of abuse in the course of counseling or from reports they receive from nursery or youth workers. It is essential for ministers to understand clearly their responsibilities under state law to report known or reasonably suspected incidents of abuse. In many states, ministers are mandatory reporters, meaning that they can be criminally liable for failing to report. A number of courts have rejected the defense made by some pastors that they failed to report abuse because they wanted to deal with the problem within the church as a matter of discipline. A few states excuse ministers from reporting abuse if they learned of it in the course of a privileged communication. Be sure to check your state law often, for this area of law changes often.

Pastoral Counseling

Many churches have been sued as a result of the sexual misconduct of ministers during counseling activities. Sadly, many of these allegations are true. However, some are false, but it is very difficult for ministers to prove their innocence since it is "my word against theirs." Your church can significantly reduce the risk of such incidents and of false allegations in a number of ways.

First, you can adopt a rule forbidding any counseling by male pastors with unaccompanied females without a third person being present. The third person can be the pastor's spouse or another staff member.

Second, prohibit off-premises counseling without a third person present, and restrict counseling on church premises. Such restrictions could include the following: (1) a requirement that opposite sex counseling occur only during office hours when other employees are present and visible; (2) limiting counseling sessions to a maximum of forty-five minutes; (3) permitting no more than four sessions with the same person. Of course, some exceptions would be in order for any of these approaches (for example, when the counselee is a relative or above a certain age).

Third, you can establish a policy that you will engage in opposite sex counseling only by telephone. This approach will be appropriate for smaller churches with no employees other than the pastor.

These restrictions will protect you and your church against three risks—inappropriate contact between a pastor and counselee, false accusations of such contact (that are difficult if not impossible to disprove), and the appearance of impropriety.

Negligent Supervision

Churches can be sued if they fail to exercise due care in the supervision of activities. The basic rule to follow here is to always have a sufficient number of trained adults present during any activity. For example, do not conduct a youth activity involving swimming or mountain climbing without an adequate number of qualified adults. If you are taking children on any water activity (swimming, boating, etc.), do you have one or more adults who are certified in CPR techniques who would be capable of assisting a drowning victim? Another problem that is common to many churches is the releasing of children from Sunday school or children's church before the adult service ends. After a parent or guardian has left a child at the church, the church generally is legally responsible for the child's safety until the parent or guardian has picked him up. If a church releases a child before the parent or guardian returns, it can be responsible for any injuries that occur. Another potential problem is releasing children in the nursery to the wrong adult. Church nurseries should establish procedures to ensure that children are returned only to authorized adults.

Copyright

Copyright law is of special significance to churches for two reasons. First, few areas of law impact churches more pervasively than copyright law. And second, copyright law involves the application of special rules that are not clearly understood by church staff members, church leaders, musicians, and even some publishers and attorneys. As a result, there is considerable confusion regarding the application of copyright law to churches. This confusion has contributed to widespread misinformation and noncompliance with the law. Such noncompliance, even if unintentional, can result in enormous financial liabilities.

The most important point to remember is this: churches are subject to copyright law, and among other things this means that a church cannot

1. make copies of copyrighted materials (including music, books, and magazines articles) without permission
2. make a "derivative work" based on a copyrighted work (such as an arrangement of a copyrighted song, or a new edition or workbook based on a copyrighted book), or
3. publicly perform a copyrighted work

Violation of copyright laws may occur in a church's music program in a number of ways. Duplicating copyrighted choral music, making audio or video recordings of church services in which copyrighted music is performed, making "chorus booklets" or similar compilations of commonly sung music, making transparencies of copyrighted music for display during worship services, copying music for an accompanist, and making bulletin inserts containing the lyrics of copyrighted music—all of these practices violate the copyright owner's exclusive right to make copies of his or her work. In addition, making changes in copyrighted music may constitute a violation of the copyright owner's exclusive right to make derivative works.

Church publications are a second major area of potential infringement. "Publications" include newsletters, bulletins, and literature duplicated for instructional purposes. Again, if such publications contain copyrighted materials that are reproduced without consent, then they will constitute an infringement on the copyright owner's exclusive right to make copies.

There are a few defenses to copyright infringement. These include permission from the copyright owner, a license, and "fair use." Also, the performance of religious music at a church in the course of religious services is exempted by law from copyright infringement. Note that this exemption applies only to the performance of religious music and not to the copying of music. The fair use exemption is limited, but in some cases will exempt limited copying if there is no commercial motivation, the portion copied is insignificant, and the copying is not a substitute for purchasing original works.

Compliance with Organizational Documents

It is important for church leaders to be familiar with their church charter, constitution, bylaws, or other organizational documents, since these documents ordinarily address many issues of internal administration. Church charters typically set forth the name, address, period of duration, and purposes of the corporation; the doctrinal tenets of the church; and the names and addresses of incorporators and directors. However, they rarely contain rules for the internal government of the corporation. For this reason, it is customary for churches to adopt rules for their internal operation. Such rules ordinarily are called "bylaws," although occasionally they are referred to as a "constitution" or a "constitution and bylaws." Church bylaws ordinarily cover such matters as (1) qualifications, selection, and expulsion of members; (2) time and place of annual business meetings; (3) the calling of special business meetings; (4) notice for annual and special meetings; (5) quorums; (6) voting rights; (7) selection, tenure, and removal of officers and directors; (8) filling of vacancies; (9) responsibilities of directors and officers; (10) method of amending bylaws; and (11) purchase and conveyance of property. Other matters that should be considered for inclusion with church bylaws (but often are not) include: (12) adoption of a specific body of parliamentary procedure; (13) a clause requiring disputes between church members, or between a member and the church itself, to be resolved through mediation or arbitration; (14) a clause specifying how contracts and other legal documents are to be approved and signed; (15) signature authority on checks; (16) bonding officers and employees who handle church funds; (17) an annual audit by independent certified public accountants; (18) an indemnification clause; (19) specification of the church's fiscal year; and (20) "staggered voting" of directors (a portion of the board is elected each year—to ensure year-to-year continuity of leadership).

Personal Liability of Church Board Members

Church officers and directors may be personally liable for their actions in several situations, including the following: (1) personal tort liability for such actions as negligent operation of a church vehicle, negligent supervision of church workers and activities, copyright infringement, and wrongful termination of employees; (2) contract liability for executing a contract without authorization (or with authorization but without any indication of a representative capacity); (3) violating one of the "fiduciary duties" that every officer or director owes to a corporation, including the duties of due care and loyalty to the corporation; (4) violating or disregarding the terms of an express trust imposed by a donor on a contribution; (5) selling securities without registering as an agent (if required by state law), or engaging in fraudulent activities in the offer or sale of church securities; (6) willfully failing to either withhold from the employee or deposit with the government federal payroll taxes; (7) approving a loan to an officer or director.

A number of states have adopted statutes limiting the liability of uncompensated directors of nonprofit corporations for their ordinary negligence. These laws do not protect officers and directors who are compensated for their duties or who engage in gross negligence or intentional misconduct.

Discrimination Laws

A bewildering number of antidiscrimination laws have been enacted by federal, state, and local governments. Many of these laws apply to the employment relationship and prohibit covered employers from discriminating in employment decisions (including hiring, firing, and benefits) on the basis of race, color, national origin, gender, pregnancy, religion, age, and disability. At the federal level, coverage under these laws generally requires a minimum number of employees plus some involvement by the employer in interstate commerce. Limited exemptions are available to religious organizations under some of these laws.

To illustrate, Title VII of the Civil Rights Act of 1964 makes it unlawful for an employer engaged in interstate commerce and having fifteen or more employees to discriminate in any employment decision on the basis of race, color, national origin, gender, pregnancy, or religion. However, the Act exempts religious organizations, including churches, from the prohibition of religious-based discrimination in employment.

A church is more likely to be subject to state and local antidiscrimination laws. However, these laws generally permit churches to discriminate on the basis of religion in their employment decisions. To ascertain the application of state and federal discrimination laws to your church, a local attorney familiar with employment law should be consulted.

Property Taxes

Every state property tax law exempts places of religious worship. It is common for state law to exempt property used exclusively as a place of religious worship. In many states, however, the exemption is not automatic. An application for exemption must be filed and approved. The states vary widely with respect to the taxability of other church-owned property. Note the following:

- *Surrounding grounds.* Some state laws specify how much of the land surrounding the house of worship is exempt. Other state laws do not address the issue, but the courts interpret the exemption of a "house of worship" to include surrounding land reasonably necessary to accommodate worship.
- *Effect of rental income.* In some states, the generation of rental income negates any exemption. Many states recognize the partial exemption principle, however, and exempt that portion of church-owned property that is not used for commercial or rental purposes.
- *Property under construction.* Generally, property under construction does not qualify for exemption.
- *Parsonages.* A parsonage is a church-owned dwelling that is used as a residence by a minister. They are exempt in many states.
- *Vacant land.* The courts have split over the tax treatment of vacant land. The majority view seems to be that such land is taxable even though it is acquired for future use as a church, unless it is used regularly for church activities (camp-outs, youth activities, recreational activities, sports, outdoor services, etc.).
- *Church-owned campgrounds.* The courts have split over the tax treatment of church-owned campgrounds. All states recognize a chapel and a reasonable amount of surrounding property to be exempt. The controversy concerns bunkhouses, residences, undeveloped land, and recreational facilities. Most courts have denied exemption to these portions of campgrounds.

Unrelated Business Income

The Internal Revenue Code imposes a tax (equivalent to the corporate income tax) on the unrelated-business taxable income of an exempt organization. The income must be generated by an unrelated trade or business that is regularly carried on. A trade or business is any activity designed to generate income. A trade or business is not unrelated merely because the earnings are used for exempt purposes. The focus is on the nature of the activity, not the use of income from that activity. The line between a taxable commercial activity and an exempt one is often difficult to define.

The term *unrelated business income* does not include

- activities performed by volunteer workers
- activities carried on for the convenience of the organization's members, students, or employees
- selling donated merchandise

Rental income is given special treatment. Note the following rules:

- Rental income from property owned debt-free is not unrelated business income.
- Rental income from property not owned debt-free (e.g., subject to an "acquisition indebtedness") is unrelated business income, in proportion to the amount of the debt, unless (1) at least 85 percent of the property (considering space, time, or both) is used for exempt purposes, or (2) the church plans to demolish the rental property within fifteen years and use the land for exempt purposes (the church must notify the IRS of its plans after five years).

It is very rare for a church to have unrelated business income. One example is the rental of a church parking lot to the patrons of neighboring businesses during the week—if the parking lot is not owned debt-free.

Payroll Tax Reporting Requirements

The term *payroll tax reporting requirements* refers to an employer's legal obligation to withhold income taxes and FICA taxes from employees' wages and to pay them (along with the employer's share of FICA taxes) to the government. All churches are subject to at least some payroll tax reporting requirements. The courts have rejected the claim that imposing these obligations on churches violates the first amendment.

The application of payroll tax reporting requirements to clergy involves two special rules that are often misunderstood:

- Clergy always are self-employed for social security purposes with respect to services performed in the exercise of ministry.
- Clergy compensation is exempt from income tax withholding, whether a minister reports income taxes as an employee or self-employed.

Use the following ten-step approach for complying with the payroll tax reporting requirements:

1: Obtain an employer identification number.
2: Determine whether each worker is an employee or self-employed.
3: Have each employee complete and return a W-4 (withholding allowance certificate).
4: Compute the compensation of each worker.
5: Determine how much income tax to withhold by using IRS Circular E (and wage and withholding allowance information).
6: Withhold nonminister employees' share of FICA taxes (unless the church filed Form 8274 and exempted itself from the employer's share of FICA taxes).
7: Deposit payroll taxes.
8: Complete and file quarterly employer's tax returns with the IRS (Form 941 or 941E).
9: Issue a W-2 to each employee; send a copy of each W-2 to the IRS along with a W-3 transmittal form.
10: Issue a 1099-MISC to each self-employed worker who was paid compensation of $600 or more; send a copy of each 1099 to the Social Security Administration along with a 1096 transmittal form.

Education

Let's conclude with some good news—through education and preventive maintenance, churches can significantly reduce their risk of being sued! You do not have to passively wait to be sued and view litigation as inevitable. Yes, the level of litigation in this country is staggering—and it is increasing. But you don't have to be a victim. By being apprised of the risks that face you and by implementing preventive practices, you can reduce significantly your risk of being sued. The bibliography at the end of this chapter lists a number of resources to assist church leaders in becoming informed about the legal issues that affect them.

Selected Bibliography

The following publications are available from Christian Ministry Resources, P.O. Box 1098, Matthews, NC 28106; telephone 1-704-841-8066.

Bloss, J. *The Church Guide to Employment Law* (1993). Addresses the application of several employment and discrimination laws to churches.

Cobble, J., and R. Hammar. The 1996 *Compensation Handbook for Church Staff.* This annual publication reviews salary data for nine different staff positions within the church, based on comprehensive survey data.

Cobble, J., R. Hammar, and S. Klipowicz. *Child Abuse Prevention Kit* (1993). Includes *Reducing the Risk of Child Sexual Abuse in Your Church,* a ninety-six-page manual addressing this critical issue, along with several pertinent forms, a one-hour audiotape, and a twenty-four-minute videotape.

Hammar, R., and J. Cobble. *Risk Management for Churches: A Self-Directed Audit* (1994). An easy-to-use, legal self-evaluation for churches.

Hammar, R. *Church and Clergy Tax Guide.* This annual publication is the most authoritative and comprehensive tax guide available for both clergy and churches.

_____. *The Church Guide to Copyright Law,* 2d ed. (1990). A complete and practical copyright reference designed specifically for churches, clergy, and church musicians.

_____. *Church Law and Tax Report.* A bimonthly newsletter apprising churches and clergy of all legal and tax developments affecting them.

_____. *Church Treasurer Alert!* An easy-to-read monthly newsletter designed specifically to assist the church treasurer.

_____. *Pastor, Church and Law,* 2d ed. (1991). The standard reference book on American church law; it contains a comprehensive treatment of hundreds of legal and tax issues that impact churches and clergy.

Meeting and Using the Media

Jeff Brawner

The American interstate system has provided advertisers with a golden opportunity to share their message with the masses through strategically located billboards. Inviting and informative signs line busy roads and interstates to inform travelers where gas, food, hotels, and interesting sights can be found. For mass communication to be effective, it is vital to know what people are looking for as well as where to look for people. The highway that will be utilized most frequently in the twenty-first century won't be an asphalt interstate—it will be an information superhighway.

For many Americans, television, radio, and computers have become more than an informational "road"; they have become daily companions. The first thing most people do when they enter their homes is flip on the lights and turn on the TV. Millions get into their cars, start the motor, then turn on the radio. Checking electronic mail has become almost as common as walking out to the ol' mailbox with the flag on the side.

If the Church is to effectively reach this sight-and-sound generation for Christ, we must utilize the same media roads much of society is using every day. The average child spends approximately 22 hours a week watching television. A recent statistical survey estimated that an adult spends 3,297 hours watching television and movies, listening to the radio, and reading newspapers, books, and magazines *per year.* Given 8,760 hours in a year, this survey showed that Americans spend over one-third of their yearly time in multimedia usage.

The reference points of most Americans are visual and auditory. In the vast majority of homes, history, literature, and art have been replaced by CNN, ESPN, A&E, the major television networks, and as many as 150 channels of viewing options. Magazines and newspapers are adapting to the ever-shortening attention span of society by offering news synopsis and quick-scan headlines. HDTV, fiber optics, interactive television, and surfing the Internet are not futuristic ideas; they are present realities that are changing society as we know it.

The good news is that God is not intimidated by the information super-highway and neither should we be. The Lord has always been in the communication business. In fact, the apostle John refers to God's Son as the *Word* (John 1:1). Throughout history we witness God inspiring His servants to use the tools of their time to spread His Word and will. From oral tradition to scribes, printing presses, radio, television, satellite, computers, and interactive media—God's servants have always taken advantage of whatever communication options were available to them.

> **" Media is there when hearts are breaking. "**

Reaching people by means of media tools will never replace personal evangelism—it can't. The single most effective tool for reaching the lost is a saved, Spirit-filled believer sharing his or her testimony with a friend. Eighty-six percent of those individuals who come to Christ do so because of a relationship with a believer. Media ministries is tailor-made to play the role of raising awareness, planting seeds, creating spiritual thirst, and affording witnessing opportunities that will inevitably arise. Media has instant and immediate access to America's homes and hearts. It is there when news is breaking; it is there when hearts are breaking. Countless testimonies of divine intervention have been documented as the Holy Spirit prompted a right message at the right moment to touch and transform a desperately hurting person. We will never win the world because we are on television or radio, but it is doubtful we will touch every person who needs to be reached without using media's "broad-casting" ability and potential.

If we are to effectively utilize the media tools of our time to touch this generation for Christ, we must understand some of the basics. When it comes to utilizing media, it's a numbers game in the strictest sense of the term. Each particular medium—be it radio, TV, or print—has an audience. For radio, it is listeners. For TV, viewers. In print, readers. Each audience—listeners, viewers, or readers—can be measured and, therefore, quantified. Radio typically sells "listeners per average quarter-hour," TV sells "household shares," and print sells "circulation."

Media as a Ministry Tool

There are three words to keep in mind when using media as a ministry tool: *relationship, research,* and *repetition.*

RELATIONSHIP

Make it a point to build a relationship with the editor of the newspaper and with the general manager and/or news directors of the local television and radio stations. They are constantly looking for stories—especially stories of local interest. It is vital to recognize that their agenda may not be the same as yours, but they are driven by the need to build and maintain their audience. Media outlets aren't interested in building your ministry, but they are interested in ways that your story might translate into boosting their viewing/reading audience.

Before contacting news outlets with a potential story, think through specific ways the story will serve their interests and needs. For example, your local news just ran a feature piece on the deterioration of the inner city, the rising crime rate, and the fear that is spreading throughout the community. Use their "bad-news" story as an opportunity to contact them about your "good-news" story—your congregation's plan to replace fear with hope. Inform them about your church's feeding outreach; let them know about the life-changing ministry your church has to prostitutes and gangs; notify the media of your people's efforts to touch the lives of children through your sidewalk Sunday schools. The media's agenda is news; our agenda is news too—the good news. Both can be accomplished if we will initiate the relationship.

Developing a relationship with the media directors in your community will break down the stereotypes they may have of you, as well as the ones you may have of them. Pray for favor and practice genuine interest and loving concern. Send news releases to the newspaper, radio stations, and television stations. Keep them brief, creative, and appealing to their audience.

RESEARCH

There is a smorgasbord of media options and opportunities in every community. Ask questions. Study the possibilities. Ask more questions. Research your market. Ask more questions.

Cable TV has changed the broadcasting landscape and opened exciting avenues of spreading the good seed of the gospel. In many markets cable access channels provide free airtime to those who will provide them with programming. In other markets cable companies have equipment and personnel to assist ministries in producing a program. James wrote, "You do not have, because you do not ask" (4:2). That biblical principle is also true when it comes to utilizing media tools in your community.

Research not only includes identifying the options and opportunities, it also includes surveying the media landscape. Here is but a sampling of the media horizon:

Radio: *Oldies Stations* that play music from the '50s, '60s, and '70s have adult listeners between the ages of thirty-five and sixty-four.
Classic Rock Stations that play music from the late '60s, '70s, and '80s have adult listeners between the ages of twenty-four and fifty-four, with a male majority or dominance.
Hot or *New Country Music Stations* have adult listeners between the ages of eighteen and forty-nine.
News/Talk Radio Stations have adult listeners between the ages of thirty-five and sixty-four.
Alternative Music Stations usually have younger listeners between the ages of thirteen and twenty-four, with a male majority or dominance.
Adult Contemporary or *Hit Music Stations* usually have adult

listeners between the ages of eighteen and forty-four, with a female majority or dominance.

Urban Contemporary Music Stations usually have adult listeners between the ages of twenty-four and fifty-four, with a black majority or dominance.

Dance or Rap Stations usually have adult listeners between the ages of eighteen and thirty-four.

Classical and *Jazz Music Stations* usually have adult listeners between the ages of thirty-five and sixty-four.

Cable: *Lifetime* is an adult female-oriented entertainment channel.

ESPN 1 and *2* are adult male-oriented channels.

CNBC is a general adult-oriented talk/information channel.

MTV is a youth- and young adult-oriented music channel.

VH1 is a young adult-oriented music channel.

E! is a young adult-oriented entertainment channel.

AMC is a general adult-oriented entertainment channel.

CNN is a general adult-oriented news/talk channel.

HEADLINE NEWS is a general adult-oriented news channel.

A&E is a general adult-oriented entertainment channel.

USA is a young adult-oriented entertainment channel.

DISCOVERY is a general adult-oriented information channel.

TNN is a general adult-oriented music/entertainment channel.

It may come as a shock to some in your congregation when you place your church spots on MTV, but remind them that young lost fish swim in that pond. Your evangelistic efforts must include identifying where hurting, broken, searching people are and then developing a strategy for reaching them on their turf.

REPETITION

The law of effective communicators is *repetition, repetition, repetition!* Strategize your media efforts in such a way that the same targeted people are exposed to your message over and over again. On the average, it takes a salesperson six attempts to persuade a prospect to say yes and purchase something. Each individual we are attempting to reach needs to be exposed to our message at least four times in a week. In a small market with a dominant local radio station and local newspaper, that is fairly easy to do utilizing a combination of television, radio, newspaper, and billboards.

In medium and larger markets, saturating an audience during prime time can be financially out of reach. However, a fruitful result can be achieved at a much more affordable price by applying *frequency* as opposed to *reach.*

Reach is achieved by advertising only where there's a big, big crowd—like the airplane dragging an Eat At Joe's banner across the lakefront on a hot summer's day in full view of a crowded beach, or a single spot on the most listened-to radio program during drive time. It can be said that those communications reached thousands of people. But what response did they generate? How many ate at Joe's, and was there response enough to make the ad buy-effective? With one shot it was probably nowhere near enough. But fly that plane over three times in the morning and three times in the afternoon at forty-five-minute intervals, beginning at 4:30 P.M., and Joe's will begin to fill up with hungry and thirsty patrons returning home from a day at the beach. The latter is an example of frequency, which when combined with reach ultimately makes communication effective.

As previously mentioned, reach is an expensive strategy. Frequency need not be. Frequency builds repetition. Therefore, a good primary strategy is frequency. And the key to frequency is *unsold inventory,* which moves us to another basic of media ministry—*timing.*

Timing in the Use of Media

In spot (or commercial) buying there are two key words—*unsold inventory.* A rate card is a station's primary negotiating tool. Perhaps you've heard the phrase "Don't pay retail, pay wholesale." A rate card is a rough equivalent to paying retail. Unsold inventory is not spoken of unless you ask, and those rates are 100 percent negotiable. By definition that is exactly what it means—i.e., commercial time that is available but remains unpurchased. To a broadcaster, unless some client contracts for it, it is strictly lost revenue. Like the baker who sells day-old bread at a significant discount, a broadcaster will do the same just to recoup something rather than waste it and get nothing.

Typically radio and TV broadcasters have an abundance of unsold inventory in January, February, July, and August. There can also be a decent amount available in September, October, May, and June as well. As the media buyer, what you are after is a guaranteed rate for unsold inventory in the following periods:

January 10—March 10
May 15—August 15
September 15—November 15

Another important phrase to be familiar with is *lowest unit rate.* The FCC has mandated that during an election, candidates can be charged only the lowest available rate per commercial. This is closely monitored because it is the FCC that grants licenses to the broadcaster. In an election year, a sales manager may tell you they have to watch how low they can go on unsold inventory because they will have to match that rate for any and all political advertising. This is absolutely true and accurate. It is not a ploy to get you to pay a higher rate. It is a matter of timing.

Hurting people are often awake when they should be asleep. They're worried, anxious, and have trouble relaxing. So it stands to reason that running spots in the evening and late night hours offers a high probability of making a connection with hurting and lonely people. As much as 66 percent of any radio and TV station's unsold inventory will be between 11:00 P.M. and 6:00 A.M., Monday through Friday, which for reaching hurting and unchurched working adults and young adults in school is a perfect match. Weekends are also great for those with economic problems. Why? People worry most about their jobs when they're away from them—evening, late nighttime, weekends.

Reaching Your Target Audience

It is not enough to know the tools and timing. To be effective in media you must identify your *target audience*. Your target audience will determine the substance, style, and placement strategy you will need to use.

SUBSTANCE

What do you want to share? The *substance* of your message will be determined by the audience you are targeting. Children, young people, singles, single parents, divorcees, senior citizens—these all have different needs, tastes, and levels of understanding. The wise communicator knows the audience and tailors the message for the listeners. This is not a matter of compromise, but of sensitivity and clarity.

STYLE

Style is a critical area of ministry. Many believers mistake *style* for *substance.* They prefer a certain style and mistakenly equate the method with the message. For some, it isn't preaching unless the message is presented in a "hellfire and brimstone" package. For others, the strong evangelistic tone turns them off—they feel as though they are being yelled at. We must present the message in such a way that it will be easy for our target audience to understand and respond to it. That requires knowing who they are and how they speak.

Focus groups can be a revealing way to determine the language our target audience is speaking. A focus group is a gathering of typical people in the demographic spectrum we are attempting to reach. We often assume we know what people want and how they speak, rather than asking and listening to them. Communication isn't *message given*—it's *message received.* If we are attempting to describe a square and the person is picturing a circle, we haven't communicated. Just because we have said it doesn't mean they have received it. The effective communicator looks for ways to make sure the message is received, and that requires a style easy for the listener to relate to and respond to.

PLACEMENT STRATEGY

Once a target audience is identified, the following questions must be asked: When will they be listening or watching? What will they be turning to for entertainment or information? It is critical to know the trends of your target audience. It requires studying the habits, tastes, and patterns of your audience, much like a fisherman knows the ways of the fish he is attempting to catch. Hunting and fishing magazines abound with insights into landing the big one or shooting the prize buck. It is amazing that hunters seem to study and know more about the prey they are hoping to kill than many believers do about the people we hope to see saved. We must be devoted to knowing the hearts and habits of those we desire to reach if we are to design an effective media strategy to reach them.

The information superhighway has become a way of life. If we use these tools of our time effectively, they can become a road used by the

Holy Spirit to lead people to Christ. It is time to use every media means available so that we might reach the masses with a message of forgiveness, healing, help, and hope.

Dealing with Change

Michael D. Comer

We no longer live in the days of "Beaver" Cleaver, when the father works, mother stays at home, the children do their chores after school, and all load up for church on Sunday morning. The information age has changed the way people work and live. The world today is not like that of our fathers. The world today is not what we learned in Bible school or seminary.

Change has drastically affected the church. In many cases we find it hard to face the fact that the environment changes. Often in our zeal to keep to an unchanging message we fail to realize we are addressing a changing world. Pastors and churches that have success realize they live in a changing world and adapt the unchanging message to that changing world. The influence of television has brought the world to rural America. In small churches, greater demands are placed on the pastor and church leaders to emulate the great parachurch ministries seen on national TV. Children who spend all week in school learning from a Macintosh computer and playing virtual computer games are no longer intrigued by a flannel board Sunday school class. Although the power of our message is unchanging, the medium of the message must change. The challenge to pastors today is how to personally deal with the pace and impact of change, how to help others deal with that change, and how to direct change in our churches.

Dealing with Personal Change

The Old Testament describes a group called the sons of Issachar. First Chronicles 12:32 says the sons of Issachar "understood the times and knew what Israel should do" (NIV). Understanding trends that impact the church and designing strategies to deal with those trends is a new skill that has become more important for pastoral leadership. Perfecting that skill requires today's minister to take specific actions to impact change personally. There are several ways that a pastor can determine impacts of change.

1. Ask God's direction and insight into the situation. Understanding change from a godly perspective and seeking divine insight into situations can dramatically affect how we respond to change.

2. Stay apprised of current events and trends by constant reading and study of multiple resources. In the past few years a number of Christian-based organizations provide data, surveys, and feedback about events that affect the local church. Book series dealing with change management directed at the local pastor are popular in community bookstores.

3. Take risks with new ideas and technology. More than likely the members of your congregation are very familiar with computers, computer graphic programs, and voice mail. The proper use of these technologies can assist in distributing our unchanging message.

4. Develop an attitude of continuous improvement. Change deals with the unfamiliar. If you are constantly striving to do whatever your hand finds to do "with all your might," you develop a mindset of quality and improvement. If you review each church event when it is completed to determine what can be done better, a mindset will develop in volunteer leadership that will constantly look for ways to improve.

5. Be a continual learner. Surveys among business, church, and community leaders have found that effective leaders are also effective and continual learners.

6. Realize that change is happening constantly but adjustment to change takes time. It has been stated by management development experts that it takes an average of twenty-one happenings to develop a habit. It takes about ten times that number (two hundred to three hundred happenings) to break a previously developed habit. Adjusting to the timing and transition of change becomes a personal challenge and requires patience.

Helping Your Congregation Deal with Change

"People don't mind change, but they do mind *being* changed." It is our responsibility as leaders to help people move beyond their comfort zone into an acceptance of change. Professional counselors are trained to assist people in overcoming dramatic change in their personal lives. It is often necessary for pastors to help congregations adjust to changes in methods of operations, changes in service order, or implementation of new ministry areas.

Although sixteenth-century writer Machiavelli turned his intellect to inappropriate uses, on one point he was right: "There is nothing more difficult to carry out, nor more doubtful of success, nor more dangerous to handle, than to initiate a new order of things. For the reformer has enemies in all those who profit by the old order, and only lukewarm defenders in all those who profit by the new order. This lukewarmness arises partly from fear of their adversaries, who have the laws in their favor, and partly from the incredulity of mankind, who do not truly believe in anything new until they have had an actual experience of it."

To assist people in accepting change, the change acceptance curve can be applied. Basically the change acceptance curve states that there are five steps individuals initiate when encountering change: (1) awareness, (2) self-concern, (3) mental tryout, (4) hands-on trial, and (5) acceptance.

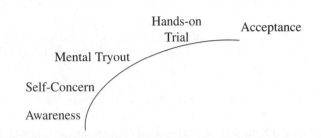

As persons find out about a particular change *(awareness),* in most cases they respond by asking how the change will affect them *(self-concern).* Sadly, in many churches people resist change because they fear it will affect their influence, or power base, with leadership or the congregation. If people can move beyond the stage of self-concern, they will find themselves thinking through how to deal with the change, what alternatives are available *(mental tryout).* Usually a rational person will move to experimenting with, trying out, some of the changes *(hands-on trial).* This may eventually move to the stage of *accepting* the change.

As people move through the change acceptance curve, there are some specific strategies that leaders can use to move people toward the acceptance of change.

Phase	Leadership Response
Awareness	Communicate
Self-Concern	Counsel
Mental Tryout	Demonstrate
Hands-on Trial	Educate
Acceptance	Support

It is important that people be informed of the change by leadership, meaning that constant communication is necessary during the awareness stage. It is much better for a board member or congregation member to hear about a change from the pastor rather than from another member of the board or congregation. During the self-concern stage, it is often necessary to spend time counseling those who will be affected by the changes. This is not consoling in the traditional sense of the word, but time spent explaining the change individually to key leaders and influencers. Spending time in this stage can assure the success of the change. Likewise, not spending individual time with key leaders and influencers can result in the failure of the proposed change.

As one moves to the mental tryout stage, the leader should demonstrate the new culture, behavior, or idea by showing what the situation will be like after the change is implemented. As people begin to accept the change, it may be necessary to reeducate the congregation on certain aspects of a change—many times leaders fail to realize that once a change seems to have been accepted, it must be constantly supported with communication, demonstration, and counseling for the change to continue. Too many times church leadership contend that a particular change has been accepted by a congregation only to see it fail because of a lack of on-going support.

At any point in the change curve, people can fall into the "land of resistance." True leadership realizes the mental model of the change acceptance curve and "baby-sits" the proposed change through the acceptance stage. Prime examples of accepting change come when a church wants to change the service times, do away with traditional ministry programs to implement fresh programs, or move into a new building.

Dealing with Organizational Change

In addressing organizational change, Chuck Swindoll noted: "Organizations tend to lose vitality rather than gain it as time passes. They also tend to give greater attention to what they 'were' rather than what they are 'becoming.' It is easier to look back into the past and smile on yesterday's accomplishments than it is to look ahead into the future and think about tomorrow's possibilities."[1]

To effectively minister in today's environment the wise pastor must not only manage change but direct it. To anticipate change and prepare for it provides proficiency in management. Leading in today's changing world requires different skills from in the past. Working closely with demanding congregations, directly communicating with boards, and providing stricter oversight of legally charged matters are but a few items today's pastor must master. To deal directly with change it is important to understand a simple but vital concept called the change life cycle.

Because it is human nature to reject most change, each change generally goes through a specific life cycle. A prime example is Moses and the Children of Israel. Before they reached the Promised Land they wandered in the wilderness for forty years. Although there were numerous theological reasons for their sojourn, moving toward a promised land usually requires a wilderness journey. This can be called the "As Is" and the "To Be."

The To Be is the vision, or dream, of your church—specifically where you want to be in five years or beyond. The To Be may be a new building, new families, new youth programs, or a better outreach ministry. The As Is is where you are today. If you are not a visionary, the To Be may seem impossible given your As Is situation. As you further define and move toward the To Be, it will require changes. Because people generally resist change, things will often degenerate before they get better. A simple drawing conveys this concept.

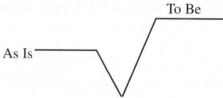

As you move toward the To Be, you may face a drop in attendance, enthusiasm, offerings, etc., because of the dramatic impact of change. Eventually you will emerge at a higher level than before. However, getting there may be a wilderness experience. Any pastor who has entered a new church or begun a building program can generally relate to this change principle. Anticipating the effects of change (i.e., the drop that may occur) can help dissuade panic.

Organizations must often reach the nadir of the life cycle before the organization begins to climb toward the To Be state. This low point is often referred to as the "valley of despair." By realizing the power of this simple concept, a decision maker will not panic or stop a project when declines occur but will implement transition strategies to help the organization move to a better state.

As leaders we must realize the power of the change life cycle. The role of the pastor/leader in directing change is to make the valley of despair as shallow and as narrow as possible. To accomplish this task and to make the valley less dramatic there are some basic change-directing steps a leader can follow.

Concepts in Directing Change

VISION

Proverbs 29:18 says that without vision "the people perish [are unrestrained]."[2] Perhaps the most important idea to directing change in an organization is a clear vision. The vision is the To Be of the organization; it is a clearly defined picture of the church operating after the changes have occurred.

It is important to differentiate between mission and vision. Simply stated, mission is why the church exists; vision is what the church is becoming. Researcher George Barna further defines the mission versus the vision of a church.[3]

Mission	Vision
Philosophic	Strategic
General	Specific
Definition	Direction
Similar to many organizations	Unique to each organization

The mission of a church is essentially the same for all churches. It is the reason we exist. For example, this is the mission of Winston-Salem First Assembly (NC):

First Assembly is a corporate body of believers in Jesus, reaching up through *worship*, reaching out through *evangelism*, reaching around through *fellowship*, and reaching in through *discipleship*.

The vision, however, is better defined; it is a picture of what the church will look like in the future. It may take the form of goals and objectives. It may take the form of picture language, concrete imagery. As an example, the administrative vision of First Assembly is shown on the following page.

Several years ago I assisted in developing a specific vision statement for a midwestern church. In a two-day workshop with the pastoral staff, church board, and church leaders, we developed a specific methodology for determining a church vision. We began with an evening of prayer, seeking God's direction for the church and the leadership. Although the weekend had been preceded with weeks of prayer, the corporate time was essential. The pastor had written a future picture of the church by dreaming in several areas: attendance, giving, evangelism, missions, children's ministry, youth ministry, etc. We began on Saturday morning with each of the church leaders writing their vision, or dream, in each of the sixteen categories. As facilitator I captured these ideas on a flip chart. After sharing the vision of the leadership, the pastor read what he had written almost two weeks before. In almost every instance it matched what the leadership had written. We used the concepts to complete a written statement of the future picture of the Assembly.

We learned several things from the vision-building workshop:

1. The pastor must hear from God concerning His specific direction for the ministry and the church.
2. The vision is "owned" by the pastor. He must believe in it and know the strategies to accomplish it.
3. Although the pastor may own the vision, the more the church leadership participates in determining that vision the easier it is to manage the change.
4. The vision must be communicated. When the vision is shared with the congregation they feel ownership and work together to accomplish the vision. Some pastors have written "I dream" articles, espousing their vision and dream for the congregation.
5. Symbolism is important. Development of a theme, logo, banners, and written materials that demonstrate the essence of the vision help people catch the momentum.
6. An action plan with strategies is important. This plan should include what is to be accomplished, when it will be accomplished, and who is responsible.

Simple words go far. If people can see a clear vision and understand its importance, change becomes easier to direct. If people are involved in the formulation and implementation of the vision, the valley becomes more shallow. If congregations can see where the changes are taking them (To Be), and they realize it is a better and reachable goal, it becomes easier to live through the valley of despair.

PARTICIPATION

Leadership specialist John Maxwell tells the story of Clyde, a deacon at his first church, a small country church. John visited Clyde's farm and

VISION STATEMENT

Administrative Area

First Assembly is a model of efficiency and effectiveness in its administrative structure and processes. Members of the administrative team realize the importance of their tasks and seek to assist both their internal customers (pastors) and external customers (members, attendees, community) with excellent quality output and a Christ-first, customer-first attitude. Outsiders often remark at the effectiveness and efficiency of the church's operations. Several larger churches have sent pastors, administrators, and staff members to First Assembly to learn from their administrative operations.

Because team members share a common goal and vision, there is an atmosphere of teamwork and congeniality. There is a constant open communication between team members, pastors, and administrators. When there are problems or conflicts, they are solved quickly, professionally, and compassionately with the help of the pastor's assistant and other team members. If there are questions or conflicts, team members often refer to the standard procedures in the First Assembly *Policy and Procedures Guide Book.*

Members of the administrative team have excellent job skills and often attend classes and seminars in order to enhance those skills. Technology classes and management seminars are offered outside the facility as well as a monthly training session offered in-house. Team members are aware of the process of constant-improvement feedback as well as the formal six-month written evaluation they receive from their supervisor. There are often special events and incentives given based on exceptional work. Team members also have get-togethers and breakaways outside work to help in building the team. Team members are constantly looking for ways to improve their work and themselves. There is an openness to share suggestions and ideas, and team members know these suggestions will be acted on promptly by the pastor's assistant.

Administrative personnel have the proper tools to accomplish their jobs efficiently. Computer problems have been minimized since all workstations carry proper software and printer connections. An electronic mail (E-mail) system has been put into place, eliminating a large amount of paper lists and memos. Calls are always answered promptly and effectively by the receptionist, who is well informed of church events. When a pastor is busy or gone, the caller is given a choice to put a message in the pastor's voice mailbox. This technology adds efficiency and ensures all messages are tracked. A new electronic scheduler helps the computer and administrative staff keep track of meetings, rooms, and meeting attendees. This technology has helped attendees to be punctual to meetings.

The work flow and processes, including communication processes, accounting processes, personnel processes, and the overall work flow have been reengineered to flow smoothly. Workers are cross trained and although their roles and responsibilities have been clearly communicated, they can easily step in when a coworker is absent or at a training session. Workload has been examined carefully and new staff have been added as needed. Some of these staff may be temporary, others may do some work from their homes. Even with the tremendous numerical growth of the church and the addition of new ministries, the work load has been distributed effectively.

There is a constant atmosphere of excitement at what God is doing at First Assembly. That excitement has infiltrated the administrative team as well. Team members look forward to going to work each day. The church has retained a "small church" feel but its business operations are conducted with a "large church" effectiveness. People are constantly asking what is the secret to such a dynamic, team-oriented work environment. The team members' response is: "Only through the help and grace of God have we been able to accomplish our vision."

while chatting with him mentioned that the church doors needed fresh paint. At the next board meeting, Clyde mentioned to the other board members that the doors needed painting and the idea was overwhelmingly passed. John Maxwell continued mentioning his vision to Clyde, who as an influencer would repeatedly communicate the ideas to the church board.

The importance of gaining participation in strategic decision making must not be underestimated. Today's pastors realize the importance of "buy-in" of the church board, but we often underestimate the importance of participation in decision making by the congregation. In today's information age society, people want more informed involvement in setting directions for their church.

Most leaders know there is a vast difference between a congregation's formal leadership of staff and its informal leadership of influencers. The influencers may have no direct leadership roles, may never show up on a church organizational chart, or may never see their names in the church bulletin. However, these influencers can determine the success of the vision and can help make the valley of despair intolerable or unimportant. The wise pastor identifies the influencers, involves them in vision determination, and communicates with them in appropriate ways at appropriate times.

COMMUNICATION

A great vision has little effect unless it is communicated correctly. Studies show that primary resistance to change comes when people do not understand the change, how the change will affect them, and what will happen after the change takes place. By calling and training, pastors are great communicators. However, communicating a dream or vision that requires change can be difficult. Both formal and informal communications should be established.

Formal communication. Annual reports that show not just finances but expansion of ministry areas are increasingly popular in both small and large churches. If your church or someone in your church has access to video production, a "vision video" showing what could happen after changes take place can help people envision a better To Be. Use of concrete imagery, word pictures, when describing changes can help.

At Winston-Salem First Assembly, we recently redirected our biweekly staff meeting away from discussing just issues, calendar dates, and attendee follow-up. Besides these discussion areas, we have implemented a status reporting process. Each department (children, youth, etc.) explains what has been accomplished in the past three months and the goals they plan to accomplish in the next three months. All other pastors and department leaders can ask questions and determine how other ministry areas extend into the reporting area. The formal communication through the written status reports has assisted in clarifying the vision and in implementing change.

Informal communication. The pastor's task is to "sell the dream" to lay leadership or pastoral staff members. Informal conversation after church, over lunch, or before and after board meetings can assist as much in clarifying the vision as pages of formal communication. Identifying influencers and change agents and communicating with these people is an integral part of implementing change in the congregation.

TRANSITION

Environment, age, background, vocation, and attitude all affect how quickly individuals react to change. Whole congregations may welcome change and quickly embrace its effects. Other congregations may react negatively and must be led gradually toward the To Be vision. Transition (defined as the rate, or pace, of change) is a vital lesson for the pastor to learn. The question becomes How soon and how much change can a congregation accept without negatively affecting the church?

A small church in the Arizona countryside had recently called a new pastor. In his zeal and attempt to "better" things at church, he made the mistake of moving the piano. The piano was moved from the left side of the platform to the right side where the sound could be better heard. On Sunday, most of the congregation was outraged. "We've never done it this way before" was the cry of the change resistance. The change was so dramatic they questioned how the new pastor could do this without asking the proper authorities. The new pastor's tenure lasted less than a year, and the piano was moved back to its original spot. Another new pastor was called. A year later, the district superintendent was asked to speak in the church. Upon arrival, the first change the superintendent noticed was the piano on the right side of the platform. The superintendent called the second new pastor aside and inquired how he was able to move the piano when the previous pastor faced such resistance. The pastor replied that he moved the piano a few inches at a time each week for one year. "At midyear the piano was practically in the middle of the platform" he replied.

The Arizona church illustrates one common theme of change. Because most people resist change, timing is important. Gradual change will result in better results, depending on the mindset of the congregation. Today's pastor must know not only *how much* change to implement but *how soon*. One too many changes can break the camel's back and lead to a call for new leadership.

The Challenge of Change

In the midst of a changing world, today's pastor must realize (1) dramatic change does and must occur, (2) true leadership calls for the management and direction of change, (3) there are models for managing and directing change, and (4) we must rely on a constant God, who never changes.

In the middle of a confusing, changing atmosphere, we look to the source of our strength and help who states that He is "the same yesterday, and today, and for ever" (Hebrews 13:8). True help in dealing with personal change, change in others, and organizational change comes when we ask for direction and strength from God our solid rock, the anchor of our soul, and the unchanging I Am.

Prioritizing the Uses of Church Facilities

Danny R. Thomas

Church facilities have gone through tremendous metamorphoses since our early days on Azusa Street. Storefronts, living rooms, open air street corners, rented halls, gymnasiums, cathedrals, and theaters have been used as gathering points to accomplish the threefold mission of the Church: edification, worship, and evangelization.

The structures have all had in common the call to house God's people. The early architects of church building went to great lengths to bring into focus, through the construction process, a tangible pronouncement of their faith in God. The great cathedrals of Europe stand as a testimony to the centrality of the church to the life of a community.

The advent of Pentecost on the plains of Kansas and at Azusa Street became the catalyst for changing the meeting house for God's people. As new bodies formed, struggling congregations sought whatever was available. Some began in homes, others in halls, still others in vacant storefronts. To provide usable space for the gathering of a growing body became paramount. As time passed, education space for teaching children and office space for pastor and clerical support demanded other facilities. With the maturation and continued sophistication of ministries, erecting buildings to facilitate all the needs of the entire congregation has gained priority.

Today facility use and plant operation consume massive amounts of pastoral energies: scheduling weddings (and rehearsals), various support groups, youth meetings, children's activities, music team rehearsals, choir practices, seasonal performances, spiritual emphasis meetings, community requests—the list goes on and on. Then adding to this, the facilities must be maintained, cleaned, and available for unscheduled use (e.g., by a church family, having lost a loved one, wanting the fellowship hall for an after-funeral potluck).

In the Assemblies of God, almost twelve thousand churches in the United States have come together in the bond of a "cooperative fellowship." Doctrinally, we are the same, yet our physical structures vary depending on congregation size, community population, and location of the church in the U.S. (e.g., colonial, New England, wood framed, country, brick, southeastern).

To accomplish the task of keeping the house of God as the tangible expression of His people to a particular community or locale, consider (1) the priority of function and the unique mission of the church, (2) the availability of volunteers or paid staff to present the facility for use either as a vehicle of worship or community outreach, and (3) the procedure for securing the facility for a given event.

To best clarify the priority use of a facility, develop a unique mission statement that reflects the application of edification, worship, and evangelization; the vision and direction of the senior pastor; and the adoption of these purposes by the congregation.

Statement of Purpose and Mission

The following suggested model can be adapted for local circumstances.

This ministry is a center and community for spiritual growth, where positive attitudes are developed, where good people become better, where hurts are healed, where lessons are learned, where friendships are developed, where marriages are strengthened, where families are bonded, where singles are valued, where the restless find peace, where love is alive, where God is understood, where eternal life is found by accepting Jesus Christ as personal Savior, and where Jesus Christ is Lord.

In that spirit the purpose of [your church name] ministries is to proclaim the gospel of Jesus Christ throughout the world as commissioned by Christ, our Lord (Mark 16:15). Every person who participates in this ministry—pastor, congregant, employee, or volunteer—is committed earnestly, wholeheartedly, and spiritually to this mission.

The mission statement guides church leaders in making decisions about facility use. When deciding if a program should have facility use, the first question asked is Does it fit the mission statement? For example, the Boy Scouts of America would like to meet weekly at the church using the educational level. *Response:* Yes, it fits as an outreach tool. But don't allow it to be seen as competition for your own boys program, rather as an open door to further minister to your community. What if the local service club asks for the use of your parking lot to set up the tent for an Oktoberfest? *Response:* No. Although the community outreach clause is applicable, the standards of Christian living established in the mission statement preclude activity that defiles the temple of the Holy Spirit. The mission statement tells everyone why we do and what we do.

Use of Facilities for Weddings and Other Events

Facility use for the celebration of marriage vows brings a unique set of requests and procedures. The suggested model at the end of this chapter can be adapted for local circumstances.

Scheduling the daily affairs and events of normal church life is a task unto itself in today's ever-expanding church facility. A growing number of congregations have Christian schools with extracurricular activities and events. As a result, internal use of the church's education rooms and shared meeting areas must be scheduled.

A simple request form that is completed by *all* the users of your church facility will save countless hours of pastoral time required when an event room is double booked.

ROOM RESERVATION AND EVENT FORM

DATE OF EVENT: _____ GROUP: _____

TIME: _____ ROOM: _____

TABLES NEEDED: Round:_____ Long:_____ CHAIRS NEEDED: Stack: _____ Fold: _____

OTHER EQUIPMENT NEEDED: _____

COMMITTEE CHAIRMAN: _____ PHONE: _____

CLEAN-UP COMMITTEE: _____
(Please fill out a separate form for sound equipment)

CHURCH CALENDAR: _____ STAFF APPROVAL: _____

COMPUTER: _____
(Please use the reverse of this form to diagram your event and describe your setup.)

The "Room Reservation and Event Form" is a handy way to pass along the request of room or area use from the group or individual to the master calendar, to the staff, and ultimately to the custodial department or volunteers doing the actual set up, tear down, and cleaning. The size of the physical structure and campus of many of today's churches demands constant maintenance and cleaning. To facilitate this, each person who serves the church body, from pastoral staff to nursery workers, must become a committee of one that picks up, cleans up, and tidies up. In addition, report forms given to a central person with the authority to expend funds to repair or refurbish an area is essential.

Reserving Equipment and Requesting Special Services

The manpower needed to keep the rooms set up is directly related to the extent of auxiliary items requested, e.g., skirted tables, platform risers, sound systems with mikes and a tape player. The request for more and more equipment and services, involving more and more man-hours, becomes a subject of great concern because of the cost of a staff person's hour of work or a volunteer's hour of time. To help the church keep expenditures in check, the group requesting space and setup must be mindful of the cost factor.

SERVICE OR EQUIPMENT REQUEST

DEPT.: _____ By: _____ Date: _____

Special Order: _____Equipment _____ Furniture _____Supplies _____Other

Services: _____Installation _____ Alteration _____Repair _____Maintenance

DESCRIPTION (Explain in detail): _____

_____

_____

_____

_____

Date Received: _____ Date Assigned: _____ Assigned to: _____

Date Ordered: _____ Vendor: _____ PO #: _____

Date Completed: _____ Comments: _____

The scheduler needs to be cognizant of the wear and tear on equipment, potential liability involved, time limitations (with respect to other groups needing the same rooms before and after an event), and, once again, how the event fits the mission statement of the church.

Vehicle maintenance, if left unattended, can become a black hole. The central person who has oversight of the plant also has the authority to remove a vehicle from service (even if it is at the last minute as a problem comes to light) or to have repairs made so that the vehicle in question is roadworthy. A daily pretrip checklist provides the church with a guideline. Have all your vehicles inspected regularly by qualified mechanics using a standard exceeding that established by your state motor vehicle department.

These are some ways for determining the use of church facilities and the equipment provided by the congregation to enable the fulfilling of our mission statement. Indeed, besides being the meeting place for His people, these facilities are also the warehouse, the production house, and the storehouse. But let us never forget, first and foremost, it is a place where we come together to meet God.

Daily Pretrip CheckList

Please complete this form before leaving the lot. This check sheet must be turned in daily, when you have completed all your runs. *Carry a cloth to wipe reflectors and light lenses during your inspection.*

APPROACH & UNDER THE HOOD INTERIOR CHECK

_____ fluid leaks under bus

_____ entrance door

_____ belts

_____ all gauges and instruments

_____ water

_____ windshield wipers

_____ oil

_____ all glass/clear/clean

_____ seats/not cut/bottoms latched

BRAKES

_____ tires tread/inflation

_____ service

_____ lug nuts/rims

_____ emergency spring

_____ exhaust system

_____ air brake recycle (at least once a week)

_____ crossing arm/eight-light system

EXTERIOR WALK AROUND

_____ interior lights

_____ battery

_____ emergency exits

_____ headlights high/low

_____ first aid kit/body fluid kit

_____ hazard lights

_____ fire extinguisher/charge/shake weekly

_____ turn signals

_____ emergency reflectors

_____ brake lights

_____ horn

_____ back-up lights

_____ body condition

Post trip walk-through: _____

AM:_____ Noon:_____ PM:_____

Activities/Field Trips:_____

BUS NO:_____ DATE: _____

DRIVER'S SIGNATURE:

_____

Wedding Rules and Regulations

1. MINISTER

The minister is eager to make your wedding an unforgettable experience, marked with spirituality, dignity, reverence, and warmth. He is available for service and counsel and is willing to assist in any way possible.

2. CHURCH CONSULTANT

The church provides a consultant to help you with your wedding plans. She will assist you in your plans, conduct your wedding rehearsal, and be in general charge of all but the pastoral services and the religious ceremony. The fee for this service is in the fee schedule and is to be paid to the consultant at the time of your first meeting with her. For an additional fee (to be determined with the consultant) she will assist in greater detail, i.e., ordering, decorating, etc.

3. MAKING ARRANGEMENTS

A. Read this material carefully. *All of it is important!*

B. Application for a desired date must be made. Forms are available at the church. No weddings will be scheduled on Sundays.

C. The rehearsal date must also be reserved by the consultant. One hour is sufficient for rehearsals if the entire party comes promptly. Ushers should be at the rehearsal to receive instructions. Only actual members of the wedding party (and parents of the bride and groom, if they wish) should be present at the rehearsal. The minister does not normally attend.

D. Attendance at the premarital seminar held at *[your church name]* is a prerequisite of all weddings held at *[your church name]* or for any wedding performed by one of our ministers held at another location. Registration is done through the church office. Seminars are offered every quarter and are held on Friday evenings and Saturdays.

E. An appointment with the pastor performing the ceremony is to be made through the secretary at the church. The marriage license is to be brought to the church secretary *no later than three days in advance* of the wedding. Please include the names of the witnesses to attend the bride and groom. (A marriage license is valid for sixty days.)

F. The chapel is appropriate for weddings of approximately 150 guests.

G. Because our church building is dedicated wholly to the Lord, those using the building must respect the property. No smoking, alcoholic beverages, or questionable language or conduct will be permitted under any circumstances, at any time or any place within the church or its premises. All music must conform to the atmosphere of reverence and be submitted in writing to the consultant one week in advance of the rehearsal date. No changes in music are permitted at rehearsal. The wedding party will be held responsible for their guests compliance with the foregoing rules. All members of the wedding party must be dressed modestly in conformity with the standards of the church. (Please confer with the consultant on the above two items.) In addition, the wedding party will be held responsible for any damages to the property or equipment. No thumbtacks or articles that would mar the building or furniture may be used. Throwing of rice or birdseed is emphatically prohibited! Food is to be confined to the reception area only. This prohibition includes the bride's room (room 312). Do not leave valuables in any room, including the groom's room (315). The church cannot be responsible for stolen items.

4. CANDLES

Candles of any nature are not permitted down the aisle. Due to fire regulations, only hurricane or votive candles are allowed from your florist. These alone are permitted in our sanctuary or chapel. *No exceptions!*

5. PICTURES

The taking of pictures of the wedding party and the wedding itself is permissible as long as it does not interfere with the ceremony. No flash pictures are to be taken during the prayer or from the front of the church during the ceremony, all of which detract from the solemnity and beauty of the occasion. However, flash pictures both of the processional and the recessional are permissible. Pictures, both in the sanctuary and the chapel, must be taken before the ceremony. These must be finished at least one-half hour before the time set for the ceremony.

6. CHURCH PROPERTIES

The wedding party is responsible for rendering assistance in rearranging church properties. They must make these arrangements in advance with the consultant. It is expected that all facilities will be left in the condition they were found in. However, for an extra fee of fifty dollars the custodian will render these services.

7. TELEPHONE

Should the bride live outside the local calling area, it is assumed that the consultant/hostess can call the bride collect.

8. RECORDING

An audio recording of the ceremony is available and will be arranged by the consultant, if desired.

9. ADDRESS

The address for the invitations should read: *[Your church mailing address]*. Please do not proceed with arrangements until you have received definite confirmation of the proposed date of your wedding.

10. COMPENSATION

As compensation for the use of the building, including heat, light, wear and tear, and for services of personnel, the following charges will be made and must be paid *in advance.*

For members and those who regularly contribute financially to the ministries of *[your church name]*, there is no charge for weddings and receptions, with the exception of custodial fees for the use of the facilities and those specifically involved in assisting and rendering services for your wedding.

Saturday night weddings and receptions are discouraged. Saturday night weddings and receptions will begin no later than 7:00 P.M. An additional fee will be required for any function scheduled after 2:00 P.M. (see fee schedule).

Honorarium envelopes, to be given to your wedding consultant at the rehearsal, will be given out at the wedding.

A. Organist/Pianist/Musicians

Separate arrangements must be made with the organist/pianist for services. We recommend that our own organist/pianist be engaged whenever feasible, and if our own organist/pianist does not play at the wedding, the substitute must be approved. The honorarium is to be the responsibility of the bride and to be determined between the bride and musician.

B. Soloist

The soloist or musicians are the responsibility of the bride. An honorarium will need to be determined between the bride and the soloist.

C. Minister

The honorarium for the minister should be commensurate with the important part he has in the service. This honorarium is provided by the groom. The suggested honorarium begins at seventy-five dollars.

D. Service

Please prepare your order of service in duplicate and give it to the consultant.
The church furnishes, if desired, the following items for your reception:
Two silver services with trays
Silver serving trays
Two silver punch bowls with ladles
Two silver candelabras
Tablecloths (Check with the hostess for colors.)

Financial Fees for Weddings

Nonmembers:

Rental of Sanctuary   _____

Rental of Chapel   _____

Rental of Foyer for Wedding   _____

Rental of Fellowship Hall   _____

Custodial fee—Sanctuary   _____

Custodial fee—Chapel   _____

Custodial fee—Foyer for Wedding (100 guests max.)   _____

Custodial fee—Gymnasium   _____

Members:

Custodial fee—Sanctuary   _____

Custodial fee—Chapel   _____

Custodial fee—Foyer for Wedding (100 guests max.)   _____

Custodial fee—Gymnasium   _____

CONSULTANT

The wedding consultant fee is one hundred dollars. We require each bride to pay twenty-five dollars upon their first appointment with the consultant. The additional seventy-five dollars is required at the rehearsal. Additional fees required for extra services are to be determined by the bride and consultant.

Authorized personnel *must* be in the kitchen to operate and facilitate the use of the kitchen equipment. The responsibility of this person is to make punch, coffee, and to clean up. For additional services there will be an additional fee. These are to be determined by the bride with the reception hostess. Check with the consultant for contact with the hostess.

RECEPTION HOSTESS

Fifty percent of the fee is required at the first appointment and is nonrefundable.

Guests up to 100   _____

Guests up to 250   _____

Guests over 250   _____

Guests 400+   _____

Setup, prepare tables   _____

Catering, etc. (more than cake and punch/coffee)   _____

Helpers   _____

Additional food served   _____

SOUND

Two sound men needed for a minimum of two hours each   _____

Lighting person for photography   _____hour

EXTRAS

Functions scheduled after 2:00 P.M. on Saturdays   _____

Tablecloths (laundry fee)   _____each

Tables (other than three serving)   _____each

Tables in balcony   _____each

Handbells (setup and director)   _____

Handling Church Finances

Paul D. Goodman

Leadership in God's kingdom involves management and oversight of His resources. Although the Lord's primary resource is people, we are called to account for all the gifts and blessings He has placed in our hands. To be less than faithful stewards would be to violate the Word of God, our standard of faith and conduct.

The church is not in business to make money. Finances are merely tools to accomplish the task of saving and shaping lives for the kingdom of God. However, this does not negate the need for careful handling and management of funds. In fact, the church should exhibit exemplary standards of financial integrity and accountability.

The pastor and official church board are generally responsible for receiving tithes and offerings, disbursing church funds, and protecting the tangible assets of the church. This needs to be clearly spelled out in the constitution and bylaws of the organization. Consider, first of all, the manner of receiving tithes and offerings.

Receiving Tithes and Offerings

The pastor is responsible for teaching and preaching scriptural principles of stewardship to the congregation. Motivated by a love for God and His people, the minister can say with the apostle Paul, "Not that I am looking for a gift, but I am looking for what may be credited to your account" (Philippians 4:17). Giving to the work of the Lord makes an investment having eternal dividends. Giving should be systematic and planned rather than erratic and emotional. At the same time, the element of excitement and joy of investing for eternity should not be neglected.

Receiving tithes and offerings should be an act of worship rather than merely a collecting time. Those who serve as ushers should be instructed to conduct themselves in a manner appropriate to worship, sparing givers the indignity of appearing more interested in the gift than in the giver. The offering time, preceded by a Scripture passage or verse relating to stewardship and accompanied by music that contributes to worship and praise, can become a meaningful part of the service.

Upon receiving the offering, ushers should immediately place the money in the hands of those responsible for counting and recording it. For security reasons this should be done in a place not readily accessible to the public. No less than two persons should count, record, and sign the offering receipt. A locked safe or other secure receptacle should be available to hold the funds until they can be deposited in the bank.

Keeping accurate financial records is a must. Generally the church treasurer is a proven, faithful member of the church board who is gifted in matters of business. Since financial bookkeeping is time consuming and calls for skills in accounting, the church treasurer may serve as oversight for someone employed for this service. When that is the case, the treasurer should still maintain a close working relationship with the bookkeeper to assure that the funds are properly handled.

A church often has a number of departments that generate income and disburse funds, so a central treasury system is definitely more efficient than having many accounts administered by various treasurers. Each department's funds are carefully recorded and accurately reported, and checks are disbursed from one central account. This not only allows the board to have better oversight of all funds, but it also reduces the chance of misappropriation.

The old ledger system of bookkeeping is fast being replaced by computer programs designed for speed, accuracy, and accessibility of information. Information regarding these programs can be found in local computer stores, but specialized programs for churches are also advertised in Christian journals and magazines. Technology has brought the price of computer hardware to within reach of any size congregation, but it is always best to find the software that will meet your needs before purchasing the computer and printer.

> **Tithes and offerings should be taken as an act of worship.**

Recording and receipting contributions must be done with accuracy, both to instill confidence in the contributors and to satisfy government requirements for charitable giving receipts. Envelope systems are employed successfully in many churches to assist in this process. Quarterly reports to contributors not only remind them to be faithful with their tithes and offerings, but are a good check and balance for the records. Individual giving records should be maintained for at least seven years in the event of IRS audits and the need for verification.

Receipting contributions other than cash requires special consideration. The church should establish the fair market value of contributed goods rather than depending on the assessment of the contributor. Generally speaking, two appraisals should be sought from persons qualified to make such judgments, and their findings should be preserved for future reference. For additional information on legal issues related to contribution receipts, the church board would be wise to subscribe to professional service organizations that offer up-to-date data valuable to the church.

Disbursing Church Funds

Monthly financial reports should be prepared by the treasurer and/or bookkeeper for the pastor and board. The reports should, at the minimum, give the breakdown of each department's income, expenses, and balance. Most boards will want general categories of expenditures identified and compared with the budget for that line item. When expenditures vary significantly from the budget, a more detailed breakdown may be requested to determine the cause.

An annual budget is a valuable tool for the officers and board of the church regardless of the size of congregation. Sometimes the board becomes the budget committee that evaluates and develops the budget for the coming year. In many cases, however, a committee is appointed by the board to evaluate the needs of the church and to report back with a recommended budget for the coming year. The board may adopt the budget as proposed or make modifications based on specific information available.

Financial reports from previous years are helpful in preparing the annual budget. As a rule, income should be projected conservatively and expenses should be projected as realistically as possible. Pastors and department leaders should be given opportunity for input to identify expenditures that may vary from the past. While it may be unrealistic to envision all that may happen to affect the budget during the year, it is a wise board that seeks to keep spending in control.

In spending the money God has entrusted to it, a church must have a vision reaching beyond the local body. If all of God's resources are kept to maintain the local church, someone is missing the heartbeat of God. Bills must be paid. Property must be built and maintained. Ministry must be compensated. But the circle of blessing can become very small if we fail to look beyond the doors of the church and community. When we handle the finances of the church, we are handling the Lord's money, and His heartbeat is for a lost world. Every church, no matter how small, should have a missions goal. There are laws of reaping and sowing that we ignore to our own detriment.

Maintaining Church Assets

Good stewardship means that church leadership holds the assets of the church in the most economically advantageous manner. Sometimes a fund will be established for a specific goal, and larger sums of money are kept for a period of time. When that happens, there should be a planned savings program in place that will yield the best interest with safety. Passbook savings accounts are notoriously low interest programs, and other instruments are available. Short-term certificates of deposits may be the wise choice when specified times are in view. If longer-term notes are desired, it would be good to look into investment programs offered by institutions within the church parent body that invest in church buildings and other worthy causes. High risk ventures should be avoided even though they have a proposed high return appeal.

Audits and Financial Reports

An annual audit is a safeguard for both the church and those responsible for the finances. In some instances the audit is performed by the board itself or by an internal church committee assigned to that task. Certified auditors are preferred in many cases because they know what to look for in the way of errors and what questions to ask to get the answers needed.

The annual church financial report should be a well-prepared statement of the income, disbursements, and balances for all of the church funds. There is a fine line between too little and too much when it comes to reporting. Too much detail can be boring and time consuming, while too little may leave questions unanswered. The treasurer and board would do well to give thought to the categories of reporting to find the proper balance. As a principle, church members should have the right to know where and how the funds of the church are spent. In a public business meeting it is sometimes wise to inform members that, should they wish more detailed information, the treasurer would be happy to meet with them in person to go over the records.

Ministerial Salaries

One area of curiosity that needs to be handled with discretion is personal income and salaries. "Just how much does he make?" is a frequently asked question. The annual report should be carefully drafted to avoid the perception of covering up, yet the church should be sensitive to the employees of the body when it comes to their personal finances. When possible, salaries and benefits of the pastors and staff may be reported together to avoid undue embarrassment or comparisons. The church board generally is responsible to establish the remuneration for those who serve the church, and their judgment should be respected.

The Internal Revenue Service has established guidelines for reporting and compensating ministerial expenses and benefits that, when properly followed, can be advantageous to the minister without additional expense to the church. Certain benefit payments, such as health care insurance or retirement investments, when made by the church directly, need not be reported as income for tax purposes. An accountable expense plan for travel or entertainment can be set up to avoid time-consuming reporting to the IRS. All of these guidelines are subject to change and must be properly administered to be of benefit, so it is wise to request the assistance of qualified stewardship consultants who are versed in tax law. The board should be willing to cooperate with their ministers to provide them the most advantageous salary and benefit package possible.

Deferred Giving

An area of financial stewardship that has often been neglected in the church is the transfer of assets from one generation to another. Frequently this is thought of as only happening at a person's death, but that is far from the complete picture. With multiplied millions of dollars changing hands annually through wills, bequests, trusts, and other forms of planned giving, the church has been relatively slow to instruct its people as to the best ways to accomplish these transitions. Taxes, attorneys, and unintended beneficiaries often dissipate the assets that could have gone directly where the benefactor wished them to go had there only been advance preparation. The pastor and board would do well to invite qualified stewardship consultants to present the benefits of planned giving to the congregation on a regular basis. Not only will the church often benefit from this, but families and relatives may also find it to their advantage.

The church should insist on accuracy and accountability in all of its financial matters. A well-planned path should be established for receiving, reporting, disbursing, and holding the funds the Lord has placed in trust with the church and its leaders. Information should be readily accessible to those who have a right to know, and proper checks and balances should be in place to protect the integrity of those who handle the money. Good budgeting should assure that the church will not fall into unexpected financial difficulty. The vision of those in leadership should always challenge the people to participate in the work that has eternal dividends.

Overseeing the Building Program

Mark Burgund

P lan, plan, plan. This is the key to a successful building program. Plan what you are going to build, and plan how you are going to pay for it. Then hold diligently to the plan.

Before an architect is hired, a building committee must be assembled. I recommend it be big enough to provide meaningful counsel but not so big as to be unwieldy. One church located on Highway 51 decided to put fifty-one members on the building committee. The church and the builder found this to be very burdensome (and incidentally there were massive cost overruns). A committee made up of only the pastor and one other person is too small to really serve its purpose of taking divergent opinions and arriving at a suitable solution. A committee of four people for small projects and up to ten for large projects seems to work best. In most cases it works best for the senior pastor to chair this committee and serve as coordinator.

Budget

When planning to build, develop an agreed price you can pay and set an upper limit that is unchangeable. Before the building is completed, this number will be challenged many times. If you are to bring your building in on budget, you must firmly hold to that upper limit. If you go into the program without firm determination to hold steady, a 10 to 15 percent overage will undoubtedly occur, and the potential is there for a much higher cost. When setting this total budget number, include an amount designated for contingencies—to handle unexpected costs without going over the original budget figure. When the contingency funds are used up, you are forced to start cutting features you originally wanted.

When compiling a budget, be specific. Some items to include are (1) the actual building, (2) site work, (3) sound and lighting, (4) landscaping, (5) phone systems, (6) fire and burglar alarm systems, (7) curtains and/or folding walls for classrooms, (8) furniture, (9) signage, (10) insurance and title company costs, and (11) interest on the construction loan (if a loan is necessary).

When considering a prospective building site, it is important to research what site work will be necessary to build on a given piece of ground. Often site work eats more of the budget than planned for. Will it require a mass soil buildup for the building to rest on? Is there proper drainage for the parking area? Where will construction connect to available sewer and water? Often bids for removing topsoil and grading the parking lot do not include respreading the topsoil over the unpaved areas or removing it from the site. This can be an unpleasant discovery late in the job. One-fourth or more of the entire budget can be spent before the building is erected. Other design and planning items include utilities, a parking lot, slab or foundation preparation, engineering fees, testing fees for compaction, surveying fees, and any street improvements on main arteries to the church site.

One church found when it tried to obtain a zoning permit that it was required to pay one-fourth of the cost of the electric stoplight that was already installed on the crossroad corner of the property. The share amounted to forty-five thousand dollars. A closer up-front check might have avoided this surprise.

> "
> **Designate an amount for contingencies—for unexpected costs.**
> "

Check local zoning laws concerning the parking lot area and frontage along the roads. Many communities are requiring huge outlays of money for "green space" in the parking lot with many trees and other plantings.

Unbelievable sums can be spent to please the sound man without the average listener sensing a difference. It is wise to identify congregations in buildings approximately the size you are building and find out what their budget was for this category (observe the lighting systems as well). There is typically a wide spread between the highest and lowest costs. Go and listen. It is imperative that your congregation have a pleasant experience listening to both the music and spoken word, but a pleasing sound does not always demand the most expensive products on the market.

Another system easily overlooked when budgeting is the phone system, and its cost can vary widely. An important aspect is its expandability. Without fail, there will be need for more phones than originally planned, and that need arises much sooner than predicted.

Stage curtains and folding walls with a high sound insulation factor are expensive. Plan these costs into your budget. In most cases it is cheaper to install these during construction than at a later date.

Do you need all new furniture or can some from your present location be used? There are companies capable of painting all the metal desks and file cabinets to match your new decor, often overnight. Magnetic powder spray-coating dries almost on impact. This can be a major cost savings. Furniture-related issues include seating, office furniture, classroom furniture, chalkboards, and audiovisuals.

Are you using pews or theater-style seating? Get bids and demonstrations of each type you consider. Visit locations where the dealers have made installations and talk to the people who use the seating.

Don't let signage be an afterthought. Whatever you decide about it needs to be included in your budget. The church sign is often the first impression a visitor has of the church. Make it a good impression.

The contractor is responsible for providing the church with a builder's risk policy having the church named as additional insured. The church also needs to alert its own insurance carrier and have the necessary coverage for the building period. If you decide to have a title insurance company handle the payouts, there will be a fee. But this is money well spent.

Forgetting to budget the construction loan interest can jeopardize the contingency line of the budget. You may decide not to include it as a budget item for the building, but it still has to be paid, even if from another fund.

Financing

When developing a plan to finance a building project, a church is wise to consider each of these alternatives.

Pay cash. This is by far the least expensive way to build.

Sell bonds or other types of notes to the people in the congregation. This usually presents a lower rate of interest than conventional financing. A drawback to this type of financing is that you must sell the bonds or notes to your congregation and later ask them to pay themselves off by contributing to a building fund. In effect, you must "sell" the congregation twice. Be aware that there are legal restrictions you must meet when doing this. If you are not using a licensed broker, be sure to contact your state securities commission.

Conventional financing requires procurement of a loan from a financial institution with repayment over a period of time. This requires a commitment on the part of the congregation to repay but does not require double fund-raising. When applying for a loan, be sure to supply the prospective lender with good historical financial data as well as intelligent, thought-out forecasts. If necessary, hire an accountant to help put this information in a form that is easily read by the lender.

Sell bonds placed through a bonding company to third parties other than your church congregation. This financing is similar to a bank loan but can be structured for a smaller repayment in the beginning and a larger repayment in the future. This is normally the most expensive form of financing with considerable up-front costs and higher interest rates. The bond company is paid a commission, often between 8 and 10 percent of the total project cost, to place the bonds. This is comparable to one to three points on a conventional note. The actual interest rate is also usually higher than it is for other financing methods.

Selecting the Architect/Builder

There are many architects that work independently from any builder, and there are those that work directly with a specific builder to offer a "design build" product where all work is done by that builder. An independent architect can be a good choice because it allows the architect to design the job without controlling influence from the builder. Also during construction, an independent architect can take a harder line with the builder to ensure that he builds exactly according to the specifications of the blueprints. An "in-house" architect can provide cost savings if he works well with your committee and no design problems arise.

Many companies specialize in church construction and build all over the country. Local architects and builders may be plentiful in your area, but they may not have experience building churches. Contractors who have built churches will be able to guide you around costly mistakes. This can be an invaluable aid if you are not fully convinced of the ultimate design and function of your church facility. A risk or downside: Out-of-town builders are often reluctant to return for problems that may arise after the building is finished.

A local architect and builder provide knowledge of building problems unique to your area. They know union labor laws and constraints, weather conditions and requirements, and the contacts with local and county officials that must be made. The building committee may need to be more diligent in communicating the needs of the congregation to a local builder and architect.

Cautions and Concerns

CHANGE ORDERS

To hold change orders to a minimum, plan in detail every area of construction. Change orders result in cost overruns. For example, a door that is not in the original plan could cost double as a change order. Many contractors bid a job very close to cost in order to get the job, expecting to make their profit through change orders. Keep a close record of each change order, including a complete description of the work and its total cost. Require contractor and owner signatures on each change order.

VOLUNTEER LABOR

Volunteer labor can be a cost savings, but it requires up-front contract agreement with the builder on how his cost will be lowered. Besides a possible cost savings, volunteer labor can also be an opportunity both for those who want to put more of themselves than just their money into the project and for those who can afford a gift of only their time and labor. In an area where there is a strong labor union presence, however, volunteer labor may be strongly opposed or not allowed.

CONTRACTS

No matter how friendly or trustworthy the contractor, the old saying "get it in writing" is not just appropriate, but essential. Misunderstandings occur even when both parties are compatible. Whenever disagreements or disputes arise, the contractor will always go back to the contract. Church leadership must be able to do the same.

Types of contracts include *cost-plus* and *guaranteed maximum price.* Cost-plus contracts require the church to pay the contractor the total cost of the building plus an agreed-upon markup for overhead and profit. The initial estimated cost of building under this arrangement will often be less than the price quoted under a guaranteed maximum price contract. Unfortunately the cost-plus contract eliminates the incentive for the contractor to keep the costs down. So the higher the cost of the building, the higher the profit he receives.

With the guaranteed maximum price contract, church leaders know what the building will cost, plus whatever change orders they sign. Under this type of contract it is important that the contractor have the financial strength to handle a loss if the costs go over the price he has quoted. If he lacks financial resources, he may walk off the job when he sees there will be no profit. Then the church would be forced to finish with another contractor, and that can be very expensive. With a guaranteed maximum price contract often you can agree with the contractor to save money off the set price if you agree to split the savings with him. This gives him an incentive to save you both money.

PAYING THE BILLS

Having all of the construction bills paid through a local title company is often a wise choice. The title company will assure that all the lien waivers have been signed and each subcontractor is properly paid. This eliminates the risk of paying construction costs twice if the contractor does not pay the subcontractors properly.

As the church makes payments before the job is completed, it is wise to hold back a 10 percent retention fee. This is a common practice and gives the opportunity to make sure everything is in proper working order before final payment is made. As a church nears the end of the job, subcontractors will start applying pressure to get the 10 percent. Once this is given up, the church has lost any leverage to get subcontractors to come back to correct inferior work. Be satisfied with the work before releasing retention funds.

Overseeing the Building

Once the actual building construction is under way, schedule regular meetings with the contractor and the subcontractors doing the work at each stage. This important step allows church leaders to be aware of any problems as they crop up, such as material delivery delays or coordination of the work schedules of individual subcontractors. Scheduling such meetings takes time but results in avoiding costly oversights. Actual supervision of the job depends on the size of the project and the expertise of the pastor and building committee. If a committee member is asked to take this responsibility, time requirements of such a task need to be considered. If it is decided that no one from the church has the time or expertise to oversee the work, hiring an owner's representative may be necessary. This person needs to have building experience, for example, a retired contractor. And whether or not he's a friend of the church, expect to offer a reasonable rate for his services.

Toward the end of each subcontractor's work and finally of the general contractor's work, make a punch list of items that need to be corrected. This is the time to be complete and very detailed. It is imperative that the work be finished before you release all the retention funds; once contractors are finished with the punch list they will expect payment.

In all the busyness of building, the congregation should stay focused on ministry and not allow the purpose of the church to become building a building. God will bless the church that keeps its focus, so that everything is done to reach the lost for Jesus Christ.

Managing Conflict

Almon Bartholomew

Conflict among the members of Christ's body is not a phenomenon of the late twentieth century. Disruption plagued the first disciples. Arguments erupted as to who would be greatest in the Kingdom. The Sons of Thunder sought the favored seats on the right and left of Jesus. Peter lost faith and returned to his fish nets, taking others with him.

The primitive Pentecostal church fared no better. Many incidents of dissension and strife are recorded in the New Testament. Something went wrong in the widows' feeding program. The church's first congress spoke to conflict over admitting Gentiles to the church. Euodias and Syntyche spread their disagreements within the church at Philippi. Divisions and contentions branded the Corinthian church. Alexander the coppersmith and Diotrophes were ego-driven troublemakers of the first order.

Considering these and other Early Church disorders, it should not be a surprise when unrest is found in today's church. Conflicts in Christ's body appear to be inevitable. Pastors and church officials must approach such occurrences with firmness and deep sensitivity. Having been involved in church conflict management on more than two hundred occasions in the past twenty years of district service, I offer more than simply an academic approach. It is an approach shaped by give-and-take in the arena of experience—it is field oriented.

Conflict Management Procedure

The following steps outline an effective management procedure: (1) inquire, (2) identify, (3) isolate, (4) innovate and implement, and (5) invigilate (watch or monitor).

INQUIRE

The first step in addressing conflict is to make thorough *inquiry*. Be a good listener. Listen to understand, not simply to reply. It is imperative to apply the apostle James' admonition, "Be quick to listen, slow to speak and slow to become angry" (James 1:19). It has been well said, "There are three sides to every conflict—your side, my side, and the right side (the truth)." Keep in mind Proverbs 18:17, "The first to present his case seems right, till another comes forward and questions him."

People practice slanting. Slanting involves selective use of the facts: Information favoring a partisan position is conveyed; the rest is ignored. Examine carefully the loaded questions and those filled with presupposition. People will try to get you leaning in their direction. A manager of conflict must constantly remember not to rush to judgment.

IDENTIFY

Having made thorough inquiry, one is now in a more favorable position to *identify* the characteristics of the conflict. Get to the essentials. It is too easy to deal with peripheral issues, never touching the nerve of the problem. As Charles Cookman, former North Carolina District Council superintendent, often said, "One must put his finger on the blister." The process may be painstakingly difficult, but you must clarify the issues. Otherwise, a Band-Aid solution may be applied to a catastrophic wound.

To identify the issue, interact with persons representing differing positions. If people believe you as arbitrator have made a premature decision, you will lose your ability to apply an effective remedy. It is imperative that the manager of conflict maintain integrity throughout the process.

ISOLATE

Whenever possible, make an effort to *isolate* the problem. Reserve time when, if necessary, the whole church is to be informed of a problem. Don't let a small fire become a raging inferno—contain it. Some years ago I was preparing to take a state examination to sell fire insurance. I remember reading in one of the manuals the difference between "friendly fire" and "hostile fire." A friendly fire will cook your eggs in the morning; a hostile fire may burn your house down. A lesson from this can be applied to conflict management: Time must be afforded for a controlled explosion, a venting, if you please. If such is not allowed within a structured framework, then a destructive, uncontrolled explosion will likely take place.

Include in this process those persons who "have need to know." This may be a very select, limited group. On some occasions it will involve the entire membership. Do not hesitate to include them if deemed necessary to bring about proper resolution.

INNOVATE AND IMPLEMENT

A good doctor knows how to both diagnose disorder and prescribe remedy. His goal of returning a patient to health rests on these two abilities. A missionary urgently requesting a decision from the national office concerning his international work failed to receive an immediate answer. Writing to the general superintendent, the missionary declared with anguish, "Your decision may hurt us, but your indecision will kill us." Management of conflict reaches a critical point when a remedy must be designed.

Innovation and *implementation* go hand in hand. I use the term *innovation* because each need has its own peculiarity, and the process of resolution must be tailored to the need. Too often we rely on the patent-medicine approach. Our Lord is the Great Physician. He addressed several maladies found in the Revelation churches. He confronted all, commended where He could, and condemned where He had to. Implementing resolutions to conflict is imperative. Avoid the snare of diagnosis without prescribing remedy.

Ask the question, Is this remedy doable? One must put to use the tools and gifts of wisdom given by God. The practitioner of conflict management must see the problem, both in its entirety and in its detailed parts. Beyond all of the application of human wisdom, we must fully rely upon the Holy Spirit's unerring wisdom. With such enablement, craft a plan for all parties to adopt and follow. If the conflict affects the whole body, your plan should include them. If the church has had limited involvement, then at some time, and in the proper forum, the church may need to be informed and brought up to date.

INVIGILATE (MONITOR)

As the process of restoration and recovery proceeds, managers of conflict are called upon to *invigilate* its progress. This means, simply, to give *vigilant* oversight to the process, to monitor it carefully. This very process may chart the course of recovery. It also provides an early warning system of potential recurrence.

Another conflict resolution process has been offered by Dr. Carl Miller of Fuller Seminary. His threefold procedure for conflict management is to desensitize, deliberate, and decide. Desensitization is the process used in cooling down the rhetoric. Deliberation is the process of examining available options. Decision involves selecting one of those options and going forward with it.

A Sample Conflicts-Management Approach

Frequently problems are camouflaged. The real difficulty is clouded by anger in the hearts of the partisans. Until this anger is dealt with, we will never be able to touch the core of the matter and bring a lasting resolution.[1] The true nature of human anger is described in James 1:20, "The wrath of man worketh not the righteousness of God" (KJV). A very literal translation reads, "An angry man doesn't do what is right before God" (Beck).

An angry person will not accept responsibility for his own actions. He will transfer his feelings to another, making it appear someone else has the embittered attitude or is guilty of wrong. A riled person misconstrues facts. Much like a drunken person who loses depth perception, the irate individual sees things out of focus. Until the resentment subsides, the original problem cannot be tackled. Heated spirits must be cooled down. This begins when a person acknowledges his behavior is reactionary and is willing in some degree to deal with his own inflamed feelings. Some basic principles must be understood.

FACTS AND PERCEPTION OF FACTS

There may be a vast difference between facts and the perception of facts. On one occasion during a church hassle several years ago, a woman said to me, "My husband gets into trouble because he tells it like it is." I responded, "Your husband may not be telling it like it is; he tells it as he perceives it to be." He might have been correct, yet he might have been somewhat in error.

Three persons can stand on three street corners of the same intersection and observe the same automobile accident. When they make their report and stand witness in court, it may appear to be three different accidents. As far as each witness is concerned, he is presenting facts honestly. It is all a matter of perspective and vantage point.

If we can bring people to the place where they will admit there is even a slight possibility they could be wrong, we will reduce the heat level. And well should we ourselves admit, "I could be in error." The structuring of facts can alter the appearance of the truth. Let us allow margin for error in ourselves and in others.

PROVOCATION AND JUSTIFICATION

It is not abnormal to react to what we consider hostile stimuli. How we react can well determine whether we are on the road to peace or war. We cannot traverse the span from the cradle to the coffin without provocation. Some things are bound to antagonize us. The problem arises when we respond to the provocation in an unchristian manner. We tend to justify our reaction on the basis of the nature of the provocation. Let us remember that no provocation ever justifies an un-Christlike response. If our rejoinder is at a carnal level, we are as guilty of offense as is the provocateur.

When was the Christian call canceled for turning the other cheek, for going the second mile, for giving the cloak and coat, for loving instead of hating, for blessing instead of cursing, and praying for the spiteful antagonizers? In more instances than not, church feuds could be settled by large applications of humility and forgiveness by all parties involved. "Be kind and compassionate to one another, forgiving each other, just as in Christ God forgave you" (Ephesians 4:32). With such doses of Christian medicine, the ill patient will soon respond with a declining fever.

METHOD AND MOTIVE

The apostle Paul speaks strongly about method and motivation in Philippians 2:3, "Let nothing be done through strife or vainglory; but in lowliness of mind let each esteem other better than themselves" (KJV). Strife is the wrong method, and vainglory is the wrong motive.

Constant agitation within the church involving matters of little consequence must be viewed as seditious. Generally such agitation is amply mixed with egocentric demonstration. The antidote is humility of mind and Christian deference to our brothers and sisters. Paul pegs it well in 2 Timothy 2:24–26: "The Lord's servant must not quarrel; instead, he must be kind to everyone, able to teach, not resentful. Those who oppose him he must gently instruct, in the hope that God will grant them repentance leading them to a knowledge of the truth, and that they will come to their senses and escape from the trap of the devil, who has taken them captive to do his will."

These, among other considerations, appear to be essential in resolving church conflict. If partisans demonstrate a willingness to submit to biblical principles and are sincere in their efforts to see harmony restored, then we are well on our way. It is when we subject church tensions to the demands of the "irresistible force" contending with the "immovable object" that wreckage and devastation come. That is an awfully high price to pay. We can't afford to insist on having our own way. Let us rather abide in Christ's beatitude, "Blessed are the peacemakers, for they will be called sons of God" (Matthew 5:9).

* * * * *

A very high percentage of conflict, both church and personal, could be resolved by a very thick application of repentance, confession, forgiveness, humility, grace, and mercy by each one on all sides of an issue. In the final analysis the scriptural principles of Christian conduct provide the best solution.

Handling Crises

Robert H. Spence

In one of His final conversations with the disciples before He went to the cross, Jesus outlined prophetically some of the experiences they would have in future days. Then He said: "These things I have spoken unto you, that in me ye might have peace. In the world ye shall have tribulation: but be of good cheer; I have overcome the world" (John 16:33[1]).

The Greek word for "tribulation" in John 16:33 is *thlipsis,* which can be translated in a variety of ways, including "pressure," "affliction," "anguish," "burdened," "persecution," or "trouble." Those words can be equated with the word *crisis.* At least two significant facts are clearly presented in the Lord's statement: (1) Disciples will experience crises in this present world, and (2) peace of mind and the peace of God are available during the crisis because of Christ's power.

The words of Jesus have application not only for those who were physically present with him on that occasion, but also for His servants today. We must acknowledge that pastors today will be called upon to handle crises. The challenge confronting a pastor is to handle these inevitable experiences in a manner pleasing to God as well as appropriate to the circumstances and people involved. The Bible contains innumerable accounts of God using men and women in times of crisis. These people have much to teach us about the correct response to unexpected events.

> **"**
> # Pastors today will be called upon to handle crises.
> **"**

Few of us will ever feel the weight of responsibility Moses felt as he faced the Red Sea surrounded by bewildered, discouraged countrymen describing Pharaoh's approaching army. But the same principles of decisive leadership can be demonstrated today. Or who could describe how Esther felt when she learned that her entire race faced annihilation, and yet her actions provide a pattern for handling a crisis that a pastor can follow today.

Crises burst on the pastor's horizon without warning. Rarely is one's schedule designed to accommodate the unexpected. A telephone call or an unannounced visitor can sweep the servant of God into the middle of a storm. Because crises do not occur in a vacuum, the pastor oftentimes, like a crew member on Jonah's boat, must cope with turbulence resulting from someone else's decision.

With frequency pastors pray for manifestations of God's power. Like Moses we petition God, "Show me thy glory." However, miracles occur because there is a need; divine healing takes place because there is sickness or injury. Crises provide the setting for a demonstration of God's power. It is indeed a mark of uncommon maturity for one to come through a crisis that has included personal disappointment and pain and be able to say with Joseph, "Ye thought evil against me; but God meant it unto good, to bring to pass, as it is this day, to save much people alive" (Genesis 50:20).

Day by day the pastor has opportunity to walk with members of his congregation who are coping with personal or family crises of every description. One must not lose sight of the fact that crises occur in the lives of people who are in the will of God as well as in the lives of those out of the will of God. The pathologist's confirmation of a malignancy or the closure of a factory eliminating employment and compromising retirement are experiences of life. They are crises to be handled.

The conscientious child of God will ask in times of crisis, What is the Lord saying to me through this? Or, What is God teaching me through this? Not only does the pastor need to apply that question to himself, but he has opportunity to share that with people he is seeking to help. Crises are not necessarily a sign of God's judgment.

Crises come in all sizes and dimensions. Some affect only one individual; others create repercussions that extend around the world. The announcement that there is a shortage of nursery workers may present the pastor with a momentary crisis as he is preparing to go to the platform to begin the worship service, but it is a situation that can be contained and addressed within minutes. On the other hand, learning that the construction company building the new sanctuary has gone bankrupt and will not be able to complete the job can create a crisis with effects that will last for years.

Some crises can be brought to a satisfactory solution for all involved while others defy settlement and will continue to generate pain and suffering for an ever-widening circle of participants.

The performance of the pastor during a crisis will affect his ministerial future. Members of the church watch him carefully to see how he handles the unexpected. Their future support will be influenced by how crises are handled.

Real or perceived, public or private, crises demand attention, and when they occur within the family of God, the pastor's involvement is essential. Handling crises will be a test of leadership and an opportunity for spiritual growth.

Regardless of size, every congregation includes members whose personal crises will be shared with the pastor. Unquestionably, many of these people turn to the pastor with the expectation that a spiritual dimension of the problem will be explored. It is imperative that the assistance received in the pastor's study be more than would be available in the social worker's office. Believing as we do in miraculous interventions in response to prayer, a crisis provides a focal point for faith and works to be combined.

> ## Crises come in all sizes and dimensions.

While the pastor's crisis ministry is often focused on those under his spiritual care, he himself is not immune to times of testing. Financial and physical crises occur in the parsonage, and the pastor's family is subject to some of the same pressures the parishioner experiences.

In the course of a week the pastor may be called upon to work with someone who has lost a job, a couple whose marriage is in crisis, a family who has lost a loved one, or someone experiencing an emotional breakdown.

As leader of the local body, the pastor may deal with crises resulting from doctrinal aberrations or congregational conflicts. In a time when litigation is so prevalent, the pastor may face lawsuits, potential or actual, involving staff or adjunct ministries of the church, such as a day-care center. And it is a rare church that has not had a financial crisis that called for strong pastoral leadership.

Knowing that crises will occur and knowing that as long as we work with people we will encounter crises, what preparation can we bring to this task? What steps can a pastor take to insure effectiveness? Some basic assumptions regarding desired pastoral characteristics are applicable, whether one is proclaiming the Word from the pulpit or working with individual members of the church in their times of difficulty. It is imperative that the servant of God establish and maintain credibility through personal honesty and integrity. The member in a crisis should have no reason to fear that difficulties shared with a staff person will be circulated among others or appear in sermon illustrations.

The pastor should be discriminating in his definition of *crisis* and not allow others to set his agenda and define *crisis* for him. Care must be taken to maintain his intention of helping people without being manipulated by those who simply want someone else to solve their problems.

Be Prepared Spiritually

A time of crisis is the ideal time to heed James' advice: "If any of you lack wisdom, let him ask of God, that giveth to all men liberally, and upbraideth not; and it shall be given him" (James 1:5). While the petition for divine wisdom may be a daily prayer, it is still appropriate to pray for special insight when engaging the complexities of human problems.

A crisis provides a unique opportunity for the servant of God. People are more open to receiving spiritual help during times of difficulty. In such times, gifts of the Spirit that have been made available for the edification of the church can offer supernatural assistance. The discerning pastor is often able to help people see that the crisis they are seeking to alleviate is not the real problem. Walking in the Spirit and ministering in the power of the Spirit enable the servant of God to be a true physician of the soul.

Spiritual preparation includes approaching problems from a biblical perspective. Scripture should be appropriately presented and discerning prayer offered. While the pastor's spiritual role and acquaintance with Scripture are vital, care must be taken to offer this assistance prudently. A hurting, distressed person needs more than the quotation of a familiar Scripture verse, a brief prayer, and a trite assurance that "everything will be all right."

Maintain the Right Attitude

In Jesus' earthly ministry, people coping with life's problems were drawn to Him. The writer to the Hebrews describes Him as being "touched with the feeling of our infirmities" (Hebrews 4:15). The parade was unending: A mother with a demon-possessed daughter, a father whose daughter was dying, sisters whose brother was deathly ill, and people like Peter who experienced a crisis of personal faith. The pastor who exhibits a Christlike attitude will find ready acceptance among his people when they are going through times of difficulty. Empathy, not sympathy, will open doors. Compassion can be sensed. The servant of God should be careful about using the phrase "I know how you feel." That statement should be made only if the pastor really knows how the person feels and has gone through a similar experience.

There are times when a crisis has developed because of misbehavior. The pastor must be careful that he handles wrongdoers without manifesting an improper spirit. The person in crisis does not need a reminder of poor judgment and bad decisions. More is needed than a pronouncement that the crisis is due to carnality or immaturity. Consideration for the feelings of all involved will open future doors of ministry. Extreme care should be taken that the pastor not appear as a know-it-all, one who has all of the answers.

When crises occur, the pastor should guard against a "woe is me" attitude. Perhaps Peter was remembering Jesus' admonition to him and the other disciples when he wrote, "Think it not strange concerning the fiery trial which is to try you, as though some strange thing happened unto you" (1 Peter 4:12). Remember, these are opportunities for God to reveal His power.

Gather Facts Carefully

The Proverbs are excellent reading for the pastor who will confront crises. Repeatedly the author counsels care when speaking. The same applies to gathering information. Pastors are shepherds, not detectives. Bias and hasty conclusions should be avoided. Learning to be a good listener—with the heart as well as the ear—will enable the servant of God to have clearer vision, seeing the individual apart from the crisis.

Allowing the person in crisis to speak freely can be most helpful at the moment and in the future. This is especially helpful when the crisis involves tragedy. Unexpected death of a family member can produce statements that seem irrational and even unspiritual. The pastor should not feel that he must answer every question or correct every distorted view of God.

If a crisis involves the discipline of staff or volunteer personnel, it is extremely important that careful documentation be maintained of conversations and remedial steps that have been offered previously. Thorough records and accurate minutes of meetings can prove to be assets of inestimable value, especially if the crisis has legal ramifications.

A pastor should be secure enough to turn to others for advice and counsel. Particularly when dealing with financial and legal crises, it is important to know one's limitations and where to find those who can provide appropriate assistance. The wise pastor knows his own strengths and weaknesses, not only in financial and legal matters but also in other areas of offering advice.

Make Decisions Deliberately

A crisis calls for decision and action. An entire congregation looks to the pastor for direction and positive steps if a crisis has occurred that involves the body. In times of difficulty, individuals seek the pastor's counsel and advice because they are looking for someone who will help them solve problems and assist in making decisions.

Finding a balance between inordinate delay and hasty action calls for wisdom. When facts are carefully gathered and appropriate counsel has been sought, the pastor must come to a conclusion and address the crisis decisively. Maintaining composure can instill confidence in those involved in the crisis. This is not to suggest that the pastor be emotionless, but rather that an effort be made to discharge responsibility in a calm and careful manner.

If the crisis involves the church, members of the board should be involved. Their involvement should be more than communication of what the pastor has done. They should have opportunity, as leaders chosen by the congregation, to share the burden of decision and offer their collective wisdom to provide solutions.

Communicate Clearly

The pastor's counsel must be clear and easily understood. Misunderstanding only compounds the problem. If the pastor is working with a single individual going through a time of difficulty, his conversation and suggestions can be more easily communicated and clearly understood than if he is working with a group.

However, crises do involve families and larger groups. When this is the case, the communication responsibility increases immeasurably. For example, if the crisis involves a problem with church finances, there should be an openness that allows involved individuals to understand the circumstances and the need. It is imperative that there be no occasion for people to think cover-up. An element of openness is being willing to admit what we do not know as well as what we do know.

In communicating decisive action there are times when the pastor's leadership role must be one of strength, standing firm for principle and for the right course of action. While honesty and forthrightness are essential, gentleness and tact should prevent bluntness and insensitivity.

There Is Life after the Crisis

Helping people solve problems and working with a congregation through a crisis can produce a feeling of satisfaction and a sense of fulfillment. Results on other occasions may not be so fulfilling. Elijah on Mount Carmel helped the nation of Israel when their crisis involved their allegiance to God. Perhaps the sound of the populace shouting "the Lord He is . . . God" was still echoing in Elijah's ears when he received the message from Jezebel threatening his life (1 Kings 18:39 through 19:2). There is no indication that the people he helped spiritually came to his defense that day. Discouraged, Elijah fled for his life only to have the Lord rescue him and help him understand more fully his ministry. In like manner, the pastor must realize that he handles crises to please his Master. Unfortunately, handling crises effectively does not make the pastor immune to criticism even from the people he has assisted.

Ministering in crisis produces stress. Prolonged involvement in complex problems can have a telling effect on the pastor's physical, emotional, and spiritual well-being. Deliberate care must be taken to deal effectively with these needs.

If the crisis has involved a congregation or personnel, the pastor should take the steps necessary to lead the congregation beyond it. Frequent references to the past can only keep people's vision focused in the wrong direction. Remember, there is life after the crisis. A past crisis could be described as a weight, perhaps one of the "weights" that the writer to the Hebrews had in mind. Lay it aside, he admonished, so that you may "run with patience the race that is set before us," helpfully adding how we might refocus our attention—"looking unto Jesus the author and finisher of our faith" (Hebrews 12:1–2).

Developing a Team of Qualified, Dedicated Staff Members

Dan Betzer

L et me simplify it: Surround yourself with people who know more about the subject at hand than you do, and then turn them loose! But as R. B. Barham witnessed, "There's many a slip 'twixt the cup and the lip."[1] All too often we make simple things very complex, and needless bureaucracy slows down the dynamic of a Pentecostal church.

I once saw a cartoon in a bait shop. A youngster about ten years old was fishing by the riverside, a mound of flopping fish all around him (which he had obviously just caught). He was using a tree branch for a pole and simple string for line. Standing next to him with nary a fish was a man with the latest in expensive fishing gear. He was growing angrier and angrier at his inability to catch anything, even as the youngster continued pulling them in. Taking pity on him, the boy suggested, "Sir, maybe your safety pin is closed." The youngster was catching more with a tree branch, some store string, and a safety pin hook than the man could catch with the complicated equipment. Pastor, the world is filled with pencil pushers and report writers. But the Holy Spirit will lead you to men and women who are "movers and shakers" for the Kingdom. This kind of staff will put your church on the front line. But you are going to have to do what Jesus told those mourning for Lazarus: "Loose him, and let him go!" The less paperwork, the better; the less bureaucracy, the more successful you will be! The more trusting you are of staff, the more your church will grow. K.I.S.S. = "Keep It Simple, Sir!"

Leadership Is Key

The creaky, old adage that no church can permanently rise above the spiritual and talent level of its pastor is valid. John Maxwell constantly emphasizes this theme of leadership. Oh, there may be a sudden burst of anointing and genius on the part of the congregation that results in growth, but without effective pastoral leadership, it will be short-lived. As goes the pastor, so usually goes the church.

Unfortunately, no pastor is perfect. Each of us has areas of ministry where we are not strong. The wise pastor understands how true this is and doesn't try to fake his way along. It is absolutely essential that a pastor honestly evaluate his own strengths and weaknesses (and if he cannot be honestly objective, then he must invite outside evaluation). While I'm aware of the ministry gifts God has given me, I know full well that I lack the ability for any number of ministry endeavors. Some balance is needed here. For example, I have never claimed to be an administrator, yet in this church of nearly thirty-five hundred members and adherents, administration is a must. Further, I do not have a keen financial mind, yet our annual budget of four million dollars demands brilliant fiscal leadership. There are yet other areas where I realize my weakness. Now consider: This congregation cannot long rise above the level of my leadership, yet I freely acknowledge there are facets of that very leadership where I am lacking. So is this church doomed? Must First Assembly muddle through without effective administration or with faulty financial direction? No, of course not! Not if the pastor develops a qualified, dedicated staff that makes up for the senior pastor's deficiencies and at the same time complements strengths. Carefully note the direction here: I do not need duplications of myself; I need men and women on my staff who have abilities I know I do not have.

> **As goes the pastor, so usually goes the church.**

I report to you frankly, after having spoken in hundreds of our churches across the nation, that many pastors hire carbon copies of themselves. These ministers are relatively comfortable with their clones, but how one-dimensional their churches are! Developing a team of qualified, dedicated staff members means honestly evaluating yourself first of all, then seeking God to bring in staff men and women who substantially broaden your ministry gifts.

These principles work in churches of any size. You don't need a large church. The concepts I share with you here were developed while planting churches in my early ministry—I didn't get them from a book! In one early church, we began meeting in the basement of our home. There was no district funding. I desperately needed help and began training laity (or bringing in experts to do so). From day one I have believed in the laity. I have found that my congregants respond to the measure of faith I show in them. I think they are wonderful and they almost invariably live up to my expectations. I often tell pastors in ministers' institutes, "Believe in your laity! They're smarter than you! That's why they're not pastoring that church." But training laity is one thing, and selecting and equipping professional staff is quite another.

Deciding Your Philosophy of Administration

Years ago I heard Dr. Robert Schuller say, "If you're going to be a successful pastor, there are three things you must settle in your own heart: (1) *What* are you trying to do? (2) *How* do you plan to do it? (3) *Why* do you even bother (motivation)?" Item three will insulate the pastor from burn-out and oversensitivity. Paul informed us he was constrained by Christ; small wonder he could stand against stonings, imprisonment, and rejection! He was properly motivated. Now how can a pastor begin to select professional staff until he has truly answered those three basic questions? Your hiring choices will depend upon those vital answers.

Just before starting a church many years ago, I asked Pastor G. L. Johnson of the People's Church in Fresno, California, to give me counsel. He responded, "Dan, first of all you must have a clearly defined philosophy of pastoral ministry. It should be written so all can read and clearly understand it." And he added, "If you don't have such a written statement, you probably don't have a clear idea what you're trying to do." Oh, how that advice helped me! Pastor, before you consider hiring staff, have a distinct concept of what you are planning to do—and how you are planning to do it.

The church I pastor has the simplest of philosophies, in fact, three words only: *Reach—Teach—Send.* The "reaching" has to do with evangelism. First Assembly is strongly outreach oriented in every endeavor. I certainly don't want staff members around me who don't share that perspective. The "teaching" has to do with training, with saturation in the Word and equipping laity to do practical ministry. I must have a staff enabled to equip. The "sending" part of our philosophy has to do with starting new churches in our area and sending out missionaries around the world. We have sent out hundreds of people to home and foreign missions, while at the same time starting three new churches in our own section. So you see, a staffer who wanted only to retain people in order to build his or her own department would not feel at home with us. You can see how the philosophy of our ministry affects the hiring of staff.

> **Pastor, before hiring staff, have a distinct concept of what you are planning to do.**

No staff member will be comfortable with a pastor for long if that leader does not know where he's going and how he plans to get there. A pastor's philosophy of leadership is usually a reflection of his or her self-image and priorities. If a pastor is a hands-on administrator, involved in every staffer's work, it will require a certain breed of worker. In my case, I employ *low-intensity management,* that is, "Hands off!" Each of my associates has ownership of his or her department. I do not saddle them with time cards, work sheets, daily reports, and other paperwork, which I consider a waste of everybody's time. I don't want to have to read them, and I surely don't want my busy people having to write them.

So how do I know what each staffer is doing? The growth and development (or lack of it) in that staffer's department is the clear indicator.

More about that when we discuss staff communication. Bureaucracy is an unpleasant word to me, so I am not going to surround myself with bureaucrats. My associate pastor, Bill Campbell, wrote for this chapter: "The freedom of First Assembly staff members to develop individual departments and ministries, the diversity of staff, and the understanding that one should take his ministry (but not himself) very seriously are all important. These ingredients encourage creativity and individuality in the organization. At the same time, there is a real sense of 'family' and 'team' that tends to keep individuality in proper balance. This prevents a disconnected conglomeration of individual ministries and gives First Assembly the ability to be a living organism that flows together to impact our city and world."

As a pastor, I see my purpose with the staff to inspire each one to be all that he or she can be and to give that person the *liberty* to carry out individual dreams for ministry. I truly want each staff member to succeed on his or her own merit, and, further, I want the congregation to love each one of them. For example, our family life pastor, George Westlake, is impacting scores of young couples for Christ. At the end of services, I see them flock around him. That thrills me! Why? Because it is the greatest indicator I know of that Pastor Westlake is successful in his assigned enterprise. If those new couples were coming to me, I would wonder why Pastor Westlake didn't have more rapport with them. That would seem obvious; however, in my travels across the constituency, I have observed many pastors who apparently are afraid for their staffs to succeed. They appear to hold their colaborers in check. The pastors display sure signs of insecurity in their own ministry and leadership and, therefore, hold their staffs at arm's length or in check.

Our youth pastor, Brad Liebe, wrote, "A staff pastor at First Assembly is allowed to dream as big as he wants—and then allowed to go after those dreams without having to go through major obstacles. The church provides the means for us to accomplish our dreams." School principal Shelton Gwaltney adds, "The senior pastor does not undermine our areas of ministry, but rather supports our leadership."

A Word of Caution

As much as I embrace the principle of low-intensity management, I understand the inherent weakness of such a system. For it to function consistently, the individual staff members and department heads must be competent, creative, cooperative, self-starting, and secure in themselves. An individual who needs a lot of direction or who does not get along well with other staff or who needs special attention from the senior pastor will not function well in this management style. But the strengths of the system far outweigh such weaknesses, in my estimation. Pastor Campbell adds, "It is refreshing to see a large church moving toward Kingdom purposes without the encumbrances of heavy bureaucracy. Thank God for the freedom to be busy with the Father's business!"

As the senior pastor of a rapidly growing congregation, I cannot afford to be bogged down with needless reports, to hand-hold aggrieved staff members, and to oversee every detail of their work. Our time is too valuable and my staff is too creative to be consumed with paperwork. Pastors, keep things simple, and let your people go!

Communication

So how does the senior pastor know what the staff is doing? Simple. Low-intensity management requires exceptional communication. Any of the eleven pastors on my staff has access to me at any time, in the office or at home. None needs an appointment. Unless I am in consultation with a parishioner, the staffers are welcome to walk right into my study. I feel this is absolutely essential.

I must explain this more fully. The ministers on my staff (both men and women) are most unusual people. Each is unique. They have strong personalities. I often lecture in ministers' institutes and encourage pastors to depart from the cookie-cutter mentality, requiring all ministers to be essentially alike. How dull such a staff would be! And how narrow a swath they would cut through a given community! I personally like very unusual people. I look for men and women not only who have character, but who *are* characters. Yet they can be cohesive as a staff.

Each staff member is hired by me personally and, further, is amenable to me. To be sure, I give our church council (our board) the opportunity to meet and interview staff candidates and would not likely go against their preferences. However, the main person the staff must answer to is the senior pastor. I do not permit any committee to hire a staff member for me. I personally conduct the interviews.

These mandates are desirable for a number of reasons: (1) Immediately we begin our communication together; (2) the staff member is made aware that he or she is accountable to the senior pastor; (3) the senior pastor becomes the buffer for his staff, avoiding the development of any embarrassing or unresolved difficulties; (4) the congregation do not consider staff as lackeys but give each one the same respect they give the senior pastor. It is vital that the congregation regard associates highly.

WAYS TO COMMUNICATE

Each Monday morning, I meet with the entire church staff for devotions and prayer. Then at 9:30, the pastors come into my study where we spend the rest of the morning together. What a time we have—talking over issues large and small, reporting, sharing dreams, praying, laughing, and seeing how each one of us fits into the overall church vision. No subject is too great or small (including sharing family or personal joys and challenges). Time is never too precious to hear the latest anecdote or joke, never too precious to pray over an expressed need. At noon, we go to lunch, even traveling together in a church van. We look forward to our Mondays together. They are fun; they are important; they are invigorating. And, oh, how those Monday sessions strengthen our cohesiveness!

I encourage pastors to lighten the load of their associates, to lift their spirits as often as they can. I spend time with these people. Some of us on the staff play golf, and we hit the links rather often. Other staff members play other sports together. Their families meet for picnics and outings. No, as senior pastor, I do not need to be involved in all these activities. I take great joy in seeing the staff and their families enjoy each other's company so much.

Each year we have a pastoral staff retreat, along with our spouses, on beautiful Sanibel Island, just off our southwest Florida coast in the Gulf of Mexico. We stay at a magnificent hotel right on the beach for three days. When we first began these retreats, years ago, I made the days a time of work and planning; however, I have relaxed that activity. The staff works incredibly hard all year. They need a relaxing break. Now we have morning prayer times together, eat our main meals together, and then hit the beaches, the boats, the links, the tennis courts, the bicycles and mopeds, and have a great time. At night, we meet in the recreation room for games. No ties, no white shirts, no suits. Staffers have told me how greatly they enjoy these days on Sanibel!

During the Christmas season, we have a huge staff party with all our children gathering for a celebration of the Lord's birth. The food is delightful. We exchange gifts (not to exceed five dollars and hopefully things that no one could possibly ever want!). Some of those gifts have gone around the horn three and four years. Laughter explodes during these times.

In case it appears that we just play, I assure you this staff works long and hard. I doubt if any of my staff puts in fewer than sixty hours each week. A thriving and rapidly growing church proves this fact. Communication among us all is a must. We keep working at it.

SECURITY

Here is an issue all too often neglected or forgotten by senior pastors: Staff members need to feel secure. Once again, quoting from Pastor George Westlake, our Family Life minister: "There is a passionate cry from staff pastors everywhere for the security of their jobs. I have witnessed staff around the country who live in frightening insecurity—of their support, and even of the job itself. This creates unrest and a critical spirit within that staff member. It is the senior pastor's role to set a table of security and support. High turnover rate, in my opinion, is largely due to a senior pastor's ineffectiveness and/or inability to lead and support his staff. The senior pastor will invariably pay the price for staff insecurities, not to mention doing the cleanup when those associates fail. There is security in support!"

Pastor Westlake is right, of course. Thus communication with staff involves not only duplicating the vision God has given to me for the church but also making sure my associates know that I love them dearly, truly believe in them, and support their role in our ministry here.

Remuneration and Benefits

If everything in this chapter is valid, then the remuneration and benefits package must reflect it. Proper respect deserves proper paychecks. I have upon occasion heard a pastor boast that he paid his staff purposefully low wages, claiming he was a good steward of God's money. Nothing could be further from truth. When wages reflect such disrespect for the worker, turnover rates are high, churches usually do not grow (at least not for long), and the moving cost of bringing in new recruits could have been used for salaries in the first place. A wise pastor and board will make their church so attractive from every angle that the staff members would be most reluctant to leave. Of course, being in God's will is the priority of any employment; however, a staff member's being in that precious will of God does not mean he or she should live on substandard pay. Jesus himself gave the policy: "The laborer is worthy of his hire" (Luke 10:7, KJV).

> ## " When wages reflect disrespect, turnover rates are high. "

Upon occasion, I have interviewed prospective staff who have immediately brought up the subject of salary. I have almost immediately dismissed them in my mind from future employment. The fact is that among the extraordinary personnel I now enjoy, not one made salary a key issue for coming on board. Each was challenged by the work here and felt God's will to come to First Assembly. Our finance committee knows well our city and its cost of living. We would never insult a staff member by attempting to get him or her to live on a substandard level. No, nobody will ever grow wealthy in our employ, but we will guarantee a respectable wage and regular contributions to future retirement.

There is great dignity in the work ethic, and there should be commensurate dignity in the remuneration offered. I entered the ministry in a church that paid me a terribly low salary. I felt so constrained by Christ to fill the ministry challenge there that I accepted their offer and God somehow brought my family through. However, that church could have easily paid twice the salary to me. One thing is sure: They got many times over their money's worth from me during those two years, and I never made wages an issue with them. I often wondered though how the board members could live with themselves when my family and I drove up to church in a battered old car that was held together with baling wire and faith, when we often wore hand-me-down clothing, when for one of our Christmases there we had no gifts under a tree, a tree we had found. I was always very proud of my call and my work, but terribly ashamed of my salary. I have made sure that none of my staff members will ever have such indignity placed upon them.

TIME OFF

Every staff member has a full day off each week (except Monday, which is staff day, and, of course, Sunday). Further, if their work is completed for the week, they need not work Saturday during the day, but they are expected at the prayer meeting Saturday evening.

Never give a staff member the feeling that you are doing him or her a big favor by giving them a day off. It is mandatory that you give it. Don't call them on the day off and say, "Listen, I know it's your day off, but . . ." (an exception would be a true emergency). That's how you lose staff members. Pastors have sometimes told me, "Well, I don't give my staffers a day off because I work seven days a week, so why shouldn't they?" "Perhaps because they're not as foolish as you" is my standard reply.

VACATIONS

People who work hard need sufficient time to unwind and rest. Vacations are mandatory for our staff. Each minister is given every consideration regarding vacations. A minimum of two weeks is given to new pastors (upon one year of service) and the number of weeks is increased with years served. Pastor, never feel that you are *giving* your staff vacation; they have earned it. I have witnessed pastors making staff feel almost guilty about going away. That is unfair! Send your pastors on their holidays with a pat on the back and orders to have a good time!

It is in the senior pastor's best interest to have those vacations staggered as much as possible so that your fighting force is not severely hampered. For example, if five of my staff left at the same time for a couple of weeks, I would certainly feel the impact. But through the years we have learned to schedule our vacations as much as a year in advance so we do not overlap each other. Thus the extremely tight and busy schedule of church life continues right through pastors' vacation times.

CONVENTIONS AND SEMINARS

In addition to vacations, I encourage our staff to attend at least one outside seminar or learning experience in their field of ministry each year. This is money well spent. The pastors come home fresh, brimming with new zeal and ideas. Each one chooses wisely those sessions desired. Occasionally it means flying a staffer from our coast to the other; however, even this expenditure returns in multiples before the year is out. If nothing else, these opportunities give confidence and assurance to each minister. (In addition, the church sends the ministers to our district councils and, on rotating schedules, to the biennial General Council.)

Several days ago, a leading educator in America sat in my office, discussing the very things in this chapter. He said, "Pastor, I see some of America's leading college presidents and administrators unable to cope with time management, staff development, and delegation of authority. These leaders could do many times more if they would just learn the fundamentals."

There is no reason to burn out. Develop that qualified and dedicated staff. Put your heart and soul into it! The returns will be manyfold and your congregation will bless you for it.

The Effective Use of Job Descriptions

E. Allen Ratta

T he effective job description consists of a dynamic set of directives that provides a framework for personnel to contribute to the overall effectiveness of a ministry. It is dynamic in that it will need to grow and adjust to changing realities. It is a framework in that it provides the general parameters and values within which leadership personnel operate without micromanagement. A job description is effective only to the extent that it advances the ministry objectives of the church. The focus of this chapter is on developing and managing effective job descriptions for church ministry. However, an effective job description is written in the following context and climate.

Prerequisites for Developing an Effective Job Description

An effective job description is not developed in a vacuum. To do so would produce a set of tasks unrelated to any sense of overall mission. This would be analogous to a factory filled with aircraft production workers forever making parts but never able to assemble them into a functional airplane. Before an effective job description can be written, two things must be taken into account: the church's mission statement and its philosophy of ministry. The pastor who aspires to develop effective job descriptions, with the potential of setting a well-functioning team on the road to achievement, will need to take into account these vital prerequisites.

A primary question must be asked. What are the major objectives of this ministry? Peter Drucker, labeled by the *New York Times* as the "founding father of the science of management," declares, "A missions statement has to be operational, otherwise it is just good intentions. . . . [It] has to focus on what the institution really tries to do . . . so everybody in the organization can say, This is *my* contribution toward the goal."[1] Before a single line of an effective job description can be written, the pastor must ask himself, and answer, some basic questions. "What am I trying to do?

What is the mission of my church?" It is only when he knows the answer to these questions that he is prepared to develop a plan of how to get there. Drucker insists, "The first task of the leader is to make sure that everybody sees the mission, hears it, and lives it."[2] A well-written, effective job description is a good beginning point to articulate and actualize the mission of the church.

Drucker takes this thought further: "The task of the non-profit manager is to try to convert the organization's mission statement into specifics."[3] This is where many pastors fall short. They know well their mission. The pastor and staff invariably believe strongly in the mission. But they fail to translate that knowledge and conviction into strategic action.

People are, in every case, the greatest strategic resource and the key to accomplishing specific Kingdom objectives. Yet all too often pastors receive little or no training in human resource management. The well-written job description is a basic tool that brings competence to such management.

The most effective job descriptions are also crafted within the context of a clear vision. Vision has been differentiated from mission by George Barna as follows, "Mission is a general statement of ministry objectives; it is philosophic. Vision is a specific, detailed statement of direction and uniqueness; it is strategic."[4] The strategic mobilization of personnel is the difference between a winning and a losing team. Every winning coach implicitly understands this principle. It is the senior pastor's responsibility to direct staff in a strategic manner. This is because he has the role of being the primary vision caster and vision is, as Barna reminds us, always strategic in nature.

Finally, corporate values are an integral part of the work environment. They often take the form of unwritten rules in congregational life. Yet they have a profound impact on the worker's ability to perform up to expectations. Alan Loy McGinnis notes, "The essential thing is that the organization has a set of standards and that the leaders enforce rigorous adherence to them."[5] An example of a corporate value is the commitment to "do everything with excellence." Adequate job performance takes on an entirely new meaning within this context. Likewise, the value that "people come first" strongly affects the climate of the workplace. Language that articulates a church's corporate values will be included in an effective job description. Corporate values written into a job description can have a profound impact on the corporate work ethic; they can build morale in the organization and create a strong sense of being on the same team.

Developing an Effective Job Description

The process of developing a job description is at least as important as the end product. An effective job description is not a bureaucratic form to be autocratically dispensed as if it alone were an adequate basis for conducting ministry. A job description that works is essentially a two-way covenant.[6] The leader commits to managing and the worker commits to fulfilling the values and obligations of the job description. Inclusive to that is a personal commitment to loyalty and to the support of one another. The pastor and the staff member covenant together, to the best of their ability, to make one another a success in fulfilling the objectives of the church. Establishing relationships of this nature will require a substantive process.

The job description that works establishes the basis of a good working relationship. It will require significant dialogue and ongoing communication for successful implementation. It has been aptly stated, "[M]ost managers know what they want their people to do. They just don't bother to tell their people in a way that they would understand. They assume they should know."[7] A proficient job description is the first step in the efficient communication of the manager's objectives.

How does one go about developing effective job descriptions? The following process can be helpful with both existing and new staff. Begin by having staff create the first draft. Ask them to write down what they actually do, what they feel they should be doing but do not have time for, and what they would like to do if they were not encumbered with existing responsibilities. Have new or prospective employees provide a description of the job as they understand it or wish it to be. Then edit their first draft and meet with them to discuss your perspective. There are several benefits to this approach.

When staff are included in the formation of their job description, it affirms the covenant dynamic of ministry relationships. The transcendent issue, in the work of the ministry, is always the will of God. Both parties need to agree that the job description lies within these confines. "Covenants require mutual agreement and communicate that the leader and staff are a team."[8] Mutual respect and commitment lie at the heart of every good working relationship.

A top-down style of management runs the risk of demonstrating the full extent of the leader's ignorance about an existing employee's actual contributions to the organization. Dispensing a written job description may make the worker feel both misunderstood and unappreciated. Getting the worker's input often heightens the leader's appreciation for the worker and his or her contributions to the ministry. The manager is likely to be pleasantly surprised at how many staff-initiated things are being accomplished in the church.

> **Begin by having staff create the first draft.**

The autocratic leader will miss many invaluable interactions with staff that both leader and staff desperately need.[9] Often the key to productivity for staff is to understand the rationale behind the leader's directives. It is critical, at the outset, for both parties to discuss and understand each other's perceptions and expectations regarding the job's requirements.

When the employee is included in the formation of the job description, it can provide critical insight into how well the temperament and gifts of the individual match the requirements of the job.[10] It is needful to discuss every line of the job description. Ask how he or she feels about each aspect of the job. One should be able to express genuine enthusiasm for 70 to 80 percent of a job's requirements or the person is wrong for the job.

Finally, this approach provides a significant training opportunity for the pastor to articulate, in practical terms, the mission of the church and his philosophy of ministry. Staff may understand the mission, vision, and corporate values of the church, but may never make the connection as to how these things relate to their specific areas of responsibility. It is the task of the leader to articulate those connections so the worker understands how specific job responsibilities can contribute to the overall ministry objectives of the church.

Elements of an Effective Job Description

There are two basic components of an effective job description: the generic and the specific. Generic items, outlined below, are general in nature and apply to all pastoral staff. They are derived from the biblically defined functions of the pastor and hold true regardless of the assigned portfolio. They also come from the mission, vision, and values of the organization. This means that the generic portion of the job description will change very little over time.

Examples of Generic Duties

Personal Duties
- Maintain a strong prayer and devotional life
- Maintain a strong family life
- Maintain priorities that promote personal and professional growth
- Practice personal evangelism

Professional Values

- Do everything with a commitment to excellence
- Maintain a "people first" perspective in all ministries
- Work with purpose and passion
- Work oneself out of a job at every opportunity
- Make people a success in Kingdom work

Professional Duties

- Work to fulfill all of the objectives of the church
- Articulate strategic vision for areas of responsibility in written form (on file)
- Craft and complete goals every month from strategic vision (on file)
- Build ministry structure to facilitate vision (structure charts on file)
- Design, promote, and implement new ministries
- Meet weekly with potential recruits
- Recruit and train people to staff new and existing ministry structure
- Disciple and grow people into greater responsibility and capacity for service

The professional duties category above incorporates what are termed the four Ps (below). No effective ministry can be sustained when any one of these components is missing. Philosophic ideas will go unfulfilled without passion. Passion will go unfulfilled without practical goals. Practical goals will go unfulfilled without people to carry them out. In other words, the lofty ideals of philosophy must find specific and practical expression for ministry to be successful. The generic portion of an effective job description, for the pastor, will include all four aspects of ministry.

The Four Ps of Effective Ministry

Components	Mechanisms	Concepts
Philosophy	Mission Statement	The Big Picture
Passion	Vision	Strategic Objectives
Practics	Goals	Measurable Action Steps
People Ministry	Structure	Human Resources

The specific components of a job description include those duties that apply to a portfolio. They are far more subject to change than the generic components and need to be developed and edited to meet the particular requirements of a work setting. Some common specifics that should be included are the date of last revision (at the top), the position title, definitions of downward and upward supervision, detailed duties and responsibilities, meetings required to attend, writing and/or speaking requirements, and office hours.[11]

The Biblical Job Description of a Pastor

The pastor's job in biblical terms is "the equipping of the saints for the work of service" (Ephesians 4:12, NASB). The pastor has the specific function of getting the other parts of the body of Christ working. It is critical to incorporate God's design for the pastor into his working job description.

Occasionally, I stand before my congregation and reiterate, "It is my job to make the day you stand before the Lord the greatest day of your life." I then go on to explain that I want them to hear the words "Well done, thou good and faithful servant" (Matthew 25:21, KJV). For many Christians, this divine praising will be the direct result of a pastor who did his job by strongly motivating them to do Kingdom work.

The effective job description for the pastor will incorporate the biblical mandate to equip laity, i.e., to recruit, motivate, train, and release people into ministry. The pastor will need to develop entirely new ministry structures. He will also need to commit a significant amount of his time to mobilizing laity.

The wise pastor, in the quest to fulfill his unique function in the body of Christ, will avail himself of every effective motivational and management tool available. A well-written job description is one such tool for equipping people (staff and laity) and releasing them into ministry. It can promote spiritual growth and the development of leadership at every level within the church.

Motivating Personnel through Job Descriptions

A job description will remain effective so long as it defines a job that adequately motivates the employee. Frederick Herzberg addresses this concept in detail in his classic article "One More Time: How Do You Motivate Employees?" With over 1.2 million reprints of the article purchased, his motivational concepts are a "must-read" for all serious managers of people. Herzberg identifies five motivational factors intrinsic to the job: "achievement, recognition for achievement, the work itself, responsibility, and growth or advancement."[12] Herzberg suggests that the motivational content of a job can be "enriched" through the application of these motivational dynamics. He offers seven principles of "vertical job loading," i.e., adding responsibilities that enhance employee motivation.[13] Three of these principles have a significant impact on pastoral ministry.

One of these significant principles is "removing some controls while retaining accountability."[14] This relates to the manner in which a job description is managed and taps into the two motivational factors of responsibility and personal achievement. Implementation of this principle requires that a pastor relinquish the need for control over every facet of the ministry.[15] Pastors who need complete control generally have an unmotivated staff.

Another of Herzberg's principles is "[giving] a person a complete natural unit of work."[16] This involves editing the actual content of a job description. A good example in the church would be to hand over in entirety the responsibilities and credit for the Christian education ministries to the Christian education pastor. This principle powerfully taps into three of the five motivational dynamics mentioned above: achievement, recognition, and responsibility. This principle requires that a pastor be secure enough emotionally to give away credit as well as responsibilities to staff.[17]

Yet another principle is "granting additional authority to employees in their activity, job freedom."[18] This involves editing the actual content of a job description and the manner in which a job description is managed. This principle again applies three of the five motivational dynamics: achievement, recognition, and responsibility. The implementation of this principle requires a pastor with flexible thinking who perceives ministry in more creative terms than traditional office hours. However, the evidence is overwhelming that most people need a good amount of structure for peak performance.[19] Ministry effectiveness will increase to the extent that a pastor can add these motivational dynamics to the crafting and the ongoing amendment of staff job descriptions.

Managing and Evaluating through Job Descriptions

No job description can be effective outside the context of a good working relationship. Relationships are seen by management leaders, even in the secular business world, as the key to the effective management of people. "Effective managers develop a relationship that allows effective performance management. It's this relationship, not the appraisal paperwork, that allows appraisal systems to work."[20]

Management leaders tell us, "For an appraisal to be effective for supervisor and employee, it must be transformed into a process of managing people everyday, not completing a form once a year."[21] Interaction and timely feedback on performance, both positive and negative, as they relate to the job description, are keys to increased efficiency. Carl George and Bob Logan use four words to define this management process: "assignment, assistance, accountability, and applause."[22] The effective job description is more than a form; it is a daily management tool. However, it is important, particularly within the confines of the nurture environment of ministry, to keep a working relationship separate from a personal relationship.[23] The evaluation of staff is one of the areas where a personal relationship may render a working relationship less effective.

Drucker states, "The executive who wants to be effective and who wants his organization to be effective polices all programs, all activities, all tasks. He always asks: 'Is this still worth doing?'"[24] If this is true of policies and tasks, how much more true is it of the instruments that manage and direct the activities of personnel. As tasks change, the job description that is an effective management and evaluation tool will need to be updated to reflect those changes.

How does a pastor fairly and objectively evaluate his staff? This can be a difficult assignment, as observed by the comments of some leading business managers. "Many managers have difficulty developing observable performance standards for such jobs as scientists, teachers, lawyers and social workers, all of whose outputs are difficult to quantify."[25] This can be an even more difficult task when it comes to the ministry. Yet objective standards are the key to the fair evaluation and development of ministry staff.

Ted Engstrom, president emeritus of World Vision International, offers one approach through his annual evaluation form for staff and board members.[26] He reviews seven performance factors: quantity of work, quality of work, knowledge and technical ability, creativity and initiative, learning ability, dependability, and cooperation. These measurements provide valuable insights into the commitment and abilities of the employee. However, if the job description is ineffective, the employee's efforts may or may not reflect any real contributions to the objectives of the organization.

Peter Drucker takes personnel evaluation one step further. He suggests that "[k]nowledge work is not defined by quantity. . . . Knowledge work is defined by results."[27] The basis for evaluation, for Drucker, centers around the question, "[W]hat has the employee contributed to advancing the objectives of the organization?" The well-written job description encourages dedicated pastoral staff to make meaningful contributions to the ministry objectives of the church.

* * * * *

The job description forged within the context of a defined mission statement, vision, and strong corporate values will reflect the ministry objectives of the church. The job description developed and implemented in concert with the employee provides the basis for effective teamwork. The job description that reflects the biblical function of the pastor will make a pastoral staff member effective in advancing the church. Pastoral staff who have been motivated through both the wise editing of the job description and a secure management style of the leader are likely to prove effective members of a ministry team. Finally, the pastoral staff person who has an effective job description that targets the actual objectives of the church and is evaluated on that basis has found a superb work environment for productivity and personal growth.

Guiding the Christian Education Program

J. Melvyn Ming

Three basic Christian education assumptions are vital for developing effective growing churches.

First, Scripture is the inspired Word of God. Everything we proclaim in Christian education ministry must have its basis in Scripture or at least be consistent with scriptural principles.

Second, Christian education exists as part of the church. Christian education is not a separate entity capable of doing "its own thing." It does not supersede the church nor replace it. Therefore, the pastor or leader should seek to integrate Christian education into a whole church strategy.

Third, Christian education cannot be divorced from evangelism. Christian education is not just the teaching arm of the church. Evangelism must occur before you can make someone who is *not* a Christian, Christlike.

Four Commitments of Disciple-Making Churches

Christian education ministry must have a clear vision of what it is seeking to do. A good example of a clear vision is the Assemblies of God program We Build People: Making Disciples for the 21st Century. This approach uses a baseball diamond as a framework for the vision.

The diamond has four goals for every individual:

1. to know Christ in salvation and be assimilated into the congregation *(membership)*
2. to grow in Christ through teaching and relationships *(maturity)*
3. to be trained as a productive member of the body *(ministry),* and
4. to find one's unique place in Christ's church as a servant/leader *(mission)*

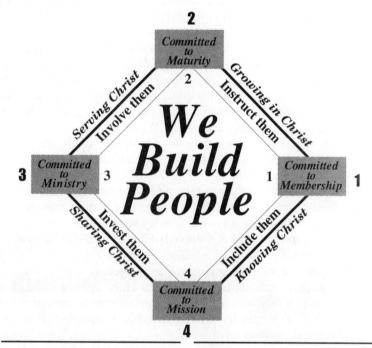

4 Commitments Disciples Make

1. Commitment to Membership
2. Commitment to Maturity
3. Commitment to Ministry
4. Commitment to Mission

4 Commitments Churches Make

1. Commitment to Include
2. Commitment to Instruct
3. Commitment to Involve
4. Commitment to Invest

Salvation is the beginning of the Christian life. It is a personal relationship with Jesus Christ. Church membership does not start the process. However, church membership is a sign or demonstration of this step. At salvation a person starts the process of growing to maturity in Christ. A person who has experienced salvation, is baptized in water, is participating in communion, and is a member of a local church has reached first base! This is a *commitment to membership.*

How do we move people toward first base? By including them in our Christian education ministries. One study found that 70 to 90 percent of Christians pointed to key relationships with friends and relatives as a very significant factor in their coming to Christ. Another study found that if people did not make at least seven friends in the first six months of attending a church, they would drop out. What is the implication of this to the Christian education ministries of a church? Every ministry, group, class, and person enrolled in a Christian education ministry must work at building relationships with people in and outside the church!

The second base is *commitment to maturity*. Here a convert grows beyond infancy and is established as a Christian. Colossians 2:6–7 says, "Just as you received Christ Jesus as Lord, continue to live in him, rooted and built up in him, strengthened in the faith as you were taught, and overflowing with thankfulness." How do we move people toward second base? By *instructing them*. This process is called many things. Some refer to it as nurturing or discipling or teaching. Whatever term we use, there is a process of development. A person begins the Christian life as a spiritual infant and must grow up. When someone comes to Christ, the Bible says there is a new creation—a baby spiritually. Paul says we should be "like a mother caring for her little children" or a "father dealing with a son" (1 Thessalonians 2:7,11).

Spiritual growth can take place one-on-one in a Sunday school class, a small group, or in other Christian education ministries offered by the church. In many ways the Sunday school is the ideal way to bring people to second base, for it is the only Christian education ministry that includes all ages.

How does someone move from second base to third base? By being equipped to minister, through the Holy Spirit and the "equipping" ministries of the church. This is a *commitment to ministry*.

When people have been saved and discipled, it is God's design for them to become involved in ministry to others. By *involving them* in ministry we give people opportunity to use the gifts and talents given to them by the Holy Spirit. This is a continuation of the discipling process but at a more advanced level, including gift development and training in specific skills.

How do people move from third base to home plate? By sharing Christ and *investing themselves* in others. Using the gifts and abilities that God has given them moves a Christian toward home plate. This is a *commitment to mission*. The Christian experiences the joy of becoming a reproducer and leading others to Christ.

The Pyramid Principle for Growth

The pyramid model was developed by David Womack. The base of the pyramid represents the ministry leadership of the church. The volume of the pyramid represents the size or constituents of the church. If the size of the church grows without broadening the base, the pressure on those in ministry leadership increases and will eventually crush them. When this happens, good people burn out and give up. Before the size can be expanded, you must broaden the leadership base so it can support greater volume. Then you increase the size. There is a continual pattern of broadening the base and increasing the size.

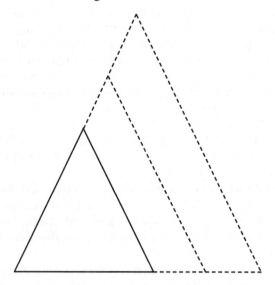

Critical Success Factor

A popular concept in leadership effectiveness is called "critical success factors." In every situation there are never more than six, and usually only three or four, critical factors that determine the difference between success and failure. What are the critical success factors in Christian education?

1. Effective Christian education ministries have *a leadership team with a vision.* Without vision and leadership, Christian education ministries tend to degenerate into nothing more than programs without significant purpose or impact. With vision and leadership, Christian education ministries are used by God to reach the lost and transform lives. Three other critical success factors flow out of leadership and vision.

2. Effective Christian education ministries are "enrollment driven." Unfortunately many Christian education ministries are attendance focused, concentrating their efforts on the attendance of those already enrolled. This usually results in plateaued or declining churches. If a church is focused on attendance, it tends to become maintenance oriented and to lose its focus on those outside the church. However, those who are outward focused tend to be enrollment oriented, to be growing, and to actually have increased effectiveness on those already attending. The infusion of new people brings about a dynamic that produces development for all.

An enrollment-driven approach also incorporates participants as well as leaders in reaching out to others. Every class or small group should have at least one empty chair to remind them that others need to be reached for Christ and spiritual maturity. A recommended enrollment policy would be to enroll the person in your ministry area who is attending for the first time and is not a member of another church. Also, enroll anytime, anywhere, anyone who is agreed.

3. Effective Christian education ministries are staffed for growth and ministry. Leadership should strive to have every class and/or group staffed with a ministry team of at least four leaders and workers. In the youth and adult areas this might include a teacher, an outreach coordinator, and two care leaders. In the children's area this might include two team teachers, a class follow-up coordinator and secretary, and a helper/follow-up worker. By using a leadership team of four or more, you ensure that every student is cared for and that the leadership team has energy to reach out to those presently not attending.

As part of staffing for growth it is imperative to provide ongoing training and development of leaders. This training may be weekly, monthly, or quarterly, but it does need to be ongoing. The familiar VHS approach to training includes three functions:

V—Vision Casting. This is a time to focus attention on the why of ministry. It includes motivation and inspiration by clarifying the vision. Leaders who are fulfilling the vision are affirmed. All are encouraged to reach out for new participants and to develop those already attending their classes and groups.

H—Huddle. This is the time for ministry coordination and pastoral care of leaders. The leaders constitute a ministry team. Plans and logistical needs are addressed. Time is provided for leaders to pray together and share their needs.

S—Skill Development. Every session should include training in one specific skill for leadership ministry. This is not the time to give a superficial overview, but a specific skill that can be implemented that week in ministry.

4. Effective Christian education ministries are organized for growth. The most effective way to develop a Christian education ministry is to establish new classes and groups. Steps include the following:

a. Define the age level and/or target group of people you want to reach.
b. Secure five to fifteen valid prospects for the new class.
c. Enlist and train four leaders for each class/group.
d. Provide the space for the group.
e. Extend invitations to the target group and begin.

Southern Baptist church growth expert Andy Anderson says, "We are not out of space, only traditional space." Effective Christian education leaders do not focus on the space they do not have, but on ways to create additional space: having multiple sessions, using adjacent buildings, using homes, having off-site classes, and having additional classes/groups at nontraditional times.

Theological Foundation

Ephesians 4:11–16 gives a biblical basis for Christian education and developing disciples.

It was he who gave some to be apostles, some to be prophets, some to be evangelists, and some to be pastors and teachers, to prepare God's people for works of service, so that the body of Christ may be built up until we all reach unity in the faith and in the knowledge of the Son of God and become mature, attaining to the whole measure of the fullness of Christ.

Then we will no longer be infants, tossed back and forth by the waves, and blown here and there by every wind of teaching and by the cunning and craftiness of men in their deceitful scheming. Instead, speaking the truth in love, we will in all things grow up into him who is the Head, that is, Christ. From him the whole body, joined and held together by every supporting ligament, grows and builds itself up in love, as each part does its work.

The church's educational ministry is done by God-called and gifted people who are given to the church (v. 11). A person is not in a ministry position by chance or accident. Nor should one be in a ministry position because he or she couldn't say no, or even only because of their natural abilities. The only reason for being in a ministry position is that the divine, sovereign, omnipotent God *called* and *placed* one in that position. "In fact God has arranged the parts in the body, every one of them, just as he wanted them to be" (1 Corinthians 12:18).

Not only does God place people in specific ministry positions, but He gives them specific gifts to perform those ministries. "We have different gifts, according to the grace given us" (Romans 12:6). First Corinthians 12:11 adds, "All these [gifts] are the work of one and the same Spirit, and he gives them to each one just as he determines." "Each one should use whatever gift he has received to serve others, faithfully administering God's grace in its various forms" (1 Peter 4:10). God not only placed and gifted these people, but he *gave* them to the church.

The purpose for gifting these people is to develop others for ministry. Ephesians 4:12 says, " to equip the saints for the work of ministry, for building up the body of Christ" (RSV). God called and gifted these people to prepare, or equip, Christians for *work.*

Notice that the measure of success is not a beautiful building or a sizable income, but people equipped for ministry. So why did God call and gift these people? To train Christians for ministry! God calls a person to leadership and gives gifts for equipping others.

The objective of Christian education is that people will become Christlike. Ephesians 4:13 speaks of "attaining to the whole measure of the fullness of Christ." The NASB has "a mature man." Unless people are becoming more like Christ, our work is in vain. This maturity in Christ is demonstrated by "unity in the faith" and "knowledge of the Son of God." How do we demonstrate Christlikeness? A mature Christian should be able to combine "truth" and "love." "Speaking the truth in love, we will in all things grow up into him who is the Head, that is, Christ" (Ephesians 4:15). Truth without love destroys. Love without truth deceives.

> ## Success is people equipped for ministry.

We are not in the baby-sitting business. We are not in the entertainment business. We are not just trying to run a program because other churches have it. No! We will gladly do those things, but the purpose is that people become like Christ. Education and training are never the end, but Christlikeness is!

The ministry of Christian education is highly theological. "We will no longer be infants, tossed back and forth by the waves, and blown here and there by every wind of teaching and by the cunning and craftiness of men in their deceitful scheming" (Ephesians 4:14).

People who are mature in Christ should be able to discern truth and detect and avoid error. We are to equip people to become grown up, "no longer infants." The ministry of Christian education cannot and should not be divorced from theology. "Be diligent in these matters; give yourself wholly to them, so that everyone may see your progress. Watch your life and doctrine closely. Persevere in them, because if you do, you will save both yourself and your hearers" (1 Timothy 4:15–16).

> **"Maturity means discerning truth and avoiding error."**

The ministry of Christian education should strengthen the church. "From him [Christ] the whole body [church], joined and held together by every supporting ligament, grows and builds itself up in love, as each part does its work" (Ephesians 4:16). "To each one the manifestation of the Spirit is given for the common good" (1 Corinthians 12:7).

Teachers are to be trained. "The things you [Timothy] have heard me [Paul] say in the presence of many witnesses entrust to reliable men who will also be qualified to teach others" (2 Timothy 2:2). How is a person qualified to teach? One way is by adequate training. Paul tells us to develop our gifts. "Do your best to present yourself to God as one approved, a workman who does not need to be ashamed and who correctly handles the word of truth" (2 Timothy 2:15). We develop our abilities through training.

Teachers carry great responsibility. James 3:1 notes, "Not many of you should presume to be teachers, my brothers, because you know that we who teach will be judged more strictly." Jesus told this parable, "'Can a blind man lead a blind man? Will they not both fall into a pit? A student is not above his teacher, but everyone who is fully trained will be like his teacher'" (Luke 6:39–40).

Parents have a teaching responsibility. The Christian education ministries of the church do not replace the teaching responsibilities of the parents (Deuteronomy 6:4–9). Rather, training parents to perform their teaching role is part of the Christian education ministry.

Pastors are to teach. We read "The overseer must be above reproach, the husband of but one wife, temperate, self-controlled, respectable, hospitable, able to teach" (1 Timothy 3:2). "The Lord's servant must not quarrel; instead, he must be kind to everyone, able to teach, not resentful" (2 Timothy 2:24).

Not all are gifted teachers, but all have teaching responsibility. "Let the word of Christ dwell in you richly as you teach and admonish one another with all wisdom" (Colossians 3:16). "By this time you ought to be teachers, you need someone to teach you the elementary truths of God's Word all over again" (Hebrews 5:12).

These insights from Scripture are not often grasped. Though not all

Christians are gifted teachers, all Christians have a teaching responsibility. These verses were not written to a select group of teachers, but to the entire body of Christ. All believers have a teaching ministry and responsibility. Being a spectator in the kingdom of God is a sign of immaturity. We must help all believers become contributors to the development of others.

* * * * *

Christian education is a vital aspect of the growing, effective church that is impacting its community. Each church must make it more than a program. It must be an integral part of reaching and developing people.

Children's Ministries

Dick Gruber

Recently in our kindergarten Sunday school class the question was posed, "What does your mom or dad do for a job?" Responses varied, as they will in a class of twenty-two five-year-old children. Some talked about offices, others homemaking, and yet others the shop or store. One boy even announced his parents never worked.

The teacher guided the discussion to the job of pastors. She asked, "What does Pastor Gruber do?" Lydia, a wild-eyed, talkative child quickly answered, "His job is to make people laugh!"

It's true; I do make people laugh, but my job title is children's pastor. I have served as a pastor and teacher to boys and girls on a volunteer and paid basis since 1975. Whether serious or on the lighter side, my desire is that each child would meet God and in meeting Him become a changed person.

Through the course of this chapter I will introduce you to children's ministries. As I do this, you will begin to comprehend the possibility in your church, large or small, for developing a quality ministry to the saints twelve years old and younger.

From a Bible viewpoint, ministry to children is as natural and common as breathing is to life. In Genesis, God says this about Abraham, "I have chosen him, so that he will direct his children and his household after him to keep the way of the Lord by doing what is right and just, so that the Lord will bring about for Abraham what he has promised him" (Genesis 18:19). This verse could have been penned for any pastor in any size church anywhere. There is a pattern established here that is repeated over and over throughout Scripture, a pattern that transcends time and works in our churches today.

The Call of the Children's Worker

God chooses leaders. Those leaders direct children to keep the way of the Lord. That direction is both verbal and active, as the leader does what is right and just. God has chosen each pastor and every church to establish credible outreach and training for children. You are chosen, as a pastor, to shepherd an ever-growing flock. The future of this flock is dependent on your good preaching and people skills. It is also imperative that young families discover and participate in viable ministries for their children.

You are chosen! Children look to you. They respect and admire their pastor. This is an inescapable honor. Abraham was to "direct his children . . . to keep the way of the Lord by doing what is right and just" (Genesis 18:19). Children's ministries begin with the integrity of the pastor. Your life in and out of the church is a testimony to every child who sees or meets you.

Your genuine concern and love for children serves as a foundation for building children's ministries in your church. Children's ministries begin with the heartbeat of the pastor. It spreads as the members of your congregation hear and see your dedication to the little ones. Like Jesus, you touch and bless the children. Like Jesus, you place importance on them from the pulpit, in the church, and in the community.

I serve with a senior pastor who lives this concept. He gives pulpit time to children's ministries on a regular basis. It is not unusual to witness him hugging and teasing children in the hallways of our church. Parents stand waiting while he places importance on their child. From time to time, I even catch my senior pastor calming babies in our nursery. His love for children is contagious. He is doing what is right and just.

Though children's ministries begin with you, continuation depends on a growing number of committed laypeople who have captured your vision. In Ephesians, Paul writes, "It was he who gave some to be apostles, some to be prophets, some to be evangelists, and some to be pastors and teachers, to prepare God's people for works of service, so that the body of Christ may be built up" (Ephesians 4:11–12).

> **Children's ministries begin with your integrity.**

Pastors prepare the saints. This inspirational, instructional, incredible task grows with every new boy or girl who enters your church. In the large church a pastor can hand off the direct development of children's ministries to a paid staff member. That staff member fulfills the role of preparing the saints, or laypeople, to minister to the children. In that setting the pastor may not directly involve himself in preparing individuals for children's ministries, but his pulpit ministry and lifestyle provide significance for children's ministry in the eyes of the people. In a way he is preparing every member of the congregation for the possibility of ministering to children.

Most pastors find themselves in a small- to medium-size church and do not have the numbers or resources to provide for a children's pastor or ministry director. In these cases trusted volunteers take on a pastoral role in organizing and preparing teachers and leaders for this vital ministry.

I began in children's ministries under the direction of the pastor's wife. Our church had a youth pastor but could not yet afford a children's coordinator or pastor. The pastor's wife oversaw the development of children's ministries. She met with us volunteer teachers and leaders on a regular basis for prayer, inspiration, and training. The children's ministry ran smoothly and was very effective. It was obvious to all volunteers that the pastor had a vested interest in this ministry.

A year later I moved three states away and began to serve in a home missions work. My wife and I co-directed the children's church and provided midweek and outreach ministries to children as volunteers under the direct oversight of our pastor. We met with the pastor two or three times a month for guidance in the development of this ministry. Our role as volunteer ministry leaders continued for two and a half years. In this setting, a church of sixty to eighty people, we had kids four through twelve years old in one children's church service. Attendance averaged thirteen or fourteen children. On Wednesday nights, I ministered to those seven through twelve, and my wife ministered to those six and younger.

> **The difference between this work and the other two was in children's ministries.**

Sunday school is important for children and adults even in the smaller church. Our pastor understood this, and from the beginning of this church there were two or three Sunday school classes for the children. Sunday school teachers answered directly to the pastor and his wife. In that small church, children had the opportunity to worship with their peers in children's church, study doctrine systematically in Sunday school, enjoy club ministries midweek, and invite friends to regular outreach services.

Speaking for two weeks in a family camp in one of our western states, I had opportunity to fellowship with several pastors. In the course of these fellowship times I discovered that three of the pastors were involved in churches that had been in existence for two years or less. Two of the works were struggling. The churches began with fewer than fifty people and had stayed right at that mark. The pastors of these churches had secular employment to support their ministries.

The third church was self-supporting, growing spiritually and numerically, and the pastor was able to give himself fully to the ministry. The difference between this and the other two churches was in their children's ministries. The pastor of the third church began Sunday school for children the day his church opened the doors. They began with one children's class, broke into preschool and elementary classes within their second month, and by the time the church was six months old had two preschool classes, three elementary classes, and a children's church. Midweek club ministries took the same priority.

Certainly the experience of three churches does not constitute a scientific survey proving the effect of children's ministries in church planting. I can't help but think, though, that a church will be blessed proportionally to the importance it places on God's little ones. Jesus said, """I tell you the truth, whatever you did for one of the least of these brothers of mine, you did for me""" (Matthew 25:40). Mark recorded this concerning Jesus' priority of ministry to boys and girls: "'Whoever welcomes one of these little children in my name welcomes me; and whoever welcomes me does not welcome me but the one who sent me'" (Mark 9:37).

Most of what I have learned about ministry to children has been caught rather than taught as I have observed my senior pastor, Rev. Jerry Strandquist. He modeled the three Ts of successful ministry: trust, train, and treat.

Trust

Trust is one of those words that doesn't always find a place in the pastor's guide to greater ministry. The pastor or layleader must trust laity with works of ministry. There is no other way to grow a children's ministry (or a church for that matter). You must trust people to minister effectively to others.

When I served in a smaller church, the circle of trust included my wife and two or three other couples. This handful of committed leaders were a blessing to the fifteen or twenty children in attendance each week. Now that I am in a larger assembly, I trust my eleven ministry coordinators and, at this moment, 156 lay volunteers serving under them. These men and women are exceptional leaders. The children of my church are growing in faith and experience.

It is also important to trust children with ministry. Children are part of the family of God *now*. They must be trusted with ministry while they are young so that when they are old, they will not depart from it. The children of your church will be the Sunday school teachers and children's leaders of your church ten and twenty years from now.

Train

It is fairly easy to trust someone in ministry for one or two weeks. They may even stay longer based on your faith and trust in them. But unless you *train* them, your teachers perish. Teachers need to constantly sharpen their skills so that the boys and girls receive the best possible ministry every time they come to the church.

Training takes a variety of forms. Modeling is my favorite. I prefer to step into the classroom setting and demonstrate with actual students the concepts and methodology I wish to see emulated by my staff. There is a place in every church for regularly scheduled staff meetings, which include vision casting, troubleshooting, and training.

Training can occur on an individual level as well. I stepped into a midweek club meeting ten minutes before starting time. The teacher was standing in a corner reading over his materials one last time. Seven or eight boys were present and in the process of making their own fun.

I asked if I could lead the boys in a presession activity. The teacher looked at me with a questioning stare and said, "No, they are not all here yet." I talked to him and with his permission led the boys in a Scripture game until the official class starting time. Discipline was restored as the boys enjoyed a presession game. The rest of the evening went well for the teacher and his group, which had grown to seventeen boys. This man had a desire to teach, but simply lacked training. I am working to train him, and his class is going to be fantastic in weeks to come.

And do not forget to train the children. It is not enough that we train them in basic doctrine and Bible facts. They need to be active in ministry. With proper training they can succeed in their early ministry opportunities, gaining confidence for later opportunities as they mature.

Treat

Treat is the final *T* of successful children's ministries. Proverbs 16:21 says, "The wise in heart shall be called prudent: and the sweetness of the lips increaseth learning" (KJV). Every worker wants to be complimented by an overseer, ministry coordinator, or pastor. Treat the saints with respect. Treat the saints as you would want to be treated. Listen to their complaints and ideas. Pray with them as opportunities arise. Send them birthday cards and appreciation notes.

Just about every book I've read on the subject of caring for volunteers discusses the concept of befriending your workers. It is hard to quit on a friend. Treat these friends the way you would treat Jesus if he was a teacher of twos in your church. The return on befriending children's workers has been massive in my experience. I cannot outserve these people. If I treat them to ice cream, they treat me to dinner. Trust them to serve. Train them in service. Treat them as a servant treats his master.

I began this chapter with a promise. I have introduced you to quality children's ministries. You have probably guessed by now that a big part of a quality program is maintaining those who serve the children. But one more thing. A children's ministry that plans to be better than mediocre must recognize the value of a child. This ministry must bless all the children, helping each one grow the fruit of the Spirit in their lives. Quality children's ministries will incorporate education and involvement for the parents of the children. It will give children basic doctrinal training, experience in Christian living, and ministry opportunities. Finally and most important, a quality children's ministry in any size church will be built on a solid foundation of prayer.

Pastor, your church can provide quality children's ministries to your community. You may have noticed that I did not mention facilities, equipment, or craft materials. Ministry to boys and girls is certainly enhanced by the quality of such aids, but relationships built between the child and Christlike teachers are the main ingredient of successful children's ministries.

Equipping Lay Volunteers for Service

John M. Palmer

Xvxn though thxrx arx forty-six kxys that makx up the ball on our nxw typxwritxr, whxn onx of thx lxttxrs isn't thxrx, it is quitx noticxablx. Just onx kxy missing rxally makxs thx diffxrxncx. Xvxn though thxrx arx a lot of pxoplx who attxnd our church, things arxn't quitx thx samx without you. Pxrhaps you say to yoursxlf, "Wxll, I'm only onx pxrson, I don't makx or brxak a program, and I'm rxally not nxxdxd. Thxy can cxrtainly gxt along without mx." But that's not thx casx. You arx nxxdxd. If our church is going to bx xffxctivx in xvangxlism, xncouragxmxnt, and disciplxship, we nxxd the activx partic-ipation and involxmxnt of xvxry bxlixvxr. Thx nxxt timx you fxxl you'rx not nxxdxd or nxcxssary in the body of Christ, rxmxmbxr this littlx arti-clx and rxmind yoursxlf, "I am a kxy pxrson in Jxsus' kingdom and all my xfforts and xnxrgixs arx nxxdxd." *Wx do nxxd xach othxr!*

We really do need each other! As the old farmer observed, "If you see a turtle on top of a fence post, you know he had some help getting there." We need each other. We pastors need our congregations, and our congre-gations need us. For us to effectively fulfill Christ's command to "Go and make disciples of all nations" (Matthew 28:19), we must work together.

God's Word gives us the perfect plan for pastors and congregations to work together. Paul outlined it in Ephesians 4:11–16, when he wrote:

> It was he who gave some to be apostles, some to be prophets, some to be evangelists, and some to be pastors and teachers, to prepare God's people for works of service, so that the body of Christ may be built up until we all reach unity in the faith and in the knowledge of the Son of God and become mature, attaining to the whole measure of the fullness of Christ.

> Then we will no longer be infants, tossed back and forth by the waves, and blown here and there by every wind of teaching and by the cunning and craftiness of men in their deceitful scheming. Instead, speaking the truth in love, we will in all things grow up into him who is the Head, that is, Christ.

From him the whole body, joined and held together by every supporting ligament, grows and builds itself up in love, as each part does its work.

"Each part does its work"—that's the key. Our churches will grow and be built up in love as we share the ministry together. It is God's intent that every believer minister. In fact, Paul teaches that the saints are to do "the work of the ministry" (Ephesians 4:12, KJV). We pastors are to "prepare God's people for works of service." So what does that mean? And how do we do that?

Enlist Volunteers

First, we need to *enlist* the lay volunteers! The greatest resources in our churches are the followers of Christ who attend our worship services week after week. But how do we get them from the pew into ministry? How do we discover and recruit them?

A POSITIVE ATTITUDE

To enlist lay volunteers, we need a positive mindset, *a positive attitude.* We must have a positive attitude about our parishioners. Most of the people in our churches want to serve the Lord; they have a heart to please God. A big reason that many of them are not ministering as they should, or would like to, is because we pastors have not inspired them to minister or shown them how to minister. Too often, when tired, frustrated, and discouraged, we pastors communicate to our people, either verbally or nonverbally, that we are disappointed in them. We sometimes even tell them that they are lazy and lack spiritual commitment. We certainly must acknowledge that some in our congregation are not as committed as they could be. And from time to time, as the Spirit leads, gentle and loving rebukes are in order. But reinforcing the negative qualities of our flock only exacerbates and intensifies the problem. It doesn't help solve it. Our people need to know that we believe in them, that we love them—no matter what they do or do not do. Our parishioners, anointed by the Holy Spirit, are our greatest resource! We need to remind them often of who they are in Christ and of what they can do for Him. We must have a positive attitude toward them. I make it a point to tell my congregation every single week that I love them. Our people respond to love.

We need also to have a positive attitude about the process of enlisting lay volunteers to minister. If we view the enlisting process as being burdensome, time consuming, or a necessary evil, we will not be effective in enlisting lay volunteers. On the other hand we ought to see the process as being an exciting opportunity. After all, we are being used by God to assist others in ministering for Him. What a privilege is ours!

As I write this chapter we are just a few weeks away from starting a Saturday evening worship service. We are beginning this service specifically to reach people whose work schedule does not permit them to attend our Sunday morning worship service. We are very excited about the prospect of reaching up to a thousand more people each week through this service.

It just so happens that we are at an in-between time with respect to children's pastors. Our new children's pastor and his family arrive the very week of our first Saturday evening service. So I have happily assumed the responsibility of enlisting men and women to minister to our babies and small children during this service. I am thoroughly enjoying the process, as I meet new people and share the ministry opportunities one-on-one with them. And knowing that I am helping them to find a place of meaningful service to the Lord is all the motivation and incentive I need. Other than spending time in prayer and the Word, very little I do is as rewarding as enlisting volunteers to minister.

> **" Very little I do is as rewarding as signing volunteers. "**

So I encourage you: Do not view the process of enlisting lay volunteers for ministry as a burden. See it as a privilege. And pursue the task with energy, enthusiasm, and excitement. In the final analysis, it is your own attitude that will make you or break you.

Henry J. Kaiser was a U.S. industrialist who founded more than one hundred companies, including Kaiser Aluminum and Kaiser Steel. From 1913 to 1930 he built dams, levees, highways, and bridges throughout the United States and Cuba. His positive attitude, enthusiasm, and can-do spirit were huge factors in his entrepreneurial success. The story is told of the time he was building a levee along a riverbank. A heavy rainstorm caused a flood, which, in turn, buried all of his earth-moving machinery and destroyed the work they had already done. After the water receded, he went out to observe the damage and found his workers glum and discouraged, looking at the mud and the buried machinery. With a smile he asked them, "Why are you so down?" "Don't you see what has happened?" they asked. "Your machinery is covered with mud."

"What mud?" he asked with a twinkle and a smile. "What mud!" they repeated in astonishment. "Look around you. It is a sea of mud." Laughing he continued, "I don't see any mud." "But how can you say that?" they asked him. "Mud is everywhere."

Mr. Kaiser, a man with an indomitable spirit and a positive attitude, then offered his perspective, "I am looking at a clear blue sky, and there is no mud up there. There is only sunshine. And I never saw any mud that could stand against sunshine. Soon it will be dried up, and we will be able to clean all our machinery and begin the project all over again."

We choose. We can see the process of enlisting volunteers as either a duty or a delight. We see either mud or sunshine. It is up to us. Our attitude makes the difference. It is true: Our attitude, much more than our aptitude, determines our altitude.

PURE MOTIVES

In addition to having a positive mindset, it is vital that we have *pure motives* as we enlist volunteers. What are our motives for enlisting volunteers to minister? What is driving us? Are we looking for people to serve just so we don't have to do the work? Are we recruiting people to minister so we can get all the slots filled? Are we enlisting volunteers for ministry because it is our job to do so? Are we recruiting so our church ministry will look better to the public? Are we simply trying to keep up with, or be better than, another church? If so, we will always struggle with this part of the ministry.

I am convinced that our motivation ought to be that we are helping individuals fulfill the call of God in their life. What has been motivating me as I have recently been enlisting volunteers for our Saturday evening service is this: I want believers to experience the joy of serving Jesus. I want them to have the opportunity of developing their God-given gifts. I want them to serve God faithfully so that some day they can hear the words "Well done, thou good and faithful servant" (Matthew 25:21, KJV).

When I asked several attendees who were not actively serving in our church to pray about helping to launch our Saturday evening service by ministering to our babies and children, my motive was to see them have an opportunity to grow through service. I want them to experience the same kind of joy I do as I minister week after week. And I have discovered that when people sense that we have their interests in mind, they are more likely to be open to the Lord's direction.

A PROVEN METHOD

In addition to a positive mindset and pure motives, we need *a proven method* of enlisting volunteers to minister. The proven method is simply Spirit-led, one-on-one recruitment.

I am not an expert in very many things. I am certainly not an expert in preaching, teaching, praying, motivating, administrating, or leading. But I am an expert in this: I know every ineffective method of enlisting volunteers. I am an expert in ineffective recruiting because I have done it so much.

In the early days of my ministry, while planting a church in Athens, Ohio, I tried every way possible to get people to minister. I made enthusiastic announcements from the pulpit about the need for people to teach Sunday school and help clean the building. I passed sheets through the congregation during the worship services, asking people to sign up to work in the nursery for the following thirteen weeks. I even did a bit of scolding and pleading from the pulpit. Unfortunately, those efforts were most often counterproductive.

When a pastor uses the pulpit to plead and/or scold, he or she degrades the high purpose of the pulpit. God has called us to preach the Word, not to scold the saints. Furthermore, regular pleading and scolding concerning personal ministry puts barriers between the pastor and the people. And besides, the reason most people don't volunteer is because they don't know what is expected; they need information.

I am embarrassed to admit it, but I have even resorted to one-on-one arm-twisting. I will never forget the Sunday morning I stood at the church door as the folks were leaving the service. Most of the twenty people who had been in the church service that morning had gone. As one woman was leaving I asked if she would teach a children's Sunday school class. She hesitated, and I just knew she was going to say no. And, sure enough, after a few seconds of awkward silence, she declined. I felt rejected and was disappointed because I felt that if she did not take the class, we wouldn't have anyone else who would or could teach it.

I am even more embarrassed to tell you my reply. Looking her straight in the eyes, I said, "I really need help with this. Could you just do it for me?" As soon as I said those words, I heard these words in my spirit, *Do it for whom?* I was instantly and deeply convicted, asked her to forgive me, and promised the Lord that I would never again twist someone's arm to do a ministry, and certainly would never ask anyone again to "do it for me." This principle now guides me: "Whatever you do, whether in word or deed, do it all in the name of the Lord Jesus" (Colossians 3:17). I can, with confidence and enthusiasm, encourage someone to minister for the Lord, but I can never again ask them to minister for me. That was a hard but valuable lesson I learned as a young pastor.

> "I'd never again twist anyone's arm to do a ministry or ask anyone to 'do it for me.'"

There is not space in this chapter to share any more of my flawed ministry recruitment techniques. I do, however, want to share the proven method of Spirit-led, one-on-one recruitment. It is a proven method because it is biblically based.

This method of enlisting volunteers for ministry begins with *biblical preaching and teaching* from pertinent Bible texts, such as, Exodus 31:1–11; Mark 10:45; Romans 12:1–8; Ephesians 4:1–16; and 1 Peter 2:1–10 and 4:10–11. Some time ago I preached a seven-week series of messages from these passages. Four of those messages were

"You Don't Have to Sit on the Bench!"
"God's Team Has No Stars!"
"God Pays His Players Well!"
"Fellowship of Christian Addicts!"

When our parishioners hear the Word of God preached with the anointing of the Spirit of God, most of them will respond. We must teach our people that as saints they are called to be priests, servants, and ministers for the Lord. Their willingness and enthusiasm to serve will grow as they understand who they are in Christ. The Holy Spirit will lead our people to minister when the Word of God becomes alive in their hearts.

In addition to preaching and teaching from the pulpit, I have found that an "Equipping for Ministry" class is extremely profitable in motivating individuals to become involved in ministry. During this thirteen-week class the students are taught the why's and wherefore's of ministering for the Lord. Well over 70 percent of the individuals who have taken this class during the last fifteen years of my ministry are involved in active lay ministry.

Once the groundwork has been laid through preaching and teaching, the next step is personal recruitment. While asking for volunteers from the pulpit may be helpful once in a while, the best long-term strategy for enlisting volunteers is one-on-one contact. Scriptures teach this principle. Elijah personally enlisted Elisha. We read, "So Elijah went from there and found Elisha son of Shaphat. He was plowing with twelve yoke of oxen. . . . Elisha went up to him and threw his cloak around him" (1 Kings 19:19). We note that Elijah went looking for someone and found Elisha. Elijah gave him an invitation and Elisha accepted.

Jesus personally recruited His disciples. He said, "'Come, follow me, . . . and I will make you fishers of men'" (Matthew 4:19). Note that Christ gave them an invitation and an incentive. Likewise, Paul's helpers were handpicked. I have discovered that individuals who are personally recruited and who respond because they sense God is leading them to do so will stay with their ministry much longer than those who are recruited using other methods.

Here are the steps I take every time I begin the process of enlisting someone for ministry.

- Define the ministry task in writing.
- Prayerfully select someone you feel can do the ministry.
- Give them the ministry description, including a brief explanation of the ministry.
- Ask them to prayerfully consider the ministry. (I don't take an immediate yes or no.)
- Set up a time to meet again.
- Find out if the Lord is leading him or her to do this ministry.
- If the individual accepts, then begin the training to do the ministry.

During the early to mid-1600s, when Cromwell was helping to lead Great Britain, there was a severe shortage of silver. He sent men everywhere looking for silver. He even sent one man to the cathedral to find this precious metal. He returned to Cromwell with this message, "The only silver in the whole cathedral is the silver the statues of the saints are made of." Cromwell tersely replied, "Then let's melt down the saints and put them into circulation." And that is what God has called pastors to do. He has raised us up to "put the saints into circulation" by enlisting, equipping, and encouraging them to minister.

Equip Volunteers

Enlistment of lay volunteers is only the first step. Additionally, we need to *equip* them to minister; that is, we need to prepare and train them. An untrained ministry team is a sure ingredient for ineffectiveness and trouble. For years I have used a fivefold training process that I learned by studying how Jesus prepared and trained His disciples.

The first step of the process is *association*. That is, we spend time with the individuals who will be ministering. Jesus "appointed twelve—designating them apostles—that they might be with him" (Mark 3:14). By spending time together, these individuals can hear our heartbeat and catch our vision. Additionally, as we get to know these individuals, we will better know how to encourage and motivate them. As the church grows it is impractical and impossible for the senior pastor to have close association with all the lay ministers, but it is imperative that someone does, because effective ministry flows out of healthy relationships.

The second step of the process is *impartation*. This is the sharing of how-to's, information concerning the doing of the ministry. This is what Jesus did when He taught His disciples to pray. He told them, "'When you pray, do not be like the hypocrites. . . . But when you pray, go into your room, close the door and pray to your Father'" (Matthew 6:5–6). He was imparting important information to them about how to pray.

We must do the same thing with those who commit to ministry in our churches. Thankfully, several of those we spoke with accepted the opportunity to help minister to the children during our Saturday evening services. Now, they will be trained by two laypeople who are well-acquainted with ministering to small children. These two individuals, one of whom is my wife, will impart the how-to's of nursery ministry and preschool children's ministry to these excited volunteers. Occasion for feeling discouraged, embarrassed, or incompetent is greatly diminished as we impart information to these who are beginning to minister.

> **"Confidence grows when delegation is done properly."**

The third step of the training (equipping) process is *demonstration*. After Jesus imparted helpful information to the disciples about prayer, He then demonstrated prayer. "'This, then, is how you should pray: "Our Father in heaven, hallowed be your name, . . ."'" (Matthew 6:9). The disciples learned how to pray by watching and listening to their Lord pray.

My wife, Debbie, is helping to train a couple of volunteers how to minister to our preschoolers during the Saturday evening service. Although they are very eager to minister to the children, they have not done it before. So Debbie will be meeting with them and reviewing the lesson. Then on that first Saturday evening she will teach the class, and they will observe. As she demonstrates how to teach, they will learn a lot simply by observing what she does. When impartation and demonstration are effectively done, ministry can be effectively learned.

The fourth step in the equipping process is *delegation*. This very important step gives the learner the opportunity of doing it under the loving and watchful eye of an experienced minister. Debbie might say to the trainees, "Next week I'll let you tell the story, but I'll be here to help you if you need it." Confidence grows quickly when delegation is done properly.

The fifth step is *supervision*. This is the step in which the ministry trainer offers helpful and constructive suggestions for the individual to improve what he or she is doing. After Jesus had sent His disciples to the surrounding towns to preach the gospel of the Kingdom, they returned "with joy and said, 'Lord, even the demons submit to us in your name.'" Jesus gave them some corrective and constructive words when He reminded them not to "'rejoice that the spirits submit to you, but rejoice that your names are written in heaven'" (Luke 10:1–19).

Perhaps you heard about the man who severely cut his hand and went to the emergency room at the local hospital. In the waiting room he saw two doors, one said Men and the other said Women. He walked through the door marked Men, went down a hallway, and saw two more doors. One was marked Over 55 and the other Under 55. Since he was in his forties he went through the door marked Under 55.

Soon he saw two more doors. One said Over Belt and the other, Under Belt. He walked through the door that read Over Belt. Lo and behold, he saw two other doors, Internal and External. He figured his was an external injury so he went through that door. As he kept walking he came to two more doors. One was marked Major and the other, Minor. Compared to other peoples' problems, he evaluated his cut hand to be minor, so he went through that door.

After going through that door he found himself out in the parking lot, just a few feet from where he had parked his car. He got into his car and went home. His wife asked, "Did they help you?" He replied, "No, but they sure are well organized."

Our churches can be very organized, but if we do not train and equip people to do the ministries God has called them to, we will find them going in and out of ministry doors on a regular basis and never really being effective and fulfilled in any ministry. No matter the ministry, whether teaching, ushering, greeting, nursery attending, or hospital visitation, it pays to train and equip. A trained lay-ministry team glorifies God and blesses many.

Encourage Volunteers

Finally, not only do we need to *enlist* the lay volunteers and *equip* them to minister, but we also need to continue to *encourage* them as they minister. We can beat drums, we can beat rugs, we can beat our friends in tennis, and we can beat eggs—but we can't beat volunteers! We must encourage them.

There are lots of ways to encourage others. I seek to encourage others by expressing my appreciation to them. Regularly I write notes of appreciation to those who are ministering in our congregation. Having thirteen full-time associate/assistant pastors makes it challenging to spend lots of time with each of them individually to encourage them. But I regularly write notes of appreciation as well as leave messages on their voice mail.

While appreciation commends the person for what he or she has done, affirmation commends people for who they are. Affirmation builds self-esteem by reminding persons of the good we see in them. Affirmation strengthens the spirit like water and sunshine strengthen the flowers and cause them to grow.

A sad and discouraged homeless man was sitting across the street from an artist's studio. The artist painted his portrait, then went across the street and invited the man to view what he had painted. At first the man did not recognize himself, for the eyes of the man in the portrait were filled with hope, there was a smile on his face, and his countenance radiated warmth, love, and confidence. "Who is it?" he kept asking. The artist simply smiled and said nothing. After a few minutes recognition began to dawn. With some hesitation he asked, "Is it me? Can it be me?" The artist replied, "That is the man I see in you." To which the homeless and seemingly hopeless beggar replied, "If that's the man you see, then that's the man I'll be." The artist's affirmation planted the seed of hope in that previously hopeless man.

I also seek to encourage the lay volunteer by being faithful in my own ministry. My example speaks silently, but loudly, to those who observe me week after week. As they see me love others and minister through the power of the Spirit, it encourages them to do the same. Too often we underestimate the power of encouragement through example.

> **Dempsey had no idea his field goal would encourage a 7-year-old boy 1000 miles away.**

A number of years ago, on November 8, 1970, Tom Dempsey kicked his way into football history with a 63-yard field goal, to help his New Orleans Saints defeat the Detroit Lions, 19–17. Mr. Dempsey was not your average kicker, because he had no fingers or toes. A specially made boot allowed him to kick the football. On that day, as he kicked the longest field goal in National Football League history, multiplied thousands watching in the stadium and on television cheered as they saw his feat.

One boy, many miles away, was especially moved. Seven-year-old Jeff Johnson watched Dempsey's kick while lying in the Kansas University Medical Center. Just three months before, a farm accident had resulted in his losing one-half of his right foot. The doctor had told his parents that he would not be able to play some sports, especially football. But that day young Jeff was encouraged, inspired by what he saw. He made up his mind then that he would someday kick field goals. Shortly after he left the hospital he began to run, then kick a football.

I spoke with Jeff shortly after his junior year at the University of Kansas. He was the first-string placekicker on the football team and during the just-concluded season had kicked several field goals over fifty yards. He told me, "When Mr. Dempsey kicked that long field goal, without any toes on his feet, I was inspired to do things I wouldn't have done otherwise."

Tom Dempsey had no idea that his immortal field goal would inspire and encourage a hurting seven-year-old boy a thousand miles away. He was just doing his job. And a boy was watching. As we faithfully, and to the best of our ability, do our ministry, we encourage and inspire others to do the same. Such is the power of encouragement through example.

The story is told of the time when Arnold Palmer met a blind golfer. Palmer was not only amazed that the man could play, but that he was so good. "What's your secret?" Palmer asked. The blind man explained, "I have my caddie stand at the hole and ring a bell. I just aim at the noise." Then he challenged Palmer to a match. The great pro, not wanting to humiliate the blind golfer, declined. But when the man said he'd play him for ten thousand dollars, Palmer changed his mind, and asked, "When do we tee off?" The blind golfer quickly replied, "Tonight at 10:30." There is no limit to what we can do for God when we have someone ringing the bell for us. And when we encourage others in their ministry, we are essentially ringing the bell for them.

We need more of our congregation to become involved in ministry. The task is formidable. Time is slipping away. Jesus is coming soon. We must evangelize and disciple our world. Thousands in our towns and cities are drowning in the sea of sin. We have to reach them, and we can't reach them alone. We can only do it as we, the pastors and our people, minister together.

Throughout the quiet streets of a fishing village that lay at the mouth of a turbulent river, a cry rang out: "Boy overboard!" Quickly a crowd gathered and anxious eyes looked out over the rushing water to the figure of the drowning boy.

A rope was brought, and the strongest swimmer in the village volunteered to rescue the lad. Tying one end of the rope around his waist, he threw the other end to the crowd and plunged into the river. Anxiously the crowd watched him breast the tide with strong, sure strokes. A cheer went up when he reached the boy and grasped him safely in his powerful arms. "Pull in the rope!" he shouted over the swirling waters. The villagers looked from one to another. "Who is holding the rope?" they asked.

No one was holding the rope. In the excitement of watching the rescue, the crowd had let the end of the rope slip into the water. Powerless to help, they watched as two people drowned because no one had made it his business to hold the rope.*

We have to hold the rope for each other! We really do need each other! God has called pastors to prepare the saints to minister. As we enlist the saints, equip them, and encourage them, our congregations will be built up so we can effectively reach our communities with the gospel of Jesus Christ.

*Taken from "Who Is Holding the Rope?" in *Decision* magazine July/August 1993, ©1993 Billy Graham Evangelistic Association, used by permission, all rights reserved.

Unit 5

Ministry to the Body

Introduction:
Priority of Ministry to the Body

Everett Stenhouse

We have all observed that many of the so-called great people of the world are, in fact, slaves, mastered by the intense race toward excellence to escape what they view as mediocrity.

Let it be said without any fear of scriptural contradiction that the truly great people in the Lord's church are those bond servants mastered by spiritual desire to help people in their struggle toward sainthood. In that high calling, greatness can indeed be found. Meaningful ministry to the body will always be a priority for the pastor with the shepherd's heart. That has always been and remains the heart of ministry.

A Divinely Commissioned Ministry

The apostle Paul esteemed his call from God as a mandate to minister to the body of Christ. He declared, "I have become its [the Church's] servant by the commission God gave to me to present to you the word of God in its fullness" (Colossians 1:25). The body can be appropriately served by the minister only as both congregation and minister give recognition to the divine commission of leadership in the Lord's church.

When the apostle Paul wrote that the Lord "gave . . . some to be pastors," he followed immediately with the reason for giving pastors-teachers: "to prepare God's people for works of service, so that the body of Christ may be built up" (Ephesians 4:11–12).

That focus must be kept clear. Pastors are God's gifts to the Church. When God gives a gift it must be assumed that the gift is of great value to the receiver. If pastors are to be of maximum value to the Church, they must direct their energies to priority ministry to the body of Christ, His church. The apostle's stated reason must be the fundamental theme underlying the pastor-teacher's well-rounded ministry to the body. This must be done despite the distracting voices inside and outside the church.

When Jesus asked Simon Peter three times about his love and devotion, Peter was crushed by the repetitiveness of the question and answered, "Lord, you know all things; you know that I love you." Jesus responded,

"Feed my sheep" (John 21:17). The Lord's response was directly related to the ministry of those who were and would be His church. A shepherd's first obligation and responsibility is to care for the feeding of the flock.

A Ministry in Servanthood

Ephesians 4:11 is the only New Testament passage where *poimen* is translated "pastor." In all other occurrences the word is rendered "shepherd." The shepherd has always been a servant to the flock. The flock gets the undivided and affectionate attention of a good shepherd.

While pastor-shepherds are servants, they are not to be considered, or to consider themselves, below the congregation. To be able to minister to the body one need not be all-wise, of superior knowledge, and able to give answers to all questions. Shepherds appointed of God will focus their best energies upon loving, caring for, and feeding the flock.

There may well be people in the congregation who are better educated than the pastor. There may be those who are vastly richer than the pastor. There may be those who live a lifestyle far different from that of the pastor. Nevertheless, times will come when any and all such people crave to be nourished by the compassion of the pastor's heart. Never, for any reason, should the value of a pastor-shepherd's ministry to the body be discounted.

Pastor-shepherds will not position themselves, nor will they allow others to position them, above the congregation. Pastors placed above the congregation do themselves, as well as the body, a distinct disservice. The ivory tower syndrome has destroyed pastors. When pastors distance themselves from the congregation, they cut themselves off from one of the principal sources of ministerial strength. Pastors are real as pastors only as they are real as people and real with people.

Nothing compares to the privilege of being received into a family circle and sharing lives and challenges of family members. The apex of ministerial respect is seen in families who make major decisions relating to their spiritual well-being only after first determining the heartbeat of their pastor about such important matters.

Pastors are to be pitied when their lack of respect for their flock allows them to become manipulators of people for some personal or ulterior purpose. Such a pastor is not to be envied.

If we will envy let us envy the pastor who throughout a half century of ministry chose not to walk onto the platform from a side door with the sound of trumpets, but was often seen long before service time sitting in the pew with an arm around a devoted parishioner, talking, praying, pastoring. That is to be envied. That defines the wonder of ministry to the body for the pastor-shepherd.

A Ministry in Discipleship

Two of the primary responsibilities of a pastor-shepherd are, first, to be a disciple and, then, to make disciples. The apostle Paul's admonition to the pastor-shepherd leadership of the church at Ephesus was "to prepare God's people for works of service, so that the body of Christ may be built up" (Ephesians 4:12). That statement from Holy Writ embodies the divine concept of discipleship. Discipleship began early in the Old Testament with this formula: "These commandments . . . are to be upon your hearts. Impress them on your children. Talk about them when you sit at home and when you walk along the road, when you lie down and when you get up" (Deuteronomy 6:6–7).

Under the new covenant our Lord said, "Go and make disciples of all nations, baptizing them in the name of the Father and of the Son and of the Holy Spirit, and teaching them to obey everything I have commanded you" (Matthew 28:19–20). "Make disciples" is central to the command. The participles *baptizing* and *teaching* are helping verbs. Whatever the pastor-shepherd does in the exercising of his gifts, whether it be teaching, baptizing, counseling, administrating, or any other pursuit in the performance of ministry, the ultimate goal must be "to prepare God's people for works of service, so that the body of Christ may be built up."

Our Lord's discourse on the seriousness of discipleship (recorded in Luke 14) makes it crystal clear that anyone wishing to follow Him must make everything else in life second to Him. Otherwise, He states emphatically, "'He cannot be my disciple'" (Luke 14:26).

Pastor-shepherds must, without equivocation, embrace the Master's demands for discipleship and be willing to adopt them as a high priority for themselves and for ministry to the body. Be reminded of the apostle Paul's words to the Colossians: "I have become its [the Church's] servant by the commission God gave me to present to you the Word of God in its fullness. . . . We proclaim Him, admonishing and teaching everyone with all wisdom, so that we may present everyone perfect in Christ" (Colossians 1:25,28).

A Personal Note

I first became a pastor when I followed my father in a pastorate in Southern California. We moved into the church parsonage, which had been emptied of all furniture and the personal belongings of my parents. The only thing left in the vacant house was a single plaque hanging on the barren wall: Impossibilities Become Challenges. It whispered to my young zealous heart. Little did I know as a new youthful pastor the significance of that brief message as it related to the pastoral ministry.

Yes, ministry to the body can break a pastor's heart; it can drain strength; it can turn hair gray. But it is the highest honor that can be bestowed upon any person by the Lord of the Church. That divine franchise is, indeed, a distinct privilege.

Relationships to Other Denominations

Don Argue

This is a *kairos* moment for the church of Jesus Christ: a time of crisis or opportunity. At the close of the twentieth century, the church exists in a world tortured by polarization, selfishness, indifference, and godlessness. Furthermore, the church in America, despite its significant influence and ministry, has been so infected by such sins that its witness and ministry for Christ is far less than it could or should be. In the face of this spiritual crisis, however, across denominational lines and throughout evangelical groups (from our vantage point with the NAE), we see a surging desire for revival and a transformation of the priorities and values of the Christian community.

It could well be that the body of Christ is ready now to allow the pastoral prayer of the Son of God in John 17:20–23 to renew itself dramatically in our lives. "'My prayer is not for them alone. I pray also for those who will believe in me through their message, that all of them may be one, Father, just as you are in me and I am in you. May they also be in us so that the world may believe that you have sent me. I have given them the glory that you gave me, that they may be one as we are one: I in them and you in me. May they be brought to complete unity to let the world know that you sent me and have loved them even as you have loved me.'"

The church of Jesus Christ is receiving a wake-up call to work together across denominational lines in a spirit of unity. Through this call to action we desire to glorify God, to strengthen our witness to those who do not know Jesus Christ as Lord and Savior, and to expand and improve our ministry to the world.

Today's Call for Action

CALL FOR PRAYER

"'Have faith in God,'" Jesus told the disciples. "'I tell you the truth, if anyone says to this mountain, "Go, throw yourself into the sea," and does not doubt in his heart but believes that what he says will happen, it will be done for him. Therefore I tell you, whatever you ask for in prayer, believe that you have received it, and it will be yours. And when you stand praying, if you hold anything against anyone, forgive him, so that your Father in heaven may forgive you your sins'" (Mark 11:22–25).

Christians are called on to pray: for unity and for the spread of the gospel. Prayer involves worshiping and praising God, calling on Him, confessing our sin and need for His grace, seeking His wisdom and counsel, interceding for others, and offering ourselves to Him and to His service.

We encourage pastors to become involved in local, regional, and national prayer endeavors. To reach our communities with the saving gospel of Jesus Christ, it is becoming more apparent that cooperative efforts among the churches are needed. Prayer agreement is the prelude to effective ministry. Today the Holy Spirit is bringing together prayer networks and prayer ministries throughout the United States. In many local communities pastors are meeting for prayer one day a month. The results have been felt in their communities.

CALL FOR REPENTANCE AND REFORM

"'If my people, who are called by my name, will humble themselves and pray and seek my face and turn from their wicked ways, then will I hear from heaven and will forgive their sin and will heal their land'" (2 Chronicles 7:14).

As Christians we should humbly and publicly follow the guidelines of 2 Chronicles 7:14 and confess that . . .

- Although we have been conscientious in our response to the mandate of the Great Commission to go and make disciples (Matthew 28:18–20; Mark 16:15), we have too often failed to live out and actualize the mandate of a loving unity that testifies to our Lord Jesus (John 13:34–35 and 17:21–22).
- Although we value unity and united Christian action, we too often do more to build our own ministries than to cooperate at winning the lost in our own neighborhoods.
- In our pursuit of faithfulness, we have too often accommodated the spirit of this world, which elevates a political correctness over the more difficult task of critical reflection and repentance.
- Although we have assented to Christian truths as embodied in our Assemblies of God Statement of Faith, we have on many occasions been unwilling to be confronted redemptively with the implications of biblical truth concerning life and faith.

We call the church to repentance, to the pursuit of revival and renewal through prayer and fasting, and to faithful obedience to God in every aspect of our lives as commanded in Scripture. We are also called to pursue the fruit of the Spirit manifested in reconciliation—to God and to each other.

CALL FOR UNITY AND COOPERATION

Jesus instructs us, "'A new command I give you: Love one another. As I have loved you, so you must love one another. By this all men will know that you are my disciples, if you love one another'" (John 13:34–35).

We call on Bible-believing churches in a community to work together diligently as a reflection of our common commitment to Jesus Christ as Lord and Savior. Furthermore, as long as truth is not compromised, believers, in a demonstration of love, can work alongside others who may not necessarily have a Pentecostal identity on specific issues. Pastors should take the lead in facilitating and supporting united evangelical endeavors that uphold the authority of the Bible, have a heart for evangelism, and desire unity based on biblical truth.

Local and Regional Action

Jesus said, "'You will receive power when the Holy Spirit comes on you; and you will be my witnesses in Jerusalem, and in all Judea and Samaria'" (Acts 1:8).

The ministry of the Church is essentially local. Therefore, we encourage pastors at local and regional levels to plan and carry out strategic cooperation in prayer, evangelism, and discipleship in order to win and keep the lost. We encourage leaders in the local church to demonstrate godly, reconciling love as in unity God's Word is proclaimed.

Pastors should use a leadership strategy that includes the following five principles for achieving cooperation without compromise:

- Focus on the absolutes of the Christian faith.
- Promote the ministry of Christ and His Word above personal ministry or method.
- Pray to raise the level of the Holy Spirit's activity in your area.
- Appreciate one another's gifts in ministry.
- Practice supportive speech and actions toward one another.

National Action

"'You will receive power when the Holy Spirit comes on you; and you will be my witnesses . . . to the ends of the earth'" (Acts 1:8).

We call pastors to lead their churches in cooperation without compromise —maintaining Pentecostal distinctives, yet standing together on the basis of the command of our Lord Jesus Christ found in John 13:34–35.

CALL FOR EVANGELISM

"Jesus came to [His disciples] and said, 'All authority in heaven and on earth has been given to me. Therefore go and make disciples of all nations, baptizing them in the name of the Father and of the Son and of the Holy Spirit, and teaching them to obey everything I have commanded you. And surely I am with you always, to the very end of the age'" (Matthew 28:18–20).

We call on the pastor and local church to work together with others according to Christ's paradigm of reconciling love on an integrated agenda of cooperative evangelism and discipleship. The implication of this call requires more than the agenda of one local church. It requires that evangelicals come together to reach the lost.

CALL FOR CULTURAL IMPACT

Jesus said, "'You are the salt of the earth. But if the salt loses its saltiness, how can it be made salty again? It is no longer good for anything, except to be thrown out and trampled by men. You are the light of the world. A city on a hill cannot be hidden. Neither do people light a lamp and put it under a bowl. Instead they put it on its stand, and it gives light to everyone in the house. In the same way, let your light shine before men, that they may see your good deeds and praise your Father in heaven'" (Matthew 5:13–16).

We call the Church to be faithful and to rely wholly on the power of God to transform our lives, our congregations, and our communities. The Church can make no greater impact on the world than in simply being the faithful, vibrant, worshiping, evangelizing, and loving community Christ has redeemed. Christians are encouraged to engage fully their dual citizenship (heaven and earth), exercising their rights and privileges freely to pray and participate in our national democratic form of government. As churches work together in unity across denominational lines, they must seek to nurture, encourage, and facilitate fidelity to the Word of God—incarnate, revealed, and proclaimed.

"To him who is able to do immeasurably more than all we ask or imagine, according to his power that is at work within us, to him be glory in the church and in Christ Jesus throughout all generations, for ever and ever! Amen" (Ephesians 3:20–21).

Back to Basics in Missions

Loren Triplett

The Bible is full of evidence that God is committed to revealing His love and to having fellowship with mankind. The stories of Scripture illustrate repeatedly that our Maker pursues every possibility of finding persons who will respond to His invitation, "Come unto me" (Matthew 11:28).

God is clearly intent on the salvation of mankind. After He went to the extreme of offering His only Son to obtain divine reconciliation, it staggers the imagination that He would depend on frail humanity to deliver His message to the human race. What an awesome mystery—God made plans to use us to explain His love to the world. We call the passages that include Christ's command regarding our task *the Great Commission.* The Pentecostal movement has always taken this mandate seriously. It is not the Great Suggestion—it is an unalterable, literal command.

Certain basic factors provide the foundation for our world vision and burden for all the peoples of the earth. They are undeniably a part of functioning Pentecostal experience. Let's review the reasons foreign missions cannot be omitted from pastoral responsibilities. Here are some of the basic factors of our Kingdom mission.

The Whosoever Factor

The basis for worldwide missions is that Jesus Christ, the Son of God, died for people everywhere. The "whosoever" factor was established before the foundation of the world. The Word of God demands that we recognize the universal love of God. It reveals conclusively His heart and purpose. "'God so loved the world that he gave his one and only Son, that *whoever* believes in him shall not perish but have eternal life'" (John 3:16). "'*Whoever* believes in Him is not condemned'" (John 3:18). "[God] wants *all* men to be saved" (1 Timothy 2:4). "The Lord . . . is patient with you, not wanting anyone to perish, but *everyone* to come to repentance" (2 Peter 3:9). "He is the atoning sacrifice . . . for the sins of the whole world" (1 John 2:2). "[Christ Jesus] gave himself a ransom for all" (1 Timothy 2:6, KJV, all emphasis added).

God's love is worldwide. With the blood of His Son, He "purchased men for God from every tribe and language and people and nation" (Revelation 5:9). It is blasphemy to try to explain away God's plan of offering salvation to whosoever believes. The perfidy of predestination leaves millions outside the reach of God's love. God has chosen to offer eternal life to whoever believes in Jesus, the Lamb slain "for the sins of the whole world."

The Perish Factor

The same "golden text" of the Bible that offers life eternal to whosoever believes also reckons with the "perish" factor. *Perish* is the often forgotten word of John 3:16. It points not to physical death but to the dreadful reality of eternal punishment.

Hell is real. It is the eternal destiny of all who do not go through the only "door"—Jesus Christ. The refrain of early twentieth-century Pentecostal preaching was "There is a heaven to gain and a hell to shun." Nothing has changed! The factor of the yawning pit of eternal damnation must never be hidden nor left out of our message. We must warn people in every nation, tribe, language, and race of the wrath to come. We must stand at the crossroads of humanity and call out to the lost; they must be told of the perish factor.

Jesus left no doubt whatsoever: "'No one can see the kingdom of God unless he is born again'" (John 3:3). And again, "'You must be born again'" to enter the kingdom of God (John 3:7).

The Master presses on in revealing divine intent to offer the great solution to human lostness by saying, "'Just as Moses lifted up the snake in the desert, so the son of Man must be lifted up, that everyone who believes in him may have eternal life'" (John 3:14–15).

Please, Pastor, do everything in your power to alert your people and your community to the hopeless consequences of rejecting Jesus. This must also be a strong factor in our "lifting up Jesus" among the nations. Their headlong rush into the abyss of their lostness can be intercepted only by their believing in the Son of God, who died on the cross for them. If He is lifted up for them to see, they can be turned from perishing and have eternal life.

Always remember and keep it fresh in the minds of your people that there are millions who have never rejected Jesus nor hardened their hearts against God—because they have never yet heard. They have never looked up to Jesus on the Cross for the healing of their sin-sick souls, because no one has explained it to them. They are lost forever unless the worldwide family of God keeps seeking the lost. We must go to the ends of the earth. We must share the good news with everyone. We must point mankind to Jesus. We must plant churches. We must never stop. The eternal plague of the lostness of humanity has a cure. How awful it will be if we do not do all within our power to reach them before it is too late.

The Obedience Factor

Oswald Chambers said it so very clearly: "The basis of missionary appeals is the authority of Jesus Christ, not the needs of the heathen."[1] We go to the ends of the earth because Jesus told us to. We bow to His authority. His Word is our command.

Matthew's Great Commission passage prefaces the command by reminding the eleven disciples that He had the authority to send them to all nations to preach, baptize, and disciple. He simply said, "'All authority in heaven and on earth has been given to me. Therefore, go'" (Matthew 28:18–19).

Mark's Great Commission passage is beautiful in its pristine clarity: "Go ye into all the world, and preach the gospel to every creature" (Mark 16:15, KJV). Neither compound words nor compound ideas are employed. It was given to be easily understood so that no believer could have the excuse of not understanding the meaning of that text. It is a simple command, an authoritative command, a repeated command, a last command, and, by Holy Spirit empowerment, a doable command. Thus, missions is not a denominational idea, nor a command born out of pity, guilt, or ambition. It is a command from Jesus Christ, our Commander-in-Chief. It is a command emphasized by the Spirit within us. That is one reason foreign missions is an integral part of our Pentecostal experience. The Spirit reminds us again and again of the teachings of the Master. That is one of the announced works of the Spirit.

Our options are obvious: either disobedience, a cardinal sin, or happy, literal obedience to the Great Commission. Oh, let us be obedient to the heavenly calling. Our true reason for doing missions is our relentless pursuit of doing the will of God. In the cause of taking the Kingdom to all peoples, we are in the perfect will of God. Second Peter 3:9 reminds us, "He is not willing that any should perish"—therefore, let us go.

The Worship Factor

The worship factor addresses the reality of how much our Heavenly Father desires to receive worship and honor from His creation—the human race. John Piper, in *Let the Nations Be Glad,* deals powerfully with this often completely overlooked factor in missions. It is a book that will help every pastor who cares about success in missions in the local church. Piper says, "Missions is not God's ultimate goal, worship is. Missions exists because worship doesn't." He goes on, "The ultimate foundation for our passion to see God glorified is His own passion to be glorified."[2]

God wants to be worshiped. He loves to be praised. He insists, "I will not yield my glory to another" (Isaiah 48:11). He will always seek to establish and display the glory of His name among all peoples. Jesus told us to do good works so that God could get more glory: "'That they may see your good deeds and praise your Father in heaven'" (Matthew 5:16). The Westminster Catechism answers the question "What is the chief end of man?" with this reply: "The chief end of man is to glorify God and enjoy Him forever."

What do you think happened in heaven when, in our own time, the Christian church was planted for the very first time in Outer Mongolia (now Mongolian People's Republic)? In that first great crusade held in Ulan Bator, the capital city of Mongolia, more than five hundred people came to know Jesus. The very first thing they were taught to do, after repenting of their sins and accepting Jesus as Savior, was to worship Him. The missionaries had translated a few praise choruses into the Mongolian language, and the words were projected onto the wall of that beautiful auditorium. It happened then in the first few minutes after new birth, eager voices of brand-new Christians were giving to God something He had never received before: worship in the Mongolian language. I wonder what was happening in heaven at that moment.

Doing the Great Commission simply increases the capacity of the human race to give praise and worship to our God. Let all the nations praise Him! That is what He wants. Our missions goal is to bring God glory and honor from every tribe, nation, people, and language. To say it another way, our reason for going to all peoples is to increase the capacity of the human race to give God what He really wants: praise, glory, and worship.

The Prayer Factor

Great Commission warriors, the "sent ones," must be people of prayer, and they must be supported by the intercession of those not called to go. Where would missions be without prayer warriors? Again, Oswald Chambers goes to the very heart of the matter when he writes, "The key to the missionary problem is not the key of common sense, nor the medical key, nor the key of civilization or education or even evangelization. The key is prayer. 'Pray ye therefore, the Lord of the harvest'"[3]

Chambers goes on to say in his next day's entry (October 17), "Prayer does not fit us for the greater works; prayer is the greater work. . . . Prayer is the battle. You labor at prayer and realities happen. What an astonishment it will be to find, when the veil is lifted, that souls have been reaped by you simply because you had been in the habit of taking your orders from Jesus Christ."[4]

The walls of atheistic Communism came down by the prayers of suffering saints on the inside of the wall and the intercessory missionary prayers of warriors on the outside. We can pray a prayer on this side of the world and things will happen on the other side. We can pray for a missionary teacher in a Bible school classroom on a distant mission field, and the Holy Spirit will be poured out in a special way upon the teaching of the blessed eternal Word. Missionaries and national preachers in hell-inspired dangers can be delivered by the hand of God through the prayers of people at distant altars. Laborers will go forth effectively to the harvest as we pray the only prayer request that Jesus left, "Pray ye therefore the Lord of the harvest, that he would send forth laborers into his harvest" (Luke 10:2, KJV).

Pastor, please, never stop leading in and teaching about the awesome power and place of intercession in the work of reaching our world. Make your church the "center of the world" from which streams divine blessing and life-changing influence to all the harvest fields of the world.

The Pentecostal Factor

According to Acts 1:8, to be Pentecostal is to be missionary. That verse clearly explains one of the evidences of the baptism in the Holy Spirit. "'You will receive power when the Holy Spirit comes on you; and you will be my witnesses in Jerusalem, and in all Judea and Samaria, and to the ends of the earth'" (Acts 1:8). A Pentecostal pastor who does not lead the church in worldwide obedience to the Great Commission is a contradiction in terms. A Pentecostal pastor will have a missionary heart and will recognize that he has been given that missionary heart by his baptism in the Holy Spirit. To be Pentecostal is to be missionary.

It is no surprise then to discover that the outpouring of the Holy Spirit at the beginning of the twentieth-century took on immediate missionary responsibilities and vision. There was a driving force within that revival that can only be explained as the energy of the Spirit. The fresh Pentecostal revival spread rapidly around the world. The Pentecostal pastor will fulfill his Great Commission responsibilities best if he understands and practices the truth of the Great Commission empowerment.

God's promise is His plan: ""'In the last days, God says, I will pour out my Spirit on all people'"'" (Acts 2:17). The Holy Spirit was given to create new awareness and new power to be witnesses both at home and to the ends of the earth. As a matter of proof, Jesus solemnly warned his newly commissioned disciples against leaving Jerusalem without the baptism in the Holy Spirit (Luke 24:49; Acts 1:4). Holy Ghost baptism is the abiding, inner power, boldness, persistence, wisdom, and anointing for every commissioned believer. Without it we are weak and useless. The Pentecostal factor claims ministry with "signs following" (Mark 16:20, KJV). The acts of the apostles is the benchmark for today. We are His action-oriented witnesses in the arena of today's Pentecostal revival. Let the pastor's heart and preaching be Pentecostal; let the home base be Pentecostal; let the "sent ones" be Pentecostal; and may all the nations of the earth be led into the continuing last-day, great Pentecostal revival. To be Pentecostal is to be missionary.

The Rapture Factor

Jesus is coming soon: "Night is coming, when no one can work" (John 9:4). This simply means that the great harvest God has made provision for must be accomplished on a shorter timeline than ever before. Consider it like this: More than half of the human race in our generation has had no explanation that salvation is through Jesus Christ, that God wants no one to perish, and that the rapture is getting closer. What we do for the great harvest must be done quickly. There is urgency in the Kingdom. Let us work then while it is still day—"Night is coming!"

"You are all sons of the light and sons of the day. We do not belong to the night" (1 Thessalonians 5:5). Night is coming! "The day of the Lord will come like a thief in the night" (1 Thessalonians 5:2). "The Lord himself will come down from heaven, with a loud command . . . and with the trumpet call of God" (1 Thessalonians 4:16).

I hear the voice of the prophet Jeremiah with his plaintive description of tragedy and hopelessness: "'The harvest is past, the summer has ended, and we are not saved'" (Jeremiah 8:20). We do not know when the last altar call will be given, nor when the last name will be written in the Lamb's Book of Life, but we know it hasn't happened yet. We are still deep in harvest—the greatest harvest in the history of humanity. Our missions task is to prepare a Bride for the heavenly Bridegroom from every nation, language, people, and tribe. The Bridegroom is on His way. What we do must be done quickly. The table is being readied and God's Word promises, "'Blessed are those who are invited to the wedding supper of the Lamb'" (Revelation 19:9).

The parable of the wedding banquet in Luke 14 really describes the commission that has been given to the church today. The master of the house ordered his servant, "'"Go out quickly into the streets and alleys of the town and bring in the poor, the crippled, the blind and the lame"'" (Luke 14:21). Finally, he sent the servant to "'"go out to the roads and country lanes and make them come in"'" (Luke 14:23). That urgency was called for because the servant kept reporting back to the master that there was still room at the banquet table. Today we must move out across the face of the earth while there is still time and room at the great Marriage Supper of the Lamb. The rapture factor is pressing us on. Jesus is coming soon.

* * * * *

None of these basic factors can be seriously challenged or discounted. They are biblically sound and undeniably the will of God for every believer and every congregation. To limit or to make optional the God-given willingness on the part of His church to accept the challenge of the Great Commission is an unconscionable act. He who would seek to show the full will of God to his flock must lead them to an effective worldview and literal obedience to the Great Commission. Let us continue to go "into all the world, and preach the gospel to every creature" (Mark 16:15, KJV).

Working with Associate Pastors: A Senior Pastor's Viewpoint

M. Wayne Benson

A senior pastor being honored for twenty years of faithful service in one pastorate said, "If I appear to stand tall today, it is because I stand on the shoulders of great men." These are the words of a man who had become aware of the effectiveness of the leadership team surrounding him. Wise is the senior pastor who discovers this early in his ministry. The effective leader is always seeking to lift others up, to recognize and honor them, to build their stature, to edify their character. The ultimate result is that the leader will also rise with the elevation of those who serve him.

The Scriptures are replete with examples of "associates" whose faith is inscribed alongside that of their leader. Jesus chose the Twelve who would walk with Him through the pages of the Gospels. Paul the apostle often made mention of the people who made him look good. These associates are so dear to the Holy Spirit that their names are forever recorded in the eternal Word of God (Matthew 10:2–4; Luke 8:1–3; Romans 16:1).

It is clear from the patterns of the New Testament that God's plan to win the world is team ministry, not the exaltation of isolated superstars. Jesus surrounded himself with disciples who would carry on His work. Faithful to the pattern, He also sent them out in pairs to do that work (see Mark 6:7). The great servant of God often stands on the shoulders of great people of God. The effectiveness of ministry is increased through a team empowered by a single vision. The mandate of discipleship is fulfilled by this plan of God to impart something "to faithful men, who shall be able to teach others also" (2 Timothy 2:2[1]). Perhaps the most important aspect of team ministry is the resulting safety it provides. Reflect on those who have had a moral failure in ministry, and you will discover that nearly all of them had stepped out on their own or had clung tenaciously to private independence. This may be the reason that the New Testament concept of eldership is always expressed in a plurality of leaders. All of us need to be accountable to someone.

There are great men and women of God who, at first glance, appear to have done it alone as they planted successful ministries or missionary works in remote parts of the world. A closer examination of their lives, however, usually reveals a support system of leaders, mentors, and friends who have had, or continue to have, a dramatic impact on their lives. I have discovered that the vision God has given me for ministry is far greater than my ability to carry it out by myself. I need the resource of the capable people God has placed beside me. Let me share with you a few insights gleaned both as an associate pastor and as a senior pastor now overseeing a staff that has grown from two to ninety-three, thirteen of them associate pastors.

Effectively Communicating Our Vision

The single most important element of effective leadership for the senior pastor is the ability to communicate ideology, philosophy, and vision to the leaders who are part of the ministry team. It is not necessary that the vision be complicated or highly sophisticated, only that it be clear. Many pastors are intimidated by the idea that they have to spell out elements of their vision, perhaps sensing the trap fallen into by many who pontificated things that God had not said or who formulated some mere man-made plan. It is good to dream, but remember: Vision is more than dreamy-eyed speculation about that TV station or retreat center you would like to have someday. Your associates need to know the basics of what you believe about the job they are doing and your philosophy about how it is to be done. They need to know how you feel the church ought to operate, what you think it should cost, how much of the budget is their responsibility if they are to effectively help you accomplish your God-given vision. These associates need to know where you are going if you expect them to lead others there with you. A resourceful, young associate will seek out a pathway to somewhere; better that it lead to the fulfillment of your vision!

The senior pastor's vision and its philosophy may be stated in various levels of detail. It may be as simple as saying "We believe the church needs to grow in the manner described in Ephesians 4" or as elaborate as an entire series over a period of months. It may be ten points scrawled on a wrinkled piece of paper carried around in the senior pastor's wallet or a finely crafted statement of purpose defined in a written volume next to the office Bible. The key is to articulate what you believe—what you believe about the operation of the church, the relationships on staff, the delegation of authority, the growth of the church, the handling of finances, the practice of ministerial ethics. Associates cannot be expected to learn these things by osmosis! Oh, they will learn them as they violate forbidden territory. And, interestingly enough, you *will* tell them these things as you correct their mistakes. But this pathway to knowledge will be strewn with experiences of hurt feelings and confidence-destroying blunders. Most experiences of this kind can be avoided by a clear understanding between senior and associate pastors at the outset of their relationship.

COMMUNICATING THROUGH A STAFF POLICY MANUAL

In a large church, such as First Assembly in Grand Rapids, Michigan, we have found that the bits and pieces of philosophical information that appeared on memos to staff or on notes from agenda meetings needed to be organized and put into a manual that could be referenced by staff at all levels of leadership. This has saved us from experiencing grief over misunderstandings and has served us as an excellent training tool for new personnel.

COMMUNICATING THROUGH A MINISTERIAL HANDBOOK

Another tool that has helped our ministers was a natural outgrowth of the policy manual, which, we found, held many specifics for the ministers that did not apply to the rest of the staff. Therefore, we developed a simple ministerial handbook that covered those areas that applied to ministers only. This little manual has built bridges of understanding among our ministers and keeps them informed of the senior pastor's expectations about items such as vacation, on-call duties, hospital visitation, outside speaking engagements, days off, and other seemingly minor issues that become "critical mass" when ignored or misunderstood.

Clear Guidelines for Effective Working Relationships

After the vision and philosophy of the senior pastor are understood, it is critical to the understanding of the church, and to all levels of leadership, that each member of the leadership team understand his or her relationship to the senior pastor, to the other members of the leadership team, and to the congregation.

A CLEARLY WRITTEN JOB DESCRIPTION

During my first twenty-one years of ministry at First Assembly, we were blessed to see 144 people answer the call to full-time ministry. For many of them, their entry point of ministry was that of associate pastor under various titles (youth pastor, music director, Christian education director, assistant pastor, etc.). Probably the greatest expression of disappointment among those with difficult initial experiences was that the senior pastor who hired them never provided a written job description. The experience often left them disillusioned and confused as they fumbled their way along, trying to guess what was expected. It is not fair to associates that they be reduced to trying to fulfill, by trial and error, an unwritten but often dogmatic set of expectations formed by a pastor or board.

EVALUATING PERFORMANCE AND STATING GOALS

Equally important to the flow of administrative understanding is a system for evaluating performance and the fulfillment of stated goals. What good is a job description if task completion is never evaluated? Every associate, especially the fledgling, needs to know how he's doing. The primary purpose of evaluation is to express appreciation and affirmation for things being done well. A secondary purpose is to provide a clear understanding of areas needing improvement or development. One word of caution to senior pastors who tend to be "prophet" types: A gentle word of encouragement will usually have a more positive effect than a harsh rebuke. And to those who tend to be "mercy" gifted: Failure to confront mistakes in a timely way will produce an entrenched path of errors and misunderstanding. Generally, in an environment of good communication, neither the affirmative nor the corrective elements of the evaluation or review will come as a surprise.

SHORT-TERM TRAINING AND LONG-TERM DISCIPLESHIP

How often has a pastor in a pinch thrust a teacher's quarterly into the hands of some unsuspecting, last-minute recruit, who is then expected to stand before a Sunday school class of junior boys and be a "teacher." The poor draftee has no experience, no training, and no supervision. No wonder that when they fail miserably, they vow never to teach again. This kind of experience undermines any impulse to volunteer; no one wants to fail, especially publicly.

Though this kind of recruitment has been eliminated from most of our churches at the lay level, at the professional level we sometimes still operate that way. It is a grave mistake to think that a Bible school curriculum or a series of required courses for ministerial credentials has provided a framework of adequate training and discipleship for our associate pastors. Knowledge of the fundamentals of ministry does not make one a capable pastor any more than passing a written test on aeronautics makes one an airline pilot. Basic skills still must be taught, flying must be experienced, piloting must be evaluated—all this with an experienced flight instructor in the right seat. Why do we assume that a new associate instinctively knows how to make a hospital call, conduct a funeral, counsel a crisis, or deliver a sermon? Rather than throw them in the water to see how well they swim, the senior pastor, or his seasoned representative, should get in the water with them. He should show them the way he does it. He should explain time-effective methods he has discovered along the way, not omitting the mistakes but making them a humorous object lesson. He should demonstrate by example the techniques, the compassion, and the heart of ministry the way he sees it. After all, that is the way the associate will be evaluated, sooner or later, formally or mentally. You will nurture a profound appreciation and bonding with a young pastor who someday will tell stories to his own congregation about how you discipled him.

Loving People for Their Highest Good

One of the simplest, and yet most profound, models for leadership is the one practiced and preached by our Lord. He summed up virtually all the Law and the Prophets with one little word: *love.* Most of what we do as leaders is not complicated if we would practice this one axiom of truth: Love those under your authority for their highest good. This can be expressed in practical, simple ways that will bring about a lasting and fruitful relationship.

LOVING ASSOCIATES AS PERSONS, NOT FOR WHAT THEY DO

Though it may be difficult to separate the professional from the personal relationship, we are obligated to see our associates first as persons, the highest object of God's love, rather than as employees whose performance enhances or hinders our vision, making us look either good or bad. I have found that if one of my associates is having a personal spiritual problem or a family or marital difficulty, they too need a pastor who cares; they too need advice and spiritual guidance. They are your sheep as much as, if not more than, any other member of the flock. In fact, the effectiveness of their ministry to the flock may well be hindered by a small problem that, left alone, could become a catastrophic failure. For that reason, one of the first questions I often ask during individual meetings with my staff ministers might be, "Hey, how you doing with the Lord?" Or, "So what's the Lord been saying to you lately?" During an agenda meeting, if I see an item at the bottom of their long agenda that reads "personal," I will often elevate that item to number one on the list. It is a simple way of saying, "You are more important than what you do."

CARING FOR THE FINANCIAL NEEDS OF THE ASSOCIATE

Wages and salaries vary widely according to demography, geography, education, experience, job description, and level of responsibility. Nevertheless, let me suggest some things that may serve as a guideline if you should be wrestling with this issue.

Your associates are your greatest resource of ministry to the body of Christ. Treat them well and you will not regret it. The congregation I pastor has a reputation for taking care of their pastors. Nevertheless, I would gladly pay them double what they now receive if we could afford it. They are professionals and should be treated with honor and dignity. Therefore, I believe I should present annually to our board the needs of and recommendations for my staff, providing credible studies on compensation levels for ministry from national organizations such as NACBA[2] or CMA.[3]

Even during austerity, when raises or bonuses are not feasible, a letter to the staff indicating the reasons for the necessary "freeze," reassuring them of your desire for their financial well-being and giving them hope for future consideration, will be appreciated as an expression of kindness and concern.

Consider the benefits you appreciate and the finances you yourself need as you review the salary and benefits package of your associates. Consider the fact that these fellow laborers may well represent your most loyal followers and be among the most sacrificial givers in the congregation. Consider also that your board may well evaluate your loyalty to staff and respond to you as you would have the board respond to them.

PROVIDING A BASE OF ACCOUNTABILITY

In a day of such fierce temptation and resulting failures, we in ministry need a base of accountability more than ever. One of the advantages of having staff pastors is the safety "in an abundance of counselors" (Proverbs 11:14). I am convinced that this safety net is not merely provided to the counselees, but also to the counselors. We need the protection afforded by a group of peers we can give an account to. In my pastorate, I have cultivated an understanding of ready accountability and a system by which we regularly examine one another's moral and ethical behavior. Each of us pastors carries a green card entitled "Just Between You and Me." On this card are seven probing questions, on topics ranging from lust to financial indiscretion.[4] We know that we have the right to ask and the responsibility to answer those questions at any time. And we know that we will inevitably arrive at the infamous last question on the list: "Have you just lied to me?" Yes, I participate as an equal in this little safeguard, for I am equally accountable to them for my moral behavior and ministerial ethics. It is certainly not foolproof, and neither does it take the place of anointed discernment that comes from a good prayer meeting with these brethren, but it does provide accountability. I am keenly aware that I "watch over [their] souls, as [one] who will give an account" (Hebrews 13:17).

Four Cardinal Points of Ministerial Relationships

Each of my staff could probably quote from memory four cardinal points of my philosophy. They are as follows:

1. LOYALTY

Above everything we know about God, He is loyal; He is loyal to His irrevocable principles, loyal to His immutable truth, loyal to His eternal promises, loyal to us (Exodus 20:5–6; Malachi 3:6; Hebrews 13:5–8; 1 Kings 8:56–57; Matthew 28:20). I expect loyalty from my pastoral staff: loyalty to God, loyalty to spouse, loyalty to family, loyalty to the church, and loyalty to me. This is not a one-way loyalty, however, one that is expected to move only up the chain of command. My associates have the right to expect loyalty from me as well.

2. FAITHFULNESS

Faithfulness is a basic requirement of anyone entrusted with the Lord's flock (1 Corinthians 4:1–2, NIV). It is the most practical expression of the Great Shepherd and can be demonstrated by anyone in the most practical ways: reliability, punctuality, good work ethic, follow-through, etc.

3. FLEXIBILITY

We have a saying among the staff at First Assembly: "Blessed is he that is flexible, for when he is bent he shall not be broken." In any church responsive to the Holy Spirit's leading, particularly a growing church, leaders must be flexible in the face of new methods, new environment, and new responsibilities (Ecclesiastes 7:10). The living, dynamic, moving church of God must not be hindered by immovable, galvanized, possessive, or rigid attitudes. For those in ministry, it is "Be ready in season and out of season" (2 Timothy 4:2).

4. COMMUNICATION

The first characteristic we learn of God, in Genesis 1, is that He is a speaking God: "God said . . ." (Genesis 1:3,6,9,11,14,20,24,26,29). We tend to recognize ministry as the speaking of many words publicly but often demonstrate poor communication privately or within our pastoral staff. Communication is the lifeblood of relationship, both professional and private. In interviewing, I have often told prospective pastors that I expect honest staff communication, which includes the responsibility to disagree with me privately and face-to-face, rather than taking a grievance with me to others (Matthew 18:15; Galatians 6:1). Likewise, they need to understand that I will exercise the same prerogative of confrontation for the purpose of correction or understanding.

Keeping Your Word

There is one source of universal frustration within relationships, and the pastorate is no exception: keeping one's word. In a sense, our word is our spirit in sound form. When we say something, we give our word. Integrity is usually measured by how we keep our word to God and to others. When we violate our word in some way, perhaps failing to follow through on it, this invalidates our leadership and frustrates those who follow. Keep your word, and others will make increasingly valuable investments of trust in your ministry.

Making a Graceful Departure

One last word of advice about the relationship between senior and associate pastors. We in the ministry are relatively quick to acknowledge that the Lord has the right to lead us where He will. Though senior pastors examine that dimension of God's will thoroughly when someone comes aboard their staff, both senior and associate pastors are often shoddy about the way someone leaves for new arenas of God's will. I am not suggesting that you have a prewritten script for resignations, but it is a good idea to provide written guidelines about your expectations during such a transition.

At the beginning of each job description for our ministers, a paragraph acknowledges the call of God as having priority over their call to serve with me. With that in view, our ministerial handbook has a section entitled "The Minister in Transition." In this section, I give details about how I would hope such a transition would be handled, from the sensing of that first nudge to the making of a public announcement. I also cover certain sensitive areas by defining what constitutes church property to be left behind and remind them of ethics in contacting former parishioners. This saves the discomfort of misunderstanding at a vulnerable time for the congregation, the senior pastor, and the transitioning minister. The last thing an associate needs in his resumé of past relationships is the wake of a poor transition. Likewise, a senior pastor wants to avoid the negatively charged atmosphere of a polarized congregation, taking sides in a dispute between him and his associate. Any associate pastor who has been afforded the honor and visibility of a ministry beside a senior pastor and who has received an education, valuable experience, and financial remuneration during that ministry should seek to leave only blessing as a legacy. Any senior pastor who has benefited from an associate's time, talent, and energy should seek to bless the minister in transition with affirmation, love, and support. The grace that brought them together should be the same grace that follows them as they part. In my twenty-one years at First Assembly, I have been blessed to work with twenty wonderful ministers, each a gift from God. Thirteen of them are still on my staff. There are not words to describe the blessing, the stability, and the reassurance that long-term, healthy "pastor-models" provide the flock of God. The Good Shepherd gave His life for the sheep (John 10:11–15). Should we do less?

* * * * *

There is no substitute for unified leadership and its ability to bring the church together as an army, marching in step for one cause, rallied around one vision. "Behold, how good and how pleasant it is for brothers to dwell together in unity!" (Psalm 133:1).

Working with Senior Pastors: An Associate Pastor's Viewpoint

Robert W. Klingenberg

For twelve years I served as associate pastor to M. Wayne Benson, senior pastor of First Assembly of God in Grand Rapids, Michigan. It was a distinct privilege as well as a quality experience. Pastor Benson afforded the best of two worlds: the greatest example of a senior pastor and personal insights from his own experience as a very successful associate pastor. Much of what I share here has been stamped upon my heart from that most rewarding chapter in my life.

Servant Yet Friend

Jesus Christ chose twelve associate pastors. There can be only one Lord, one Master, and one Head. Two heads on anything is a freak. Likewise, there can be only one chief pastor in any church; all the other pastors must follow him. When Jesus Christ found one He wanted as His associate, as in the case of Philip, He said, "'Follow me'" (John 1:43[1]).

So the senior pastor of any church, as he represents Jesus Christ the Chief Shepherd of the sheep, must say to his associates, "Follow me." It is an absolute equivalent. Therefore, it is of the very essence of associate pastoring to have the fervent desire and total commitment to fulfilling the senior pastor's vision. Only when the associate pastor comes to serve the senior pastor will he be free to fulfill his sacred calling and not be a standing contradiction to his title. Not only will he be free to fulfill his calling, but he then will also be immeasurably blessed for it. That principle is found in the words of Jesus when He said, "'If anyone serves Me, let him follow Me; and where I am, there shall My servant also be; if anyone serves Me, the Father will honor him'" (John 12:26).

Frankly, if more associate pastors understood these principles, the length of associate pastoral terms would increase. Associate pastors would then understand that they are not in that position to pursue their own agenda, but to find great satisfaction and total ful-fillment in doing what the senior pastor senses to be his God-given vision. The associate pastor must be an extension of the senior pastor's hands—that is his call-ing. I have heard associate pastors say to their senior pastor, "I'm not going to commit myself to fulfilling your vision until I am sure that I can agree with all of it." Or again, "I don't want to talk about that now, we'll talk about it later." Not only should such an associate be fired, he should have never been hired. He is an out-law and a rebel and has no right to the high and honor-able title of associate pastor. An associate pastor is a servant of his senior pastor, and a servant is to embrace

> " **Associate pastor— to fulfill the senior pastor's vision.** "

his master's commands even if he does not understand at times the rea-sons for them.

However, if that is all there is to the senior pastor–associate pastor rela-tionship, then it would be both unbiblical and unhealthy. If all that the associate pastor received from his leader were commands and directions, the servant would grow very distant from his master. That is why Jesus said, "'No longer do I call you slaves, for the slave does not know what his master is doing; but I have called you friends, for all things that I have heard from My Father, I have made known to you'" (John 15:15). You see, effective orders and healthy obedience require an uncommon friend-ship, lest the associate pastor feel disassociated and not much like a pas-tor at all. The senior pastor must treat his associates as colleagues and friends, not as slaves or inferiors. The pastoral staff must know their senior pastor's heart, what he has heard from Jesus Christ, where he is going, and why he is going there. All of that is exactly how Jesus did it with his "associate pastors." A servant, on the other hand, is not informed of his master's intent or the reasons for his directives. Associate pastors who have that kind of relationship with their leader work as foreigners under the same church roof. Though they are at the same location, it is only as strangers at best.

Friend to friend is a most extraordinary relationship. Friends are made privy to matters that are shared with no one else. Friends are allowed not only into each other's heads, but into each other's hearts. That is exactly why Jesus could say to his disciples, "Many prophets and righteous men desired to see what you see, and did not see it; and to hear what you hear, and did not hear it" (Matthew 13:17). Again, he indicates the sacred priv-ilege that was entrusted to them when he told them, "'To you it has been granted to know the mysteries of the kingdom of God, but to the rest it is in parables; in order that seeing they may not see, and hearing they may not understand'" (Luke 8:10). The disciples of Jesus lived on the level of a sacred trust, a level foreign to all others. For Christ, friendship with His associates took precedence over leading them as His followers. This is precisely why we are told about Abraham, "He was called the friend of God" (James 2:23). The reason Abraham could be called the friend of God was because he was treated as one. There was an intimacy and exclusive familiarity between God and Abraham. When God had decided to destroy Sodom, He could not hide His plans from Abraham, for true friendship would not have allowed such concealing. The Bible presents that great friendship to us in that instance in these words, "And the Lord said, 'Shall I hide from Abraham what I am about to do?'" (Genesis 18:17).

We must hasten to add that Jesus Christ did not convey His heart or His head through some senior disciple to the other disciples. In the ranks of Christ's associates, there was no such thing as a bona fide senior associate pastor. Jesus Christ neither shared His heart nor conveyed His head through some representative. No one can be a friend by proxy or an effective leader through a deputy.

Pastors First, Specialists Second

We must make a careful distinction between noun and verb. As stated in a recent issue of *Homiletics* magazine, "What do adjectives do? They modify nouns. Adjectives modify things that are larger and more important than they are. Adjectives are ornaments and lights you hang on nouns so that nouns become more alive and meaningful."[2] It is helpful to understand that adjectives are like decorations on a Christmas tree. However, nouns are the Christmas trees themselves.

In the title "associate pastor," *associate* is the adjective and *pastor* is the noun. The adjective *associate* is but a descriptive, while the noun *pastor* is the very definition. Far too often the associate pastor comes into the church known as an adjective and not a noun. Then, depending upon his particular associate role, he or she is immediately viewed as an associate specialist in music, evangelism, Christian education, counseling, or whatever. Sad to say, in the eyes of many church people his specialty associate position becomes the noun, and his pastoral role becomes the adjective, or less. The senior pastor and his congregation must make it clear that we are not bringing in pastoral associates, but rather associate pastors. That simply means that every associate pastor must first of all be known and honored for his pastor's heart, and not for his associate specialty (whatever that might be).

Noun is of the essence, and the noun *pastor* means "shepherd." Sheep need a shepherd. The senior pastor, therefore, should first of all pray for and secure *pastors* in his staff-building process, not associates. The entire pastoral staff should be comprised of men and women who love sheep, who desire to feed sheep, who enjoy giving guidance to sheep, and who want to lay down their lives for the sheep. A shepherd's heart must always be first and foremost in members of the church pastoral staff. That is in distinct contrast to what has evolved in many church staffs today—

pastoring in the associate role has become a weak idea at best. Sheep must be the associate pastor's top priority, not a limited option. That way, associate pastors will not first of all use sheep as a means to an end but will minister to them and sacrifice for them as ends in themselves. Sheep do not exist to make the associate pastor's portfolio successful; rather, the associate pastor, like all pastors, exists to enable sheep to be successful in their walk of faith.

Associate pastors must be taught by senior pastors how to be shepherds. However, the senior pastor should never do that as a superior but as an equal. He is dealing with pastors just like himself, and not primarily as associates or adjectives. Therefore, he must not coerce and domineer but rather confer and deliberate with his associates as treasured pastoral resources. Every senior pastor needs heads and hearts besides his own. In isolation there is not only loneliness, but great weakness as well. The knotty problems that senior pastoring encounters in today's complex society require counsel from colleagues whose insights may even be greater than his own and whose pastoral concerns are certainly no less. I think that is exactly why we read these words in the Bible: "Where there is no guidance, the people fall, but in abundance of counselors there is victory" (Proverbs 11:14). In short, if I had been told ten years ago what problems and perplexities and perversions I would be counseling today, I would not have believed it. The situations are so serious, so intricate, so labyrinthine, that to have friends and fellow pastors surrounding you is like the fresh supply of troops and armaments brought to a wearied general who at times feels himself about to give up and yield to the enemy.

The senior pastor must make certain that for his associates the words of Scripture are being fulfilled, "A man's gift makes room for him" (Proverbs 18:16). Each specialty ministry, each unique gifting, whether musical or educational, whether visitatorial or administrative, everyone must be embraced as indispensable and vital to the church's health and effectiveness. However, the first concern of the associate pastor must not be that the sheep make room for his gifts, but rather that his pastor's heart always makes room for the needs of the sheep. The church's great need today is not for experts in their field but for shepherds in His fold.

Every associate pastor must develop and possess as his real specialty the art of shepherding. The senior pastor must train his assistants in all the basic disciplines of the pastoral calling: preaching and teaching the Word of God, counseling and giving guidance to the wayward, ministering comfort and healing to the sorrowing and the sick, and teaching associate pastors how to bring sheep into the fold. Anything less than that disqualifies the associate pastor from his noun status. Then all that you have left is an adjective! An adjective by itself enhances nothing.

The Commander, the Company, and the Commission

If the senior pastor and his fellow pastors are to discover their definitive calling, they must do so in the light of Christ and His staff of twelve associate ministers. If that calling is to become clear and accurate, a careful search of the New Testament will quickly reveal that Jesus and His disciples were more like a commander and his company of soldiers than just a teacher and his students. Jesus Christ, who came into the world to do spiritual warfare against the powers of darkness and set the captives free, is like a commanding officer dispatching his small company into a universal conflict. We know it as the Great Commission.

At first, the disciple's mission was somewhat limited. Jesus sent forth the Twelve with these instructions, "'Do not go in the way of the Gentiles, and do not enter any city of the Samaritans; but rather go to the lost sheep of the house of Israel'" (Matthew 10:5–6). Then just before His ascension, He universalized the scope of His mandate and said, "'All authority has been given to Me in heaven and on earth. Go therefore and make disciples of all the nations, baptizing them in the name of the Father and the Son and the Holy Spirit, teaching them to observe all that I commanded you; and lo, I am with you always, even to the end of the age'" (Matthew 28:18–20).

The heartbeat of every pastoral staff vision must be evangelism. There should be no greater burden on the heart of a pastoral staff than the salvation of the lost through Jesus Christ. If Jesus could not help but weep over Jerusalem, then no one is qualified to be a senior pastor who cannot do the same for his parish. For that matter, no one should fill the position of associate pastor who is unable to regularly shed tears for perishing humanity.

> **No one unable to regularly shed tears for perishing humanity should fill the position of associate pastor.**

I was divinely favored to be able to copastor with a senior pastor who was constantly leading his staff and church on an evangelistic expedition. His vision was always filled with fresh strategy for adventuring into new territory to win the lost for Christ. The atmosphere in weekly staff meetings was always clear, urgent, and very sharp. We were saturated as associate pastors with a vision from our senior pastor that the greatest harvest of souls was just before us. We were blessed with a leader who never allowed us to think for one moment that we had arrived, thereby allowing no room for lethargy or self-congratulation. Never before had I met, and perhaps never again will I meet, a pastor who could inspire such furious onslaughts against Satan's strongholds.

But it is work, very hard work. That is why Jesus commands us, "'Beseech the Lord of the harvest to send out workers into His harvest'" (Matthew 9:38). I have found that it is easy to bring a sinner to an altar for salvation. Why? Because it is God who makes converts, that is His part, and that makes it easy for us. The difficult part is making disciples out of those converts, and that is our obligation. Our Commander Jesus Christ never commissioned us as His company to add numbers or members to the church. Rather, He told us to make disciples, that is, produce those who swear total allegiance to Jesus Christ and obey everything He commanded. There are so many forces that seek to draw the new convert away from discipleship and back into darkness. Jesus says to us, "'I send you out as sheep in the midst of wolves'" (Matthew 10:16). We must take

Him seriously, for shepherds well know that, given enough time, one wolf is able to destroy an entire flock of sheep. Shepherds, therefore, must be trained and must train others how to protect the sheep by equipping them for spiritual warfare.

The greatest thing that a senior pastor can do for his fellow ministers is to manifest a burning love for the sheep, especially for the lost and those who were once part of the fold but have wandered off. No service is too menial, no time is too inconvenient, no effort too great, and no sacrifice too painful to show people that Jesus loves them. The greatest remembrance of my senior pastor is the ecstatic joy that he manifested over one sinner being saved. Likewise, it comes as no surprise that his biggest tears were shed for wandering sheep who had been deceived by Satan and bitten with his infectious venom of rebellion. I never realized that a man could be so broken over a wandering sheep. Then, when the wanderer, like the prodigal son, came back home, under the leadership of our senior pastor, the church would have a party. The greatest legacy that my senior pastor gave me was that he became the embodiment of these words in Scripture, "'He got up and came to his father. But while he was still a long way off, his father saw him, and felt compassion for him, and ran and embraced him, and kissed him'" (Luke 15:20).

In summary, what's most important in a senior pastor's relationship with his colleagues is not the sound of his words but the light of his life. In this regard, I am reminded of this little story. A man who previously had no doorbell decided to buy one that ran on a battery. But it was not long before his wife turned it off because her nerves could not stand the noise it made throughout the house every time it rang. Not wishing to waste the battery, the man put it in a lamp in his workshop, but the light was so faint that he could not use it. Later he asked an electrician why the battery could produce such a noise through the doorbell and yet be insufficient for a light. The electrician told him it takes much more power to shine than it does to make a noise![3]

Mercy toward Imperfection

I've always maintained that the Lord Jesus Christ is much easier to please than people. True perfection is far more tolerant of imperfection than is human perfectionism.

How gently Jesus dealt with His staff, especially in the midst of their most glaring imperfections. As Jesus neared that final and most painful hour of His life, He desperately needed the prayerful support of His disciples. Considering the enormity of His burden, His request was not at all that unreasonable: He simply asked that they sit up and pray with Him. You know what happened! They slept instead, numbed in those moments to all concern for their Master. His rebuke was mild as He asked, "'You men could not keep watch with Me for one hour?'" (Matthew 26:40), as if He felt their embarrassment more than His own agony. In effect He covers for them, which is not surprising, for as Peter (most appropriately) tells us, "Love covers a multitude of sins" (1 Peter 4:8). In fact, He who is perfect love makes an excuse for His associates and says, "'The spirit is willing, but the flesh is weak'" (Matthew 26:41). This is as if to say, "I know that you love Me, I see inside your hearts; therefore, I forgive your failing and am merciful and understanding toward your physical weakness.

Thank God for senior pastors who gently point out to their associates the requirements of ministry. But also, thank God for senior pastors who are quick to pardon their associate pastors and who manifest great tolerance for the weaknesses and shortcomings of the flesh.

The Bible tells us to speak the truth in love. As a former associate pastor, just a word to senior pastors, of which I am now one. Speak the truth in love, and remember we can always stand a lot more of your love than your truth. That is something every good senior pastor should bear in mind. Christ did!

Planning for Church Growth

J. Don George

C hurch growth begins with a basic understanding of and commitment to the Great Commission. Jesus said, "Go ye into all the world, and preach the gospel to every creature" (Mark 16:15[1]). Jesus furthermore said, "Go ye therefore, and teach all nations, baptizing them in the name of the Father, and of the Son, and of the Holy Ghost: teaching them to observe all things whatsoever I have commanded you" (Matthew 28:19–20). Jesus finally said, "Ye shall receive power, after that the Holy Ghost is come upon you: and ye shall be witnesses unto me both in Jerusalem, and in all Judea, and in Samaria, and unto the uttermost part of the earth" (Acts 1:8).

The Great Commission helps us understand that God's desire for His church is growth. Surely we can see that the Church's failure to grow is displeasing to God. The will of God concerning the lost is clearly revealed in Scripture. "The Lord is . . . not willing that any should perish, but that all should come to repentance" (2 Peter 3:9). Jesus said, "As my Father hath sent me, even so I send you" (John 20:21).

Great growth characterized the Early Church. The Jerusalem church in the first century experienced remarkable growth. In fact, the church grew from 120 in the Upper Room to 3,120 in just one day. Luke declares, "They that gladly received his word were baptized: and the same day there were added unto them about three thousand souls" (Acts 2:41). A short time later, Luke records, "Many of them which heard the word believed; and the number of the men was about five thousand" (Acts 4:4). Still later, the authorities said to the disciples, "You have filled Jerusalem with your doctrine" (Acts 5:28).

It must be clear, to even the most casual observer, that the Early Church in Jerusalem was experiencing great growth. Such growth must surely have delighted the heart of God. God wants His church to *grow up, grow together,* and *grow out.*

To grow *up* implies that the Church is becoming more mature in faith and Christian practice. "They continued steadfastly in the apostle's doctrine and fellowship, and in breaking of bread, and in prayers" (Acts 2:42).

To grow *together* implies that God is working through His body, not just through individual members who isolate themselves from others. "All that believed were together, and had all things in common" (Acts 2:44).

To grow *out* implies outreach. The Church must break beyond its self-imposed barriers and reach out to society beyond its own borders. The Church must be relevant to its culture. In Jerusalem, the Early Church was "praising God, and having favor with all the people. And the Lord added to the church daily such as should be saved" (Acts 2:47).

Although there are several vital elements necessary for the growth of the local church, there is one aspect that stands out above all others. One singular ingredient is absolutely essential for church growth. The necessary ingredient is not prime location, spacious facilities, state-of-the-art equipment, professionally trained singers and musicians, academically accomplished teachers, or even powerful Bible preaching. Great churches have been built, and continue to grow, without the ingredients that some would feel are indispensable for church growth.

> " **The essential element for church growth—vision.** "

What is that essential element without which no church can grow? The answer—*vision!* Great churches are not built without vision. Local churches do not continue growing without vision.

Many believe the greatest single tool to reach the world and expand the church today is a well-articulated and easily understood vision. "Where there is no vision, the people perish" (Proverbs 29:18).

Vision is necessary for *purposeful involvement* in God's kingdom. The loss of vision results in the loss of a sense of purpose and destiny. Vision gives meaning and purpose to otherwise mundane assignments. Vision is the channel through which creative ideas and energy flow. Vision to a local church is like banks to a river.

Vision is necessary for *moral discipline.* Without vision people tend to become undisciplined. We do not live godly lives because we are godly. We live godly lives because we desire to fulfill God's purpose. Our nation's Founding Fathers were willing to sacrifice because they had a vision. Abraham left Ur of the Chaldees because he had seen the vision.

Vision is necessary for *endurance.* We endure because of our vision of Jesus. The Bible says, "For the joy that was set before Him endured the cross, despising the shame" (Hebrews 12:2, NKJV). Moses "endured as seeing Him who is invisible" (Hebrews 11:27, NKJV).

Vision is necessary for *success.* Without vision the work we do for God will, at best, be uninspired, ineffective, mundane, average, and of little consequence. Inspiration and faith, so necessary for success, result from vision.

Planning for growth involves six aspects. Consider this acrostic:

V isibility
I nsight
S trategy
I mplementation
O utreach
N urture

Visibility

Visibility within the community is essential for a church to grow. A church may achieve visibility through a prime location, beautiful building, media outreach, or in a variety of other ways. It is possible, however, to become visible to the community with none of these advantages. There are basically three things the community should know about the local church: (1) the church exists, (2) the location of the church, and (3) the identity of the church.

The first two items can be achieved through publicity. A church can advertise in the local newspaper, the local radio and television stations, the telephone yellow pages, door-to-door literature distribution, etc. The third item can be achieved through public relations. Word of mouth is by far the most effective means of letting the community know about the church. When the people start talking about what God is doing through His church, the crowds will come and the church will grow. The personal testimony possesses unparalleled powers of persuasion.

Insight

The local church must possess insight into the unique personality and needs of its community. Hindsight enables one to know about the past. Foresight enables one to be aware of future events. *Insight,* however, gives understanding of the present. Insight into a community's personality and needs is more important than either hindsight or foresight.

Each city or community has its own cultural mores. The wise pastor will become familiar with the local business, social, and political power structure by becoming involved in community affairs. The public school system, civic clubs, community projects, and youth activities provide excellent opportunities for the local pastor to become involved with his community.

Methods of effective outreach and ministry will vary from one community to the next. The method and style of outreach that is highly effective in one community may not be the most effective in another. Insight, therefore, is an essential element in planning for growth.

Strategy

"Which strategy of growth should be utilized in this community?" This question must be answered by the pastor and local church leaders. God can reveal the most effective growth strategy for each church. Every God-given vision must be accompanied by a God-given strategy. Strategy sometimes comes moment by moment as we follow God one step at a time.

Joshua announced to the Israelites, "Sanctify yourselves: for tomorrow the Lord will do wonders among you" (Joshua 3:5). When the priests walked into the Jordan, one step at a time, the waters parted and formed a corridor the people could pass through. We cannot do the *work* of God apart from the *wisdom* of God. Who we listen to is all-important in designing a strategy of growth. "Blessed is the man that walketh not in the counsel of the ungodly" (Psalm 1:1).

Although God's people may be outnumbered, they will never be out-smarted as long as they seek God's wisdom. Gideon, Joshua, and Jehoshaphat heard from God and employed God's wisdom in winning great victories.

Involve the people in planning the strategy. In the church I pastor, we presently have more than six hundred people involved in strategizing for growth for the next five years. Thirty-one committees of twenty persons each are involved in designing a strategy that we believe will enable Calvary Temple of Irving, Texas, to grow from five thousand to ten thousand in the next five years.

Study Commitees of Calvary Temple

Adult Christian Education	Athletic Ministry
Bus Ministry	Calvary Christian Academy
Care Group Ministry (Elementary)	Children's Ministry
Children's Ministry	Communications/Public Relations
(Nursery/Preschool)	Elder's Ministry Facilities
Counseling Ministry Evangelism	Fine Arts Ministry
Finance/Fund-Raising	Hispanic Ministry
Food/Clothing Ministry	Men's Ministry
Master's Commission	Prayer Ministry
Missions	Security/Traffic Control
Prospect Follow-Up	Single Adult Ministry
Senior Adult Ministry	Ushers/Hostesses/Hospitality
Staffing	Women's Ministry
Video/Audio Ministry	Young Couple's Ministry
Young Adult Ministry (College, etc.)	Youth Ministry

Each committee has a chairman, vice-chairman, and recording secretary. The committees meet monthly throughout this year. After one year, each committee presents a strategy for growth in their area of study. The schedule of the committee meetings each month is as follows:

7:00–7:15 P.M.	General Session (All committees meet together for challenge and instruction from the senior pastor.)
7:20–8:30 P.M.	Committee Meetings (Each committee meets in a separate room.)
8:35–9:00 P.M.	General Session (All committees meet together for reporting and final inspirational challenge by the senior pastor.)

This year is a year of study and strategizing. The next four years we will implement the strategy of growth in each department of the church.

Implementation

Once the local church has seen the vision and has designed an insightful strategy of growth, it is then time to implement the strategy. It is reasonable to expect those who are involved in designing the strategy to also be involved in the implementation of the strategy. We expect those who are designing our growth strategy at Calvary Temple to lead the way in putting the strategy into practice. Plans on paper are of little value. The plan must be implemented.

Plans, of course, must be pragmatic. Make great attempts. Be willing to try something new. Dare to take risks. But when it is clear that a particular program isn't working, have the courage to set the program aside and move on to a different plan. Jesus cursed the unproductive fig tree. Maintain only those programs that produce. Bury the dead programs and allow God to create something new, exciting, and productive.

The successful implementation of a growth strategy depends to a large extent upon the involvement and motivation of the pastor. Motivation is the key to successful implementation. People get involved in the things they genuinely desire to be a part of. The best motivation is internal. The skillful and motivated pastor can create an atmosphere in which people become highly motivated. The pastor must convince the people that he believes the chosen strategy of growth will be productive. The pastor creates the climate where internal motivation blooms. He reminds the people that God will respond to obedience. "If ye be willing and obedient, ye shall eat the good of the land" (Isaiah 1:19).

Some people are hesitant to get involved in church programs and ministries for a number of reasons:

Fear of failure. In the Parable of the Talents, fear of failure caused the wicked servant to fail completely.

Feelings of inadequacy. Quite possibly, some people have confused humility with an inferiority complex.

Threat of new situations. Some who are happy with the old wine are convinced the new wine can't be nearly as good.

Danger of disenfranchisement. If the church grows, certain people may no longer feel useful or important.

Cost of change. With church growth comes new demands on time, talent, and treasure.

The wise pastor identifies the factors hindering the involvement of the people and attempts to overcome them.

Outreach

The church that plans for growth must have an aggressive strategy of outreach. No church that does not involve itself in attempts to reach the lost beyond its own borders will grow. The command of Jesus is "Go!" He commands us to go into the streets and lanes of the city; into the highways and hedges; to the poor, the lame, the halt, and the blind; to the lost sheep of the house of Israel. "Go . . . and compel them to come in, that my house may be filled" (Luke 14:23).

Outreach ministry opportunities are limitless in our day. Let the church reach out through home fellowship groups, bus ministry, literature distribution, radio and television ministry, hospital visitation, convalescent homes and retirement centers, athletic teams, weekly or seasonal mailings, newspaper stories and ads, telephone ministry, musical productions, and special events. Every city or community has its own outreach possibilities through such events as fairs, rodeos, auto races, athletic events, parades, festivals, flea markets, cultural celebrations, jails, prisons.

We must take the gospel to those outside the walls of our church facilities. To be effective fishers of men we must place the net on the outside of the boat. The late Thomas F. Zimmerman, general superintendent of the Assemblies of God for many years, often said, "God has called us to be fishers of men, not keepers of the aquarium." The supermarket manager often places the same item in three or more locations throughout his store because he knows that the greater the availability of the product, the greater will be his sales. Let us take the gospel to people wherever they are.

Nurture

The growing church will indisputably be a place of nurturing. Good spiritual food, a loving environment, and an atmosphere of friendship and concern are characteristics of the nurturing church. In today's impersonal society, it is vital that the church maintain a personal touch. When people come to church, they must be convinced that they are special.

A child grows by eating food. His digestive organs break down the food into basic elements of nutrition. Through the bloodstream, the body assimilates these nutrients, creating new muscle, bone, and skin. In like manner, the church grows. It matters not how many people come into the local church as long as it is able to assimilate them into its life.

Newcomers must feel comfortable and welcomed in the church. The church I pastor has been known for more than twenty years as "the church that love is building." At Calvary Temple in Irving, Texas, we say to everyone, "We love you just the way you are."

People must always be more important to the local church than *programs* or *property.* The growing church will develop a people-oriented ministry rather than a program-oriented format. Jesus said, "I will build my church" (Matthew 16:18). The growth of the church is a natural result of the promise of Jesus. It is natural for the church to grow. When the body is healthy, the church grows both numerically and spiritually. Growth does not depend upon a magic formula.

It is so simple. Get the church well. Dare to see the vision. Become visible to the community. Design an insightful growth strategy. Then implement the strategy through outreach and nurturing. Get ready for something good to happen. Make plans for growth. Expect an abundant harvest, and God will help you. Increase will occur!

Growing from a Pioneer Church to a Multistaff Church

Dan Secrist

I watched them, curiosity mixed with dread, as they approached my front door. I greeted the three men as they filed into my front room—smiles that looked strained, body language that betrayed too much confidence. Why were they here on a Sunday afternoon? Two of them had resigned as leaders in the church just the past week, and the other man, the third board member, was now sitting down with them saying, "Pastor, we need to talk with you." I felt my pulse quicken as they began their presentation.

They were kind but confident, and in a few minutes it was done: "At first we thought the new church was a good idea, and maybe it was. We wanted to help you get it started, but now that it has been going for several months [there was a pause], well . . . we've been praying together this afternoon, and we believe the Lord has told us the church is to close. We just came to tell you that." They prayed for me and left.

They were not malicious, they were friends. They simply saw no future in our efforts and wanted out—the sooner the better. It would be easier for them if the whole thing ended, and we could all say it was a nice idea whose time just had not come. We had spent a lot of hours together over the previous nine months and labored hard to get a new work started. They had prayed, they kept the books, they led worship, they visited people with me, and they were faithful. Now it was over.

It is hard to start a new church. I wept.

After nine years in missions, my wife, Sue, and I had returned to the States with the dream we felt was from God: we wanted to pioneer a church. We didn't want to build on another's foundation and have to undo a lot of philosophy and programs before we could get things going. We wanted an unencumbered start. Further, we were convinced that new churches were the best way to see God's kingdom grow because new churches attract new people, and the more preaching points there are in an area, the more penetrating and diverse is the impact of the gospel. Besides all that, hadn't God spoken to us to start a new church? I was pretty sure—at least I thought I knew the voice of God.

More than once I reflected on the story of the animals on a farm that had just been transferred to a new owner. The chickens said to the pig, "Hey! Let's welcome the new farmer with a great breakfast of bacon and eggs." The pig looked at the chickens and said, "That's easy for you to say; it's only an offering. For me it's total commitment!" Starting a church was not just an idea or a hobby, it was our whole life, and we believed God wanted it to succeed.

Over the next several days I spent considerable time praying and meditating. I drove the back roads, prayed, and wept as I sought God for direction. My wife and I went to the district office for counsel, and I talked with a number of fellow pastors and trusted friends. What should we do?

By the next Sunday we had what we believed was the word from the Lord, not a cocky confidence but an assurance of what we were to do: Don't close the church, the vision is from God. Ask all those who remain to declare themselves as charter members and sign their names to commit to the new church. Meet with all the men every Saturday for a men's breakfast and fellowship. Include them all in some of the decision making. Have the midweek meeting in our own home for a time.

What did we learn? Be prepared for battle! Satan doesn't want to see new churches started or the kingdom of God grow, and he will use every means possible to divert good people and bring turmoil and discouragement. If we had not the confidence that God had spoken (and confirmed His leading to us in several ways), we might have surrendered at that point.

The People Who Pioneer

Many people left during the first year. Even though we started with seventy-six people on the first Sunday, by the end of the year we had settled down to about fifty regulars, and not many of them were the ones that started with us. Most of the attendees from the first months moved on. I discovered this is quite typical of new church plantings: Very few of the original visionaries become long-term supporters. The early pioneers, for the most part, are not settlers. They are important in that they are risk takers and adventurers, willing to try the unknown—thank God for them! But once the church begins to take on patterns, they typically drift away.

The owner of the funeral home we were renting for our church came to me one Sunday just before service (really a great time for bad news!). "We'll give you about two months and you have to leave." What a shock! We had nowhere to go and no money to spend on higher rent.

However, this crisis gave God the opportunity to relocate us and give us enough floor space to begin Sunday school. What a difference that made. Out of that problem we discovered a principle that truly is universal: Our impossibilities are God's opportunities for miracles. That theme and that mindset served to carry us through many other challenges. Why focus on the problem? Be innovative and look for the solution. God always has an answer if we are willing to wait on Him long enough to get it.

Today we are a church of several hundred with four full-time pastors and numerous support staff and volunteer pastors, but it did not happen overnight. In fact, there were several more dragons of crisis to face, and each one had its unique set of formidable teeth!

The People Who Leave

"Pastor, we really love the church, and we love you, but our teenage son has no friends here and he wants to go to Central Church across town. We do hate to leave, but we don't want to lose our children. We'll be praying for you and this church but attending over there." Rather than try to talk them out of it, I prayed with them, blessed them, and let them go. I often announce that our church is to be like a bridge: open at both ends—easy to get on and easy to get off. However, when people do get off, our prayer is that they will have advanced in their walk with God. Our goal is to build God's kingdom, not ours.

In a pioneer church, you cannot have all the programs and ministries of an established church—and that will frustrate some people. Others don't think it is growing fast enough and are not willing to wait around to be part of the solution. Their perceived needs are not met. Frustration grows in their hearts and sooner or later they leave.

It is part of the price of ministry to have people you truly care about walk away from you, and that hurts. But God is more interested in our character than in our comfort, and character is developed in the dark times. You dare not look back, but look to Jesus and the future He has planned for you. If you keep the vision before you of a strong and viable ministry and keep your heart right before God, He will bless, you will grow, and the church will grow.

Week by week and month by month they continued to appear: young couples with no children or else young school children, and older folks whose kids were grown and gone. We were alert to the fact that youth groups are slow to form, and our church was no exception. Youth go where youth are, and we had no youth group yet—only three teens all from the same family. If they would only stay long enough for others to see them, then the others would stay, too, and we could get a youth ministry going!

God provided our answer in the person of a young man who felt called to be a youth pastor. "Pastor Mark," as we called him, was willing to work for a minimal salary—just because of God's call. He would support his family with supplemental secular employment until we could employ him full time. If our theory was right, this new staff person (if he is truly called of God to this place at this time) would attract enough new people in time to put him on salary.

The People Who Are Paid

How wise is it to hire staff before growth? It is either that or wait until you have the income stream sufficient to support more staff. Most churches never seem to have enough money to spare, so they never add more staff. We were fortunate this first time to find someone willing to make a personal sacrifice, and it paid off as the youth group burst into life. However, the next two staff members added were definite steps of faith. Did we have the money to hire them? Not really. Other things were sacrificed to hire them, but in a short time their ministries had touched so many lives that the church grew and the financial pressure was minimized.

The Christian life is a life of faith. If we always look to the bank account for our direction, where is the faith? Peter stepped out of the boat into the water while it was still roiling. He didn't wait for the calm before exercising faith. He merely said, "'Lord, if it's you, tell me to come to you on the water'" (Matthew 14:28). The life of faith is a lot more exciting because it is full of unknowns—and I believe that is exactly where God wants us. As we walk by faith into the future, praying and listening to His voice, there is uncertainty—even fear at times. (Almost every pastor I know who leads an expanding ministry experiences occasional fear.) Yet no great spiritual venture is ever accomplished by money, skill, and administrative prowess alone. God wants to be the hero of His church. He will honor our faith in Him.

Hiring staff is a step of faith—not just because it stretches the finances, but bringing a new person into the mix of leadership always involves risk. Will he or she fit our church? Will conflicts arise because of a different philosophy of ministry or because of different methods? And where should this new person come from? Serious prayer and careful interviews are important!

> **"**
>
> **If we always look to the bank account, where is faith?**
>
> **"**

Most of the hired staff should come from within the local church. These people already understand the philosophy and share the history and subculture of the church. They have trained under the present leadership and have already established strong relationships. They should easily slide into position if you have properly prepared them and the congregation for the changes.

Should you ever hire from outside the church? Of course! Outsiders give fresh perspective and ideas that can be a real blessing and help. But too many outside hires can give you more diversity than is healthy for the church. Our research and experience indicate that no more than 25 to 30 percent of your staff should come from outside your local church for optimum health and momentum.

The actual staff structure will vary from church to church because each church is unique in setting, size, subculture, and budget. Lyle Schaller in *The Senior Minister* suggests that every staff person should see his or her role as a valuable member of the team, not as the overseer of a separate kingdom, and should be driven by group goals, not individual goals. He then offers eight principles that have been very useful to us: Build a staff that will (1) function as a team, (2) achieve the productivity of a highly decentralized staff, (3) relate to one another as supportive members of a caring family, (4) be motivated by identical visions of what God is calling your church to be and to do, (5) recognize their interdependence and the necessity of mutually reinforcing goals and activities, (6) minimize the natural drift toward becoming a hierarchy, (7) benefit from healthy internal competition but not become a network of rivals, and (8) offer challenging, fulfilling, and satisfying experiences for everyone on the staff.[1]

The People Who Grow

The majority of churches in the world are small—somewhere under one hundred in attendance, and most of them stay that way year after year. As we studied church growth, we did learn principles that were helpful, but we also observed something else: Many "growth churches" use principles that directly contradict one another! We finally concluded that there really is no universal formula—no pat answers. However, we do believe God wants His church to grow.

The Great Commission is actually very clear and simple: Make disciples, i.e., devoted, obedient followers of the Lord Jesus Christ. If what we are doing does not change lives, then we should drop it. God can bless only what contributes to His purposes. Putting time and effort where it counts will certainly give you a better chance to grow.

Recently I did a staff training on "Allocative versus Innovative Thinking." Allocative thinking says, "Resources are limited. Since there is only so much money in the pot, we must apportion it very judiciously: Cut wherever necessary and try to give a fair share to each department." If the problem is defined in shortage terms, people naturally feel more comfortable with an allocative planning model. Just defining a problem tends to move us toward an allocative approach in order to ration what are perceived to be finite resources. So in a church, if we see the budget as a limit, we will never have faith to go beyond what exists today.

The innovative approach says, "What are the other options? What are the possibilities? What if finances were not limited? Is God able to do miracles?" One approach says, "Cut back and don't burn out your people." The other says, "Include more people and expand the ministry opportunities!" One says, "Pay off the mortgage." The other says, "Start new ministries, go to multiple services." One starts with the problem, the other starts with the vision. One looks to the past, the other looks to the future.

I remember a small church I worked with in Spain. I first noticed it while walking down the street in Madrid one evening: There were large spikes sticking out of the door from top to bottom. It looked like a fortress! Evidently children used to pound on the door during services and disturb the small band of faithful worshipers. So they drove huge spikes from the inside of the door clear through the wood, and the sharp points greeted you as you approached the door. Then a new pastor came. He didn't just take the spikes out of the door, he opened it and welcomed the children. Before long, there were kid's clubs, crusades, Sunday school, and other activities that attracted those "little nuisances" right into the kingdom of God! In the process of winning the children to Jesus, the pastor solved the problem of kids banging on the door during worship. Observe the innovative approach: As the attendance grew, there were more resources to expand the ministry, remodel the old building, draw ever-larger crowds, and accomplish the real task of the church.

Innovation is vital if a church is to grow. More people leave a church because of boredom than for any other reason. However, our innovation must not abandon the fundamentals of Jesus' directives, nor our culture, nor our sociology. We have learned that many traditional programs (such as Sunday school and Sunday morning gatherings) became traditional because they work! Today, there is a growing movement toward the use of high-tech drama, video, and illustrated sermons in our churches. These can be very helpful supports to the presentation of the gospel, and we do use them—but in a limited way. I hope these glamorous methods do not degenerate into gimmicks and substitutes for the preaching of the Word. Preaching is important! Visual stimuli such as television, movies, and dramas appeal to the emotions, while language appeals to the mind. There was a reason why Jesus said to go and preach the gospel.

The Pastor Who Leads

Every organization is the lengthened shadow of a single man or woman. That is true for churches as well as for secular organizations. Each church has its own personality and, to some degree, its own subculture. Who is that person at the top who casts such a shadow of influence? In a healthy church, it is the senior pastor.

Lyle Schaller in his book *Effective Church Planning* says, "The vast majority of lay-controlled congregations tend to be small in size and/or declining in numbers. In nearly all large and rapidly growing congregations the decision-making processes are heavily influenced by the pastor."[2]

In the early days of the church, leadership was much easier. I simply made all the decisions, announced them, and that was it! As other people were added to leadership and the church grew, decision making became much more complex: You float the ideas out first, you consult with other leaders for input, and then you present them more formally. Finally, you are able to implement them if you win people to the vision. Deacons, staff, department leaders, and informal leaders all need to feel they are part of the team and help carry out the new vision for the church. You cannot lead without their help. The truth is, if you have good counsel from these people, you will end up making better decisions, and they will support you in the process.

God does not lead His people through committees. He speaks to a leader, and the leader leads the flock. God can and does use committees sometimes. (The Lord knows we have enough of them; if He wants anything done He sometimes has to use a committee!) But if I read the Bible correctly, His method is to speak to a man, then use that man to communicate the message to the rest of the people.

On the other hand, anyone who has ever heard from God must beware of the messiah complex, or thinking a person becomes more important because God has spoken to him or her. The fact that God has spoken does not make one more important at all. Such a person just happened to be the one God chose to speak to. Each person has a place in the kingdom of

God, and the position of pastor is one of several called to serve the flock.

As I traveled the world as a missionary, I watched for common threads in healthy churches. There were many, of course, but one that stood out to me was that the pastors were all long term in the local church. It takes years to build credibility and relationships in a community. It seems ironic that we tell the people of the church, "Be faithful to attend the services of the church. Join us, become a member and don't be a church hopper. It is important for you and for your children to plant your roots deeply and have a home church." Then every few years the pastor himself feels "the call" and moves on. After several such violations of integrity, the people begin to doubt the sincerity of their leaders and are less and less willing to commit to the next pastor. In their minds are honest questions, *How long will you stay? You ask us to be loyal to you; can we trust you to be loyal to us?* When we answered God's call to start a church, I asked my wife, "Are you willing to stay for the next twenty to thirty years in this place if God so leads us?" She agreed.

> **We say don't be church hoppers, but every few years we feel 'the call' and move on.**

I'm not saying that a pastor can never change churches or leave a community. I well understand that there are times when a pastor needs to leave a place: For many reasons, it can be best for both the pastor and the church to get a fresh start. What I see as harmful is the constant turnover of pastors in a given church; it leads to stagnation, lack of direction, and cynicism.

Early on, I asked God for direction as to who I was to become. Over many weeks of intensive introspection, prayer, and meditation, I developed twenty-three "life principles" that define who I want to be. These give me guidelines for choosing priorities and principles for living out my life. Decisions are much easier when I know what I stand for and have a written set of guidelines for my life. These are not a list of rules, but concepts that apply broadly to the canvas of my whole life. Let me share ten of them. I seek to

1. *Love God with all my heart, soul, and mind* (Matthew 22:37). Seek God's will in every area of my life. Practice the presence of God. Seek to bring Him glory in all I do and say (1 Corinthians 10:31). No matter the consequences, be a man of God above all else. Find my identity in Him.

2. *Love my neighbor as myself.* First my wife, then children, then extended family, local church, other Christians, then all people. I will try to earn the goodwill of everyone I meet. While the greatest need of every life is an intimate relationship with God, I will try to promote that relationship without damaging the self-esteem of others. I will try to be kind to and understanding of those who disagree with me; cause others to feel important; serve the largest number of people that I effectively can.

3. *Love myself.* I will not be harsh or tear myself down when I fail. I am still a child of God and loved by Him. I will do all I can to secure a sense of personal worth and be generous with private praise when I have

done something well. I will keep a positive attitude toward myself while recognizing that all my blessings come from God.

4. *Maintain a daily quiet time.* For the rest of my life, I will strive for a daily time of solitude with God for prayer, Scripture reading, meditation, and planning so that I may have His direction and blessing in the achievement of the worthy tasks He has called me to.

5. *Demonstrate integrity.* I will be forthright, honest, and fair with everyone and avoid hidden agendas by making only clear statements I can wholeheartedly support. I'll keep my word and be someone others can trust: sincere always, consistent, and dependable.

6. *Maintain a disciplined lifestyle.* The small decisions reveal the kind of person I am becoming. "Don't put things down, put them away." I will get up at a regular time. I will do the toughest tasks first and whatever is left will seem easier.

7. *Maintain good health.* Be consistent in exercise, careful in diet (eat regular, balanced meals), and get eight hours sleep. Some stress is necessary for motivation, but I will reduce or eliminate things that cause distress.

8. *Make ministry a lifestyle—discipleship.* I must never separate what I am from what I do. I must integrate the truths I learn and pass them on to others. I must develop many quality relationships so I can grow and help others to grow.

9. *Grow intellectually.* Keep curious about everything. I will record what I learn so as not to lose it. Stay alert. Read widely, research, and meditate. Compare all knowledge to Scripture. Read the Scriptures daily. "Talk with sinners and think with saints." Study true heroes. "Blessed is the man who finds wisdom, the man who gains understanding" (Proverbs 3:13).

10. *Build the local church.* "Wherever you are, be there with all your heart." I will always be an active member of a local church and build up the body of Christ, encouraging and inviting others to come. I will pray for it and support it with cheerful giving of time, talent, and money.

Everything of value in life flows from who you are, not what you do, so I keep my list handy and refer to it often.

As pastors, we find it easy to compare ourselves with others who are either more or less "successful" than we are. There is a subtle urge to compete. Joseph M. Stowell in *Shepherding the Church into the 21st Century* says we should not compete; that is carnal. "Carnality engenders in our hearts an environment of fear, positions us in defensive postures, and makes our ministry a forced function of our calling rather than a spontaneous expression of our growing unhindered love and intimacy with Christ."[3]

An understanding of Ephesians 4:11–15 gives us a way to measure our ministerial success with its target of preparing people for works of ministry, unity, maturity, and the likeness of Christ. Personal success, Stowell says, is a matter of living out our lives according to God's expectations and standards in undaunted routine faithfulness. Only rarely does the spectacular make us successful; rather, it is the regular, ongoing faithful cadence of our lives in terms of our commitment to Him that makes the difference. Our purpose is to glorify His name and to enrich eternity, not to glorify ourselves and enlarge our kingdoms.

The Leaders We Train

I'll never forget the board meeting that began my education: A young attorney sat in the board meeting listening, writing occasional notes on his yellow pad. The tension was high, as often it had been since three men had been elected to form the first official board of our pioneer work. Led by the lawyer's questioning—as if in a courtroom setting—the pressure rose. He was displeased, irritated. Finally it came: "Gentlemen," he dropped his pen on his legal pad for emphasis, "I am through. And [he turned to the Christian education director] as soon as the Sunday school year is over, I'm giving up my class. Pastor, tomorrow morning you'll have my letter of resignation on your desk."

The board member in charge of Christian education cleared his throat calling for attention. "I don't feel I can serve on the board any longer either. This is my resignation too."

For months I had watched the tide of tension rise. Why couldn't we work together? We had the same goals and purpose, the same doctrine. Yet no sooner had we put a Band-Aid on one situation than another would erupt somewhere. Must conflict be a part of church life?

Pastoring a growing church necessitates constant paradigm shifts. The way you function changes often because the church is changing often. If you do not continue to grow and change, the church will stop growing and changing. All change is perceived as loss to someone, and loss is typically met with resistance and anger. Change must be managed, not just allowed to happen.

A vital ingredient of growth is training—anticipating the changes and preparing people for them. Out of desperation, I developed a training course for the new deacons over the next several months. It was then I realized that I had many assumptions that were not necessarily understood by others. After one particular deacon training retreat, a new deacon came up to me and said, "Pastor, I have been a deacon in two other churches before I came here. I never really knew what a deacon was supposed to do. Now I think I know." That was encouraging!

From that point on, our deacon meetings took on a new flavor, and for the past eight years, I have found my board to be one of the most supportive and inspirational groups in our church. I look forward to meeting regularly with this group of high-caliber, spiritually mature individuals. These men are among my closest friends.

We now have training courses for everything! Our new members class, for example, uses a series of booklets we developed that explain the reason for membership; the history, philosophy, and doctrines of the church; the expectations we have of new members; and a test for giftedness. It is filled with inspiration as well as information and is spread out over four sessions, although it could easily be expanded to many more. People are shown a ladder of growth and development so they have direction for their lives as they join the church. We must create a sense of destiny and importance in our work for the Lord.

I like what Abe Lincoln is reported to have said: "A river becomes crooked, following the line of least resistance. So does man. I'll study and get ready, and then maybe my chance will come." We try to prepare people before issues become problems by instilling vision in them for a positive future as they walk with God and grow as members of our church. Aspire to quality in everything. Generate the best quality you can with what you have. You may not have much to start with, but people can be trained.

Another innovation is that deacons are no longer elected by popular vote. This may not be the American way, but it is the scriptural way. Now a carefully selected screening committee, led by the pastor, prayerfully reviews all nominees for office and presents only the qualified and approved to the congregation. Then, after prayer, the names are drawn by lot, and we believe God honors the process with His choice. This takes all the political machinations out of leadership selection and gives the deacons a deeper sense of destiny, for God has chosen them, not man.

Helping people find their place in service to the Lord through His church is really what pastors are called to do. Inspire them to hear from God and get their own vision for the ministry they are called to. It is exciting indeed to discover new talent that may have previously lain dormant and then to release those people to develop, grow, and reach others. There is always a sense of risk, to be sure, but it is absolutely essential that we give people room to fail. We dare not overcontrol God's flock. Let people test the edges of their talent and ministry, and they will breathe new life into any church. Just be there to encourage, give some help, and pick them up if necessary!

Finally, we must recognize that all of our planning, labor, and innovation can never replace the truth of 1 Corinthians 3:6–7: "I planted the seed, Apollos watered it, but God made it grow. So neither he who plants nor he who waters is anything, but only God, who makes things grow."

Special Services

Jerry A. Strandquist

Sunday morning is a special time in the life of the church. Fifty-two times each year, every seventh day, we have another Sunday to lead God's people in a worship experience. If we include the Sunday night service and the midweek prayer and Bible study, we have a challenging task before us to keep the services vibrant and alive, not only for our people but also for us as leaders. What can we do? Is it possible to become stale and boring even with the greatest story ever told and the joy of a relationship with Jesus Christ, the Creator of the universe?

This calling to lead people to know Jesus Christ and encourage growth in their walk of faith is both a privilege and an honor. Our responsibility is to plan and conduct the service under the divine direction of the Holy Spirit, allowing worshipers, saved and unsaved, happy or depressed, young or old, rich or poor, an opportunity to meet with the great loving God. He is the only One who can begin to meet the diverse needs represented at each service.

> **Good services don't just happen. They are birthed through diligent planning and prayer.**

Because the Church is an ever-changing organism with high and low moments, we must grasp, highlight, and use key times in the life of the Church. All we need to do is follow the Church calendar as a guideline for special annual emphases, such as Christmas and Easter.

Each church will have its own days needing special recognition, such as anniversaries, evangelistic crusades, and missions conventions. All of us are creatures of habit, but our congregations can tire of the limited variety in the order of the worship service. I called my eldest son, who is away at college, and asked him about the morning service at the church he attended. He responded, "Same old, same old," which meant it was just like the last few weeks or months. Now I know criticism is typical of youth, but adults have said the same about church: no change, no spice, no spirit, too predictable, no variety. Does God work in only one way? Is He limited in creativity, or are we just too lazy or lacking in our own creativity to bring new life and excitement to the worship experience?

The success of the worship service is in direct proportion to the preparation in the days and weeks before. Good services don't just happen. They are birthed through diligent planning and prayer. With a focused approach, we can have far greater impact, with long-lasting results.

I like to think we are in the middle of a construction project and God, the Architect, has appointed us to be project managers. Like the wise builder in Matthew 7:24–27, we are constructing something that will last. I am to be a good steward of that which He has entrusted me, His church. As the project manager, I must insure that everything in our services builds on the foundation of Jesus Christ. A beautiful home has interesting windows, and a vibrant service will also have "windows" that create interest. However, the windows only highlight the main structure, the message of Christ's redemption and His power to change lives. I am to diligently lead so that His church will be able to stand when the storms come, because the church's foundation is the rock.

Planning and the Church's Purpose

The purpose for our existence as a church needs to be very clear. This will help us plan our services. To know our mission and how we are going to fulfill it is important in our planning. Here are a number of questions that we have asked ourselves as the leadership of our church in

Bloomington, Minnesota. Use them to help define your purpose as a church; your answers will impact how you plan each service.

- What is the purpose for our meeting together?
- Who decided what the purpose should be?
- Does the leadership know our purpose?
- Has the purpose been shared with the church?
- Can the purpose be clearly explained and stated?
- If we have a purpose statement, does it need to be updated?
- Do our actions line up with our stated purpose?
- Can we notice any trends in a review of last year's services?
- Have we planned for missionaries and evangelists?
- How much time do we give to planning?
- Who should be a part of the planning process?
- What time of the year should the planning take place?
- Should we have a yearly plan? Six months? Two years?

Every fall we have a planning meeting for the coming year. I bring together a small group of people who are directly involved in the worship service, such as those who are responsible for our music, plus other creative visionary people from the church who can add insight to our planning process. This committee can be as large or as small as you want it to be. The members need to be appointed by the pastor for no longer than a year, with the possibility of reappointment. Their assignment would be threefold. First, support of the pastor's vision and purpose; second, accountability in making sure the worship experience stays true to the stated purpose; and, third, insight that will help fulfill this purpose creatively.

Planning should be done in a casual setting, with plenty of time for prayer and dialogue. We review last year's themes and important days in the life of the church. We look at past services and note what was successful. We then determine what we will continue to do and what will be discontinued because of ineffectiveness. I love this time of planning because we can control the calendar and our programming.

The worship experience should be planned with the same attention to detail that we would give if we invited guests to be entertained in our home. The house would be cleaned, a table decorated, a menu planned, food prepared, and we would dress appropriately in anticipation of the guests. We need to remind ourselves we are about our Heavenly Father's business. His people, those who are hurting and looking for hope and encouragement, as well as seekers, will be joining us. Most important, God is with us, and we want to honor Him with our very best preparation.

> **The purpose for our existence will help plan our services.**

When I first came to Bloomington Assemblies of God Church to assume the senior pastorate, I had been influenced by the great church in Barrington, Illinois: Willow Creek Community Church pastored by Bill Hybels. This "seeker-driven" church focused on reaching the unsaved

Mary's and Harry's of our world. Its purpose is to reach those who don't know Christ by removing any barrier that would keep them from hearing the gospel. Because of my desire to see the lost come to a saving knowledge of Jesus Christ, I encouraged the leadership of Bloomington Assemblies of God Church to seriously consider becoming a seeker-driven church. After a time of trial and error, we came to acknowledge that we were most comfortable with our Pentecostal roots yet would remain very "seeker sensitive" in our own approach rather than being seeker-driven. We would give time for worship, pray for the sick, encourage the gifts of the Holy Spirit during worship, and have altar calls. Assuming that visitors would be with us every Sunday, we would look for opportunities for brief teaching moments about the gifts of the Holy Spirit, altar calls, and worship, reassuring first-time visitors that what they were experiencing was based upon the Word of God.

Just recently I asked a young couple applying for membership in our church what attracted them to Bloomington Assemblies of God Church. She was brought up as an atheist and he, a Lutheran. Both replied, "When we come to Bloomington, we see and sense that God is here."

Once we had established our style, planning became a lot easier. I would divide the year into four sections, starting with January: January to Easter would be our first quarter; Easter to June, our second; July to September 1, our third; and September to Christmas, our final quarter.

January to Easter

January to Easter is our time of reflection. With the beginning of the new year and setting of new goals, a prayer emphasis is timely; January has a theme of prayer and fasting. We plan morning and evening prayer meetings in the church, each department schedules special times of prayer, and home-centered prayer meetings take place throughout the week in care group settings. During this period, we plan corporate times of prayer within the church as a whole. Friday all-night prayer services and Sunday evening prayer and praise services are times of directed prayer for the needs of our church body, our community, and our world. I will preach on prayer and often include a prayer seminar during this period with a prayer evangelist or teacher. One year we encouraged people not only to pray but also to fast during the first forty days of the year. Some fasted a meal a week, some a day or two of the week, others fasted for a week, and one fasted the entire forty days. We just asked everyone to participate in some way. Today entire ministries are devoted to prayer. At your local bookstore great resources are available to help in teaching on prayer and finding creative ways to lead people in prayer.

February, the month when our thoughts turn to love, is a great time for a family life seminar with a sweetheart banquet. A series of messages on relationships (from how to have healthy relationships to strengthening our present relationships) is always a contemporary need. This same theme is carried out in our Wednesday night adult program, featuring classes dealing with marriage, parent and child relationships, healing broken relationships, etc.

In March we are preparing for Easter. We have used the 50-Day

Spiritual Adventure, which is published by The Chapel of the Air Ministries.[1] Chapel of the Air provides printed resource material, which is used as a personal devotional guide and follows a central theme, leading towards the Easter celebration. Eight topics are covered each week and supported by the sermon. The topics are always relevant and our people have enjoyed working through timely biblical subjects together. Also, many of our people come from church backgrounds that include a Lenten season. We find the 50-Day Adventure a "Lenten-type" vehicle that helps bridge the gap between their traditions and ours.

Easter to June

Easter usually is celebrated in the month of April. A high percentage of our community will attend church at Easter, so it is a prime time to capture their attention. Some of those who visit have no church background or are just looking to attend a new church. Yearly we give several performances of an Easter pageant that dramatizes the message of the Cross. We always give people an opportunity to receive Jesus Christ as Savior during the pageant. Advertisements announcing the Easter pageant and our Sunday Easter worship service will be purchased in the local newspaper. The ads are written both to grab the attention of the reader and to address their need of a Savior. Several weeks prior to Easter, our church family is given the opportunity to purchase a flower (lily, mum, tulip, or hydrangea) in memory of a loved one. These plants and flowers decorate the sanctuary for Easter. On Easter Sunday our bulletin contains an insert listing the memorial, and the flowers are taken home following the Easter service. All the music and the sermon will focus on the resurrection of Jesus Christ.

July to September 1

The three summer months are given special attention in our planning. We have found through experience that people will search for a new church in the summer months. Because it is summer, many of the people in the congregation are on vacation, and we all become more relaxed. There is a freedom to modify some of the things we do during the year. For instance, if your choir dismisses for the summer, put together a small worship team. Vary the worship team: one Sunday use only men, another Sunday a family, a youth ensemble, or children. They not only could help with the worship but could also provide the special music. I am always looking for ways to involve our people. Each week use different laypeople to read the Scripture, pray, and receive the offering. This is a great time to train people. Take time to rehearse with them; they need to know where they should stand, which microphone to use, and when during the service they will participate.

Each year we have a patriotic service the closest Sunday to the Fourth of July. The church is decorated with our American flag and red and white flowers. Some years we have used one large American flag, with red, white, and blue ribbon strategically placed in the sanctuary; other years, many smaller flags have been used. Again, variety in decorations helps keep your celebration fresh. Patriotic songs or a musical is sung by the choir and a patriotic message given, emphasizing our Christian responsibility to our nation. We recognize all those who have served our country by having them stand when their branch of service is mentioned. We have also invited key Christian community leaders to come and address our congregation and to share a short testimony. Our mayor is one of the outstanding Christian gentlemen in our community and has given a clear witness of his relationship to Jesus Christ. We have extended the invitation to others even when we don't know much about their faith, but they can speak about our country for a few minutes and then we pray for them and thank them for their service to our community.

Our community has given us permission to have some of our Sunday night services in a park adjacent to the church property. Neighbors have joined us during our singing and have stayed to hear the testimonies and the preaching. We try to use these times for church fellowship and follow the service with refreshments. We have served ice cream one night, watermelon another, and even have had corn on the cob. New families have found these opportunities invaluable for making new friends in the church family. Children on blankets, older people in their favorite lawn chair, and planes coming in for a landing at the nearby airport have all added humor and vitality to these special Sunday evenings.

Doing everything we do for the glory of God means we try to pray and plan and serve to the very best of our ability. The summer schedule includes recruiting and training our workers for the fall program.

September to Christmas

September to Christmas is a time for "reaping the harvest." Vacations have ended and the students are back in school. A back-to-school emphasis encourages our students to pray for their schools and look for opportunities where the Holy Spirit will use them in making a difference on the local school campuses. We have used a youth evangelist to speak to our congregation and students and many times have been able to schedule him for assemblies in our local schools. This draws young people who would not normally attend church to our services in the evenings. We encourage our youth sponsors to lead the youth in times of prayer and committing themselves to making a difference in their world. Our youth department sponsors a back-to-school prayer retreat.

We will commission all of our Sunday and midweek workers on a Sunday morning by having them stand during a commissioning prayer. We ask our workers to make a commitment for one calendar year.

For us, the month of October is given to missions. The entire building is decorated to help set the tone for our convention. Missionaries are invited one year in advance to come and share in one of our services or to participate in a home fellowship group. We use the yearly theme published by the Division of Foreign Missions. Beautiful banners and posters, along with missions bulletins, are available by simply writing or calling the Division of Foreign Missions. This month is planned by our missions committee, made up of a combination of staff and laypeople who have a passion for missions. This committee meets monthly to consider missions

Special Events We Have Held

January

Prayer emphasis. Week of prayer. Men's prayer breakfast. Women's prayer retreat.

February

We Love Kids Banquet—a banquet just for kids! The printed menu includes items that kids love: hot dogs, macaroni and cheese, and ice cream. The children sit at tables and are served by the parents dressed up as clowns, etc. A local children's pastor is brought in to speak. He will dress as a character, use puppets, or share a great object lesson for the children.

Cabin Fever Banquet. This becomes more inclusive, for the entire church family, than a sweetheart banquet. With the weather in Minnesota, we look for any excuse to get together, using it as a time for the leadership to say thank you to our many volunteer workers.

The Annual Business Meeting. We moved the annual business meeting to Sunday night because God's business should be conducted in a spirit of worship and thanksgiving. I know this is not always possible, but we have found it to be a wonderful way to encourage new families to attend. It is a time for reporting the wonderful results of the past year, passing positive resolutions, and creating a prayerful setting for the election of any new leaders. We have also served a meal at the business meeting or have had refreshments following the conclusion of business. This again creates a family atmosphere and encourages unity of purpose and fellowship.

March or April

Seder—the Jewish celebration of the Passover. We have invited a Jewish Christian to conduct a family-style Seder, complete with the meal, or demonstrate the Seder, without the meal. Many of our people are unfamiliar with the significance of the Passover meal in light of the revelation of Jesus Christ.

May

Kids musical. This usually happens on Sunday night. The children have rehearsed a musical on Wednesday nights and present it to the congregation in either a full concert, or they will provide special music for a morning or evening service. Sets are created, drama is presented, and many family and friends visit. This is a great opportunity to reach people for Christ who are coming to see, for example, a favorite nephew or granddaughter perform.

June

Graduate Recognition Service. We recognize the most recent graduates from high school and college. Sunday morning they will parade into the service in their caps and gowns and sit on the front pew. During the service they will be asked to stand when their name is called, and they will step to the front of the church, where they will be given a gift. The graduates remain standing while the pastor prays a prayer of blessing over them. Both music and message are directed to the graduates and their families.

needs presented to them by letter or personal request from a missionary. Many times a missionary will meet with them personally to share a need. The committee also plans the missions convention and appoints committees to handle various responsibilities of the convention. More recently we have given each department (youth, children, music, etc.) and adult Sunday school classes a country. It is their responsibility to decorate a table and an area, to procure the food for their featured recipe item, and to serve it at our "Taste of Missions." Servers are dressed in the garb of their country, and it is fun to see ownership develop as they make their country's booth the best they can. Last year over eight hundred people ate their way through the many taste locations in our building, accompanied by a variety of musical groups, including everything from a harpist to a jazz band. Many of the top missions churches are more than happy to share the great ideas they use in presenting missions in creative ways.

Someone with a recent answer to prayer will be featured during the Thanksgiving service. Usually we have an exciting answer to prayer from someone in the youth group, a child, or an adult. We ask them in advance to prepare a testimony. The service includes testimonies, worship, and a closing word of thanksgiving. Often we feature a benevolence offering and encourage our people to bring a food item for an inner city ministry.

Christmas is a time of regional traditions. Some areas will have a Christmas Eve service while others feature a Christmas Day service. With our strong Lutheran population, we find a traditional Christmas Eve candlelight service attracts both our people and those in our community without a church. Candles, music featuring our brass or strings, traditional Christmas carols, and a nativity scene with narration are all components of this service. Each year we endeavor to present the nativity scene in a unique way: We have incorporated it into the carols, using a dramatization and even "Christmas card" scenes. Entire families come together, and we emphasize participation by the congregation. The service must have the Christmas story read from the Scriptures. The sermon may contain visuals or even an illustrated sermon for the children's sake. In our community, most of the families leave the church for Christmas dinner and then open gifts, so the service must not last more than an hour.

> **Practical Steps to Make an Event Happen**
> 1. Appoint a committee to be responsible for the event.
> 2. Appoint a chairperson for the committee.
> 3. Set a budget.
> 4. Make sure all important steps are covered in a job description for the committee. Determine who is responsible for publicity, decorating, food, programs, and music.

Key Questions

What is the purpose of the Sunday morning, Sunday night, and Wednesday night services? What is the purpose of the Sunday School of the Bible? These are tough questions, but they need to be asked. Why do we do what we do? Is it done because of tradition, or is there a valid purpose for what we do? We took time in our planning meeting either to come up with good answers for "why we do what we do" or to stop doing it. These are the conclusions we came to:

1. *What is the purpose of the Sunday morning service?*
   a. Behavioral preaching; all preaching should translate into under-

standable behaviors that conform to the image of Christ.
   b. Worship God corporately; grow in the Word.
   c. Inspiration.
   d. Entry point into our church; most people visit a church on a Sunday morning.
   e. Public recognition of faith steps: salvation, water baptism, communion, baby dedications, healing, baptism in the Holy Spirit.
   f. Opportunities for prayer and ministry.
2. *What is the purpose of the Sunday night service?*
   a. Building community
   b. Ministry to the body
   c. Relationships
   d. Fellowship
3. *What is the purpose of the Wednesday night activities?*
   a. Training
   b. Skill building
   c. Intercessory prayer
4. *What is the purpose of the School of the Bible?*
   a. Systematic Bible study
   b. Doctrinal emphasis
   c. Communication of needs
   d. Smaller community opportunities

Planning and conducting special services does take special time and effort. But the rewards and benefits are worth the extra outlay of church and staff resources. Your church can be the beneficiary of spiritual and numerical growth as you provide these vehicles for the Holy Spirit to use in touching lives for the Kingdom.

Building Community Goodwill toward Church and Pastor

Zenas J. Bicket

Good community relationships are essential if the church is to be a growing church. Unfortunately, some congregations prefer the comfort of the status quo. No new members means the influence and power circles are not disturbed. But Scripture nowhere places a premium on the Christian community remaining comfortably undisturbed. The Great Commission says nothing at all about maintaining "ease in Zion."[1] Without qualification or reservation come the marching orders, "'Go into all the world and preach the good news to all creation'" (Mark 16:15). The commission includes more than foreign missionary service. The community in which God has planted the congregation is part of the world that needs to be reached. In fact, "hometown" comes first in the sequence: Witnesses in Jerusalem first . . . Judea and Samaria next . . . and finally "'to the ends of the earth'" (Acts 1:8).

What constitutes the community the local church is to reach? The exact definition may vary from the rural town to the large suburban area. For the purposes of this chapter we will use an all-inclusive definition. The community consists of people sharing some common interests and living in the same general locality. Even within the larger cities, there are fairly distinct communities. These may be represented as racial, religious, cultural, or economic communities. The church should extend open arms to members of all these subcommunities, but experience indicates that local churches usually attract persons with interests and backgrounds similar to the predominant makeup of the existing congregation. Fortunate, indeed, is the church that has a healthy mix of all the subcommunities so that the outreach can be more diverse and effective.

No matter how eloquently the gospel message is delivered, it is ineffective if it is not heard. "How can they believe in the one of whom they have not heard?" (Romans 10:14). So the question naturally follows: How can we get the unsaved to listen to the message? We must earn the right to be heard. The community will listen to the pastor and congregation toward whom they feel goodwill. When outsiders are persuaded that a church has the total welfare of the community at heart, they will listen when the pastor speaks.

Gaining community goodwill is absolutely essential if the church is to fulfill its mission. There is no place for a complacent attitude, one which says, "We're here, and we preach the gospel every week. When they need us they will come." Not so! When members of the outside community need help, they go to those who have given a loud and clear signal that they want to help. And wanting to help is demonstrated as the church and its members go into the community with Christlike love and compassion.

Attitude toward the Community

A positive attitude toward the community is crucial for both the pastor and the church. It takes only one visit to a church for a guest to decide that the church is indifferent, exclusive, or antagonistic toward outsiders. To fulfill its mission, the church must view the community with love, concern, and genuine interest.

With all the demands on the pastor's time, there are a multitude of excuses for not putting out the effort to be involved in the community. There are sermons to be prepared and books to be read. Counseling and ministering to the membership is more than a full-time task in itself. It is so easy to remind members of the congregation how they ought to be out in the community touching lives. But the pastor, too, must be out in the community for two good reasons: to serve as a model for his church and to represent the church to the community in a way that individual members can never do it.

To project a good image for the church and to gain the goodwill of the community, the pastor must avoid a holier-than-thou attitude. The community is to be won to Christ, not bludgeoned into submission. An enthusiastic pastor and congregation, rather than being apologetic for the church's doctrine and behavior, will speak with pride of their church, its doctrine, and its people. Such enthusiasm is contagious. People needing help are drawn, not to people who are depressed with their own problems, but to positive Christians who testify of what God has done for them in their struggles. A pastor and congregation solidly sold on their church will make outsiders believe the same about the church.

Many churches, especially small churches, minister to a narrow segment of a multicultural community. The extreme of this narrowness is a church in which one extended family provides the majority of membership and controls decisions and directions on a strongly partisan basis. In one sense the local church should be multicultural; in another sense it should not. No church can truly call itself Christian if it refuses to witness and win to Christ any specific ethnic group; on the other hand, the church has only one Bible, one message, one Lord and Savior. Though the message is singular, the people who need the message come from many ethnic and cultural backgrounds. The church has an obligation to them all.

As persons from varied backgrounds accept the message of salvation and become part of the local church, they do not become overnight exactly like the old-timers with their time-honored traditions. A large dose of patience and compassion must be prescribed for the Great Commission church reaching out to the entire community. It is understandable that established church members have feelings of apprehension when new and very different people become a part of the congregation. How should the old-timers relate to these outsiders? To assuage their feelings of being threatened, they should be taught, as a mark of their trust and love for God, to think of other cultures as vehicles through which the gospel can be expressed. The first-century Jewish Christians were stretched almost to the breaking point when God began bringing Gentiles into their fellowship. But today's congregation needn't face such stress; they have the benefit of the Jewish Christians' example, and we can prepare them to minister to a multicultural society. Can we, with the help of the Holy Spirit, rise to the same largeness of heart to embrace as Christian brothers and sisters those who come from backgrounds far different from our own? The multicultural nature of the community must always be much in the mind of the pastor and congregation who are determined to win the lost of the community.

> **The multicultural nature of the community must be kept in mind if it is to be won.**

A seminary professor who had previously pastored both small and large churches for over twenty years told his students who were anticipating pastoral ministry: "If I were a pastor, whether I wanted to or not, I would plunge into community affairs. First, I would study the community. I would find out who the people are and what they need. I know they need Christ, but possibly they need bread, too, and will not believe the stories of my Jesus who fed the hungry until they see that concern expressed through me."[2]

Such enthusiasm and concern for the community, and for all of its subcommunities, is a good start for any pastor accepting the spiritual leadership of a church.

Goodwill through Integrity and Good Reputation

Religion and business may seem to be mutually exclusive, but, in fact, there is a close relationship between the two. The businessperson without integrity is a blight in the community. A minister without integrity in business matters is a blight on the reputation of the church and the Lord he represents.

Nothing brings the minister more quickly into community disrepute than to be known as a bad financial risk. It is naive to think that a single unpaid bill is known only to the businessperson to whom the debt is owed. The business community shares information about deadbeats. And when a minister or a church is delinquent, the news travels doubly fast. Churches and pastors may be tempted to think that as religious entities they should be given special consideration for when they pay their bills. But God's children hold themselves to a higher, not a lesser, standard.

One minister's lack of integrity in paying bills promptly reflects not only on his congregation and his Lord but on the entire ministerial profession. Pastors who have left town with a trail of unpaid financial debts have made their successor's task extremely difficult. Such irresponsibility has sometimes been justified by claiming that God has promised to provide, so He will take care of those to whom the debt is owed. The debt, however, is not God's. True faith in God's promise to provide will foster accountability and a determination to personally pay the debt. The exercise of faith for provision is the responsibility of the one who incurs the debt, not the lender of the credit. Charge accounts and installment purchases are not wrong in themselves. But they have gotten many a person into irresponsible and sinful behavior. One's motto should be "I must pay as I go; and if I can't pay, I won't go." Bankruptcy may be legal, but it does not promote goodwill. Even if an individual, minister or layperson, declares bankruptcy, the moral obligation to repay a debt remains. The name of the Lord and the reputation of His church are at stake.

The pastor's integrity must also extend to public and private statements. Never should a minister make unfounded or questionable statements. At all cost, one must avoid a credibility gap. When a minister has a reputation for integrity, the community will respect his taking a stand and making moral statements even when they disagree with him on the specific issue.

The pastor must also demonstrate integrity in keeping promises and appointments. Each appointment is a promise, a promise to be kept with promptness. Contacts with key community business and civic leaders lay the foundation for future ministry opportunities. If a luncheon or office appointment is made, the pastor should be there as promised. The acquaintance visit should be respectful of the time limitations of the community leader. An informal agenda of two or three items the pastor wishes to mention will leave the leader with the awareness that the Lord's servant is businesslike and professional. Opportunity will eventually come for the pastor to share the spiritual burden he has for the community. The brief agenda might include the pastor's desire to be an involved member of the community, an offer to assist in any way compatible with the mission and ministry of the church, and a promise to support the leader with regular prayer.

In some smaller communities, ministers may be offered discounts on certain purchases or professional services. But never, never, never should the new pastor ask for a discount. God's servant cannot gain goodwill for the congregation, the ministry, and the Master by begging (as it will be perceived). If a discount is voluntarily offered, it should be generously acknowledged. If a pastor should ever face a sudden financial emergency, a loan may be the only immediate solution. But businesspeople or professionals in the congregation should never be placed in the awkward circumstance of having to say no or to make a loan that was not wholeheartedly extended. The privacy of the transaction would more than offset the relatively small amount of interest charged by the bank. The opportunity to establish a relationship with a community leader may also turn out to benefit the Lord's work in the community.

Though the pastor may meticulously honor these admonitions, members of the congregation with less awareness of propriety may ask the pastor to cosign for a loan. The pastor who attempts this kind of compassionate assistance will learn that it obligates and hampers an otherwise effective ministry. The pastor who finds it difficult to say no might respond, "All of my ministerial training advised pastors never to become involved in such joint alliances." Declining in this manner, along with some suggestions that might help the member solve a financial problem in another way, will win more friends in the long run—or avoid unnecessarily losing friends.

Goodwill through Service to the Community

To what extent should the pastor be involved in community and civic affairs? Must one work actively to correct society's wrongs? Are the blights of alcohol, drugs, gang activity, pollution, immorality, pornography, and racial injustice merely talked about from the pulpit (if mentioned at all)? Or is one obligated to participate in removing these injustices and wrongs? Of course, one should not forsake a heart gospel for a social gospel. But does an emphasis on the changed heart absolve the minister of responsibility for seeking a changed society?

Jesus called His followers the salt of the earth. Salt must touch some other substance before it can season or preserve. Even though the preaching of the gospel leaves little time to spearhead a variety of social causes in the community, the pastor should with his presence cooperate in attempts by the community to solve its social problems. The minister's voice as the messenger of God can speak with much authority and influence. Possibilities for involvement are many: serving on the school board, participating in PTA and civic clubs, cooperating with United Way and blood bank drives, and accepting appointments to head community improvement efforts. If the senior pastor is unable to participate in such activities, an associate might be able to represent the church.

The pastor and church can more quickly gain the goodwill of the community by love, concern, and compassion than by rudely crusading against evil in the community. One must always keep priorities in proper perspective. Winning the soul of the abortionist is more important than registering your opposition; more abortionists, prostitutes, and swindlers have been won by a quiet, loving witness than by violent crusades against their evil practices. There is, of course, a time to crusade, but let it be when God unmistakably commissions, as He did the Old Testament prophets, a prophetic, denunciatory ministry. Even so, the prophet's message was never accompanied with violence. When a message of judgment must be preached, a broken heart is the best source of the judgmental word.

As the pastor surveys ways to gain community goodwill through humble service, he will not be disappointed. Every community needs more volunteers. And working on committees, giving presentations, and public speaking are all opportunities for meeting people in the community. Those blessed with much—and Christians are blessed with so much—must give some back. To meet people who need relationships with a church and the Christ of that church is just an added opportunity of volunteer efforts. One moderate-size community holds an annual Good Community Fair, where booths of nearly one hundred organizations that use volunteers describe their programs. Many of these organizations function in areas related to the ministries of the church: e.g., hospice, Salvation Army, hospital auxiliaries, senior adult programs, nursing homes and senior centers, street missions, Alzheimer's Association, and Alliance for the Mentally Ill.

The church and its pastor should be especially concerned about the youth of the community. Waiting around every corner for an opportunity to ensnare our youth are the drug pushers, the gang leaders, and the purveyors of pornography. Crusading against these evils may have some value, but time spent in programs providing activities for youth not yet caught up in the wiles of the devil is much more effective in changing society. Involvement in community youth programs will send a strong message to the youth of the church: The pastor cares about you and what could happen to you; the pastor wants God's best for you.

The pastor will serve the community well and gain goodwill in the process as the community perceives a strong effort from the church to protect community values and morality. Television, cable, and local entertainment threaten to obliterate all vestiges of moral standards and behavior. But it takes more than one voice to stand against advertisers and organized purveyors of filth. A cooperative effort of several churches and church groups will let the community know that the religious leaders and their congregations are concerned—and praying. But pastors must be aware of the possible outside interpretation: that the churches are attempting to make everyone conform to Christian standards of conduct. Although we desire that everyone know Christ and serve Him faithfully (cf. 1 Corinthians 7:7), we can never force people to be inwardly righteous. They can be restrained by laws passed by a majority of legislators, but crusading churches should make it clear that they seek only to protect innocent youth and preserve family virtues for the welfare of the entire community. Spitting accusations at reprobate drug dealers and pornographers will not win them to Christ. Yet the community, and hopefully even the reprobates, will be touched by a compassionate, Spirit-prompted concern for the future of the children and the community. Boycotting the products of companies that support immoral entertainment is sometimes necessary. But again, concern rather than vindictiveness should be the face presented to the community.

There are so many ways a community can be improved, and involvement of the pastor and church in some of them will gain goodwill. The community will appreciate a church whose youth group accepts responsibility for cleaning up litter along the highway. Making the neighborhood more beautiful is not necessarily a spiritual exercise, but it can gain goodwill so that the message of salvation can be heard. Supporting the creation of parks and recreation facilities in deprived neighborhoods is another means of community improvement. The pastor and church need not find new projects to initiate. Every average community has leaders discussing things that can and should be improved. By listening to public discussions and reading the editorial page of the newspaper, the pastor can write notes of support and volunteer help for those projects that let the community know the church has the neighborhood, community, or city at heart.

We must never let happen in our Pentecostal churches, however, what has happened in many old-line churches. What they began as involvement to reach the community can become the end rather than the means to the end. Such churches have slipped into preaching a social gospel, and their lack of growth proves it. Tragic indeed is the Pentecostal church that is neither growing nor touching the community. But touching the community with a heart of compassion for the souls of the community will result in a growing church.

Goodwill through Cooperation

In every effort to gain the goodwill of the community, we must always remember our mission. Like the salt that seasons and preserves, we are to change the community, not join in its failings. But to wrap our righteous robes around ourselves and refuse to work with other Christians, whether or not they know salvation as we know it, just because we are opposed to ecumenism is a neglect of our commission to reach the world. We can join with non-Pentecostals to combat social evils. But we must never sacrifice our distinctive beliefs and experience for the sake of cooperation. A Pentecostal with an up-to-date empowerment by the Holy Spirit should be able to keep a focus on mission without compromise or concession. Cooperation with other churches for the sake of a better community is not evil ecumenism.[3]

If the theological distinctives present insurmountable difficulties, then nonreligious agencies headed by Christians can be an excellent way of making contacts and building community goodwill. Volunteer work with organizations like family services, friends of the library, and the public schools can eventually provide pastors or church members an opportunity to influence decisions on spending funds or choosing curriculum. Community members who applaud a voice for morality will feel goodwill and appreciation toward the church whose pastor upholds high standards of morality and ethics.

Volunteer community leaders often receive more criticism and abuse than appreciation. The servant of God cannot support decisions that violate basic morality and virtue. But a note of appreciation when moral decisions are made and a polite expression of regret when decisions undermine community morality will influence future decisions of the leaders. When there is a good relationship between the church and community leaders, some pastors have scheduled a City Employees Honor Day. If appropriate, county employees could be invited as well. Generous expression of appreciation for making the community a safe and wholesome city could be followed by a sermon on Proverbs 14:34: "Righteousness exalteth a nation: but sin is a reproach to any people" (KJV).

> **"The pastor with a generous and loving heart toward nearby churches will find local efforts blessed."**

Several Assemblies of God or Pentecostal/Charismatic churches in a community may seem competitive. The pastor with a generous and loving heart toward neighboring congregations and fellow ministers will find God's blessing on local efforts. Any changing of membership from one church to another always has potential for misunderstanding. Stealing members from other churches should be avoided at all cost. But to resist cooperative efforts to reach the community because of a fear of losing members to a cooperating church is extremely shortsighted.

A Pentecostal pastor has a special message to share with non-Pentecostal churches in the community. In this time of a renewed move of the Holy Spirit, many spiritual leaders and laypeople are looking to pastors of Pentecostal churches for assistance in receiving a new spiritual experience. Pentecostal pastors or churches so busy with internal programs that they cannot minister to outside groups will have to answer to God for the neglect. The opportunity to minister to non-Pentecostals must be earned by a spirit of friendliness and cooperation. An isolationist attitude does not bring invitations to share the baptism in the Holy Spirit with hungry hearts. If a Pentecostal church and its pastor have gained the respect and goodwill of the community, non-Pentecostals who are searching for a fresh reality will find it easy to visit a friendly and open spiritual counselor.

The growth of the charismatic movement in the traditional churches and in independent assemblies has brought the classical Pentecostal pastor some new concerns as well as opportunities. Lack of sufficient doctrinal background in some of these groups has brought abuses. But abuses cannot be allowed to stifle the true ministry of the Holy Spirit. From the 1973 General Council Minutes come these wise words:

Marks of the genuine moving of the Holy Spirit include the following: (1) Emphasis on worship in spirit and in truth of almighty God; (2) recognition of the person of Christ—His deity, His incarnation, and His redemptive work; (3) recognition of the authority of and hunger for the Word of God; (4) emphasis on the person and work of the Holy Spirit; (5) emphasis on the second coming of Christ; (6) emphasis on prayer for the sick; and (7) emphasis on sharing Christ in witnessing and evangelism.

The Assemblies of God wishes to identify with what God is doing in the world today. . . . We do believe in the institution of the church. We trust the Holy Spirit to bring the members of Christ's body into a true unity of the Spirit. . . .

The Assemblies of God does not place approval on that which is manifestly not scriptural in doctrine or conduct. But neither do we categorically condemn everything that does not totally or immediately conform to our standards. No genuine spiritual movement in church history has been completely free of problems or above criticism. The Pentecostal movement of this century has experienced its problems relating both to doctrine and conduct. Spiritual maturity leads to a balanced life which will bear the fruit of the Spirit while displaying the gifts of the Spirit.

We place our trust in God to bring His plan about as He pleases in His sovereign will. It is important that we find our way in a sound scriptural path, avoiding the extremes of an ecumenism that compromises scriptural principles and an exclusivism that excludes true Christians.[4]

Goodwill through Avoidance of Partisan Politics

What should be the pastor's role in local, state, or national politics? The admonition Jesus gave His followers is easy to quote: "'Give to Caesar what is Caesar's, and to God what is God's'" (Matthew 22:21). But how does the verse transfer into the pastor's relationship with the everyday working of the government of his community, state, and nation? Those to whom the pastor ministers should first be challenged to be dedicated Christians; then they should be encouraged to be conscientious citizens. To this extent the pastor is involved in politics.

The pastor, of course, cannot overtly support partisan political causes even though he has his personal preferences. At the very least the pastor should encourage adult members of the congregation to participate in the election process and set an example by casting an informed ballot. The pastor's involvement in politics and government should be restricted to issues rather than personalities. The minister, of course, is obligated to speak out on moral questions, no matter what the political implications may be. Without mentioning names, one can directly address the scriptural principles being violated. The pastor must respect the fact that the congregation will include believers of differing political persuasions. It is for this reason that no party or candidates can be endorsed. Entirely proper, however, is the dealing with issues involving moral principles and the encouragement of all members to know how the various candidates stand on such moral issues.

The pastor who respects the appropriate limitations on political activity will be regarded by the community as a spiritual leader rather than a political figure. Though there may be disagreements on which candidates best represent Christian virtues and values, the faithful pastor will gain the goodwill of an entire community for standing strong on moral issues but avoiding political involvements.

Goodwill through Creditable Public Relations

Public relations is nothing more than keeping the community aware of the church and its activities, goals, and achievements. An effective public relations program does not require a large budget. Even a small church can solicit favorable interest in its activities. The pastor in any case must develop some expertise in public relations, supervising the overall operation of the program. The entire congregation also should know they are involved in public relations work for their church, even though they do not write news stories or prepare advertising copy for the media. The pastor should be aware of the different types of public relations activity and use each appropriately.

Advertising is a paid announcement in print or on some electronic media. Because the advertiser pays for the service, the content and form of the message can be controlled.

Publicity is the free attention a church receives because of its involvement in activities of general interest to the local community. A news story about the church may be written by a media reporter, or the church itself may send a press release to the media. Only to the extent the church controls the event being reported can it control the content of the news story. Since no payment is made to the media for publicity items, the media organization has the final word on how the event is reported.

Promotion is the advancement of the church through both advertising and publicity. Promotion is the ultimate goal of an effective public relations program.

The public relations image of the church should be contemporary without sacrificing the respect that properly belongs to a religious institution. A visit to a public library will produce ideas and examples that catch the public eye. Hiring the services of a media designer who understands the mission and nature of the church could be money well invested. Drawing on current resources for ideas will help the public to perceive the church as able to meet today's needs with up-to-date answers. The Bible is always up-to-date, but we bring people to the Word in the way the times demand.

The correspondence that comes from the pastor or the church office creates a public impression. Is the church office careful in using correct spelling and grammar? If so, maybe the pastor and people can be trusted to be accurate in what they preach and teach. Are the media presentations contemporary? Has the church found that a web page on the Internet superhighway can be used to reach the millions of Internet subscribers? If so, viewers seeing or hearing about the church's use of the latest technology will assume that the message delivered with contemporary means will also meet contemporary problems.

Broadcast media are excellent means for reaching the local community. But the approach should be more than another talking head delivering a sermon. The already-reached Christians may listen or watch with interest, but to reach the outsiders who need the message of salvation, the approach must be different. A program should be carefully planned and timed. It should have plenty of illustrations that will hold attention. One central idea or emphasis is better than a hodgepodge of ideas. Theological discussion should be saved for the Sunday school class or midweek service. Speak in a person-to-person tone, keeping the tempo brisk and lively. Sinners can be converted through a broadcast, but generally the church should look on its media activity as building goodwill so the community can be reached with the salvation message. The Holy Spirit can lead the pastor to the right balance of goodwill and good news.

Goodwill and Good Growth

Never should a pastor or a church seek community goodwill for the sheer pleasure of being well thought of. Never should the servant of the Lord be simply a people pleaser. Our sole aim should be to please our Master in what we do. Some people misinterpret the words of Jesus when He said, "Woe to you when all men speak well of you" (Luke 6:26). Trying to get everyone to speak well of us is quite a task. To achieve such human favor would necessarily mean forfeiting God's favor. But it is improper exegesis to turn the statement of Jesus around to read, "Woe to you if you don't have everyone speaking evil of you." God's people are not told to invite persecution and ill will. It certainly will come if we follow Christ completely, but we are not to seek it.

The apostle Paul must have captured some of this spirit of attracting goodwill when he said, "I have become all things to all men so that by all possible means I might save some. I do all this for the sake of the gospel, that I may share in its blessings" (1 Corinthians 9:22–23). Still today, God's servants and people must do whatever it takes to win the lost. The church with that burden will be a growing church.

Relating to Community Leaders

Warren D. Bullock

The Pentecostal pastor's maximum effectiveness is dependent on seeing himself as pastor to his community or city. He must see himself as more than pastor only to those who come to church each Sunday. His pastoral role extends beyond the four walls and stained glass windows of his church building. Since Jesus taught that "the field is the world" (Matthew 13:38), a narrow, restrictive view of the pastoral function will run counter to Jesus' broader view of the task.

Some pastors limit their ministries by misunderstanding the apostle Paul's definition of the pastor-teacher. In outlining specific "people-gifts" from Christ to the church, Paul says, "It was he who gave some to be . . . pastors and teachers" (Ephesians 4:11). The function of the pastor-teacher is "to prepare God's people for works of service, so that the body of Christ may be built up" (v. 12). So the pastor may argue that his only job is to prepare the Christian to do the work of the ministry. After all, the shepherd does not bear sheep, only sheep bear sheep. Therefore, when he has trained the congregation in their task, his own task is completed.

> **Some leaders will be won to Christ only by the pastor.**

However, Paul is not attempting in Ephesians 4 to provide an exhaustive list of what a pastor is to do. He confines himself to that which will bring about "unity in the faith and in the knowledge of the Son of God" and will result in the body of Christ becoming "mature, attaining to the whole measure of the fullness of Christ" (v. 13). Beyond these important goals will be a ministry that focuses on a lost world that must be reached not only by the congregation but by the pastor too.

Persons of influence generally hold other influential persons in high esteem. Because of the pastor's respected position, community leaders will be open to the building of a relationship that can result in positive, spiritual dividends. Some of these leaders will be influenced or won to Christ only by the pastor.

The ministry of Jesus provides a model for wide influence among diverse leaders. Jesus did not live in an ivory tower, isolating himself from people. You cannot read the Gospels without having the sense of being in a crowd. Jesus taught that the essence of Christianity was the building of relationships, first with God and then with our neighbor (Mark 12:30–31). To follow Christ's example, the pastor will develop a consistent, growing relationship with Him, out of which will flow a life of building relationships with others. From relationship comes the right to speak into another's life, particularly about spiritual matters.

Among the community leaders with whom the pastor will develop relationships are public school educators, elected political officials, newspaper editors, funeral directors, doctors, attorneys, CEO's, and bankers. His motivation for reaching out to these leaders must not be with the idea of using them to further his own or the church's ends. Rather he will touch their lives with their best and eternal interests in mind. In the spirit of Christ, he will seek to serve rather than to be served. That he and the church may also benefit from the relationship is simply a by-product of that service, not its goal.

Public Relations

Public relations, as the name implies, is the building of relationships with the general public. When tied to the church and its mission, public relations gives visibility to the church for the purpose of reaching the community for Christ. Newspaper advertising, direct mail, television and radio spots, and high profile special events may all serve to develop relations with the public, which in turn may provide an audience for the presentation of the gospel. However, these approaches to building relationships tend to be somewhat impersonal. The public is more likely to identify with a person than with an institution, especially the church. Most often that person is the pastor.

When I pastored Calvary Temple in Seattle, Washington, it was known as "the church by the freeway." About seventy blocks from downtown Seattle and about twenty blocks from the University of Washington, situated right by the I-5 freeway, the brick church with the white cross became a familiar landmark. If people decided to attend, it was easy to find. But its location alone did not determine whether or not they attended.

If I introduced myself to key leaders as the pastor of Calvary Temple, they identified the church by the freeway with a person. That person/ pastor smiled, was friendly and approachable. He seemed genuinely interested in them. He didn't act as if he were better than them. If they later decided to go to church, would they come to Calvary Temple because of the effective advertising and media blitz, or would they come because they had identified the church with a person they would like to get to know better, even if he was a preacher?

In some cases this principle of identifying the institution with a person is reversed. Business and political leaders often place value on a person based on the organization he or she is associated with. That value may be determined by what the organization, in effect what the pastor, can do for them. However, if the church has established a good reputation over the years, the pastor benefits from that reputation, even if he has only recently taken the pastorate. In either case, the church and its pastor can exert significant influence on people in key community positions.

> **The public is more likely to identify with a person than with an institution.**

As a general rule, the smaller the community, the greater the opportunity for influence among leaders. Conversely, the larger the community, the more difficult it is to build relationships with leaders. Having served both in the Greater Seattle metropolitan area and in Spanaway at the suburban/rural outskirts of Tacoma, Washington, I found the opportunity for impact was greater in the latter than in the former. In Seattle I was one pastor among hundreds. In Spanaway I pastored the largest church in the area. Consequently doors of opportunity frequently opened to me in Spanaway that never opened in Seattle.

Whatever size community God has called us to, we must take the initiative to meet leaders. Make an appointment to meet the mayor. Schedule time with the superintendent of schools. Introduce yourself to the editor of the local newspaper. Join Rotary or Kiwanis in order to rub shoulders with the influencers of the city. Don't wait for them to come to you. They won't. You must go to them.

Politics

To put the term *politics* in the same sentence with the *Pentecostal pastor* seems contradictory. Politics smacks of influence peddling, moral relativism, mud-slinging elections, and expediency in place of principle. The Pentecostal pastor stands for positive influence, moral absolutes, voting one's conscience, and living by biblical principles. The art of political compromise is unknown to the man or woman of God. So sharp is this dichotomy that the pastor's tendency will be to avoid anything or anyone connected with politics. But a great opportunity will have been missed.

John Pollock chronicles the ability of evangelist Billy Graham to be a friend to politicians without being political.[1] Reverend Graham has met with presidents, emperors, prime ministers, and other national leaders around the world. His integrity, candor, keeping of confidences, and evident concern for each leader have helped him to have spiritual influence in political circles most ministers could never enter. His associations with world leaders have not led to personal compromise but have allowed him to be Christ's representative to important decision makers. While Billy Graham has a unique international role to play, the pastor can play a similar role in the local community.

When one is at opposite ends of the political spectrum from elected officials, the tendency may be to attack and criticize them. The wise pastor will know how to distinguish between confronting issues on the basis of moral principle and challenging leaders who hold objectionable points of view. To dishonor an official and his position in order to argue for and establish an honorable principle is a contradiction. Once a pastor attacks an elected official personally, the opportunity for continued spiritual influence is ended. You cannot win to Christ those you are vilifying. No matter how much you may disagree with their stance on the issues, you must not allow worldly methods and attitudes to destroy a future opportunity for dynamic Christian witness.

Watch for decisions and actions the official can be commended for, and then write or phone your appreciation. Such positive reinforcement can often have a greater long-term impact than actively taking opposing positions. The church should not be known only for what it is against, but also for what it is for. Unfortunately many churches develop an "anti" reputation, which hurts their influence in the community.

When a church I pastored decided to start a Christian school, we determined that it was not going to serve as a protest against the public school system. In fact we met with the public school administrators to express support of their schools and to explain that our church school was being established to provide an alternative to the public school. We were not opposing them and the work they were doing. In fact, we would do all we could to assist and undergird them in their challenging responsibilities. My own children attended public school and would continue to do so.

The response from these educators was positive and open. We continued to encourage our church people to be actively involved in the parent-teacher fellowship and other opportunities to provide Christian influence. My personal contacts with the superintendent of schools through the weekly Kiwanis luncheons were also an important factor in maintaining a healthy relationship with the school system. Later our church became the primary site for the annual baccalaureate service for graduates and their families.

Politics? The world might call it that. But the Pentecostal pastor sees it as building relationships with people of influence in the community. Again the goal is not to enhance the pastor's reputation but to give spiritual help to leaders, who in turn make the decisions that can change the community.

Prayer

Prayer is the pastor's single most effective tool for impacting community leaders. Personal access to such leaders is often severely limited, but prayer knows no limits. Guarded walls of suspicion and antagonism are not easily breached, except through prayer. Prejudices against the church and/or hostility toward God himself are intimidating opponents, but not to prayer. Prayer invades impregnable hearts, softens rock-hard spirits, and pushes intransigence toward God.

The pastor will lead his people to pray for those in positions of authority out of obedience to Scripture. Paul's exhortation to Timothy is to us as well: "I urge, then, first of all, that requests, prayers, intercession and thanksgiving be made for everyone—for kings and all those in authority, that we may live peaceful and quiet lives in all godliness and holiness" (1 Timothy 2:1–2).

Ronald Hastie pastored in Olympia, the capital city of Washington State. Some years ago he began a pattern of prayer with his congregation at Evergreen Christian Center that continues to this day. In the Sunday bulletin he would list key leaders: denominational, educational, political, missionary, etc. In the morning service he would then lead his people in prayer for these leaders. The following week he would send a letter to each of those they had prayed for, stating that the congregation of Evergreen Christian Center had them on their prayer list. No political position was advanced, no requests were made, and no favors were asked. Prayer was the focus. Needless to say, in a city where the state legislature grapples with the issues of the day, such a letter regarding prayer was well received.

Long before "prayer walks" were publicized, the Holy Spirit led me to begin walking around blocks of Seattle, praying. I began by walking the blocks immediately surrounding the church and then over time expanding the territory. As I prayed for each home and each business I walked by, I found my burden for the city increasing. In addition, my passion for the lost intensified. Without forethought, I found myself praying for the leaders of the city not only while I was walking but while I was driving or showering or shopping. I came to know our city better than I ever had and discovered new insights about its spiritual darkness and depravity. The capacity to identify evil strongholds increased, and thus I knew better how to pray for my city and its leaders.

Two unforgettable prayer experiences relating to city leadership have been burned into my memory. While in prayer one morning, a question rose unbidden from my spirit. I had not anticipated it nor been thinking about it. It was this: "What one person in Seattle, if he or she were to find Christ, would have the greatest spiritual impact on the city?" Just as quickly as the question had come, the name and face of a well-known, high-profile leader came to my mind. Then I felt the Spirit's prompting, *That's the person you need to intercede for.* So I did. I cannot say that I have yet seen the answer to my prayers, but I continue to pray with the confidence that I am praying in the will of God.

The second experience was similar in that I sensed clear and specific direction as to how to pray. That is not surprising since the Word promises that "the Spirit helps us in our weakness. We do not know what we ought to pray for, but the Spirit himself intercedes for us" (Romans 8:26). My experience has been that this help from the Spirit comes not only through praying in the Spirit, but by the Spirit helping me to know what to pray for with the understanding. Such was the case in this experience, as I heard the Spirit's directive, *Pray for a change of leadership at the top of city government.* A few weeks later the mayor announced his intention not to seek reelection. My prayers alone did not create the mayor's decision, but I do believe they played a part.

Prayer is an unbelievably powerful weapon for good. Without it every effort of the pastor to exert strong influence on community leaders will be annulled. Prayer can easily open doors that the pastor may unsuccessfully try to knock down without prayer. A pastor who comes from the prayer closet aglow with the Spirit will find favor with people in high and low positions whom he could never impact otherwise.

The Pentecostal pastor has the advantage of being Spirit filled, Spirit anointed, and Spirit led. The Holy Spirit will use him to touch the lives of people in authority. The fruit of such ministry may grow slowly and imperceptibly, but it will grow! And the leader, the church, and the community will be better for it.

Changing Pastorates

Ron McManus

All of us have experienced the emotion of wanting to resign our pastorate on Monday mornings. Maybe you are like the pastor who every Monday drove out to the edge of town, past the city limits, just to get the feeling of what it would be like to leave town. Even when we get past those momentary feelings, we have to acknowledge that determining God's will, plan, and purpose for our ministry—including how to make a smooth transition in pastorates when that seems wise—represents one of the most crucial times in life.

In this chapter, we want to explore (1) how to determine God's will in making a pastoral change, (2) what must be considered in the transition or passing of the baton from one leader to another, and (3) how to begin ministry in a new place—effectively!

Determining God's Will

Pastors can sometimes suffer because of decisions made in the emotion of a moment. A premature or ill-advised decision can lead to a lifetime of regret. How do we sort through all the things going on in our ministry so that we can hear the voice of God and respond to the prompting of His Spirit? Before resigning a pastorate, it is vital to ask ourselves several important questions.

Have I fulfilled the vision God put in my heart when I came here?

Remember the excitement of being selected as the pastor of a body of people who had expressed their confidence in your leadership and their desire that you lead them? There was excitement at the potential of this open door of ministry. It is important to look back on those moments and evaluate the things God put in your heart regarding the church, its ministries, and your role. If you made the move in the will of God to come to this place of ministry, have you fulfilled what God called you to do?

I remember as a student in Bible college wrestling with the will of God. I was not sure about my calling to pastoral ministry. I remember a professor who counseled me on one particular day and changed my understanding about God's will. He said to me, "Do you believe you are here right now at college in the will of God?" My response was yes. Then he said these words: "Then you're already in the will of God. The important thing now is to continue to walk sensitively to the Holy Spirit and the Lord will direct your steps."

I firmly believe that if God has brought you to a place of ministry, you are already in the will of God; to make a move, then, will require God's releasing you from the original vision He gave you or assuring you that you have fulfilled the mission He called you to accomplish in that local church.

John Maxwell says,

> No man can measure the burden that God has given him; he can only respond to it. When God gives you a burden you must stay at a work because it is God who has given you that burden; but when the burden leaves, it is time for you to leave. However, just because the burden is beginning to leave does not mean it is time to leave. Before a leader begins changing his location, he must examine why his burden is leaving. If there is a valid reason his burden is leaving, then he can leave geographically. If he can't give a valid reason for his burden leaving then he has to go back to the Word of God, to prayer, to repentance, and repeat the first works.[1]

Am I allowing my emotions to dictate my decision to leave?

One of the great problems in the ministry is burnout. Many of us come to points of physical and emotional distress where we do not feel able to function any longer in the setting of our present calling. I remember vividly a time in my own life when this was the case. We had just completed a major four-year building program at our church. We also conducted a capital stewardship program to raise two million dollars. During the last two years of the building program, our church had five Sunday services. Many Sundays I ministered in all five services. By the time we moved into our new facilities, my emotions were completely spent. I didn't even want to show my friends or colleagues through our new facilities. I hated the place and the building. My temptation, as is the case for many pastors after a major building program, was to resign and leave. Fortunately, I did not allow my emotions to dictate that decision, although the temptation was extremely great. It has been eight years since that building program, and I remain pastor of the church. How grateful I am I did not jump ship when my physical and emotional state had quit. Some of the most productive ministry of my life has happened since that time.

Does the Lord want to stretch my life personally where I am now?

Many pastors have been in the ministry over twenty years, but their ministries are only two or three years old because they change churches every two or three years, repeating the same sermons and style of ministry over and over again. To remain in one place of pastoral ministry requires personal growth and stretching. Often we do not want to move outside our comfort zones. The Lord places us in specific points of ministry that require our own personal growth and development. We must resist the urge to move on to greener pastures and decide to grow where we are planted. A dear saintly veteran minister said to me one time, "If you will take care of the depth of your ministry, God will take care of the breadth."

Am I allowing a few people to cause me to lose perspective?

Probably one of the greatest gifts in the ministry is perspective. If the enemy can cause us to lose perspective, wrong decisions will result. In my church body there are a minority of people who are negative about whatever leadership is seeking to accomplish. It is important to keep in perspective the number of people who seem to resist your leadership. Sometimes we become overwhelmed by this small group of people and ignore the vast majority who love us, support us, and are praying for us. We should never allow people nipping at our heels to influence decisions regarding our ministry or the direction of the church.

Am I running from a problem that the Lord has called me to address?

Some churches have a history of specific kinds of problems. Churches that change pastors every three or four years have a problem that needs to be addressed. If you were to ask a district superintendent, he would tell you that most of the problems in local churches are the result of mistakes made by leaders. They may not have been made by the present pastor and are possibly due to situations with a pastor from many years ago, but the lay leadership of the church determined they would not allow themselves to be hurt again in that particular way. In many situations, healing comes to a church body through a pastor who remains faithful and committed in the face of long-standing structural or personality difficulties in the local church. Running from the problem is not the solution. The Lord is looking for a leader who will remain faithful, continue to love the people, and help them work through the problems or difficulties that have stifled their growth and kept them from fulfilling the mission God called them to as a church.

How will my family be affected by a move now?

One of the most sensitive points in making a change in ministry relates to the pastor's family, especially the children. As a parent, you must be responsive to where they are and how a move will affect them. If it is God's will for you to move, the Lord is able to work in their lives, enabling them to accept the move. On the other hand, there may be times when a child is not responsive; it still may be God's will for you to move. In any case, it is vital that you remain open in your communication with your children and do everything possible to make the move easy for them.

Dealing with Transition

If you are able to answer these questions successfully and are convinced God is leading you to change your place of ministry, the next important question is, How do I make this move so my present ministry does not suffer and assure that my future ministry will be effective?

A graceful exit is essential. It recognizes when a job or a relationship is over. It involves leaving the past without denying its value or importance and believing that every exit is also a new entry.

John Maxwell states, "When you leave properly, many things happen. You will grow as a believer and as a leader. The work you leave will continue to grow. The work to which you are going will grow. The body of Christ will grow. Your friends will grow because you will take them with you as you communicate your dream to them."[2]

How you communicate a resignation to a congregation affects not only how they evaluate your ministry with them, but prepares them to accept and respond to new leadership. In resigning, the first step is to communicate to the church board your decision. This is best done in person; however, it is important that you submit a written resignation as well.

The written resignation gives you an opportunity to articulate your feelings regarding what God has spoken to you about your move as well as to affirm the church, which He has allowed you to lead for a time. This written resignation should then be communicated to the congregation in a Sunday morning service. I have discovered over the years that if a resignation is read early in a service, for all practical purposes, the service is over. I recommend that a resignation not be communicated until the message has been preached and an altar response given.

It is important in resigning to communicate effectively to the people who have loved and supported you so they do not feel you are rejecting them. Throughout your ministry, it is important that you communicate a Kingdom perspective to your congregation. Over the years in my pastoral ministry, many associates have come and gone. We have been able to help our congregation keep perspective because we have a worldwide view of the kingdom of God and recognize our role in it.

Many church boards do not know how to move through this transition time and begin the process of selecting a new pastor. If they will allow, it is important for you to give them some guidance in how to structure the transition process. Also encourage them to talk with the district superintendent. The superintendent has valuable years of experience in the pastoral selection process and can be very helpful to a church board.

Many pastors leave churches with a great deal of emotional baggage. All of us have experienced hurts in the ministry; it is important to put behind us the events and emotions that may have accumulated. Whatever you need to do to make things right with individual members of the congregation, do it; do everything in your power to leave with a clean slate. This is extremely important for you, far more important than it is for the congregation you are leaving. Any emotional baggage you carry into a new pastorate will immediately influence and cripple your effectiveness. My parents have been in the ministry nearly fifty years. I have watched them go through many struggles and hurts in numerous pastorates over that time. It is exciting to see them in their seventies and still effective in ministry because they refused to carry emotional baggage from the hurtful experiences in pastorates. I cannot overemphasize how important this release is to your effectiveness in the ministry and the well-being of your spouse and family.

One of the temptations when leaving a pastorate is to receive phone calls from past parishioners and to be invited back into the area for numerous occasions. Unfortunately, many problems have arisen with former pastors visiting parishioners, which puts both the former pastor and the parishioner(s) in a vulnerable position, open to criticism, with the new pastor. Following is a list of guidelines and procedures that are important to consider after having left a church.

1. The former pastor should sever all ties with church operations.
2. The former pastor should contact parishioners only after notifying the current pastor and receiving his approval.
3. The former pastor should not return unless he receives an invitation from the current pastor.
4. The former pastor should not take advantage of former parishioners when passing through by stopping to spend the night or receiving love offerings from them, but should make contact with the new pastor of the church when planning to visit any of the members.
5. The former pastor should not pursue relationships with former parishioners after leaving the church.
6. The former pastor should refrain from giving any advice or counsel to former parishioners.
7. The former pastor should not preach funerals or weddings or perform any other pastoral ministry for former parishioners unless the current pastor gives the invitation.
8. If living in the same community, the former pastor should if at all possible attend another church.

In other words, when you leave—leave.

For the new pastor coming in, it is important that you leave a written overview of several areas of church ministry, beginning with the finances. Make sure financial reports are in order so the new pastor can readily see the financial standing of the church. If there are commitments that have been made but not reflected in the financial reports, include them in the overview so the new pastor will not be blindsided by financial commitments the board and the pastor have made that are not a part of the ongoing financial report. This overview should include documents of the church: the constitution, the bylaws, and any other documents that relate to the ministry. This will allow the new pastor to get a feel for the legal aspect of the ministry and to read through the official documents on properties and buildings.

Minutes of the last annual business meeting can also be of tremendous help to a new pastor. The pastor can see any unfinished business discussed in the annual church meeting; he can immediately be abreast of congregational concerns and specific discussions that have taken place. All these things will allow the new pastor or pastoral candidate to gain an understanding of where the church is. It will also demonstrate a very positive attitude toward your leadership and your organization of the ministry.

One of the critical struggles in the pastoral transition comes in churches that have associate pastors. It is my firm belief that pastoral staff work for the pastor. There are differing views in various churches, but I believe pastoral teams work together most effectively when there is one boss and one person the staff is responsible to.

When the pastor resigns, the pastoral staff member(s) should resign also. This doesn't mean they have to leave immediately; they may stay during the transition period. But the new pastor should be given the right to select those who will serve with him or her in the pastorate. This is the only way that loyalties and commitments can be made to the senior pastor. It is important that a church board understand these dynamics. Many problems have risen with associates during transition periods because the associates felt they should become the pastor of the church or because they were not loyal and committed to the new pastor's leadership. These problems can be avoided if associates understand that they work for the pastor and their tenure is up when the pastor resigns. If the new pastor selects them or chooses to keep them on the pastoral team, that is fine, but it should be the new pastor's prerogative.

Beginning in a New Place

Candidating for a church can be an interesting experience (to say the least). Several factors enter into the candidating process. Prior to meeting with the church board or pulpit committee, it is important to get proper information to assist in that meeting. First, you need a copy of the constitution and bylaws of the church. This will tell you the prerogatives and assignment of the pastor and allow you to see how the selection process has been established. Second, it would be helpful to have a copy of the financial statement of the church, letting you know if there have been financial problems in the past and how solid the financial footing is at the present time. Third, it would be helpful to have a copy of the church's mission statement, if there is one. These are specific areas you will want to discuss with the board or pulpit committee in your initial meeting. Most committees feel that the meeting is for them to find out everything they can about you. However, it is important for you to let them know you also need information about them so you can effectively evaluate whether or not your ministry would fit with their goals and objectives as a church. You will want to hear them articulate their desires for the church in the future. What are the things they feel are critical issues being faced by the church at the present time? What kind of pastor do they think would be most effective in their local body? What are they looking for in a shepherd? It is then very important to share your philosophy and vision for ministry. Is there a compatibility between what you believe God has called you to do and what this congregation really needs and desires?

On the Sunday of my election to my present pastorate, at the conclusion of the Sunday evening service and prior to the vote, I had an open forum time with the congregation, allowing them to ask questions of me and to give me a chance to share my philosophy of ministry with them. It proved to be a very important session. This allows people personally to hear your heart for ministry and your vision for the church. Set time limits on the session. Take thirty minutes or so to do this prior to the vote, so the exchange does not become lengthy or allow one or two people to dominate the conversation. In my case, the forum resulted in a 98 percent vote.

> **" Spend your first year getting to know the people. "**

The beginning of a ministry in a new congregation is affectionately referred to as the honeymoon. It can last for up to a year. Many ministers say they have been at a church for ten years and are still on their honeymoon. Essentially, the honeymoon is a time when people have not had a chance to form negative opinions about the pastor; the absence of criticism allows a new pastor to establish some things that would later on probably be more difficult. However, be very careful during this period not to make major changes in any dimension of the ministry. I believe the first year specifically should be spent in getting to know the people and letting them experience your love for them. The first year in a new pastorate is a wonderful time to do some specific training, especially with the church board. During the first year of my present pastorate, I had three overnight retreats with the members of our board, which allowed me to share more specifically my vision for the church, allowed us to plan and prepare for the future of the ministry, and gave us a special time to knit our lives together in a bond of love. This is extremely important for the future of the ministry. It has been said that if you are leading people and no one is following, you are simply taking a walk. The days are gone when strong, autocratic leadership could demand that people follow without question. It simply will not happen in today's culture. Effective pastors must spend time in building consensus, training and equipping leadership, and then walking with them into the future.

Your attitude toward the former pastor's leadership is very important during this process. All new pastors find things they feel were inadequate in the previous pastor. It is a mistake to point these things out to the board or to members of the congregation. Your responsibility is to be positive toward the previous leader. The people who loved the former pastor will love you for that, and those that didn't even like the previous leader will respect you for not being negative toward leadership. It is a win-win situation for you to be positive in your public as well as private expressions about the previous pastor's ministry.

Your role in beginning at a new place is critical. The first year in a pastorate establishes patterns that a pastor will live with into the future. One thing the Lord impressed upon me when I became the pastor of a new church was that I would make my "own bed of hay." Potentially the Lord was saying that what you establish as priorities for the ministry in the first year are the priorities you will find yourself living with long term. For example, if you build a ministry on hype, then that's what you have to continue. If you build it on discipleship, then that will be the hallmark of your ministry there. If you build it on evangelism, that will be a priority that will continue. This means that the first year in a new pastorate is extremely important. Make sure you establish biblical priorities you are prepared to live with in that pastorate. If you do, they will stand you in good stead throughout your time of leadership in the local church.

What Is Biblical Counseling?

Wayde I. Goodall

I am often asked the question, "What is Christian counseling?" Or "What do you mean when you say we should counsel people biblically?" Are we talking about just using Scripture when we talk to people? Do we ever deviate from the truths found in the Bible when counseling others? There is some confusion on the subject. I have known people who must use a Scripture verse whenever they give advice. I have known people who seem to use the Bible as a weapon and actually repel people rather than help them discover how much God loves them and wants to help them. God can show caring pastors marvelous ways to help those in need—unique ways that are creative and right to the point.

Recall, for a moment, the way David's counselor Nathan confronted him about sin in his life. The Bible tells about the devastating sin that David was involved in, having committed adultery with Bathsheba. It appears that David was going to try to just forget it when he was informed by her that she was pregnant. David had a real dilemma on his hands, not to mention what Bathsheba was facing. David felt he needed to cover his sin and devised a plan that would get her husband killed. He asked his military leaders to place Bathsheba's husband, Uriah, in the front line of battle, then withdraw support from him, allowing the enemy to kill him. David's plan worked. Uriah died in battle. He was a good man, a good husband, a dedicated soldier, and a loyal citizen. After his death, David was free to marry Bathsheba. Even though she was pregnant, David was evidently able to conceal that matter as well. David was home free—or was he?

Obviously David had forgotten that God was watching his every step. God saw the lust, lies, adultery, murder, pride, and rationalization (2 Samuel 12). David permitted a barrier to rise between him and God. He didn't want to face his problem and make it right. Every step of the way David could have stopped. He could have stopped when he began to lust for Bathsheba or before he issued his invitation to adultery. A person can stop sinning at any point, make things right with God, and begin again. It is the enemy of our soul who makes us think we need to continue along the path of sin, covering our tracks. He is the one who holds us slave to that course.

David's problem seemed to be over, but God remembered. God spoke to David's friend and counselor Nathan. Somehow, God filled Nathan in on all the details and on how He felt about the failure of his leader. God also told Nathan to speak to David in a confrontational way and warn him. Nathan loved God and he loved his friend David. His dilemma was that David could continue to deny the problem and even possibly have Nathan killed for such an accusation. Nathan must have also felt something that every true friend needs to feel: A friend's eternal soul is more important than an earthly friendship. It is better to win a friend to Christ and help him get his relationship right with God than to keep the friendship.

Nathan thought of a unique way to confront David. He began with a story:

> "There were two men in a certain town, one rich and the other poor. The rich man had a very large number of sheep and cattle, but the poor man had nothing except one little ewe lamb he had bought. He raised it, and it grew up with him and his children. It shared his food, drank from his cup and even slept in his arms. It was like a daughter to him.

> "Now a traveler came to the rich man, but the rich man refrained from taking one of his own sheep or cattle to prepare a meal for the traveler who had come to him. Instead, he took the ewe lamb that belonged to the poor man and prepared it for the one who had come to him."

> David burned with anger against the man and said to Nathan, "As surely as the Lord lives, the man who did this deserves to die! He must pay for that lamb four times over, because he did such a thing and had no pity" (2 Samuel 12:1–6).

David had pronounced his own judgment.

When Nathan knew David understood the point of the story, he said, "'You are that man!'" (v. 7). After a further rebuke and warning from God, Nathan informed David about how God was going to discipline him. Then David said, "'I have sinned against the Lord'" (v. 13). Nathan gave his friend God's message: "'The Lord has taken away your sin. You are not going to die. But because by doing this you have made the enemies of the Lord show utter contempt, the son born to you will die'" (vv. 13–14).

The story is tragic, but the lesson on how to confront is brilliant. Only God could have given Nathan this plan. Sometimes ministers need an original plan from God as they sincerely endeavor to help those they care about.

In counseling people, spiritual leadership needs to understand some basic biblical principles of counseling. Following are the ten important ones.

1. *Holiness and mental health are synonymous.*

The more stable people become as Christians and the more they understand how to apply the truths of God's Word to their lives, the better mental health they will have. Walking in the ways that God has designed simply works.

Jesus said; "I have come that they may have life, and have it to the full" (John 10:10). God wants people to have a fulfilled and healthy life, free of mental confusion. He has given us His Word for our direction. The principles and truths in the Bible will help people, not harm them. David said, "How can a young man keep his way pure? By living according to your Word" (Psalm 119:9). "Your Word is a lamp to my feet and a light for my path" (Psalm 119:105). When pastors give God's counsel through His Word, they offer something that helps not only spiritually but emotionally and mentally as well.

2. *Counseling should not just meet the needs of people, it should also help them find relationship with God.*

Hardships or discipline in one's life can be God's way of bringing a person into proper relationship with himself, an act of love on God's part. Pastoral counselors can't take away the pain in people's lives, but they can help them learn from their pain. Understanding the need to be sensitive and compassionate, pastors can look for ways to help people grow through their negative experiences. The writer of Hebrews says:

> Endure hardship as discipline; God is treating you as sons. For what son is not disciplined by his father? If you are not disciplined (and everyone undergoes discipline), then you are illegitimate children and not true sons. Moreover, we have all had human fathers who disciplined us and we respected them for it. How much more should we submit to the Father of our spirits and live! Our fathers disciplined us for a little while as they thought best; but God disciplines us for our good, that we may share in his holiness. No discipline seems pleasant at the time, but painful. Later on, however, it produces a harvest of righteousness and peace for those who have been trained by it (Hebrews 12:7–11).

With every painful experience in life, valuable lessons can be learned.

3. *Combining the Spirit of God and the Word of God in the people of God helps people grow.*

As we grow in Christ and begin to understand and apply the Word of God to our lives, the Holy Spirit helps us understand our place in Christ and what God has done for us. Fellowship with a group of believers in a local church is also necessary. People need people to encourage them in the faith. If ministers are trying to help persons with needs, the greatest thing we can do for them, after listening and showing understanding, is to introduce them to Jesus Christ. As pastors, we must help them read and study the Bible daily and get them plugged in to the church and all it offers.

When I meet with people I often call my time a "divine appointment." I want to introduce them to their Creator God and help them know the God who loves them and will meet all of their needs. I want them to understand that God has given us a Book, the Bible, that explains His ways and how He has designed people to operate. I also want them to know that there are places where His children gather frequently to hear from His Word and worship Him in concert. I want to do this not only because I believe this is God's will but because I sincerely feel that this is what every human being needs to grow spiritually.

4. *People experience satisfaction from life only when they are in proper relationship with Christ.*

People who continue to seek the world's way of satisfying their deep inner longings (with such things as wealth, material possessions, immoral sexual satisfaction, etc.) are only satisfied temporarily and will never fulfill their deepest needs. Only a relationship with God through His Son Jesus Christ can satisfy.

Bishop John Taylor Smith, the former chaplain general of the British Army, told of preaching in a large cathedral using the text from John 3:7, "Ye must be born again." In order to drive it home, he said: "My dear people, do not substitute anything for the 'new birth.' You may be a member of a church, even the great church of which I am a member, the historic Church of England, but church membership is not new birth and 'except a man be born again he cannot see the kingdom of God.'" The rector was sitting at his left. Pointing to him, Smith said, "You might be a clergyman like my friend the rector here and not be born again, and 'except a man be born again he cannot see the kingdom of God.'" On his left sat the archdeacon in his stall. Pointing directly at him, Smith said, "You might even be an archdeacon like my friend in this stall and not be born again, and 'except a man be born again he cannot see the kingdom of God.' You might even be a bishop, like myself, and not be born again, and 'except a man be born again he cannot see the kingdom of God.'"

Then Smith went on to tell that a day or so later he received a letter from the archdeacon, in which he wrote: "My dear Bishop: You have found me out. I have been a clergyman for over thirty years, but I had never known anything of the joy that Christians speak of. I never could understand it. Mine has been hard, legal service. I did not know what was the matter with me, but when you pointed directly to me and said, 'You might even be an archdeacon and not be born again!' I realized in a moment what the trouble was. I had never known anything of the 'new birth.'"

He went on to say that he was wretched and miserable, had been unable to sleep all night, and begged for a conference, if the bishop could spare the time to talk with him.

"Of course, I could spare the time," said Bishop Smith, "and the next day we got together over the Word of God and after some hours we were both on our knees, the archdeacon taking his place before God as a poor, lost sinner and telling the Lord Jesus he would trust Him as his Savior. From that time on everything has been different."[1]

Billy Graham often speaks of an empty void in every human heart. The void can be filled only by Jesus Christ. There is no substitute. Try as they might, people are only truly satisfied in life when they are in proper relationship with Christ.

5. *The Lord doesn't necessarily take away painful experiences in life, or memories of those experiences (e.g., parental mistreatment, death of a loved one), but the Lord sensitizes believers through painful experiences and uses them to help others who are struggling or hurting.*

Scripture says, "Praise be to the God and Father of our Lord Jesus Christ, the Father of compassion and the God of all comfort, who comforts us in all our troubles, so that we can comfort those in any trouble with the comfort we ourselves have received from God" (2 Corinthians 1:3–4). The ministry of Teen Challenge has found that ex-drug addicts are uniquely able to help people who struggle with drug problems. Their program has one of the highest success percentages (for people in their program staying off of drugs) of any drug program *in the world*. Governments are requesting Teen Challenge's involvement in their countries because of their success rates. The secret of Teen Challenge is basic: Introduce a person to Jesus Christ. Then through prayer, lots of love, and the removal of the person from his (drug infested) environment he is set free from his tragic problems. They understand that when a person with a cocaine problem is set free by coming to Christ and learning new habits, that person also has a unique ability to help others with the same problem. Why? Because the God of comfort has comforted him and he in turn can comfort others with that same comfort. What a truth to understand! People who have gone through an abusive experience can get comfort from our compassionate God and help other abused people. People with an alcohol problem can do the same. Bereaved people can receive comfort from God and, in time, help other bereaved people. The memory is always present but the Lord takes the pain from it, and it is only a memory. With the memory, people can become more sensitive to others and reach out to them.

> **"It is never proper to counsel contrary to the Word of God."**

6. *Scripture is always right.*

No matter what feelings or emotions indicate, it is never proper to counsel contrary to the Word of God. People often think they can get away with an affair without being hurt, when the Scripture teaches the opposite (e.g., Proverbs 6:27—"Can a man scoop fire into his lap without his clothes being burned?"). Some think that the Bible permits divorce for whatever reason, when in fact it does not. One should always obey Scripture when counseling. On occasion I have been tempted to find a way that would accommodate what people want to do, even though the Bible counsels against it. I have been tempted because people can present their problems with such emotion, such sincerity. Sometimes people say they want a divorce because they don't love their spouse any longer; they are very unhappy and want to start over in a marriage with another person. Even though my emotions tempt me to tell them to do as they want, I can't yield, for to do so would be contrary to the counsel of God. I have counseled homosexual people who sincerely felt that God created them that way and they had no choice in the matter. Even though their argument was full of sincerity and emotion, I knew it was not valid. God does not create people to be homosexual. The homosexual lifestyle is a choice—a very wrong choice. And people can be free from it—with God's help. How do I know that? Because Scripture teaches this fact in numerous places.

> **" It is the counselee's responsibility to do the right thing. "**

Scripture is always right. Pastoral counselors can be completely confident that God knows what He is talking about. He has created us and He has given us a blueprint for living, His holy Scripture.

7. *The counselee is always responsible to do what is right.*

It is the minister's responsibility to tell a person biblical truth, but it is the individual's responsibility to act and do the right thing. If a counselee decides not to follow biblical counsel, the minister is not in a position to help much beyond what has already been counseled. Each of us is responsible for our own behavior; each of us decides to do right or wrong, to obey or disobey. There are times when people truly do not know what to do, but once they understand what the Bible requires, they need to make the scriptural choice.

A pastor should not feel guilty when the person being counseled decides not to accept the counsel. People cannot be locked in a room until they make the correct choice (that is, unless they are criminal; then society can put them in prison). Ministers present the truth, try to encourage the counselee to do the right thing, give support and encouragement in the right direction, and then let the person make the decision. If the right decision does not follow, the pastor is at an impasse. Ministers can (and should) keep loving and praying for the person. Ultimately, though, people are responsible for their own behavior.

8. *The counselee is capable of choosing a biblical, Christ-honoring response to his or her problem.*

Whatever one's problem might be, there is a response that would honor Christ. We can choose to glorify Christ in all of life. When facing a new day or decision, it is good to ask: "What would Jesus do?" There have been times in marriage counseling where a couple just do not have the motivation to try any longer. They want to quit because it would be easier that way. Neither rhyme nor reason will convince them to try a little harder. During these times I have often asked the question, "Would you try a little more for Jesus?" "Would you hang in there for the glory of God?" "Would you be willing to make the decision that Jesus Christ would be the most pleased with?" People are capable of choosing to answer these questions in the affirmative.

9. *Every individual, no matter what the personal problem might be, is a person of worth, made in the image of God.*

People are valuable. Whether they are guilty of homosexuality, incest, murder, child molestation, or whatever their sin or problem might be, they have value in God's eyes. God loves them and has created them for His glory. Christ desires to change human beings, no matter what their lifestyle has been, or is. God can change and help with every kind of problem people face. There is hope for everyone. We in ministry need to look beyond the behavior and see how badly the Lord would like to help each individual.

10. *All truth is really God's truth.*

At times medical science declares it has discovered a new way to help people, a new medicine, a new vaccine, or a new counseling technique. If it is truth (and sometimes it is not), it originated with God. Humans just haven't noticed the solution or truth until now. New stars are routinely discovered in the universe. Do these stars belong to the person who discovered them? Did they just come into existence? No, the stars have always been there because God put them there. New microorganisms are found frequently. Are they really new? They have always been there. If a medical doctor can help a person through his or her expertise, then we should be grateful for this. Thank God for His truth whenever it's discovered. If individuals we are trying to help need medical attention, we should refer them to a competent physician. If they need psychiatric help, we should encourage them to work with a psychiatrist who will counsel without violating a client's spiritual convictions. All truth belongs to God, and we thank Him for it.

* * * * *

These ten principles are divine principles. They will work to bring healing and health as ministers reach out through counseling to those in need.

Personal Counseling in the Power of the Spirit

Donald Lichi

The faithful pastor serves the local congregation in a number of important roles: a general practitioner, scholar, interpersonal relations specialist, community problem solver, educator, preacher, priest (one who leads in liturgy and presides at rites), organizer, administrator, and pastor (including counseling, visiting, and other forms of social care). Research indicates that the Assemblies of God pastor works an average of fifty hours per week, of which approximately 9 percent (four hours) is spent in counseling activities.[1]

There are many textbooks and other excellent resources on counseling techniques. It is not the purpose of this chapter to duplicate or replace them; rather, it is my intent to focus solely on the relationship of the pastor-counselor to parishioners, especially its challenge to counsel in the power of the Holy Spirit.

The Pastor As Counselor

In our highly complex world, to cope with the rigors of daily living people are turning to mental-health counseling in increasing numbers. Despite the fact that numerous delivery sources are available (professional counselors, psychologists, psychiatrists, social workers), the majority of people prefer counsel from their pastor. Indeed, the trend to seek the pastor first for mental-health concerns has remained relatively constant for over three decades.[2] Why is this so? Typically the pastor is more accessible than mental health professionals and already enjoys a relationship with parishioners. Thus the pastor has a natural entry into their homes and lives at the predictable transitions of life (e.g., birth, marriage, death), as well as in times of family or personal crisis. Writing on the topic of the pastor's role as a counselor, Dr. Richard D. Dobbins points out that "introducing people to Jesus remains the primary evangelistic mission of the Church (Mark 16:15)" and that the primary pastoral mission of the church is to save as much as possible of the "saved person's Kingdom potential."[3]

Pastors are regularly confronted with a similar magnitude and complexity of mental-health problems as those generally seen by mental health professionals. These include issues such as

- matters of faith
- sexual problems
- depression
- anxiety/worry
- parenting issues
- school/career/job guidance
- family problems
- alcohol or drug use
- premarital and marriage counseling
- bereavement

Many pastors, faced with the types of problems listed above, desire additional training in biblical counseling. While the necessity for specific training in counseling seems obvious, the pastor must first seek the development of the spiritual gifts as a prerequisite to effective Spirit-led counseling.

The Uniqueness of Counseling in the Spirit

The awareness of and reliance upon the power of the Holy Spirit constitute the distinctive of the Pentecostal pastor involved in Christian counseling. But what makes Christian counseling *Christian?* There is a vast difference between a Christian who practices counseling and counseling that is truly Christian, biblical, and Spirit empowered. Dr. Gary Collins, a pioneer and leader in Christian mental health, offers the following definition of Christian counseling:

Attempts to define or describe Christian counseling tend to emphasize the *person* who does the helping, the *techniques* or skills that are used, and the *goals* that counseling seeks to reach. From this perspective the Christian counselor is:

- a deeply committed, Spirit-guided (and Spirit-filled) servant of Jesus Christ
- who applies his or her God-given abilities, skills, training, knowledge, and insights
- to the task of helping others move to personal wholeness, interpersonal competence, mental stability, and spiritual maturity.[4]

Following the above model, the challenge set before the pastor is three-fold: (1) What is personally required if the pastor is to counsel in the power of the Holy Spirit? (2) What techniques and skills should the pastor acquire in order to counsel in the power of the Holy Spirit? (3) What desired result or model of "health" is sought in the life of the counselee?

The Spirit-Filled Pastoral Counselor

God desires that the pastor have *a well-trained mind* and *a Holy Spirit-governed heart* (1 Corinthians 12:12ff.). To truly counsel in the power of the Holy Spirit is to have a heart, mind, and soul that desperately seek after God. The pastor needs a God-awareness, the fruit of a heart given to study and prayer. His life should exemplify and model an active attempt to draw upon the resources of the Holy Spirit before, during, and in between counseling sessions.

To counsel with the mind, heart, and power of the Holy Spirit, the pastor must *walk* in the Spirit. Through the baptism in the Holy Spirit, the pastor is sensitized to the *charismata,* the extraordinary demonstrations of divine presence and power granted to the Christian by the Holy Spirit. However, only an *ongoing relationship* with the Holy Spirit will yield a familiarity with the workings and ways of the Holy Spirit. Scripture clearly instructs the pastor to be highly disciplined in body, mind, emotional expression, interpersonal relationships, and in the cultivation of a rich inner life. Balance in the physical, intellectual, emotional, social, and, most important, the spiritual areas of life will enable the pastor to avoid burnout in the ministry.

The spiritual disciplines of the Christian life are described by Richard Foster in his classic book *Celebration of Discipline.* In this important study, Foster describes the following spiritual disciplines:[5]

- *Inward disciplines*—meditation, prayer, fasting, and study
- *Outward disciplines*—simplicity, solitude, submission, and service
- *Corporate disciplines*—confession, worship, guidance, and celebration

The sole purpose of the spiritual disciplines is to bring us to a place before God where the Holy Spirit's presence transforms us into the very image of Christ (Romans 8:26–29). As Foster notes, "The Spiritual Disciplines are a way of sowing to the Spirit . . . they can only get us to the place where something can be done; they are God's means of grace."[6]

The pastor must be serious about developing the "holy habits" that bring him into a transforming relationship with the Holy Spirit. Too often pastors confuse their work *for* God with their walk *with* God. William Law (1686–1761) wrote that if we are going to pray for the Spirit of God, "we are to make that Spirit the rule of all our actions"[7] Our lives should be as holy as our prayers.

This is not to imply that additional training in counseling is not necessary. Indeed, the pastor is well advised to read books, attend seminars, and, if possible, pursue additional formal training in biblical counseling. Considerable benefit can be achieved through more formal studies in the behavioral sciences. If we accept that *all truth is God's truth,* then we also realize that at times truth is "happened upon" (discovered), operationalized, and developed by the unregenerate who may not acknowledge or give glory to God (see Romans 1). However, the pastor who is grounded in the Word of God can confidently delve into the behavioral sciences, determine what lines up with Scripture, and allow discovered and operationalized truth to serve the believer in the counseling relationship.

Here is an example of how "truth" has been discovered or operationalized by the unregenerate. Several years ago while in the midst of doing my doctoral research, I came across an article whose authors claimed to have made a startling discovery about how to eliminate stealing behavior in children. Via several research studies, the authors determined that if a child was required to make restitution over and above what was stolen, the stealing behavior would be greatly diminished in the future. Of course, knowing what Scripture has to say in the Old Testament (Leviticus 6:1–5) about stealing and restitution, I had to chuckle. The authors had simply "discovered" truth. They did not invent truth. Thus the behavioral sciences can assist the pastor in operationalizing truth for the benefit of the Christian counselee.

Remember, the Holy Spirit will not contradict God's written Word. Indeed, the Holy Spirit will only confirm the Book He wrote (Mark 12:36; 2 Timothy 3:16–17; 1 Peter 1:11; 2 Peter 1:21). While study in the behavioral sciences can be profitable, the wise pastor will take the same approach as the Berean Christians, who were commended because they were diligent to search the Scriptures "every day to see if what Paul said was true" (Acts 17:11). A trustworthy source of formal training in the behavioral sciences is the curriculum of Berean University of the Assemblies of God. It offers both undergraduate and graduate counseling programs that are theologically consistent with a Pentecostal perspective. Spirit-filled counseling is nothing short of applied sanctification!

Required Techniques and Skills

Christian counseling is both a sacred trust and a therapeutic relationship between the pastor-counselor and the parishioner-counselee. Gerard Egan states, "Helpers are effective to the degree that their clients, through client-helper interactions, are in a better position to manage their problem situations and/or develop the unused resources and opportunities of their lives more effectively."[8] Dr. Richard Dobbins has often noted that the pastor is in a unique position to powerfully influence a person's horrifying images of God, crippling ideas of self, destructive habits, and hurts from the past. In addition to promoting healing, the pastor helps the counselee develop the divine potential God has for his or her life.

The word *therapy,* from the Greek *therapeuto,* implies that healing occurs in the context of a healing relationship. God brought healing to us by becoming incarnate in our world. Similarly, the Spirit-empowered pastor employs the gifts of communication to faithfully administer God's grace (1 Peter 4:10). Through accurate empathy, the pastor becomes deeply involved with the counselee. The pastor identifies with the counselee's pain, while at the same time offering hope, comfort, direction, confrontation, and opportunity for growth. Think of the impact this kind of healing relationship can provide!

Can a pastor effectively counsel and simultaneously be in an attitude of prayer? Can we listen with our heart of compassion and at the same time be talking to God the Holy Spirit? Yes! But we have to be disciplined in order for this to be accomplished. Keeping one's heart in an attitude of prayer throughout the counseling session is admittedly a difficult task, but don't give up or quit trying! A wise variation on a familiar saying observes, "Anything worth doing is worth doing *wrong* until we learn to do it *right!*"

> " **The word therapy implies a healing relationship.** "

The name Jesus used most often to refer to the Holy Spirit, *parakletos,* has been variously translated "advocate," "comforter," "helper," and "counselor." The pastor entering into a counseling relationship will no doubt minister in each of these ways. The pastor must be motivated to display the same qualities as Christ, the Wonderful Counselor (Isaiah 9:6).

Jesus knew what it meant to live (and counsel) in a way that brought the eternal power of the Holy Spirit into the needs of the hurting and powerless. Scripture records that He would not break off the wounded reed, nor would He squash the smoldering wick (Matthew 12:20). Rather, He embraced what was and made it better. He modeled the unhurried ability to listen. He was compassionate, yet He positively confronted hypocrisy. Jesus communicated love, forgiveness, and a confidence that the counselee could change. By dying for us, Christ communicated that we are of great worth. He knew the difference between acceptance and approval. He accepted people and at the same time disapproved of their sinful behaviors. He faithfully warned of the consequences of destructive life choices.

Jesus, full of the Holy Spirit, also met people in crisis situations. He confronted with compassion:

- The rich young ruler, in an existential crisis, asking what must I do to inherit eternal life
- Zacchaeus caught in a career crisis
- The woman caught in adultery and facing a moral crisis
- Mary and Martha facing the crisis of the death of their brother Lazarus
- Nicodemus facing a spiritual crisis

The parishioner comes to the counseling session expecting to hear from God's servant and to gain God's wisdom and counsel about matters of personal concern. A wavering, inconsistent message will lead to an unreliable, lukewarm, circumstantial conscience in the life of the counselee. A pastor who consistently reveals the mind of the Spirit to the counselee will help build a more reliable conscience in that counselee.

Both Joseph and Daniel were called upon to offer counsel. Both prayed often about the counsel they were giving, and both were known as men in whom the Spirit of God dwelt. So too, that pastor who by conscious, moment-by-moment choice surrenders, responds, obeys, yields, and is sensitive and pliable in God's hand will be known as a man in whom dwells the Spirit of God. The very same Holy Spirit that indwelled and empowered the prophets and apostles is present now in the life of the Spirit-filled pastor!

The Product of Holy-Spirit Counsel

Counseling in the power of the Spirit will produce the fruit of the Spirit in the pastor and the counselee (Galatians 5:16–26). The pastor knows that true freedom occurs as one's lifestyle conforms to that which the Holy Spirit seeks to produce. With boldness and clarity, the pastor urges the counselee to make the kinds of life choices that avoid immorality, self-centeredness, addiction, etc.

What is the result of living a life empowered by the Spirit? A clear and compelling answer appears in Eugene H. Peterson's paraphrase of the Bible, *The Message:* 'He brings gifts into our lives, much the same way that fruit appears in an orchard—things like affection for others, exuberance about life, serenity. We develop a willingness to stick with things, a sense of compassion in the heart, and a conviction that a basic holiness permeates things and people. We find ourselves involved in loyal commitments, not needing to force our way in life, able to marshal and direct our energies wisely" (Galatians 5:22–23).[9]

In sum, the Spirit-guided pastor exhorts the counselee to live a serious, practical, passionate, and godly life.

The Spirit-filled pastor will experience a love for the things God loves and a hatred of the things God hates. He will be grieved over the things that grieve the Holy Spirit. For example, the Holy Spirit grieves over such things as forgetting God (Deuteronomy 32:18), whining and grumbling (Numbers 14:27), putting God's patience to the test through conscious disobedience (Exodus 16:28; Psalm 78:41), and a continued lack of faith and trust (Numbers 14:11; Psalm 78). Additionally, as Ephesians 4:30–32 points out, the Holy Spirit is grieved over how Christians behave toward one another. He also grieves when He sees false pride, hypocrisy, injustice, and legalism (2 Corinthians 3:6).

On the other hand, the pastor counseling in the power of the Holy Spirit should anticipate breakthroughs in difficult counseling situations. When there seems not to be a right or best answer or when the process seems stuck, the pastor will depend on the Holy Spirit to provide discernment or to suggest areas of inquiry and options previously not considered. The Holy Spirit provides power, teaches, leads, comforts, and convicts of sin. The pastor counseling in the power of the Holy Spirit will be the conduit for the Spirit's ministering to the counselee. The pastor should encourage the counselee to let the Holy Spirit have access to his or her entire life: healing of past wounds, empowerment for the present struggle, and hope for a glorious future.

* * * * *

If the pastor's heart is right, if a desire to minister is present, if the training is in place, and if there is a consistent walk in the Spirit, the inevitable result will be godly counsel in the power of the Spirit. The pastor desiring to counsel in the power of the Holy Spirit must desire two things: to be like Jesus and to respond instantly to the unction of the living Holy Spirit. There simply is no other way to meet the many needs of parishioners.

Maintaining Vision for a Lifetime

John Bueno

aving been born and reared in a missionary home, I came to realize that much of the mystery and romanticism traditionally attached to the ministry was not a part of my heritage. Feeling the call of God on my life and concluding my studies at Bethany Bible College, I had decisions to make regarding God's will for my future. I had two full-time offers to be a part of the ministerial staff in two different churches, but I didn't feel at ease with either of these propositions. I consulted with my godly parents, and they told me that it was much more important to know what God wanted for my life than for me, at that juncture, to pick out what was best for my future.

After much consultation with the Lord in prayer, I decided that I would accept neither of these offers but go to the church where the pastor who had guided me through my teenage years was in the midst of a difficult struggle in his most recent pastorate and had asked me to assist him. There was no financial remuneration for this ministry, and it meant that I would have to seek secular employment to support myself during those first months and years of ministry. Looking back on that experience, I feel that God helped me to learn some of the great principles of maintaining vision for a lifetime. It was during those months and years that God began to build in my own heart the principles that I would like to share in this chapter. Naturally, there are many things that could be said relating to this important topic, but I want to share just four of the main principles that have guided my life over almost forty years of ministry, the great majority of them being overseas.

Take Life in Small Segments

One of the great truths Jesus taught regarding our experience in life is found in Matthew 6:34: "Do not worry about tomorrow, for tomorrow will worry about itself. Each day has enough trouble of its own." It wasn't long after my first experience in ministry that I received a phone call from Melvin Hodges, then the Division of Foreign Missions field director for Latin America and the Caribbean. He asked me if I would consider going to El Salvador on a temporary assignment. I asked him how long "temporary" meant, and he responded by saying that it probably would mean two years unless the mission was accomplished sooner than expected. That temporary assignment lasted twenty-eight years, and I can see God's hand upon every decision that was made at that juncture in my life. However, if Brother Hodges would have asked me to go to El Salvador for twenty-eight years, I don't know whether I would have had the courage and spiritual stamina to say, "Yes, I will go for a lifetime."

One of the great principles of maintaining a lifetime vision is to do God's work and follow His will one step at a time. It is sometimes difficult to see a whole lifetime ahead of us. The challenges and the difficulty of the Great Commission seem overwhelming at times. If we look down the road too far, we sometimes may faint out of fear and uncertainty. There is a reason why Jesus asked us to take life in twenty-four-hour compartments. I have known many people who have failed in their efforts for the Master simply because they tried to cross the bridge before they reached the river. There are some people who are always looking at the negatives and the impossibilities of the future; however, if we ask God for grace and stamina to do His will and purpose today, He will also give us the strength and courage for the days ahead.

> **If we look down the road too far, we sometimes may faint out of fear and uncertainty.**

It was the prophet Zechariah, in speaking of Zerubbabel's effort to rebuild the temple, who asked this question: "'Who despises the day of small things?'" (Zechariah 4:10). Often we look at the scope of the task and wonder what can my little part do to change things? How can my life make a difference when the responsibility and the task is so great? We look at our limited talents and wonder if what we do will really make a difference in the Kingdom. The example of Zechariah should be an inspiration to all of us. We too start with what we have and must be faithful in the responsibilities God gives us even though they do not seem to be important at the time. The building of the foundation of our ministry and our service to the Master often starts with small and apparently insignificant things. If we are faithful in the first small responsibilities God gives us and do our work faithfully before the Master in the time ahead of us, God will map out the master plan and strategy for our entire lifetime. We can't see the lifetime scope until we are first willing to start with the small rudimentary things and, as God leads us, move into other areas of ministry. One of the tragedies of many lives today is that they seek to accomplish a lifetime of service in just a short period of time.

Life gives us in God the stepping stones that will enable us to serve our Master over a lifetime.

Keep Plodding

Not all of our life experiences are exhilarating or stimulating. We can't live in ecstasy every moment of our lives. Much of our commitment to Jesus Christ is simply faithful plodding in the difficult, as well as in the victorious, times. Some people live in frustration because they think exhilaration and joy should fill every moment of their lives. Difficult times provoke questions of whether or not they are in the will of God. Some pastors prematurely leave the ministry, discouraged because they are not seeing the results they envisioned in the beginning. My first nine years in El Salvador were difficult ones. There was not great growth, and revival did not come immediately. I had gone to every seminar on evangelism and church growth I could find. I tried to learn the strategies and plans that would bring revival and growth to our church, but all seemed to no avail. One year followed after another, and the constant voice of the Spirit in my own heart was that I should just keep plodding.

It was not easy; I felt my life slipping away with no apparent results. But the principle I learned during those nine years has certainly been a tremendous blessing to me over the long haul. Sometimes it is just putting one foot in front of the other and being faithful in the responsibilities God has given us. It is true that God gives great victories and wonderful moments of joy and exhilaration, but if we look through Scripture we see that the great men and women God used were people willing to keep plodding even in the difficult times. Space will not permit us to recount the stories of Abraham, Moses, and Noah, but if we reflect on their lives, we will see men who accepted God's word as fact and kept moving even when outside circumstances didn't confirm their vision and their call. Years and years went by before they saw the fulfillment of God's promises in their lives. This does not mean we should take a fatalistic view of life and say, "Whatever will be, will be." It simply means that we take God at His Word and keep walking with Him in true faithfulness, always conscious of the fact that He is leading us. Whether we feel good or not does not alter God's promises. Outward success is no proof of a lifetime vision. God is always faithful to His Word and He will bring to pass in due time the vision He has placed in our hearts.

Be Yourself

While being yourself might seem simplistic, it is vital to keeping your vision for a lifetime. We often try to imitate other ministries that seem so glamorous and so effective. But how many people have succumbed to discouragement simply because they tried to imitate someone else's vision or ministry? When absorbed in delusions of grandeur, we are not willing to begin with the small things; we want to see the glorious fulfillment immediately and without a true reflection of our talents and dedication to the Master. Jesus taught in the Parable of the Talents (Matthew 25:14–30) that the importance of service to God was not how many talents we had but what we did with the talents that He gives us. The one-talent person cannot be expected to do all of the things that a five-talent person can do. I believe that one of the great principles in ministry is that we recognize God has given everyone unique abilities and talents in His service. When we place them at God's disposal, He can greatly multiply and use them for His glory. Some of the great catalysts for revival in history have not been the five-talent people, but rather one-talent people who simply did what God asked them to do and didn't try to imitate what He was doing through someone else.

We often hear the statement that so-and-so is the Billy Graham of Latin America, of Europe, or of wherever. I don't believe God wants another Billy Graham. While all of us admire the great things that God has done through this great man, God does not want to make carbon copies of Billy Graham. Every one of His servants is unique. We are asked to fit into the overall plan simply by placing our talents at His disposal. Discouragement and frustration come when we try to do or be something we aren't, when manipulation and deceit are used to promote our vision, when we are not truly submissive to God's will and purpose in our lives, when jealously or bitterness comes into our lives simply because we have not enjoyed the measure of success that others have. If we could see God's heart and know His real purpose for ministry, we would change our approach and with true humility before God say, "Lord, you know the limitations and the strengths of my life. Use them to the utmost so that I can be a true servant of Jesus Christ."

Be Sensitive to God

This leads me to the last and maybe the most important principle of ministry I have learned over the years. In looking through God's Word and even at the lives of contemporary servants of the Master, the temptation is to search for formulas or man-made programs that brought success. It is surprising how many people want an easy three-step way to fulfill God's purpose in their lives. When I was pastoring a church of over twenty thousand in San Salvador, everywhere I went people wanted to know my "formula for the growth." When I would try to share the principle of awareness and sensitivity to God's voice and will, they seemed to be greatly disappointed. Generally speaking, people want some easy formula that when followed step-by-step will guarantee success.

Throughout the period of the Bible, men and women were used of God simply because they were willing to hear His voice and feel the touch of His Spirit on their lives. Even in our day the great servants of Jesus Christ are not noted for their enormous talents or intellect; they are simply people who are willing to hear God and to respond to what He wants for their lives. This is not as easy as it sounds, for we are often caught up with the business of life and all of the management techniques available to us to maximize our time and energy. While many of these principles are excellent and can be of great assistance, we will lose our primary focus if we don't learn the principle of the quiet times with God—the moments when He speaks to us and confirms through reading His Word and through prayer that He indeed is guiding our lives. There is one prayer I express almost every day of my life: "Lord make me sensitive to Your will today. May I not rely on the principles of men or on ideas that are successful for others, but may I know Your will and may I respond to what You want me to do in my service in Your kingdom."

Down through the years there have been times when that voice seemed to be silent. Those were the most difficult days of my life because I felt weak and helpless without the guidance and strength of God's will and voice. It was only when I stopped everything and determined to know His will and purpose for my life that I felt once again the satisfaction of Christian service. Frustration and defeat come to our lives when we miss God and His will for our lives. The more sensitive we are to His voice, the more successful we will be in His service. A lifetime commitment to Jesus requires true sensitivity to His will and purpose.

Going back to the words of Zechariah, we see God's plan once again in the life of His servant. "The word of the Lord came to me: 'The hands of Zerubbabel have laid the foundation of this temple; his hands will also complete it. Then you will know that the Lord almighty has sent me to you. Who despises the day of small things?'" (Zechariah 4:8–10). The God who enables us to lay the foundations in the beginning, when it seems so small and inadequate, is the same God who allows our hands to complete the work in His time and purpose. The beauty of Christian service is knowing that what God allows us to begin He also allows us to complete. A lifetime of God-inspired vision is the greatest service any human being could possibly render.

Unit 6

Spirit-Anointed Worship

Introduction:
The Priority of Ministry to God

Thomas E. Trask

Hezekiah was twenty-five years old when he succeeded his father, Ahaz, as king. Ahaz, a diabolical leader, had made molten images for the Baals and had even sacrificed his sons in fire (2 Chronicles 28:2–3). When Hezekiah became king "he did right in the sight of the Lord," setting Israel on a righteous course. "In the first year of his reign, in the first month, he opened the doors of the house of the Lord and repaired them" (2 Chronicles 29:3[1]). For the next several weeks, Hezekiah cleaned out the house of the Lord. Then he brought in the priests and the Levites and instructed them: "Now it is in my heart to make a covenant with the Lord God of Israel, that His burning anger may turn away from us. My sons, do not be negligent now, for the Lord has chosen you to stand before Him, to minister to Him, and to be His ministers" (2 Chronicles 29:10–11).

Hezekiah's instructions to the ministers were threefold: (1) God had chosen them to stand before Him; (2) they were to minister to, or serve, God; (3) they were privileged to be God's ministers. The same message comes to God's ministers today.

God has chosen you to stand before Him. We in the ministry are to stand in the gap. As leaders we are responsible for bringing people to God, but, even more important, we must realize that we stand personally before Him and are to be examples to our families and those we serve. Our lives—dedicated and obedient to Jesus Christ—are to be exemplary and reflect integrity, righteousness, and complete surrender to our living Lord. Paul instructed Titus, "In all things show yourself to be an example of good deeds, with purity in doctrine, dignified, sound in speech which is beyond reproach" (Titus 2:7–8).

In his biography of George Whitefield, Arnold Dallimore wrote: "I have endeavored to give my portrait of Whitefield both reality and depth. I make known, not only his accomplishments and abilities, but also his foibles and his mistakes. I must confess, however, that I had almost wished his faults had been more pronounced, lest by reason of their fewness and feebleness, I should be charged with favouritism."[2]

What a compliment if, when looking at our lives, people cannot find any sinful faults! Not only are we responsible to stand before God and the people now, but a day will come when we will have to give an account of our ministry. John Bunyan said, "At the day of doom men shall be judged according to their fruits. It will not be said then, 'Did you believe?' but, 'Were you doers or talkers only?'"[3]

Is there an awareness in your life that you now stand before God? He is ever present—aware of our thinking and the condition of our hearts. We stand before Him and His holy nature, and His incomprehensible love should radiate from us and affect everything we do in the precious calling we have.

> ## We are serving not just a denomination.

Then, we are "to minister to Him" (2 Chronicles 29:11; "to serve him," KJV). Hezekiah said, "It is in my heart to make a covenant with the Lord" (v. 10). A statement often used by early Pentecostals, but misunderstood by many, was "I'd rather burn out than rust out." Philosophically, this statement meant, "I'm going to serve the Lord with all my heart and passion." I believe this is what Jesus was referring to when He said, "Thou shalt love the Lord thy God with all thy heart, and with all thy soul, and with all thy mind" (Matthew 22:37, KJV).

Loving God means serving and obeying Him. Hezekiah made a covenant to obey God because of his great love for Him. He understood that if he was going to be a follower (and a leader), he was required to serve the Lord with all his heart and might. Our ministry is not just a job but a sacred calling. We do what we do because God has chosen us for this role in His kingdom (see Acts 20:28). When we understand this we will have greater confidence and a sense of God's help.

Dr. Martyn Lloyd-Jones, one of the tremendous preachers of this century, said:

> The greatest danger for me, the greatest temptation for me, is that I should walk into this pulpit twice next Sunday because it was announced last Sunday that I would be doing so. Of course, it is right that a man should not break his contract. It is right that a man should not break his word. . . . Yes! But that I am simply doing it because, well, another Sunday has come and I am announced to preach twice, and I must preach two sermons, that is external service. I am not doing it "in my spirit." Oh! When a man does it in his spirit, it is because there is something in the very depths of his being that calls it out.[4]

We are involved in a sacred service to our Master. What a responsibility! What an honor! Daniel Webster said, "The most important thought I ever had was that of my individual responsibility to God."[5] We in pastoral ministry must understand that we are serving not just a denomination but the entire kingdom of God. While we are grateful for our Fellowship and God's blessing on it, there is a much larger picture: We are serving the Lord as ministers in His kingdom.

Finally, we have the privilege of being "His ministers" (2 Chronicles 29:11). All that we do is to be ministry to the Lord—our worship, praise, adoration, dedication, commitment, talents, and abilities are to minister to the Lord. It is amazing that God not only accepts but greatly enjoys praises from frail, fallible human beings.

The Psalmist said the Lord "inhabits" the praises of His people (see Psalm 22:3, KJV). He dwells, or lives, in those praises. Just as human beings appreciate sincere gratitude and kind remarks from others, so God enjoys the sincere praises of His people, their gratitude and thanksgiving. He not only deserves these praises but, in a wonderful way, will inhabit them.

We minister to the Lord not only by our obedience and service but by our thanksgiving. From my deepest heart I pray, "Lord, You've been so wonderful to me. Thank You. I praise You. I adore You. I exalt You because of Your faithfulness to me and the privilege You have given me to minister this precious gospel."

Charles H. Spurgeon said: "Doth not all nature around me praise God? If I were silent, I should be an exception to the universe. Doth not the thunder praise Him as it rolls like drums in the march of the God of armies? Do not the mountains praise Him when the woods upon their summits wave in adoration? Doth not the lightning write His name in letters of fire? Hath not the whole earth a voice? And shall I, can I, silent be?"[6]

Hezekiah experienced the joy of ministering to the Lord. From this perspective he said, "Do not be negligent now, for the Lord has chosen you to stand before Him, to minister to Him, and to be His ministers" (2 Chronicles 29:11).

As ministers (pastors, missionaries, evangelists, teachers), our first calling is to minister to the Lord and to keep our hearts and lives right with God. We are to point the people we serve to our living God and adore our living Lord with our praises. Of all people, we who have been called should minister to Him.

Making Place for Pentecostal Distinctives

James K. Bridges

There are distinctive differences between a genuine Pentecostal worship service and the ordinary congregational worship service in most churches today. While there may be some surface similarities, the basic differences will be found in leadership attitudes, congregational involvement, purpose and focus of the meeting, intensity of worship, and often the duration of the meeting. But more important will be the manifestations of the Holy Spirit as described in 1 Corinthians 12 and 14.

When we speak of making place for Pentecostal distinctives, we are not just putting new wine into old wine skins. We are not just adding a few new parts to an old order. Pentecost is God's new order of worship whereby we are enabled by divine strength to worship God "'in spirit and truth'" (John 4:24[1]); Jesus said, "'The Father is seeking such to worship Him'" (v. 23). The coming of the Holy Spirit on the Day of Pentecost has liberated the church to worship God as He so desires that we do.

Pentecostal worship is New Testament worship. Under the guidance of the Holy Spirit himself, it complies with and is subject to the Word of God. Pentecostal worship should be the worship of any church naming the name of Christ. As General Superintendent Thomas E. Trask says in *Back to the Altar,* "The Pentecostal church was never supposed to be a branch of Christianity but the very trunk of the tree."[2] Pentecostal worship enables the church to honor the Triune God, to exalt our Lord Jesus Christ as Savior of the world and Head of the Church, to edify the Church, and to let the power and presence of God be manifested on the earth through the Holy Spirit.

Pastoral Responsibility

The great majority of churches today have on staff ministers of music or song directors who are called worship leaders. But ultimately the final responsibility for the worship of the church belongs to the pastor. Building a worshiping mood in the congregation, creating an atmosphere in which souls stand awestruck in the presence of their Creator, is a cardinal part of the preacher's task.

In a Pentecostal worship service the leader must worship and participate just like everyone else. He must be a first partaker of the fruit. There is no place for a preacher who sits on the platform like a coach on the sidelines and just observes. You can tell if a pastor is involved with worship. If he is constantly whispering to others with small talk or if he is moving about the platform trying to get things together that should have been done before the service started, he has not learned how to worship God and will be of little value to the church as a Pentecostal worship leader.

Pentecostal worship requires Pentecostal leadership. A pastor who is not Spirit-filled will not know how to respond when the Holy Spirit begins to manifest His presence in a service. Such pastors are often unaware of their responsibilities or the significance of their role as a worship leader. Accomplishing the divine intentions that the Lord has designed for a church service must be the pastor's ultimate goal when he steps into the pulpit to lead the worship service.

Blessed is the congregation whose pastor is at home in the presence of God. The minister who is spiritually uptight, unsure of himself, and fearful that things will get out of control will create an atmosphere of tension and bondage among the people. It is a leader's responsibility to give the people a sense of security that all is well and that if something extraneous affects the service, he will maintain adequate control. It is also the duty of a leader to be at home with the things of God, whether it be the manifestations of the Spirit or the demonstrations of the believers. The anointed, prepared leader will be able to discern the genuine from the pseudo and will lead the people away from extremes, using maturity and tact.

WORSHIP LEADER ATTITUDES

A Pentecostal worship service doesn't just happen. To a great extent it requires a wise pastor who knows how to preside under the auspices of the Holy Spirit, providing for the balance, variety, and participation that a New Testament assembly should have.

The attitude with which a minister begins the service sets the level of worship that will occur. Services begun with light, flippant attitudes, manifesting irreverence for the presence of God, often never rise above that level of lightheartedness, thus grieving the Holy Spirit and hindering a genuine meeting with God. An attitude and mood of praise, faith, joy, hope, love, and holiness is a work of the Holy Spirit in the worship leader. What a challenge and what a privilege to see the moods of doubt, despair, hopelessness, fear, and fault-finding dispelled by the power of God's Word and God's Spirit.

PENTECOSTAL ORDER

The pastor responsible for conducting a Pentecostal worship service should spend considerable time studying 1 Corinthians 14. Valuable instruction is given concerning the objectives, conduct, and components of worship when "the whole church comes together in one place" (14:23). The mature leader well understands the admonition of the apostle Paul: "Let all things be done decently and in order" (14:40). This instruction deals directly with the way a body of believers are to conduct themselves in a worship service. Nothing sidetracks or derails a worship service like disorder and the confusion it brings. Confusion, Paul states, is not authored by God and has no place in the assembly (14:33). The chaos of disorderly services not only creates confusion among the members, but also causes the community to lose confidence in the church and its leadership. Rather than being held in esteem as sane, spiritual people, they are looked upon as mad (14:23), dangerous religious quacks.

The apostle Paul set forth for us, by way of contrast, an ideal Pentecostal worship service, where scriptural order prevails and the purposes of God are accomplished. In such a service all are ministered to according to their needs—believers, the unlearned (uninformed, possibly those not baptized in the Spirit), and unbelievers (14:24). Operating in the Spirit and according to the Word of God assures the presence of God in the midst of the people and a genuine worship experience (14:25).

For the sake of order, Paul limited the number of messages in tongues with interpretation (14:27). This would prevent excessive use of the gifts and allow for other manifestations and ministries of the Spirit, e.g., the messages of the prophets (14:29). Even the instruction regarding married women was for avoiding confusion, brought about when a wife in the women's section would call out a question about the sermon to her husband in the men's section (14:34–35). The church still needs to maintain order in its meetings to insure the presence of the ungrieved Spirit.

Components of Worship

The apostle Paul gives us an understanding of things that are important to a Pentecostal worship service: "Whenever you come together, each of you has a psalm, has a teaching, has a tongue, has a revelation, has an interpretation" (1 Corinthians 14:26). So Pentecostal worship should include singing, teaching, preaching, messages in tongues and interpretations, and special insight into the knowledge of Christ (although the apostle was not intending this list to be exhaustive).

It is vitally important that we realize each component of our worship service must fit together harmoniously, and all serve the highest purpose. Several times Paul sets forth the goal: "Let all things be done for edification" (14:26). Each part of the service should assist in the goal of building up the body of Christ. Anything less is unworthy of a place on the order of service.

Items making up an order of service for a Pentecostal worship service should flow together smoothly with a sense of continuity. They should not appear to be a loose sequence of unrelated items. We need to scrutinize the ingredients of our worship services to determine how scriptural they are and whether they add to or take away from the worship. For example, the place given to announcements should be of concern to many pastors. Sometimes announcements consume entirely too much time and are inserted at the most inopportune times. One appropriate way of handling announcements is to print them in a bulletin distributed by ushers. But please don't insult your people by reading them from the pulpit. Another approach is to present them just before you begin the worship service. Whichever way, see that announcements do not interrupt the flow of worship and hinder the moving of the Holy Spirit.

SPIRIT-PROMPTED SINGING AND MAKING MELODY

The Church was given a song on the Day of Pentecost and continues to sing it today. The Lollards filled England with their singing. The Roman Catholic Church complained that Martin Luther had sung many more people into Protestantism by his hymns than he ever preached into it by his sermons.[3] "The Wesleyans announced by their singing that a new epoch in Christian history had dawned."[4]

Anointed singing that involves the entire congregation is one of the distinctive marks of Pentecostal worship. Choirs, soloists, and instrumentalists are important to the worship service. However, our most important singing is that which is done by the congregation.[5] Something is seriously wrong in a Pentecostal worship service when the congregation has lost its song and has surrendered it to a delegated few. "From the days of the apostles to the last church revival, it is true that when the Spirit of God moves mightily, the people burst into song."[6]

Ephesians 5:18–19 speaks of singing born of the Spirit: "Be filled with the Spirit, speaking to one another in psalms and hymns and spiritual songs, singing and making melody in your heart to the Lord." There will be times when the believer is guided by the Holy Spirit to sing in the Spirit. Paul's reference to "spiritual songs" may be singing in the Spirit. The apostle refers to his own distinctive experience in 1 Corinthians 14:15—"I will sing with the spirit [sing in unknown tongues], and I will also sing with the understanding [sing in a known tongue]."

It is incumbent on our musicians to create moods with their instruments and songs that move the heart to freely worship the Lord Jesus Christ in a Pentecostal atmosphere. We should question songs with minor chords designed to create an eerie mood of "divine presence," which is more worldly than spiritual. Also, the church should be cautious about spiritualizing Jewish national folk music as some sort of sacred biblical style the church should embrace. Equally critical is the attempt to copy the sounds, styles, and appearances of the world's music and singers.

The Pentecostal church must not lose its song in the Spirit. It must keep its singers and musicians at the foot of the Cross, where the spirit of entertainment and all show of the flesh can be crucified. C. E. Jefferson wrote, "Music may convert itself into a peacock and exist only for the sake of display. Display in the house of God is abominable, and music when used for display, instead of being an angel to build up, becomes a devil to tear down."[7] If it is not stopped, the crass commercialization of gospel music and the imitation of this world by gospel singers will cause the Holy Spirit to withdraw from the church.

PENTECOSTAL PRAYER

The apostle Paul was a man of prayer. He understood prayer at all levels of need. He spoke to the Ephesians about "praying always with all prayer and supplication in the Spirit" (6:18). To the Corinthians he wrote, "I will pray with the spirit [in an unknown tongue], and I will also pray with the understanding" (1 Corinthians 14:15). Paul's knowledge of prayer and the church's desperate need to be a praying church led him to show the Romans how great must be the believers' reliance on the Holy Spirit: "The Spirit also helps in our weaknesses. For we do not know what we should pray for as we ought, but the Spirit Himself makes intercession for us with groanings which cannot be uttered" (Romans 8:26).

Spirit-inspired prayer—in the forms of confession, petition, thanksgiving, supplication, praise, and intercession—is a distinctive that has given Pentecostal worship its power and attraction. People seeking God in earnest, "holding on to the horns of the altar," have been the reason revival has come to their church. Robert Murray McCheyne reported that when revival came to Dundee, Scotland, there were thirty-nine prayer meetings going on in his church at the time.[8] Nothing reveals a church's true character like the quality of prayer being prayed in its services. Much of our praying is done in such a perfunctory manner that it would never qualify for the praying James directs the church to do (James 5:13–18): Pentecostal leaders must know how to pray *the prayer of faith*. It is "the effectual fervent prayer of a righteous man" that avails much (5:16). This is Pentecostal praying and it will make a difference in the worship service.

Let the pastor be known as a person of prayer. In nothing should we be more like Jesus. A praying Pentecostal pastor will beget a praying Pentecostal church. It is time for all Pentecostal churches to return to the days of scheduled prayer meetings, before and after services, for men, for women, for youth, and for children.

While Charles Spurgeon was in France trying to recover his health, he wrote his London congregation regularly. One of his letters included the pleading of his shepherd's heart, urging his people to be faithful to the church and especially to the prayer meetings, which he considered to be the reason for the success of his great church.[9] It is time for the Pentecostal church to wait upon God!

PENTECOSTAL PREACHING

One of the most important elements of a Pentecostal worship service is the proclamation of the Word of God. The Word must have a primary place in the order of worship. We can all identify with J. Sidlow Baxter's anger when, after sitting through a string of preliminaries (which included boring announcements, extended lifeless singing, and two choir arrangements done so poorly that they added nothing to the service), he was handed the service at sixteen minutes to noon to deliver a message from God to His people. He exclaimed, "O how wrong it is!" Such a condition in the churches of his day prompted Baxter to title his book *Rethinking Our Priorities.*[10]

Pentecostal preaching is such a vital part of our worship that we must never allow it to become a slave to any trends, techniques, or teachings that compromise its powerful proclamation of the full gospel. Some ministers are too prone to jump on a popular religious idea and become imbalanced even to the point of falling into error. Many preachers will stand in the Bema judgment before the Head of the Church and have no satisfactory answer for why they failed to preach all of the truth of the Word of God.

And to preach a sermon as an end in itself and dismiss people from the service without expecting or allowing a response from them is a sure indication that the minister has lost the Pentecostal enduement of the Spirit. We must avoid the temptation to preach sermons just for the sake of sermons, with no faith nor expectation of reaping a harvest for the Lord. Pentecostal preaching under the anointing of the Holy Spirit will produce fruit. The Word of the Lord will not return void.

READING THE WORD OF GOD

Often missing in the order of service is the reading of God's Word. This omission speaks loudly to the declining reverence for the Holy Scriptures and to the rushed programs filled with fast paced activity that simply leave no room for the Word of God to be read.

The foundation and plumb line for all our worship are in the Holy Scriptures. After giving the treatise on the manifestations of the Spirit in 1 Corinthians 14, the apostle Paul concludes, "If anyone thinks himself to be a prophet or spiritual, let him acknowledge that the things which I write to you are the commandments of the Lord" (14:37). It is truly an ignorant person who rejects the Bible as the inspired, infallible, and inerrant Word of the Living God. Paul exhorted Timothy, "Till I come, give attention to reading, to exhortation, to doctrine" (1 Timothy 4:13). We understand the "reading" was most likely a reference to the public reading of Scripture. Pentecostals must reconsider the importance of publicly reading the Word of God in our worship services and find creative ways of making this an effective part of our order of service.

C. E. Jefferson wrote, "Drench your church in the spirit of the Bible. Read it like a man of prayer. Keep alive in men's hearts reverence for the Bible as a whole. Resolve, then, to read the Bible generously to your people."[11] And, in another place he wrote, "Read the Bible to your people without comment. Do not dim its light by your assumptions. Let it shine undarkened by your interpretations. Do not quench its fire by your suppositions. Let it radiate its heat, and who knows how many hearts may be melted."[12]

PENTECOSTAL MANIFESTATIONS

The Pentecostal worship service is known for manifestations of the Holy Spirit, such as speaking in tongues, interpretation of tongues, and prophecy (Spirit-inspired utterance in one's own language). As we come to the threshold of the twenty-first century, we observe that these phenomena are widespread in more churches, countries, and peoples than they were at the beginning of this century, when the Pentecostal movement had its beginning.

As long as we obey the Word of God and stay open to the moving of the Holy Spirit, we will enjoy the manifestation, or gifts, of the Holy Spirit in our worship services. May we keep the words of 1 Thessalonians 5 ever before us: "Do not quench the Spirit. Do not despise prophecies. Test all things; hold fast what is good" (5:19–21).

The apostle Paul in 1 Corinthians 14 gives us vital teaching regarding the manifestations in our worship services:

1. Everything we say and do and any manifestation of the Spirit should be for the building up of the church (v. 26).
2. The gift of prophecy is so helpful because it is Spirit-inspired utterance in a language everyone can understand. So desire to prophesy (vv. 1,3).
3. The gift of tongues is valuable. Never forbid to speak in tongues. Paul enjoyed the gift more than anyone in the church (vv. 18,39).
4. But the only way for tongues to edify the whole body is if they are interpreted. So if you use the gift in church, pray to interpret. No doubt Paul used the gift privately to great advantage, and so should we (vv. 13,27–28).
5. Prophecy as described in the New Testament and prophecy from the Old Testament prophets are not of the same standing; prophecies spoken in the congregation as well as messages in tongues must be judged by the church (v. 29). They are not equivalent to the Holy Scriptures (v. 37).

6. When the gifts are used properly we can expect people to be convicted of their sin, recognizing the presence of God and surrendering their hearts to Christ (v. 25).
7. The regulations the apostle placed on the gifts were to prevent excessive use and provide for balance in the worship service (vv. 27–30).

PENTECOSTAL DEMONSTRATIONS

Pentecostal worship services have been known for physical demonstrations. But they must always come spontaneously, in response to a mighty moving of the Holy Spirit in the service. As believers have sought God around the altars, experiences such as falling prostrate before the Lord, being slain in the Spirit (falling down under the influence of the Spirit), strong crying and tears, holy laughter, and jumping or running have occurred. Such demonstrations have never been planned or scheduled, as has become a pattern in more recent times.

The Pentecostal worship service has plenty of freedom for physical demonstration within the boundaries of the Word of God, within which the worship leader is responsible to keep the congregation. Just as we need balance in the Spirit to keep us from excesses, even more so do we need balance in the flesh, or the physical. In Pentecostal meetings there is always the danger of people allowing their zeal to slip into carnality. And there is always the danger of becoming imitators of extreme practices. Pentecostal worship leaders must ever be on guard against emotional fads, which will usually run their course when the excitement has worn off.

Ultimately, the Pentecostal church must judge its worship by what is happening inwardly rather than outwardly. Jesus told us that the Holy Spirit's coming would mean that He who had been with us will now be in us (John 14:17). It is the mighty Pentecostal power at work in us that will make our worship meaningful and effective.

Notice again that when Paul describes the power of a Pentecostal worship service (1 Corinthians 14:25), it is not the physical demonstration of a person falling on his face that is the essential item; it is the recognition of the presence of God, acknowledgment of an inner need, and worship of God. It is essential that we keep the proper focus and balance in our worship services so that the will of God through the Holy Spirit will never be hindered by the improper intrusion of the human element.

"'To worship,' said William Temple, archbishop of Canterbury from 1942 to 1944, 'is to quicken the conscience by the holiness of God, to feed the mind with the truth of God, to purge the imagination by the beauty of God, to open the heart to the love of God, and to devote the will to the purpose of God.'"[13] For such to happen will take more than what goes on in the average church service today. This kind of worship can take place only in a Pentecostal worship service where the Word of God is honored and preached in its entirety, where the Spirit of God is allowed to superintend the meeting, and where the people of God are open and obedient to hear what the Spirit is saying to the churches (cf. Revelation 2 and 3).

Before You Step into the Pulpit: Sermon Preparation

H. Maurice Lednicky

Powerful, effective sermons are mandated of every person who delivers the Word of God. But such sermons do not just mysteriously appear. Even one's giftedness does not insure dynamic preaching. Great Bible preachers are committed to the foundational principle that God's Word alone is the basis for all that pertains to spiritual birth, development, and life in Christ. "Faith comes by hearing, and hearing by the word of God" (Romans 10:17[1]).

Homiletics, or sermon preparation, is important for the minister who wants his message (1) to be biblically correct, (2) to emphasize truth with a relevant application, and (3) to be presented in a clear, understandable manner. Time spent in study and preparation affords the minister confidence to speak with God-given authority. "Saturday night specials" (my classification of last-minute sermon preparation) hardly ever have the quality or depth to produce life-changing responses in the hearts and minds of hearers. "The longer you are in the ministry, the more disciplined effort it takes to preach with freshness and vitality."[2]

After an especially enthusiastic preacher had spoken, a woman was telling her friend about the great message she heard. The other woman excitedly asked the theme of the message. After several attempts at recalling the preacher's subject, she said, "I don't remember what he said, but I really liked the way he said it." Enthusiasm is an excellent quality for preachers, but it must not be mistaken for either the anointing of the Holy Spirit or assurance of biblical truth.

Every preacher should take advantage of any opportunity to improve preaching skills. There are scores of excellent volumes on this subject by various authors. Like any other discipline of life, diligent effort is constantly demanded of those who desire a fruitful pulpit ministry. It is in the privacy of being alone with God and His Word that the "message" reaches the heart. Preparation for public presentation is but the transitional step from the prayer closet to the pulpit.

Some key elements worthy of consideration in regular sermon preparation are noted here. Obviously, this is not an exhaustive list. Hopefully, some ideas will germinate and assist you in maximizing your God-given capabilities for "rightly dividing the word of truth" (2 Timothy 2:15).

Be Spiritually Prepared

Although the significance of personal spiritual preparation for ministry is adequately covered in unit 1, it cannot be overstated. If we simply give lip service to being a man or woman of God, it matters little how well the technical skills have been honed. Preaching is not the product of a few hours in the study each week; it is the outflow of a lifetime in relationship with Christ. It is in the secret place with Him that we receive truth into our spirit and mind. Here the Holy Spirit illuminates the Word. Proper understanding of scriptural relevance to contemporary need must be at the heart of every message. Principles can then be made applicable to daily living.

Understand the Scripture Passage

View the big picture first, that is, the whole Word of God. Then, concentrate on a particular passage. Even here, it is important to have a clear understanding of the historical setting of the book the passage comes from (i.e., to whom written, under what circumstances, when, etc.).

For example, Paul wrote the letter to the believers at Philippi from prison in Rome. This was one of the churches he founded on his second missionary journey. Even though not a wealthy congregation, they had lovingly and sacrificially given to his physical needs. Responding to their generosity, he wrote them a very personal letter of thanks. With just this tiny bit of background information, the theme of "rejoicing" found throughout the letter now becomes quite significant.

In today's society, there is great emphasis on continuing education. For the spokesperson of God, the private disciplines of prayer and study must be a way of life, as if it were a continuing-education course. There are no shortcuts. The apostles understood this. "'We will give ourselves continually to prayer and to the ministry of the word'" (Acts 6:4).

Use Reliable Resources for Assistance

1. *First and foremost is the Bible itself as a resource.* Investigate related passages throughout Scripture that speak to the text (subject) under consideration. Many study Bibles (e.g., Full-Life Study Bible, Thompson Chain) are helpful in connecting companion verses. An exhaustive concordance can offer quick and reliable assistance. Today's computer software packages advance a plethora of possibilities for Scripture study.

2. *Use of various translations can be valuable.* Most preachers have a personal preference of a translation for the pulpit; however, one of the easiest ways to gain a broader perspective on a passage is to examine several translations simultaneously. The most commonly known and read among believers include the King James Version (KJV), New King James Version (NKJV), New American Standard Bible (NASB), New

International Version (NIV), *The Amplified Bible* (AMP), and *The Living Bible* (a paraphrase). The serious student will quickly locate several other lesser-known versions that offer additional insights into Scripture.

A word of caution: Word usage changes from generation to generation. A specific translation should never be used to defend a particular position that does not agree with the whole teaching of Scripture. In light of our understanding of scriptural authority, it seems unnecessary to warn the minister against compromising the propositional truth of the inspired Word of God.

3. *Word study volumes are numerous and often provide even further insights into the meaning of words and passages.* Even though one has not had the privilege of learning biblical languages, with a bit of diligence great truths can be discovered. This is fascinating and becomes a marvelous treasure hunt. An investment of time here will, at the very least, contribute great inspiration to the preacher's personal enrichment.

4. *Commentaries often compile homilies and thoughts from various authors.* By examining several writers, it is possible to find a spark of inspiration. However, it is wise to avoid relying heavily on another's inspiration.

A personal library is one of the preacher's most valuable resources. Even with limited finances, the dedicated servant of the Lord will find ways to expand the sources that provide deeper insight. Quality books are a worthy investment. It has been said that the person who never quotes will never be quoted. Perhaps of even greater significance is that through careful study of the Word and the writings of those who give full authority to Scripture, the minister will almost always avoid being caught up in faddish or false doctrines. With so many conflicting voices in highly visible ministries, it is absolutely imperative that we have a clear understanding of what we preach. What a sacred trust has been given to those whose call is to the pulpit!

Choose Illustrations Carefully

The purpose of an illustration is to bring a spiritual truth into the arena of daily life. Jesus was a master at using illustrations. To a people whose lives revolved around agriculture, He spoke of sower and seed, of sheep and shepherds, of wheat and tares. Why? So they could comprehend the higher principle that otherwise might have escaped them.

The first consideration is that an illustration must be appropriate. It must be appropriate for the pulpit, the occasion, and the audience. It must also serve to enhance the scriptural truth presented—or it can only be described as filler for the message. Personal illustrations used with humility can be very effective. The hearers identify with the preacher, many having gone through similar experiences.

Humor can often serve to emphasize a point. However, one must be sensitive to the feelings of others so that humor does not become offensive. Perhaps self-effacing humor is the safest choice. Being able to laugh at yourself almost always raises the level of appreciation others have for you.

Determine the Appropriate Style for the Occasion

There are various definitions identifying sermon "type"; for the most part sermons have been broadly categorized as topical, textual, and expository. In his classic on sermon preparation, *The Making of the Sermon,* T. Harwood Pattison provides this simple definition: "the topical sermon, in which the theme is especially prominent; the textual sermon, in which more regard is paid to the words of the text; and the expository sermon, in which, as a rule, a longer portion of the Bible is taken as a basis for the discourse."[3]

Expository preaching is preferable for the pastor who is speaking to the same audience repeatedly and over an extended period of time. This will insure that the message is truly Word centered and that there is a systematic progression in preaching the "whole counsel of God." Some homileticians strongly insist on expository preaching as the only valid way to communicate God's Word. With this I must strongly disagree. Other styles have specific value and unique appeal for various occasions.

For example, in presenting a series of messages on a particular societal problem (e.g., the breakdown of the family), a topical approach to each segment of the subject may be quite effective. Variety, including illustrated sermons and other creative approaches (audience participation, use of audio or video) may gain an attentive ear from a very discriminating culture.

Organize Your Thoughts

The first priority is to develop a thesis statement. What do you want to say? Reduce it to one or two sentences. If you were to read the Scripture passage, state the theme of the message, and then sit down, would the congregation be able to clearly identify the main truth? Very seldom does the "scattergun" approach serve the messenger's purpose. Before you begin an outline, see the conclusion!

Next, select the subthemes, or points, of the message. While it has been a rather standard practice that sermons should have no more than two or three major points, this is certainly not a hard and fast rule. In expository preaching the passage itself will most often determine the number of points to be considered. Individuality, scriptural maturity of the audience, the truth being emphasized, the length of time available, and the context of the meeting (e.g., banquet, youth rally) must all be factored in when determining organizational content.

Each of your points, constituting the major parts of the outline, should govern the material included under them. However, the entire sermon should be interrelated, each succeeding point building on the previous one and sequentially moving toward the desired conclusion. By carefully constructing the outline, the preacher avoids the pitfall of needless repetition and aimlessly wandering away from the subject. One man joked that the problem with Pentecostal preachers was that they took a text and departed from it!

If the minister maintains strict discipline in staying with the subject in his study, he will never need to worry about straying in the pulpit. I must pause here a moment. This is not the stifling bondage of a mechanical process. The message, not the method, should ultimately influence the hearer to move toward God. However, the better prepared the man or woman of God is, the less it will seem that he is laden down with "Saul's armor." As the speaker feels at liberty, the level of communication with the audience will dramatically improve.

Every Spirit-anointed preacher has enjoyed the enriching experience of digressing from a previously prepared outline at the Spirit's leading. And we pray often to be open channels of divine blessing. This is truly wonderful, but far different from the person who attempts to manipulate a congregation of worshipers simply because he is not prepared to minister the Word.

Some choose to preach from a manuscript; others prepare a detailed outline; still others employ only brief notes. A gifted few can preach powerfully without the assistance of any written notes. Again, personal ability and preference should be the guide. The point is to use whatever means necessary to communicate effectively in the pulpit.

In *Principles for Preachers,* Jesse Moon indicates that preaching notes should be comprehensive enough to include

1. The title or subject
2. The Scripture reference or text
3. The proposition
4. A transitional sentence from introduction into the body
5. Main divisions and subdivisions
6. Transitional sentences from one main division into the next
7. A concluding résumé
8. A final application
9. A statement of invitation
10. A reference to an appropriate invitational song[4]

File the Finished Product

You will want to maintain a record of what you preached, as well as when and where it was preached. Incidentally, I find it helpful to put the date, location, and specific service right on the sermon outline. Then I retain a hard copy as well as one in the computer file. (An insurance agent suggested that I do this and keep them at different locations in case of a fire, theft, or vandalism.) With an appropriate filing system, it is easy and helpful to review and evaluate preaching patterns. Referring to previous outlines can be quite enlightening. Additionally, segments of a particular study (e.g., eschatology, Bible characters) can be useful in a future message that includes Scripture references or biblical illustrations previously studied in depth.

Sermon preparation is not the task of a few hours per week. It is the commitment of a lifetime. The God-called, Spirit-anointed man or woman has no greater privilege or responsibility than proclaiming eternal truth. If the preacher is to deliver the only message of redemption and hope to depraved humanity, surely it is worth his very best effort. Never approach the pulpit unprepared. Skillful sermon preparation alone does not make great preachers . . . but it surely does help!

The Altar Call and Congregational Commitment

David Cawston

Having been born into a Spirit-filled Christian missionary family, I felt the "family plan" qualified me for a personal relationship with God. Little did I realize that one day I would personally have to make the decision to invite Jesus Christ into my heart. I had cut my teeth on the front pew of a church and had listened to hundreds of my father's sermons. I could remember so many of his powerful illustrations, and I had seen many of his altar calls. Like most preachers' kids, I thought those invitations were intended for everyone else but me. After all, I had never done anything that would qualify as bad in the eyes of others. Compared to so many of my friends, my sins didn't seem that serious. Later in life, I learned that there must come a time when God makes real a person's need of salvation.

My conversion experience came at the most unusual time. I was thirteen years old and attending one of our denominational conferences. At the conclusion of the evening service in a football stadium, the speaker gave an invitation for people to receive Jesus Christ as Lord and Savior. The convicting power of the Holy Spirit was so heavy upon me that I felt like the worst sinner who ever lived. When asked to raise my hand I responded. As the speaker came to the second phase of his altar call, he invited all those who had raised their hands to come forward. I remember thinking, *What will my parents think? They think I've been a Christian for years!* Just then a gentleman sitting behind me placed his hand on my shoulder and said, "Son, if you want to go forward I will go with you." It was like a dam had broken. I cried my way to the altar, personally responding to the call of the Holy Spirit to invite Jesus Christ into my life. Much to my surprise, both my parents told me that they had been waiting for a long time for me to make that decision.

Ever since that moment I have always believed in the importance of altar calls. It has been a commitment of my ministry to give an altar call at every service whether I think it is appropriate or not. I have always been amazed that no matter what I am preaching on, someone in the congregation accepts Christ. Not long ago I was meeting with my altar workers coordinator before a Sunday morning service. When he heard that I was preaching on tithing that morning, he looked dismayed. I said, "John, watch and see if there are not as many or more people saved today." At the end of the service that morning eighteen people made a commitment to Jesus Christ. Altar calls are nothing more than allowing God to complete what He has been doing in the hearts of people. It doesn't make any difference what the topic of the sermon is, the Holy Spirit is present and accomplishing His work.

At one time I pastored a large church that presented an outstanding Christmas production each year at our community's performing arts center. The tickets were fifteen dollars per person and the production was sold out for five performances to fifteen thousand people. When I first took the church, I learned that the people in leadership of the musical were hesitant to include any type of opportunity for a decision for Christ in the program. The rationale was that these people had paid to come to the production and, therefore, an invitation might offend and drive them away. But what was the purpose of a Christmas musical if we didn't conclude with a personal invitation to receive the Christ of Christmas? I assured all the parties that I would tastefully give an opportunity for people to receive Jesus Christ as Savior towards the end of the performance. To the surprise of all, over three hundred people invited Christ into their lives during those performances. The invitation became an integral part of the annual production and never adversely affected the attendance in the years that followed.

> " **It has been a commitment of my ministry to give an altar call at every service.** "

If Christ is the Head of the Church, let us give Him His rightful place by allowing the Holy Spirit opportunity to draw people to Him. If you will make a commitment to give altar calls, God will reward your faith with people who respond. In one church I pastored the altars had been removed. I replaced them and told the board that I would be giving an altar call for salvation at the end of every service. Their response was one of surprise. They said, "We haven't had anybody saved at our altars for a long time." I assured them that people would respond in time if we would continually give them the opportunity. Sure enough, within just a few weeks people were coming to the altar to receive Jesus Christ, and the church was beginning to grow. People began to invite their neighbors and friends to church because they realized that we would help them win these people to Christ by giving an altar call at the end of each service. The altar call allows the Holy Spirit to do His job of convicting people of sin and drawing them to forgiveness through Jesus Christ. He partners with us as we give Him opportunity, and the Lord adds to the church daily such as should be saved.

Biblical Background of the Altar

The altars of the Old Testament were very significant, places where people had a personal encounter with God. It wasn't that God didn't speak to them at other times and places, but there were specific times where decisive commitments and covenant relationships were made and an altar was built.

Abram built an altar to the Lord after leaving his homeland in Ur of the Chaldees (Genesis 12:7–8). He had just arrived in the land of Canaan, and the Lord appeared to him at Bethel to make a covenant. The covenant was in response to Abram's faith to put his complete trust in God by obeying Him. God promised to give Abram the land of Canaan. Abram returned to this same altar to meet God again after an eventful side trip to Egypt (Genesis 13:4). Here the principle is established that the altar is the place where a person meets God. Abram returned to the place where God had spoken to him and again called on His name. From this point on in Scripture God could be approached at an altar. It was through the altar experiences that Abram became a friend of God. His friendship with God ultimately led to the altar of sacrifice on the mountains of Moriah, where God asked him to offer his only son Isaac.

We can see the development of the significance of the altar all the way through the time of Moses to the altars of the tabernacle. It is then that definition is more fully given as the Lord asks Moses to build two altars. One was the altar of sacrifice, where the sin offerings of Israel were presented daily before the Lord. The other was the altar of incense, which represented the prayers of Israel continually coming up before God. Both images speak to the purpose of the place set aside as an altar in our churches today. This is a place where people can come to God for forgiveness and present themselves to Him in a covenant relationship. It also is a place where they can continually renew that covenant by ongoing communication.

> **"**
> # Here the principle is set that the altar is the place where one meets God.
> ****

The altar is a designated place to meet God, and the altar call defines a time to meet Him. People need to be led to decisions and times of renewal. We are all experts in procrastination. Unless challenged to commitment either by difficult circumstances or by Holy Spirit anointed leadership, we tend to put off finalizing our decisions.

Jesus, in His only documented full sermon (Matthew 5 through 7), concluded by bringing his listeners to a point of decision. He taught that there is only one entrance gate into the kingdom of Heaven and that it is difficult to find. Then He addressed the fact that words alone are not important, but it is actions that really count. Finally, Jesus told the story of two men who built houses, one on sand and the other on rock. When the storms of life came, the house on the rock was the only one that stood firm. People must examine which kind of house they are building. It is time to make a decision.

On another occasion (Luke 18:18–23) a rich young ruler approached Jesus and asked to follow Him, but Jesus told him to sell all that he had and give the money to the poor. It was a point of decision, but the young ruler walked away because the price was too great.

The apostle Peter at the conclusion of his sermon on the Day of Pentecost brought his listeners to a point of acceptance or rejection. After declaring the death and resurrection of Jesus Christ and the empowering of the Holy Spirit, Peter gave his altar call: "'Repent, and let every one of you be baptized in the name of Jesus Christ for the remission of sins; and you shall receive the gift of the Holy Spirit. For the promise is to you and to your children, and to all who are afar off, as many as the Lord our God will call'" (Acts 2:38–39[1]). This is one of the most powerful altar calls of all time. There were three thousand souls saved on that one day!

Paul the apostle shared his testimony with King Agrippa in a private meeting and concluded with such a powerful altar call that Agrippa said to Paul, "'You almost persuade me to become a Christian'" (Acts 26:28).

Purpose of the Altar Call

The altar call should bring people to a decision. To put it in sales terminology, it is to "close the deal." What salesman would present his sales pitch and then walk away after the presentation without attempting to make the sale? Every time the gospel is proclaimed, we need to bring closure by giving an opportunity for people to accept or reject the offer.

First, this opportunity allows the Holy Spirit to do His work. Jesus said of the Holy Spirit, "'When He has come, He will convict the world of sin, and of righteousness, and of judgment'" (John 16:8). God the Holy Spirit partners with you in presenting the gospel to make real the life-and-death decision about salvation. He speaks to the heart of the listener and convicts him of his sin and his need of a Savior.

It is interesting to talk to people who have responded to an altar call for salvation. More often than not they did not hear specifically what was being preached, but rather they responded because of their need of forgiveness and a relationship with God. The awareness of their need of salvation was brought about by the conviction of the Holy Spirit. As I stated earlier, I have preached on many different topics but have always had people receive the Lord. The Holy Spirit was doing His job of convicting, and by giving an invitation I was allowing Him to complete His work. If we believe in the Holy Spirit's power to draw men and women to Christ, we need to give Him opportunity to work by bringing them to a point of decision.

Second, the altar call speaks to the believer that God is alive and working in the Church. Every time I give an altar call, my congregation is encouraged in the Lord. Recently I had a parishioner come to me and share an experience he had had in a nearby college of another fundamental denomination. The professor was teaching a class on evangelism and asked the students about the number of people being saved in their churches. After several students had reported very low numbers during the last year, this young man, surprised at the minimal impact of the other churches, reported a figure of several hundred. The professor and class were astounded. The student, encouraged to be a part of a church that was reaching the lost, explained that at every service an altar call was given and people came forward to receive Jesus Christ. I believe the significant difference in our church and theirs is the altar call.

Third, the altar call provides an avenue for many people to be involved in the birthing and discipling process. I always have a well-trained team of altar workers who work with me. They have the opportunity personally to lead people to Christ. They are well-trained in personal evangelism and make sure that every person who comes forward receives one-on-one counseling and prayer. The joy that this ministry brings to their own spiritual lives is immeasurable. The personal touch is also important in the beginning of the discipleship process: The altar workers bridge the gap between the trip to the altar and the attendance of a new believers class for helping these new converts move into discipleship. The enthusiasm of the altar workers is infectious for the whole congregation!

Fourth, the fact that the altar call is an important part of every service focuses our congregation on the purpose of the Church. Too often churches fall to the level of being simply another organization or club that we belong to. We forget that the mission of the church is not to make people comfortable but to equip them for the work of the ministry. The purpose of that ministry is only one thing: to keep reaching people for Jesus Christ! Our task is not complete until everyone is reached. Regularly giving an invitation keeps this purpose in focus. Your congregation will join you in the mission if you will train them and assist them. Over 90 percent of the people that come to our church come as a direct result of a personal invitation from someone in the congregation. If your people know that an invitation for salvation will always be given, then you are assisting them in their evangelistic efforts. Many times people come to me before a service, concert, or special event and tell me that a friend or relative has come with them, and they are praying for that person's salvation. Every altar call is an opportunity for us to partner with the Holy Spirit to accomplish the Great Commission.

Providing the Opportunity

It is vitally important that you conclude every sermon, talk, or presentation with a very clear and simple opportunity for people to respond for salvation. They need to know they are sinners but that does not keep God from loving them. In fact, He has always loved them and desires a personal relationship with them. That is why He gave His Son Jesus Christ to die for them. Jesus Christ paid the price for their sins, and they can now come to God by accepting what Christ has done. In fact, He is knocking at their heart's door now. All they have to do is to open that door by acknowledging their desire to receive Jesus and He will come in and forgive their sins and establish that personal relationship with them. Remember, salvation is simple! We complicate things. To see how simple the response can be, look at the response of the thief on the cross to Jesus: "'Lord, remember me when You come into Your kingdom'" (Luke 23:42).

There are many ways for people to respond to your invitation. One of the most common is to have them raise their hands. I use this method most frequently in a service. It gives an opportunity for an initial response of corporate prayer, and then I can follow that up with an invitation to the altar for personal ministry. It also allows my altar workers to watch for those who raise their hands so that if they do not come forward, an altar worker can move to that individual after the service and talk one-on-one.

Sometimes I ask those who wish to receive Jesus Christ to lift their eyes while others' eyes are closed and to make eye contact with me. That way we can agree together as I corporately pray for them. I have used this method at banquets and in other events when there was no opportunity for personal ministry. I ask those who respond to tell the person they came with of the decision they made.

> **" There are many ways for people to respond. "**

I have often used response cards. In situations when we have a tight service schedule because of multiple services and not enough altar time, I provide a spiritual response card that people can fill out and leave in a designated place on their way out so we can follow up with personal ministry later. This method has also been effective.

At large gatherings such as concerts and Christmas or Easter presentations, I have enclosed a response card in the program to receive feedback on the performance or to add their name to a special concert mailing list. I usually draw the audience's attention to this at the opening and have them fill out this information. Then at a designated point in the presentation, I give a simple challenge to receive Jesus Christ as Savior and ask them to pray silently with me as I pray for all. After the prayer, I ask them to mark their card or just tear the corner off of their card as a signal to me that they prayed to receive Christ. I usually tell them that I would like to send them a book as a gift to help them in their walk with the Lord. I request that they leave their cards on the seat or hand them to an usher on the way out. The response to this approach has been excellent, and I have seen thousands accept the Lord this way.

The congregation's attitude toward the altar time is extremely important, requiring training from the pulpit about the significance of this part of the service. It is not a prelude to the benediction. It is a time when the Holy Spirit can apply what He has been saying during the service; it is God's moment of personal speaking. To the unbeliever it is about their salvation. To the believer it is allowing the seed of God's Word to be planted in their hearts so that the enemy does not steal its truth before it has been applied. When the invitation to come to the altar is given, I request that the altar workers move out with the unbelievers. In a Billy Graham Crusade, have you noticed that the altar workers come forward with those responding to the invitation? This primes the pump. Many people are afraid to make the first step forward, but if there are others coming from the audience, then the unbeliever is not afraid to move with them. This method provides support for the unbeliever. And if the altar workers have an identification badge, it is easy to pair them up with those needing prayer.

Likewise the atmosphere is extremely important at the altar time. As people bow their heads and the accompanists begin to play, I am giving the invitation and focusing on those who are raising their hands. I always find it important to have music playing or being sung while the actual invitation is being given. It helps people focus on what is happening instead of on any movement that might be taking place. The music should be strictly at a background level when you are talking, or it will be distracting rather than helpful. The song being played or sung should be a familiar chorus or hymn so that believers can worship while unbelievers are responding. The Billy Graham Crusades have always used the hymn "Just as I Am." The *Revivaltime* radio broadcast used the song "There's Room at the Cross." The significant factor is to use something that is familiar to your people.

The most important thing after the altar call for salvation is the follow-up! Whether that follow-up is in person or by mail, it must be done. Ten percent of the process is bringing the person to a point of decision while 90 percent is discipling them. I have used follow-up teams that visit every person who made a decision for Christ. These visits don't take long, but they familiarize us with where the individuals live, what their needs are, and confirms their commitment to the Lord. It also gives us an opportunity to invite these new believers to a class specially designed for them. The teaching team of the new believers class also make a telephone contact with the new convert after the initial visit. Their responsibility is to see that the new convert attends the class. The new believers class lasts only twelve weeks, and its curriculum is designed so a person can enter at any time and leave after having completed a twelve-week cycle. This builds a bridge to other ministries and classes of the church to insure that we can continue the discipling process with each new convert.

A Final Word

I have spent most of this chapter discussing altar calls for the purpose of bringing the unbeliever to commitment because I believe that this area is seriously neglected in our churches today. Having spoken in hundreds of churches across the nation, I have noted an absence of this kind of altar call. I challenge you to return to the purpose of the church. The church is a place for the birthing of people into the Kingdom as well as a place for the celebration of faith and commitment of the believer.

Your commitment to the altar call will have a tremendous multiplying effect upon your church! Your people will be excited about people being saved. They will partner with you in bringing their friends and family members to church. Your water baptismal services will increase. In fact, there have been times in my ministry when we had water baptism every Sunday as a result of the number of people being saved. Your people will grow in maturity and commitment to reaching the lost. The ministries of the church will grow as you meet the needs of these new believers. Your church will continue to grow as the Lord adds to your congregation daily.

Achieving Variety in Pulpit Ministry

H. Robert Rhoden

E very pastor knows the power of a deadline. It seems every time we turn around, it's Sunday. Wasn't it just yesterday you last preached, and now another sermon preparation stares you in the face? No other single activity will make a greater impact on your effectiveness in ministry than preaching. When churches in our Fellowship are searching for a pastor, they still refer to a *pulpit* committee. Although other factors contribute to the success of our pastoral leadership, we recognize the priority we must give to preaching. Good preaching does not come easily, it is hard work. People vote on us every week with their feet and their pocketbooks, often in response to our preaching.

Charles G. Finney forever changed the face of American preaching. He introduced creative elements such as story telling, personal experience, humor, and persuasive appeal in his proclamation of the gospel. Those elements endure in homiletical practice today.

Factors that Influence Sermon Preparation

The dictionary defines a *factor* as "something that actively contributes to the production of a result." The minister who ignores certain factors will speak to congregations that are not listening and will answer questions that people are not asking.

AUDIENCES

Michael Sack provides an excellent concise analysis of the four audiences the minister faces in a heterogeneous congregation.[1] (See sidebar.)

TELEVISION

Television has become the dominant medium of communication in our society. In the United States we have more television sets than we have

The Multiplex Congregation

Understanding the four audiences you face:

GENERATION X

WHO THEY ARE
- 16 to 25 years old
- "Feed me" generation
- Low self-esteem
- Retreat from world into small groups

WHAT THEY NEED
- Unconditional acceptance
- Very short list of what's really important
- Written reinforcement of key concepts (e.g., a spiritual notebook)

Want to be needed

BUSTERS

WHO THEY ARE
- 25 to 35 years old
- "Why me?" generation
- Don't like crowds or mingling with other generations
- Skeptical of guarantees

WHAT THEY NEED
- Relationships
- To create a better world
- To talk things over with peers

Wants real relationship

BOOMERS

WHO THEY ARE
- 35 to 50 years old
- "Entertain me and earn me" generation
- Faddish, intellectually lazy
- Looking for spiritual definition

WHAT THEY NEED
- Talk about meaning, self-definition, and worth
- New church models
- Media

Want to be sought after

OLDER ADULTS

WHO THEY ARE
- 50 and up
- "Need me and show me" generation
- Possess skills and money
- Want to do something worthwhile

WHAT THEY NEED
- In preaching, positive examples of older adults
- Appreciation

Want respect - consult me

people. With the average person watching eighteen-thousand commercials a year, information is being dispensed in twenty- to thirty-second visual time frames. Communication experts tell us that speeches, therefore, should develop a thought in a three- to six-minute segment and then transition to another segment with the next thought. The presence of TV has moved us from a reading culture to an oral/visual culture. Television is story, and the people who watch television are story people. It is a challenge to have the congregation think sequentially in this visual/story age. We, therefore, speak in terms of relationships rather than just propositional truths. This gives the sermon the flavor of being grounded in people's lives. We are coming full circle, for Jesus used this method by telling parables.

Planning for Variety

My challenge as a pastor was preaching three times a week. On the one hand I struggled with subject matter. Equally frustrating was the unfulfilled expectation that the congregation would remember the material and put it into practice. The solution for me came in turning to the yearly church calendar and adapting it to a Pentecostal church. We used what was appropriate for us.

For preaching, one might think through the calendar year in the following manner:

January. January is a great month to teach on goals or stewardship of time, talent, and treasure.

February. Since February includes Valentine's Day, it is the ideal month to speak about marriage and family.

Easter and Lent. The forty days prior to Easter are called Lent on the church calendar. Rather than avoiding these liturgical customs or criticizing them, why not seize this time as an opportunity to teach on sanctification. I found that people from other traditions appreciated understanding the real meaning of giving up something if it will help one to become more like Christ.

Pentecost. From Easter to Pentecost is perfect for teaching on life in the Spirit. One can teach on the fruits and gifts of the Spirit as well as the power for witnessing that comes with the baptism in the Spirit.

Mother's and Father's Days. Mother's Day and Father's Day are special opportunities to touch families with the themes of love and responsibility.

July. One might use a theme of freedom for special emphasis on the Sunday nearest July 4.

August–September. A September series I did on "Managing Life" was very popular. The four patriarchs of Genesis provided perfect material for this series. Abraham managed his life by faith, Isaac by love, Jacob by grace, and Joseph by a dream.

October. The last Sunday in October is Reformation Sunday. What a great opportunity to preach on justification by faith and to set the day in its historical context. It enhances the service to sing "A Mighty Fortress is our God," making special note of the verse that declares "the spirit and the gifts are ours."

Veterans Day and Memorial Day. These special days are opportunities to touch the military people of the community. The themes of authority and honor bring a warm response at these times.

Thanksgiving. Thanksgiving rivals any holiday of the year for me. It would be tragic to miss this opportunity to remind the congregation of the biblical admonition to give thanks and to set the historical context of this national holiday.

The Advent season. The four Sundays prior to Christmas can be a prime time to connect with people in the congregation who have liturgical backgrounds and to expand the thinking of those unfamiliar with the church calendar. It can also provide an opportunity for them to invite their friends to church. Here are four Sundays to preach the four biblical cardinal doctrines: Jesus is our Savior, Jesus baptizes us in the Holy Spirit, Jesus is our Healer, and Jesus is our coming King. The Isaiah 9:6 passage is made for the Advent season—Wonderful Counselor, Mighty God, Everlasting Father, and Prince of Peace.

The foregoing is intended to be suggestive rather than comprehensive. The concept of preaching in a series with attention to special days creates a pattern for learning and living that I believe in.[2]

SERMON PREPARATION QUESTIONS

1. What is the main point of this sermon?
2. If I weren't the pastor, would this sermon interest me?
3. Am I communicating in concepts that are easy to understand?
4. What response do I expect from the congregation?
5. If I were in the congregation, would I want someone to speak to me in this manner?
6. What components, e.g., quotes, humor, illustrations, add variety to the message?
7. How long is this sermon? A good sermon need not be long; a bad one shouldn't be.[3]

VARIETY IN COMPONENTS OF THE SERMON

Every sermon has three basic components: the beginning, the main points, and the ending.

Beginning

It is critical that we develop variety in the way we begin sermons. People who "channel surf" give each program a seven-second opportunity to capture their attention before switching to another channel. Audiences watching a speaker in person are slightly more charitable. Nonetheless, they use the same "remote-control mentality." The speaker should be aware of a variety of techniques for gaining congregational attention.

A quote. Use a line from a famous person or a dramatic line from a current news article.

A rhetorical question. "How many people have ever been in a storm? Today we are talking about surviving the storms of life."

An unusual fact. "Have you ever tasted a nice cool, refreshing Coke? Congratulations! So have hundreds of millions of other people all around the world. And it's all Robert Woodruff's fault. Well, not all his fault, but he is largely to blame. You see, Woodruff, head of Coca-Cola for over fifty years, had the audacity to tell his staff in 1941, 'See that every man in uniform gets a bottle of Coca-Cola for five cents wherever he is and whatever it costs the company.' When World War II ended, he went on to say that in his lifetime he wanted everyone in the world to have a taste of Coca-Cola. Talk about vision! With careful planning and a lot of persistence, Woodruff and his colleagues reached their generation around the globe for Coke."[4]

I used this story as an introduction to a missions sermon. After giving the opening sentence, I paused, took a sip from a can of Coca-Cola, and proceeded. One man in the congregation had his camera that day. He jumped up and surprised me by taking a picture as I stood in the pulpit drinking from the can. Needless to say, it was a major attention-getter!

Humor. Old and widely circulated jokes tend to make the listener think the rest of the sermon might also be stale. A personal humorous experience or something invented on the spot grabs audience attention far better. A friend of mine who often had the congregation laughing remarked, "We laughed a lot, but I didn't tell a single joke—only stories about life."

A story. This is perhaps the most used introduction. Make sure the story leads into the main point of the sermon.

Main Points

Three points is a good number for the body of a sermon. Regardless of the number of main points, having variety in the way we divide the material is most essential to good preaching.

One of the most popular styles is to begin each heading with words that start with the same letter (e.g., *purpose, plan,* and *power*) or sound (e.g., *cynicism, psyche,* and *sin*).

Using the *Who, What, When, Where, Why,* and *How* questions is another style.

Putting the first three letters of the alphabet together is also effective. When I taught on sharing one's faith in a public meeting, I used the ABC's of sharing—Audible, Brief, and Christ-centered.

Whatever one does to provide hooks the congregation can hang their memory on, it should have variety and creativity.

Ending

As the speech passed the one-hour mark, the crowd lost patience and began leaving. Not deterred, the speaker droned on. Finally, only one person remained in the audience. In appreciation, the speaker leaned over and said, "I would like to say in conclusion, Sir, that you are a gentlemen." "You are wrong, mister," the man replied. "I'm the next speaker." Knowing when and how to conclude is critical to every sermon. If we have focused on the question, Exactly what do I want the congregation to do? then the conclusion should lead to a response.

Summarize your major points. Someone has said if you use this age-old method, then keep it light, bright, and tight. Do not repeat the sermon.

Ask a question. For example, Isn't it time we stop talking about it and do it? Or, If this isn't the answer, what is?

Tell a dramatic story. Again make sure the story connects with the main point of the sermon.

Make the last line one of your best lines. "Clinton Lacy of West Richland, Washington, achieved the world record for sermon length in 1955. He preached 48 hours and 18 minutes, using texts from every book of the Bible. Eight persons stayed to the end. Not knowing how to stop is not as destructive as not knowing when to stop. But pilots who end their flights by shutting off the engines instead of making a smooth connection with the ground tend to have fewer passengers on their next trip."[5]

VARIETY IN SERMON STYLE AND CONTENT

Each minister has a favorite theme that filters into each sermon. No matter where I start in a sermon, at some point the theme of hope will surface. Variety in style and content is not intended to affect our personal spiritual formation, which is inextricably linked to our favorite life theme. By *style* I mean evangelistic or teaching and by *content* I mean topical or expository.

Evangelistic Style

For the pastor who is called to edify the saints, developing an evangelistic style may be a great challenge. While every sermon in some way points to salvation, the Holy Spirit at special times can place upon the pastor a particular message with the primary purpose of reaching the unsaved. A dedicated prayer time for each sermon will make room for the Holy Spirit to guide toward evangelism when unsaved persons are in the congregation. Recently, while I was visiting a church on Sunday morning, the pastor, an outstanding teacher of the Word, focused his message on the lost. You could sense the burden of his heart. Many responded to the invitation. The ultimate key to variety is the direction the Holy Spirit provides during prayer and preparation.

Teaching Style

It is not unusual for us to draw a sharp line of distinction between preaching and teaching, that is, between *kerygma* (public proclamation) and *didache* (ethical instruction). We draw that distinction from the summary of Jesus' Galilean ministry in Matthew 4:23—Jesus went about all Galilee *teaching* and *preaching*. While these two activities are ideally conceived as distinct, both of them are based upon the same basic facts. The *kerygma* proclaims what God has done, while the *didache* teaches the implications and applications of this proclamation for Christian conduct.

With this understanding, we define teaching in a formal sense as a process of communicating selected information in a created environment through a variety of methods. Our pulpit teaching, therefore, provides an opportunity to speak instructively. The apostle Paul's answer to problems and controversies, like the misuse of spiritual gifts, was not more liturgy to stifle human manifestations but teaching to guide and guard against abuse.

Problem solving is one teaching style. Ask the questions, How did we get into this mess? What went wrong? Then present a solution and ask people to respond with a decision to correct the problem. Baby Boomers love this how-to approach.

Dealing courteously with controversy is another teaching style. Stuart Briscoe says we can preach controversial topics without picking a fight by (1) turning the heat off and the light on, (2) doing our homework, (3) touching the funny bone, (4) giving balanced treatment, and (5) considering pastoral needs.[6]

Topical Handling of Content

The challenge of topical preaching is to make sure it is not just a compilation of stories, quotes, etc. Topical preaching should be as biblically based as any other type of preaching. It needs the same amount of study. Careful exegesis is mandatory to maintain the integrity of consistent biblical preaching.

I struggled as a pastor with preaching/teaching the congregation 52 different things each year (or 104 if you add Sunday night, or 156 if you include Wednesday night). For me, it was impractical to expect a congregation to learn that many different things or to assume I could adequately prepare material on so many subjects. Since repetition is the first law of learning, I chose as a general practice to pick one topic or theme a month with the hope that the congregation could learn twelve things a year. While the people of the congregation had to decide the effectiveness of this approach, I interpreted their feedback to be positive.

Expository Handling of Content

I am persuaded that all preaching should include careful exegesis. The traditional approach to expository preaching is to take a book of the Bible and preach through it. It is much easier to use the "through-the-book" approach with smaller books of the Bible. May I suggest some other approaches.

Character study. Studying the lives of Bible characters like Abraham, Joseph, Esther, Ruth, Samuel, Peter, and Paul helps the congregation to identify these Old and New Testament characters as real people, especially when we do not hide their failures.

Great passages of the Bible. Teaching the Ten Commandments, the Twenty-Third Psalm, the Beatitudes, and the Lord's Prayer will renew these familiar passages in people.

The Sermon on the Mount. This material almost preaches itself and is familiar even to people who are young Christians. It touches subjects that are timeless and transcultural.

The miracles. The seven miracles in the Gospel of John beautifully teach that Jesus was the master over quality, distance, time, quantity, nature, circumstance, and death.

These suggestions are intended to plant seeds. Your list will grow as the Spirit guides you to the truth you are to preach. (I intentionally use *truth* rather than truths because one will never run out of material when he or

Good Reading for Good Preachers

Good preachers are voracious readers. Here is a selected biblical preaching bibliography for those who are pressing on in their quest to be an anointed and skilled messenger.

Berkley, James D. *Preaching to Convince.* Dallas: Word Books, 1986.

Dudurt, Michael, ed. *Handbook of Contemporary Preaching.* Nashville: Broadman, 1993.

Dynamic Preaching (monthly magazine published by Seven Worlds Corporation, 321 Troy Circle, Knoxville, Tenn., 37919).

Larsen, David L. *The Anatomy of Preaching.* Grand Rapids: Baker Book House, 1989.

Lloyd-Jones, D. Martyn. *Preaching and Preachers.* Grand Rapids: Zondervan Publishing House, 1972.

Miller, Calvin. *Marketplace Preaching.* Grand Rapids: Baker Book House, 1995.

Miller, Donald G. *Fire in Thy Mouth.* Nashville: Abingdon Press, n.d.

Robinson, Haddon W. *Biblical Preaching.* Grand Rapids: Baker Book House, 1980.

Rodd, Clarence, ed. *We Prepare and Preach.* Chicago: Moody Press, 1959.

Stott, John. *Between Two Worlds.* Grand Rapids: William B. Eerdmans Publishing Co., 1982.

Torrance, Thomas F. *Preaching Christ Today.* Grand Rapids: William B. Eerdmans Publishing Co., 1994.

Wiersbe, Warren. *With the Word.* Nashville: Thomas Nelson Publishers, 1991.

she preaches the truth. The one who is merely looking for truths to preach will eventually experience a famine of inspiration.)

In conclusion, we look again at Gardner Taylor, the "pulpit king." Two of his statements capture the essence of what it means to be a proclaimer of God's Word with variety and creativity. "There's no excuse for the preacher if he or she is not speaking to people for God—a presumptuous undertaking, to be sure, but one that we are called to do. And unless that is done I don't think preaching has occurred."[7]

In response to the question, What makes a great preacher? Taylor said, "In the book of Ruth, Naomi says, 'I went out full, and I've come back empty.' . . . That's the story of life. It's also the story of preaching; we must keep ourselves full so we can empty ourselves in the pulpit."[8]

Planning the Worship Service in Concert with the Spirit

David Lim

The worship service is the most important time of the week for the local church. It reveals the church's philosophy of worship, purpose, direction, and caring. It is in microcosm what the church does all year long. It is the church's signature, saying to all, *This is what we are—our values, our thrust, our essential being.*

Each church must think through its calling, its convictions about spiritual gifts, and its part in the greater body of Christ. Otherwise, Sunday services will merely be times to gather, to come to programs. Such programs may be routine or may reflect innovative and contemporary ideas, but no conviction, direction, or supernatural power will be evident. A child once wrote a note to God: "Dear God, we had a great service last Sunday. I wish you'd been there!" We can have programs, rituals, innovations, and sermons, but at the same time we can miss God.

The church should be a place where people come in order to go out— a place to learn God's mandate, to minister life to fellow believers, to encounter God afresh, to face trials and challenges with divine strength, to be the Church incarnate in society. A church full of life and vitality attracts people and motivates its members to touch others.

This chapter has six parts. The first part, "Exalt God Alone," gives the basis of our entire ministry. The five that follow tell us how to exalt God in the worship service.

Exalt God Alone

Before coming to Grace Assembly in Singapore, I earnestly prayed to hear a word from God. What did He want to do through the church? His only response was, *Give God the glory—or else!* At first I thought it was God's word to stay humble. Only later did I realize the awesome implications of that word. My whole ministry had to glorify God, or I had no ministry left! Serving under an awesome, holy God, no human feels adequate or dares boast. Ministry is holy! The glory of God became a philosophy that influenced every program. Our method cannot reflect human ingenuity alone, but God's ways of fulfilling His plan. Grace Assembly is a multicultural, multilingual congregation. Perspectives and methods differed greatly. Our church had to seek God's method; we had to do His work by His power. This meant a personal commitment of prayer, normally two to three hours per day, and a commitment to move the entire congregation to pray. The pastoral staff has a weekly prayer meeting to pray for services, outreaches, and needs. At congregational prayer meetings we take time to focus on ministries and outreaches of the church. During music rehearsals, musicians immerse the worship ministry in prayer.

God's glory must be revealed to the nations, so we must develop a strong missions program. Giving God glory means that, in good times or difficult times, we exalt Jesus! Through that, individuals will learn how to find victory and glorify God. And since our lives are to be living sacrifices to God, we had to learn how to glorify God in our worship.

Encounter God through Celebration

Worship is giving glory to God unconditionally, lovingly, and obediently. Its most important focus is a dynamic, life-changing encounter with God. True, God meets needs and answers prayers as they are mingled with worship. And worship may provide good feelings. But if these are primary motivations, worship has become self-centered. Our one desire should be to please God in worship; then God may heal hurts, melt stubborn hearts, touch us for service, or challenge us to deeper faith. Our people must know we are on holy ground. No flesh can stand in His presence!

Worship must unite the congregation so it may move forward as one. As a multilingual congregation, we have separate language services. In our English services we try to have at least one hymn to bring young and old together at a point of worship. The young need to appreciate the depth and majesty of the hymns. The older ones need to sense the dynamic encounter, celebration, and victory of the choruses. The issue is not whether we should have all hymns or all choruses. Interestingly, our Chinese congregations prefer more hymns, some songs with Chinese melody, mixed with contemporary choruses translated into Chinese. Yet, their worship is vibrant and meaningful.

Music should progressively lead us into the throne room of God, into the Holy of Holies. An excellent pattern of songs begins with a call to worship and leads to celebration, thanksgiving, praise, and adoration; then in the Holy Place we can hear God speak and share His heart's desire with us. The call to worship may be a hymn, such as "All Hail the Power," or a chorus, such as "I Will Enter His Gates." We plan for one or two peaks of worship. Usually worship will peak at the point of praise or adoration with a hymn like "How Great Thou Art" or a chorus like "Majesty." Then the congregation *knows* they can release powerful praise to God. This can free Christians to allow the Spirit to minister through them with the gifts. Moments of revelation can happen as God impresses people with a word, a song, an exhortation. One should move from the horizontal to the vertical, rather than jump back and forth from one to the other: At the point of adoration, the call to worship is out of place.

Each service should have a consistent pattern. If you use different song leaders each week, they must learn to follow a general pattern. This gives the congregation a sense of security and direction about what is happening next. I prefer the worship leader primarily to lead singing, flowing from one song to another; a song leader who follows his own style—singing songs he prefers, commenting on each verse, and reading poems and articles—interrupts the flow of worship.

Choose worship leaders who know how to lead undistracted, sincere worship. Accompanists and back-up singers need to be strong musically and spiritually. They set the pattern. Let others gain experience in other settings; Sunday worship services are not practice times for new leaders.

Pentecostal worship reflects the expectancy that God can speak at any moment to anyone. When people experience God afresh and anew, they will testify to the glory of God. Strong worship becomes one of the greatest motivations towards evangelism. It allows God to do divine surgery on wrong attitudes, inner hurts, and wrong practices. When we touch God, we can never be the same.

Empower Ministry through Spiritual Gifts

Gifts are not optional. They are integral to Pentecostal ministry. Teaching on the gifts gives a safety framework so your people will *know* how to exercise, apply, and evaluate the gifts. Lead them step-by-step from theory to practice. Show them how to be sensitive to the Spirit daily. I help staff and board members listen to the Spirit in a season of prayer prefacing every staff and board retreat. Then they share what God is laying on their hearts. They see how God confirms their words through what others share.

Model sensitivity. A leader leads by example. He prays for the sick, comes against Satan's trickery, and reflects a lifestyle of faith in God. He daily finds joy in the Lord and hears from the Lord in intimate conversation. He grows in his knowledge and understanding of spiritual things. He relies increasingly on God to do the work in and through his life. He is not afraid to pray for one or more gifts of the Spirit to be manifest to confront needs. This modeling is most important if people are to learn sensitivity to spiritual gifts.

Model readiness. A leader must prepare to share a word from the Lord before asking the congregation to do so! Sometimes leaders inadvertently dampen the move of the Spirit instead of encouraging it. If they ask the congregation to share words God gives them and no one responds, then people feel God did not speak to them. This discourages others from sharing. If the leaders themselves are prepared to share, this will encourage others to hear from God too. Before and during each service, leaders should ask God what He wants to emphasize during that service.

In fact, when a gift of tongues is exercised, the leader must take the responsibility to have the interpretation if no one else does! If the prime purpose of tongues is to praise and worship God, then tongues and interpretation are given to encourage a congregation to see the greatness of God and worship Him freely. Leaders should know what the Spirit is saying for a given service and be prepared to interpret the tongues. Then, if someone else gives the interpretation, the leader can confirm that indeed this was what the Spirit said to him also! This greatly encourages everyone.

Proper evaluation liberates. When leadership is confident, unafraid to evaluate and encourage the move of the Spirit, the people will not fear fanaticism and will allow the Spirit to work on their lives. Teach from Scripture. Show what God is saying to the church.

We can dampen the exercise of gifts by legalistically, suspiciously viewing each manifestation. If you must correct, do it gently in the spirit of love, affirming the positive and moderating the negative. For example, what if there are four expressions of tongues and interpretation? In my early days as a pastor I would have declared the fourth expression to be carnal. Now I take a more pastoral approach. I always affirm a person whom God touches! This encourages others. There are many possible reasons a fourth expression was given. Horizontal words of exhortation, warning, and challenge should have been ministered as prophecies rather than tongues and interpretation. In the enthusiasm of the moment, one may bubble over with the fresh touch of God. When God impresses a truth on someone, other sensitive believers will also be inspired by the same truth. Perhaps the sharer lost count or is a beginner in sharing gifts. None of these reasons is carnal! Use this as an opportunity to teach on gifts positively. I might say, "The primary purpose of tongues and interpretation is to point people towards greater worship of an awesome God. Paul feels that normally three utterances in tongues with interpretation should be sufficient to encourage a congregation to praise God. Today God touched a brother to affirm other aspects of the greatness of God. How many of you also sensed the Spirit saying something similar to these utterances? You see, God is also speaking to you! Next time, others of you may also share! Now, some of these words could have been given as prophetic utterances, because of their horizontal ministry to build the body of Christ. Don't just wait for tongues, begin to minister what God puts on your heart!"

> **"When leadership is confident, people let the Spirit work."**

Evaluation is not always negative. We can affirm the positive. Where two or three share, evaluate what God is saying to your church. Show what the Bible says. Lack of evaluation will cause confusion; people will not know what to accept or reject. Normally I do not criticize a person publicly unless doctrinal matters arise or confusion develops among the people. If I need to correct further, I will call that person during the week to give more detailed teaching and to encourage his part in the body of Christ. Do not sound reactionary or negative. Lift up Jesus!

Enable God's People through Preaching

There is no substitute for leadership from the pulpit. It is an awesome responsibility. The pastor must evaluate where his people are spiritually and where he can lead them if he builds the proper foundation. Not all pastors are outstanding orators, but all communicators must know and work to their strengths. Use guest speakers when they will do something unique for your people.

The introductory comments before preaching are crucial. People come to church to hear good news. Create an awareness of what the Spirit has been doing. Did someone receive Christ during the week? Has someone found deliverance from bondage or healing? Did someone manifest a gift? Has God done a special work on a mission field? Featuring these moments suggests direction to the congregation; it tells them your priorities. They rejoice in the goodness of God. It tells them that their church is alive and that you are sensitive to the Spirit.

A sermon cannot tell people all they need to know on a subject. Sermons bring awareness, point out key issues, simplify their parameters, and point to Jesus as the authority and answer. Use other training times to develop a subject in depth. Sermons bring the impact of God's Word to the entire congregation.

You should overprepare. Sunday is the tip of the iceberg. What goes on below makes all the difference. The focus in Grace Assembly is the Sunday morning service and the cell meetings that are held throughout the week. Thus, on average I need fourteen to twenty hours to work on a Sunday morning sermon. For a midweek service I approach preparation more spontaneously and topically. I find the spontaneous approach a refreshing change and yet profitable for my people.

Read as thoroughly as time will allow. If you pick up one meaningful illustration or insight, it may help to punch the point home. Choose commentaries that give differing perspectives. Though my first love is exposition of Scripture, my starting point is congregational needs. Believers need practical teaching for spiritual victory, for conquering temptations, for strengthening family relationships, and for developing exemplary Christian behavior. Show them *how* to live for God or you have not preached!

As you grow, your people will grow. Each Sunday sermon is crucial. Envision how that message can change their lives that week and how it will affect their families and jobs. A baseball player who swings a bat must envision the follow-through of his swing. A football player envisions the follow-through of his blocking or kicking or tackling. Just so, a preacher must see beyond Sunday. Walk through your sermon so that each point will help attain these goals. Know the sermon so well that it is part of your life and its flow is deeply imbedded in your spirit. Does every point flow to the major point? If it does not, file it for future use. Will teenagers grasp the truth? Will the mature grow by it?

My main points are illustrated on overhead transparencies. I work through at least ten to twelve drafts of my sermon, praying through each point. Breakthroughs in hearing what the Spirit says, in communicating the Word, in clarity of understanding, and in the ultimate response of the congregation happen in further revision. Often I ask colleagues for input on my sermon outlines. They can point out needed improvements. Perhaps I could state my points more sharply, or the flow is not there, or there is too much content (I have been a Bible college and seminary teacher!).

Reserve Saturday night for prayer and final revisions. We have eight services each Sunday. Normally I am only in the three or four larger services. Yet I intercede for each service and pray through the sermon again. I pray that God will touch lives and release souls from bondage.

Because I have prepared thoroughly, I am not centered on self or on the sermon. I am free to be Spirit-centered and people-centered. Before preaching, I scan the congregation one by one at appropriate points and pray for each one. *What is each one's need today, Lord? Please meet it!* My congregation knows I am not just checking who is present or absent. I have made considerable eye contact even before the sermon begins. Even when shaking hands with parishioners I pray a quick prayer for them. I wish to be a vessel through whom the Spirit flows to meet their needs.

With preparation, prayer, sensitivity to the overall direction of the church, and hearing what God wants to say for each service, there is an air of expectancy. God will touch lives and people will receive practical, life-changing teaching.

Exhort for Response

The heart of a Pentecostal service is the time for response. Some respond while singing, others in hearing the sermon, and yet others in ministry from fellow Christians. The preaching of the Word is vital, but it is the response to the preached Word that gives us our cutting edge. We plan the whole service for response to the Spirit of God!

Always give opportunity for people to come to Jesus. By giving an altar call for the unsaved, you sound a strong message that winning lost souls is a major emphasis. Give opportunity for rededication, personal ministry, and prayer for the sick. By asking those in several categories of need and commitment to come forward, no one needs to feel singled out. Train altar workers to look over the audience to see who raises their hands for each appeal. The focus is not on in-depth counseling at the altar, because the time and circumstances are too limiting. Rather, obtain basic information and focus on ministering spirit and life to them. Select altar workers who are truly prayer warriors, who believe in the miracle-working power of God. At the close of the altar time, give the entire congregation time to respond in celebration to the Lord! Cell groups may discuss Sunday messages in practical application. This is also a form of response.

Envision the Spirit's Total Purpose

Spirit-led planning of worship services focuses on the overall picture, not just one Sunday at a time. David Mohan, pastor of the great New Life Assembly of God in Madras, India, fasts ten days at the beginning of the year to hear God's leading. This church is built on prayer and fasting. They immerse each service, Sunday activity, and outreach in prayer. Periodically, I take three-day fasts to clear the mind, cleanse the soul, conquer the enemy, and clarify the vision. Knowing the direction God is leading the church gives meaning and impact to all we do as a congregation and to our worship services. A Sunday service can be taken in isolation, week by week, or it can be in the context of what the Holy Spirit is doing in your assembly.

Some pastors set their church calendars according to what they want to preach, without regard for the direction of the church and needs of the congregation. What is God's word for your church this year, or even five years from now? You need not share that vision in detail with the congregation because it may scare them! Do not promise the congregation what must be in the sovereign hand of God alone. But you must know the appropriate time to lead them strongly in areas of praise, prayer, missions, inner healing, spiritual warfare, gifts of the Spirit, faith, practical lifestyle, or family life. That sense of vision allows the congregation to move in concert with the Holy Spirit. The people will strongly sense the vision.

Do everything in line with the church's overall vision, philosophy, and direction. Early in January, attract your people to the vision God gives to you for that year. I usually plan two series of Bible exposition annually, in addition to other topical series. The Scriptures I use will depend on the needs of the people and the burden God places on my heart. Topical series normally continue for four to six weeks. Exposition may take longer. I grow as I research new materials. Topics can be developed with some depth and emphasis. Members of the congregation sense direction and invite friends for specific services. In planning for the year, I keep eight to ten Sundays free; should the Spirit change our direction, I can change. Of course, I work with standard dates of our church year: Chinese New Year, Good Friday, Easter, Christmas, and national holidays.

> " **Spirit-led planning focuses on the overall picture.** "

The vision must be clear. How will our services impact the congregation? In turn, how will they impact their friends and the community? What contribution does each service make to the growth and direction of the church? Does it glorify God, both immediately and long term? Does it stretch our faith and challenge our walk? That vision must transform your life first if you expect it to transform your church.

If you plan a midweek meeting, the same principles apply. Can people expect to encounter God? What is the purpose of the meeting? If it is prayer, are you leading them and teaching them in genuine intercession? This gives framework and focus, so people know how to hear from God. This is more than just planning everything around a theme—you provide the leadership; you hear from God first.

You may ask, why all this work for Sunday services or prayer meetings? And I respond, where else do you have the privilege to see so many adherents and outsiders? Where better can you teach people interdependence? Where can you best multiply your effectiveness? Each one of your congregation may touch twenty to forty people that week. The potential is staggering. Here you can model the victory of the Christian walk and the ministry of gifts. These are crucial hours. Either they will hear from God, or they will not. They will hunger for God and find answers to their needs or go away empty. They will either touch their neighbors or reflect a watered down, defeated Christianity. Flow with the Spirit—not because this is impressive, but because a desperate world needs to see those who have encountered the true and living God!

The Place of Music in Congregational Worship

Paul Ferrin

All of the time and effort we spend in music in our services should point toward the ministry of the Word. Everything the minister of music, choir director, or worship leader does should prepare the hearts of the congregation to receive the Word of God. It has always been my goal to hand the service to my pastor on a silver platter, whereupon he can immediately begin his ministry without sensing the need of any further preparation before the Word.

People come into our churches from all walks of life and with many varied needs. There is no possible way to anticipate the heartaches, the burdens, the sadness, the loneliness, and the frustration that fill the lives of our church family. The time of corporate worship can bring the congregation to the One who provides relief, comfort, forgiveness, and love to those who open their hearts to receive.

Nothing surpasses great congregational singing. It raises the adrenaline. It lifts to the heavenlies. It creates a surge. Vince Lombardi, former coach of the Green Bay Packers, would order his professional football athletes to stand on their locker-room tables and sing at the top of their voices. It created an atmosphere of victory! Lombardi's teams won many championships.

The total investment of message and music should move the unrighteous towards righteousness. The sanctuary is not a concert hall; it is the arena where the struggle against sin and defeat is the first priority. First Samuel 16:23 tells how anointed music can drive away tormenting spirits: "David took a harp, and played with his hand: so Saul was refreshed, and was well, and the evil spirit departed from him" (KJV[1]). When anointed music begins to flow in a service, heartaches, burdens, sadness, loneliness, and distress begin to flee. There is a great desire to move toward the altar. My father-in-law, a very godly man, was converted as a teenager while anointed singers sang

> Drifting carelessly with the tide,
> Drifting over the waters wide,
> With no Captain your course to guide,
> Drifting over life's sea.
>
> *Chorus:*
> Drifting, drifting, no port in sight!
> Drifting far from the gospel light;
> Lest you go down in the stormy night;
> Drifting over life's sea.[2]

This lonely teenager, who had been on his own since the age of ten, could not wait for the altar call but got up from his seat during that song and made his way to an old-fashioned altar. Many others followed in that service.

Ministering Together

The choir, instrumentalists, and soloists are partners ministering together, for there are no stars in God's kingdom. A music department cannot minister effectively if there is dissension, jealousy, and criticism. When musicians stand to minister, they must have a fresh anointing each time. God has chosen to work through people. He does not just anoint songs or messages. If messages were in themselves anointed, we could stand and read the sermons of John Wesley or Billy Sunday, and the results would be accomplished. Great messages and great songs must be delivered by someone with a fresh anointing. God anoints the messenger! We need a fresh touch from God every time we walk out on that platform. In fact, we dare not go without it. "It is God who makes both us and you stand firm in Christ. He anointed us" (2 Corinthians 1:21, NIV). The one who created us and knows us best—our faults, our failures, everything about us—is now anointing us for service.

Jesus himself, echoing Isaiah 61:1, said, "The Spirit of the Lord is upon me, because he hath anointed me to preach [sing] the gospel to the poor; he hath sent me to heal the brokenhearted, to preach [sing] deliverance to the captives, and recovering of sight to the blind, to set at liberty them that are bruised" (Luke 4:18, KJV). With the anointing, anything can happen during the ministry of music. Without it, we have a musical performance that leaves one cold and unmoved. When one sings or plays under the anointing, people are saved, sick bodies are healed, and the brokenhearted and lonely are touched. The time is too short and the message too vital to play church.

Pastors and staff members must often become involved in music ministries in the church, yet they feel totally inadequate to perform the duties required. The following comments can encourage them and you to step out in faith and watch God perform miracles through music ministry. Paul's confidence came from God: "I can do all things through Christ who strengthens me" (Philippians 4:13). James gives us some very helpful advice: "If any of you lacks wisdom, let him ask of God, who gives to all liberally and without reproach, and it will be given to him" (James 1:5). *The Living Bible* states it this way: "If you want to know what God wants you to do, ask him, and he will gladly tell you, for he is always ready to give a bountiful supply of wisdom to all who ask him; he will not resent it."

There are many examples in Scripture where God did not step in and get involved until an individual had first acted in faith. Exodus 4:2–4 is the familiar story of Moses having a conversation with the Lord. The Lord asked him, "'What is that in your hand?'" And Moses replied, "'A rod.'" And then the Lord said, "'Cast it on the ground.'" That seemed like a simple request, and Moses did as he was told. But as he cast it on the ground, the rod became a serpent, a hissing snake, and Moses did exactly as I would have done. He fled! Then the Lord said to Moses, "'Reach out your hand and take it by the tail.'" A little more difficult request! When Moses did as he was told, when he actually took that snake by the tail, it became a rod in his hand. The miracle did not take place until Moses had it by the tail.

The same principle was seen when the ark of the covenant was being taken across the Jordan (Joshua 3). The waters that came from upstream did not stand "in a heap" until the soles of the priest's feet were wet. They had to get their feet wet before the miracle took place. When Elijah requested the widow to use the last of her flour and oil to make him a cake, he told her that the bin of flour would not be used up, nor would the jar of oil run dry (1 Kings 17). When she obeyed, there was flour and oil from a miracle source. How much better that was than baking a little cake, eating it, and dying. But before she received the miracle, she had to make a cake for Elijah.

> **The choir, instrumentalists, and soloists are ministers together, for God's kingdom has no stars.**

When God has called us to do something, we are to do as Elijah did at his "pity party" in the cave or as Peter did when Jesus, walking on the water, said to him, "Come!" We must get out of the cave, out of the boat, out of our little place of security, and keep our eyes upon Him, not on the circumstances around us. When we do that, we cannot fail. It is important that our time of congregational worship should be very meaningful and with as few distractions as possible. Anything that takes our thoughts away from the Lord keeps us from accomplishing our ultimate goal. I have seen such distractions when slides shown on a screen were not changed at the proper time or perhaps the wrong slide was projected. Misspelled words on a slide, wrong chords, inappropriate key changes, or the choosing of choruses and hymns that have nothing whatever in common can be distractions.

Achieving Flow in the Worship

The key word is *flow!* Much preparation is essential to accomplish this flow. The theme or type of service must be considered. The pastor's sermon title or a series theme is often a good place to begin. At other times the theme will be established by the season of the year or by a revival or missions emphasis. Other themes such as healing, prayer, praise, worship, the Holy Spirit, the Second Coming, the Blood, or the Love of God can be the basis of a worship service.

The musician or worship leader should look at the musical preparation time just as a pastor looks at his message preparation time. Just as the pastor sits down with his Bible, concordance, and sermon-help books and prayerfully prepares his message, I begin with my hymnbook, praise and worship chorus books, Bible, recordings, and other worship-planning material and seek God for His leading. Perhaps I have a "seed thought," a hymn or a chorus that is the source from which God begins to flow in my heart, giving me everything needed to make the worship time flow together.

Not only the theme, but key signatures, time signatures, tempo, and the overall feel should all be taken into consideration. Some people think a good medley is five songs all in the same key regardless of theme or feel. It is usually appropriate to sing two or three choruses of one tempo instead of going from slow to fast and back to slow, giving a roller-coaster sensation. You may wish to begin with some up-tempo choruses and move on to a slower, worshipful one. Or perhaps begin with soft, easy choruses and move up to a big stately one, such as "How Great Thou Art."

Hymns and choruses can blend and flow together if consideration and planning are given to theme, keys, and feel. An example of this could be as follows:

"All Hail King Jesus" in the key of F.
Using a D7 modulate to the key of G for "All Hail the Power."
Following the final verse, using an E-flat, modulate to the key
    of A-flat.
"Lift Up Your Heads" or "Majesty" could be used in A-flat.

Variety Adds Spice

Variety is certainly an important ingredient in musical ministry, not only in the type of music we use, but with the people who sing and play the music. We must always keep in mind that people from all walks of life make up our church family. They all have their own individual musical tastes. Over thirty-eight years of church ministry has afforded me the opportunity to encounter choir members with extreme likes and dislikes in musical styles. There have been those who would have been happy if we sang nothing but the sacred classics. However, just a few seats over would be a choir member who loved southern gospel. A few rows back was a member who thought the finest gospel music in the world was written by John W. Peterson, and next to him was an advocate of the old hymns. The minister of music has the task of bringing everyone together where they can all sing and enjoy various types of music. I have always said, "No matter what your taste in music is, if you will attend my church for one Sunday (morning and evening), you will hear something you like. Too much of any one thing, no matter how great, will become boring, old hat. Every style of music has *something* to say. It is the same with the congregation! Many would prefer the old hymns and gospel songs, while others would like a steady diet of contemporary praise and worship choruses. We must always remember that God is not as concerned with *what* we sing as He is with the condition of our heart *when* we sing.

Another important part of having variety in our music is the choice of who sings or plays that music. While the choir is the backbone of the music department, from that all-important group can come solos, duets, trios, quartets, mixed ensembles, as well as ladies and men ensembles. The same can be said of the instrumental part of your music program. As you build your church orchestra, you can also bring the same variety of instrumental groups. The more people you can use, the greater the variety you will achieve and, at the same time, the more people you will give opportunity to use their vocal and instrumental talent to glorify the Lord.

Involvement in Other Ministries

It is important for those who are involved in and committed to music ministry to be involved in other ministries of the church as well. Music leadership must also be spiritual leadership. When the music portion of a service is concluded, those involved should not consider themselves through. They, along with the pastor, are planting seeds that will be harvested at the time of the altar call. Someone has said, "You can't lead people in worship if you are not first a worshiper." I have observed the music ministry of the famous Brooklyn Tabernacle choir on several occasions. I have always noticed that those who sing are the first to pray with those who have responded to the altar call.

My mother-in-law, who is now with the Lord, often told me how the choir director in the early days of the Pentecostal church in Denver, Colorado, would line up the choir before a service and ask each one individually, "Do you have the victory?" If they could not answer in the affirmative, they would be asked to step aside and not proceed into the choir loft for that service. Somehow, he realized the importance of *ministry* and how it was impossible to minister if every choir member was not where one should be in a relationship with God.

Make Yourself Ready

Finally, let me say how very important it is to prepare yourself for the task before you. God will help! He will bless and anoint your efforts and ministry. However, He expects us to study and learn to do all we possibly can to prepare ourselves. One very helpful source for anyone in music ministry is attendance at as many conferences as possible dealing with one's particular area of music. Some conferences may even be local, where the expense could be kept to a minimum. A tremendous amount of help and inspiration comes from networking with others who are involved in like ministry. There are many helps you can subscribe to, including music packets from the various publishers, as well as magazines, newsletters, and books.

Perhaps it would be advantageous to attend classes at a university or Christian college in your area. If you are really serious about honing your craft, even private lessons would help tremendously. Don't be afraid to seek help from those inside or outside your church. There might just be an accompanist in your church who has knowledge about key signatures and modulations to help you in planning your praise and worship time.

The Power of Music Ministry

There are many scriptural references in the Old Testament regarding the use of music to usher in the presence of God. Read some of them in 2 Chronicles 5:11–14; 7:6; and 29:25–31. In modern times, great revivals and church services have used music as an effective tool. Famous evangelists have had their musician coworkers, such as Billy Sunday and Homer Rodeheaver, D. L. Moody and Ira Sankey, Billy Graham and Cliff Barrows, and Kathryn Kuhlman and Dr. Arthur Metcalf.

Never before in history have we seen the tremendous variety of music coming from a large number of Christian composers. We also have a plethora of instruments, especially from the electronic keyboard, which can create every sound imaginable as part of a music ministry in our churches.

May we choose music and present the gospel message in every service so that God will be worshiped and magnified. Everything we do must be done to the glory of God!

Conducting Prayer Meetings that Reach the Throne

James D. Marocco

A prayer meeting recorded in Acts 4:24–31 one could say touched the throne of God. Luke tells us in Acts 3 of a lame man, sitting by the temple gate called Beautiful, who was miraculously healed in the name of Jesus through the ministry of the apostles Peter and John. The miracle caused such a stir that Peter and John ended up preaching to a large throng that gathered. Arrested by Jewish leaders distraught over their preaching in the name of Jesus, they were ordered not to preach in that Name again. Upon being released, their first act was to gather the church for a prayer meeting—this is the prayer meeting described in Acts 4.

Luke describes its results: "The place where they were meeting was shaken. And they were all filled with the Holy Spirit and spoke the word of God boldly" (Acts 4:31). Their prayers were answered by God's dramatic intervention. They had, as the writer of Hebrews described, approached "the throne of grace with confidence, . . . and receive[d] mercy and . . . grace to help . . . in . . . time of need" (Hebrews 4:16).

Corporate Prayer Must Be Seen as Efficacious

From this passage, insights can be extracted that will help us to conduct effective prayer meetings. The first of these insights is that corporate prayer must be seen as efficacious. It is an understatement to say that the apostles were motivated to pray. But (were they living today) the threat of persecution could have just as easily provoked them to form a political action committee, instigate a riot, or engage in many other activities. The first thing they did, however, was to gather the church and pray. Why? They believed prayer could truly change things.

Before a group prayer meeting can be effective, there must be a common belief that what is taking place will actually change the course of history. Too often prayer meetings degenerate into nothing more than another religious meeting. Faith is absent, and without it the prayer meeting is a waste of time. Charles Finney, the great evangelist of the 1800s, in describing his conversion experience, expressed how angry he got over being in a prayer meeting with people who were just going through the motions, who did not really believe God would do something.

We must believe that prayer moves the hand of God. The apostle Paul believed this and consistently asked people to pray for him. One such request is found in Romans 15:30: "I urge you, brothers, by our Lord Jesus Christ and by the love of the Spirit, to join me in my struggle by praying to God for me." To the apostle Paul, prayer was vital to life in God. He not only had the churches pray for him, but he prayed for the churches. The intensity of his praying is reflected in his words to the Thessalonians: "Night and day we pray most earnestly that we may see you again and supply what is lacking in your faith" (1 Thessalonians 3:10). Prayer then, from a biblical perspective, is crucial. It is the means God has chosen to release His power in the world. Those gathering for prayer must be reminded of this so they can pray in faith.

Corporate Prayer Should Be Persevering Prayer

Another important thing to remember is the necessity of persevering in prayer. In Luke 18 Jesus uses the example of the perseverance of a widow as a way of encouraging His disciples not to give up praying. Consider this scene:

> For a moment you are standing outside and it is a very cloudy day. The clouds are dark and foreboding. As you pray, the clouds part and the sun's rays behind the clouds, which had been there all along, now begin to shine on you. Prayer to me is like that. It is allowing God's power to be directed upon a given situation. The clouds represent demonic powers that attempt to hinder. The mistake that we make is the belief that my intense prayer in the past resolves all the problems for the future. No, what happens is that

when we cease praying the clouds move back into place, hiding the sun. The spiritual realm is dynamic, and prayer must be ongoing if one is to sustain victory and allow God's power to continue to affect their situation. That is why Jesus, in Luke 18, gave us the parable of the widow and the unjust judge and states, "men ought always to pray and not to faint." We must overcome a western mind-set that tends to see prayer as a waste of time since nothing visible is being accomplished immediately.[1]

Persevering in prayer is faith in action. It is walking in the pattern of Jesus who at Gethsemene prayed the same thing three times (Matthew 26:39–44). Therefore, it is important for the leader to remind those praying not only of the efficacy of prayer, but also of the necessity to persevere in prayer.

Corporate Prayer Should Be in Unison

This brings us to another major insight on how to conduct an effective prayer meeting: "When they heard this, they raised their voices together in prayer to God" (Acts 4:24). Not only must we see perseverance in prayer and see it as efficacious, but we must pray in agreement.

From the passage, agreement seems to encompass two areas. The first is the unity of audible prayer: "They raised their voices." They prayed out loud together. Pentecostals in the early 1900s understood the importance of this kind of praying; the church in prayer could be heard many blocks away. Over the years, Pentecostals have lost this unique prayer distinctive, becoming more contemplative in prayer. I am a good example of the shift. My father prayed very boisterously. I would say, "Dad, why do you pray so loud? God is not deaf!" He would answer me with the remark, "He is not nervous either!" My concept was that silent, meditative prayer was just as appropriate.

However, two things began to draw me back to the importance of verbal prayer that my Pentecostal forefathers instinctively practiced. The first was the discovery that prayer in the Old and New Testaments was primarily out loud. In the story of Hannah (1 Samuel 1:12–14), Eli, the priest, thought Hannah was drunk because she was praying without making a sound. Usual prayer was out loud. We see the same understanding in Jesus' words in Matthew 6:6: "When you pray, go into your room, close the door and pray to your Father." Since prayer was out loud, in order for one to pray effectively in secret, one would need to get alone. Jesus' Parable of the Pharisee and the Tax Collector states, "The Pharisee stood and prayed thus with himself" (Luke 18:11, KJV). However, some expositors argue for the actual reading, "The Pharisee stood by himself and prayed thus." Since prayer was out loud, the publican could probably hear, though some distance away, the prayer of the Pharisee. This changes the whole nature of the parable, making an even more dramatic contrast between the prayers of the Pharisee and the publican.

A second thing that drew me to the importance of audible prayer was becoming a part of Dr. Cho Yongii's Church Growth International board and having numerous occasions to observe the Korean members of his church, the Yoido Full Gospel Church, pray together. On one occasion, I had the privilege of addressing the delegates to the 1987 Church Growth

International Conference in Seoul, in a special meeting at Prayer Mountain. My talk was sparked by a comment I overheard one delegate make to another during one of the services at the Full Gospel Church in Seoul. He asked, "Why do people pray that way?" He was referring to the very vocal and vigorous expressions as the entire congregation prayed together. (Their praying is so powerful it sounds like a giant waterfall. One cannot be in the sanctuary when the people are praying without being moved.) As I prepared for my talk, I came to the conclusion that Korean Pentecostals had maintained the correct biblical way to pray: audible corporate prayer. Western Pentecostals, on the other hand, sold their birthright for acceptability with evangelical brothers and sisters. In so doing we lost the corresponding release of power that went with this kind of praying. It is no wonder that the Yoido Full Gospel Church is the largest church in the world with over seven hundred thousand adult members. Dr. Cho sees this kind of praying, which they call "praying through," as the foundation for phenomenal growth.

> " **Pentecostals have lost this unique prayer distinctive.** "

My conclusion was further strengthened by an understanding of the Hebrew worldview: To the Hebrews, God is known by what He does and says, not by an abstract theological conception. God's heart is also expressed by His words and deeds. As for His creation, Jesus points out, "'For every idle word men may speak, they will give account of it in the day of judgment. For by your words you will be justified, and by your words you will be condemned'" (Matthew 12:36–37, NKJV).

Added to this is the Hebrew perspective that words are powerful. God created all that exists by speaking it into being. To the Hebrew made in God's image, words spoken had a great effect. Jesus states, "'Whoever says to this mountain, "Be removed and be cast into the sea," and does not doubt in his heart, but believes that those things he says will come to pass, he will have whatever he says'" (Mark 11:23, NKJV). Given this understanding of the Hebrew worldview, it is no wonder audible prayer was so important. As one prayed aloud, his words were being judged and weighed by God and were also having a powerful impact.

Corporate Prayer Should Have a Common Focus or Pattern

A second area of agreeing in prayer is not only praying out loud, but praying together along the same lines or for the same thing. Jesus states in Matthew 18:19, "'If two of you on earth agree about anything you ask for, it will be done for you by my Father in heaven.'" *Agree* is a key word in this verse. The actual Greek word is *symphoneo* (*symphony* in English). It clearly indicates a group of people praying out loud according to a similar theme. A symphony is the perfect illustration, because it consists of different instruments (people) playing different notes (prayer), but they all flow in harmony, making one sound to God.

This, then, brings us to another insight from Acts 4: Only one prayer is recorded. Now, this could be viewed in a number of ways. It could have been a prayer like those in the Psalms in which one leads and all the others repeat what the leader says. Or Luke may have recorded the gist or pattern of their prayer. Everyone prayed their own prayer, but along the same lines. They all declared God's sovereignty, prophetically described the situation they were in, and prayed for God's power to be manifested.

I believe we are seeing here a pattern of prayer similar to that which Jesus taught His disciples, traditionally called the Lord's Prayer. If so, a pattern of prayer can be a tool by which to lead an effective prayer meeting. This can be done in a number of ways. The one I use most *is* the Lord's Prayer. I dissect it into its three main parts: praise, God's concerns, and our concerns. It can be expanded and developed to deal with a number of important issues affecting the church and the individuals praying. Another pattern that has been suggested is the tabernacle prayer, made popular by Dr. Cho Yongii.[2] Another way is by taking a particular Psalm and praying the pattern found in it like the apostles did here in Acts 4. Another pattern is praying the prayers of the apostle Paul.

Beyond a pattern of prayer, some have found visual reminders a helpful tool for guiding group prayer. Some use banners listing various themes or needs, which certain people pray for when drawn to the banner by the Holy Spirit. Others have people with various needs stand as others gather around them and agree with them by specifically praying for the stated need. Some use maps of given places or other visual helps to pinpoint a given prayer need. All of these help the group to flow together throughout the prayer time.

Pentecostal Prayer Is Spirit-Anointed Prayer

A final insight from Acts 4 that helps us conduct effective prayer meetings is that of recognizing the work of the Holy Spirit. Luke states in Acts 4:31—"They were all filled with the Holy Spirit." The Holy Spirit desires to pray through us as well as to use us to be the means by which our prayers are answered. "The Spirit also helps in our weaknesses. For we do not know what we should pray for as we ought, but the Spirit Himself makes intercession for us with groanings which cannot be uttered. Now He who searches the hearts knows what the mind of the Spirit is, because He makes intercession for the saints according to the will of God" (Romans 8:26–27, NKJV). In an effective prayer meeting we must express our dependence on the Holy Spirit and ask Him to manifest himself by leading the prayer time. The greater sensitivity we have to His promptings, the more effective our praying will be.

Conducting a prayer meeting that reaches the throne of God must begin with all participants knowing that their praying is efficacious. We must be willing to persevere, to pray through. We must pray in agreement through audible corporate prayer, praying together for the same thing. We must utilize a pattern of prayer or visual helps to unite those praying so we flow together. Finally, the Holy Spirit must be acknowledged and allowed to manifest himself. Then we can expect to have prayer meetings that, like the one in Acts 4, reach the throne of God.

Maintaining Sound Doctrine and the Flow of the Spirit

Jerry McCamey

One day I had a very real learning experience at a gas station just a few blocks from my office. I stopped to drop off a flat tire for repair. I stuck my head in the station door and asked if I could leave the tire and pick it up later. I thought this would give the needed time to repair the flat, and I would not have to wait. I was totally taken back when the attendant informed me, "We don't do that kind of work here!" I checked the station's sign to be sure I had not accidentally pulled into a fast food restaurant. Sure enough, I was at a nationally known gas service station.

That was a quick reminder of just how specialized we have become these days. Not long ago we could take our car to the service station and say, "It's broke. Fix it!" Whatever was mechanically wrong was soon detected and repaired, no matter what the problem. These days we take the car one place if we have a muffler problem, another for brakes, some place else for transmission difficulty, one place for gas, and still another for an oil change.

This specialty syndrome also holds true with food service. There once was a time when you could go into the cafe and order a wide variety from the menu. Now, if you want a hamburger you go to McDonald's. For a taco, it's Taco Bell. If you crave chicken, you head for Colonel Sanders. All fish lovers must find their way to Long John Silvers. My family, many times, has to make three or four stops on the way home to satisfy all appetites. This trend in food and car service industries is all fine and good. It presents no problem of any major proportion to me or to anyone else. We gladly accept it for the convenience it brings.

What I find alarming is the growing number of pastors and churches that are falling prey to this "specialist" mentality. Many churches seem to involve themselves only in areas of ministry that they either enjoy or find particularly easy. We have "Word" churches, "praise" churches, "fire and brimstone" churches, "love" churches, "body" churches, "outreach" churches, "family" churches, "disciple" churches, and the list goes on. In response to many of the hurting people whose needs or problems may not fit into a particular specialty, many churches would have to say, "Sorry, we don't do that kind of work here."

In these last days the church needs to be a place of healing and refuge for whosoever—no matter what the need. We must insist on being a church of balance. We can and must rediscover that we can have the unchanging, sound doctrine of the Word of God and still flow with the wind and spontaneity of the Spirit.

Jesus said to the woman at the well, "God is a Spirit: and they that worship him must worship him in spirit and in truth" (John 4:24[1]). In these words, I find the blueprint for maintaining sound doctrine *and* the flow of the Spirit in one's church. The Lord was simply telling this woman at the well and those of us today caught up in the "tradition versus freedom in the Spirit" debate that we are wasting our time.

Any advocate of being Spirit-led who does not absolutely insist on everything lining up with the Word is clearly in error. The same is true of anyone claiming to be doctrinally sound, yet having forgotten that being spontaneous and led by the Spirit is completely solid doctrine. It's not a question of one or the other. It's a matter of spirit *and* truth!

This great truth is repeatedly underscored throughout the Bible. Let me share some examples of how the balance of the Word and the flow of the Spirit constitute the only way to serve and worship God.

Salvation—Sound Doctrine and a Work of the Spirit

"If thou shalt confess with thy mouth the Lord Jesus, and shalt believe in thine heart that God hath raised him from the dead, thou shalt be saved. For with the heart man believeth unto righteousness; and with the mouth confession is made unto salvation" (Romans 10:9–10).

A person must confess with the mouth that Jesus is Lord; he must speak it out. All else becomes secondary to the lordship of Jesus Christ. But a person can say "Jesus is Lord" a million times and still not receive salvation. When this confession is joined with the belief in one's heart that God raised Jesus from the dead, then the glorious light of salvation shines, and new life is breathed into that person. The confessing is the truth element; the work of the Spirit in response to believing faith represents the spirit element.

Relationship with the World—In Spirit and in Truth

"Come out from among them, and be ye separate, saith the Lord, and touch not the unclean thing; and I will receive you" (2 Corinthians 6:17). "Go ye into all the world, and preach the gospel to every creature" (Mark 16:15).

The Word is emphatic in its teaching of separation from sin and the things of this world. The Scriptures also strongly commission each believer to reach every creature in this world. To accomplish these two imperatives we must again utilize the tandem tool of "spirit and truth." We must learn to be *in* this world, but not *of* it. The children of God must understand that they are in this world, or they will ignore the hurting of those around who are desperately in need. Yet, at the same time, we must set our affection on the things above.

As God hates adultery and murder but loved David, so must we learn to hate sin and love the sinner. Again, this can be done only by understanding that they who worship God must do so in spirit and in truth.

Godly Service—In Spirit and in Truth

"Jesus saith to Simon Peter, Simon, son of Jona, lovest thou me more than these? He saith unto him, Yea, Lord; thou knowest that I love thee. He saith unto him, Feed my lambs. He saith to him again the second time, . . . [and] the third time, Simon, son of Jona, Lovest thou me? And he said unto him, Lord, thou knowest all things; thou knowest that I love thee. Jesus saith unto him, Feed my sheep" (John 21:15–17).

We are taught in 2 Corinthians 5:17 that when a person accepts Jesus Christ as Lord and Savior, he or she becomes a new creature. This is accomplished through the work of the Holy Spirit known as regeneration. The Lord changes us from the inside out. Many try to start on the outside, but that can never produce salvation since our righteousness is like "filthy rags" (Isaiah 64:6). But we also err in not allowing what God has done on the inside to change the outside, how we walk and talk. Jesus went to great lengths to emphasize this to Peter. The Lord clearly expects our inner being's love for Him to dominate our flesh in serving Him. We cannot serve our way to Jesus Christ, but our love for Him will cause us to *work and serve Him.*

James, in stressing this same principle, went so far as to say, *"Even so faith, if it hath not works, is dead, being alone"* (James 2:17, my emphasis). Here we see spirit and truth expressed in both faith and works.

Stewardship—In Spirit and in Truth

"Bring ye all the tithes into the storehouse, that there may be meat in mine house, and prove me now herewith, saith the Lord of hosts, if I will not open you the windows of heaven, and pour you out a blessing, that there shall not be room enough to receive it" (Malachi 3:10). "Every man according as he purposeth in his heart, so let him give; not grudgingly, or of necessity: for God loveth a cheerful giver" (2 Corinthians 9:7).

The needed balance of spirit and truth cannot be seen any more clearly than in these two verses. We are commanded to pay our tithes. This is not optional. Yet, the Lord wants us to go beyond just the doctrinal truth of this principle and move into the spirit of *cheerful* giving.

Church Worship—In Spirit and in Truth

"Let the word of Christ dwell in you richly in all wisdom; teaching and admonishing one another in psalms and hymns and spiritual songs, singing with grace in your hearts to the Lord" (Colossians 3:16).

One of the most prominent battlegrounds in this "specialty" issue of either sound doctrine or the flow of the Spirit can be seen in the clear lines drawn in our praise and worship. If it were only a matter of style, there would be no problem. There always has been and always will be room for churches to take on different personalities and preferred styles. But much of what we see is not a simple matter of preference. In many cases, believers in this same family of God (remember, there is only one Body) have decided to label and judge any praise and worship that differs from theirs as not of God. This cannot and must not be. Why? Because it is wrong. Hymns that convey truth and sound doctrine and choruses that reflect our emotions and spirit are both not only acceptable, but needed. We must always maintain the great hymns of the church, declaring such sound doctrines as the Cross, heaven, the Blood, healing, and the rapture of the Church. But there must not be a neglect of choruses. Many times these choruses are a personal response to Jesus' still-asked inquiry, "But who do you say I am?" These choruses, or "spiritual songs," are the expressions of our soul and our heart. Often they are the personalization of the doctrinal truths we embrace.

If we are truly honest, we have to admit that our real problem is not hymns versus choruses or traditional versus contemporary. It is the beat and/or style we take exception to. Remember, neither 4:4 time nor a syncopated, militant beat is found in the Bible. As a matter of fact, there is no specific beat or time that we must embrace or be limited to. Some may prefer southern gospel, others enjoy contemporary, while some want country, the list continuing into a wide and vast variety. Let's all commit to following Psalm 103:1 and bless the Lord with all that is *within* us and not worry so much about what's *without*. Let's allow God to be the final judge of what He receives as a sweet savor unto himself. It would also be good for all of us to read Romans 14 again to help keep our focus on our relationship with our Master, rather than being hindered by what we view as unacceptable styles of others.

Not Forsaking Sound Doctrine

Some churches have experienced conflict and division over what constitutes spirituality and the move of the Holy Spirit. Members of the congregation, and sometimes the spiritual leader, are attracted to highly visible ministries of prominent evangelists. Unusual manifestations are either elevated to evidences of spirituality or condemned as fleshly exhibitions prompted by autosuggestion. What is the conscientious pastor to do? We strongly desire the move of the Spirit in the congregation, but we also want revival to be authentic and lasting, not a passing fad.

When the congregation is divided over the legitimacy of the manifestations, the pastor must, more than ever, preach the Word—and only the Word. We must not allow enthusiasts to make manifestations into marks of spirituality, condemning those who do not participate as unspiritual or quenchers of the Spirit. But neither should those who feel uncomfortable condemn those who respond with outward manifestations, as long as there is no overt disobedience to Scripture. The test of a genuine move of the Spirit is the spiritual growth that comes from the experience. Are souls genuinely saved and are believers transformed and energized to a deeper commitment to Christ? If so, we must let God be God. But in all the uncertainty and controversy, the pastor must be equally conscientious in defending sound doctrine (the truth) and inviting the genuine move of the Spirit, who cannot be restricted to moving as people judge proper because of previous spiritual experience. The Pentecostal revival of the twentieth century fractured many of the molds constructed by old-line denominations. When God moves, we must be close enough to recognize His presence and cooperate with what He is doing in the world.

The maintaining of sound doctrine and the flow of the Spirit is an absolute must for every pastor, believer, leader, church, and movement. If we focus on truth only, we can get in a rut and become tunnel-visioned. The result of this imbalance will be that we become inflexible and quench the flow of the Spirit. If our sole emphasis is flowing with the Spirit, we will have no foundation and will ultimately come crashing to a halt. The result will be devastating.

Let's be pastors who are not specialists but general practitioners. We need full-service Christians and full-service churches who worship in spirit and truth. We must maintain sound doctrine and the flow of the Spirit so that our full-service God can do all things for all people. "Whatsoever ye do in word or deed, do all in the name of the Lord Jesus, giving thanks to God and the Father by him" (Colossians 3:17).

Pentecostal Preaching

Ernest J. Moen

What images run through your mind when you hear the phrase *Pentecostal preaching?* I hear a mighty rushing wind sweeping through the auditorium. Electricity crackles in the air and builds to a rising crescendo of fire. It sends a trembling through the limbs of those poised on the edge of their seats, their faces enraptured by the inspired words of the speaker. The speaker? He is dripping from the exertion of his preaching, his hair and tie askew, his face alternately glowing and distorted, the words tumbling out of his mouth as fast as he can say them. There's a fire blazing in his eyes, a reflection of the Pentecostal fervor planted within him by the Holy Spirit. His words are divinely inspired, easy to understand, powerful in context. They have the power to drive a stake through the heart of a sinner until he is doubled over in agony and crying out for forgiveness. That is Pentecostal preaching!

Let me take you with me down memory lane where C. M. Ward at Lake Geneva Bible Camp practiced the art of true Pentecostal preaching before the inevitably packed auditorium. At the apex of his sermon on hell, he would walk to an old upright piano on the platform, lift the lid, and pull out a picture of Adolph Hitler. "Let me take you out of hell," he would say to the picture. Then one by one in a thundering voice he would identify the distinctive moments in Hitler's vile history. All would relate to Christianity. The verdict rendered, he'd consign Hitler back to perdition. On various occasions, he did the same with Stalin or Caesar or Napoleon. The audience was with him at every breath, every pulse, every step. Multitudes of souls poured out of their seats and up to the altar at the conclusion of his sermons.

> " **The difference goes beyond emotion.** "

Then there was Robert Fierro relating the plight of the Mexican orphan children. In heartbreaking detail, through tears, he would describe their misery. I went out of that meeting with an empty wallet, unable to withhold anything from that missionary appeal. Ivan O. Miller is another prime example of a Pentecostal preacher. When in his Puritan manner he explained the life of Christ to the student body of North Central Bible College, his ideal of holiness made me feel like a moral leper crying for purity of personal power over sin.

What are the elements of Pentecostal preaching? Is it distinct from other kinds of preaching? Is there a difference in style or substance from sermons delivered in the traditional church or even the evangelical church? I contend it goes far beyond emotional factors. I observe three distinctives that relate to Pentecostal preaching: the anointing, the sermon structure, and preaching for results. But before we define the styles and structure of the Pentecostal sermon, let's look at the introduction.

There are three basic purposes for a sermon introduction: to gain attention, to present the proposition or theme, and to create interest. Exercise great care in your introductory comments. Be careful to avoid repetition. Avoid ad-libbing—the result could be an offensive remark that wasn't well considered. Don't read the text from several different translations—it gets boring. And don't take too long to get to the body of your message.

Anointed Pentecostal Preaching

Pentecostal preachers especially should understand and experience the anointing. The timeworn phrase "Better felt than telt" is on the mark. I had a college professor by the name of T. J. Jones who would say to the class, "You can always tell a preacher who's been baptized in the Holy Spirit." I am sure he was referring to the anointing.

The Bible has a multitude of examples of the anointing for service and ministry. David said, "I have been anointed with fresh oil" (Psalm 92:10[1]). The Lord told Aaron, "You shall anoint them, consecrate them, and sanctify them, that they may minister to Me as priests" (Exodus 28:41). Leviticus 10:7 says, "'The anointing oil of the Lord is upon you.'"

ANOINTED TO SERVE

In being anointed to serve, we are sanctified. The Hebrew word for *sanctify* means "to set apart, consecrate, dedicate." We are set apart to minister to (serve) one another. By God's Spirit we worship, doing priestly service in a spiritual temple. We do that spiritual service by the presence and power of the Holy Spirit in our lives.

ANOINTED TO SANCTIFY

"Moses took the anointing oil, and anointed the tabernacle and all that was in it, and sanctified them" (Leviticus 8:10). The holy anointing oil made everything it touched holy. First John 2:20 says symbolically, "You have an anointing from the Holy One." There is a sense of awe in both the hearer and the speaker. We are possessed by His holy presence. We are holy in His holiness, loving in His love, strong in His strength, tender in His tenderness, and calm in His peace. The anointing "gives us insights and instructs us how to put the truth into action in a way no mere human teacher could."[2]

In my Scandinavian heritage, the word *unction* (*smera* in the Swedish Bible) means literally "to be rubbed in." When we were children, our mother rubbed Vicks VapoRub into our chests when we had bad colds. The sanctifying anointing of the Holy Spirit spiritually rubs a supernatural presence into the mind, the heart, the tongue, and the entire congregation.

ANOINTED TO SEE

Christ's counsel to the lukewarm church of Laodicea was "Anoint your eyes with eye salve, that you may see" (Revelation 3:18). Only those who have been divinely called to ministry may experience this. There are times when, while sitting on the platform or even in the middle of a sermon, the mind of a preacher is pierced by heart-searching truths that will astound the congregation. At those moments, the Holy Spirit will touch those who have grown cold in their walk with God, those who have committed sin. God's Word will be applied without personal comment or identification. The penetrating power of the Holy Spirit, the anointing, reveals the spiritual condition of the inner being.

ANOINTED TO STAND

"He who establishes us with you in Christ and has anointed us is God" (2 Corinthians 1:21). The word *establish* here means "to make firm or steadfast." Hearing anointed preaching Sunday after Sunday provides stability, firmness, and steadfastness in the walk of faithful Christians.

Preaching the gospel without power is ineffective. It was said of the early apostles, they "preached the gospel . . . by the Holy Spirit sent from heaven" (1 Peter 1:12). While pastoring First Assembly of God in Rockford, Illinois, I had a fine couple, Bill and Susan Hall, who were very gifted and anointed in their music. If I sensed I needed a special touch that morning, just before I preached I would call them down from the choir. "Bill and Susan, will you come and sing 'The Spirit of the Lord Is Now Upon Me?'" This beautiful Scripture chorus is taken from Isaiah 61:1, "The Spirit of the Lord God is upon Me, because the Lord has anointed Me To preach good tidings to the poor; He has sent Me to heal the brokenhearted, To proclaim liberty to the captives, And the opening of the prison to those who are bound." I can affirm that each time it was sung there would come upon the congregation an earnestness of prayer for the pastor, an open heart, a receptivity in the body, and a hunger for God's

Word to come forth. I shall never forget the impact that their ministry had upon the church. The anointing of the Holy Spirit is valid and affirming.

ANOINTED TO SAVE

Because Saul was to be set apart as the king of Israel, the Lord told Samuel, "Thou shalt anoint him to be captain over my people Israel, that he may save my people" (1 Samuel 9:16, KJV). The preacher, too, is set apart and anointed to bring the message of salvation to the people through anointed Pentecostal preaching.

ANOINTED TO PREACH

The entire Book of Acts is full of examples of preaching followed by Spirit-initiated results. In Acts 2, three thousand were saved. In Acts 4, five thousand believed. In Acts 6, "the number of the disciples multiplied . . . and a great company of the priests were obedient to the faith" (6:7, KJV). In Acts 9:35, "All who dwelt at Lydda and Sharon . . . turned to the Lord." In Acts 11:21, "A great number believed and turned to the Lord." In Acts 13:44, "Almost the whole city gathered to hear the word of God." In Acts 14:1, "A great multitude . . . believed." In Acts 14:21, "They . . . preached . . . and made many disciples." In Acts 16:5, "The churches were strengthened in the faith, and increased in number daily." In Acts 17:6, Paul and Silas were identified with those "who have turned the world upside down." And in Acts 18:8, a synagogue leader believed "and many of the Corinthians, hearing, believed." In Acts 19:20, when the gospel was preached in Ephesus, "The word of the Lord grew mightily and prevailed.

ANOINTED FOR VICTORY

Isaiah 10:27 says, "The yoke shall be destroyed because of the anointing" (KJV). In Pentecostal preaching, one should not lose sight of the fact that there is a clear objective to the sermon. God's people come to church with grievous burdens. Think of those who are recently divorced, the excessive drinker whose sin is hidden, the marriage that is failing, the teenager who is starting the road to drugs, a deacon's daughter engaging in premarital sex, and on and on. Problems by the hundreds are before the preacher. When the anointing of the Holy Spirit comes upon the sermon, victory will be announced. It has been said that in every major battle there is a fifteen-minute period where the tide can swing toward victory or defeat. The moment of anointing is a moment for victory.

Before Pentecost, Peter was uncertain: "'Lord, if it is You, command me to come to You on the water'" (Matthew 14:28). But after Pentecost, he was "Scripture certain." Have you ever heard greater anointing than the sermon in Acts 2? Before Pentecost, Peter was self-motivated—he cut off the ear of the servant of the high priest. But after Pentecost, he exalted Christ. Before Pentecost, he was cowardly and denied his Lord. After Pentecost, he was courageous in the boldness of the Spirit (Acts 4:13). Before Pentecost, he was swearing when he denied his Master (Matthew 26:74). But after Pentecost, he was praising God (Acts 4:24). Before

Pentecost, he was warming himself at the enemy's fire (Luke 22:55). But after Pentecost, he had the inner fire of the Holy Spirit's baptism (Acts 2:14). Victory flows from the anointing of the Holy Spirit. The spiritually dead are raised to life. Consider Peter's Pentecostal sermon: "When they heard this, they were cut to the heart, and said to Peter and the rest of the apostles, 'Men and brethren, what shall we do?'" (Acts 2:37). Pentecostal preaching that is effective and well-received is characterized by a special enduement, an unction, an anointing of the Holy Spirit.

ANOINTING THROUGH PRAYER

The anointed Pentecostal preacher spends long sessions waiting on the Lord. Little prayer means little power in preaching. Much prayer, more power. There is a definitive equation between prayer and the anointing. As our prayers go up, the power comes down. All preachers have had the miserable experience of preaching without the anointing. Then all of us have had the joy and sheer ecstasy of the touch of God, something from another world, that enabled articulation, thought processes, and verbal expression beyond our own human ability. Thank God for the anointing of the Holy Spirit!

Many years ago, as a young man in my late teens, I recognized the call of God upon my life. I became serious about it and began preparing for my calling. I am eternally grateful to the evangelical church, for it was there that I learned the gospel, was saved, baptized in water, and called to preach. I am intensely committed to preaching the birth, life, death, resurrection, ascension, and soon return of our blessed Christ. The gospel songs are a part of my psyche; I learned them in Sunday school and church. When I became sincere in my quest for the Holy Spirit's power and release upon my life through the baptism of the Holy Spirit, I had a profound experience.

One day, my pastor requested that I go for a ride far into the fertile fields of northwestern Minnesota. Ostensibly, he wanted to show me his new Buick. But he soon expressed his greater concern that I was going to leave the fellowship of the evangelical world and move into the Pentecostal community. The strength of his appeal was this: Pentecostal preaching is shallow and there are very few theologians in the Pentecostal church. While we can all attest on occasion to our own unique experiences of both truths, we also recognize that we have outstanding theologians who have hammered out a solid, biblical belief system for us. In addition to that, I would stake claim that there is nothing that compares to a well thought-out, well-prepared, prayed-over, anointed Pentecostal sermon. It holds your attention. It feeds your soul. It stimulates your mind. And most of all, it moves your will toward God. The Pentecostal pastor is acutely aware of human need, the Holy Spirit having shown where to go in the Scriptures to solve deep-seated human problems. Pentecostal preaching is often mass counseling.

Pentecostal Preaching Styles

Before mentioning a few styles used in Pentecostal preaching, I note that reading is a prerequisite for preaching! Reading a single good book having good counsel and good principles will make life a success. Many a young person has started off on a career of honor and usefulness by reading a good book. One English cleric declared that Shakespeare and the Bible had made him an archbishop. John Wesley claimed that Thomas à Kempis' *Imitation of Christ* and Jeremy Taylor's *Holy Living and Dying* determined both his calling and his character. Henry Martyn was made a missionary by reading the lives of David Brainard and William Carey. Alexander Pope was indebted to Homer for his poetical inspiration. Goethe became a poet as a consequence of reading Goldsmith's *The Vicar of Wakefield.* Carey was moved to minister by reading *The Voyages of Captain Cook.* The lives of George Washington and Henry Clay awakened aspiration in Lincoln's soul that led him on to his fortune. The signers of the Declaration of Independence were men of literary persuasions. As children they had fed mentally upon the Bible, *Pilgrim's Progress,* and Josephus. Reading creates thinking. Reading fosters the art of thinking. Patrick Henry thirsted for knowledge and found a way of satisfying the desire by reading. The same is true for the preacher. He must read to be alert. It will create thought.

EXPOSITORY PREACHING

In exposition, the minister takes a portion of God's Word and expands on its truth. Many pastors like to preach verse by verse, a Book of the Bible, or the entire Bible. The composition and flow of expository preaching has many components. One of them is *explanation* or *information.* Know the Word. Know it doctrinally and historically. Know it devotionally and practically. This appeals to the mind, the heart, and the will. In the study of God's Word, look for information—the history, the facts: who, what, where, and when.

Then look for *illumination.* This is the doctrine. What are the truths? Then comes *incubation,* the devotional, the meditation that becomes a part of the heart. And then there is the *incarnation,* that which is practical and living. *Imagination* is also involved. In summary:

Information—*what does it say?*
Illumination—*what does it mean?*
Incubation—*what is its practical application?*
Incarnation—*how can I live it?*
Imagination—*how can I say it to my people?*

Then there is the proper organization of the Word for best delivery and reception by hearers. We do not preach to impress, we preach to express. In communication, we arouse, we alarm, we explain, we convince, we remind.

Today's seminary professors appeal to students for more expository preaching. I may be wrong, but it seems that the evangelical pastor is perhaps more deeply committed to expository preaching than is the Pentecostal preacher. I recall an experience in a church I pastored in Minnesota. A young evangelical pastor just out of seminary lived at the edge of the parking lot of our church. He had been there for about a year and a half and had been taught to preach expository sermons. He started with the Book of Genesis. One Saturday morning, he appeared in my office weeping and said, "I'm in Genesis 23, and there's nothing there that my people need tomorrow morning. I have to preach, and I don't know what to tell them. My professor told me to preach through the Bible, and I'm stuck already." I told him to return to his study, get on his knees, then preach and give to his congregation fresh manna from heaven's oven. He did and built a great church.

Nonetheless, expository preaching requires great effort. You must read the passage using a number of translations. You must feel the atmosphere of the passage. Repeat words and phrases to yourself. Do not discount first impressions. Analyze and study this portion of Scripture. Watch for persons involved, events that occurred, words that are used, historical context, the doctrines involved, the illumination of cross-references, the problems presented, and the practical lessons.

If you are skilled at collective thought, expository preaching has many advantages. It saves time. You know where you're going. You don't have to hunt and peck for a text for next Sunday. It forces the pastor to study and plan. It lays the foundation for future sermons. And it encourages your people to be good Bible students. It will help build a thematic approach in hymn selection and the objective for the entire service.

> **"A pastor's personality and the length of the expository series are closely related."**

A pastor's personality and the length of the expository series are closely related. Donald Gray Barnhouse could preach for years on the Book of Romans and maintain and increase the interest of his congregation. I have discovered that a series of five to six weeks duration is most effective for my own personality. One summer I tried to preach through the Book of Revelation. I did well until I got into the woes, the trumpets, and the vials. I found those middle chapters an absolutely unwieldy task. I couldn't wait, nor could my people, until I got into Revelation 18 to 22. We needed victory, not drudgery, and it took a long time, well over three months, to get there. Haddon Robinson makes a helpful distinction between exegesis and exposition: "Exegesis is the process of getting meaning from the text, often through noting the verb tense or where the word emphasis falls in the original languages. That's what you do in your study as you prepare. But it's seldom appropriate in a sermon on Sunday morning. In fact, an overuse of Greek or Hebrew can make us snobs."[3] Charles Spurgeon expressed a similar attitude. The people in the marketplace cannot learn the language of the academy. So the people in the academy must learn the language of the marketplace. It's the pastor's job to translate.

SPECIAL OCCASION SERMONS

Though some ministers steer clear of sermons for special occasions, such sermons have been of great value in my pastoral ministry. Even in my past work as district superintendent, I tried to fit the sermon to the occasion—anniversaries, church dedications, patriotic days, ordinations, funerals, plus the obvious holidays. No doubt others can be added to this list.

I always like to think of a Pentecostal preacher as one who preaches so people will want to come back and listen again. There are ways to accomplish this. Are you relevant? Are you talking about current events in the context of authentic Christianity? Can you relate the statements of Jesus to the values of this age? What biblically significant event in the news has everyone talking? I can remember preaching a sermon when Jimmy Carter was elected president entitled "Now that Our President Is Born Again." Prophecy preaching has eluded the Pentecostal church in the last twenty-five years.

TOPICAL PREACHING

Few of my Pentecostal peers agree with me, but topical preaching holds appeal for me. Robert Schuller is a topical preacher. One can do Bible biographical preaching, a study of outstanding personalities. Scriptural topics are legion. Doctrinal sermons can be topical, and even theological and doctrinal sermons have topical overtones. Series preaching can be topical. Clarence MacCartney's preaching of his series sermons was always topical. There were the great soldiers of the Bible: Joshua, the soldier after whom Christ was named; Saul, the soldier who fell on his sword; David, the soldier with a broken heart; Gideon, the soldier with a broken pitcher; the soldier who preached at the cross; Cornelius, the first soldier to come to Christ; Christ, the last Conqueror, on His white horse.

Or how about the businessmen of the Bible: Lot, the man who made it in real estate; Esau, the man who made it in cereals; the rich fool, the man who made it in warehouses; the man who made it in iron chests; the head treasurer, Judas, the man who made a corner on sin; and Jesus, the man who made a corner on souls. The Bible often uses the word *remember,* which would make a good topical series. "Remember now thy Creator," "This do in remembrance of me," etc. Think of the topics of the day such as the immoral invasion of the movie and television industry, the impact of rock music on our culture. If I were pastoring today, I would preach extensively on the assault on the family from a biblical perspective. I would talk about the deterioration of culture. These are all topical venues.

EVANGELISTIC PREACHING

Throughout our history, the Pentecostal church has been known as a voice from the pulpit calling for repentance. From tent meetings to brush arbors to revival meetings to street meetings, the voice of the preacher has been central. I am discerning a subtle shift, and we are losing the evangelist's touch. Some believe that the pastoral pulpit is exclusively for discipleship. Granted, our people need to grow, but I dispute the idea that evangelistic preaching is shallow. If you research the sermons of Charles Spurgeon, D. L. Moody, R. A. Torrey, or Billy Sunday, the cry to the lost is filtered through all the content material without sacrificing one bit of faithful doctrine.

Before we jettison our flavor of evangelism in pulpit ministry, we would do well to rethink our history. I am not yet willing to discard the idea that the midweek service is designed for teaching and prayer. Sunday morning can be reserved for both discipleship training and appealing to the lost. Some feel that Sunday morning should be used exclusively for evangelism and Sunday nights only for discipling. But where the pastor is strongly committed to Sunday night, Sunday nights still flourish. I find it in the district I served, and I find it across the country. This means that the evangelistic sermon has priority in the planning and style of the pastor. If it is accompanied by good music and inspiration, it will appeal both to saint and to sinner. There should be much thought and preparation for a contrast to Sunday morning. The two services cannot be the same.

I observe that strong pastors of large soul-winning churches feed the sheep on Sunday morning. My counsel would be to find a bridge three-quarters of the way through the sermon where you can move from feeding the sheep to throwing out the net. The bridge is the key, and it can be done. For instance, wherever preaching takes us, there is a vantage point to connect to the unsaved. I feel strongly on this issue because we are losing the fervor of preaching to the lost. We can learn to design our sermons to have relevance to the spiritually unconditioned. Noah's ark, Abel's sacrifice, Moses' rod, Jacob's staircase, and a hundred other images speak both to the saved and the unsaved.

My appeal is to be orthodox, doctrinally correct, and biblically centered in evangelistic reading. Political correctness is even changing historical data. A textbook writer tells teachers to be skeptical of scientific accounts of how humans first arrived in North America because science reflects "logic" instead of Indian myths. Or a New Jersey teacher explains to fourth graders that Christopher Columbus was not a heroic explorer who discovered America but a "murderer" who stole it. This is having profound effect on biblical dogma as liberal theologians pick up this attitude, redefining and diluting the plain meaning of Scripture. Evangelistic preaching teaches us that we are not to be culturally driven but culturally relevant from a biblical perspective.

Preaching for Results

Every sermon demands a summons. Every appeal demands a verdict. The sermon must produce action. "Multitudes in the valley of decision" should be true every Sunday morning. There are those who say public invitations have no place in this sophisticated age. Ask Billy Graham about that. Others say invitations should be extended in a personal, private setting. But if it is right to ask an individual to repent, why not ask a whole audience to do the same? The public appeal goes hand in hand with the personal appeal. Is it right for us to take the time to explain the gospel in the sermon, exhort listeners to receive it as a gift of God's grace, and then dismiss the people without giving them an opportunity to respond? I think not! Hebrews 13:10 says, "We have an altar." Unfortunately the altar call is gradually being phased out in many churches. I think this is due to fear of failure, a fear of receiving no response. Subtly, we might believe the altar call isn't necessary.

There have been times during my preaching when I felt in my spirit that a certain couple or individual would respond as I moved into the altar call. Sure enough, that's what happened. I did my best to reassure them that they wouldn't be asked to join the church, to donate money, or otherwise do anything that would embarrass them. But I would say, "Without a single exception, there's no one in this room who hasn't privately prayed to God. You've asked for forgiveness. You've asked for help in a time of trauma. You have mumbled a weak prayer as you left the doctor's office. Everyone has prayed a prayer in private. Matthew 10:32 states that we should do this before men. Now is the time. Raise your hand and slip to the nearest aisle, and I will help you pray this prayer in public."

> **Preaching for results is crucial. The sale isn't made until the name is on the dotted line.**

Preaching for results is imperative. No salesperson makes the sale until the name is on the dotted line. No track star wins the race until the finish line is crossed. No halfback wins the ball game until the ball is over the goal line. The sermon has been preached; the saints have worshiped; the choir has sung; the offering has been collected. Now is the time to pull in the net. There's something about standing on top of the winner's platform at the Olympic Games and hearing the national anthem. There's something about responding to Christ in public that affirms the greatest decision of our lives. A wedding is public. A graduation exercise is public. The response to the public appeal is psychologically therapeutic. We respond openly to the nudge of the Holy Spirit.

Our general superintendent is very concerned about discipling after conversion—water baptism, baptism in the Holy Spirit, church membership—and rightly so. I have observed that where there is a pattern of altar calls, the other results will naturally follow. The congregation will be brought to respond to public appeals. One year I felt a great burden for unsaved husbands of Christian women in our church. I gave an altar call one Sunday night for every wife of an unsaved husband to come forward and have the church pray with them. One hundred and ten women flocked to the altar. We did not win one hundred and ten men to Christ, but to my knowledge thirty-eight did come to Christ in the following year. A year later, we acknowledged the conversions during a special service. It was a high night in Zion! The choir members wore tuxes and formals, the testimonies were hand-picked, the wives told of life in the home with an unsaved husband. Then the husbands came down the aisle to stand by their wives and told what life is like after conversion. I've been in great services over the years, but none compare with the tide of love and emotion of that memorable night.

The conclusion of the sermon and the preparation for the appeal must be well thought out and prepared in advance. I love to keep the choir on the platform. They will help with the invitation hymn. The pianist and organist need to know when to slip unobtrusively to their instruments. Knowing how to move from the conclusion of the sermon into the appeal is a true art form.

How do you extend the service without annoying the congregants? We have all experienced abuse. Yet if this is a part of a church's persona, the congregation also desires response and results. To the pastor, I would say, "Never be discouraged." Peter preached and three thousand came forward. That's a pretty good response. Stephen preached and he got stoned.

There is nothing like Pentecostal preaching. It is fire in our bones. It stimulates every nerve. It's of the same spirit that makes little children skip and run when they could walk, or the lamb frolic in the green meadow in spring. It's an elixir, a tonic for the diseased, discouraged, and destroyed. God restores and renews through the anointed flow of the Holy Spirit.

In 1970, while pastoring in Minnesota, I was asked by a dear friend to preach a fellowship meeting. Another Christian organization, which had a broadcast network throughout Minnesota, asked me to record a month's daily broadcasts. I threw all my sermons into a large attache case, went down to southwestern Minnesota, and preached the fellowship meeting before driving the 170 miles back home. By the time I arrived, I was weary to my bones. I left my sermons in my unlocked car overnight, and when I went to retrieve them the next morning, my briefcase was gone. I rushed into the house, thinking I must have taken it inside. It wasn't there. Word spread, and it was the biggest news in this country town. I was interviewed on the radio station. I got a call from the sheriff, a member of a traditional church, who said, "I hope it was my pastor who stole them because he could use Pastor Moen's sermons." The UPI picked it up. One woman drove every country road in the county looking for my sermons. My wife says I went into a depression. I felt my life's work was gone. I walked through the gravestones in the cemetery at the end of my block, looking for my sermons, thinking someone had thrown them in there. One of the deacons said to me, "Pastor, we're so glad you lost your sermons. You're preaching better than ever, and now we can hear from God." That was twenty-six years ago. God is faithful. I have a full supply of sermons again.

Pentecostal preaching? I believe it's the answer for this age. We can turn the spiritual atmosphere from *apostasy* to *apostolic*. Forgiveness of sins is heart and center of Peter's promise in Acts 2:37–39. Pentecostal preaching will be both the core circle and circumference of the latter-day outpouring.

Making Announcements Count

Rob Carlson

Last winter I sat in awe, as from the front row of the auditorium I listened and observed our symphonic orchestra play during each of our Singing Christmas Tree performances. The music was beautiful; at times it was peaceful and elegant, and at other times very aggressive and attacking. The strings, winds, brass, and percussion all played in exquisite harmony. Each instrument played a strategic and important part. As I sat back and enjoyed the teamwork and precision of the orchestra, I was impressed by one intriguing fact: The rest is as important as the note. The oboe's solo was beautiful, but it was equally beautiful when it counted five measures of rest while the harp played. The triumphant sound of the trumpet was victorious and uplifting, but when the trumpets counted ten measures of rest and were silent while the strings played, I found the trumpets equally beautiful. Whether playing five measures of beautiful, melodic, purposefully written notes, or counting five measures of beautifully calculated rests, the result was superb.

Making announcements count is a similar process. The rest is as important as the note. A worship service can be greatly impaired by thoughtless, purposeless, nonstrategic announcements. Many announcements I have witnessed and heard through the years have sounded like trumpets screaming obnoxiously when they were to be counting five measures of rest allowing the violins to play quietly. The main worship experience (Sunday morning for many of us) should be as thoughtfully planned, strategically prepared, and purposefully coordinated as any orchestration or symphony. Our services must be saturated with prayer and sensitivity to the leading of the Holy Spirit, but this in no way excuses thoughtlessness, purposelessness, or sloppiness. For years we have contended "spontaneity is next to godliness" or "just go with the flow." In all reality we are saying, "I really didn't take adequate time to prepare, plan, practice, and pray for the most important hour of the week in the lives of my people." Remember, we get only one hour each week with some of our people. No one wants the Holy Spirit to break into our services and overwhelm us in revival more than I do. But I think that while we pray for revival we should also pray, "God, lead me as I prepare a deeply spiritual and meaningful service for the beautiful people you have sent me and who are depending on me and this worship experience. Lord, I want to be faithful to pray hard, prepare hard, and plan hard, and in so doing provide a service that leads people into incredible worship of the King of kings and the application of His Holy Word." Announcements are not exempt from this process. They should not be tacked onto or added into the service. They need to be thoughtfully planned. Why? Because we cannot afford to waste the time of people who are hungry and thirsty for God. We cannot mess around, play around, or stumble around unprepared and call that blessed. People fill our pews at every worship service who are beaten and bruised spiritually, emotionally, mentally, financially, physically, and relationally. Every part of the worship service must lift them up and point them to Jesus. We must give our absolute best to the Lord as we prepare every aspect of our worship experiences. As much as I enjoyed the beautiful symphonic orchestra, I value a thoroughly planned, well thought-out, prayer-saturated worship service even more.

Following are several ideas for you to consider as you make sure that your announcements are a purposeful part of the worship "symphony" experience.

There Are Times to Rest and Not Play

Most churches produce a weekly bulletin. I think this is wise. An attractive, attention-getting, informative, thorough, and accurately written bulletin listing key events and announcements is vital to making announcements count. All important announcements should be placed in print multiple times in advance of the event they are trumpeting. Let's face it, repetition is the key to retention, and if an announcement is placed in the written bulletin only once, many people will not see it. Most people scan the bulletin and miss some announcements with each reading. Thus, I suggest promoting key events four weeks in advance and running the bulletin ad for four weeks. This may seem like overkill, but making announcements is basically promoting. And if an event or cause is worthwhile, you will want to promote it well so that maximum participation is insured.

I follow four rules when it comes to counting measures of rest (not playing), not verbally stating a particular announcement. Most announcements are worthy of being placed in print in the weekly bulletin. It is vital, however, that an appropriate person is designated to edit the bulletin for clarity, accuracy, and propriety before it goes to print each week. The bulletin should be positive and as motivating as it possibly can be. Here are my rules:

1. *Don't read the bulletin to people.* I have been a part of worship services where an inordinate amount of time and attention was given to reading through the bulletin. I was both bored and insulted. What a waste of time! After all, I can read the bulletin for myself. Some argue, "People

can read but they won't. We need to read it to them." Nonsense. Train your people to read it for themselves. We have more important things to do in our services. Let's be realistic, the Lord is counting on us to be good stewards of the time we have with our people for corporate worship. We need to spend as much time as possible in celebrating the Lord and His Word.

2. *Don't make a verbal announcement if it's not in print.* Most events or ministries that need to be promoted have a variety of who, what, where, when, and why details that are necessary to effectively communicate the event. It is much better to draw the attention of the congregation to the written details than to take extra time to verbally articulate all of the details. Besides, many people may be very interested but will forget the details. If they try to write down the details, they will not be prepared or have time when the announcement is verbally stated. It is a courtesy and a sign that proper planning has taken place for all important announcements to be in print. After all, if the event or ministry is worthwhile, than it deserves the forethought of a well-written bulletin ad.

3. *Don't make a verbal announcement just because someone forgot to put it in the bulletin.* The Sunday morning pulpit must not and cannot become the place where we solve problems created by the poor planning of department heads. If someone forgot to place an ad in the bulletin, they just forgot. And more times than not the best thing we can do is let the event suffer and not rescue it by pumping it from the platform. Quite frankly, if an event has not been adequately promoted in the bulletin, it probably should not be verbalized, because it is very likely that the entire event is poorly planned. Maybe the whole event needs to die in silence. Many pastors know what it feels like to get bombarded by well-meaning department leaders or staff members just before service time with announcements that just *have* to be made. The timing and request are both inappropriate.

As the pastor, I am responsible for leading a meaningful, spiritual, uplifting, and challenging worship service. Consequently, the "Rob's Announcements" segment of our services are limited to two announcements each week. Pastoral staff members lobby for their cause, but in the end I select the announcements that I believe are most valuable for the whole church to hear. Rob's Announcements are then followed by a time of greeting that is always full of energy. It is our goal to make sure that the praise and preaching times of our services are dynamic. But we also want our promotion time to be dynamic as well. Limiting verbal announcements in number, promoting them in print, following announcements with an energetic greeting time, and, finally, making sure that the announcements relate to the majority of the congregation are key factors to making announcements count.

4. *Don't make verbal announcements that do not relate to the majority of listeners.* If an announcement does not pertain to the listener, he or she will turn the announcer off. This results in wasted time and unproductive ministry in the lives of those who are turned off. Making sure the announcements that are given are promoted effectively and relate to most of the listeners is vitally important. For example, an announcement for

seven committee members to meet Monday night should not be given in the public worship service. Those seven people should be contacted individually. I realize that emergency meetings sometimes have to be called. But even when this happens, the whole body can be involved by asking them to pray, making the announcement and the event relevant for everyone. Emergencies, however, are the exception.

In the end, announcements are about dispensing information and promoting meaningful ministry. And every worthwhile ministry endeavor needs to be promoted heavily through the mail, in the bulletin, over the telephone, in person, via departmental newsletters, etc. Promoting the ministries of the church is very, very important. But the Sunday morning worship service is about promoting Jesus Christ and drawing the attention of every listener to Him and His hope-filled and life-changing Word. We must keep our priorities clear and not allow *anything,* not even announcements, to take away from praising God and preaching His Word.

Having said that, I do believe there are many ways we can effectively communicate announcements in the worship service. Our goal is to *make announcements count,* i.e., make them effective and productive. So how do we turn announcements from mediocre to motivational?

There Are Times to Play and Not Rest

Just as the rests are vital to the exquisite music of the symphonic orchestra, so are the notes. In fact, without the instruments playing their notes there wouldn't be any beautiful harmony to enjoy. When the brass, strings, winds, and percussion do play, however, they are concerned with playing the right notes at the right time with the right volume and at the right tempo. Let's look briefly at the tone, timing, volume, and tempo of making announcements count. Again, the orchestra must prepare itself to be effective, and so must we.

1. *Tone.* When announcements must be verbally communicated, they do not have to be boring or unimaginative. In fact, with a little creativity, they can be both memorable and motivational. Selecting the most effective way to make an announcement is a little like choosing the best note to play. There are many notes to choose from, and there are many ways to make an announcement. An announcement should set the tone for the event it promotes. For example, instead of reading an announcement that informs the congregation concerning the missions program of the church and the upcoming missions convention, why not consider:
   a. *A Two Minute Missions Moment.* Invite a missionary to attend the worship service, wearing clothing from his part of the world, and conduct a scripted and rehearsed two-minute interview.
   b. *A Missions Parade.* Recruit people from your congregation to wear clothing and carry flags from various parts of the world. Have them march into the sanctuary and to the platform as a tape of energetic music and important information is played.
   c. *A Missions Multimedia Presentation.* Tell your missions story using music, slides, and/or video projection. Collect slides or

video footage from all your missionaries and have someone in your congregation weave them together into a powerful missions message. There are gifted people in every congregation whose technical and creative skills go untapped because we choose to read announcements. Make your announcements count! Get your people involved!

d. *A Missions Live Telephone Conversation.* A simple telephone hookup and brief platform conversation with a missionary half-way around the world can help set the tone for the upcoming missions emphasis.

2. *Timing.* As in so many things we do, timing is crucial when it comes to making announcements count. Promoting the right event, at the right time, and in the right way can mean the difference between a successful event or an unsuccessful one.

a. *Every Turkey Bring a Turkey.* As we promote benevolence, mercy ministry, and social concern within our congregations, proper timing can turn apathetic listeners into passionate participants. For example, people are touched with the needs of others around the holidays. We don't want to manipulate the emotions of our people, but we do need to train them and mobilize them to care for others. When you communicate to your congregation that you are linking arms with the churches and agencies in your community to care for twenty-five hundred needy families who will go without food at Christmas, consider carrying a turkey to the platform and challenge everyone to bring turkeys to the service the following Sunday.

b. *Human Video on Human Need.* As winter approaches, consider having your students perform a human video with captivating background music. Follow it up with an appeal for people to provide warm blankets for the gospel mission and those in need.

c. *Presentation.* Call people forward who are involved in a ministry or who in some way illustrate what you need to communicate. For example: If you are appealing to your congregation to "adopt" a Navy family (we live near a Navy port), invite a family from your congregation who has recently adopted a Navy family and ask them to come forward and escort their fully uniformed and newly adopted Navy friends to the front. Introduce both families to the congregation and encourage others to sign up at the information center to adopt their own Navy family. Much of what we learn we learn visually. Give people the visual with the audio as much as possible.

3. *Volume and Tempo.* The conductor knows just how and when to make the orchestra crescendo and decrescendo. He knows how and when to pick up the pace and when to slow things down. When we promote ministries, there are times we need to be loud, energetic, and fast moving. There are other times when we need to be soft, contemplative, and slower paced.

a. *Ministry March.* If it is Church Ministries Day and you are preaching on "every believer a minister," plan to conduct an enthusiastic ministry march. Ask all the leaders of every ministry in your church to create a banner and recruit their ministry teams. At the appropriate time of the service, hand out a ministry opportunity survey and ask those seated in the sanctuary to get involved in God's work. Start your carefully selected marching music and let the march begin! The congregation will witness banners, ministries, people, teamwork, camaraderie, and more. It's one way to promote ministry in a memorable way.

b. *Ministry Fair.* Before your people even come into your sanctuary or worship center they can witness announcements. Television monitors in the foyer can convey important information, table displays can prompt participation, and the information center can provide fliers and sign-up opportunities. On Church Ministries Day, for example, you could even set up a ministry fair in the lobby or in another prime location. As people enter they will see table after table of church ministries on display, each with involvement opportunities communicated clearly. Nicely decorated tables, balloons and streamers, and effectively displayed posters, pictures, and promotional materials can be used to employ "unemployed" believers. What a powerful visual announcement even before people enter the worship center!

c. *Drama.* An effective drama can be used to drive home a message on an upcoming divorce-recovery workshop or parenting seminar or ministry to aging parents class or any support or recovery group. An effective drama can quietly bring a tear to the observer's eyes, while sincerely communicating an important ministry opportunity.

You Can Do It!

Announcements are all about effectively promoting ministry and mobilizing God's people to participate in ministry. The choice is yours. You can read the bulletin and make your announcements miserable and mediocre. Or with a little creativity, planning, and sensitivity, you can make your announcements memorable and motivational. You can make your announcements count!

The orchestra conductor works hard to make sure every instrument is ready and prepared to communicate beautiful music. As pastors, we too have beautiful music to communicate; it's called good news! Announcements do not have to detract from praise and preaching. With a little imagination and preparation they can communicate the incredible and effective need-meeting ministries of the church, while promoting upcoming events and encouraging participation. As long as we count our measures of rest and play the notes where written, we will make our announcements count! Let the symphony of praise and preaching and promotion begin!

Unit 1:
Priorities in the Pastor's Life

Introduction: Priorities in the Pastor's Life

[1]All Scripture quotations in this chapter are from the New King James Version unless otherwise indicated.

[2]Ralph Turnball, *The Best of Dwight L. Moody* (Grand Rapids: Baker Book House, 1971), 51.

Accountability Groups for Pastors

[1]Clarence Jordan, *The Cotton Patch Version of Matthew and John* (New York: Association Press, 1970).

[2]For a more complete discussion of continual accountability, see Robert E. Coleman, *The Master Plan of Evangelism* (Westwood, N.J.: Fleming H. Revell Co., 1963), 94–101.

[3]The areas involve the interrelationships of church members, church leaders, younger and older believers, husbands, wives, parents, children, masters, slaves, and governmental officials. See Harvey Herman, Jr., *Discipleship by Design* (Springfield, Mo.: DHM College Ministries Department of the Assemblies of God, 1991), lesson 4,4.2.

[4]From a survey in *Discipleship Journal* 72: 42. ©1992 by The Navigators. Used by permission of NavPress. All rights reserved.

[5]Eugene H. Peterson, *Working the Angles* (Grand Rapids: William B. Eerdmans Publishing Co., 1987), 4.

[6]See also the excellent interview with Lloyd John Ogilvie, "Keeping the Drive Alive," *Leadership* 10, no. 3 (1989): 16–22.

[7]Dallas Willard, *The Spirit of the Disciplines* (New York: Harper & Row, Publishers, 1988), 187, 188.

[8]Following the death of my first wife, I entered a grief recovery program. Each evening we began by renewing our commitment to a covenant of confidentiality. One person would read aloud a statement something like this: "We believe that total personal honesty and group confidentiality are essential to the process of recovery from loss. We therefore agree to be totally honest as we share and to protect one another by absolute confidentiality. To indicate that this is our commitment, we lift our hands in agreement and pledge." On each occasion we literally raised our hands in the air and looked around the room for several seconds. We were all signaling clearly to one another: You can trust me. I will enclose you with my confidence. It is safe to be totally honest with me.

[9]Dietrich Bonhoeffer, *Life Together* (New York: Harper & Row, Publishers, 1954), 98, 101. This entire book is germane to this theme. Chapter 5 ("Confession and Communion") offers much practical wisdom and is worth careful reading and lengthy meditation.

[10]The following formula calculates the number of relationships possible in any group. It amply illustrates the need to restrict the size of any accountability group. "X" represents the number of persons in the group.

$X^2 - X \div 2$ = Number of relationships

Thus a group of four is 16 minus 4 divided by 2 = 6 relationships. A group of 5 has 10 relationships and a group of 6 has 15 relationships. A group of 7 has 21!

[11]Various books list questions such as these. See for instance the suggestions in Gordon MacDonald's *Rebuilding Your Broken World* (Nashville: Oliver-Nelson Publishers, 1988), 203–4; and H. B. London, Jr., and Neil B. Wiseman's *The Heart of a Great Pastor* (Ventura, Calif.: Regal Books, 1994), 228, 229.

[12]Jerry Jenkins, *Focus on the Family,* June 1993.

The Pastor and His Devotional Life

[1]All Scripture quotations in this chapter are from the New American Standard Bible unless otherwise indicated.

[2]Noah Webster, *American Dictionary of the English Language 1828* (San Francisco: Foundation for American Christian Education, 1967).

[3]Moshe Dayan, *Living with the Bible* (New York: William Morrow and Co., 1978), 195–98.

[4]E. M. Bounds, *Power through Prayer* (Grand Rapids: Zondervan Publishing House, 1962), 42.

[5]Arnold A. Dallimore, *George Whitefield, God's Anointed Servant in the Great Revival of the Eighteenth Century* (Westchester, Ill.: Crossway Books, 1990), 14–16.

[6]Betty Lee Skinner, *Daws* (Grand Rapids: Zondervan Publishing House, 1974), 38.

[7]Bud Greenspan, *100 Greatest Moments in Olympic History* (Los Angeles: General Publishing Group, 1995), 107.

The Pastoral Marriage

[1]Sherri L. Doty, "Credentials, Marital, and Ministry Status by Gender," *Assemblies of God Ministers Report* (Springfield, Mo.: Gospel Publishing House, 1995).

[2]At the time of this writing, 3.4 percent of Assemblies of God credentialed ministers were engaged in foreign missions and 1.4 percent were under home missions appointment.

[3]Donald M. Joy, *Bonding: Relationships in the Image of God* (Dallas: Word Books, 1985), 59.

[4]Ibid., 31.

[5]Wayne Warner, "A Study in Longevity," *Assemblies of God Heritage* 15, no. 3 (fall 1995): 26–28.

[6]Raymond T. Brock, *Parenting the Elementary Child* (Springfield, Mo.: Gospel Publishing House, 1995), ch. 6 passim.

[7]Dwight H. Small, *Christian: Celebrate Your Sexuality* (Old Tappan, N.J.: Fleming H. Revell Co., 1976).

[8]Raymond T. Brock, "The Deception of Affairs," *Pentecostal Evangel,* 24 April 1988, 6, 7, 15; Raymond T. Brock and Horace C. Lukens, Jr., "Affair Prevention in the Ministry," *Journal of Psychology and Christianity* 8, no. 4 (1989): 44–55.

[9]David Augsburger, "The Private Lives of Public Leaders," *Christianity Today* 31, no. 17 (1987): 23.

[10]Tim Stafford, "Great Sex: Reclaiming a Christian Sexual Ethic," *Christianity Today* 39, no. 14 (1987): 31, 45. Page 45 shows the following:
Have you ever sought professional counseling for sexual temptation?
Laypersons: Yes 7%, No 93%; Pastors: Yes 10%, No 90%. (Source: CTI Research).

Working with All Kinds of People

[1]Proverbs 15:1 (KJV).

[2]Some concepts in this chapter are taken from Hal Donaldson and David P. Donaldson, *The Velcro Church (*Sacramento, Calif.: LEAD Ministries, 1993).

The Pastor, His Office, and His Schedule

[1]Quoted in Richard I. Winwood, *Time Management: An Introduction to the Franklin System* (Salt Lake City: Franklin International Institute, 1990), 13.

[2]Ibid., 74.

[3]Max Lucado, *In the Eye of the Storm: A Day in the Life of Jesus* (Dallas: Word Books, 1991), 97–98.

[4]Archibald Hart, *Focus on the Family Presents Pastor to Pastor with H. B. London, Jr.,* vol. 1, *Budgets and Burnout* (Colorado Springs: Focus on the Family, 1993), audiocassette.

[5]These items may be found at a local office supply store or Christian retailer. Or order from the following: *The Franklin Day Planner* (Franklin International Institute, Inc., P.O. Box 25127, Salt Lake City, Utah 84125-0127). *The Daytimer* (Daytimers, Inc., P.O. Box 27000, Lehigh Valley, Pa., 18003-9859; 1-800-225-5005). *The Christian Service Planner* (Spirited Communications, 1838 Ellinwood Road, Baltimore, Md. 21237).

[6]Dianna Booher, *Clean Up Your Act! Effective Ways to Organize Paperwork and Get It Out of Your Life* (New York: Warner Books, 1992), xvi.

[7]Winwood, *Time Management,* 125–26.

[8]Martin John Yates, *Hiring the Best: A Manager's Guide to Effective Interviewing* (Boston: Bob Adams, 1988), 18.

[9]Ibid., 20.

The Pastor's Study

[1]Richard E. Orchard, "The Pastor and His Preaching-Teaching," in *And He Gave Pastors: Pastoral Theology in Action,* ed. Thomas F. Zimmerman, G. Raymond Carlson, and Zenas J. Bicket (Springfield, Mo.: Gospel Publishing House, 1979), 158.

Expository Preaching

[1]Portions of this chapter appeared in George O. Wood's article "How Expository Preaching Helps the Church," *Enrichment,* summer 1996, 26–30.

[2]Hugh Thomson Kerr, quoted in George W. Peters, *A Biblical Theology of Missions* (Chicago: Moody Press, 1972), 209.

[3]Space does not permit me here to retell the drama and pathos of Livingstone's story. You can find it on your own in a sermon by Frank William Boreham, "David Livingstone's Text," in Andrew W. Blackwood, *The Protestant Pulpit* (Grand Rapids: Baker Book House, 1977), 164–65.

Back to the Word in Our Preaching

[1]This chapter is reprinted from "A Return to Biblical Preaching," from the book *Back to the Word: A Call to Biblical Authority.* ©1996 by Gospel Publishing House, Springfield, Mo. Used by permission.

[2]All Scripture quotations in this chapter are from the New American Standard Bible unless otherwise indicated.

[3]Henry Ward Beecher, quoted in George Sweeting, *Great Quotes and Illustrations* (Waco, Tex.: Word Books, 1985), 28.

[4]George Sweeting, *Great Quotes,* 34.

[5]Thomas E. Trask and David A. Womack, *Back to the Altar: A Call to Spiritual Awakening* (Springfield, Mo.: Gospel Publishing House, 1994).

Unit 2:
The Pastor's Personal Life

Introduction: The Pastor's Personal Life

[1]Charles H. Spurgeon, *Lectures to My Students* (Grand Rapids: Zondervan Publishing House, 1954), 17.

[2]Phillips Brooks, *Lectures on Preaching* (Grand Rapids: Zondervan Publishing House, 1871), 99.

[3]All Scripture quotations in this chapter are from the New King James Version unless otherwise indicated.

[4]Richard Baxter, *The Reformed Pastor,* ed. Hugh Martin (London: SCM Press, 1956), 63.

[5]Spurgeon, *Lectures to My Students,* 8, 9, 18.

[6]Eugene Stock, *Practical Truths from the Pastoral Epistles* (Grand Rapids: Kregel Publications, 1983), 177, 178.

[7]Donald C. Stamps, ed., *Full Life Study Bible* (Grand Rapids: Zondervan Publishing House, 1992), 1908.

[8]Warren W. Wiersbe, *Be Faithful* (Wheaton, Ill.: Victory Books, 1983), 44.

The Character of the Lord's Servant

[1]Carmen Wassam, "Pirates in the Church?" *Pentecostal Evangel,* 1 September 1991, 10. According to Wassam's article, a church can keep from violating copyright laws by using music on which copyright protection has expired or by purchasing a *blanket license.* "A blanket license authorizes churches to make copies of music for congregational use. A license from Christian Copyright Licensing, Inc., for example, allows churches to print songs in bulletins and songbooks, produce slides and transparencies, make customized arrangements, and record worship services for tape ministry (as long as tapes are sold only on a cost-recovery basis). Churches that obtain a license from CCLI for a modest fee based on church size have authorization to use songs owned by more than 400 Christian publishers."

[2]It should be noted that for the pastors of many small churches, the issue is not so much the possibility of excess income but rather the need for basic maintenance. The church board and congregation have a responsibility to see that the pastor is given proper honor, esteem, and necessary income. Not to do so is in itself a character flaw. But the focus of this study is the character of the minister. The love of money and material possessions can be just as much a problem for the underpaid as for the overpaid minister. Those who lack can sometimes envy those who have more. Grasping for more, even if it is not attained, can be just as much a character flaw as seeking more than is needed.

[3]Ralph M. Riggs, *A Successful Pastor* (Springfield, Mo.: Gospel Publishing House, 1931), 54.

The Unique Struggles of Today's Pastor

[1]The full text of this account can be found in Robert H. Schuller, *Your Church Has a Fantastic Future!* (Ventura, Calif.: Regal Books, 1986), 183–89.

[2]Jay Kesler, *Being Holy, Being Human* (Waco, Tex.: Word Books, 1988), 163.

[3]H. B. London, Jr., and Neil B. Wiseman, *The Heart of a Great Pastor* (Ventura, Calif.: Regal Books, 1994), 22.

[4]Calvin Miller, *The Empowered Leader* (Nashville: Broadman and Holman Publishers, 1995), 22.

[5]W. A. Criswell, *Criswell's Guidebook for Pastors* (Nashville: Broadman Press, 1980), 330.

[6]Author unknown.

[7]Quoted in Ralph G. Turnbull, *A Minister's Obstacles* (New York: Fleming H. Revell Co., 1946), 147.

The Minister's Wife

[1]It is understood that speaking of the minister's spouse as a wife can be interpreted as an expectation that all ministers are men. The General Council of the Assemblies of God has officially declared that women are fully accepted as ministers eligible to fill any offices in the church. This chapter, written by the wife of a minister, recognizes that the majority of pastors currently are men. Rather than a wife speaking to other ministers' wives, this chapter focuses on male ministers. However, many of the concepts presented can be applied to a minister's spouse of either gender.

[2]Walter Wangerin, Jr., *As for Me and My House* (Nashville: Thomas Nelson Publishers, 1987), 85–87. Used by permission.

[3]All Scripture quotations in this chapter are from the New King James Version unless otherwise indicated.

[4]The incidents from the lives of Martin and Katie Luther are drawn from William J. Petersen, *Husbands and Wives* (Wheaton, Ill.: Tyndale House Publishers, 1989), 34.

[5]Ibid., 116.

[6]Ibid., 92.

[7]Ibid., 130.

[8]Henri Nouwen, *Seeds of Hope* (New York: Bantam Books, 1989), 18, 19.

[9]Ibid., 21, 22.

Coping with Financial Pressures in the Family

[1]Adolph Bedsole, *The Pastor in Profile* (Grand Rapids: Baker Book House, 1958), 124.

Staying Healthy in the Ministry

[1]Allan C. Reuter, "Stress in the Ministry: Can We Fight Back?" *Currents in Theology and Mission,* August 1981, 221–31.

[2]Woodrow Kroll, *The Vanishing Ministry* (Grand Rapids: Kregel Publications, 1991), 16.

[3]All Scripture quotations in this chapter are from the King James Version unless otherwise indicated.

[4]Bernard Grun, ed., *The Timetables of History,* 3d ed. (New York: Simon and Schuster, 1991), 473.

[5]James Patterson and Peter Kim, *The Day America Told the Truth* (New York: Prentice-Hall, 1991), 94–173.

[6]Edgar W. Mills and John P. Koval, *Stress in the Ministry* (Washington, D.C.: Ministry Studies Board, 1971).

[7]Gary W. Kuhne and Joe F. Donaldson, "Balancing Ministry and Management: An Exploratory Study of Pastoral Work Activities," *Review of Religious Research* 37, no. 2 (December 1995): 147–63.

[8]Ibid.

[9]Brother Lawrence, *The Practice of the Presence of God,* trans. John J. Delaney (Garden City, N.Y.: Image Books, 1977), 16–17.

[10]*New Catholic Encyclopedia,* 1967 ed., s.v. "Lawrence of the Resurrection," 569.

[11]Kenneth W. Osbeck, ed., "Amazing Grace," *101 More Hymn Stories* (Grand Rapids: Kregel Publications, 1982), 101.

[12]Richard D. Dobbins, *Your Feelings . . . Friend or Foe?* (Akron, Ohio: Totally Alive Publications, 1994). Readers may call EMERGE Ministries at 1-800-621-5207 to order this book.

[13]William C. Nichols, *Marital Therapy: An Integrative Approach* (New York: Guilford Press, 1988), 11ff.

[14]"Divorce Rates for Clergy Match Laity?" *Beacon Journal* (1 July 1995): A7, A8.

[15]Eugene H. Peterson, "The Good-for-Nothing Sabbath," *Christianity Today,* 4 April 1994, 34–36.

[16]Kroll, *The Vanishing Ministry,* 43–47.

[17]Brent B. Benda and Frederick A. DiBlasio, "Clergy Marriages: A Multivariate Model of Marital Adjustment," *Journal of Psychology and Theology* 20, no. 4 (1992): 367–75.

[18]Ibid., 367.

[19]Ibid.

[20]Philip Goldberg, *Executive Health* (New York: McGraw Hill Publications/Business Week Books, 1978), 25.

[21]Gordon MacDonald, *Ordering Your Private World* (Nashville: Oliver-Nelson Publishers, 1985).

[22]Etta Saltos, "The New Food Label as a Tool for Healthy Eating," *Nutrition Today* 29, no. 3 (May/June 1994): 20.

[23]Allen Nauss, "Ministerial Effectiveness in Ten Functions," *Review of Religious Research* 36, no. 1 (September 1994): 58–67.

[24]H. Newton Malony and Richard Hunt, *The Psychology of Clergy* (Harrisburg, Pa.: Morehouse, 1991), 136.

Handling Stress and Avoiding Burnout

[1]All Scripture quotations in this chapter are from the New American Standard Bible unless otherwise indicated.

[2]Quoted in George Sweeting, *Great Quotes and Illustrations* (Waco, Tex.: Word Books, 1985), 42.

[3]Robert Freeman, quoted in Sweeting, *Great Quotes,* 42.

[4]Johannes P. Louw and Eugene A. Nida, *Greek-English Lexicon of the New Testament: Based on Semantic Domains* (New York: United Bible Societies, 1988), 308.

[5]Thomas Carlyle, quoted in Sweeting, *Great Quotes,* 212, 213.

[6]Neil T. Anderson, *Victory over the Darkness* (Ventura, Calif.: Regal Books, 1990), 126.

[7]Ibid, 127.

[8]Ibid., 127–134.

The Pastor's Person, Possessions, Habits, Moods, and Leisure

[1]Items in this list without Scripture references are observed as general characteristics of Jesus' earthly ministry.

[2]Richard Gaylord Briley, *The Seven Spiritual Secrets of Success* (Nashville: Thomas Nelson Publishers, 1995).

[3]Recommended reading: John T. Molloy, *Dress for Success* (New York: Warner Books, 1975).

Continuing Education to Meet Changing Needs

[1]John Gardner, quoted in the *Executive Speechwriter Newsletter* 9, no. 6.

[2]David Womack, ed., *Pentecostal Experience: The Writings of Donald Gee* (Springfield, Mo.: Gospel Publishing House, 1993), 21.

[3]David Linowes, quoted in the *Executive Speechwriter Newsletter* 9, no. 5.

[4]For a challenging book on the changing workplace, see Peter Drucker, *Innovative Entrepreneurship* (New York: HarperCollins Publications, 1985).

[5]Edward De Bono, *New Think* (New York: Avon Books, 1967). Used with permission.

[6]Ibid., 19–21.

[7]Ibid.

[8]For a delightfully entertaining and unique way of looking at the great diversity of America's divisions, see Joel Garreau, *The Nine Nations of North America* (New York: Avon Books, 1982).

[9]Isidro Lucas, *The Browning of America* (Chicago: Fides Claretian Publishers, 1981).

[10]One of many sources for good cross-cultural communications is Stele Ting-Toomey and Felipe Korzenny, eds., *Cross-Cultural Interpersonal Communication* (Newbury Park, Calif.: Sage Publications, 1991).

[11]For a good source on time in America see Edward T. Hall, *The Dance of Life* (New York: Anchor Books/Doubleday, 1983).

[12]Esther Wanning, *Culture Shock USA* (Singapore: Time Book International, 1991), 3–5.

[13]Ibid., 3–5.

[14]For a good study on this topic see Kenneth R. Johnson, "Black Kinesics: Some Nonverbal Communication Patterns in the Black Culture," in *Intercultural Communication: A Reader,* ed. Larry Samovar and Richard Porter (Belmont, Calif.: Wadsworth Publishing, 1972), 181ff.

[15]Mary J. Collier, "Nonverbal Sensitivity," *International Journal of Intercultural Relations* 13, no. 3: 287–302.

[16]For an excellent treatment of using a given culture's beliefs and values to best convey the gospel (called *redemptive analogies*), see Don Richardson, *Peace Child,* 3d ed. (Glendale, Calif.: Regal Books, 1976), and *Eternity in Their Hearts* (Ventura, Calif.: Regal Books, 1981).

Sexual Ethics in the Ministry

[1]This chapter has been adapted from Wayde Goodall's article "Sexual Ethics in the Ministry," *Advance,* fall 1995, 52–55.

[2]V. Raymond Edman, quoted in George Sweeting, *Great Quotes and Illustrations* (Waco, Tex.: Word Books, 1985), 105.

[3]"*Leadership* Family and Ministry Survey Summary," *Leadership,* July 1992, 13.

[4]J. Holroyd and A. Brodsky, "Does Touching Patients Lead to Sexual Intercourse?" *Journal of Professional Psychology: Research and Practice* 11 (1980): 807–11.

[5]"*Leadership* Family and Ministry Survey Summary," 13.

[6]All Scripture quotations in this chapter are from the New American Standard Bible unless otherwise indicated.

[7]R. Folman, "Therapist-Patient Sex: Attraction and Boundary Problems," *Psychotherapy* 28 (1991): 168–73.

[8]Gary Collins, *Excellence and Ethics in Counseling* (Dallas: Word Books, 1991), 66, 67.

[9]Ibid., 67.

[10]"*Leadership* Family and Ministry Survey Summary," 17.

[11]Ibid., 18.

[12]Cocounseling is team counseling. For example, a husband and wife, or the pastor and a deacon, may counsel together with a client.

[13]T. Gutheil, "Borderline Personality Disorder, Boundary Violations, and Patient-Therapist Sex: Mediocolegal Pitfalls," *American Journal of Psychiatry* 1, no. 46 (1989): 600.

[14]Transference refers to the client's unconscious, excessive emotional response to the counselor.

[15]D. Benner, ed., *Baker Encyclopedia of Psychology* (Grand Rapids: Baker Book House, 1985), 242.

[16]K. Pope and M. Vasquez, *Ethics in Psychotherapy and Counseling: A Practical Guide for Psychologists* (San Francisco: Jossey-Bass, 1991), 110–11.

When the Pastor Needs Professional Help

[1]Although women ministers are subject to the same stresses as men, the references in this chapter are to "he" and "him" rather than "he and she" or "him and her" because the experience of EMERGE Ministries in counseling ministers is primarily with men.

The Pastor As Shepherd

[1]*New International Dictionary of New Testament Theology,* 1971 ed., s.v. "Shepherd."

[2]See Rick Warren, *The Purpose-Driven Church* (Grand Rapids: Zondervan Publishing House, 1995).

[3]Phillip Keller, *A Shepherd Looks at Psalm 23* (Grand Rapids: Zondervan Publishing House, 1970), 35.

[4]Rev. Glen Cole, pastor emeritus of Capital Christian Center, Sacramento, California.

[5]Keller, *A Shepherd Looks at Psalm 23,* 35.

[6]J. Robert Clinton, *The Mentoring Handbook* (Altadena, Calif.: Barnabas Publishers, 1991), 17–23.

Unit 3:
Preparing for Revival

Introduction: Revival Is . . .

[1]All Scripture quotations in this chapter are from the King James Version unless otherwise indicated.

Implanting Mission and Vision in Others

[1]All Scripture quotations in this chapter are from the King James Version unless otherwise indicated.

[2] Henry David Thoreau, *Walden* (New York: The Modern Library, 1950), 288.

Seven Steps to a Pentecostal Revival

[1]*Software Toolworks Multimedia Encyclopedia,* s.v. "Revival" (Danbury, Conn.: Grolier Electronic Publishing, 1992).

[2]All Scripture quotations in this chapter are from the King James Version unless otherwise indicated.

[3]Author's definition.

[4]*Grolier Multimedia Encyclopedia,* s.v. "Reformation" (Danbury, Conn.: Grolier Electronic Publishing, 1995).

[5]James Burns, *The Laws of Revival,* ed. Tom Phillips (Wheaton, Ill.: World Wide Publications, 1993), 24.

[6]Tom Phillips with Mark Cutshall, *Revival Signs: The Coming Spiritual Awakening* (Ventura, Calif.: Vision House, 1995), 84.

[7]Habakkuk 2:4; Romans 1:17; Galatians 3:11; Hebrews 10:38.

[8]Nehemiah 4:2; Psalms 85:6; 138:7; Isaiah 57:15 (twice); Hosea 6:2; 14:7; Habakkuk 3:2.

[9]There is some controversy about whether this passage was in the original Gospel of Mark because it is missing in some ancient texts. However, without it the Gospel would end abruptly on a negative statement. In addition, it is written in the same style as the rest of the book, it is consistent with the rest of the New Testament, and the content would not have been written at any other age then that of the first-century church. It is not uncommon for the first or last pages of ancient manuscripts to be lost.

[10]Jack Deere, *Surprised by the Power of the Spirit* (Grand Rapids: Zondervan Publishing House, 1993), 66.

Developing a Prayer Ministry in the Local Church

[1]Paul E. Billheimer, *Destined for the Throne* (Ft. Washington, Pa.: 1975), 17.

[2]Ibid., 17, 18.

[3]Ibid., 101.

[4]R. A. Torrey, *How to Find Fullness of Power* (Minneapolis: Bethany Fellowship, 1972), 82, 83.

[5]Ibid.

[6]Andrew Murray, quoted in Dick Eastman, *Change the World School of Prayer Manual* (Colorado Springs: Every Home for Christ, 1992), D–119.

[7]Leonard Ravenhill, *Why Revival Tarries* (Minneapolis: Bethany Fellowship, 1959), 29.

[8]All Scripture quotations in this chapter are from the New King James Version unless otherwise indicated.

[9]John R. Mott, quoted in Edwin Harvey and Lillian Harvey, *Kneeling We Triumph* (Chicago: Moody Press, 1974), 20.

[10]E. M. Bounds, *A Treasury of Prayer,* comp. Leonard Ravenhill (Minneapolis: Bethany Fellowship, 1961), 92.

[11]E. M. Bounds, *The Weapon of Prayer* (Grand Rapids: Baker Book House, 1975), 64.

[12]Every Home for Christ annually produces a very meaningful World Prayer Map

specifically for this purpose. It includes a unique 31-day prayer guide for the nations which, when used systematically, helps the user pray for every country on earth each month. For information on obtaining quantities of this map write: Every Home for Christ, P.O. Box 35930, Colorado Springs, CO 80935.

[13]Ravenhill, *Why Revival Tarries,* 154.

[14]Bounds, *A Treasury of Prayer,* 89.

[15]Billheimer, *Destined for the Throne,* 104.

Revival through Prayer and Fasting

[1]All Scripture quotations in this chapter are from the King James Version unless otherwise indicated.

[2]A copy of this book is in the British Museum in London, England.

Planting a New Congregation

[1]David J. Hesselgrave, *Planting Churches Cross-Culturally* (Grand Rapids: Baker Book House, 1980), 135.

Evangelizing a Community

[1]All Scripture quotations in this chapter are from the New American Standard Bible unless otherwise indicated.

Mobilizing Men and Women for Outreach

[1]All Scripture quotations in this chapter are from the King James Version unless otherwise indicated.

Training and Commissioning Elders and Deacons

[1]In small churches, the roles of elders and deacons may be filled by the same group of persons.

[2]The twenty italicized points are quoted from Gene A. Getz, *The Measure of a Man* (Ventura, Calif.: Regal Books, 1985), passim.

The Gift of the Evangelist: A Pastor's Perspective

[1]All Scripture quotations in this chapter are from the New King James Version unless otherwise indicated.

[2]"Total Church Evangelism Strategy," report presented by the Total Church Evangelism Strategy Committee to the General Presbytery of the Assemblies of God, Oklahoma City, Okla., 5 August 1987.

The Gift of the Evangelist: An Evangelist's Perspective

[1]Richard Armstrong, *The Pastor as Evangelist in the Parish* (Philadelphia: Westminster Press, 1990), 33, 34.

[2]Billy Graham, *A Biblical Standard for Evangelists* (Minneapolis: World Wide Publications, 1984), 81.

[3]Although the evangelist is described throughout this chapter as a man, the Pentecostal church has been blessed over the years with many anointed women evangelists. The priorities, in either case, are still the same, with appropriate adjustment for the situations of a woman minister.

[4]Graham, *A Biblical Standard for Evangelists,* 99.

[5]Sterling Huston, "Preparing an Evangelistic Event," in *The Calling of an Evangelist: The Second International Congress for Itinerant Evangelists,* ed. J. D. Douglas (Minneapolis: World Wide Publications, 1984), 237.

[6]W. E. Biederwolf, quoted in George Sweeting, *The Evangelistic Camp* (Chicago: Moody Press, 1955), 19.

Signs and Wonders

[1]Leon Morris, *Spirit of the Living God: The Bible's Teaching on the Holy Spirit* (London: InterVarsity Press, 1960), 64–65.

[2]All Scripture quotations in this chapter are from the King James Version unless otherwise indicated.

The Priority of Revival

[1]All Scripture quotations in this chapter are from the King James Version unless otherwise indicated.

Unit 4:
Effective Accountability

Introduction: Accountability to the Fellowship

[1]All Scripture quotations in this chapter are from the King James Version unless otherwise indicated.

[2]Application for Ordination Certificate, General Council of the Assemblies of God, form no. 737-006.

[3]Documents and printed materials regarding these areas of information are available from the General Council of the Assemblies of God (Springfield, Missouri), its related agencies, and the respective district council offices.

[4]From *Ministerial Ethics and Etiquette* by Nolan B. Harmon. Second rev. ed. ©1987 Abingdon Press. Used by permission.

A Long-Range Plan for the Church

[1]All Scripture quotations in this chapter are from the New King James Version unless otherwise indicated.

Working with Church Boards

[1]Max DePree, *Leadership Is an Art* (New York: Dell Publishing, 1989), 34–35.

[2]Bruce W. Jones, *Ministerial Leadership in a Managerial World* (Wheaton, Ill.: Tyndale House Publishers, 1988), 130.

[3]Jim Buchan and Marcia Ford, "How Many Hours Should a Pastor Work?" *Ministries Today,* July/August 1995, 22.

[4]Madeleine L'Engle, *Walking on Water* (Wheaton, Ill.: Harold Shaw Publishers, 1980), 23.

[5]Ibid.

[6]Ibid., 30–31. Used by permission of Harold Shaw Publishers.

[7]Peter Drucker, *The Effective Executive* (New York: Harper and Row, Publishers, 1966), 1.

[8]J. Robert Clinton, *The Making of a Leader* (Colorado Springs: NavPress, 1988), 168–71.

Conducting the Church Board/Business Meetings

[1]All Scripture quotations in this chapter are from the King James Version unless otherwise indicated.

[2]*Robert's Rules of Order,* revised by Darwin Patnode, may be ordered from Gospel Publishing House, Springfield, Mo., order number 03-2334.

[3]Zenas J. Bicket, *The Effective Pastor* (Springfield, Mo.: Gospel Publishing House, 1973), 137, 138.

[4]John C. Maxwell, "Getting Your Church Board on Board," *Enrichment,* fall 1996, 86. Portions of this article have been adapted and are used by permission.

[5]Ibid., 84–86.

Knowing and Using the Legal System

[1]To illustrate, Rule 505 of the Uniform Rules of Evidence, which has been adopted by several states, provides:

(a) *Definitions.* As used in this rule:

(1) A "clergyman" is a minister, priest, rabbi, accredited Christian Science Practitioner, or other similar functionary of a religious organization, or an individual reasonably believed so to be by the person consulting him.

(2) A communication is "confidential" if made privately and not intended for further disclosure except to other persons present in furtherance of the purpose of the communication.

(b) *General Rule of Privilege.* A person has a privilege to refuse to disclose and to prevent another from disclosing a confidential communication by the person to the clergyman in his professional character as a spiritual adviser.

(c) *Who May Claim the Privilege.* The privilege may be claimed by the person, by his guardian or conservator, or by his personal representative if he is deceased. The person who was the clergyman at the time of the communication is presumed to have authority to claim the privilege but only on behalf of the communicant.

Dealing with Change

[1]Charles Swindoll, quoted in *The Church Resource Book* (El Cajon, Calif.: Injoy Ministries).

[2]All Scripture quotations in this chapter are from the King James Version unless otherwise indicated.

[3]George Barna, *The Power of Vision: How You Can Capture and Apply God's Vision for Your Ministry* (Ventura, Calif.: Regal Books, 1992).

Managing Conflict

[1]Almon Bartholomew, "Hot Potato 101: A Primer for Church Conflicts," *Advance,* November 1983. The material is suggested as an introduction to conflict management for groups or individuals needing such help.

Handling Crises

[1]All Scripture quotations in this chapter are from the King James Version unless otherwise indicated.

Developing a Team of Qualified, Dedicated Staff Members

[1]R. B. Barham, quoted in Bergen Evans, ed., *Dictionary of Quotations* (New York: Avenel Books, 1968), 638.

The Effective Use of Job Descriptions

[1]Peter F. Drucker, *Managing the Nonprofit Corporation: Principles and Practices* (New York: HarperCollins Publications, 1990), 4.

[2]Ibid., 45.

[3]Ibid., 5.

[4]George Barna, *The Power of Vision: How You Can Capture and Apply God's Vision for Your Ministry* (Ventura, Calif.: Regal Books, 1992), 37.

[5]Alan Loy McGinnis, *Bringing Out the Best in People* (Minneapolis: Augsburg Press, 1985), 56.

[6]Anne Marie Nuechterlein, *Improving Your Multiple Staff Ministry: How to Work Together More Effectively* (Minneapolis: Augsburg Press, 1989), 33.

[7]Kenneth Blanchard and Spencer Johnson, *The One Minute Manager: The Quickest Way to Increase Your Own Prosperity* (New York: Berkley Publishing, 1981), 66.

[8]Nuechterlein, *Improving Your Multiple Staff Ministry*, 33.

[9]Ted W. Engstrom, *The Making of a Christian Leader: How to Develop Management and Human Relations Skills* (Grand Rapids: Zondervan Publishing House, 1976), 60.

[10]Peter F. Drucker, *The Effective Executive* (New York: Harper and Row, Publishers, 1966), 76–79.

[11]Judith A. DeLapa, "Personnel World: Job Descriptions That Work," *Personnel Journal* 68, no. 6 (June 1989): 156.

[12]Frederick Herzberg, "One More Time: How Do You Motivate Employees?" *Harvard Business Review* 65, no. 5 (September/October 1987): 113. Note: More than 1.2 million reprints of the article have been purchased, which exceeds by over 300,000 the next closest article ever printed in the *Harvard Business Review*. Reprints of this article can be ordered by calling (617) 495-6192; article reprint #87507.

[13]Ibid., 114.

[14]Ibid.

[15]Ted W. Engstrom, *Your Gift of Administration: How to Discover and Use It* (Nashville: Thomas Nelson Publishers, 1983), 85.

[16]Herzberg, "How Do You Motivate Employees?" 114.

[17]Frank R. Tillapaugh, *Unleashing the Church: Getting People Out of the Fortress and Into the Ministry* (Ventura, Calif.: Regal Books, 1982), 115.

[18]Herzberg, "How Do You Motivate Employees?" 114.

[19]Lyle E. Schaller, *Getting Things Done: Concepts and Skills for Leaders* (Nashville: Abingdon Press, 1986), 256–58.

[20]Craig Eric Schneier, Arthur Geis, and Joseph A. Wert, "Performance Appraisals: No Appointment Needed," *Personnel Journal* 66, no. 11 (November 1987): 83.

[21]Ibid., 84.

[22]Carl F. George and Robert E. Logan, *Leading and Managing Your Church* (Old Tappan, N.J.: Fleming H. Revell Co., 1987), 111.

[23]Nuechterlein, *Improving Your Multiple Staff Ministry*, 39.

[24]Drucker, *The Effective Executive,* 106.

[25]Schneier, "Performance Appraisals: No Appointment Needed," 83.

[26]Bob Biehl and Ted Engstrom, *Boardroom Confidence* (Sisters, Oreg.: Questar Publishers, 1988), 255–56.

[27]Drucker, *The Effective Executive,* 7.

Guiding the Christian Education Program

[1]David A. Womack, *The Pyramid Principle of Church Growth* (Minneapolis: Bethany House, 1977). Used with permission.

Unit 5:
Ministry to the Body

Back to Basics in Missions

[1]Oswald Chambers, *My Utmost for His Highest* (14 October entry) (London, England: Simpkin Marshall, 1934), 288.

[2]John Piper, *Let the Nations Be Glad* (Grand Rapids: Baker Book House, 1993), 15, 40.

[3]Chambers, *My Utmost for His Highest* (16 October entry), 290.

[4]Chambers, *My Utmost for His Highest* (17 October entry), 291.

Working with Associate Pastors: A Senior Pastor's Viewpoint

[1]All Scripture quotations in this chapter are from the New American Standard Bible unless otherwise indicated.

[2]National Association of Church Business Administrators, 7001 Grapevine Highway, Suite 324, Fort Worth, TX 76180-8813.

[3]Christian Management Association, P.O. Box 4638, Diamond Bar, CA 91765.

[4]The following seven questions have been adapted from Dave Carder, interview with James Dobson, *Focus on the Family,* radio program, 26 March 1993. Dave Carder is assistant pastor of First Evangelical Free Church of Fullerton, Calif.

1. Have you been with a woman anywhere this past week that might be seen as compromising?
2. Have any of your financial dealings lacked integrity?
3. Have you exposed yourself to any sexually explicit material?
4. Have you spent adequate time in Bible study and prayer?
5. Have you given priority time to your family?
6. Have you fulfilled the mandates of your calling?
7. Have you just lied to me?

Working with Senior Pastors: An Associate Pastor's Viewpoint

[1]All Scripture quotations in this chapter are from the New American Standard Bible unless otherwise indicated.

[2]"The Five Adjectives of a Noun Christian," *Homiletics,* October /December 1995, 28.

[3]Wim Malgo, "The Birth of Jesus Christ," *Midnight Call,* December 1995, 6.

Planning for Church Growth

[1]All Scripture quotations in this chapter are from the King James Version unless otherwise indicated.

Growing from a Pioneer Church to a Multistaff Church

[1]Adapted from Lyle E. Schaller, *The Senior Minister* (Nashville: Abingdon Press, 1988), 70.

[2]Lyle E. Schaller, *Effective Church Planning* (Nashville: Abingdon Press, 1979), 54. Shaller's many books are thought-provoking resources on church growth and church life.

[3]Joseph M. Stowell, *Shepherding the Church into the 21st Century* (Wheaton, Ill.: Victor Books, 1994), 70. The character of the pastor is foundational to healthy and long-lasting growth in any church.

Special Services

[1]More information can be obtained from The Chapel of the Air Ministries, Box 30, Wheaton, IL 60189-0030.

Building Community Goodwill toward Church and Pastor

[1]Even in the Old Testament, the leaders of God's people were expected to be active and contributing to the spiritual and physical welfare of the congregation: "Woe to you who are complacent in Zion, and to you who feel secure on Mount Samaria, you notable men of the foremost nation, to whom the people of Israel come!" (Amos 6:1).

[2]W. McFerrin Stowe, *If I Were a Pastor* (Nashville: Abingdon Press, 1983), 40.

[3]Donald Gee (a gifted preacher, teacher, and writer in the earlier days of twentieth-century Pentecost) recommended that Pentecostals infiltrate the ranks of liberal churches. He reasoned that there was enough power in Pentecost to change the liberals rather than Pentecostals being changed by the liberals. Instead of following his suggestion, classical Pentecostals refused to have anything to do with the liberal churches. As the twentieth century has unfolded, many of those churches have had pockets of charismatic renewal. One wonders if the Pentecostal message would have spread more rapidly if Gee's suggestion had been followed. Gee, of course, would not countenance any compromise of Pentecostal theology or experience. He saw the apostle Paul taking on the philosophers and idol worshippers through the mighty power of the Holy Spirit.

[4]Spiritual Life Committee's report to the 1973 General Council of the Assemblies of God, *General Council Minutes* (Springfield, Mo.: Assemblies of God, 1973), 80–81.

Relating to Community Leaders

[1]John Pollock, *Billy Graham: The Authorized Biography* (New York: McGraw-Hill Publishers, 1966), ch. 29.

Changing Pastorates

[1]John Maxwell, *When to Quit* (El Cajon, Calif.: Injoy Life Club, audiotape, vol. 10, no. 1).

[2]John Maxwell, *When to Move in Leadership* (El Cajon, Calif.: Injoy Life Club, audiotape, vol. 5, no. 6).

What Is Biblical Counseling?

[1]George Sweeting, *Great Quotes and Illustrations* (Dallas, Tex.: Word, Inc., 1985), 222, 223. Used with permission.

Personal Counseling in the Power of the Spirit

[1]Research conducted by the author.

[2]Gerald Gurin, Joseph Veroff, and Sheila Feld, *American View of Mental Health: A Nationwide Survey* (New York: Basic Books, 1960). Richard A. Kulka, Joseph Veroff, and Elizabeth Douvan, "Social Class and the Use of Professional Help for Personal Problems," *Journal of Health and Social Behavior* 20: 2–17.

[3]Richard D. Dobbins, "A Basic Approach to Biblical Counseling" (unpublished manuscript presented at a seminar, Akron, Ohio, 1995).

[4]Gary Collins, *The Biblical Basis of Christian Counseling for People Helpers* (Colorado Springs: NavPress, 1993), 21.

[5]Richard Foster, *Celebration of Discipline* (New York: Harper and Row, Publishers, 1988), v.

[6]Ibid., 7.

[7]William Law, *A Serious Call to a Devout and Holy Life* (New York: Everyman's Library, 1967), 2.

[8]Gerard Egan, *The Skilled Helper: A Problem-Management Approach to Helping,* 5th ed. (Pacific Grove, Calif.: Brooks/Cole Publishing Co., 1994), 5.

[9]Eugene H. Peterson, *The Message* (Colorado Springs: NavPress, 1993), 470.

Unit 6:
Spirit-Anointed Worship

Introduction: The Priority of Ministry to God

[1]All Scripture quotations in this chapter are from the New American Standard Bible unless otherwise indicated.

[2]Arnold A. Dallimore, *George Whitefield: The Life and Times of the Great Evangelist of the Eighteenth-Century Revival,* vol. 1 (London: Banner of Truth, 1970), 15.

[3]John Bunyan, quoted in George Sweeting, *Great Quotes and Illustrations* (Waco, Tex.: Word Books, 1985), 156.

[4]Martyn Lloyd-Jones, quoted in Tony Sargent, *The Sacred Anointing: The Preaching of Dr. Martyn Lloyd-Jones* (Wheaton, Ill.: Crossway Books, 1994), 31, 32.

[5]Daniel Webster, quoted in Sweeting, *Great Quotes,* 41.

[6]Charles H. Spurgeon, quoted in Sweeting, *Great Quotes,* 191.

Making Place for Pentecostal Distinctives

[1]All Scripture quotations in this chapter are from the New King James Version unless otherwise indicated.

[2]Thomas E. Trask and David A. Womack, *Back to the Altar: A Call to Spiritual Awakening* (Springfield, Mo.: Gospel Publishing House, 1994), 80.

[3]J. Sidlow Baxter, *Rethinking Our Priorities* (Grand Rapids: Zondervan Publishing House, 1974), 167.

[4]Charles E. Jefferson, *The Building of the Church* (New York: Macmillan Co., 1910; reprint, Grand Rapids: Baker Book House, 1969), 135 (page citation is to the reprint edition).

5Jack Hayford, John Killinger, and Howard Stevenson, *Mastering Worship* (Portland, Oreg.: Multnomah Press, 1990), 50.

6Jefferson, *The Building of the Church,* 135.

7Ibid., 137.

8Andrew A. Bonar, ed., *Memories of McCheyne* (Chicago: Moody Press, 1958), 419.

9Charles H. Spurgeon, *The Metropolitan Tabernacle Pulpit,* vol. 31 (Pasadena, Tex.: Pilgrim Publications, 1973), 60.

10Baxter, *Rethinking Our Priorities,* 162.

11Jefferson, *The Building of the Church,* 147.

12Ibid., 143.

13John MacArthur, *The Ultimate Priority* (Chicago: Moody Press, 1983), 147, quoted in Erwin W. Lutzer, *Pastor to Pastor* (Chicago: Moody Press, 1987), 90.

Before You Step into the Pulpit: Sermon Preparation

1All Scripture quotations in this chapter are from the New King James Version unless otherwise indicated.

2Bruce Mawhinney, *Preaching with Freshness* (Eugene, Oreg.: Harvest House, 1991), 27.

3T. Harwood Pattison, *The Making of the Sermon* (Philadelphia: American Baptist Publication Society, 1941), 53.

4Jesse K. Moon, *Principles for Preachers* (Duncanville, Tex.: Star Graphix, 1975), 112.

The Altar Call and Congregational Commitment

1All Scripture quotations in this chapter are from the New King James Version unless otherwise indicated.

Achieving Variety in Pulpit Ministry

1Michael Sack, "Brain Scan of America," *Leadership* 16, no. 4 (fall 1995): 31. Used with permission.

2Adapted from H. Robert Rhoden, "Sunday Potpourri versus Biblical Topical Preaching," *Enrichment,* summer 1996, 56–58.

3Ibid., 58.

4Thomas Oliver, *The Real Coke, The Real Story* (New York: Random House, 1986), 17, 20–21, 23–24.

5Herb Miller, *Speaker Skills* (Lubbock, Tex.: Net Press, 1995), 14.

6Stuart Briscoe, "You Had to Bring It Up," *Leadership* 16, no. 4 (fall 1995): 61–65.

7Gardner Taylor, "Timeless Tension," *Leadership* 16, no. 4 (fall 1995): 21.

8Quoted in Edward Gilbreath, "The Pulpit King," *Christianity Today* 39, no. 14 (11 December 1995): 28.

The Place of Music in Congregational Worship

1All Scripture quotations in this chapter are from the New King James Version unless otherwise indicated.

2E. E. Hewitt and B. D. Ackley, "Drifting" (Nashville: Rodeheaver Co., copyright renewed 1945, p.d.).

Conducting Prayer Meetings that Reach the Throne

[1]James Marocco, *You Can Be a Winner in the Invisible War* (Kahului, Hawaii: Bartimaeus Publishing, 1992), 55, 56.

[2]In "tabernacle prayer," the various objects in the tabernacle dictate an aspect or emphasis of prayer: e.g., *the altar*—confessing and expressing thankfulness for Christ's sacrifice; *the laver*—praying for cleansing through the Word; *the lampstand*—putting on the full armor of God and inviting God's power into one's life; *the altar of incense*—interceding for family and friends; *the table of showbread*—claiming God's will and direction for one's life; *the mercy seat*—praying in the name of Jesus; *the ark*—praying for the greatest needs in one's life.

Maintaining Sound Doctrine and the Flow of the Spirit

[1]All Scripture quotations in this chapter are from the King James Version unless otherwise indicated.

Pentecostal Preaching

[1]All Scripture quotations in this chapter are from the New King James Version unless otherwise indicated.

[2]Stanley M. Horton, *What the Bible Says About the Holy Spirit* (Springfield, Mo.: Gospel Publishing House, 1976), 121.

[3]Haddon Robinson, Bill Hybels, and Stuart Briscoe, *Mastering Contemporary Preaching* (Portland, Oreg.: Multnomah Press, 1989), 57.

Scripture Index

OLD TESTAMENT

NEW TESTAMENT

Subject Index